

CasaXPS Manual 2.3.15

CasaXPS Processing Software for XPS Spectra

Casa Software Ltd.

NO WARRANTY

Casa Software Ltd. does its best to ensure the accuracy and reliability of the Software and Related Documentation. Nevertheless, the Software and Related Documentation may contain errors that may affect its performance to a greater or lesser degree. Therefore no representation is made nor warranty given that the Software and Related Documentation will be suitable for any particular purpose, or that data or results produced by the Software and Related Documentation will be suitable for use under any specific conditions, or that the Software and Related Documentation will not contain errors. Casa Software Ltd. shall not in any way be liable for any loss consequential, either directly or indirectly, upon the existence of errors in the Software and Related Documentation. The Software and Related Documentation, including instructions for its use, is provided "AS IS" without warranty of any kind. Casa Software Ltd. further disclaims all implied warranties including without limitation any implied warranties of merchantability or fitness for a particular purpose. CasaXPS should not be relied on for solving a problem whose incorrect solution could result in injury to a person or loss of property. The entire risk arising out of the use or performance of the Software and Related Documentation remains with the Recipient. In no event shall Casa Software Ltd. be liable for any damages whatsoever, including without limitation, damages for loss of business profit, business interruption, loss of business information or other pecuniary loss, arising out of the use or inability to use the Software or written material, even if Casa Software Ltd. has been advised of the possibility of such damages.

Acknowledgements

Casa Software Ltd would like to thank all those providing data and offering enlightening discussions leading to the current state of the CasaXPS software and manual. It is a humbling experience to work with so many knowledgeable people and the author would like to express gratitude to all concerned.

Contents

Getting Started with CasaXPS

CasaXPS is downloaded from the Web in a zip file. The zip file includes the executable program file and also configuration files essential for the correct functioning of the program.

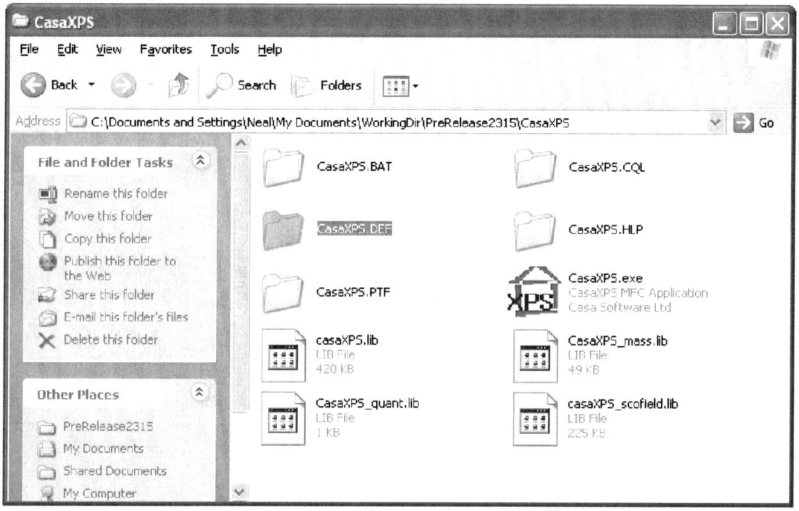

The CasaXPS.exe file must reside in the directory with the configuration files. To place an icon for CasaXPS on the Desktop, a shortcut should be created. Drag the shortcut onto the Desktop.

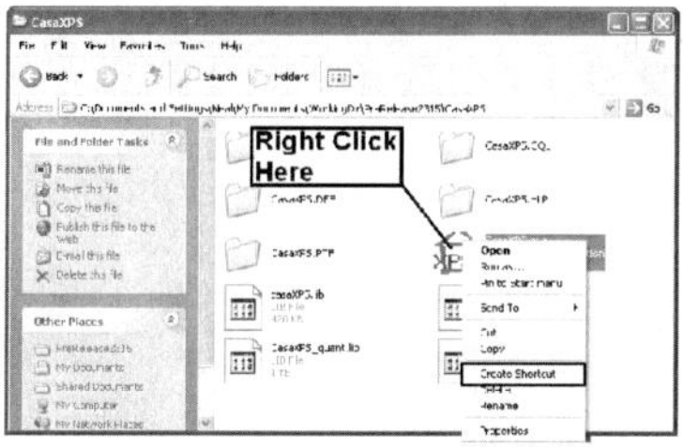

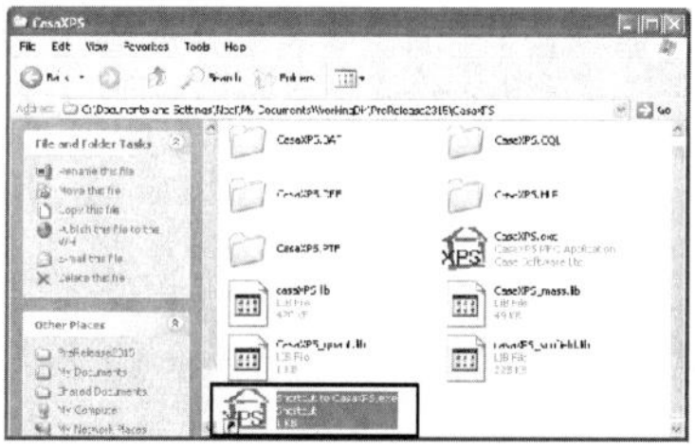

Licensing CasaXPS

The license information for CasaXPS appears at the top of the End User License Agreement (EULA). Two strings from the EULA must be copied and pasted exactly as given into the About Dialog of CasaXPS before pressing the Update License pushbutton.

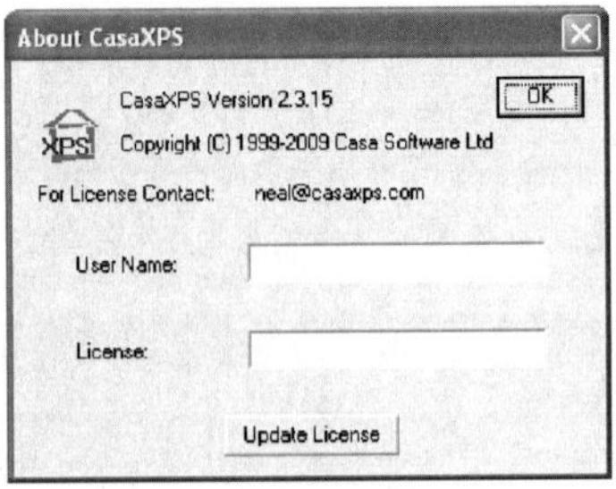

Once the license information is accepted, the title bar of the CasaXPS main window displays the Username string. Without a license, CasaXPS functions in demo mode only.

Opening a VAMAS file

The native file format used by CasaXPS is ISO 14976 VAMAS ASCII format. To open a VAMAS file:

1. Select the Open option on the File menu or use the Open toolbar button.

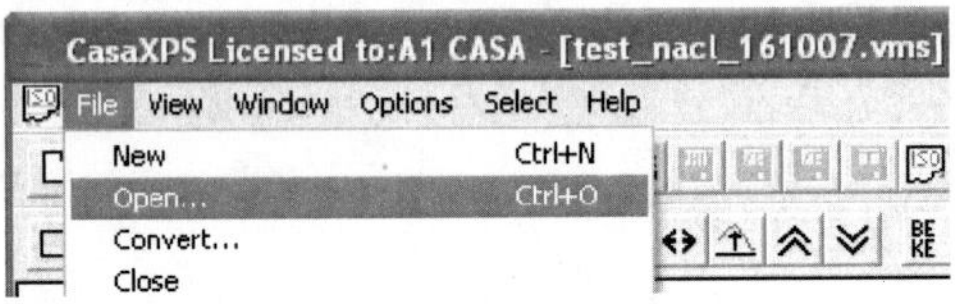

2. Browse the directories using the File dialog window and select a VAMAS formatted file.

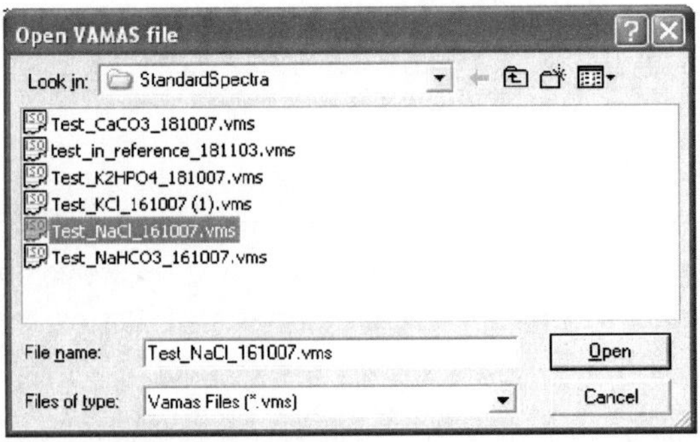

The selected file opens in an experiment frame.

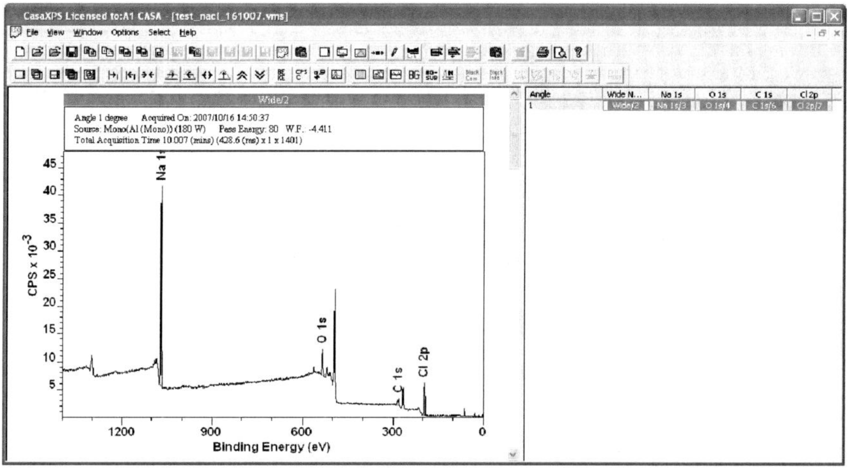

Displaying Spectra

A VAMAS file may contain one or more spectra. The spectra are held in data blocks within the VAMAS file and these data blocks or VAMAS blocks are displayed in the right-hand pane of the experiment frame.

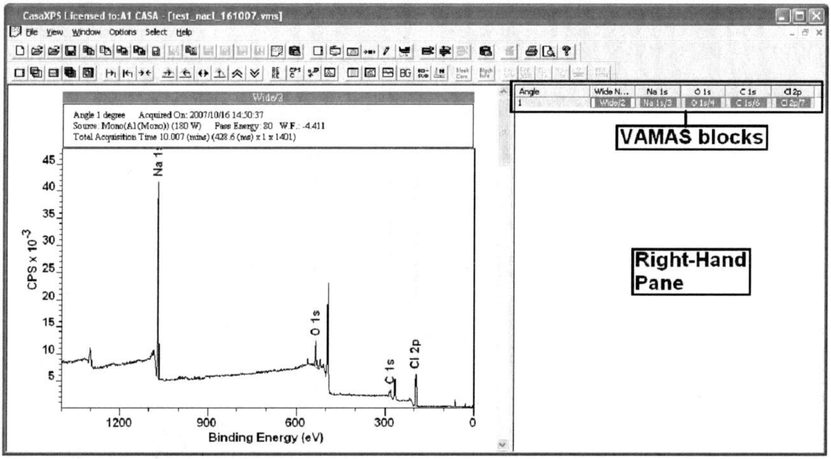

Displaying spectra involves selecting one or more VAMAS blocks in the right-hand pane before pressing the display toolbar button.

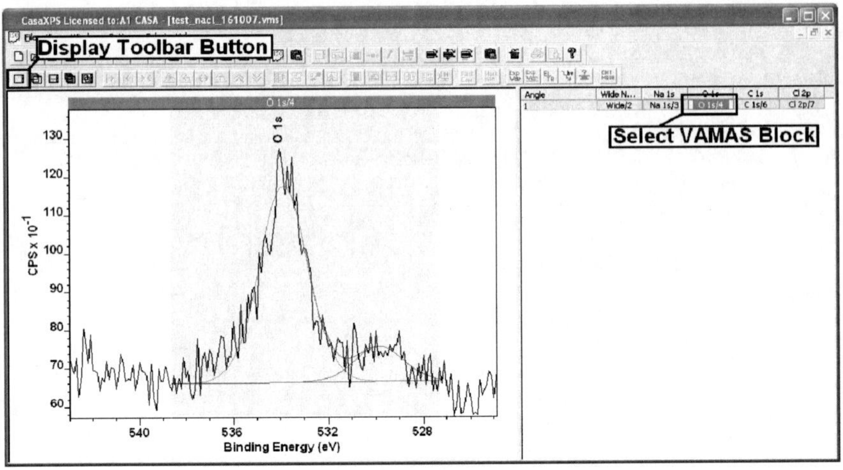

The left hand mouse button is used to select a VAMAS block in the right-hand pane. A single click of the mouse selects the VAMAS block beneath the cursor, while double-clicking the mouse caused the VAMAS block beneath the cursor to be selected in the right-hand pane and also displayed in the left hand pane.

Overlaying Spectra

Spectra within an experiment frame are overlaid by first selecting a set of VAMAS blocks in the right-hand pane before pressing the overlay toolbar button.

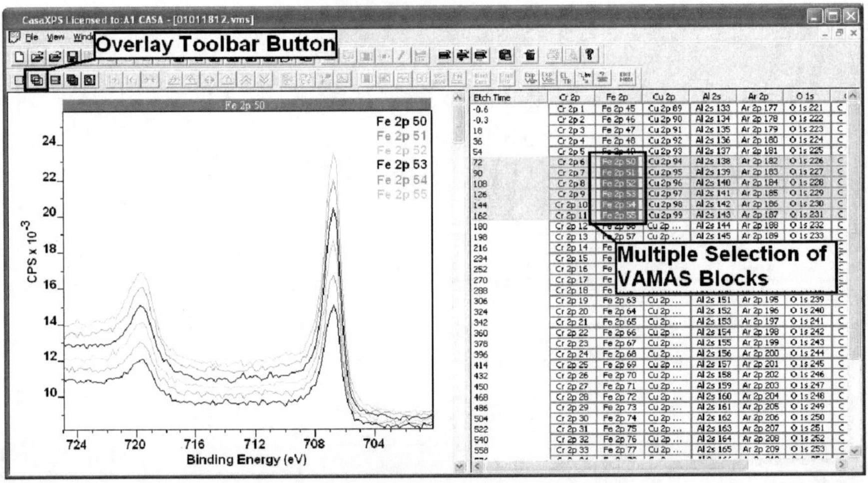

Multiple selections of VAMAS blocks are achieved using a combination of mouse actions coupled with the use of the Shift and Control keyboard keys.

To select a contiguous set of VAMAS blocks:

Select the first VAMAS block in a range.

Hold the Shift key down and select the last VAMAS block in the range.

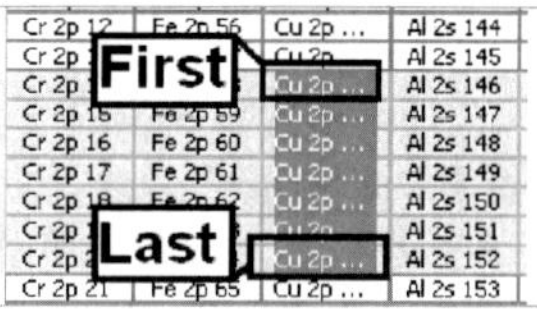

To add VAMAS blocks to a selection:

Hold the Control key down and select a VAMAS block in the right-hand pane.

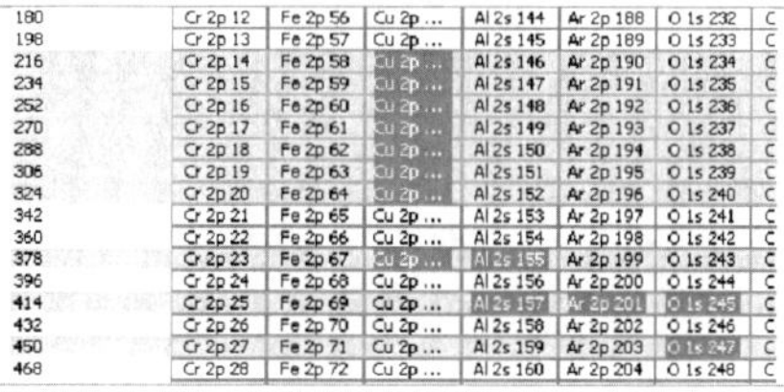

Measuring Peak Intensities

Quantification is performed on the Quantification Parameters dialog window.

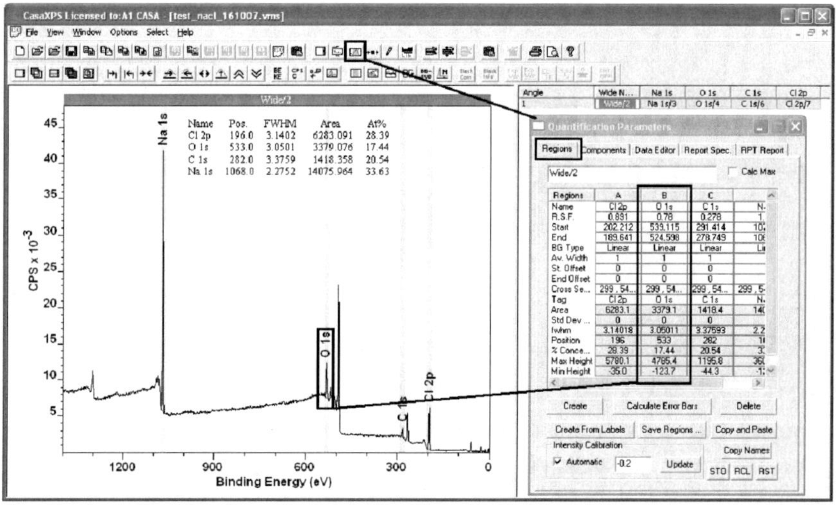

Each peak used to measure the composition of a sample requires a quantification region. The quantification region defines:

1. The name associated with the peak e.g. O 1s.
2. The relative sensitivity factor (RSF) for scaling the raw peak area.
3. The start and end energy limits over which the peak intensity is to be measured.
4. A background type specifying the algorithm for calculating a background curve on top of which the photoelectric peak sits.
5. An average width representing the number of data channels used to determine the intensity of the background at the two energy limits specified by the start and end fields.
6. A percentage offset for each of the start and end limits specifying a reduction in the computed background intensity at these limits.
7. Additional parameters available for use with a subset of background types.
8. A TAG string used to identify a region.

Quantification reports based on regions are displayed over a survey spectrum using the Regions property page on the Annotation dialog window.

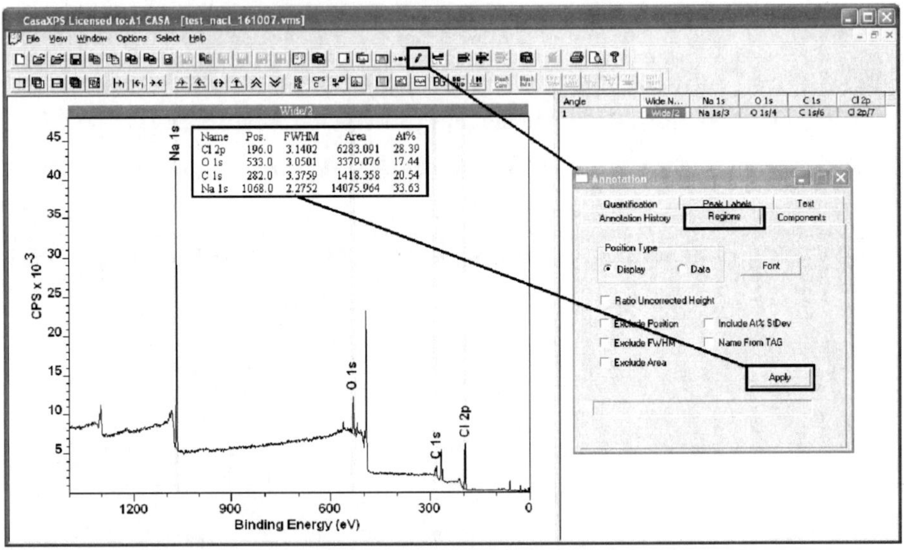

Peak models are created using a quantification region to define the background and synthetic lineshapes defined using the Components property page on the Quantification Parameters dialog window.

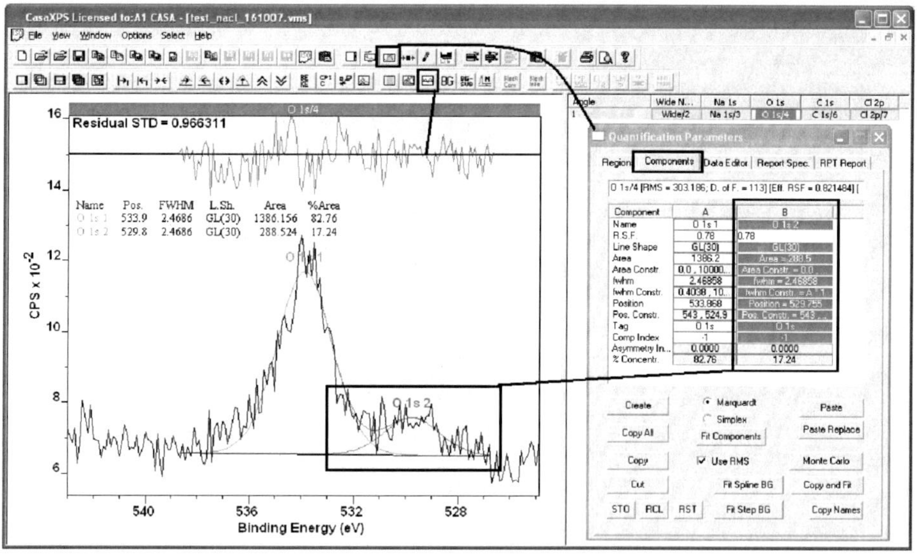

Components are synthetic lineshapes defined in terms of:

1. Component name e.g. O 1s 2.
2. A relative sensitivity factor (RSF) used to scale the raw peak area.
3. A lineshape specifying the functional form for the component e.g. GL(30) or SGL(20).
4. The raw area of the component peak.
5. A constraint for the raw area of the component peak.
6. Full width at half maximum FWHM for the component peak.
7. A constraint for the FWHM.
8. The position of the component peak.
9. A constraint for the component position.
10. A TAG string used to link regions and components for quantification purposes.
11. A component index used to group components for operations and display.

The component parameters are displayed over the data as a table using the Components property page on the Annotation dialog window.

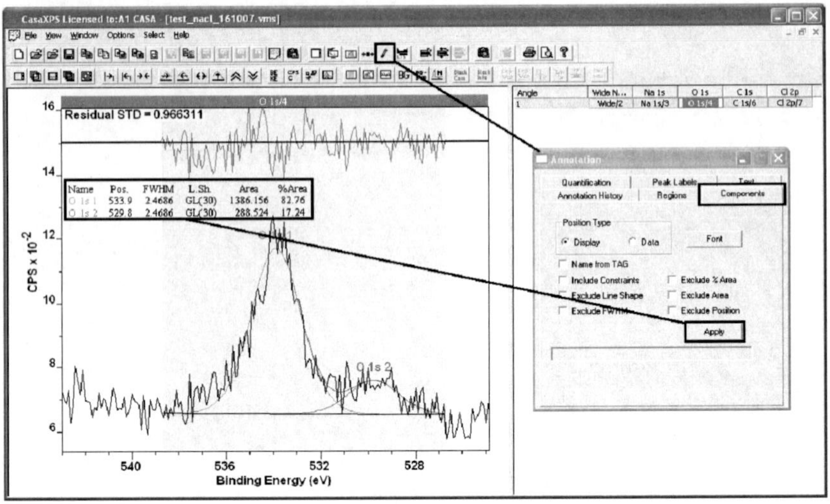

Quantification results based on quantification regions and components are generated for export using the Report Spec property page on the Quantification Parameters dialog window.

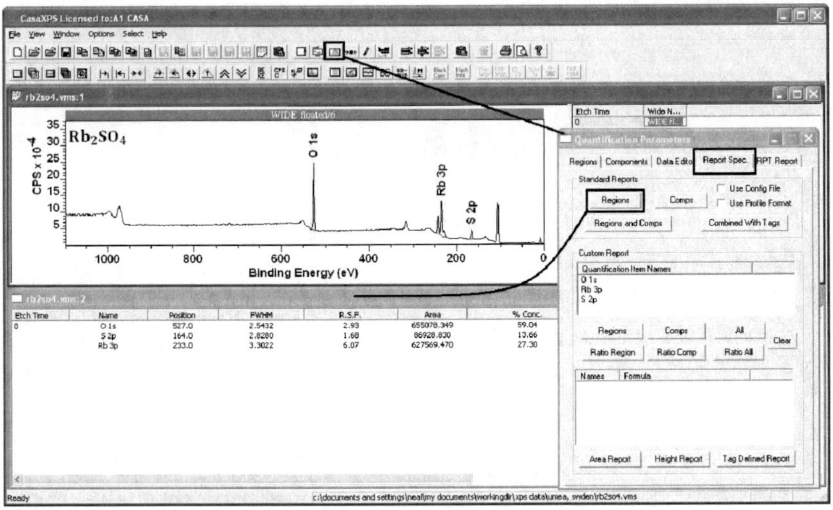

Quantification reports generated from the Report Spec property page are based on the selection in the right-hand pane of the experiment frame. The text based report generated by selecting one or more VAMAS blocks and pressing the Regions button, for example, is exported via the clipboard using the Copy toolbar button.

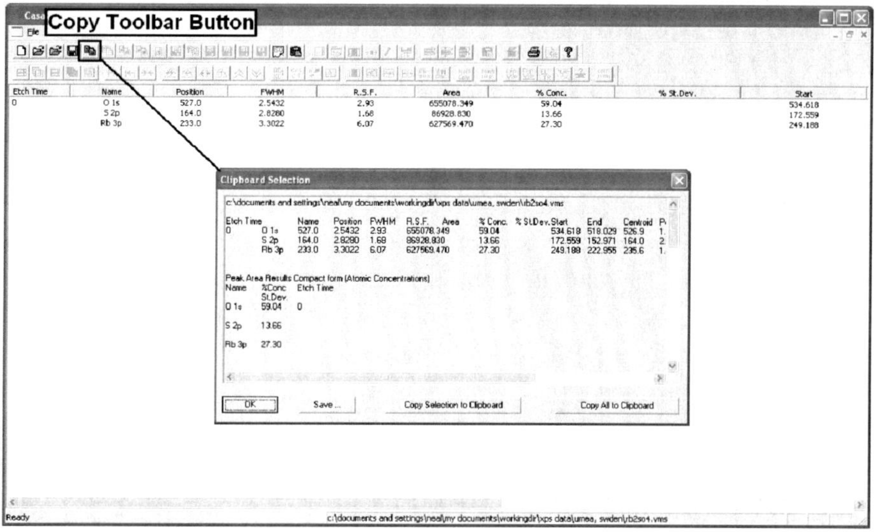

The quantification table is place on the clipboard and may be pasted into a spreadsheet program or any other program capable of accepting text via the clipboard.

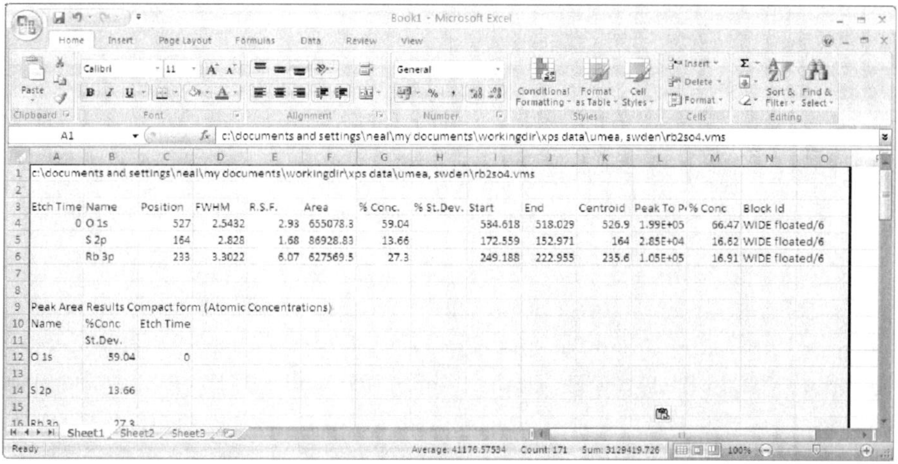

Working with Spectra

The following sections describe features in CasaXPS using typical tasks to illustrate options available to the user.

Quantification using Survey Spectra

Elemental composition for a surface is typically determined from survey spectra. A survey spectrum measures the count rate over a wide range of energies using a relatively low energy resolution with high sensitivity. In most cases the survey spectrum provides the basis on which more detailed high resolution narrow scan spectra are acquired.

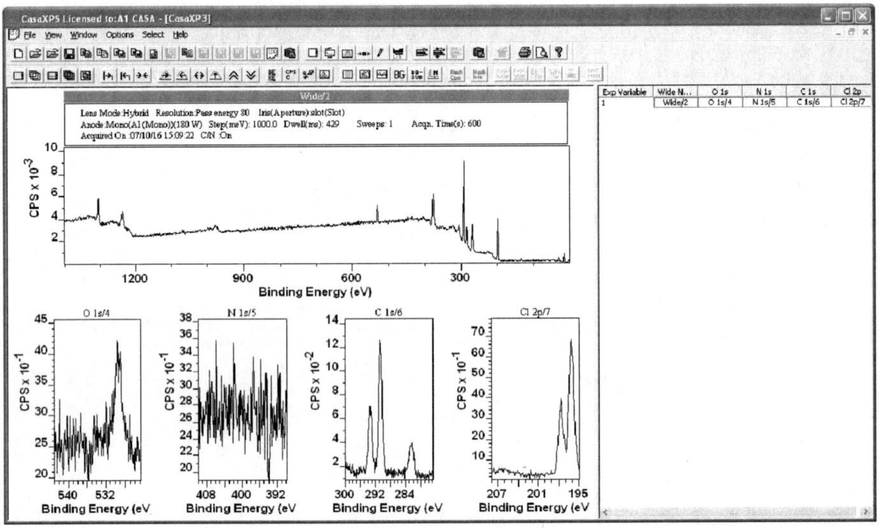

A survey spectrum does not include the detailed peak structure seen in the high resolution narrow scan data, but provides the context for peaks in the energy spectrum. The information in the survey spectrum includes all the related transitions and background shapes vital to understanding the sample. Identification of peaks is performed using the, so called, element library.

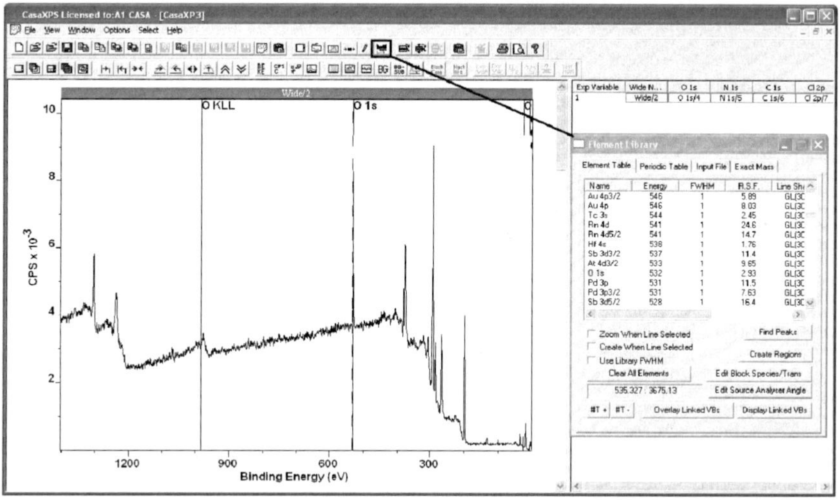

The element library is a list of transitions for both photoelectric and Auger peaks. The element library provides information about peak positions and more importantly maintains a set of relative sensitivity factors used to quantify the peak areas in terms of surface composition. The library also relates peaks due to transitions within a given element, thus selecting one transition in the element table results in markers appearing on the data for all the transitions for the element selected.

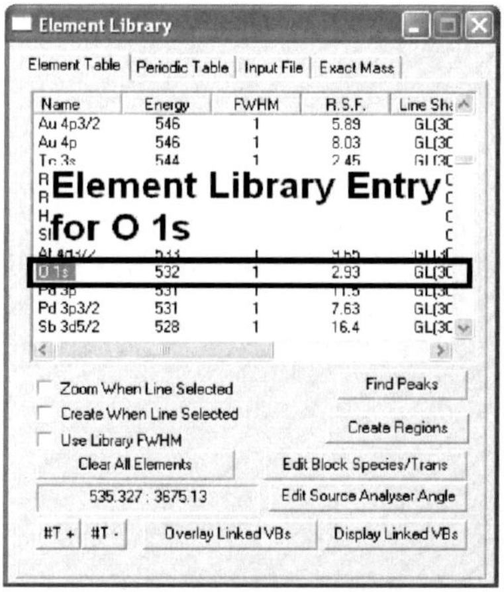

Element markers can be placed on the display via the Element Table property page or the Periodic Table property page of the Element Library dialog window.

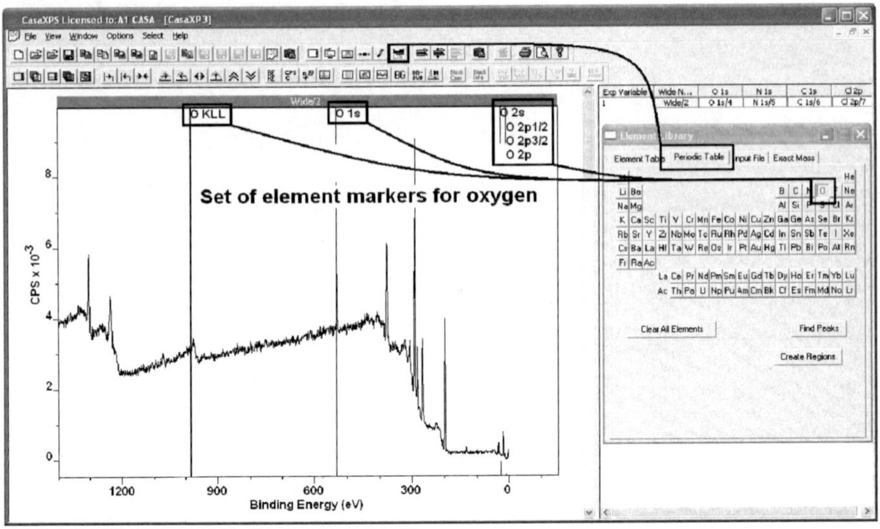

The element library is an ASCII file located in the same directory as the CasaXPS.exe executable file named CasaXPS.lib. If no entries appear in the element table the executable and library files are not in the same directory as required. The element library is essential for quantification of XPS data therefore it is important the directory structure in the CasaXPS zip file is maintained intact. The most common reason for a lack of an element library within CasaXPS is that the CasaXPS.exe has been moved to the Desktop, thus separating the executable from the element library file. To avoid this problem, always create a shortcut for the CasaXPS program file and move the shortcut onto the Desktop rather the program file itself.

A first step in quantifying a survey spectrum is to identify the elements by assigning each peak to an element. On occasion, peak positions may be offset in energy due to charging of the sample. It is both comforting and informative to adjust the peak positions to the expected energies for the transitions assigned to the peaks. Energy calibration is performed using the Spectrum Processing dialog window.

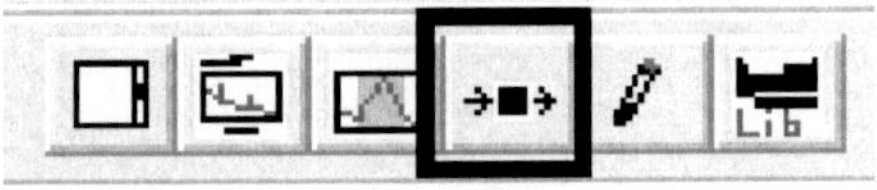

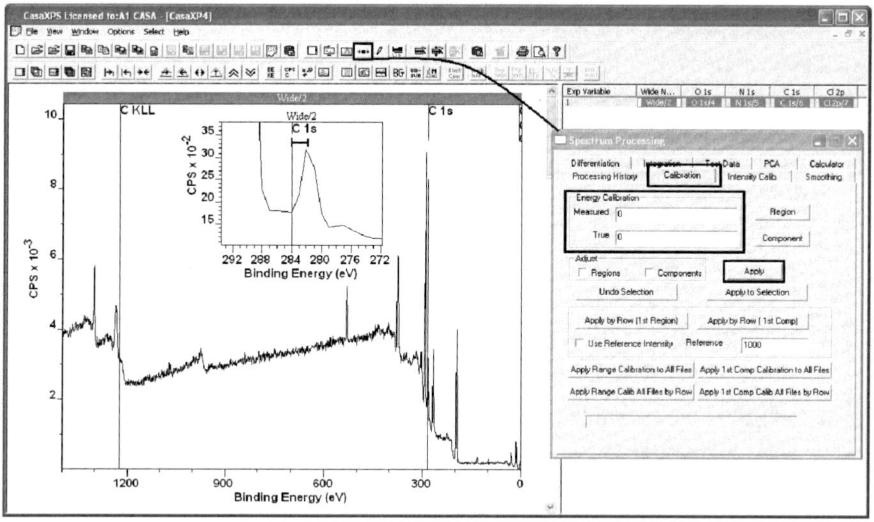

Energy calibration is performed using the Calibration property page on the Spectrum Processing dialog window. The case of calibrating a single survey spectrum is the simplest calibration operation since a survey spectrum represents a complete set of photoelectric transitions maintained within a single VAMAS block. The energy shift determined for the correction based on one peak necessarily corrects all the peaks in the VAMAS block. For the current example data, identifying the carbon 1s transition, assuming the peak is predominantly contamination and therefore expected to appear with binding energy of 285 eV, allows the a calibration to be performed. Specification of two energies indicating the measured binding energy for the C 1s peak and the true binding energy assumed to be 285 eV is sufficient to determine the shift in energy required to position the measured peaks in binding energy. Calibration of a single VAMAS block displayed in the active tile is performed by pressing the Apply button on the Calibration property page.

The peak position in the data before calibration is entered in the Energy Calibration section of the Calibration property page either manually or alternatively using the cursor and mouse.

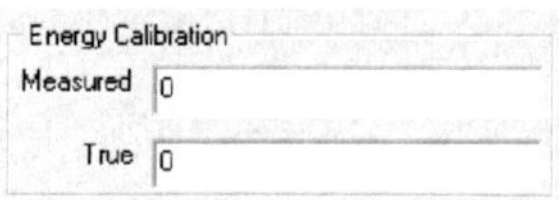

The Measured field is updated each time the cursor is located over the left-hand pane of the experiment frame and the left mouse button is clicked.

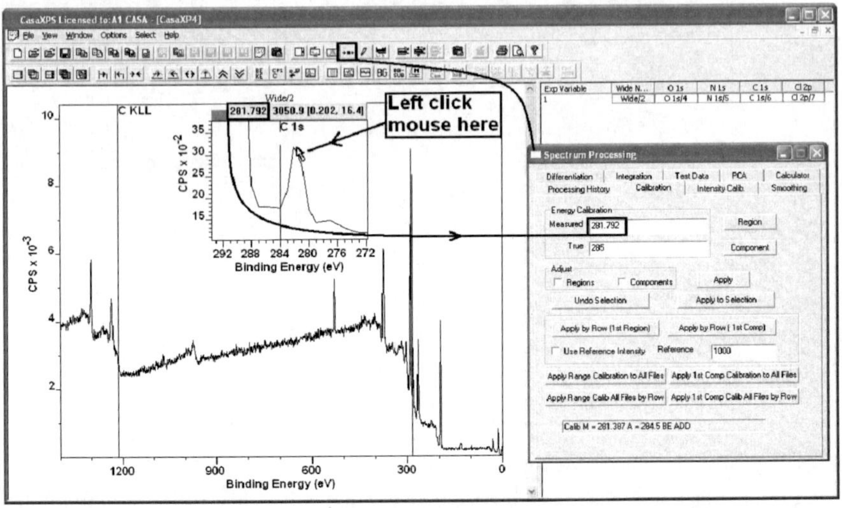

To complete the calibration, a value is entered into the True text-field before pressing the Apply button on the Calibration property page. An entry specifying the calibration parameters is entered on the Processing History dialog window and the energy scale is shifted by the difference between the Measured and the True energies entered on the Calibration property page.

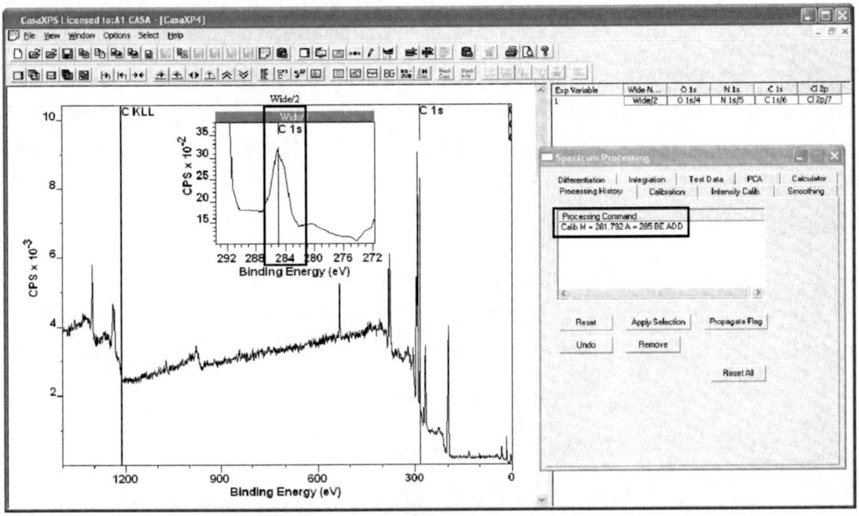

The Apply button on the Calibration property page only affects the active VAMAS block in the active tile. To apply the same calibration to a set of VAMAS blocks, the Apply to Selection button is used instead. The Apply to Selection button calculates a shift based on the parameters on the Calibration property page and applies the same shift to all VAMAS blocks selected in the right-hand pane of the experiment frame. The use of the Apply to Selection button will be discussed in detail for the example below in which high resolution narrow scans are energy calibrated.

Elemental composition of survey data requires the linking of peaks to transitions in the element library. Connecting peaks to transitions permits RSF scaling information to be added to the quantification regions used to calculate peak intensities. Quantification regions for survey spectra are therefore best created via the element library, particularly because a survey spectrum, by nature, is a collection of peaks from a variety of transitions and therefore the VAMAS block cannot include knowledge regarding a peak's origin. High resolution spectra, in contrast, are acquired under circumstances where species and transition information are available, either due to prior acquisition of a survey spectrum or sample knowledge. The creation of quantification regions for survey spectra is performed using a combination of the Element Library and Quantification Parameters dialog window.

The element library provides not only a means of identifying peaks in the data but once a set of element markers are displayed over the survey spectrum, regions can be created based on the element markers where a region is created for each element indicated. By pressing the Create Regions button on either the Element Table or the Periodic Table property pages regions are created for each element using, as a default, the transition with the largest RSF. The transition used to create these regions can be explicitly defined using a configuration file, but in the absence of a configured transition, the largest RSF determines which peak is used to quantify an element.

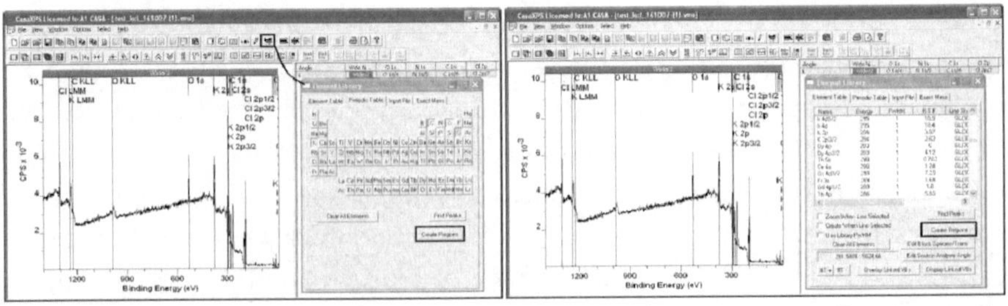

The current example is potassium chloride (KCl). Four quantification regions created based on element markers for oxygen, carbon, chlorine and potassium are added to the VAMAS block for the survey spectra and an annotation table equivalent to a table created by the Regions property page of the Annotation dialog window is added too.

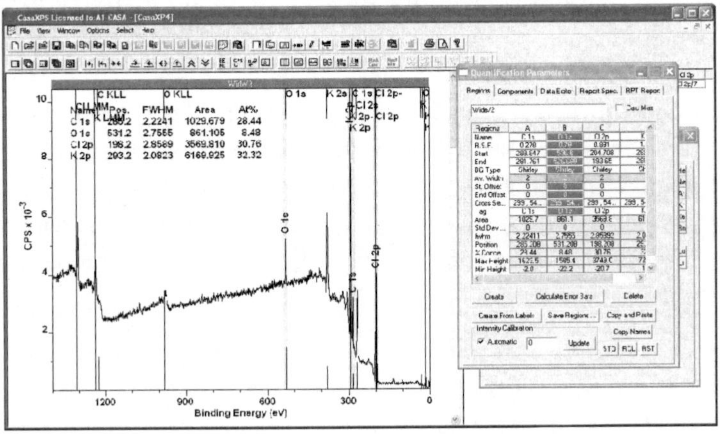

The regions are created using the name and RSFs from the element library combined with the parameters last used to create a quantification region. If for example on pressing the Create Regions button the regions are created using the background type Shirley, but for the data in question a linear background is deemed to be appropriate. Editing the background type for one of the regions using the Quantification Parameters dialog window and recreating the set of regions using the element library mechanism results in a new set of regions now utilising the newly used linear background type.

To alter a parameter in the regions such as the background type:

1. Alter the background type on one of the existing regions.

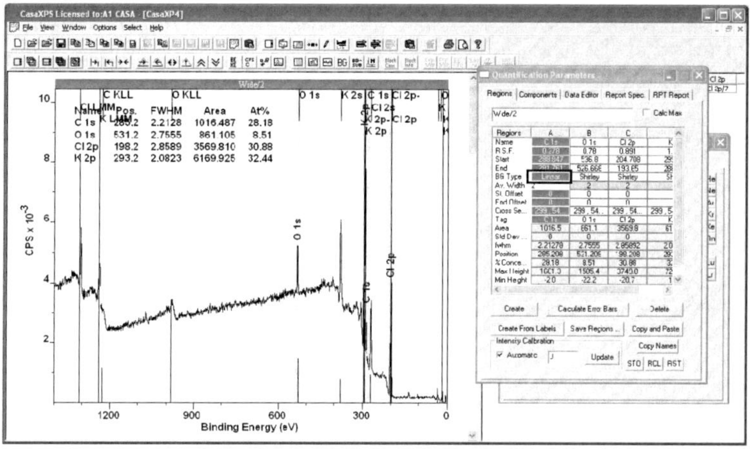

2. Re-create the regions using the element library and the current set of element markers.

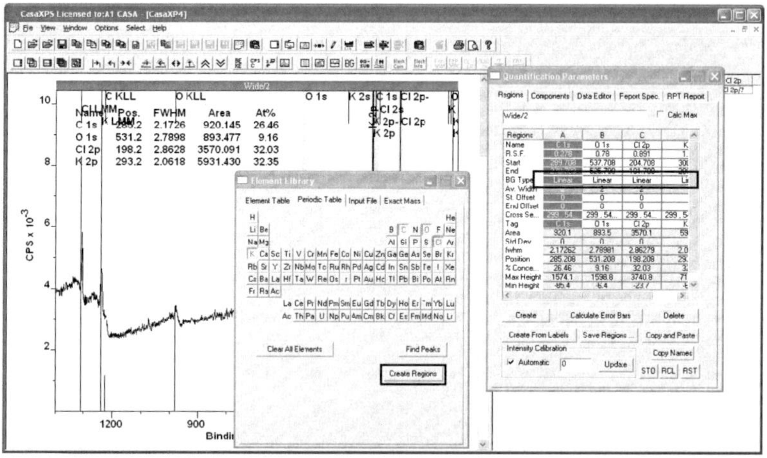

The same two steps will permit other region parameters not extracted from the element library to be similarly adjusted.

It is always wise to visually inspect the regions used in the quantification. Often the background limits may need adjusting and confirmation that the correct RSF for the peak identified has been used. A useful tool for inspecting the regions is via the zoom list for the active tile. The display tiles in the left-hand pane provide for reducing the intensity and energy display limits using zoom boxes defined via dragging the cursor over an area of the display tile.

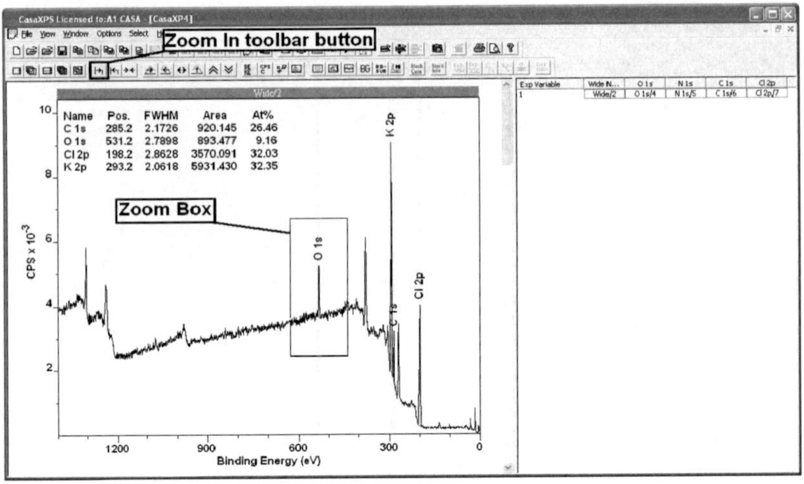

Either clicking inside the zoom box or pressing the Zoom In toolbar button cause the display to expand the zoom box to fill the display area of the tile.

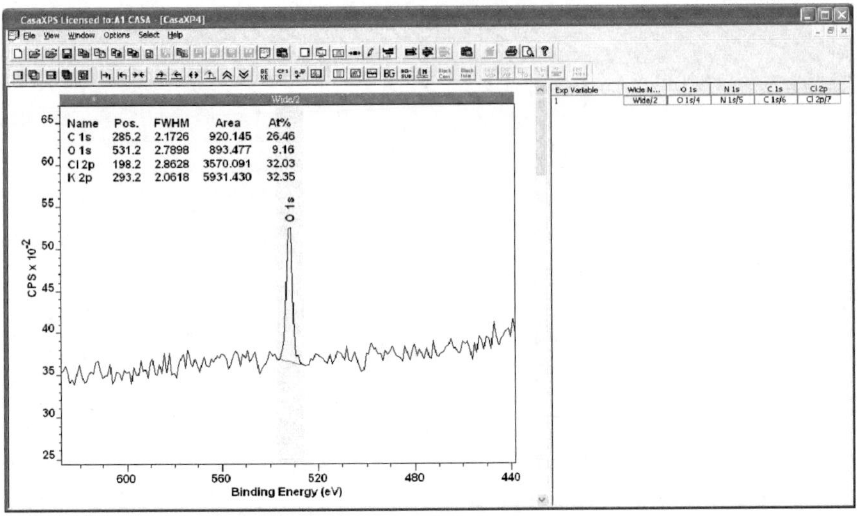

To return to the previous zoom state, the Zoom Out button can be pressed. Each time a zoom box is used to alter the display state, the dimensions of the zoom box are placed on a zoom list. The Zoom Out toolbar button actually cycles through the set of zoom states previously defined by the zoom actions. To reset the current zoom list to the full range of the intensity and energy scales the Reset toolbar button must be pressed.

Zoom In

Zoom Out

Reset Zoom List

While the region limits can be examined via a sequence of zooming in followed by zooming out then zooming in again, a mechanism employing the zoom reset facilitates the inspection of the regions by placing a set of zoom states onto the zoom list based on the current set of regions refined on the data displayed in the active tile. Pressing the Reset toolbar button causes the display to return to the full view of the data. The Reset toolbar button also loads a set of zoom states onto the zoom list so that by pressing the Zoom Out toolbar button the display is switched between intervals about the region energy limits. To inspect the regions it is therefore simply the case of pressing the Reset toolbar button followed by repeatedly pressing the Zoom Out toolbar button. If the Region property page is top-most on the Quantification Parameters dialog window, the region limits are easily adjusted under mouse control.

The sequence of display states cycled through using the Reset and Zoom Out toolbar buttons for the KCl data are as follows:

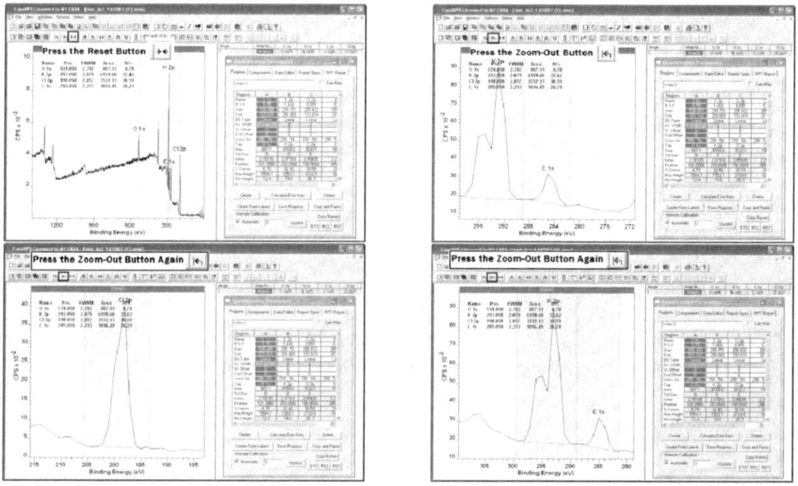

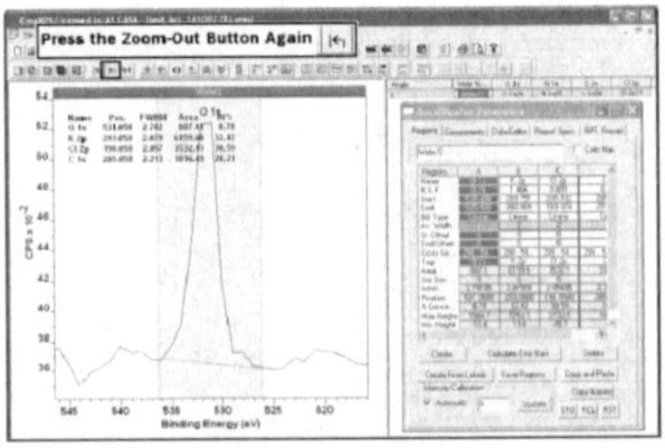

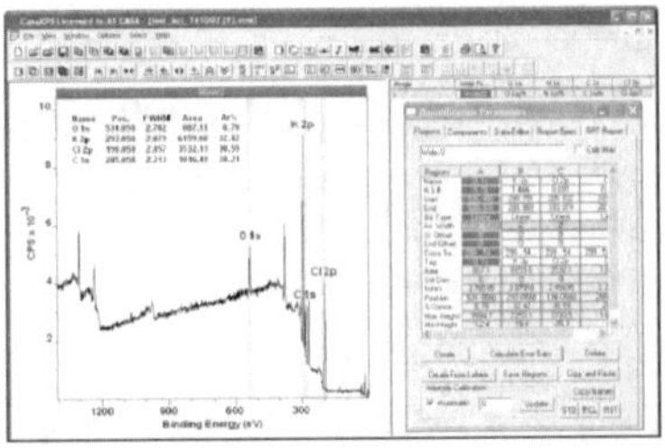

Following a complete cycle through the regions defined on the data displayed in the active tile, the tile display returns to the state initially invoked by pressing the Reset toolbar button. At this point each region will have been reviewed and potentially adjusted to the point that the quantification table over the display may be considered valid.

The accuracy for the atomic concentrations relies on the precision with which the peak areas are calculated and also the validity of the relative sensitivity factors used to determine the quantity of material responsible for the measured peak intensity. The uncertainty due to the appropriateness of the sensitivity factors cannot be measured based on the data available to CasaXPS; however provided the counts per bin are supplied in the VAMAS file and the instrument from which the data are acquired obeys Poisson statistics, the uncertainty in the precision can be estimated for regions and added to a quantification report. The technique for measuring the precision in the calculation is based on a Monte Carlo procedure.

Adding a column to the regions report annotation involves first re-creating the region report using the Annotation dialog window with the tick-box enabled on the Region property page with the label Include At% St Dev. The second step is to press the button on the Regions property page of the Quantification Parameters dialog window labelled Calculate Error Bars. Once the calculation is complete, the %St Dev column values for the atomic concentrations are added to the quantification report displayed over the data in the left-hand pane.

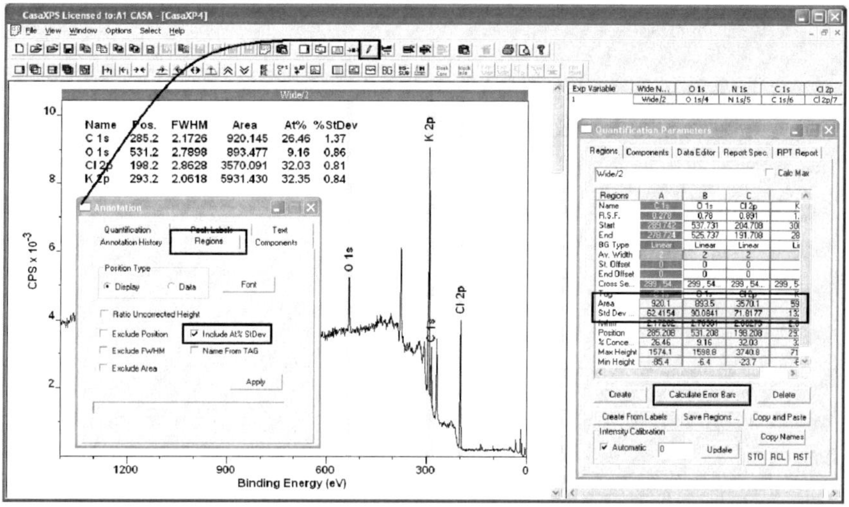

Adjusting the regions annotation involves deleting any annotation table already displayed over the data. The Annotation History property page provides the means of deleting and adjusting annotation defined on a VAMAS block.

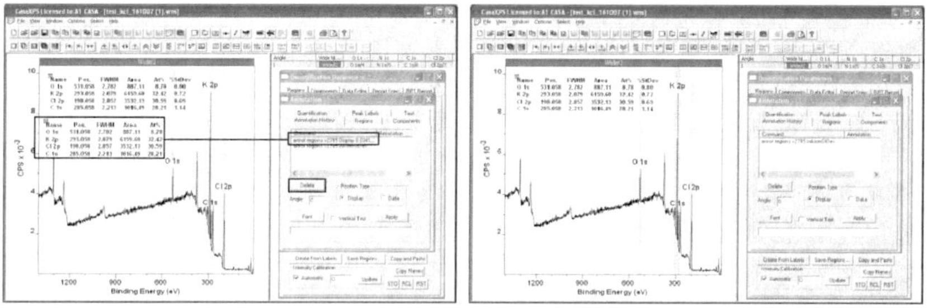

Factors influencing the quality of the XPS information are appropriate RSFs for a given background type and the stability of the background with respect to noise in the data. Any analysis performed using a standard library of sensitivity factors can only realistically hope for type B scenario, where measurements are repeatable, but not necessarily producing the correct values. Type A scenario is only possible for materials for which RSF are measured from standard samples. Ideally the grouping of results in Type B would be achieved centred on the true value.

Type A

Poor precision better accuracy:

Noisy data with poorly defined background limits but well defined RSFs.

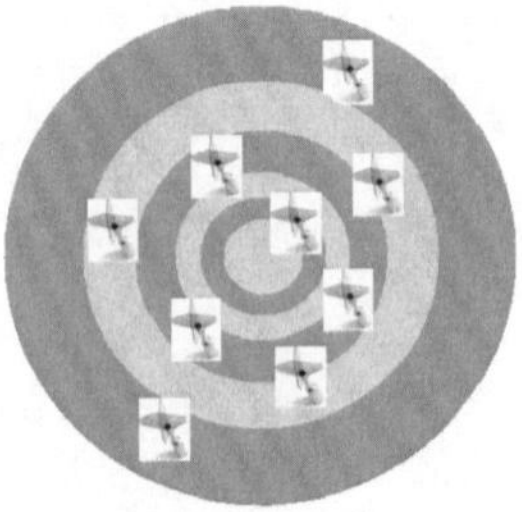

Type B

Good precision poor accuracy:

Good signal-to-noise but inaccurate RSFs

The first objective for most analyses is therefore to achieve repeatability for identical samples. Acquisition times are typically selected to achieve good precision, however photo-ionisation cross-sections for some materials or sample damage due to exposure to x-rays force less than idea signal to noise ratios in practice. It is therefore important to optimise the precision possible for a given set of data and to this end the average-width region parameter can enhance the precision achieved.

The Av Width region parameter provides a means of improving the stability of the background with respect to noise in the data.

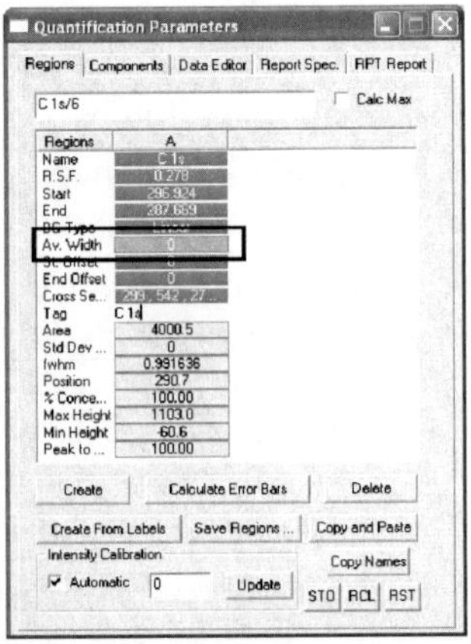

The key point is that the location of the background with respect to the spectral data should be independent of the data channels corresponding to the start and end energy parameters. For noisy data, if a single data channel specifies the intensity of the background at either extreme of the region interval, the background calculation may produce significant differences simply due to the choice for these region limits.

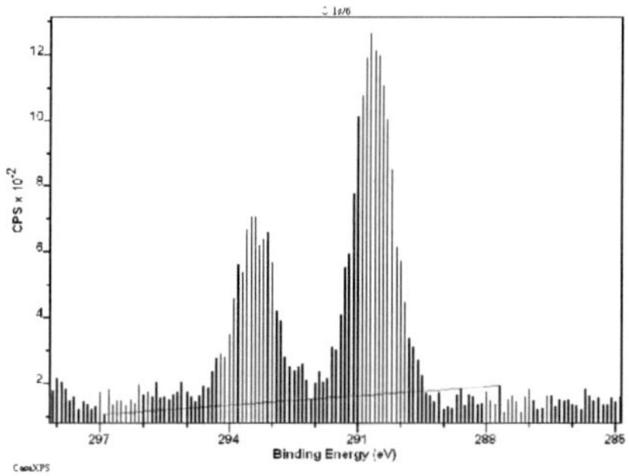

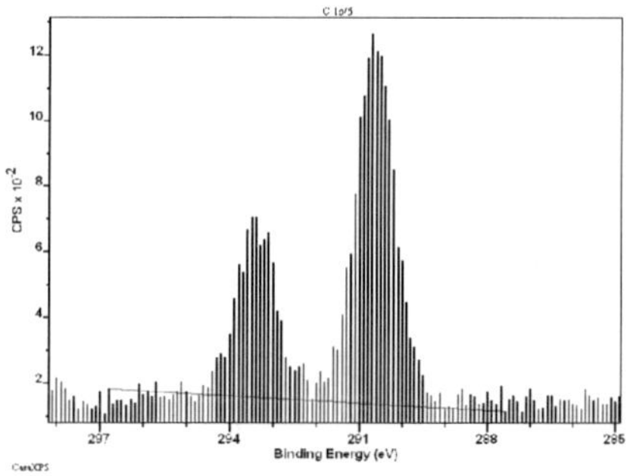

An Av Width of zero results in a single data channel defining the intensity for the background at either end of the region. A linear background for these data moves from a negative gradient to a positive gradient based on simply shifting the region energy limits by one data channel. Since the peak intensity is measured using the background subtracted counts per second, it is clear that the computed area and therefore atomic concentrations are, under these circumstances, subject to unnecessary error.

A remedy is to introduce a non-zero Av Width parameter. The Av Width parameter specifies the number of data channels to the left and right of the data channel which would otherwise be used in isolation to specify the background intensity at the region limits. Thus, an Av Width of 3, say, would specify the background intensity at these limits to be calculated from seven data channels. Three to the left of the data channel determined from the region limit, the data channel determined from the region limit itself and three more data channels to the right, making a total of seven data channels.

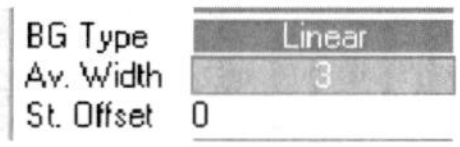

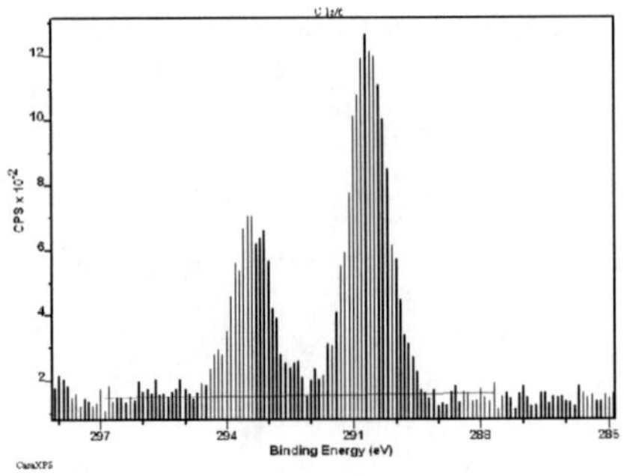

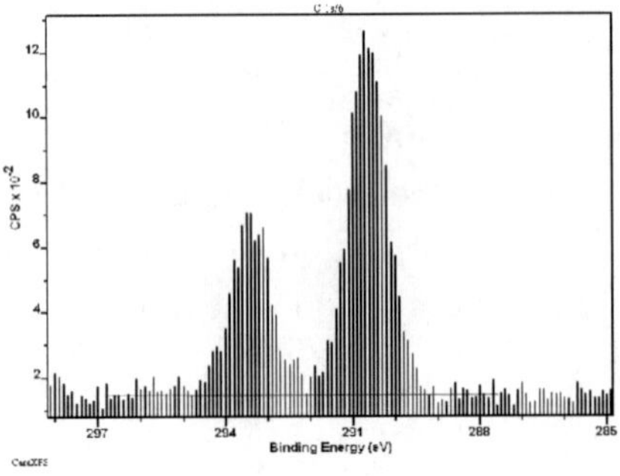

The background intensity at the region limits is now very insensitive to the noisy in the data. Moving the region limits by one data channel returns an almost identical linear background.

While smoothing the data before quantification provides an alternative approach to averaging the intensities from a limited range of data channels, data smoothing alters the shape and resolution of the peaks, therefore is unattractive when creating peak models. Employing the Av Width parameter is preferable to smoothing the entire spectrum.

The intensity calculated from the data channels specified by the Av Width parameter may be determined in one of two ways:

1. A simple mean average over the data channels specified.
2. Fitting a polynomial to the data channel intensities in a least squares sense.

The default method used to calculate the background intensities can be configured at start-up, or switched using the Av Width field on the Regions property page of the Quantification Parameters dialog window. A more detailed description of these features appears in following sections, but for now it is sufficient to know that the Av Width parameter can significantly improve the precision for computed concentration values.

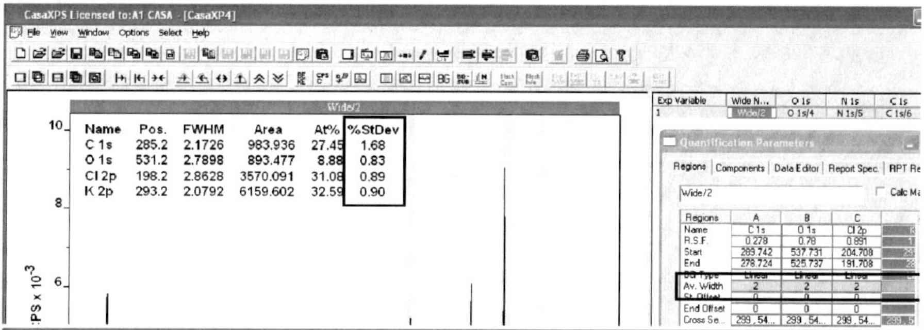

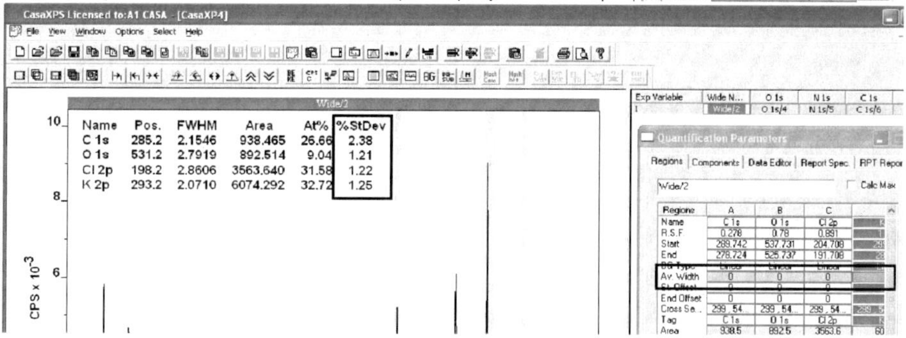

For the above example, the Av Width method calculates the background intensity by fitting a polynomial to the range of data channels. The colour for the background to the Av Width field indicates which algorithm is employed. A plain background to the Av Width field indicates the mean average algorithm is in use.

High Resolution Spectra

Once the composition of a sample is known, narrow scan spectra acquired with higher energy resolution are often used to investigate the chemical state for the elements at the surface. Reducing the pass energy improves the energy resolution but reduces the count rate; hence the need to measure the intensities over reduced energy intervals. The KCl data file includes a survey spectrum measured with pass energy 80 together with four narrow scan spectra using pass energy 20 for a Kratos Axis Ultra.

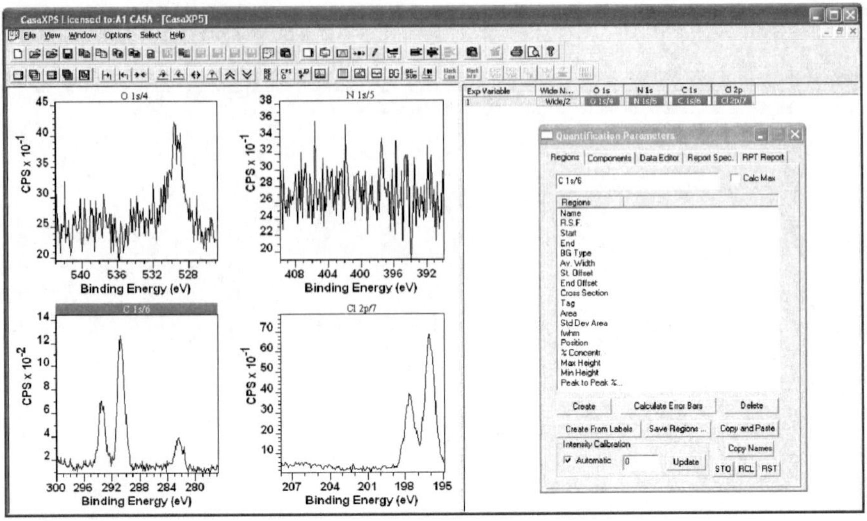

Using pass energy 20 to acquire the interval containing the chlorine 2p doublet resolves the doublet nature of the 2p transition. The same energy region from the survey spectrum fails to produce the clarity for the two chlorine peaks.

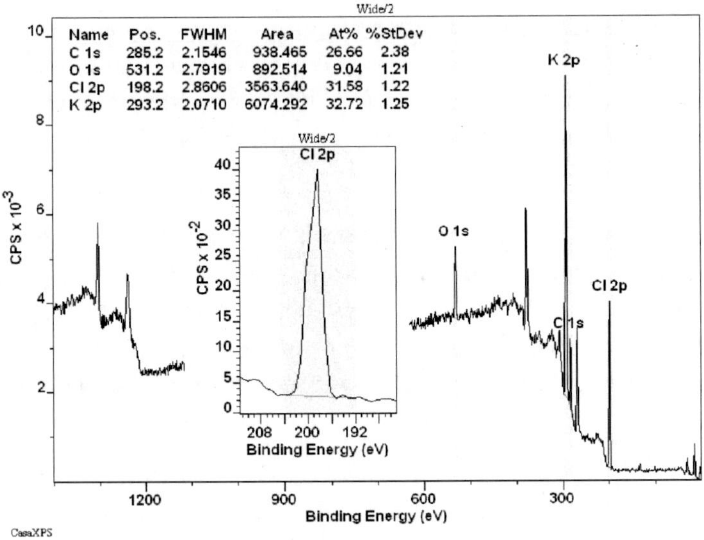

These two ways of visualising the data are achieved using tile display options based on regular arrays of display tiles in the first case and an inset tile to provide a closer view of the Cl 2p peaks in the survey spectrum.

Changing the Number of Tiles per Page

The number of tiles per page is determined by the Page Tile Format dialog window.

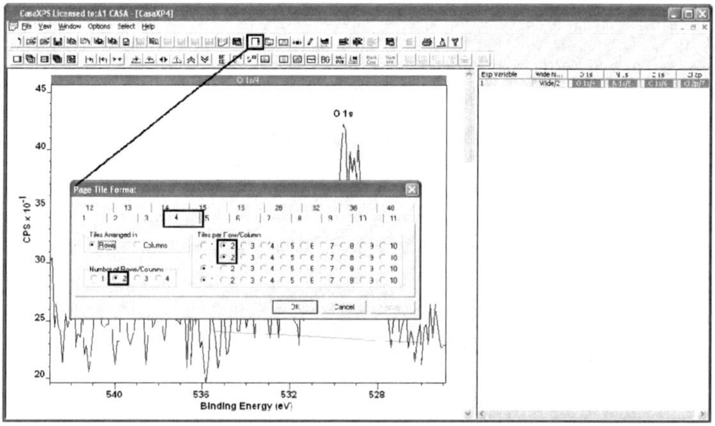

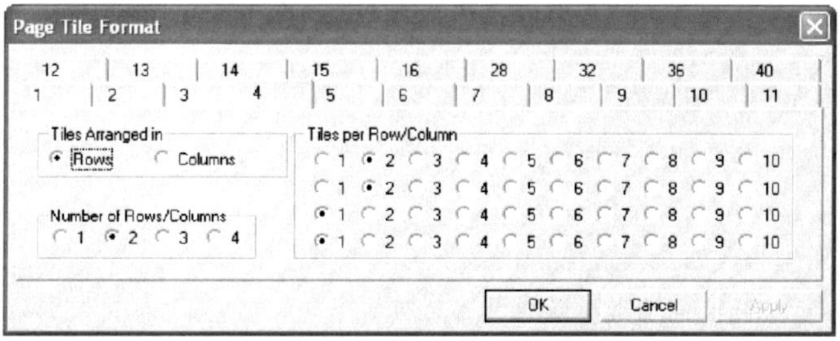

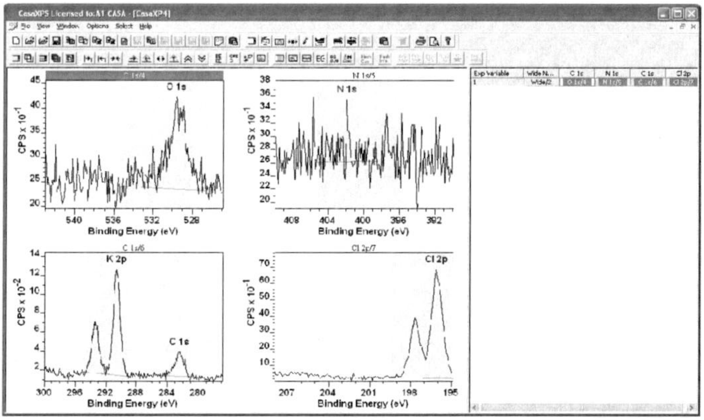

A set of property pages offer predefined arrays of display tiles in terms of the number of rows in the array coupled with the number of tiles within in each of four possible rows. The number of rows and number of tiles per row may be switched to define the array in terms of columns using the **Tiles Arranged in** radio buttons.

By organising the radio buttons on the Page Tile format dialog window as follows the four narrow scan spectra are arranged in two columns, where the first column displays three tiles and the second column contains a single tile:

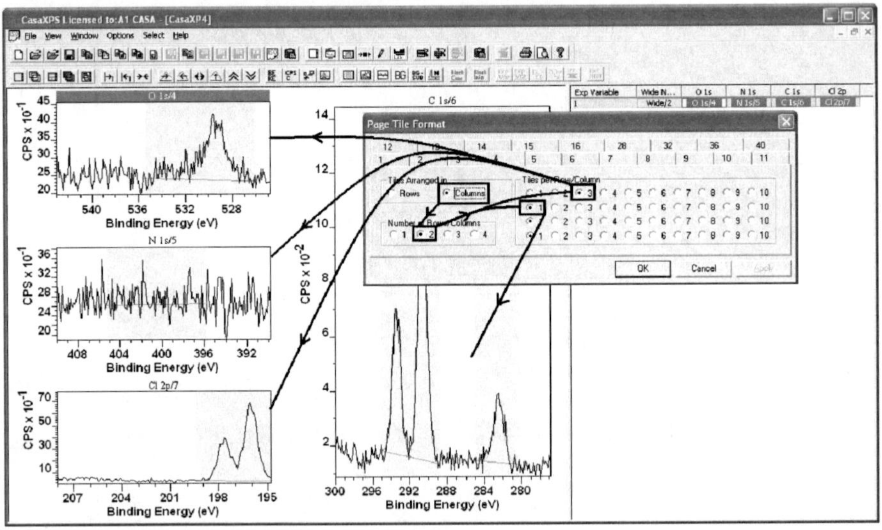

Inset Tiles

The alternative to a regular arrangement of tiles is to use the inset tile mechanism. The most common use for inset tiles is highlighting one or more intervals of interest in a survey spectrum.

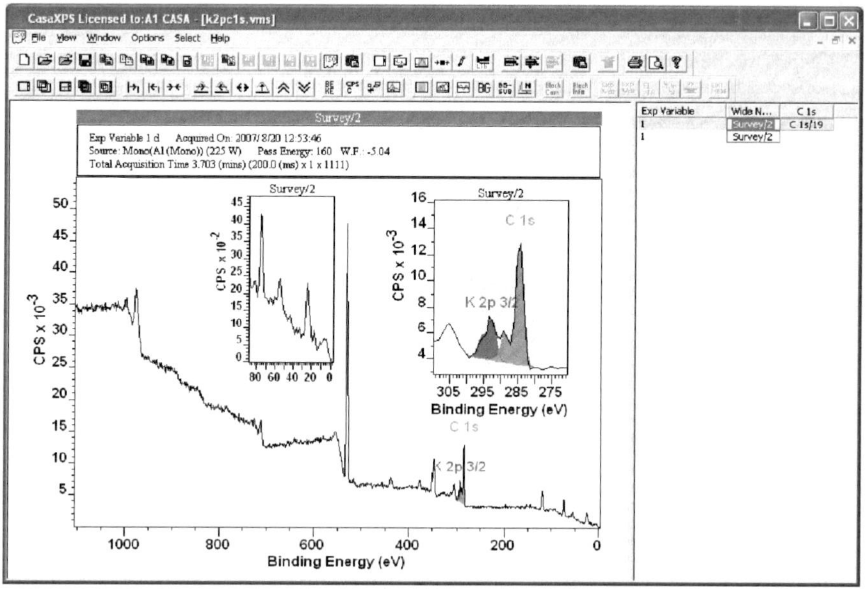

An inset tile is created by using the mouse to drag a zoom box over the data in the active tile followed by pressing the Insert key on the keyboard. The data below the zoom box appears within the inset tile created when the Insert keyboard key is pressed.

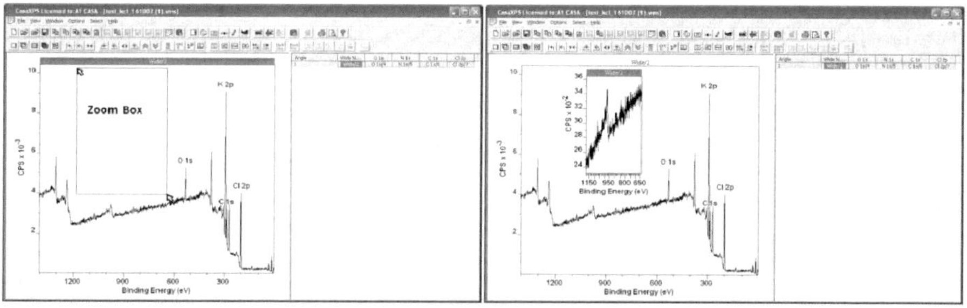

Data displayed in an inset tile is manipulated identically to data displayed in the parent tile. Zoom Out and any other of the toolbar buttons for adjusting the display ranges can be used to display the desired peak information.

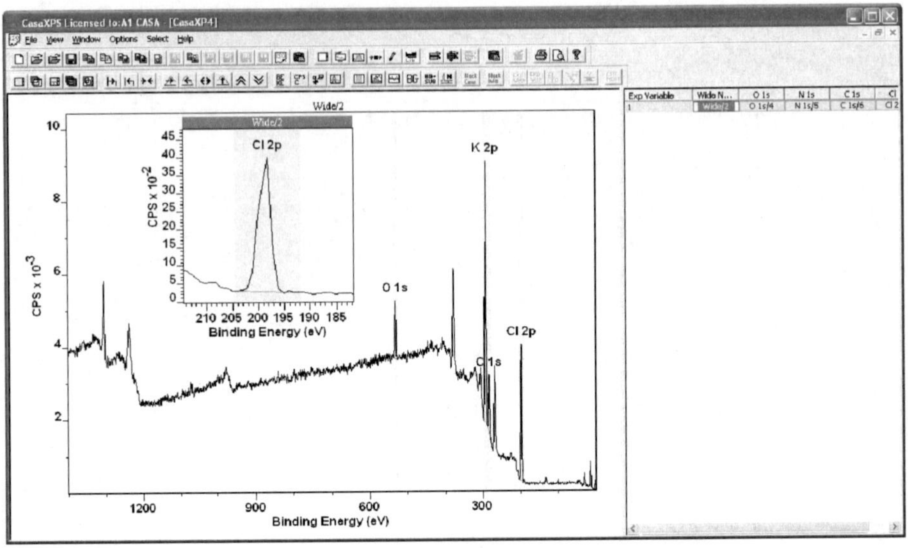

The tile with focus, including the inset tiles, can be used to manipulate data via the toolbar buttons or any dialog window. Logically, there is no difference between an inset-tile and any other tile appearing in the left-hand pane; regions and components respond to adjustments within an inset tile in the same way as adjustments made when the parent tile has focus. Further, data from any VAMAS block in the right-hand pane can be displayed in an inset tile. Focus is transferred to any tile by left-clicking the mouse with the cursor inside the tile. The title for the data in a tile becomes highlighted once focus has been acquired by the tile, at which point a VAMAS block from the right-hand pane is inserted into the tile by first selecting the VAMAS block in the right-hand pane, before pressing the Overlay toolbar button.

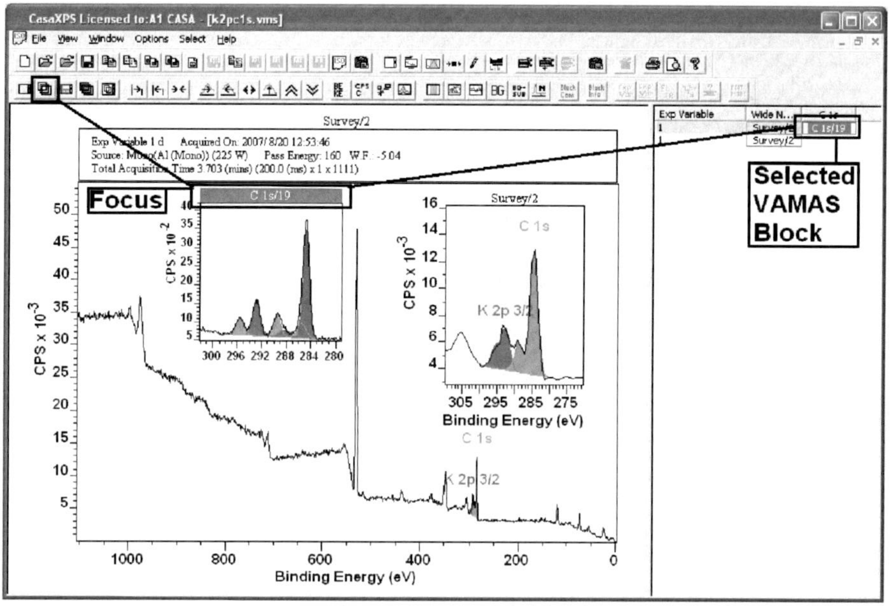

Creating Regions for Narrow Scan Spectra

The approach used to create regions for survey spectra, while available, is less appropriate for narrow scan spectra. The principal difference between survey spectra and narrow scan spectra resides with the targeted nature of the narrow scan spectra where peaks are assigned to a transition within a specific element. A survey spectrum represents all transitions from elements in the surface of the sample. In general, since narrow scan spectra can be assigned to a specific transition, information about the transition is potentially included in the VAMAS block maintaining a narrow scan spectrum.

The KCl example illustrates a set of narrow scan spectra for which element/transition fields are assigned to the four narrow scan spectra. The caveat is the C 1s VAMAS block. While the VAMAS block assigned the element/transition C 1s does indeed include the carbon peak, the proximity of the K 2p peaks to the C 1s energy means the two transitions are both included in the spectrum labelled C 1s.

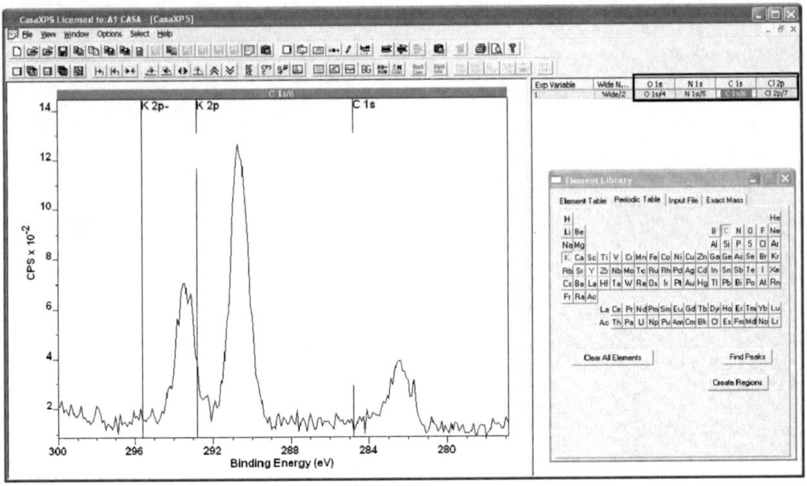

Whenever high resolution narrow scan spectra are assigned the correct element/transition VAMAS fields, a toolbar button offers a means of creating quantification regions. Regions are created by selecting the VAMAS blocks in the right-hand pane before pressing the Add Regions toolbar button.

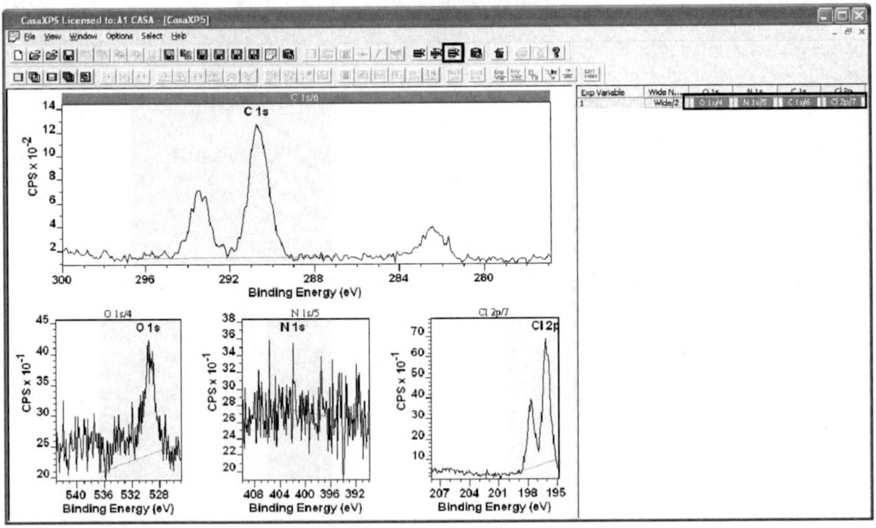

One region is created per VAMAS block selected in the right-hand pane. The RSF and name assigned to the regions is determined from the VAMAS block element/transition fields. Other region parameters are based on the last used values for these parameters. While regions have been created for each of the four VAMAS blocks in the KCl VAMAS file, the set of regions are less than perfect.

The most obvious error is the C 1s region has been positioned over the K 2p doublet. The largest peak in the narrow scan spectrum is included in the region interval and since the K 2p intensity exceeds the C 1s intensity, the region is determined for the K 2p peaks rather than the true C 1s peak. Regardless of whether the correct peak was associated with the element/transition fields in the VAMAS block, a narrow scan spectrum containing more than one transition will typically require manual adjustment following pressing the Add Region toolbar button.

The first step in rectifying the error is to move the region from the K 2p peaks to span the C 1s peak. Invoking the Quantification Parameters dialog window with the Regions property page top-most enables a pair of vertical locators at either end of the quantification region. If the cursor is placed midway between the vertical markers and dragged, the region limits are both shifted by the same amount and therefore the current region is shifted by these actions until the region spans the C 1s peak only. Note that the RSF extracted for the region is based on the C 1s assigned for the narrow scan spectra and as such is correct for the C 1s peak intensity.

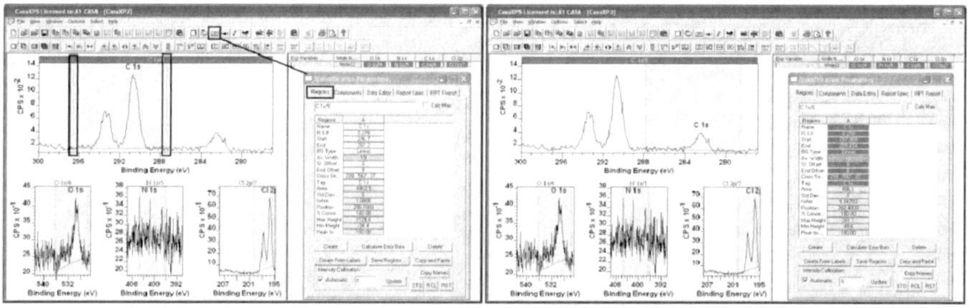

A region must be manually created for the K 2p doublet peaks:

1. Zoom into the K 2p doublet peaks.

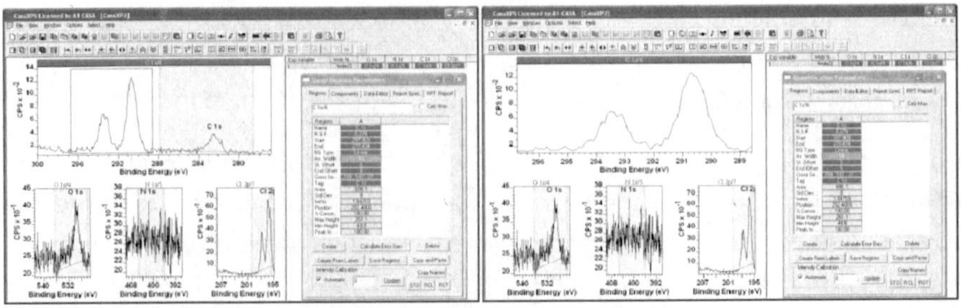

2. Invoke the Element Library dialog window and select the K 2p transition using the Element Table list.

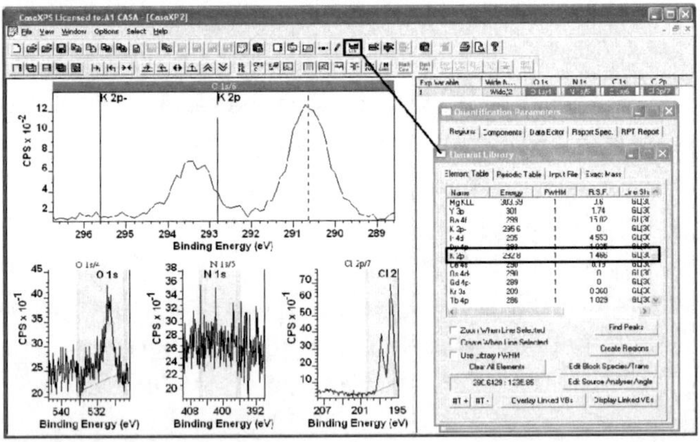

3. On the Regions property page of the Quantification Parameters dialog window press the Create button.

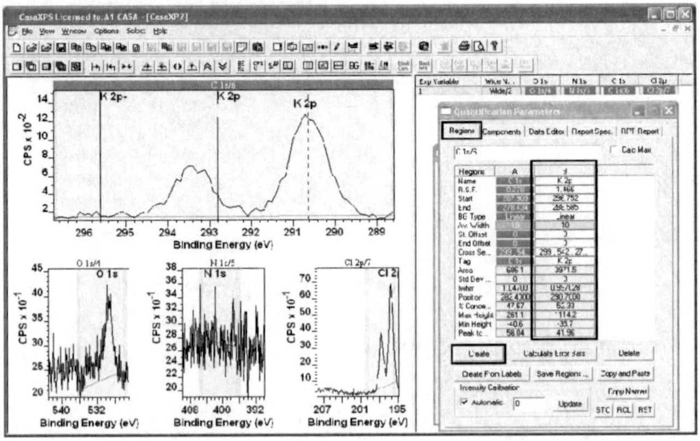

The region created on pressing the Create button extracts the name and RSF based on the transition selected via the element table.

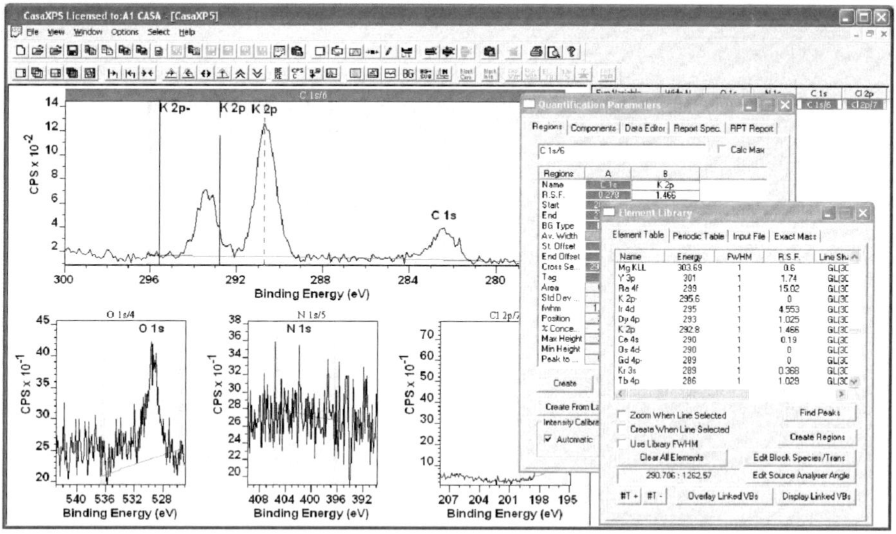

The O 1s narrow scan region highlights a further issue, namely, the background is poorly defined even though the Av Width field is set to 10. An Av Width of 10 should produce a very stable background definition, however the background automatically calculated for the data appears poor. The problem with the background results from a feature of the Av Width. If there are insufficient data channels at either end of the region limits to compute the background based on the specified number in the Av Width field, then rather than progressively introducing a reduced number of channels in the averaging process, the approach is to switch to just one data channel when determining the background. If a problem exists and it is significant, the precision of the background is either as good as requested or as bad as possible, with nothing in between. The intension is such problems should be obvious rather than attempting to hide these errors. The solution is to adjust the region limits to ensure the specified Av Width can be calculated. This involves positioning the region limits so that there are more than 10 data channels available for use at either end of the energy interval for the region.

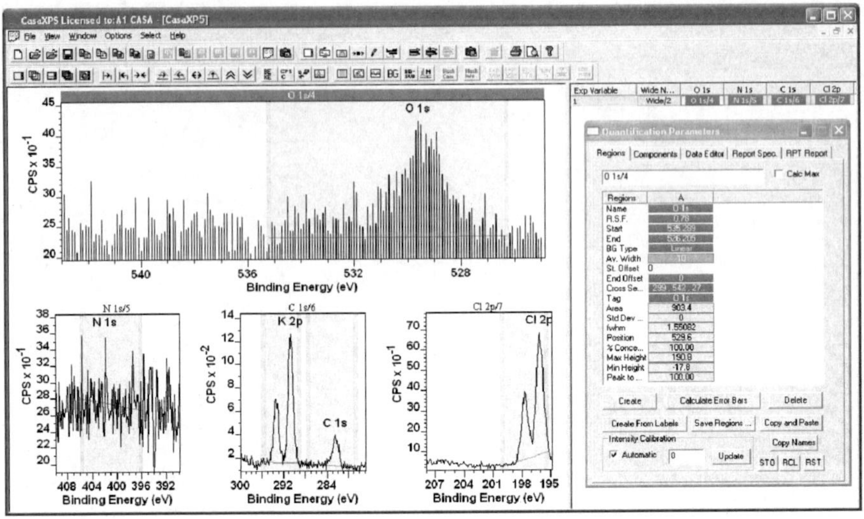

While the problem with the O 1s background can be solved, a similar problem with the Cl 2p data cannot be solved in terms of Av Width adjustments. The difference for the Cl 2p data is that the acquisition window failed to include sufficient data channels to lower binding energy of the peak envelope.

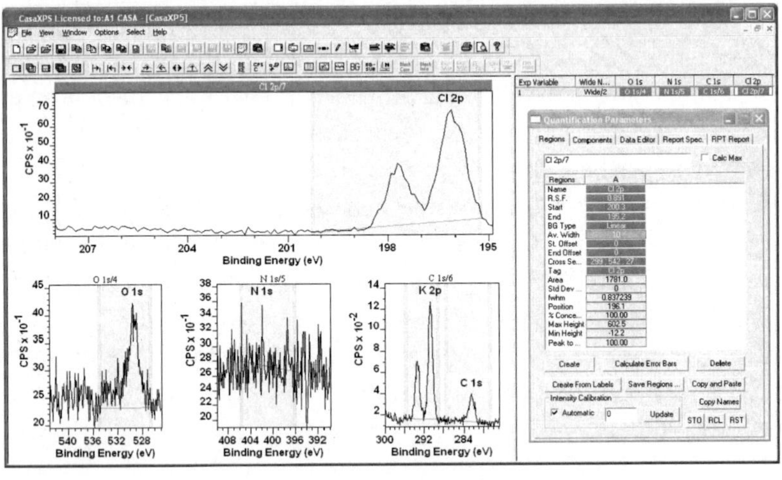

For the case of the chlorine peaks, the background type linear needs to be changed to one not relying on both end limits. One possible solution is to switch to the background type Min and adjust the energy interval to accommodate as much of the peak structure as possible.

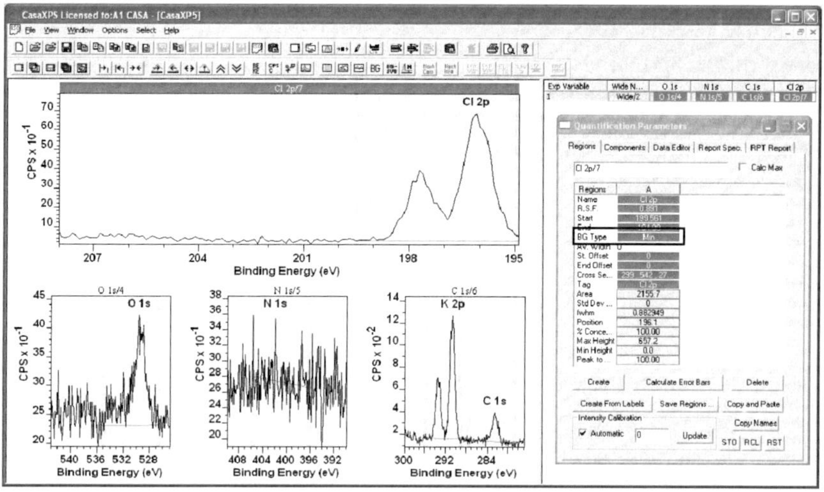

The background type Min simply places a horizontal background level with the minimum intensity in the region energy interval. For this example the solution appears good, based on the relative intensity of the two peaks for Cl 2p the minimum background can be justified.

Doublet peaks are a feature of XPS spectra. A given electron configuration results in a range of quantized (for core level solid state materials) energy levels. These energy levels may split to form related energy levels under the influence of spin-orbit interactions and for sufficiently large elements these spin-orbit energy differences are apparent in the XPS peak structure. For the case of potassium chloride, both elements are sufficiently large to exhibit spin-orbit splitting due to transitions involving the emission of a 2p electron. Potassium chloride offers an example of a diatomic molecule where the initial state is clearly a singlet ground state. The doublet nature of the XPS peaks assigned to K 2p and Cl 2p are due to the doublet nature of the excited ions, where the final state is available with two possible energies. According to theory, these two energy levels are formed from a set of degenerate states, where the number of degenerate states allocated to each of these two observable energy levels depends on the total angular momentum quantum number (j-j coupling notation) $\boldsymbol{j = l + s}$, where $\boldsymbol{l}$ is the orbital angular momentum number and $\boldsymbol{s}$ the spin angular momentum quantum number. For the emission of an electron with p ($\boldsymbol{l}$ = 1) angular momentum, the final state offers two energy states, $\boldsymbol{j}$ = 1/2 and $\boldsymbol{j}$ = 3/2, in the proportion 2(1/2) + 1 to 2(3/2) + 1 or simply stated the expected intensity ratio of 2p doublet peaks is 1:2. Both the

K 2p and the Cl 2p doublets obey the relationship between the intensities for the $2p_{1/2}$ and the $2p_{3/2}$ peaks.

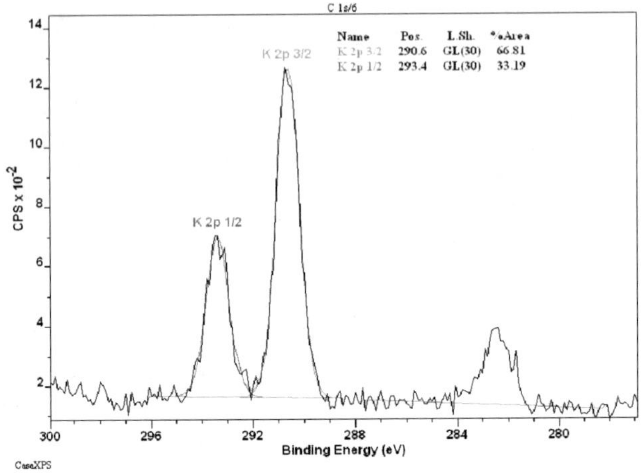

photon energy = kinetic energy + binding energy + (work function +sample bias)

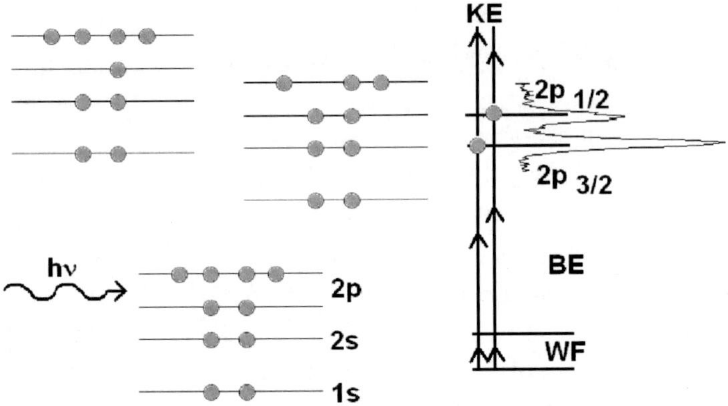

Calibration of Binding Energy Scale for Narrow Scan Spectra

The basic equation for the photoelectric effect modified for XPS includes terms which explain the reason peaks appear at energies different from values reported in the literature. The sample, when placed in the vacuum chamber of an XPS instrument is either electrically connected to the instrument, or electrically isolated and therefore allowed to change potential relative to ground. In either case, the electrons emitted from the surface must overcome a potential barrier to enter the vacuum. The measured position of the peak, as a result, is not absolute but relative to the energy required by an electron to break free of the sample surface. To position the XPS peaks with respect to a binding energy scale, the calibration procedure involves a simple shift in energy. For sets of narrow scan spectra, the assumption usually employed is all data acquired under the same sample charge state are calibrated by applying the same energy shift to each narrow scan spectrum. The shift is typically determined using the position of a know peak and applied to the appropriate set of spectra.

Energy calibration for sets of narrow scan spectra are performed using the same mechanism used to calibrate a survey spectrum; the only difference is the shift calculated for one spectrum is applied to others in the VAMAS file. The spectrum for which a peak position is known is displayed in the active tile. The Calibration property page on the Spectrum Processing dialog window again provides the means of applying the energy shift based on the selection in the right-hand pane of the experiment frame.

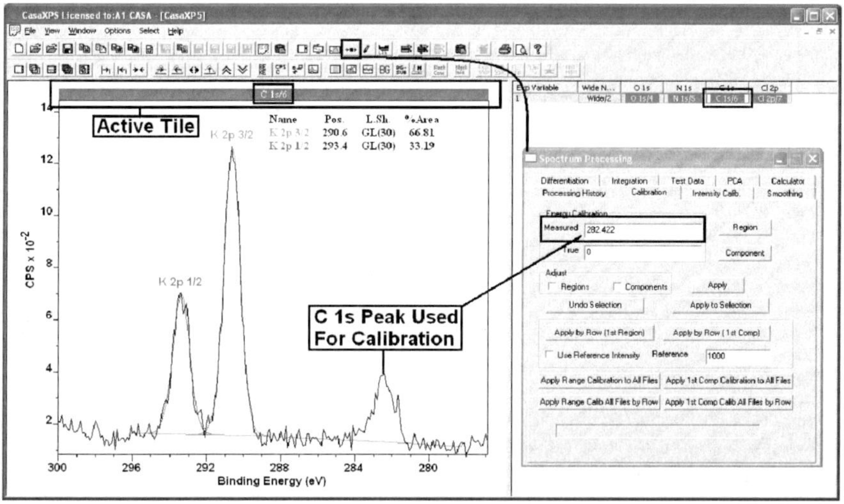

The expected value for the C 1s peak is entered in the True field on the Calibration property page and a selection in the right-hand pane of all VAMAS blocks for which the sample bias experienced during the acquisition of the C 1s peak also applies. For the KCl sample, the O 1s, N 1s and Cl 2p narrow scans are selected in addition to the C 1s VAMAS block.

One further consideration is the action associated with the regions and components already defined on the data. When the energy shift is applied to the spectra, the regions and components may or may not be shifted also. Since the regions and components are placed on the data prior to calibration of the energy scale, it is appropriate to shift both the regions and components. Tick-boxes on the Calibration property page control these shifts associated with the regions and components. On pressing the Apply to Selection button with the tick-boxes as shown below results in the peaks, the regions and the components defined on the K 2p doublet all moved by the same offset in energy as the spectrum. The energy shift calculated from the C 1s peak is also applied to the selected O 1s, N 1s and Cl 2p VAMAS blocks.

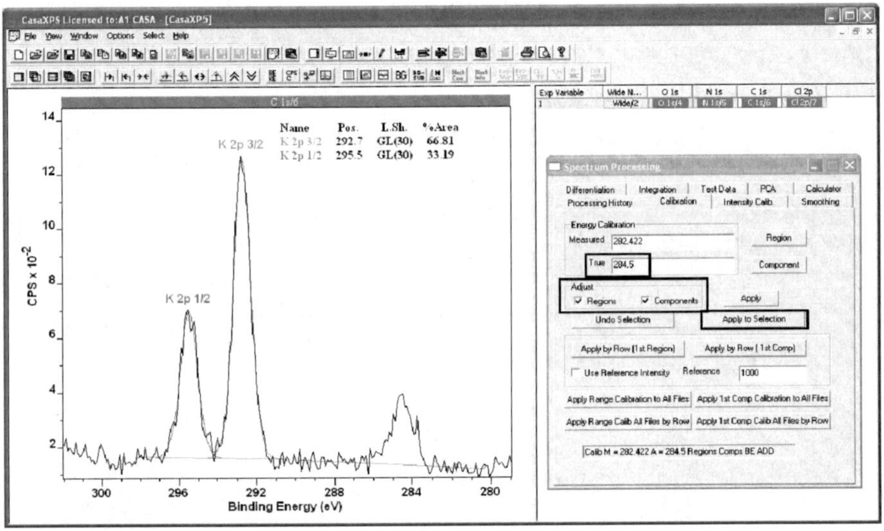

The use of the Adjust Regions and Components tick boxes for individual files is almost always appropriate.

The circumstance in which the regions and component may not need shifting with the data arises if regions are propagated to the data from another source file from which the calibration used to create the regions would not be appropriate. If the Region and Component tick-boxes are left un-ticked, the data can be made to move into line with the propagated regions.

The Measured energy used to specify the energy shift can be obtained from several sources. The most direct is via the cursor and the mouse left-hand button. A position in the left-hand pane indicated by the cursor when the mouse button is pressed is loaded into the Measured text-field. Alternatives to the interactive method include using a region defined on the data prior to calibration.

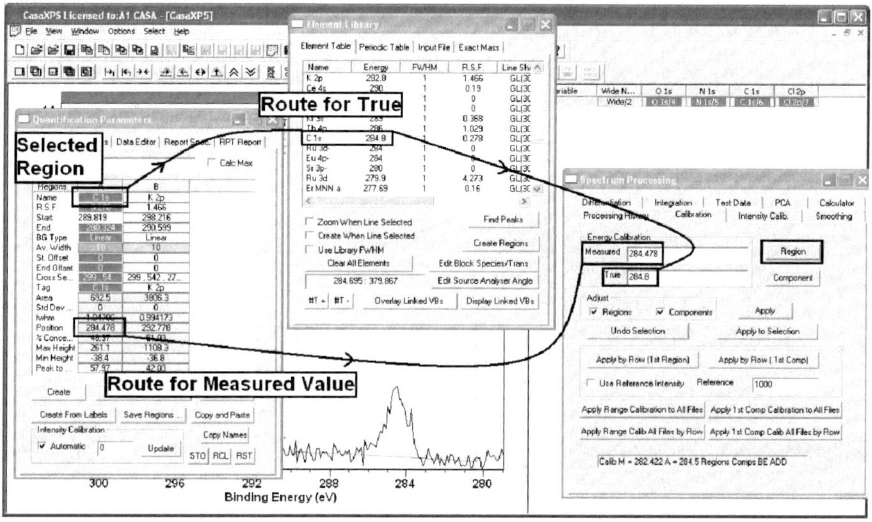

The procedure involves the Regions property page on the Quantification Parameters dialog window, the element library and the Region button on the Calibration property page. The Element Library dialog window is not required for the procedure; nevertheless the name field in the selected region on the Regions property page, if specified to match an entry in the element library, causes the energy from the element library to update the True text-field. When the Region button on the Calibration property page is pressed, the position for the largest peak in the selected region on the Regions property page is entered for the Measured energy and provided the name field for the region matches an element library entry, the True field is also updated at the same time. Once these text-fields are specified, the calibration of the data proceeds as described above.

Often the energy calibration is dependent on the position of a component in a peak model. For example the C 1s peak expected to be positioned at 284.8 eV, say, is not found in isolation and therefore to identify an accurate position of the peak a three component model is required. Once such a model is created for a piece of data, the calibration procedure equivalent to the one based on a region can be performed now based on a component rather than a region. The Components property page offers a means of selecting a component. When a component is selected and the Component button on the Calibration property page is pressed, the Measured and True values are again updated based on the position of the selected component and the element library entry matching the name field for the selected component.

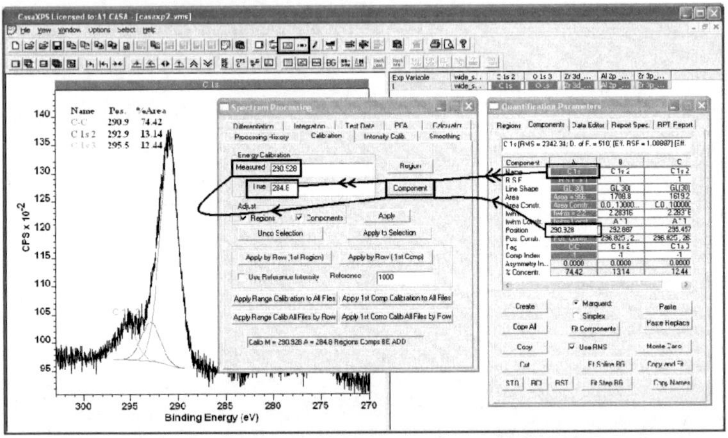

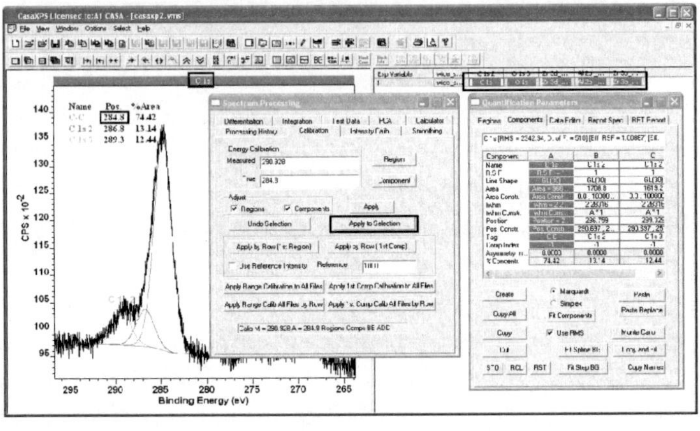

Once again, the selected VAMAS blocks are all calibrated with respect to the chosen component. Making an appropriate selection in the right-hand pane prior to pressing the Apply to Selection button on the Calibration property page allows a set of related spectra to be calibrated in one action. The Processing History property page is used to confirm the calibration for each VAMAS block is as intended.

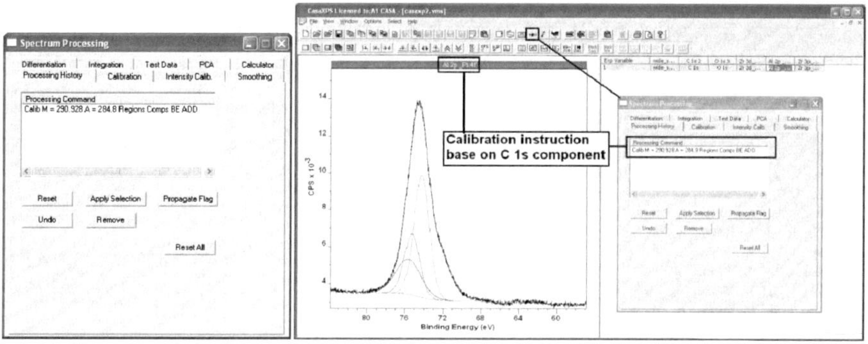

The Calibration property page includes options for use with sets of spectra from differing sample potentials. Such data requires a means of calculating the appropriate shift for each charge state. These features will be described elsewhere.

Quantification of Narrow Scan Spectra based on Regions

The discussion so far regarding the KCl spectra is focused on energy calibration and defining regions. The objective in preparing the data is to create a quantification report capable of expressing the essential characteristic of the XPS data. Samples are compared based on these quantification tables.

Quantification of narrow scan spectra is performed using the Report Spec property page on the Quantification Parameters dialog window.

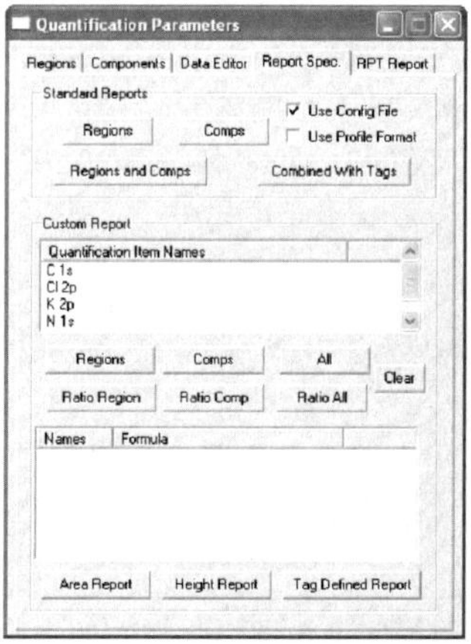

The buttons on the Report Spec property page act on the data selected in the right-hand pane of the experiment frame. The key to successfully quantifying narrow scan spectra is ensuring the VAMAS blocks containing the data from the same experiment appear in the same row in the right-hand pane.

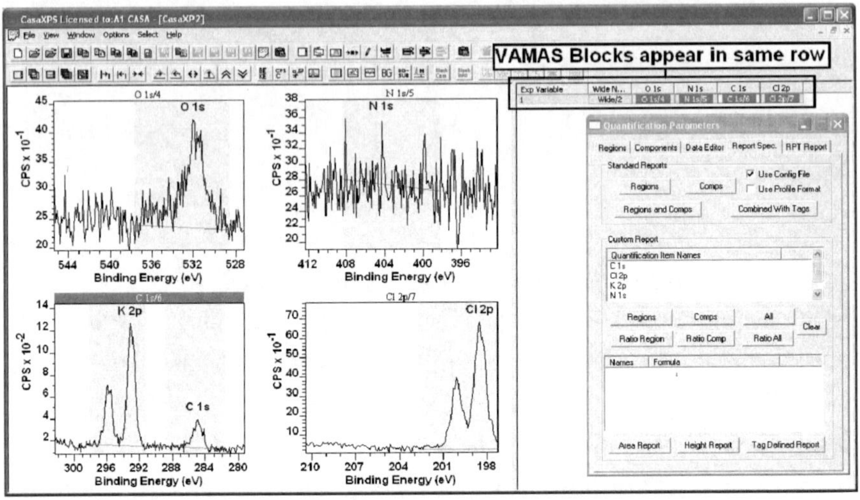

VAMAS files generated from modern instrumentation typically appear with the correct VAMAS field assignments to ensure the data are aligned as required in the right-hand pane. In the event the data blocks do not appear in the same row, options in CasaXPS permit the re-organisation of the VAMAS blocks. Organising the VAMAS blocks in the right-hand pane involves assigning the same experimental variable to each VAMAS block involved in the quantification and, by adjusting the species/transition fields for each spectrum the blocks are arranged in the right-hand pane in separate columns. Several options are available to aid the organisation of the VAMAS blocks in the right-hand pane. These will be addressed in a separate section of the manual.

A typical quantification table is generated using the Standard Report options on the Report Spec property page.

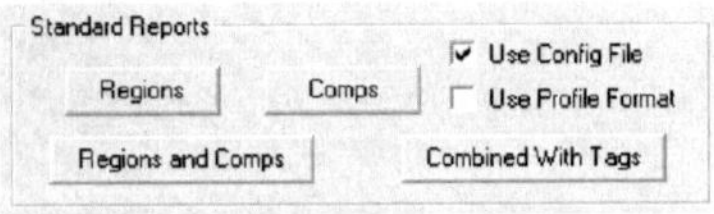

To generate a standard report from a set of narrow scan spectra:

1. Define regions for each peak used in the quantification of the sample.
2. Select the VAMAS blocks in the right-hand pane.

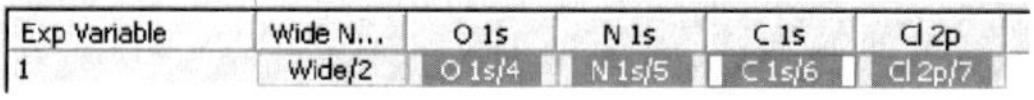

3. Invoke the Quantification Parameters dialog window and select the Report Spec property page.

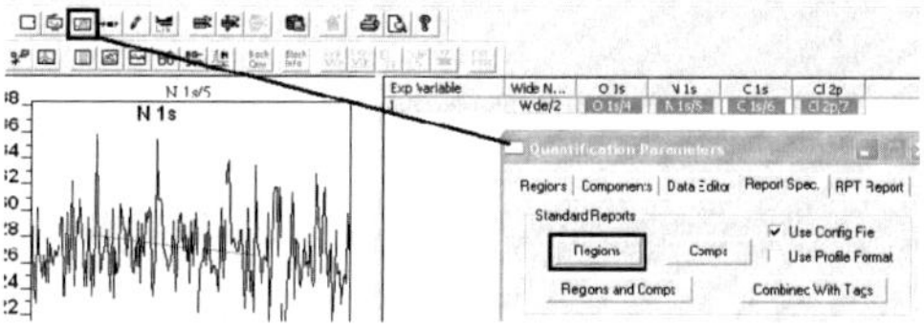

4. Press the Regions button in the Standard Report section.

Version 2.3.15 of CasaXPS includes a new option for choosing from a range of configuration files defining the format for the standard report. If a directory named QuantTables exists in the CasaXPS.DEF directory, a list of files from that directory is offered in a dialog window.

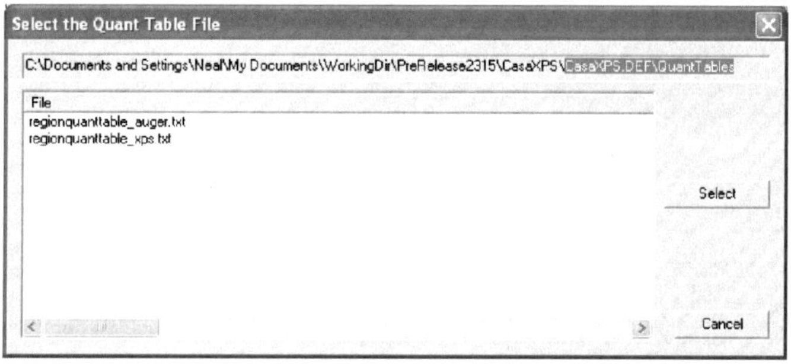

If the QuantTables directory does not exist, the previous RegionQuantTable.txt file located in the CasaXPS.DEF directory is used to format the text report.

A configuration file specified by either method is used only when the Use Config File tick-box is ticked.

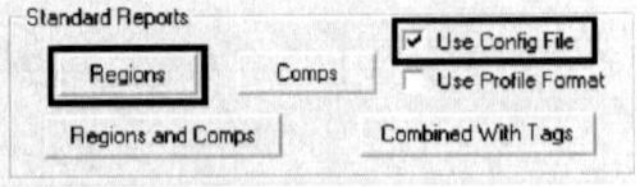

The consequence of selecting the Regions button from the Standard Report section is a new window appears showing the quantification table within CasaXPS.

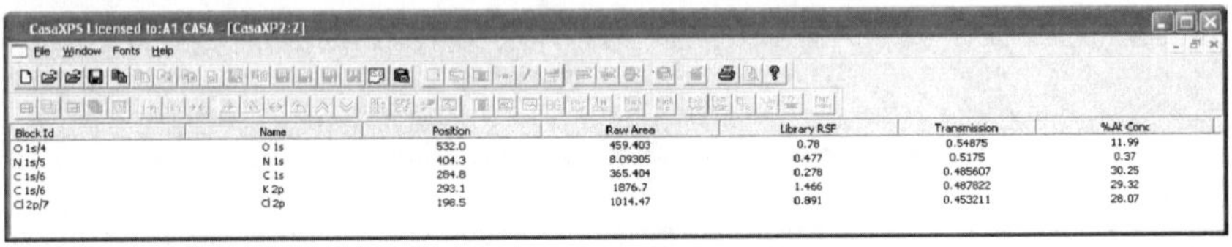

The data displayed in the quantification report may be printed as text:

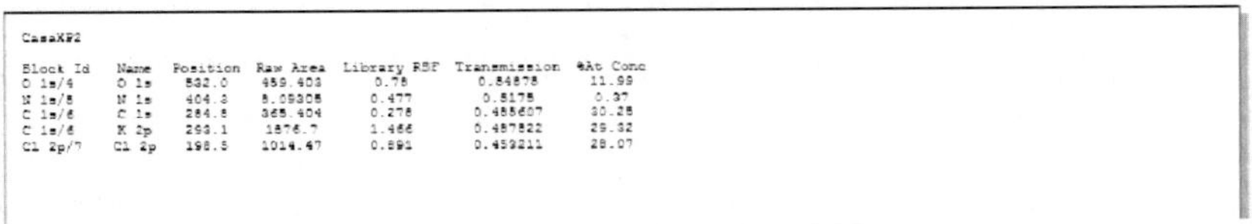
CasaXP2

Block Id	Name	Position	Raw Area	Library RSF	Transmission	%At Conc
O 1s/4	O 1s	532.0	459.403	0.78	0.54875	11.99
N 1s/5	N 1s	404.3	8.09305	0.477	0.5175	0.37
C 1s/6	C 1s	284.8	365.404	0.278	0.485607	30.25
C 1s/6	K 2p	293.1	1876.7	1.466	0.487822	29.32
Cl 2p/7	Cl 2p	198.5	1014.47	0.891	0.453211	28.07

Or the text report placed on the clipboard: 

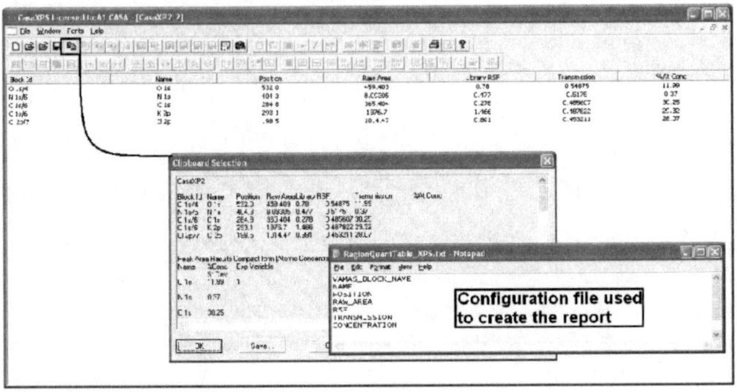

Creating a Peak Model

Quantification is also possible based on intensities measured using synthetic peak shapes. Examples of peak models have already been used to illustrate points relating to quantification regions, but a discussion relating to the creation of these peak models was deferred until now.

To begin with, the case of doublet peaks serves to illustrate how information about peaks can be used to construct a peak model. Consider a narrow scan spectrum measured over a doublet pair from the Cr 2p transition.

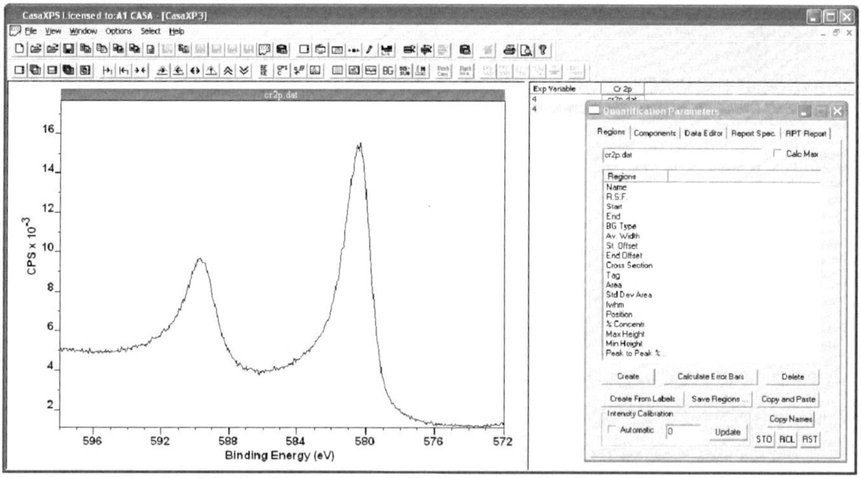

Doublet peaks represent a transition from the initial state for an atom to a final state, where the final state is split by spin-orbit interactions due to the unpaired electron in the p sub-shell. The combination of angular moment for the electrons in the final state produces two excitation paths to near identical states in the proportion 2:1 for the emission of an electron with p symmetry. To be explicit, states with total angular moment 1/2 are half as common as states with total angular moment 3/2. Further, the energy difference caused by the spin-orbit interaction is characteristic of a chemical state for the chromium. Doublet peaks can therefore be modelled using parametric constraints for both peak area and relative position. Chromium also illustrates a feature of metallic XPS peaks, namely the peaks exhibit pronounced asymmetry.

To construct a peak model, the first step is to create a background on top of which the synthetic component peaks are located.

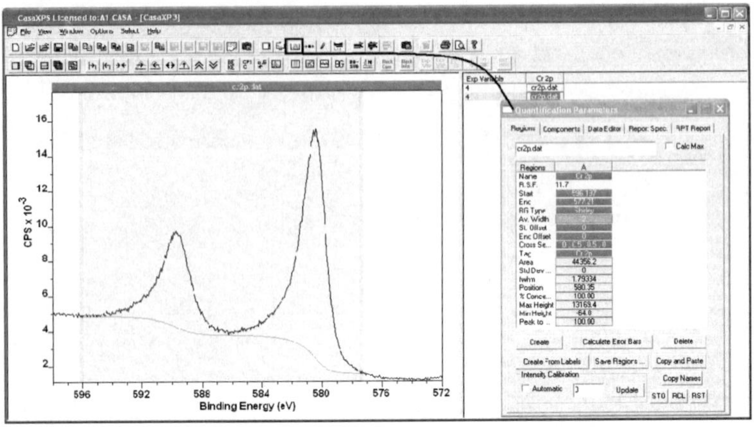

For the particular data in this example a Shirley background type is used to span both peaks in the Cr 2p doublet pair. An Av Width set to two helps to stabilise the background shape with respect to noise in the data. Just as with quantification based on regions alone, a well defined background significantly improves the precision for the calculation of peak intensities measured with synthetic peaks.

The Components property page on the Quantification Parameters dialog window provides tools for creating component peaks.

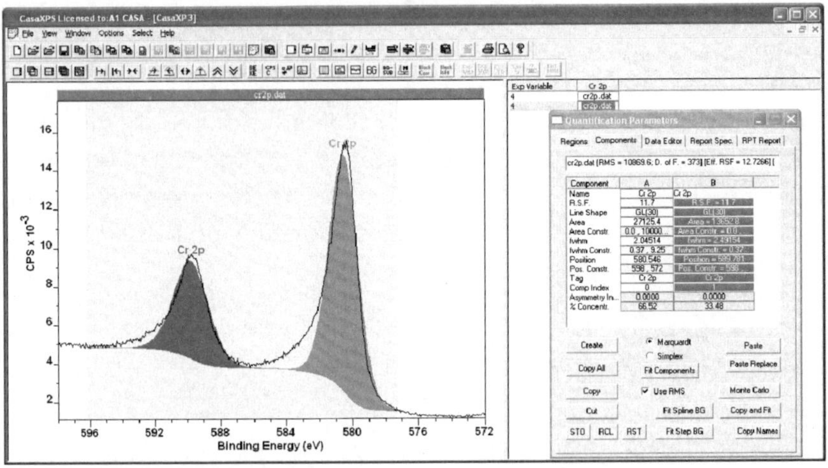

The VAMAS block in the example is assigned the correct species/transition fields for the doublet pair, namely, Cr and 2p respectively. Since these species/transition strings match an entry in the current element library for the transition Cr 2p, pressing the Create button twice on the Components property page causes two Gaussian-Lorentzian peaks to be added on the display with the appropriate RSF and lineshape as defined by the element library. The Components property page displays each component as a column of parameters specifying the position, peak area and FWHM.

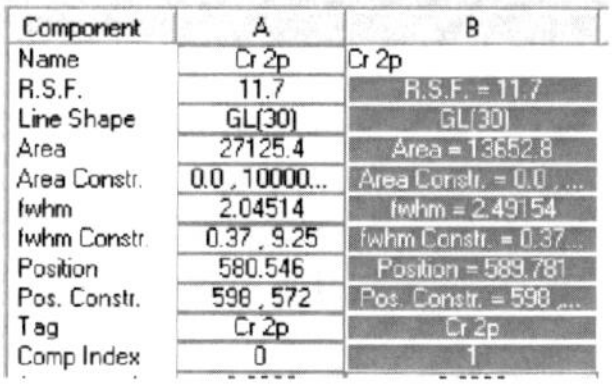

These three parameters are optimised by pressing the Fit Components button.

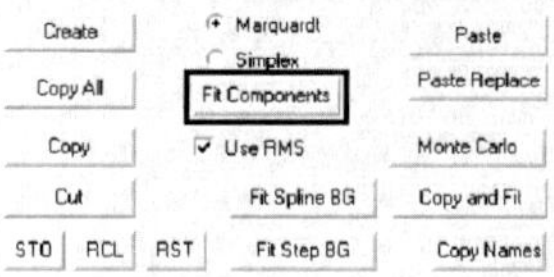

The key to obtaining a good peak model is restricting these optimised parameters to ensure the least squares criterion returns a physically meaningful solution. For a 2p doublet-pair, a physically meaningful solution involves ensuring the ratio of the peak areas is 2:1. Parameter constraints are initially specified in the form of an interval:

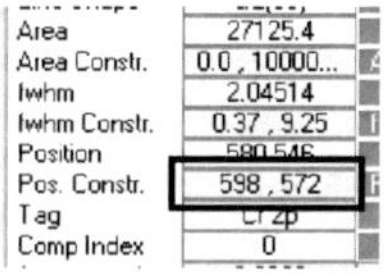

Alternatively the constraints can be specified as a relationship between the corresponding parameter in a different component. Each component appears on the Components property page as a column and each column is headed by a button labelled alphabetically.

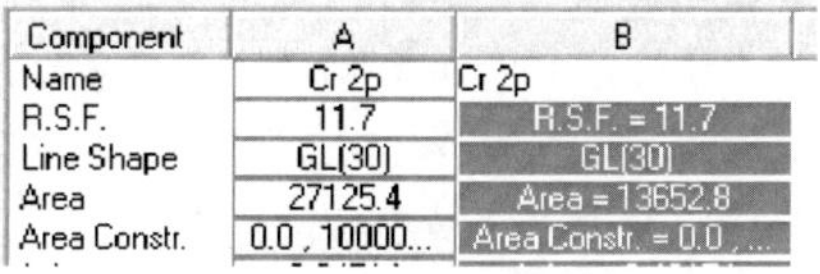

Maintaining the area relationship for the Cr 2p doublet involves entering an area constraint using the alphabetical character above the column of component parameters. To ensure the peak area for the component in column B is half the peak area of the component in column A, the Area Constr. field in column A is changed to **B * 2**.

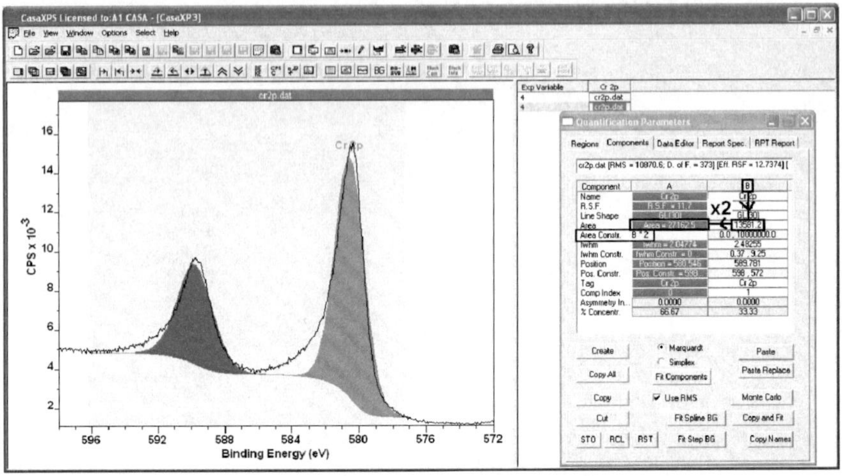

Similarly, if the offset in energy between the doublet peaks is known, the position constraint can be used to enforce the correct energy separation of the peaks.

Component	A	B
Name	Cr 2p	Cr 2p
R.S.F.	11.7	R.S.F. = 11.7
Line Shape	GL(30)	GL(30)
Area	27162.5	Area = 13581.2
Area Constr.	B * 2	Area Constr. = 0.0 ...
fwhm	2.04774	fwhm = 2.48255
fwhm Constr.	0.37 , 9.25	fwhm Constr. = 0.37..
Position	580.546	Position = 589.781
Pos. Constr.	598 , 572	A + 9.2348
Tag	Cr 2p	Cr 2p

The most important input to a peak model is the lineshape. The Cr 2p exhibits asymmetry in the peak shapes thus a Gaussian-Lorentzian lineshape will struggle to model the data envelope. Introducing an asymmetric lineshape provides a means of modelling the data more precisely, however in doing so introduces an uncertainty into the peak intensity calculation. These issues are dealt with in detail elsewhere (***Walton et al ISBN 978-0954953317***). It is important to understand that for any functional form which integrates to infinite, the peak intensity is dependent on the parameters used to specify the lineshape and therefore most asymmetric lineshape when used to measure intensities require calibration.

Gaussian-Lorentzian lineshapes do integrate to finite area, hence the practice of modelling data using blends of these two functional forms. Nevertheless, for peaks such as the Cr 2p doublet, modelling a pair of peaks using Gaussian-Lorentzian lineshapes produces a far from satisfactory approximation to the data envelope. To accommodate asymmetric peak shapes whilst retaining a functional form with finite area, two Lorentzian based lineshapes introduced in version 2.3.14 and extended in version 2.3.15 of CasaXPS offer a means of modelling peaks such as the Cr 2p lines. The LA and LF lineshapes are described in detail elsewhere, but essentially use a Cauchy functional form raised to a power and convoluted with a Gaussian. Asymmetry is introduced by varying the value for the power across the maximum of the Cauchy function. The LF lineshape extends the LA lineshape by introducing a damping parameter which limits the extent over which the asymmetry extends, but in every other respect the two lineshapes are the same.

The Lorentzian lineshape with FWHM *f* and position (in kinetic energy) *e* is given by

$$L(x\!: f, e) = \frac{1}{1 + 4\left(\frac{x-e}{f}\right)^2}$$

The basis for both the LA and LF lineshapes is

$$LA(x\!: \alpha, \beta, f, e) = \begin{cases} [L(x\!: f, e)]^{\alpha} & x \le e \\ [L(x\!: f, e)]^{\beta} & x > e \end{cases}$$

The lineshape parameter entered on the Components property page for the asymmetric Lorentzian is LA(α, β, *m*), where *m* is an integer between 0 and 499 defining the width of the Gaussian used to convolute the *LA* functional form.

LF(α, β, *w*, *m*) is identical to the LA lineshape with the exception that the specified values of α and β are force to increase to a constant value via a smooth function determined by the width parameter *w*.

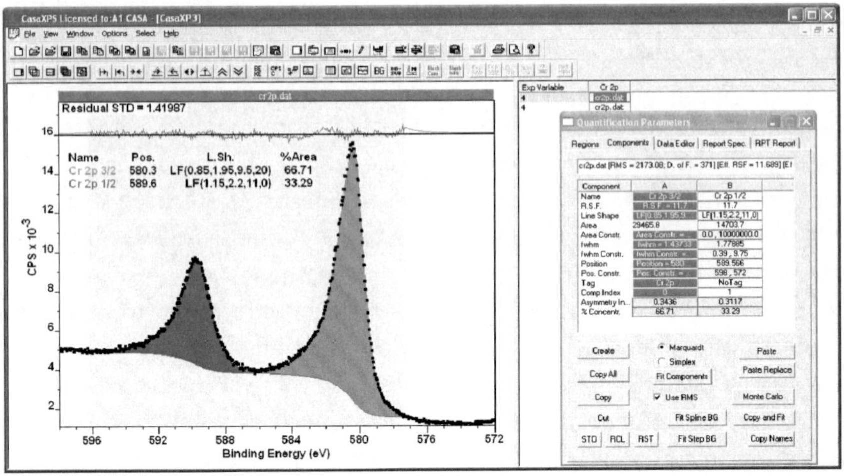

Note that for a model based on the LF lineshape, the relative intensities for the Cr 2p doublet pair are achieved without constraints. There is an element of luck in achieving the expected ratio for the peaks in a doublet pair. The principal reason being the uncertainty associated with the background type used to approximate the scattered electrons. It is difficult to claim any practical background type generates the correct background and since the background also has an influence on the lineshapes the apparent agreement with the theoretical ratio is somewhat fortuitous. Scofield cross-sections calculated for the Cr 2p doublet peaks for photons of energy 1486.6 eV suggest the ratio should be 1.93:1. Since the doublets represent electronic states with slightly different energy, and therefore different eigen-value and wave function, the calculated intensity ratio may well differ from the 2:1 ratio determined by simply counting total angular momentum states using the expression 2j+1.

The Cr 2p spectrum represents a relatively simple example of a peak model. The data suggests two asymmetric peaks are required, although there are no guarantees more peaks are not involved in the construction of the data, but the very least that can be said is that the data envelope alone does not support the use of more than two peaks in the peak model. In is however reasonably common to find complex data envelopes for which peak models are constructed. A spectrum for CeO_2 is interpreted using five doublet pairs for the Ce 3d transition.

V. Matolín, M. Cabala, V. Cháb, I. Matolínová, K. C. Prince, M. Škoda, F. Šutara, T. Skála and K. Veltruská, A resonant photoelectron spectroscopy study of Sn(Ox) doped CeO2 catalysts, Surf. Interface Anal. 40 (2008) 225–230.

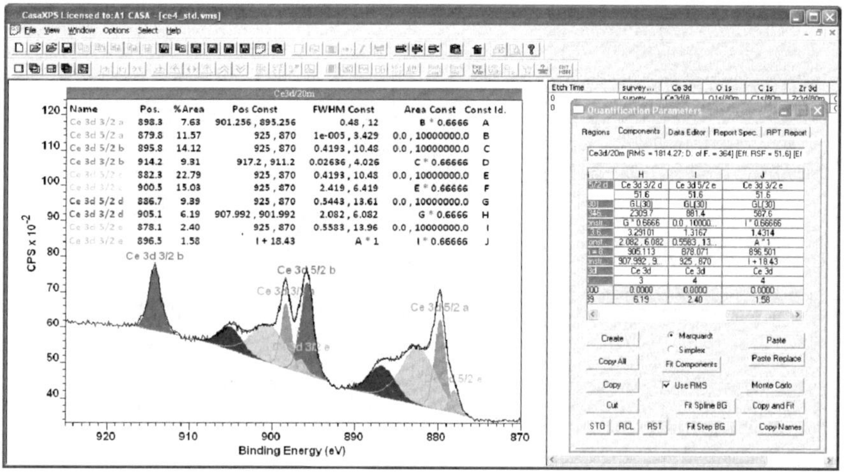

The constraints used to interpret the Ce 3d spectrum are listed using the Components property page of the Annotation dialog window. 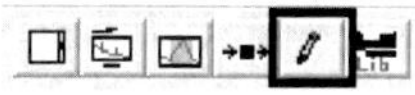

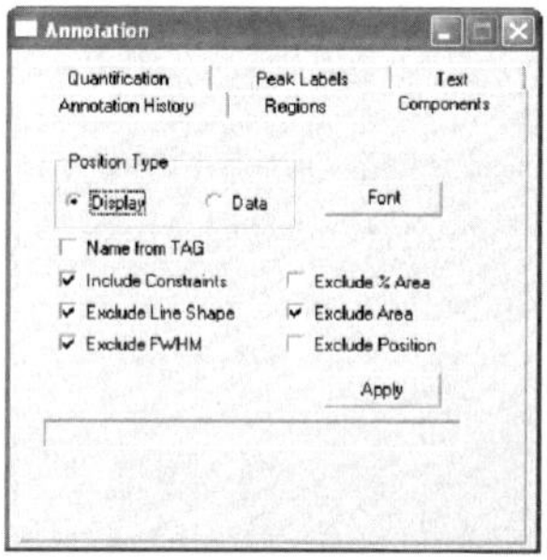

Doublet peaks resulting from the emission of a d-orbital appear with intensities in the ratio 2(3/2)+1:2(5/2)+1 or 2:3. Without these constraints, a peak model for data such as these would fail to obtain a physically meaningful description based on ten synthetic peaks optimised in a least squares sense. Even with constraints applied to the fitting parameters, without corroboration from other sources, a peak model based solely on data such as these can lead to problems. The model developed for CeO_2 based on one spectrum when applied to data acquired from a different sample from a different instrument tests the generality of the model:

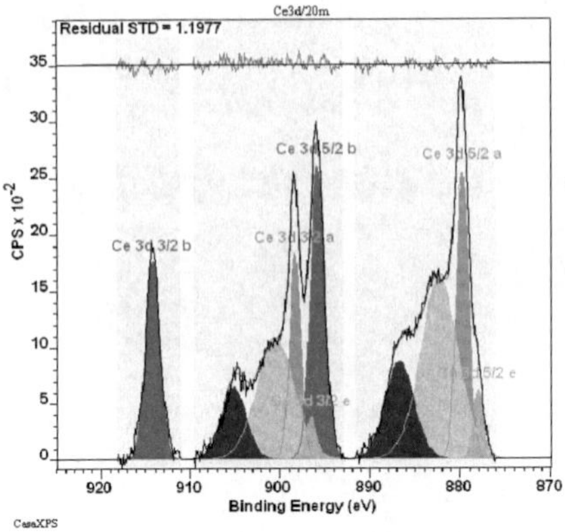

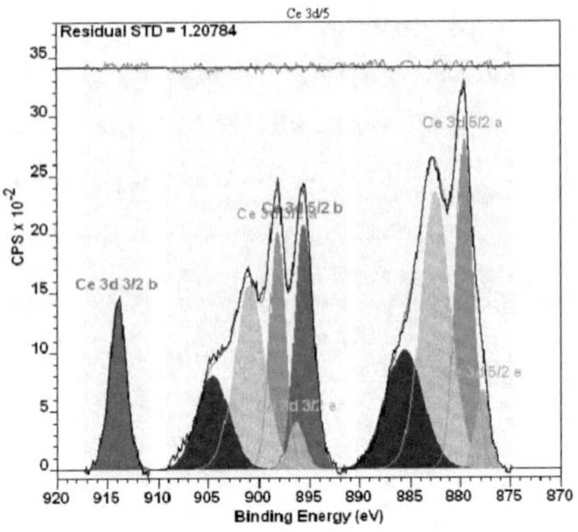

Successfully constructing a peak model relies on iteratively building peaks with constraints until a stable model satisfies the data envelope and the physical context for the data. A good place to start is in the literature. A series of publications provide background to the use of doublet pairs in the CeO_2 model:

V. Matolín et al. Surface and Interface Analysis. 40 (2008) 225–230.
J.P. Holgado et al. Applied Surface Science 161 (2000) 301–315
L. Cossarutto et al. Applied Surface Science 126 (1998) 352–355
Yu.A. Teterin et al. Journal of Electron Spectroscopy and Related Phenomena 88-91 (1998) 275-279
M. Romeo et al. Surface and Interface Analysis,. 20, (1993) 508-512

The first step requires the specification of the background to the peaks. The survey spectrum for the CeO_2 sample illustrates clearly the problems associated with the background selection.

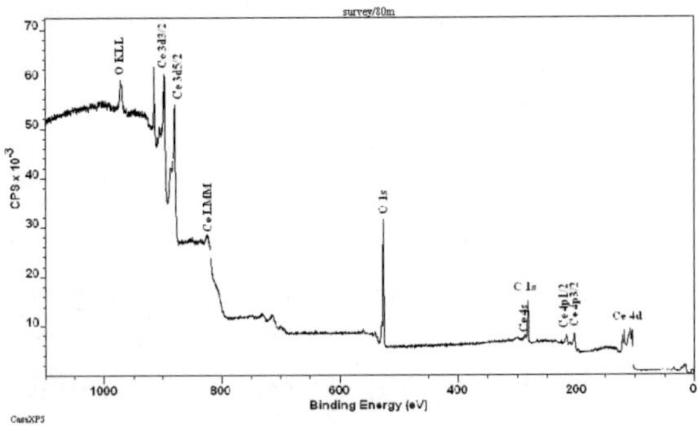

The step in the background is complicated by the multiple peaks associated with the Ce 3d transition. A Shirley background is often the choice made in the literature, however for peak envelopes such as Ce 3d, the multiple overlapping peaks means that the definition of a Shirley background is not unique. The Shirley algorithm is only truly defined for a single peak. When more than one peak contributes to the data shape the number of ways the Shirley algorithm can be interpreted is large. CasaXPS actually includes several variations on a theme for calculating a Shirley background. Since the Shirley background has no inherent theoretical basis and the implementation is uncertain, for the current example a simple linear background applied to three regions provides an understandable and repeatable means of removing a background contribution from the data.

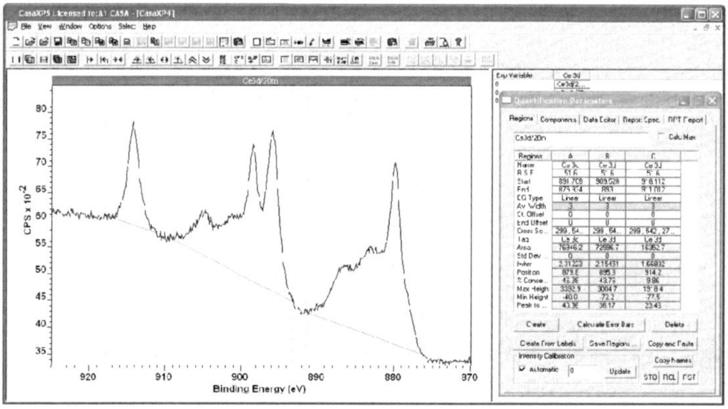

The first peak created using the Components property page is placed on the data at a position to reduce the largest variation in the data. If the Components property page is top-most on the Quantification Parameters dialog window, the newly created peak can be moved to a new position under mouse control. Place the cursor at the peak maximum and drag the cursor to a new position.

Point at the peak max:

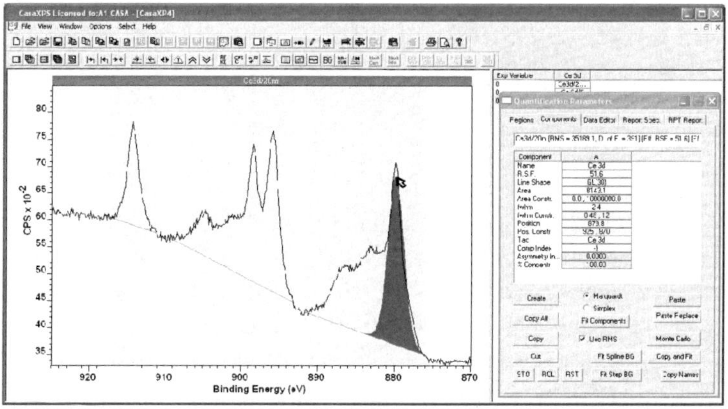

Drag the cursor by holding down the left-mouse button:

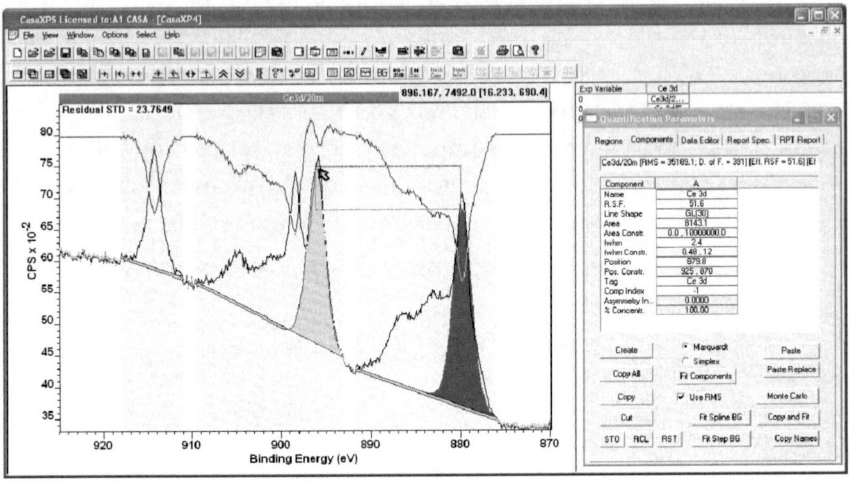

The peak position changes to the new position once the left-mouse button is released:

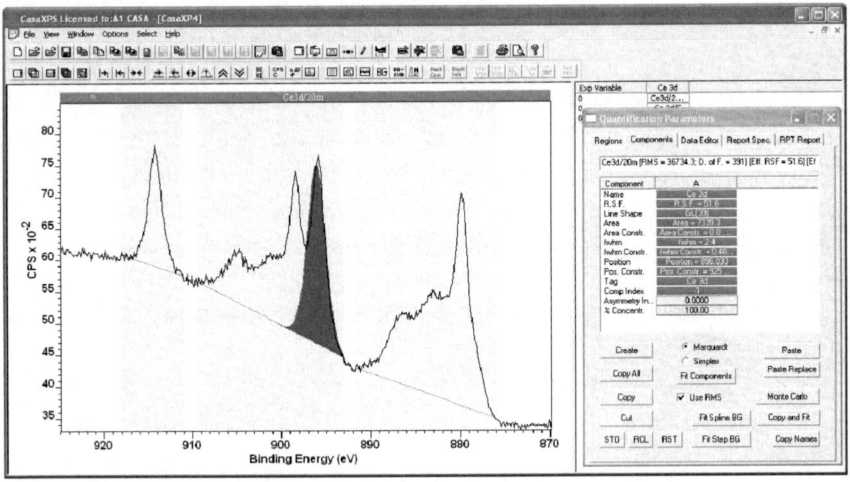

Both the peak position and peak height are adjusted by placing the cursor at the top of the synthetic peak. Similarly, placing the cursor at the side of the peak, about half way down, causes the FWHM and height to adjust under mouse control. If the Shift keyboard key is also held down during the drag action, only the FWHM changes. Note that if the FWHM changes without the height also adjusting, the peak area will alter from the initial value. Without the Shift key modification to the drag action, the FWHM and height adjust to ensure the peak area is maintained unchanged.

Place the cursor at the side of the peak and hold down the left-mouse button:

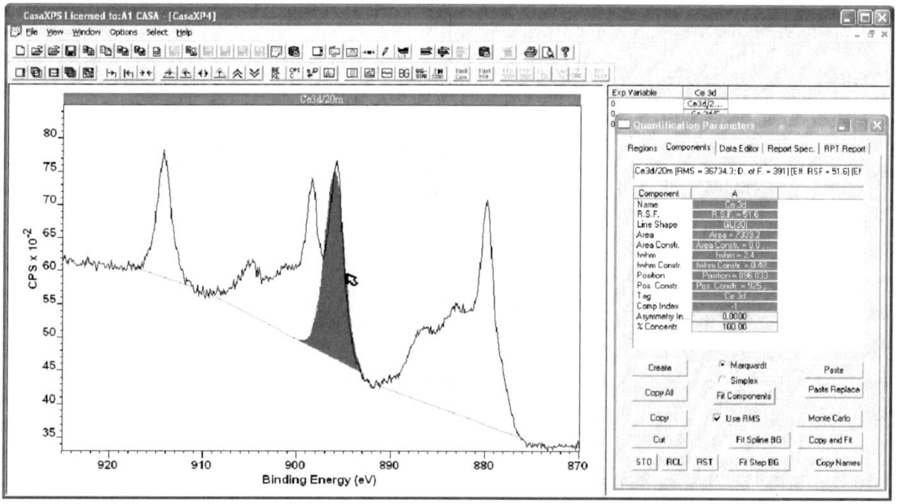

Drag the cursor to a new position. The height and FWHM adjust.

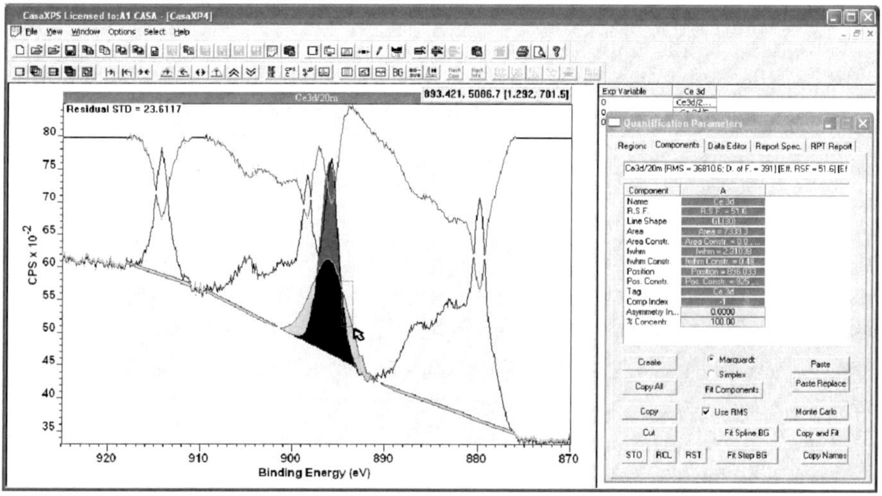

Release the left mouse button to update the FWHM and area parameters for the component:

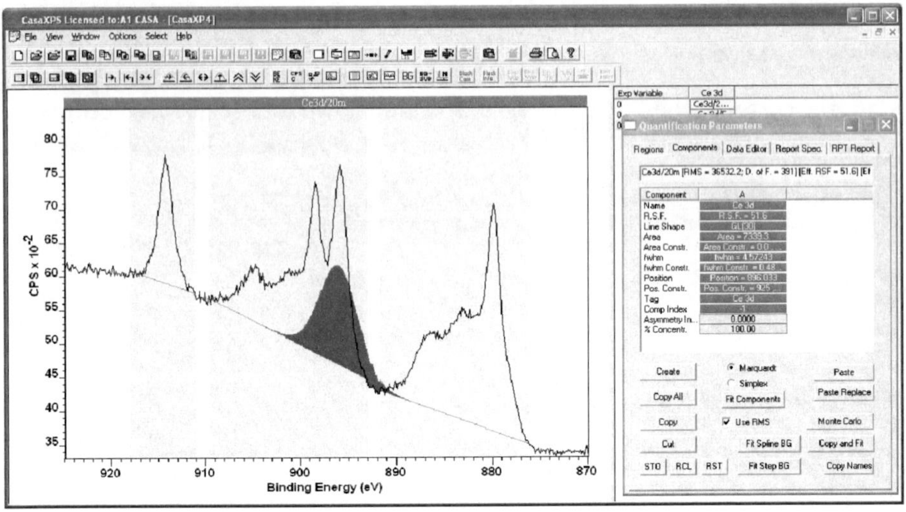

If the Shift keyboard key is held down during the drag operation, the height of the peak is unaltered by the drag action. Starting with the cursor at the side of the synthetic peak, hold down the Shift key and begin dragging the cursor to a new position using the left mouse button:

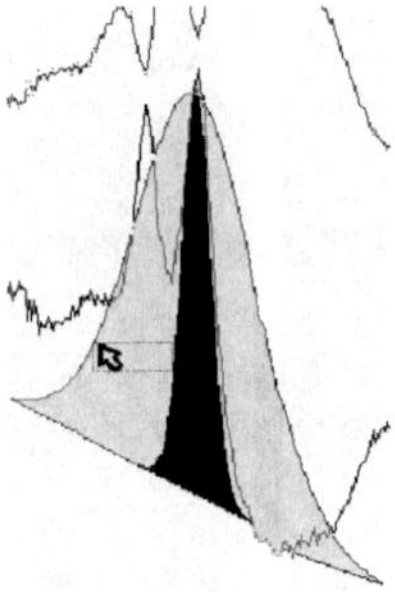

Doublet pairs resulting from electrons with d angular momentum are typically separated by characteristic energy differences. The structure for the Ce 3d envelope becomes clearer on observing the consistency of spacing for the four most prominent peaks. A feedback box appears when the cursor is dragged across the active tile. The values displayed during the drag process represent the position of the cursor in terms of energy and intensity, and the displacement for the cursor from the initial position of the cursor when the drag operation began. While these two doublet pairs for Ce 3d arise from different chemical states for cerium, the energy difference between the peaks for a given doublet pair should not deviate significantly.

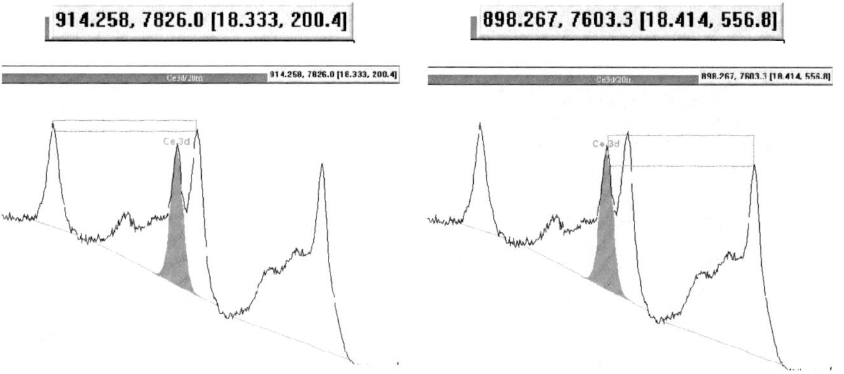

The pairing above guides the placement of the next peak created for the model.

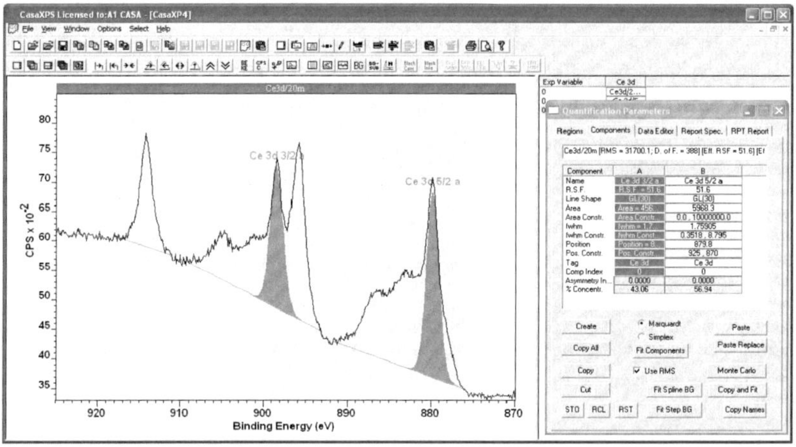

At this point in the construction of the peak model, the relationships between the peaks for a 3d doublet, when introduced in a rough manner, can help to add further doublet pairs to the data. The *2j+1* relationship for the relative peak intensities between peaks in a doublet pair suggests an area constraint in the proportion 3:2 is appropriate for the $3d_{5/2}$ and $3d_{3/2}$ components. Similarly, the current separation calculated from these initial positions for the two peaks provides a guide for peak separations for other pairs of doublet peaks. A position constraint computed from the current peak positions is introduced by entering the alphabetic character heading one component on the Components property page into the position constraint field for another component followed by pressing the enter key.

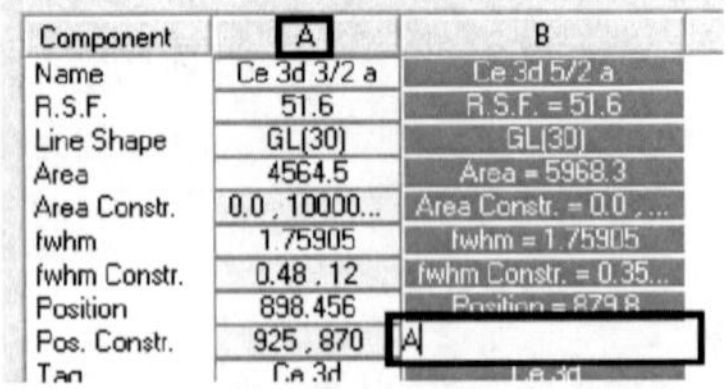

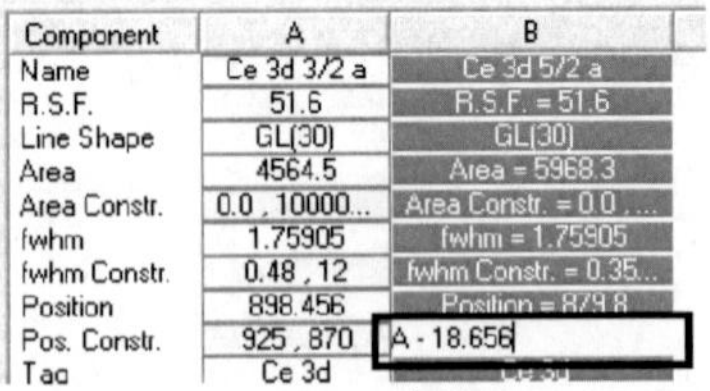

The format for a position constraint involves specifying a component using the alphabetic characters heading the columns of parameters displayed on the Components property page. An offset in energy between two peaks is specified by entering a character followed by the value for the offset. If no offset is entered with the character, the offset is calculated from the current positions for the two peaks involved. For the case of these two Ce 3d peaks, the positioning of the peaks is rough and therefore the offset is rough too. Nevertheless, since the peak model is expected to entail five doublet pairs, at this stage of building a peak model, the objective is to provide a means of copying and moving peaks in doublet pairs. To this end, an area constraint of the form A*1.5 entered into column B on the Component property page helps to link the doublet peaks further. These constraints, if required, can be released later in order to provide sufficient flexibility to fit the model to the data.

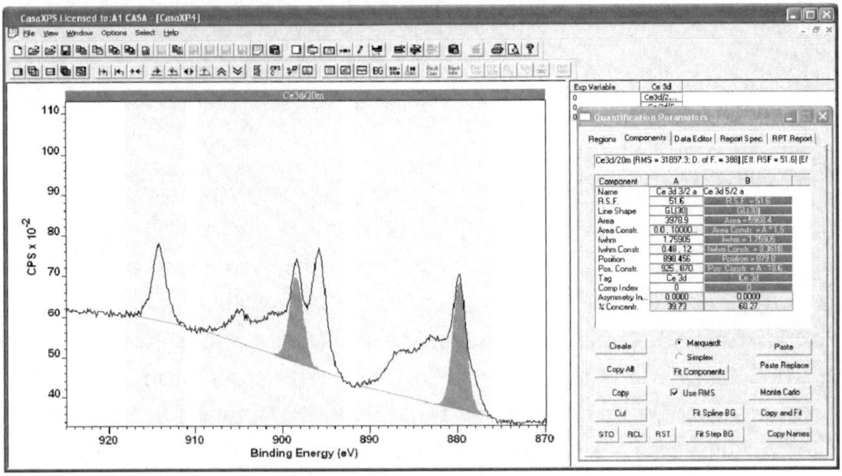

The advantage of applying these constraints is clear when the Copy button on the Components property page is followed by pressing the Paste button. The Copy button places a copy of the component currently selected on the Components property page onto an internal clipboard to CasaXPS. Also, any components linked to the selected component are also added to the clipboard. Any constraints linking the selected component to the additional components are maintained within the set of components copied to the clipboard. The result of pressing the Paste button is two components are added to the components for the data.

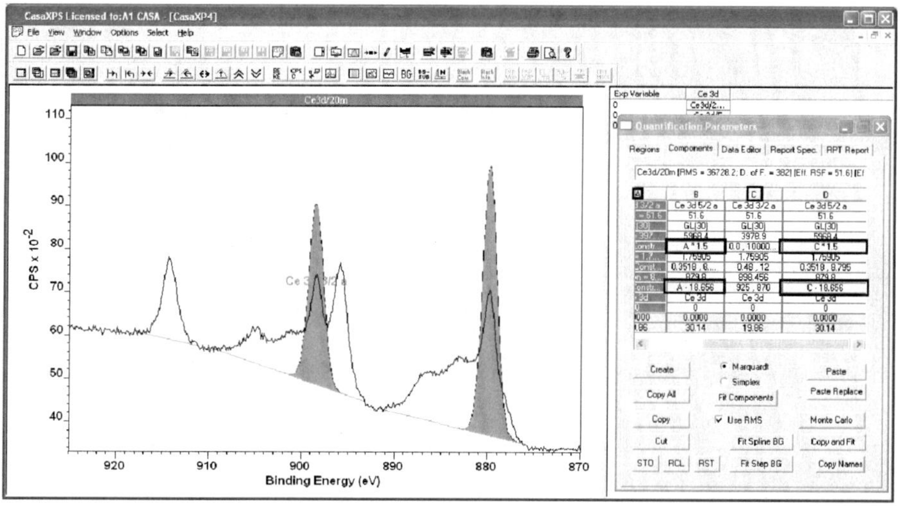

The new components are identical to the initial pair of components with the exception that the constraints relate to the new column characters. Using the cursor to point at the top of the controlling peak in a constrained pair of peaks causes both peaks to move as a unit.

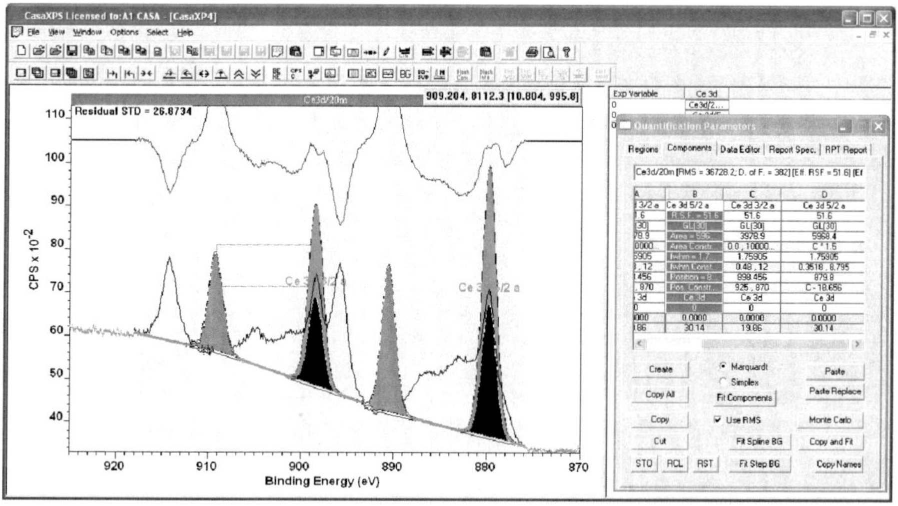

Since the initial doublet pair were defined in terms of both area and position constraints by referencing the 5/2 peak to the 3/2 peak, the controlling peak with respect to these constraints is the 3/2 peak.

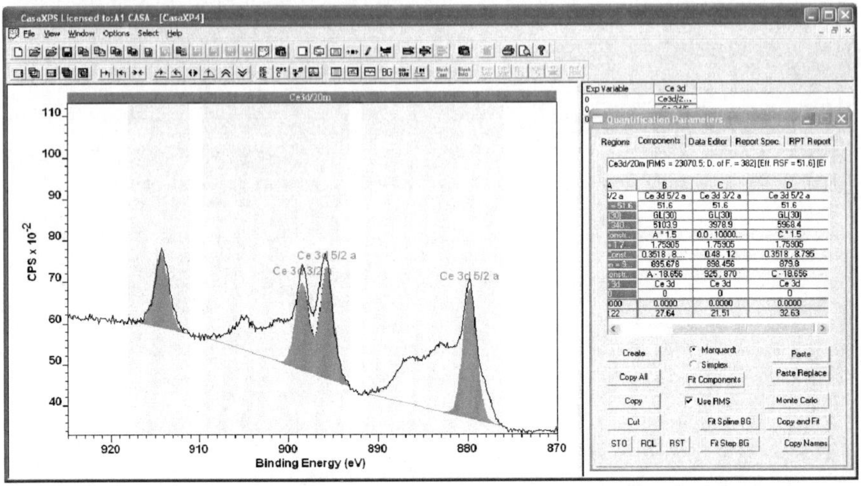

The display mode used for the components is currently set to colour the components using the Comp Index field as defined on the Components property page.

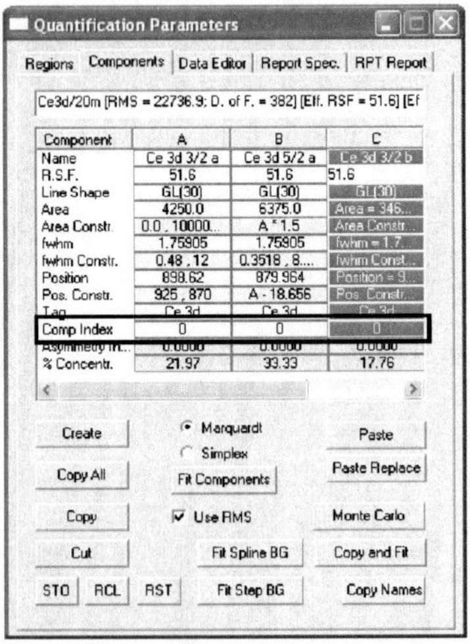

When a new component is created, the Comp Index field is set to -1. The values for the Comp Index are in the range 0 to 15 and correspond to the palette of colours used to display the components.

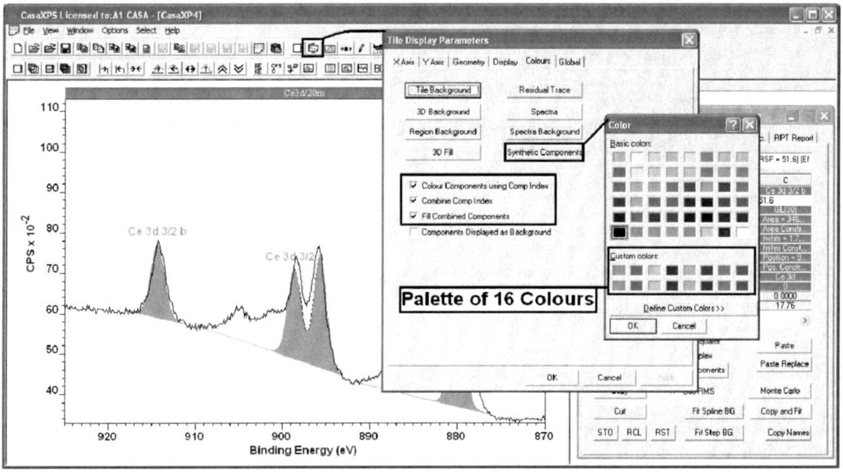

The initial pair of components prior to pressing the Copy button on the Components property page was assigned a Comp Index of 0 for each component. When pasted to create two new components, the Comp Index is retained as 0, hence all the peaks are filled with the same colour. Changing the Comp Index in the two new peaks to 1 illustrates both the difference between the two doublet pairs and also the connection between the peaks within a doublet pair.

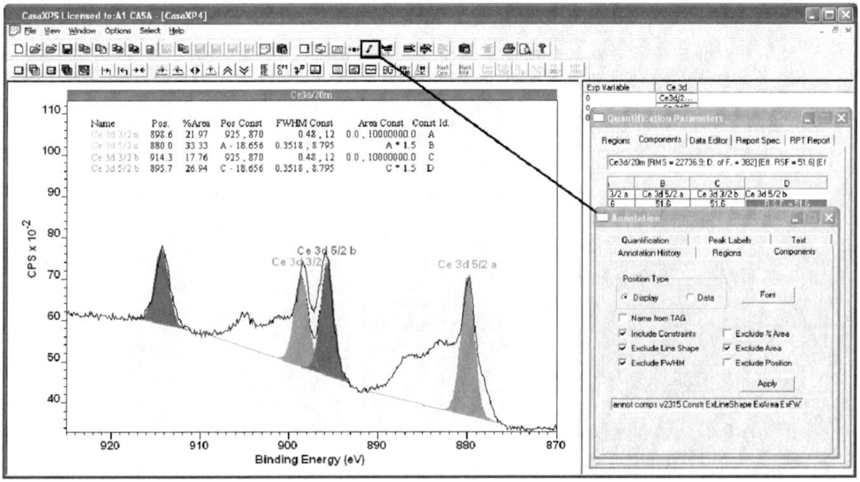

The components on the CasaXPS clipboard can be pasted three more times and each time moved to a new position appropriate for the five sets of doublets expected for the data envelope.

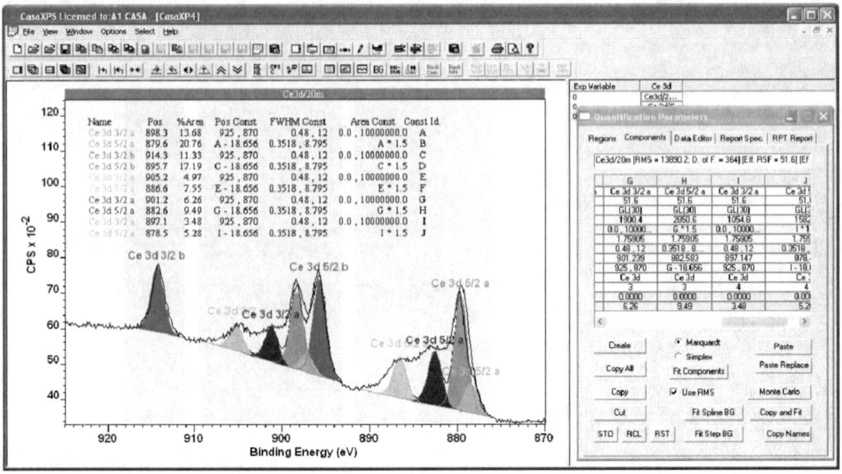

So far the peaks are located using the mouse only. No optimisation is performed at this stage in the modelling process. As the peak model stands, while the area constraints are reasonable, the position constraints are poorly defined. If the Fit Components button is pressed on the Components property page the results are disastrous.

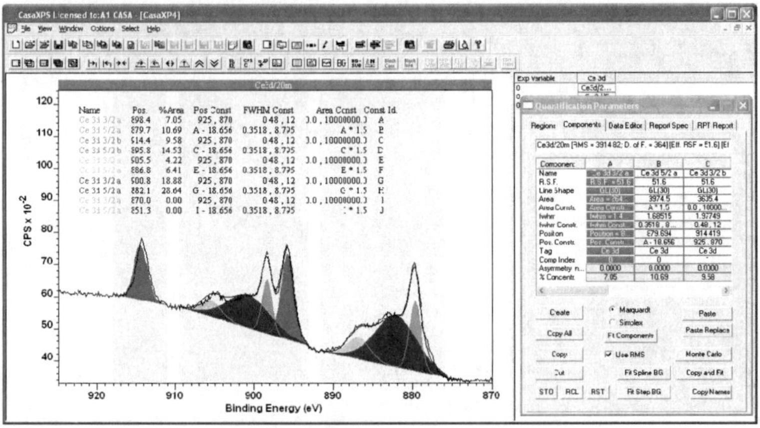

The positional constraints force the least squares optimisation to accommodate the data envelope with non-physical peak shapes in terms of FWHM, resulting in a zero area for one doublet pair. Fortunately all in not lost; the state of a peak model is saved to a list of peak models each time the Fit Components button is pressed. To recover the state prior to pressing the Fit Components button, press the RCL button at the bottom of the Components property page.

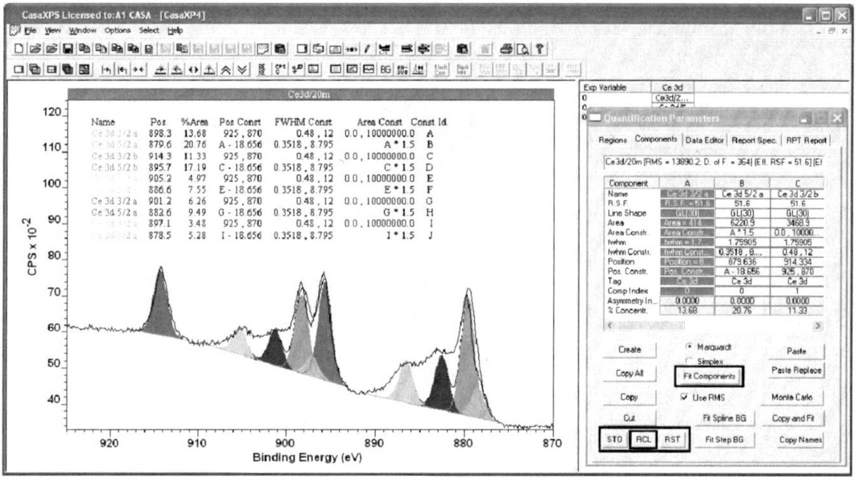

At any time during the modelling process, the STO button stores the current state of the peak model without performing an optimisation step. It is therefore possible to maintain a list of acceptable interim peak models, which can be returned to by pressing the RCL (recall) button. A third button RST (reset) clears the list of peak models.

The position constraints were the source for the poor optimisation step, therefore having returned the state of the peak model to an intermediate form, these position constraints can be adjusted to permit a better least squares solution. The simplest solution is to release the position constraints to allow the position parameters to vary independently during optimisation. A quick way to return a constraint to an interval about the current value is to enter into the constraint field the # character followed by a numerical value.

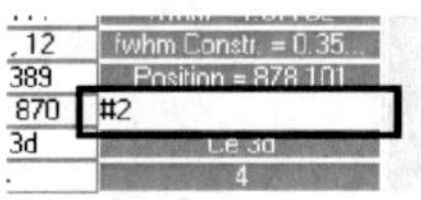

Optimisation of the peak parameters following releasing each position constraint using #2 results in a new least squares solution involving non-zero area values for all doublet pairs.

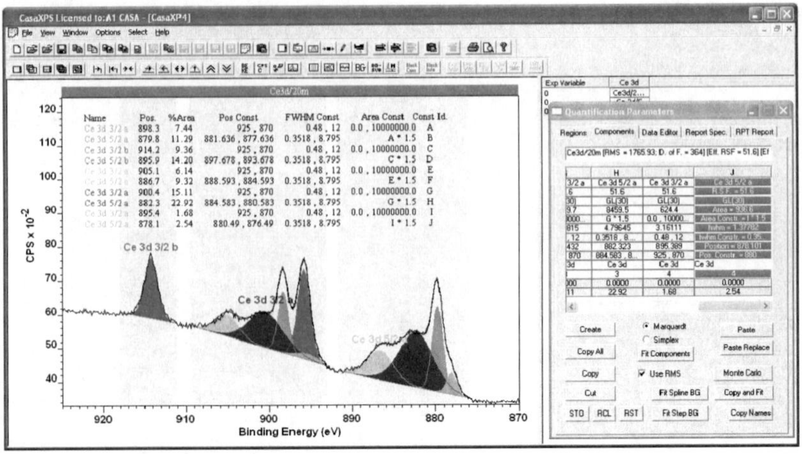

While the peak model looks more acceptable, one further anomaly can be rectified using the FWHM constraints. The set of doublet pairs are all characterised by FWHM in close agreement between the 3/2 and 5/2 components with the exception of the smallest doublet pair. Introducing constraints for the FWHM before refitting the data produces a more realistic solution.

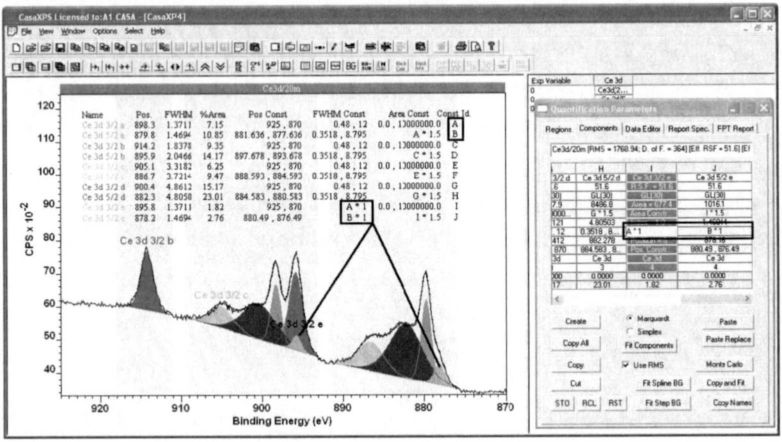

Exporting Peak Models in Graphical Form

Creating a report for a sample typically involves transferring the data to word processing software. The simplest way to transfer a peak model into another software package is via the clipboard. The graphical information can be placed on the clipboard as a bitmap of size explicitly defined via a dialog window. The Copy toolbar button provides a means of placing a bitmap of the active tile onto the clipboard, where the size in pixels of the bitmap is specified on a dialog window.

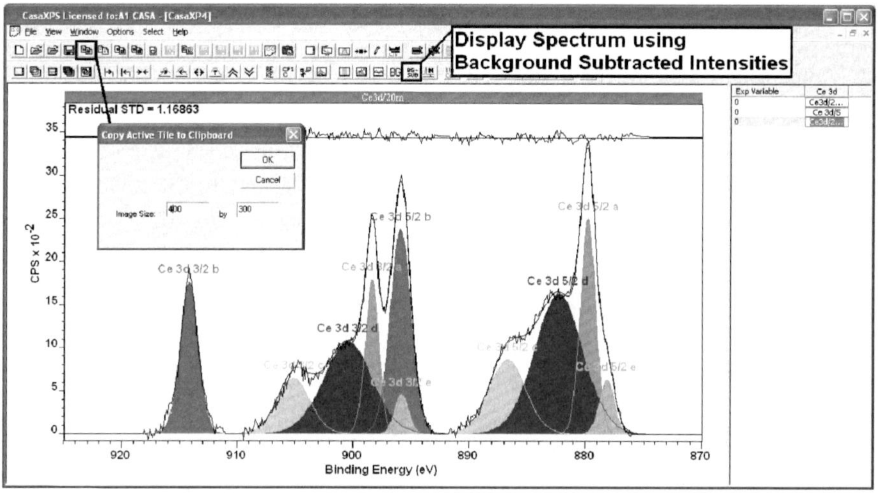

After placing a bitmap on the clipboard, the graphic of dimensions specified on the dialog is pasted into other applications by selecting the Paste option (usually Control+V).

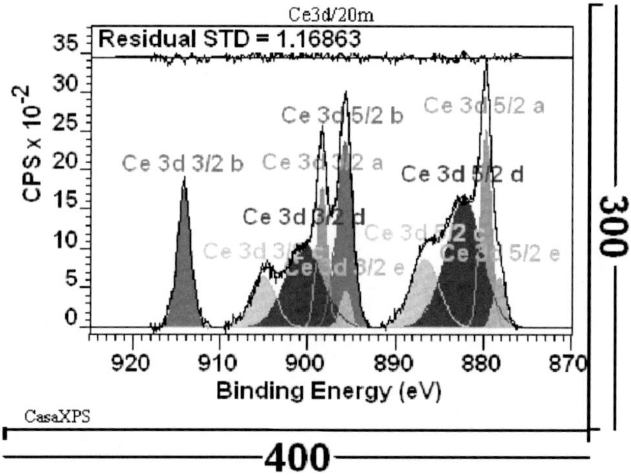

The Copy toolbar button draws the active tile into a bitmap. An alternative is to select the Copy Page of Tiles toolbar button.

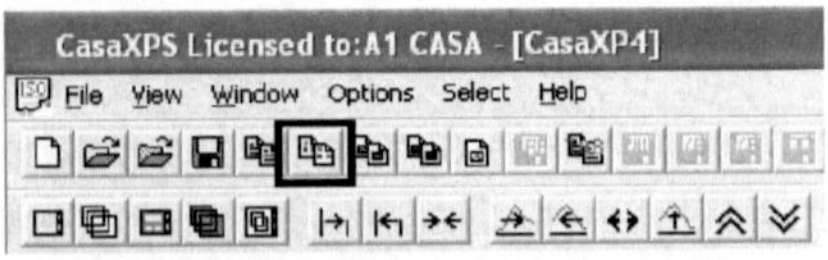

A bitmap of dimension equivalent to the left-hand pane in the experiment frame is used to draw the set of tiles. If the number of VAMAS blocks displayed in the left-hand pane exceeds the number of tiles per page, a scroll-bar appears to the right-hand side of the left-hand pane. The tile format visible in the left-hand pane is repeated for each set of tiles grouped according to the tile page format specification. One tile within the set of tiles is always selected as the active tile. When the Copy Page of Tiles toolbar button is pressed, the set of tiles belonging to the same format grouping as the active tile is placed on the clipboard.

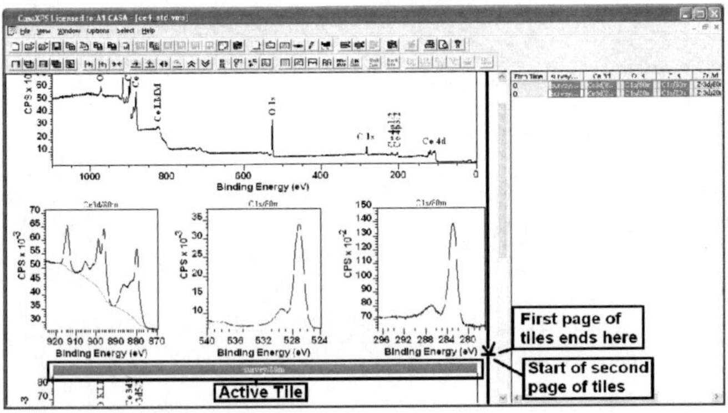

The tiles from the page just visible are placed on the clipboard as a consequence of the active tile belonging to the second page of tiles. The clipboard when pasted into Word appears as follows:

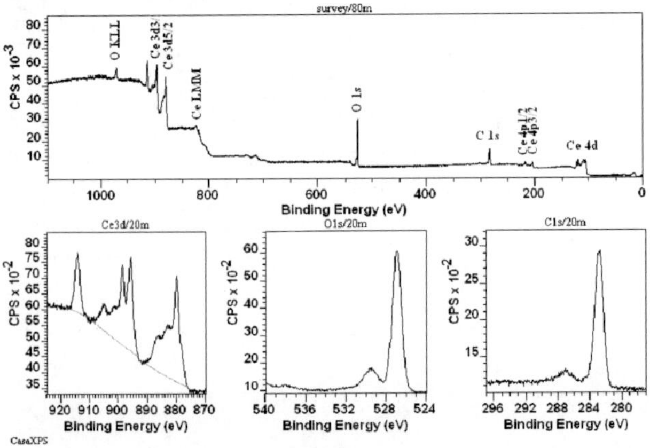

Additional toolbar buttons offer export via enhanced meta-file format EMF. While the files are typically small compared to bitmap files, the EMF format represents a sequence of drawing instructions and these drawing instructions must be interpreted by the software displaying the EMF file. Historically, EMF files are unreliable and not very portable, but nevertheless provide a means of exporting data as a sequence of tiles in a relatively compact form:

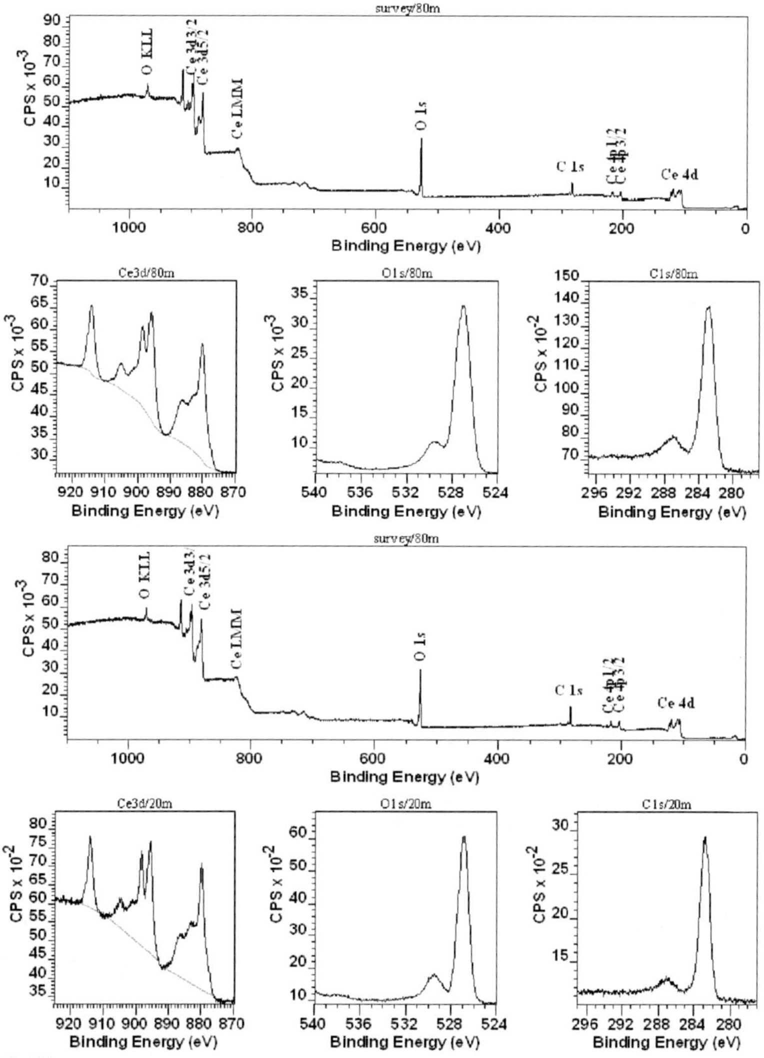

The above tile format is identical to the set of tiles maintained by the scrolled list in the left-hand pane of the experiment frame. Exporting the data using the Copy Page of Tiles toolbar button is only capable of placing one of these sets of four spectra on the clipboard. The EMF Scrolled list toolbar button copies the entire set of tiles to the clipboard. The only question remaining is whether the software to which the EMF data is moved displays the graphics correctly. It should be pointed out that the EMF file above displayed correctly in Word 2007, but failed when converted to PDF format via Word 2007 PDF export option. In general, the EMF export route is not recommended but can on occasion be useful.

Exporting Peak Models as ASCII Data

On occasion exporting a peak model in the form of numerical ASCII data is desired. The Save TAB ASCII to Clipboard toolbar button provides a means of taking the peak model in numerical format through the clipboard. Any program capable of recognising text on the clipboard can paste a table of TAB spaced columns of data representing the energy values in both kinetic and binding energy, the spectral data, one column per synthetic component in the peak model, the background intensities and the total synthetic envelope.

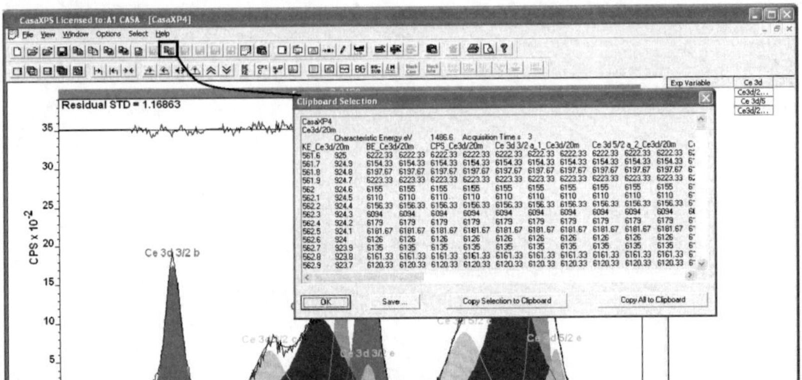

The Clipboard window in CasaXPS offers a route to saving the data to file, however the clipboard provides a convenient means of transferring the peak model to other programs. Excel, for example, accepts the data on the clipboard, where the TAB delimited causes the columns to appear in separate cells in the spreadsheet.

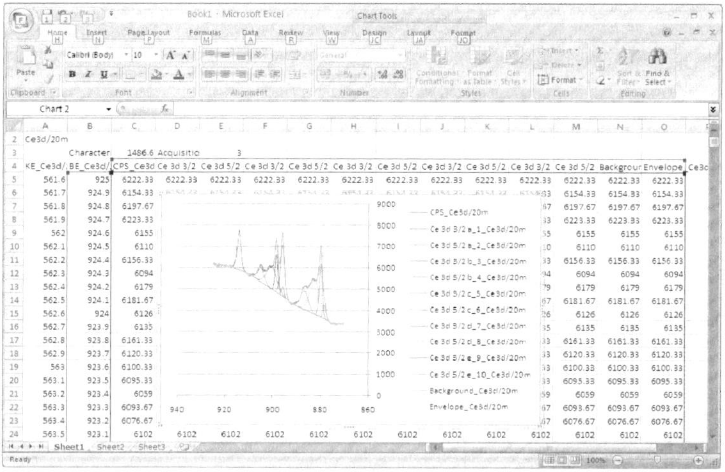

The source for the peak model placed on the clipboard via the Copy TAB Spaced ASCII to Clipboard toolbar button is the active tile. Only one peak model at a time can be placed on the clipboard. For situations where many peak models require exporting, an alternative route via a text file allows any peak model defined on VAMAS blocks selected in the right-hand pane to be exported to file.

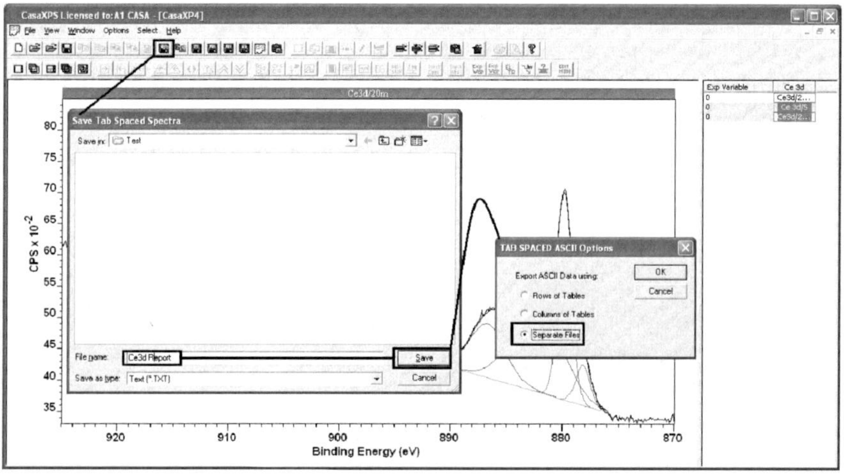

The peak models from the VAMAS blocks selected in the right-hand pane are exported as ASCII files in one of three formats:

1. Rows of tables, where each new peak model appears as a table positioned horizontally in the resulting file.

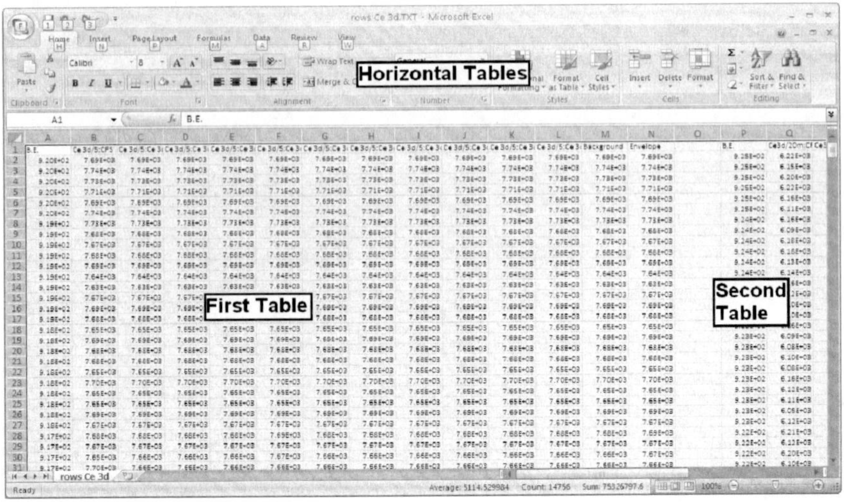

2. Columns of tables, where each peak model appears as a table positioned vertically one table after the other.
3. Separate file; a file is created for each peak model plus a master file in which the list of files created are listed.

After exporting peak models using separate files, the directory includes files containing tables with names created from the specified filename concatenated with sequential numerical values; one per selected VAMAS block. A text file with the name as specified in the File dialog window lists the set of table tiles created by the operation.

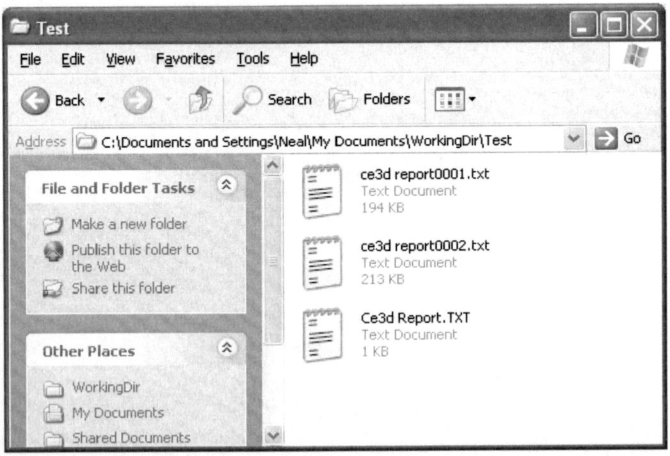

The list file appears as follows:

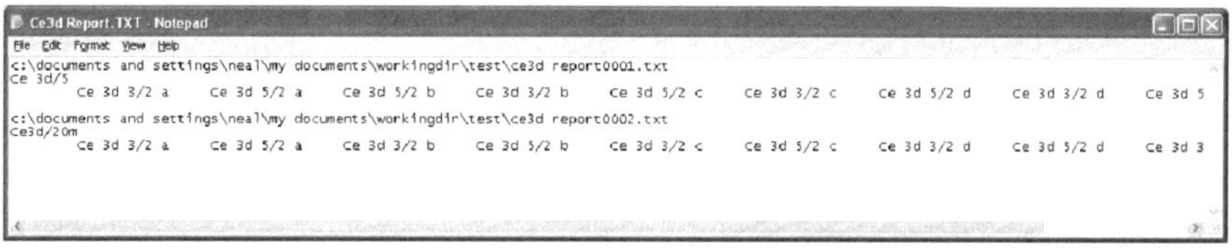

The individual files containing the peak models include two tables: one offering kinetic energy and counts, the other binding energy and counts per second.

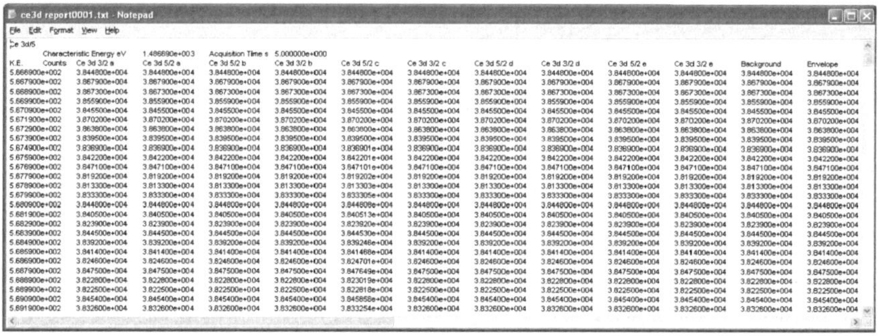

Quantification based on Components

A good example of where components are essential when attempting to quantify a sample is a surface containing antimony and oxygen.

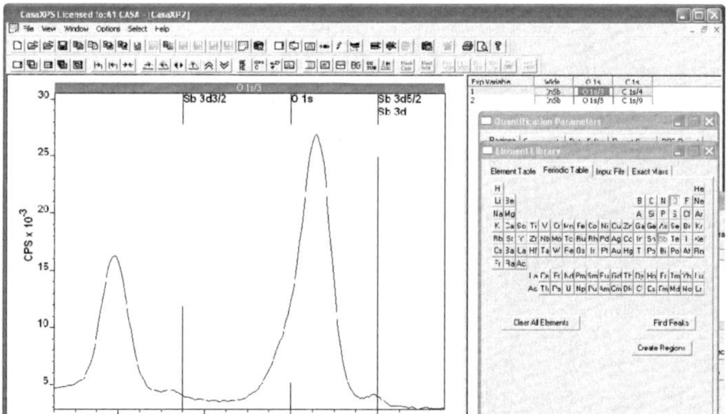

Oxygen and antimony create interfering peaks for the O 1s and chemically shifted Sb $3d_{5/2}$ transitions. While antimony might be measured using one of the many lesser antimony transitions, the options for oxygen are limited.

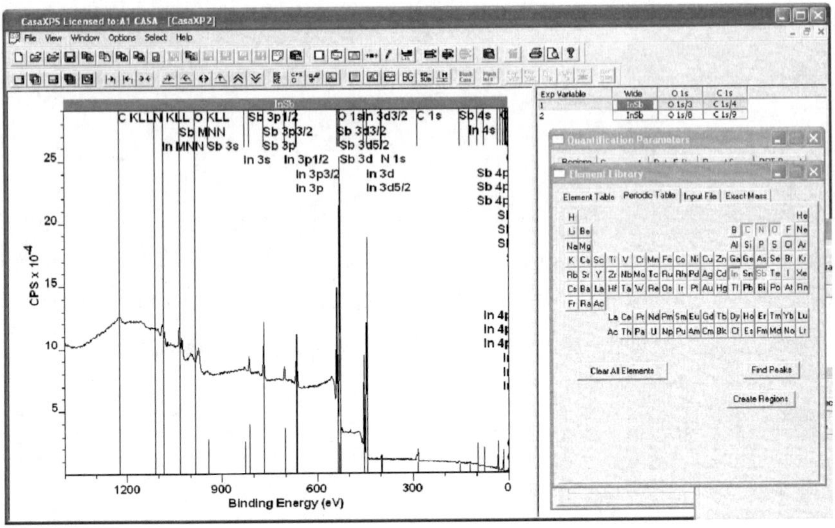

Separating the overlapping O 1s peak from the Sb $3d_{5/2}$ peak is central to obtaining quantification information about the sample composition. The experiment includes a VAMAS block assigned the element/transition O 1s, but in reality the spectrum is comprised of two doublet pairs from the Sb 3d transition and at least one O 1s peak. For the purposes of the current quantification, which is content to obtain elemental information, the O 1s transition will be treated as a single peak. The proposed peak model is therefore constructed from five components, four of which can be constrained to obey the relationships for d sub-shell spin-orbit splitting, namely, the intensity ratio of $3d_{3/2}$ to $3d_{5/2}$ is 2 : 3. The anomalous ratio of the peaks in the O 1s spectrum can be assessed using the Custom Report on the Report Spec property page and a pair of quantification regions.

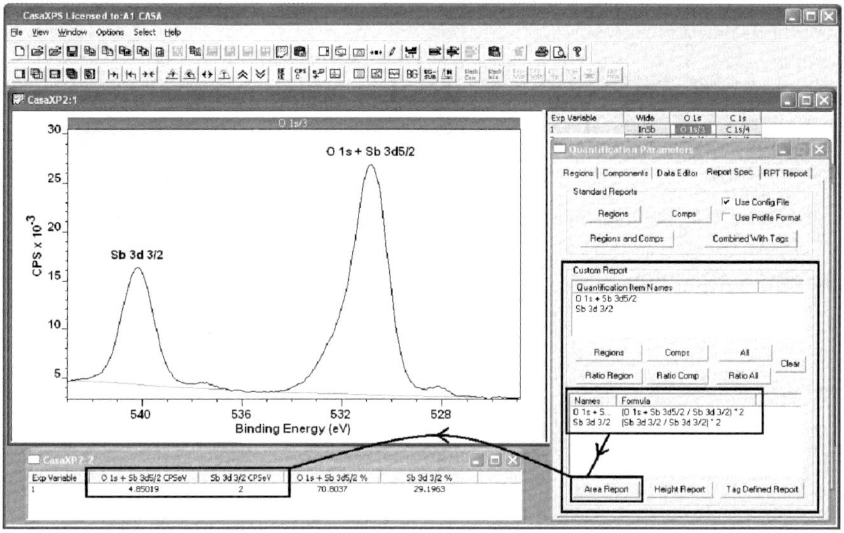

A ratio of 4.85:2 suggests the region associated with the Sb $3d_{5/2}$ peak has an excess of signal compared to the Sb $3d_{3/2}$ strongly implying the presence of an addition peak to accompany the Sb $3d_{5/2}$ transition.

While a peak model could be developed using the pair of regions with linear backgrounds, defining similar equivalent backgrounds for the survey spectrum might be a problem, and since the VAMAS file relies on the survey spectrum for a full quantification of the sample (the narrow scan spectra do not include indium spectra) it is important to use options that equally apply to survey spectra. The broader peaks of the lower resolution survey data make the region limits difficult to define in an equivalent way to the better resolved higher resolution data.

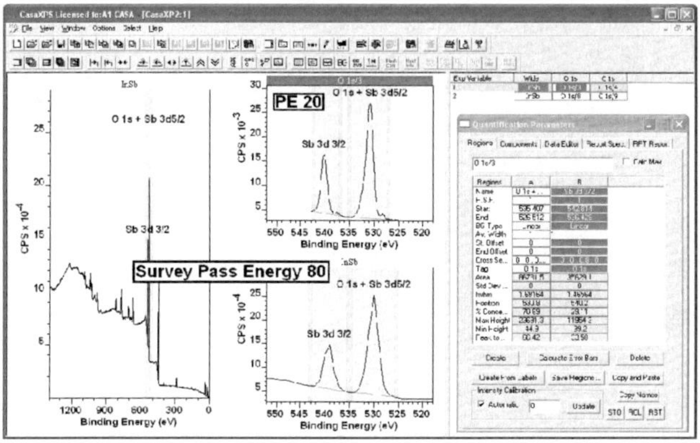

The solution employed for these circumstances is to define the background using a Tougaard 2-parameter universal cross section spanning all the peaks in the Sb 3d doublet. The background defined using the Tougaard algorithm is relatively insensitive to resolution of the peaks and therefore, in this case, more transferrable between the data acquired using different pass energies.

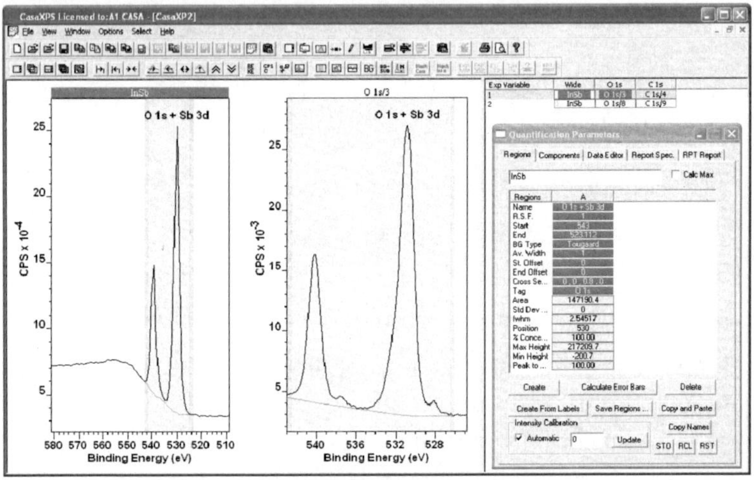

The peak model for the O 1s + Sb 3d region is created based on the data in the VAMAS block containing the high resolution spectrum.

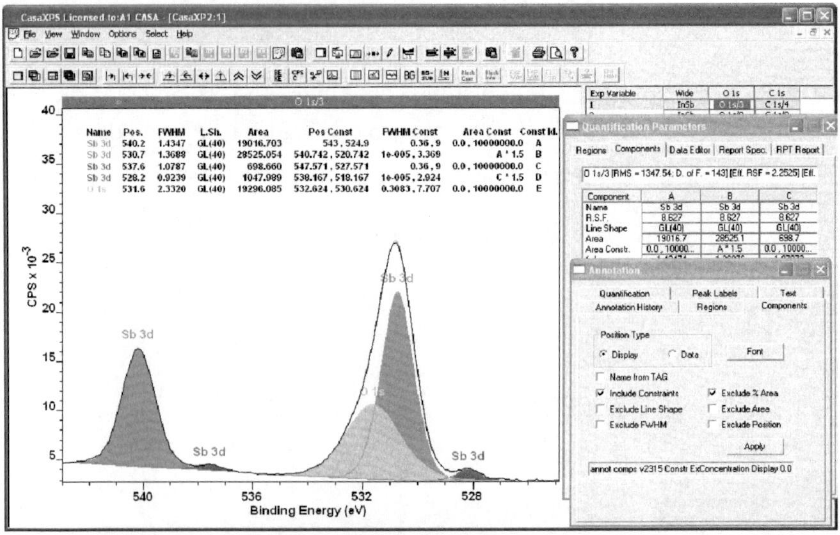

The primary source for controlling the area determined for the O 1s peak is the constraint imposed on the $3d_{3/2}$ and $3d_{5/2}$ antimony doublet peaks. Without these constraints the intensity for the O 1s peak would be highly correlated with the Sb $3d_{5/2}$ peaks and therefore the uncertainty in the area determined for the O 1s would be relatively large compared to the constrained peak model. The significance of these constraints is that the area calculated for the Sb $3d_{5/2}$ peaks are linked to the well defined area for the Sb $3d_{3/2}$ peaks.

While the high resolution data offers a means for constructing a peak model, the file as supplied must use the low resolution survey spectrum to perform the quantification of the sample. To employ only high resolution spectrum would require data for an indium peak and also the N 1s peak. Since these data are not available with corresponding acquisition conditions as the O 1s/Sb 3d and C 1s spectra, the survey is the only source for the indium and nitrogen. Due to issues with changing acquisition conditions, regardless of transmission correction, a quantification using data from different acquisition modes (lens functions/pass energy) is not recommended. Given a peak model prepared on a high resolution spectrum, the essential structure of the peak model can be encapsulated by imposing additional constraints and transferring the heavily constrained model to the survey spectrum. The survey data is then used to fit the peak model. A quantification report based on the survey spectrum yields the desired result, where regions are used to compute the intensities for carbon, nitrogen and indium while the oxygen and antimony are calculated from the fitted components. The following describes how these results shown below are achieved. An alternative approach based on effective RSFs and tagged regions and components provides a direct link between the survey spectrum and the high resolution data without the need to fit peak models to relatively sparse survey data. These techniques based on tags will follow later in the discussion.

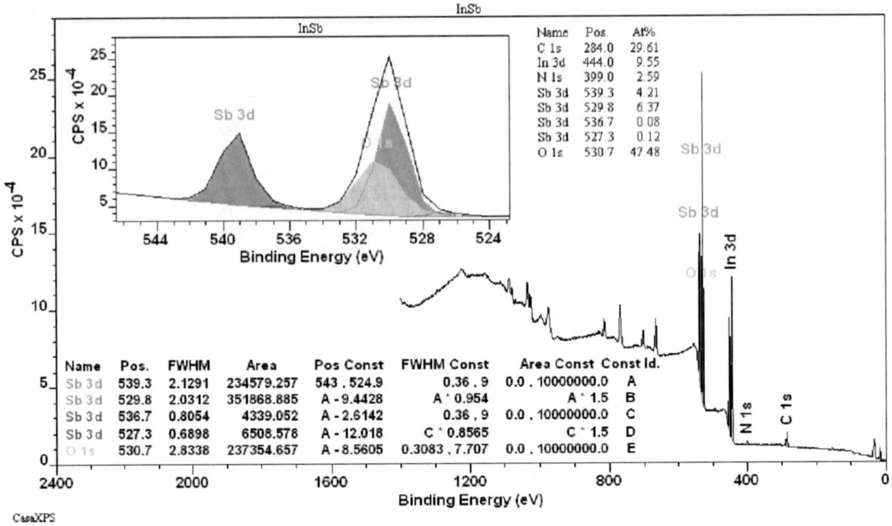

A Closer Look at Developing a Peak Model for InSbO

The data file includes a survey measured with pass energy 80 and two narrow scan spectra acquired at pass energy 20. These acquisition parameters were used to repeat a measurement from a different position on the sample; hence the VAMAS file contains six VAMAS blocks. The two distinct measurements are assigned different experimental variables and so appear as separate rows in the right-hand pane.

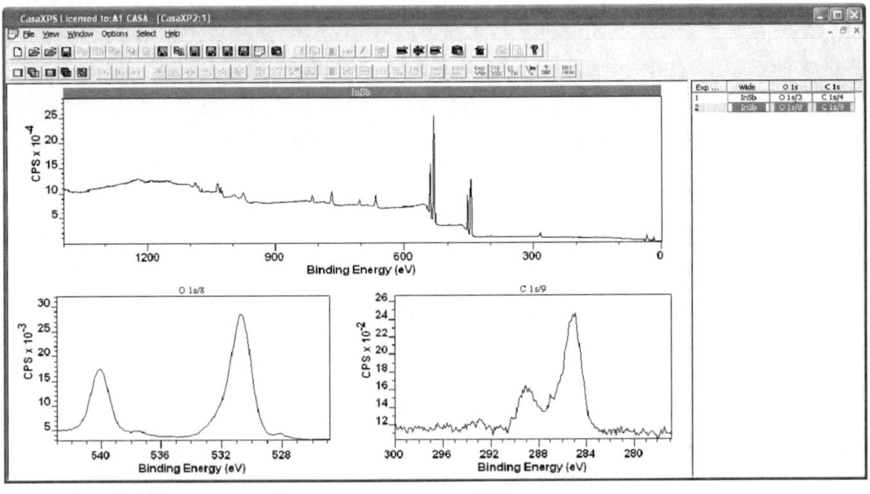

Since the spectrum assigned the element/transition O 1s is in reality O 1s + Sb 3d, elemental quantification of the surface requires a peak model for these data, the results of which will be transferred to the survey spectrum in order to complete the quantification. Once the quantification for one measurement is complete, the analysis performed in terms of regions and components may be propagated to the second measurement, thus avoiding the need to repeat the same analysis manually.

The peak model for the O 1s + Sb 3d data envelope is prepared using the narrow scan spectrum:

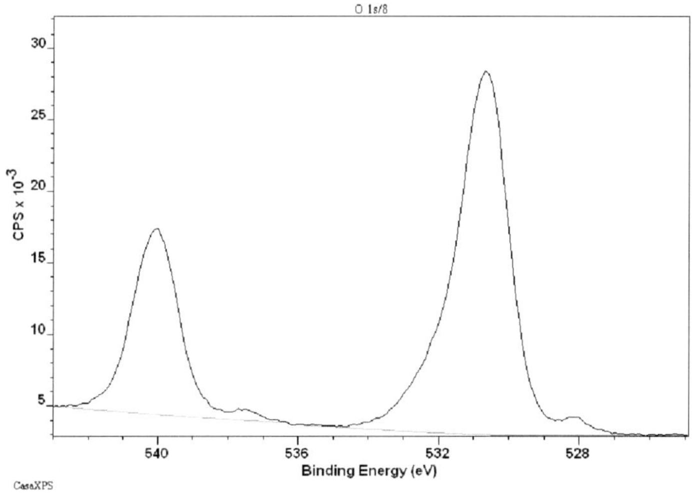

Pass energy 20 data clearly shows the nature of the Sb 3d doublet where visual inspection suggests two pairs of doublet peaks are required. Further, the stronger asymmetry in the Sb $3d_{5/2}$ peak implies the presence of the oxygen peak to the left of the Sb $3d_{5/2}$ peaks. Data such as these may be far more complex in structure than these simple observations can reveal, but for the purposes of an elemental analysis a relatively simple model is sufficient. Specifically, if the constraints ensure the Sb $3d_{3/2}$ intensity is mirrored in the Sb $3d_{5/2}$ envelope, then the signal unaccounted for by these Sb 3d peaks must represent the O 1s signal.

After creating a Tougaard background as described above, the process of creating components via the Components property page on the Quantification Parameters dialog window can begin. On pressing the Create button on the Components property page, a new peak is positioned on the data.

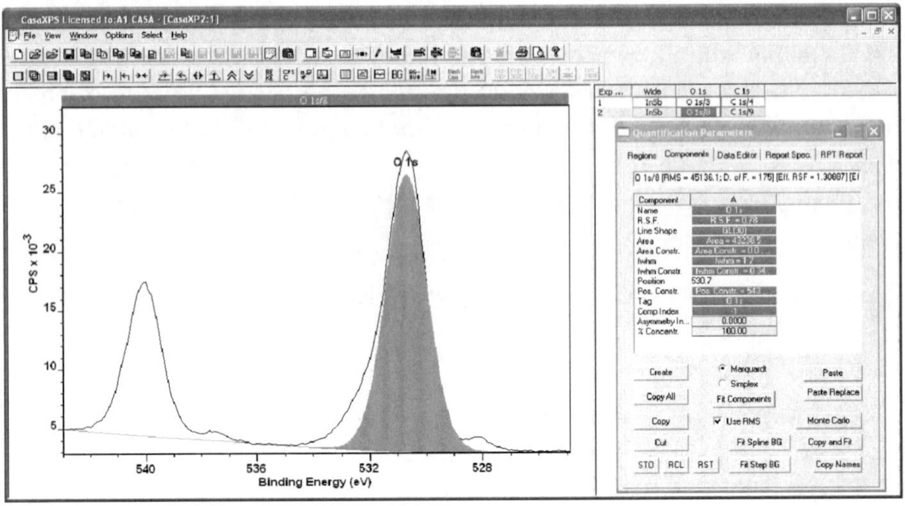

Note that, while the new peak is positioned based on the maximum in the background subtracted data, the name and RSF are retrieved from the element library based on the element/transition fields assigned to the VAMAS block. Since Sb 3d is the dominant intensity in the data, the peak is positioned consistently with an antimony peak. The data, however, are assigned the element O and transition 1s and therefore the new component is named O 1s with corresponding RSF. The antimony peaks are more obvious in the data, therefore creating antimony peaks first would be the natural order. The name and RSF for the initial component must be updated with the appropriate RSF for the quantification of Sb 3d. Updating information from the library is achieved by entering into the name field for the component the # character followed by the name field used in the element library. The appropriate RSF for the component corresponds to Sb 3d, therefore the name field should be specified as #Sb 3d.

On pressing the enter key, the # character is removed from the name field and the RSF and lineshape from the library entry matching the string entered are updated in the component fields:

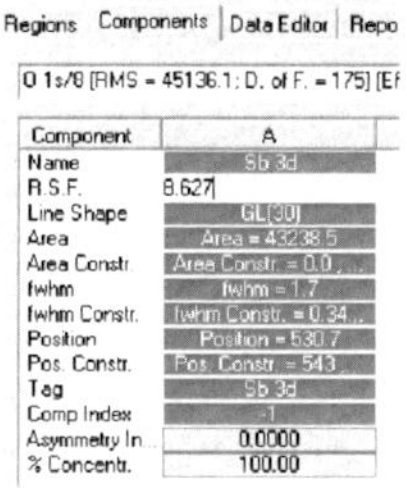

The intensity for antimony will be measured using all the antimony peaks, therefore regardless of which peak in the doublet pair the component represents, since the intensity will be summed over all the component peaks, the RSF for the combined doublet should be used. A common mistake is to assign the RSF for doublet peaks based on the individual peaks in the doublet. The result of using all the peaks in the quantification, yet with RSFs assigned for spin-orbit relative intensities of the peaks is to incorrectly double the concentration for the material in question.

Creating the component peaks directly from the element library ensures the correct name and RSF are used in the component. The Element Table property page combines with the Component property page of the Quantification Parameters dialog to create components based on selecting the name field from the element table on the Element Library dialog window. A component is created each time a name field is selected whilst the tick-box Create When Line Selected is enabled.

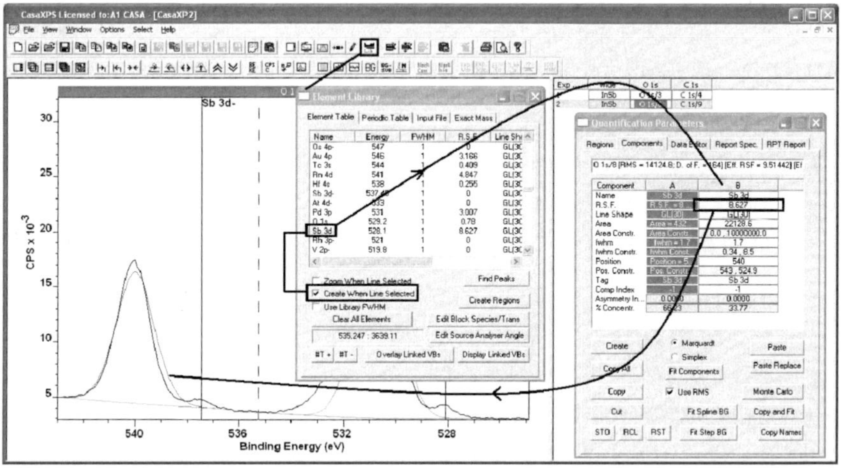

The Sb $3d_{3/2}$ peak, in theory, is 2/3 the size of the Sb $3d_{5/2}$ peak. Imposing the area constraint and adjusting the constrained peaks using the mouse actions described above offers the first evidence of the O 1s peak.

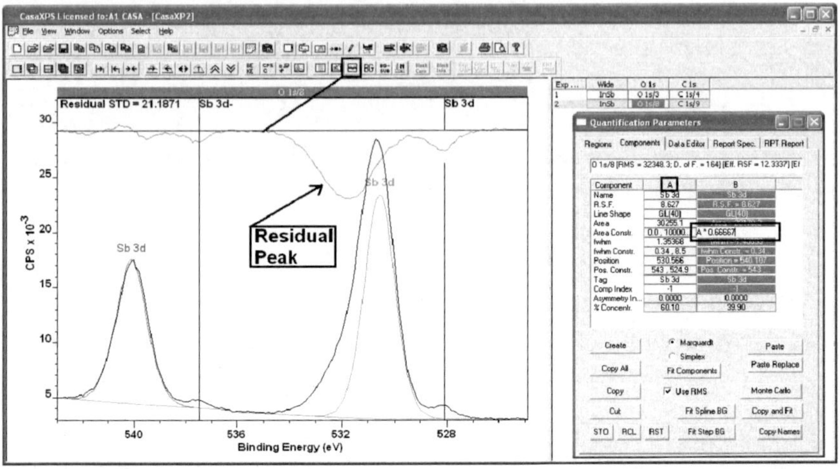

Before creating the O 1s peak, taking a copy of the two components currently defined offers a means of adding a pair of peaks subject to the same area constraint and assigned the appropriate RSF for the Sb 3d transitions. Pressing the Copy All button on the Components property page places a copy of literally all the peaks defined so far onto an internal clipboard. The constraint of interest is the area constraint, but linking the current peaks using the position constraint provides a convenient means of moving both peaks as a unit. Ultimately, the position of these peaks is better determined once all the peaks are added to the peak model, so the position constraint entered for only two peaks will need to be released later.

A simple way to copy the two peaks with a position constraint whilst retaining the original peak model is to first add the two peaks without a position constraint to the stored list of peak models. Press the STO button on the Components property page.

The two components are added to the peak model list exactly as found. Once stored, the position constraint is added by entering A into the position constraint field in column B.

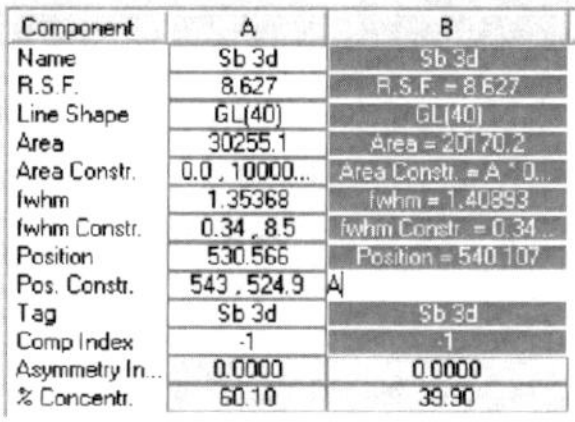

Component	A	B
Name	Sb 3d	Sb 3d
R.S.F.	8.627	R.S.F. = 8.627
Line Shape	GL(40)	GL(40)
Area	30255.1	Area = 20170.2
Area Constr.	0.0 , 10000...	Area Constr. = A * 0...
fwhm	1.35368	fwhm = 1.40893
fwhm Constr.	0.34 , 8.5	fwhm Constr. = 0.34...
Position	530.566	Position = 540.107
Pos. Constr.	543 , 524.9	A
Tag	Sb 3d	Sb 3d
Comp Index	-1	-1
Asymmetry In...	0.0000	0.0000
% Concentr.	60.10	39.90

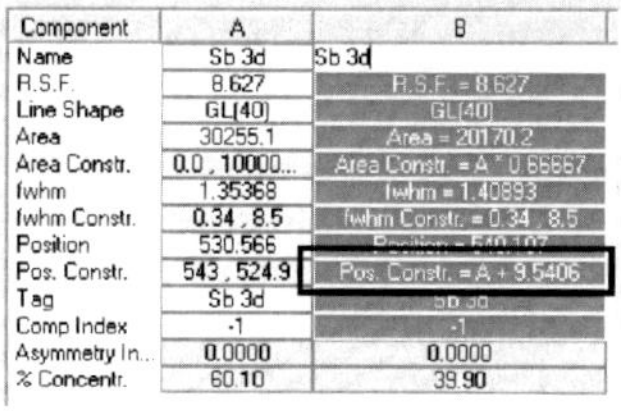

Component	A	B
Name	Sb 3d	Sb 3d
R.S.F.	8.627	R.S.F. = 8.627
Line Shape	GL(40)	GL(40)
Area	30255.1	Area = 20170.2
Area Constr.	0.0 , 10000...	Area Constr. = A * 0.66667
fwhm	1.35368	fwhm = 1.40893
fwhm Constr.	0.34 , 8.5	fwhm Constr. = 0.34 , 8.5
Position	530.566	[illegible]
Pos. Constr.	543 , 524.9	Pos. Constr. = A + 9.5406
Tag	Sb 3d	Sb 3d
Comp Index	-1	-1
Asymmetry In...	0.0000	0.0000
% Concentr.	60.10	39.90

The difference between the two peaks is calculated from the current positions. At this point the two peaks are placed on the CasaXPS component clipboard by pressing the Copy All button.

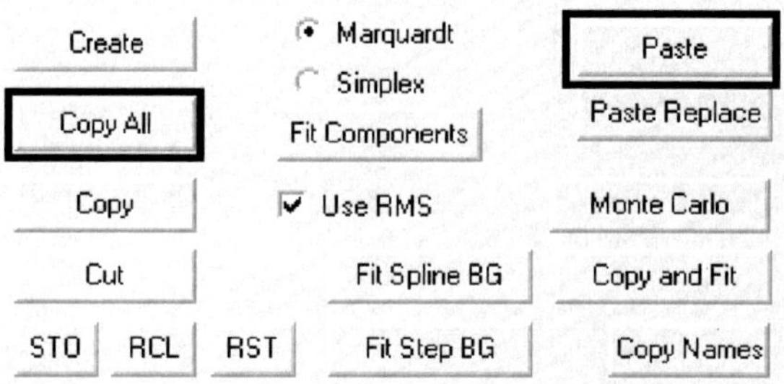

The original pair of peaks is recovered from the stored peak models by pressing the RCL button. To add another pair of peaks including an additional position constraint, press the Paste button on the Component property page. These two new peaks are moved as a unit due to the position constraint and can be adjusted to account for the small Sb 3d doublet to lower binding energy of the larger Sb 3d doublet.

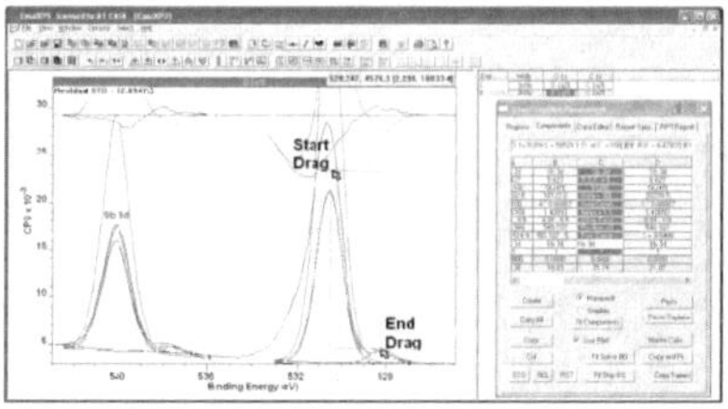

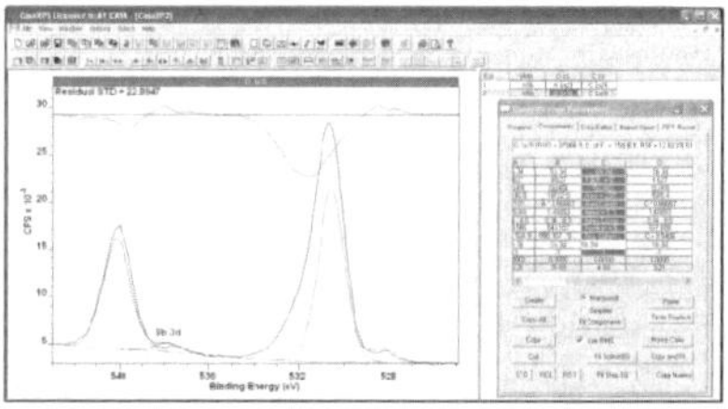

The Copy All and Paste buttons causes two identically positioned doublet pairs to exist. The original two components constrained by the area alone will be in columns A and B on the Components property page. The two new peaks will appear in columns C and D. When the mouse is used to move components, the cursor placed at the top of the component in the left-hand pane grabs the first component in the order of the alphabetical column headers A, B, C, D. As a result of this ordering, the cursor, by default, grabs the Sb 3d peak in column A. The new peaks are always added to the end of the list of components. To ensure the newly added component is grabbed by the drag action, hold the Control-key down before pressing the left-mouse button. With the Control-key held down, the component selected will be the component with the highest alphabetical character located where the cursor is placed in the left-hand pane. Confirmation of which component is selected is provided by the Component property page. The component chosen by the mouse action is highlighted in the table of component parameters. To observe which component is selected by the Control-key and mouse, rather than dragging the mouse, simply left-click at the location at which a drag operation is desired. The highlighted component will change to reflect the click selection.

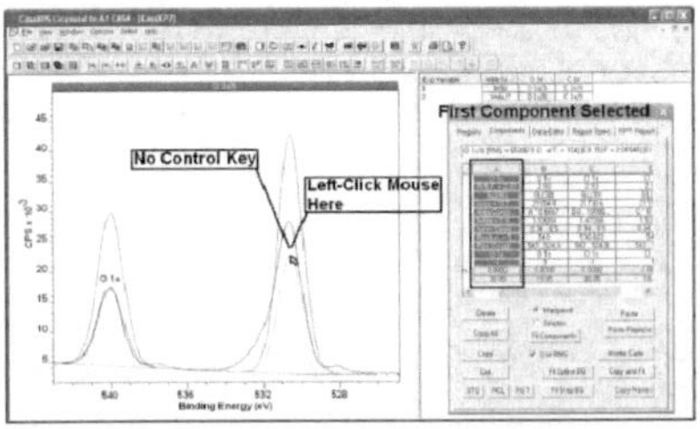

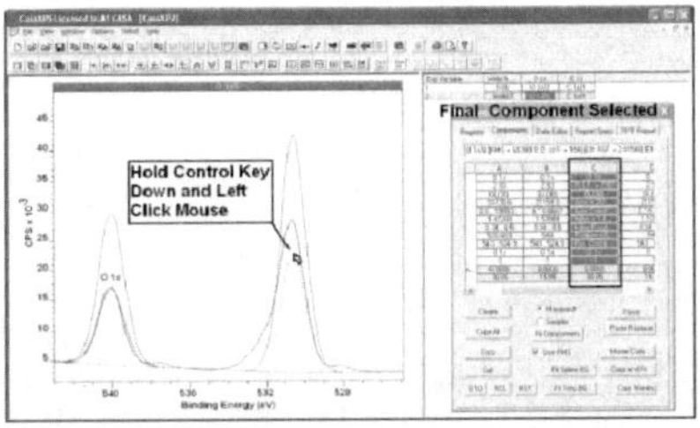

Once all the Sb 3d peaks are assigned, the position constraint used to move the minor doublet pair into position can be released using the # character applied to the constraint field. When entered into a constraint field, the # character followed by a numerical value causes the constraint to be updated based on an interval about the corresponding parameter value plus and minus the value entered together with the # character.

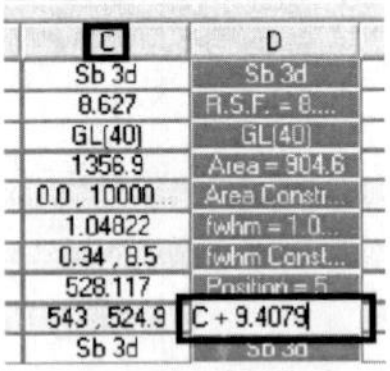

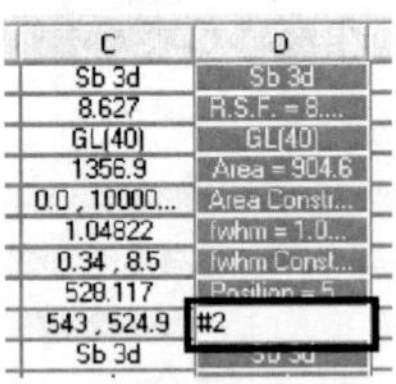

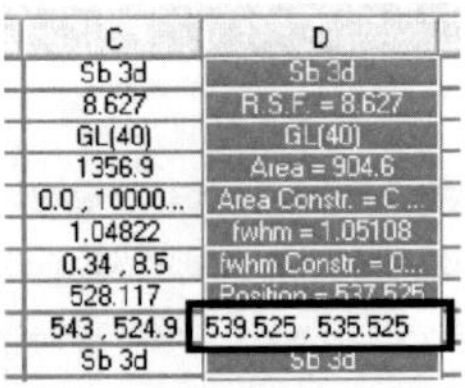

The # character combined with a numerical value can be applied to the area and FWHM constraints too. Also to fix a parameter, simply enter the # character into the corresponding constraint field and press the Enter key.

The four peaks representing the Sb 3d signal positioned on the data account for all but a peak structure assumed to be the O 1s peak.

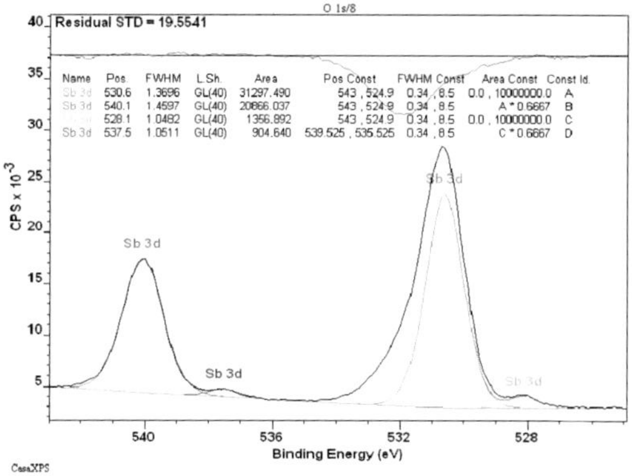

Adding a single GL(40) peak and fitting the five component model to the data produces the model used earlier.

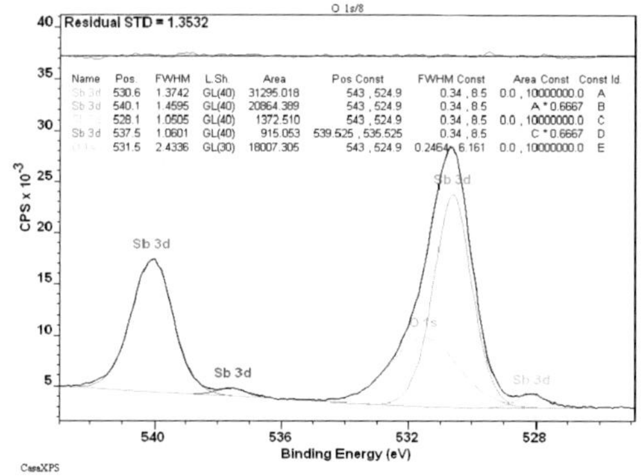

The refined nature of the five component peak model achieved for the PE 20 data would not be possible based on the PE 80 survey data.

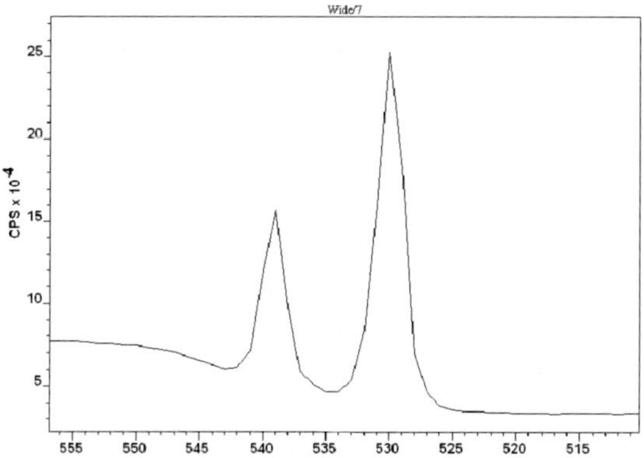

Nevertheless, the PE 80 data will be used for the elemental quantification and so the refinements of the PE 20 peak model, after encapsulation in constraints, are transferred to the PE 80 data to achieve the goal of quantification using components and regions based on the survey spectrum. Initially, the entire peak model from the PE 20 data is completely constrained in terms of relative position, relative FWHM and relative area for the five components. Once fully constrained, the peak model is copied using the Copy All button on the Components property page and pasted onto the survey spectrum.

To fully constrain the position, a keyword *link* is entered into a position constraint field:

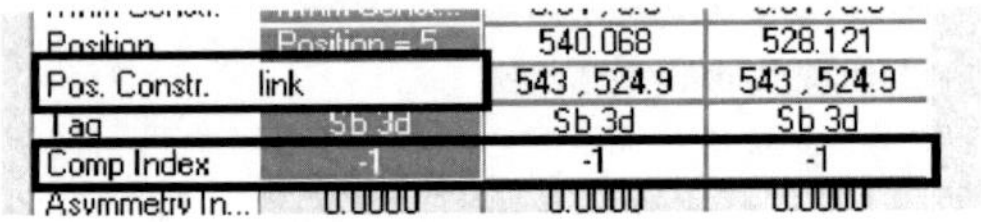

All the components with the same Comp Index field are constrained to be the energy offset determined from the current positions for the peaks relative to the component for which the keyword was entered.

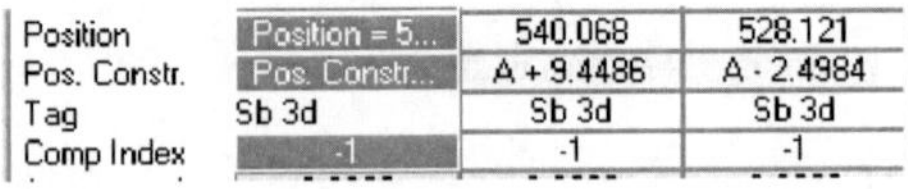

Since the FWHM for PE 80 data is expected to be greater than for PE 20 data, the FWHM for the model must be allowed to adjust when fitting to the survey data. The relationship between the FWHM for the components within a doublet pair should remain within reason in the same proportion in the PE 80 data as the PE 20 data, therefore a constraint, which turns out to be necessary, is applied to the FWHM between components within the doublet pairs based on the relative FWHM determined from the PE 20 data.

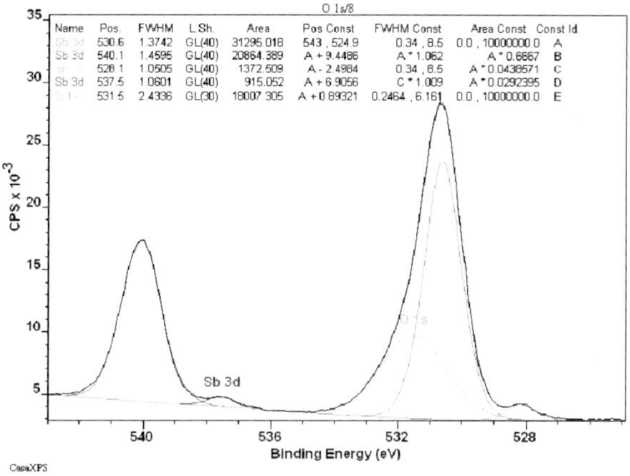

Placing the constrained peak model onto the CasaXPS component clipboard by pressing the Copy All button, then displaying the survey spectrum in the active tile before pressing the Paste button transfers the peak model to the survey.

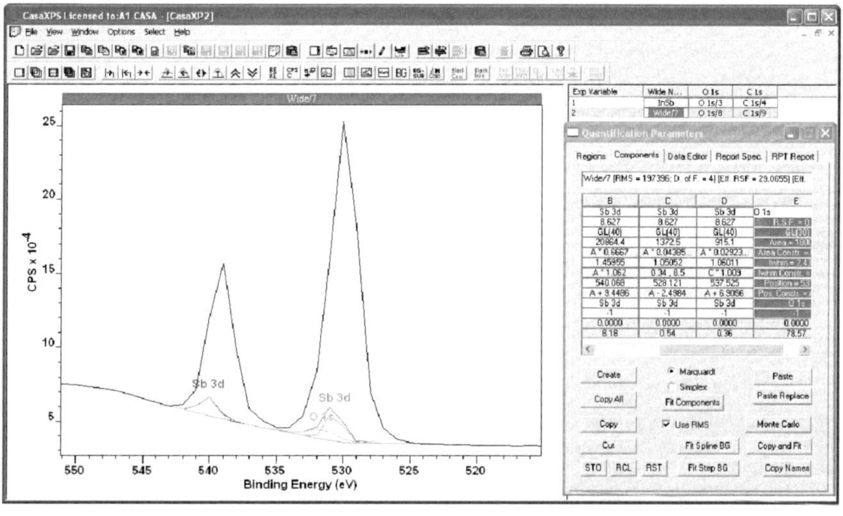

Without constraining the peaks as described above, pressing the Fit Components button would be unwise. The optimisation routines require the peak model to be close enough to the intended data envelope to prevent the solution finding an alternative local minimum to the problem defined so well by the PE 20 data. On occasion adjustments via the mouse or peak parameters may be required before attempting the optimisation step. The constraints introduced in this example are sufficient to guide the least squares solution. Pressing the Fit Components button, for these data and the given peak model, results in a very acceptable solution for the survey O 1s + Sb 3d region. Note that a region based on a Tougaard background must be defined for the survey spectra and adjusted to accommodate the new peak model.

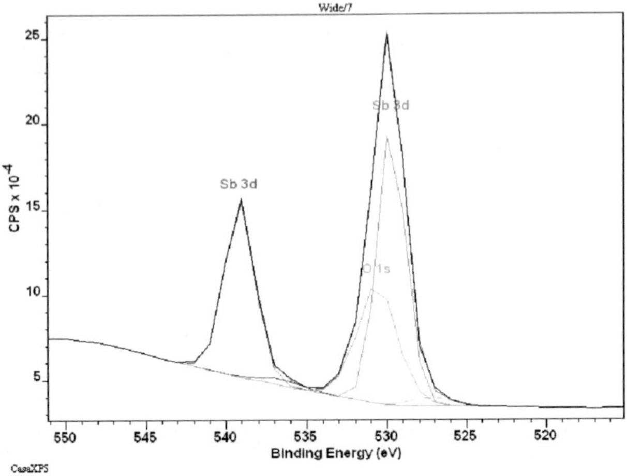

Quantification based on the survey spectrum also requires the definition of regions for indium, nitrogen and carbon. Since a region and components are already defined on the survey data, the task of adding three new regions presents the opportunity to describe a method for creating regions from peak label annotation.

Peak Label Annotation and Creation of Regions

The state of the quantification process for the survey data is as follows:

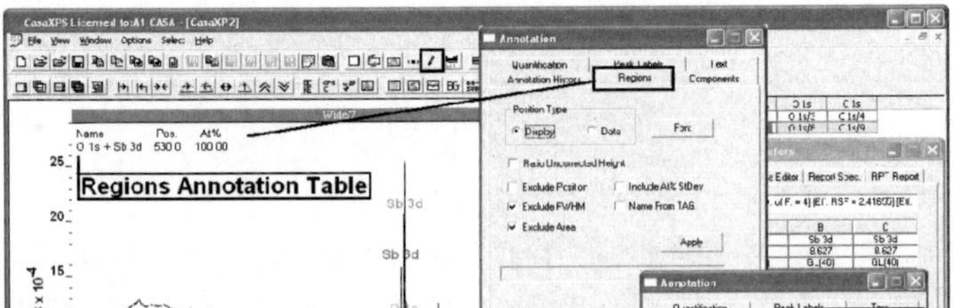

Displayed over the survey spectrum are two tables corresponding to annotation for regions only and components only. These types of annotation are created using the Annotation dialog window. Tables created from either the Regions property page or the Components property page on the Annotation dialog window represent information extracted directly from the spectrum for which the annotation is defined.

If regions are already defined on a spectrum and it is wished to retain these regions, creating regions via the Element Library dialog window is not an option, since the Create Regions buttons on the Element Table and Periodic Table property pages will delete existing regions before recreating regions based on the element markers. An alternative to creating the regions using the Regions property page and the element table, which is also a perfectly good approach, the job of annotating peaks and also creating regions can be combined in one step as follows.

The Annotation dialog window includes a property page entitled Peak Labels.

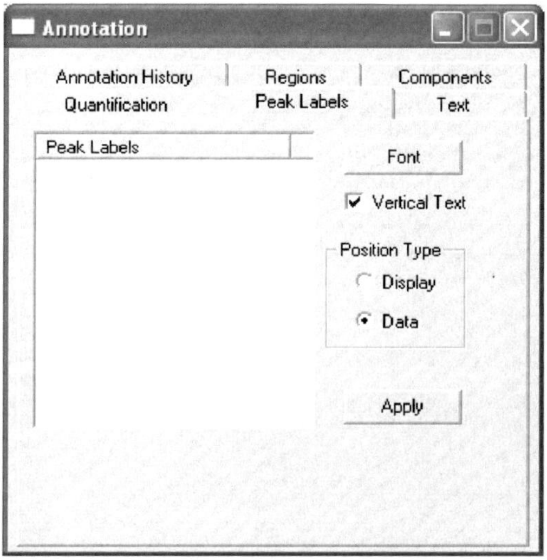

The Peak Labels property page interacts with the element library. Placing peak markers on the survey spectrum for an element also enters the names for the peak markers into the table on the Peak labels dialog window.

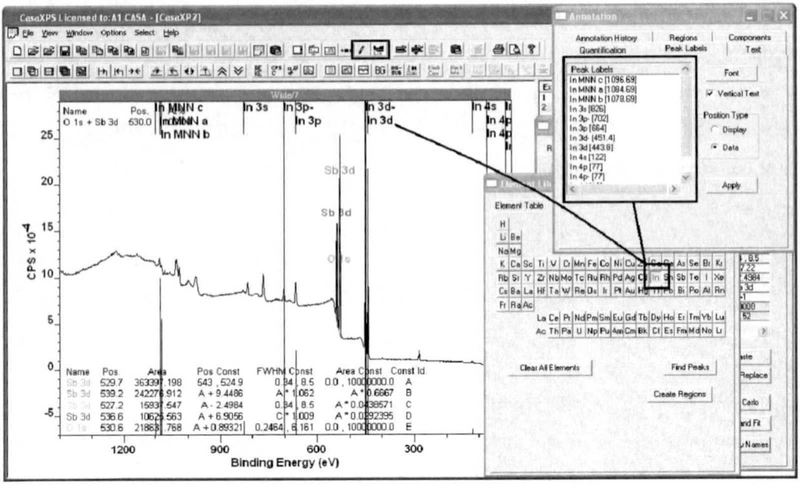

The table on the Peak Labels property page are selected using the mouse and the Control key to add more than one label selection to the table. On pressing the Apply button, the Peak Labels property page adds text labels to the spectrum in the active tile.

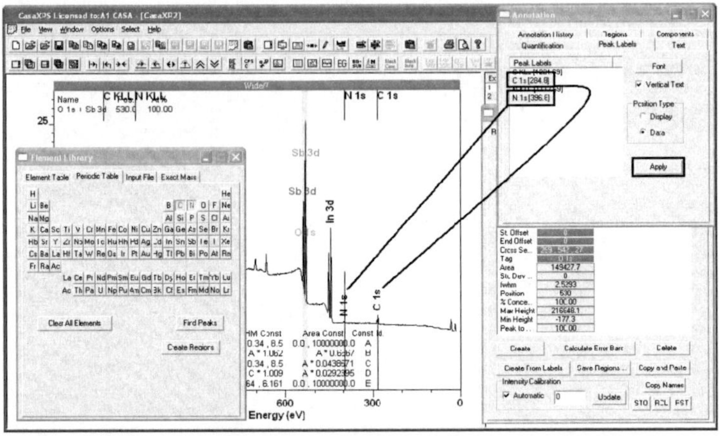

The Annotation History property page list the set of annotation defined on the data in the active tile. The peak labels listed on the Annotation History property page are used to create regions via the Regions property page of the Quantification Parameters dialog window. The Create From Labels button on the Regions property page creates a region for each piece of annotation designated as *annot text peak* using the name to extract the RSF from the element library.

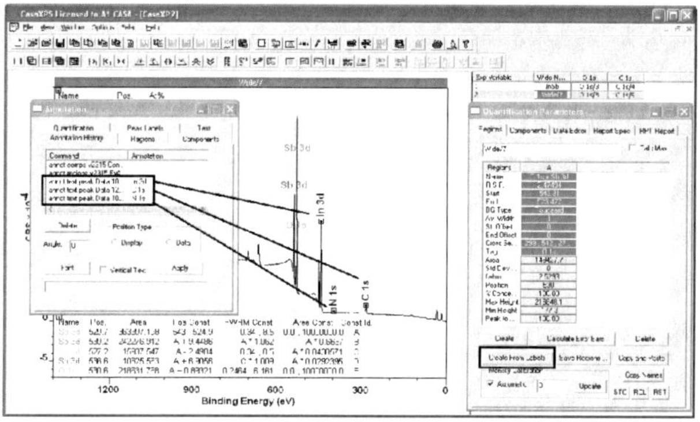

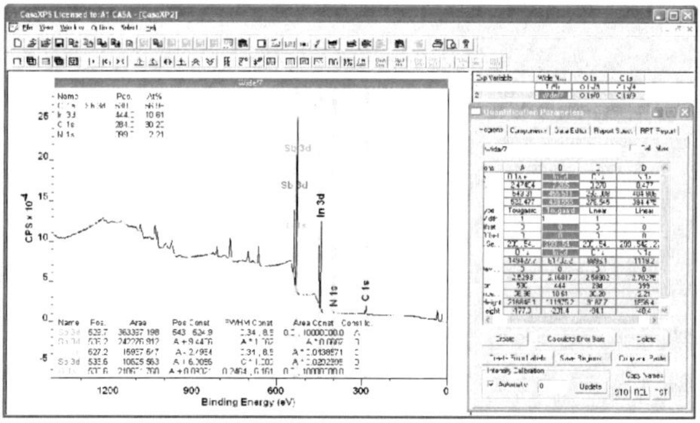

The annotation table offering quantification based on regions is worth noting. Since the O 1s peak overlaps with the Sb 3d doublets, the library RSFs cannot be used to scale the intensity for these combined peaks measured using a single region. Rather than displaying erroneous atomic concentrations, the region quantification table displays a partial quantification of the sample, achieved by supplying an effective RSF for the region representing both oxygen and antimony. The effective RSF is calculated from the PE 20 spectrum peak model and displayed in the text-field at the top of the Components property page:

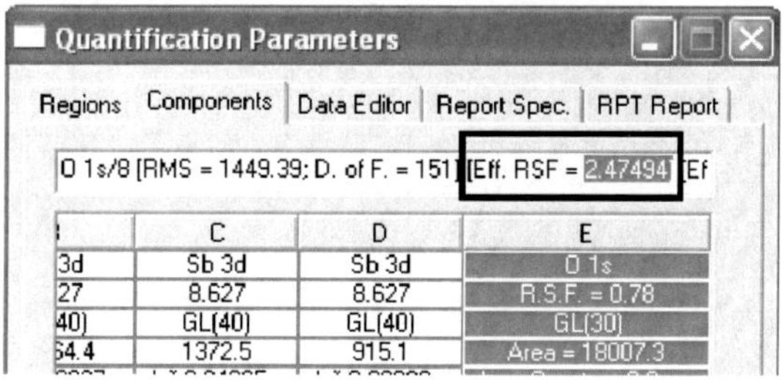

The effective RSF is calculated from the RSFs used in the peak model and the relative intensities of the component peaks. The effective RSF calculated for the data in the high resolution spectrum is used in the region for the same interval defined on the survey spectrum. While the atomic concentration for oxygen and antimony are yet to be fully resolved, the effective RSF allows the correct atomic concentrations for nitrogen, carbon and indium.

Quantification based on regions alone employing an effective RSF for the oxygen/antimony region:

Name	Position	Raw Area	RSF	Transmission	%At Conc
O 1s + Sb 3d	530	854453	2.47494	5.71817	56.98
In 3d	444	433883	7.265	5.31048	10.61
C 1s	284	33045.9	0.278	3.71464	30.2
N 1s	399	5441.34	0.477	4.86165	2.21

Following quantification based on regions and components, the fully resolved quantification table appears as follows:

Name	Position	Raw Area	RSF	Transmission	%At Conc
Sb 3d	529.7	363397	8.627	5.71817	6.86
Sb 3d	539.2	242277	8.627	5.76044	4.54
Sb 3d	527.2	15937.5	8.627	5.70972	0.3
Sb 3d	536.6	10625.6	8.627	5.74776	0.2
O 1s	530.6	218632	0.78	5.7224	45.63
In 3d	444	433883	7.265	5.31048	10.48
C 1s	284	33045.9	0.278	3.71464	29.81
N 1s	399	5441.34	0.477	4.86165	2.19

Quantification based on regions and components is obtained via the Report Spec property page. The survey spectrum must be selected in the right-hand pane before pressing the Regions and Comps button.

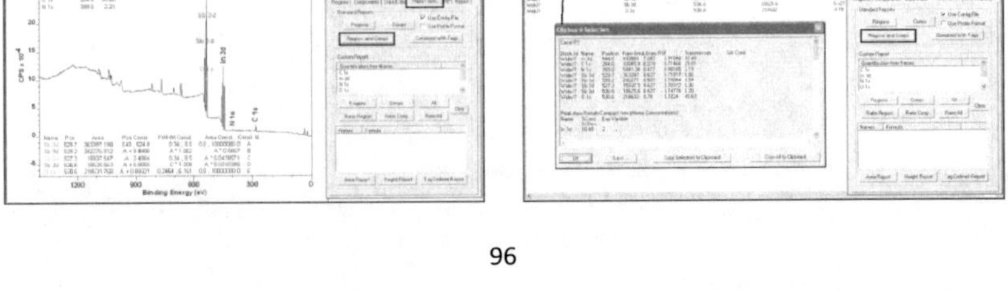

The report generated by pressing the Regions and Comps button is placed on the clipboard via the Copy toolbar button (or Control-C) and pasted into a spreadsheet program using Control-V.

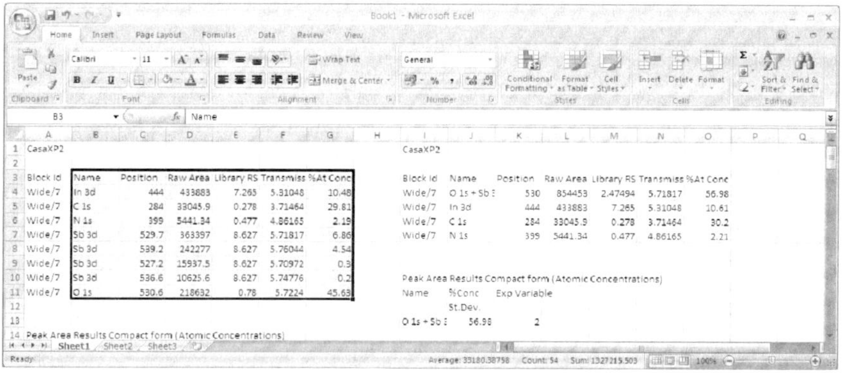

Some Notes on Displaying Spectra

Each tile displayed in the left-hand pane maintains a set of display parameters. These display parameters include fonts, colours and display options specific to a tile. The primary source for the display parameters is the Tile Display Parameters dialog window.

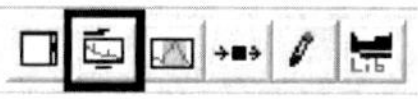

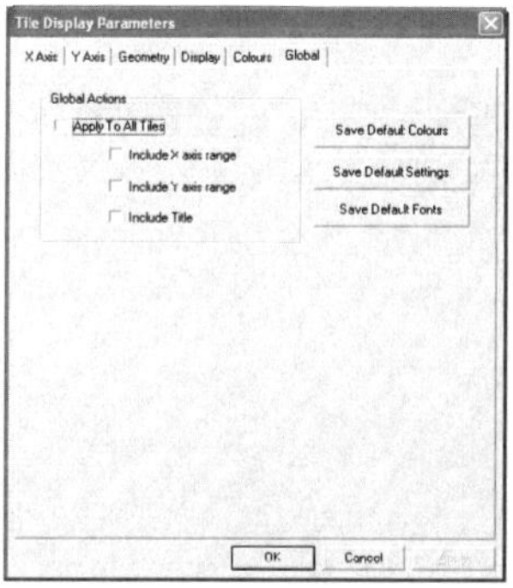

The Tile Display Parameters dialog window consists of property pages managing different aspects of the tile display options. Once a set of display options are prepared and applied to a tile, these parameters are saved to a configuration files via the Global property page. The configuration files are located in the CasaXPS.DEF directory and are used to reinstate the tile options when next CasaXPS is started.

During the discussions in this manual relating to peak models, various display options have been used. Some of these display techniques employed will be described in more detail.

When a tile is created to display a spectrum in the left-hand pane, the set of display parameters used to visualise the data are maintained as a template. The template is initialised on starting CasaXPS via the configuration files or in the event of no configuration files by hard coded settings. Each time the display parameters for a tile are updated from the Tile Display Parameters dialog window, the set of display options are saved to the template and used to display the next piece of data entered into a tile. The appearance of the next tile created therefore depends on the appearance of the last set of parameters used to update the template.

In addition to the Tile Display Parameters dialog window, the display settings are adjusted using buttons on the toolbars. These toolbar options also update the tile display template.

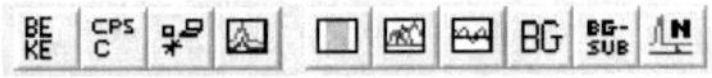

When preparing a report, the display of data from an experiment may involve multiple tiles in various arrangements where each tile utilises different display settings.

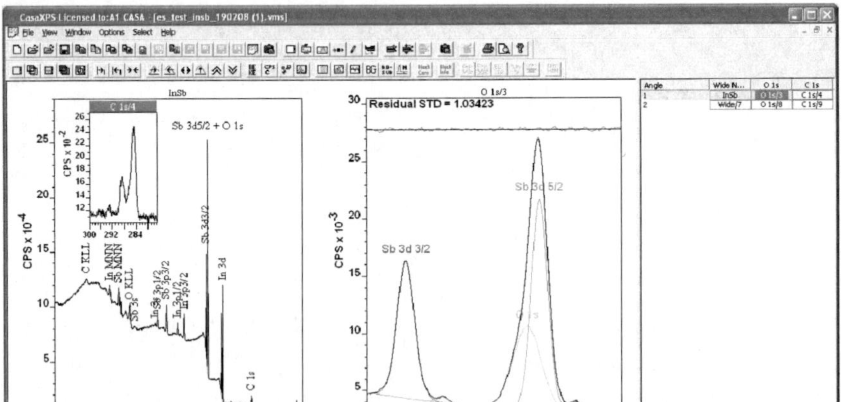

The tile format created for a particular data file may be required at a later time. Without taking action, the next time a VAMAS block is selected and displayed these carefully prepared display settings are lost. A given state of the display in terms of both number of tiles and tile display parameters are saved either to disk or to a temporary template, and at a later time the file or template restored as required. Saving a tile format file or a temporary template based on the current display is achieved using the Options menu.

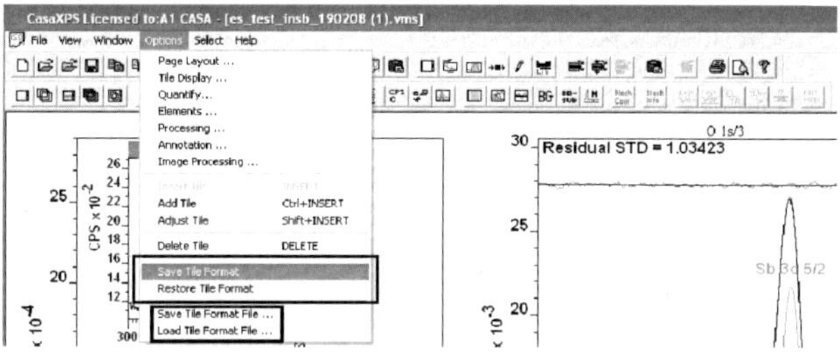

A previously saved template is restored via the Options menu. Thus a format typically used for processing data is transformed to the format used to print the results.

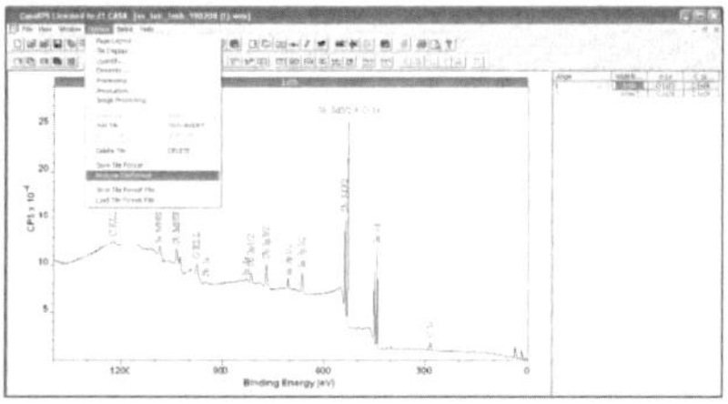

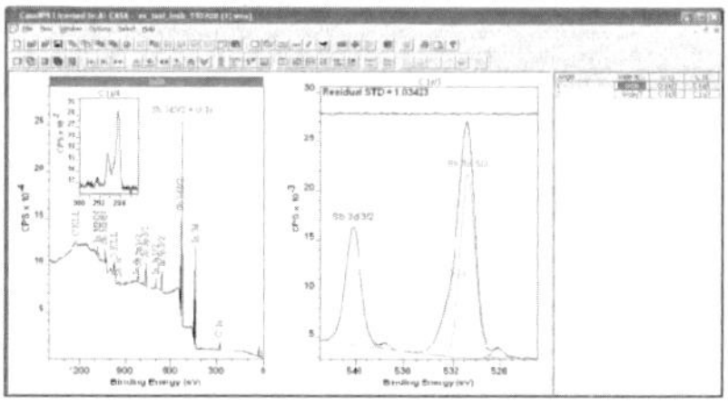

The tile format template option is only available until a new format is stored or the current CasaXPS session ends. A more permanent means of saving a tile format is to create a tff file from the Options menu. These files are ASCII files containing the display parameters used to visualise the data and, once the corresponding VAMAS file is available in an experiment frame, can be loaded to reset the display back to the desired state.

Some Notes on Displaying Components

A variety of tools are used to display components in a peak model. The default display options for components colour the components sequentially based on the palette of Custom Colours as displayed on the Color Dialog window invoked from the Colours property page of the Tile Display Parameters dialog window.

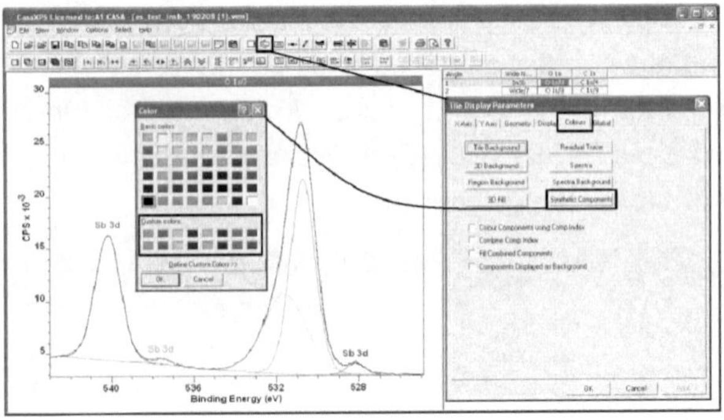

The palette of custom colours is indexed top left to top right, then bottom left to bottom right. The indices therefore run from 0 to 15.

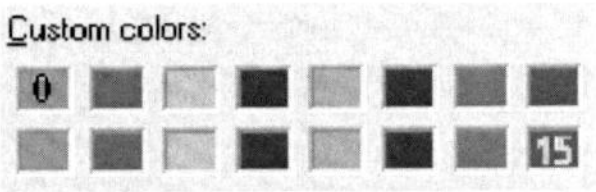

The indexed colours are used to alter the appearance of the components under the control of the tick boxes on the Colour property page and the Comp Index field as defined on the Components property page of the Quantification Parameters dialog window.

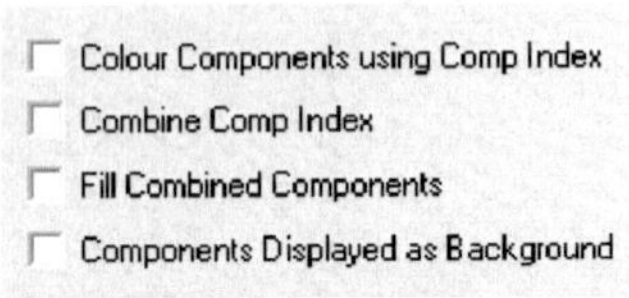

Tag	Sb 3d	Sb 3d	O 1s
Comp Index	0	0	1
Asymmetry In...	0.0000	0.0000	0.0000

When a component is created, the Comp Index field is set to -1. For the case of the Sb 3d peaks the Comp Index can be assign the same value for components belonging to a doublet pair, when coupled with ticking the box labelled Colour Components using Comp Index on the Colours property page, the tile displaying the peak model colour codes the peaks according to the Comp Index fields with respect to the index numbers for the Custom Colour palette.

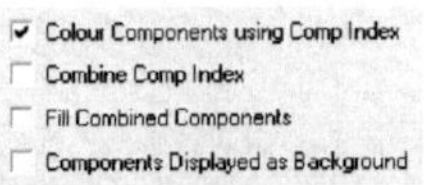

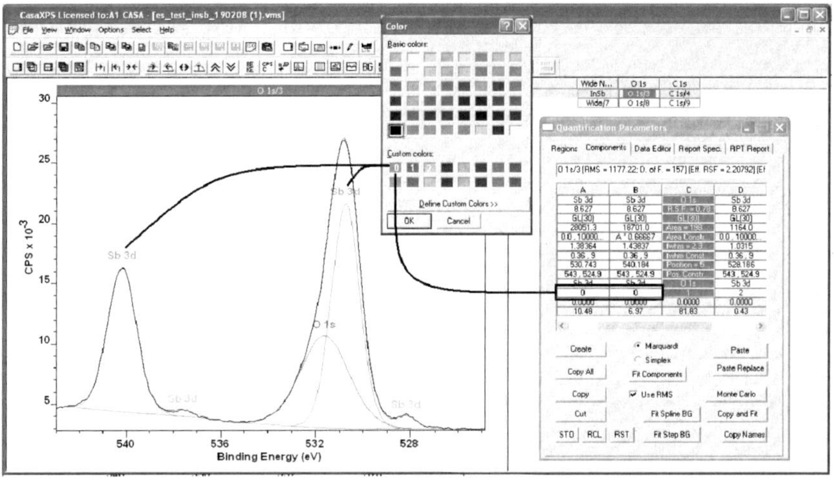

A further change in the display aimed at highlighting a relationship between two or more peaks is achieved by also ticking the Combine Comp Index tick-box:

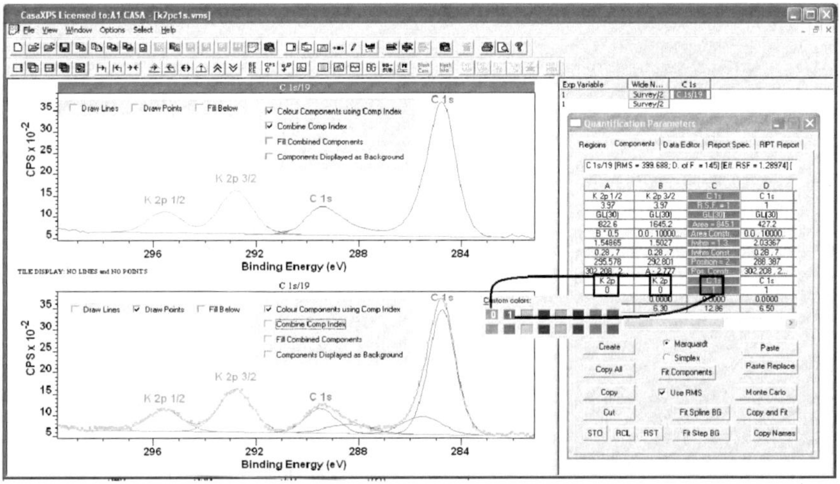

Two further display options for components include (top tile) filling the combined peaks using the Comp Index to determine the colour for each component and (bottom tile) filling the combined peaks based on the Comp Index, but where the individual components are coloured using the default colour indices. Note, the Comp Index for the two sets of components is altered to 14 and 15. The components are coloured using the default index sequence 0, 1, 2, ... therefore changing the Comp Index to 14 and 15 allows the fill colour to be controlled independently of the default component colours.

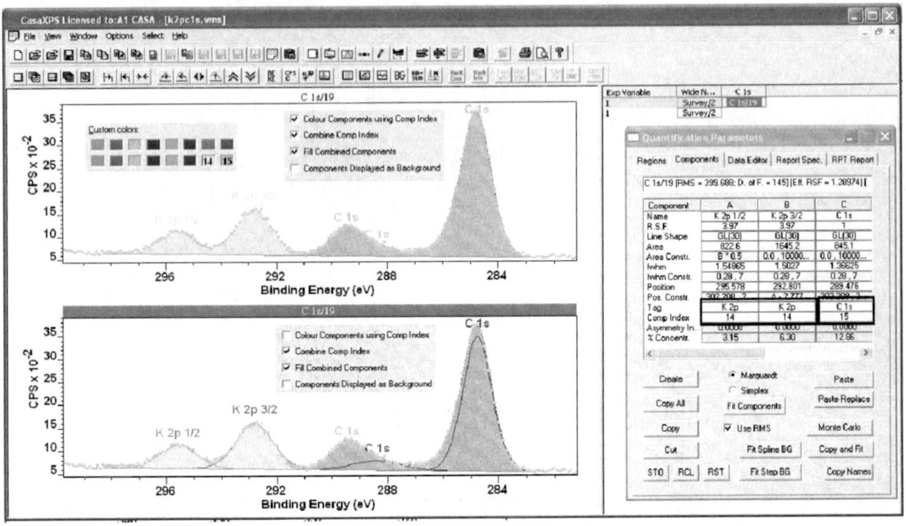

Quantification Based on TAGS

The quantification performed using regions and components applied to the pass energy 80 survey spectrum was possible because the survey data included sufficiently well behaved peaks for the Sb 3d/O 1s region to permit a meaningful peak fit. For data acquired at a lower energy resolution or for which the overlapping peaks are less well defined, the peak fitting approach applied to the survey spectrum may yield a less reliable quantification. In situations where peak fitting to survey data is inappropriate, the quantification method based on TAGS offers a means of recovering a full quantification from a survey spectrum containing overlapping peaks. The TAG method also requires a high resolution spectrum for the energy interval containing the overlapping peaks, however rather than transferring the peak model to the survey spectrum, the peak model is used to allocate intensity measured from the survey spectrum to the peaks identified in the high resolution data.

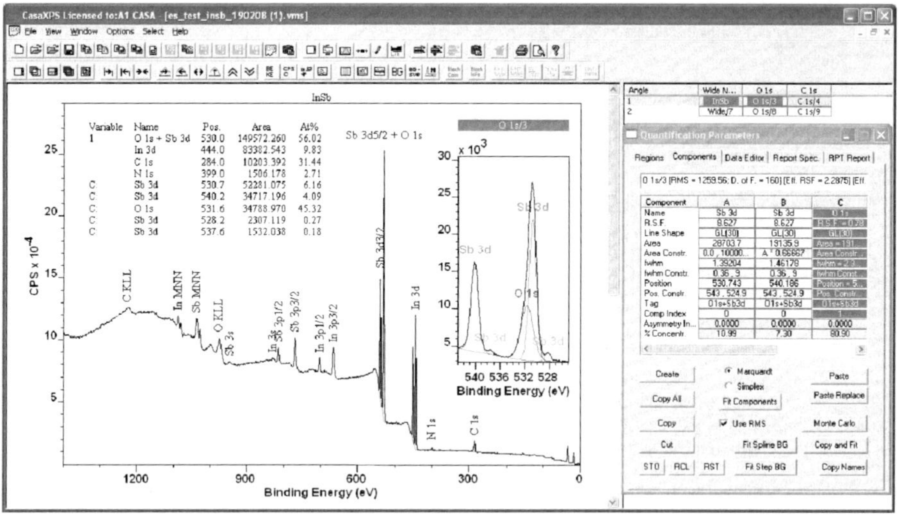

The same procedure as described earlier is employed for creating a peak model on the narrow scan spectrum over the oxygen/antimony interval. Once again, the effective RSF from the high resolution data must be calculated and entered for the region on the survey spectrum equivalent to the region used to model the high resolution data. The same set of regions defined on the survey spectrum for indium, carbon and nitrogen are also required and when combined with the O 1s + Sb 3d region assigned the effective RSF, a partial quantification in terms of regions is available for the survey spectrum. The steps so far are identical to the steps described earlier. At this point, however, the TAG field for each region and component is used to link together quantification information from different VAMAS blocks. Specifically, the quantification region for the O 1s/Sb 3d peaks must be assigned the same TAG field as each component defined on the high resolutions O 1s/Sb 3d spectrum.

A TAG field is simply a string other than the string NoTag. The only significance of the string entered for the regions and components is that the strings should be unique for each region used in the quantification and the TAG fields for the components in the peak model are exactly the same as the TAG field in the equivalent region on the survey spectrum. In the current example, the components defined on the narrow scan spectrum are assigned the string O1s+Sb3d. The exact same string is entered for the equivalent region on the survey spectrum.

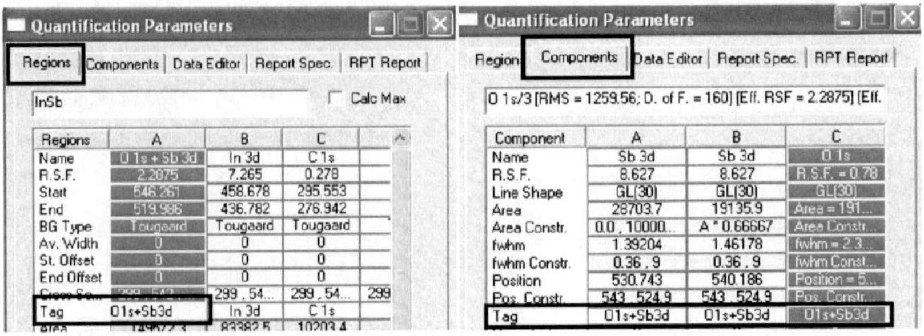

Note that the peak model on the narrow scan spectrum also includes a region. The TAG field for the region on the narrow scan region should be set to NoTag. If the current TAG field is deleted and the Enter key pressed on the keyboard, the field is updated with the appropriate NoTag string.

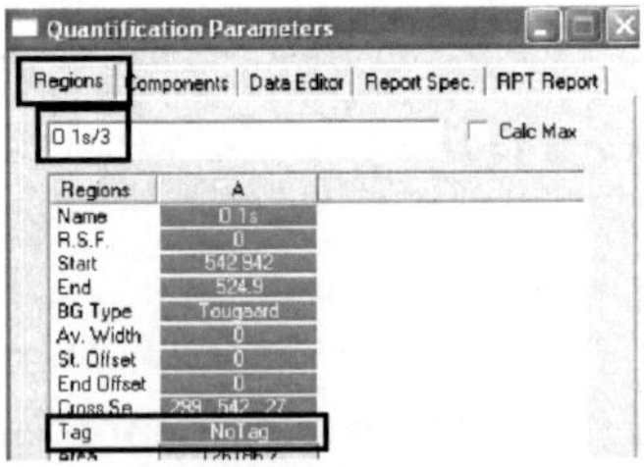

Once the TAG field are appropriately defined for survey and high resolution data, the Report Spec property page provides the means of creating a quantification report offering the partial quantification in terms of regions from the survey plus a further decomposition of the intensity for the O 1s / Sb 3d region proportioned in accordance with the relative intensities of components from the high resolution spectrum.

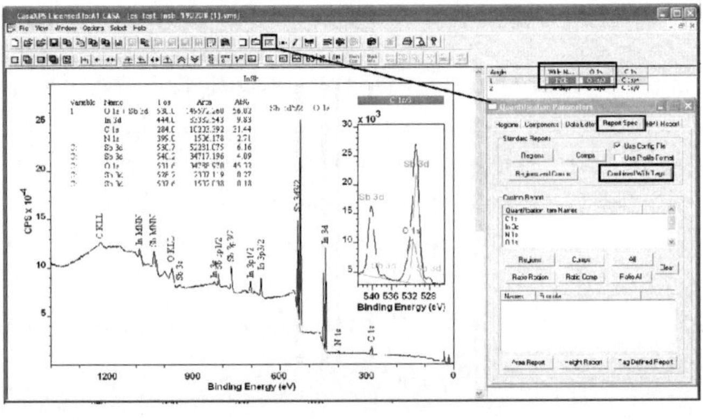

Before pressing the Combined With Tags button on the Report Spec property page, both VAMAS blocks containing the survey and the O 1s/Sb 3d data must be selected in the right-hand pane.

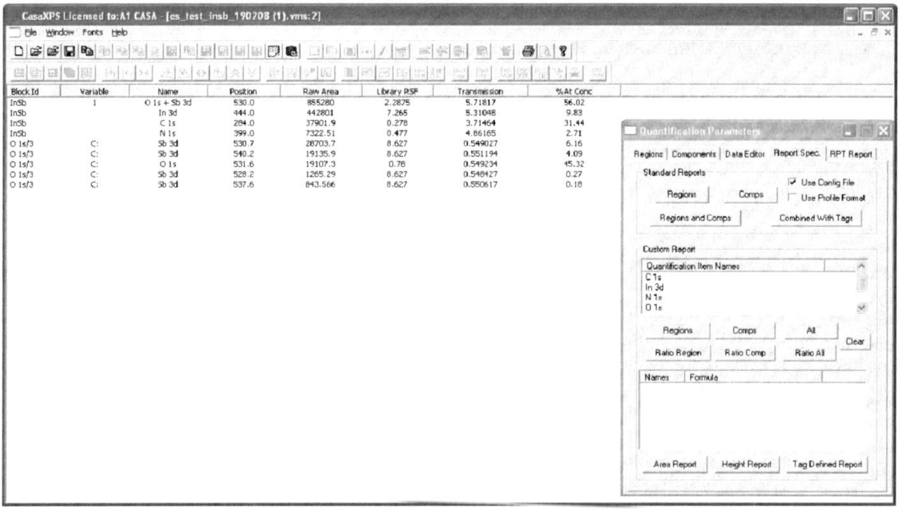

In this example, the format for the quantification report is specified by a configuration file located in the CasaXPS.DEF/QuantTables directory.

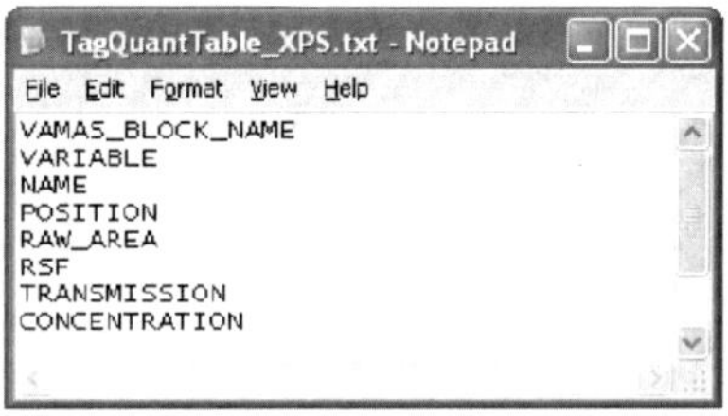

The configuration file is prepared to highlight the source for the quantities determined by the TAG report. The first column lists the VAMAS block from which the information in each row derives. The second column displays the experimental variable common to all the VAMAS blocks contributing to the quantification report. Rows marked with a C: derive from component values, with the exception of the atomic concentration which derives from a combination of the survey data region with the same TAG string as the components from the high resolution spectrum. The component intensities are used to calculate the fraction of the atomic concentration from the survey region associated with each of the components in the peak model sharing a common TAG string.

Propagation of Regions and Component involving TAGS

The data file contains two measurements of identical nature. The processing performed on the first row corresponding to the experimental variable value equal to 1 can also apply to the second row with experimental value of 2. Propagation of these processing steps reduces the effort in performing the equivalent analysis for both measurements. Propagating the processing for the survey and O1s/Sb 3d spectrum regions and components is achieve by overlaying the survey and VAMAS block assigned element/transition fields O 1s in the active tile. Overlaying VAMAS blocks in the active tile offers a means of specifying more than one source VAMAS block and permits the propagation of processing to the set of selected VAMAS blocks guided by the Match Species/Transition option. The Propagate and Match toolbar button performs the transfer from the source VAMAS blocks to the target VAMAS blocks, designated by the selection in the right-hand pane, based on the element/transition fields in the VAMAS blocks.

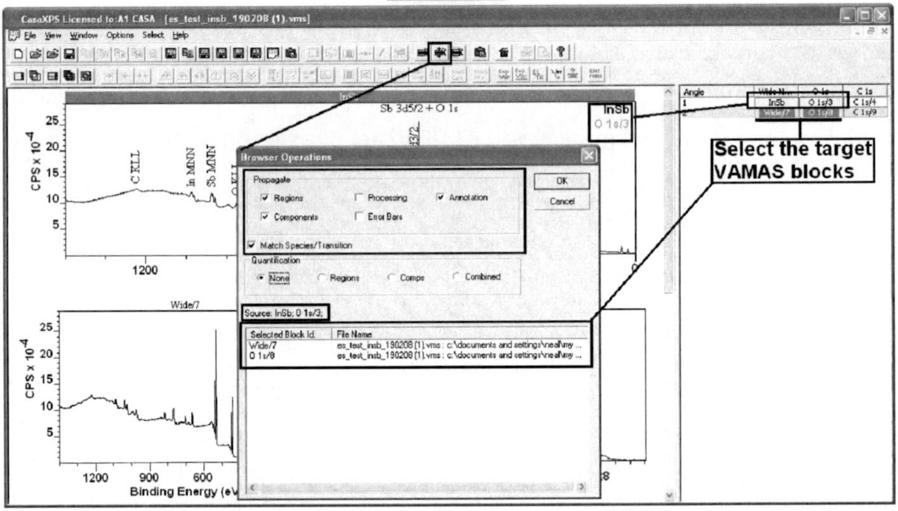

After propagation of regions, components and annotation, the survey and O 1s VAMAS block are updated with the same regions as the two source blocks. There is one remaining issue related to the effective RSF for the data in the second row. The effective RSF is calculated based on the peak model and since the data to which the peak model is fitted in the second row is potentially different from the first row, the effective RSF is most likely different too. It is therefore important to update the effective RSF for each row before moving to generating the full quantification report.

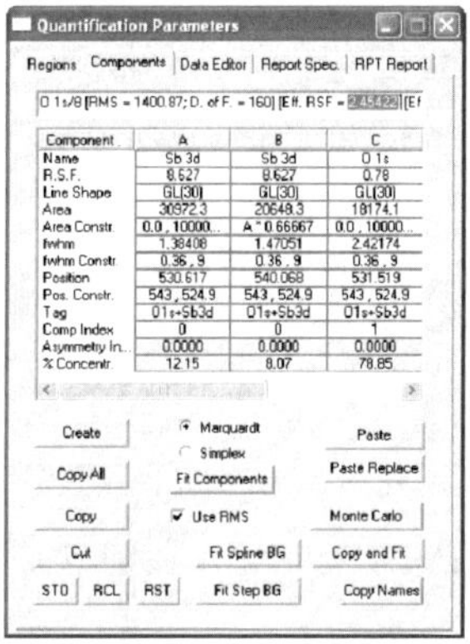

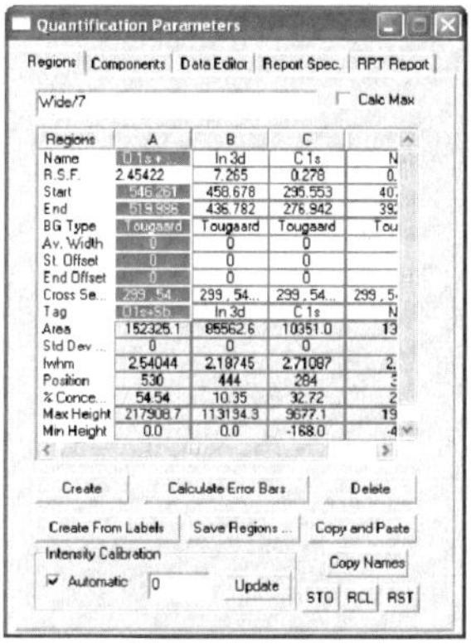

The advantage of using the TAG mechanism is in obtaining more precise quantification from survey spectra including overlapping peaks. The disadvantage is that each measurement must be updated manually with the appropriate effective RSF. The potentially less precise method based on fitting the peak model to the survey data does not rely on effective RSF values determined from the narrow scan data, and therefore the propagation step is sufficient to transfer all information required for the quantification step and as a result quantification is much more efficient using peak models fitted to the survey data than when employing the TAG mechanism.

Once the spectra in both rows are updated appropriately, a quantification report including both sets of spectra is obtained by selecting in the right-hand pane all the VAMAS blocks for which regions and components are defined before pressing the Combined With TAGS button on the Report Spec page.

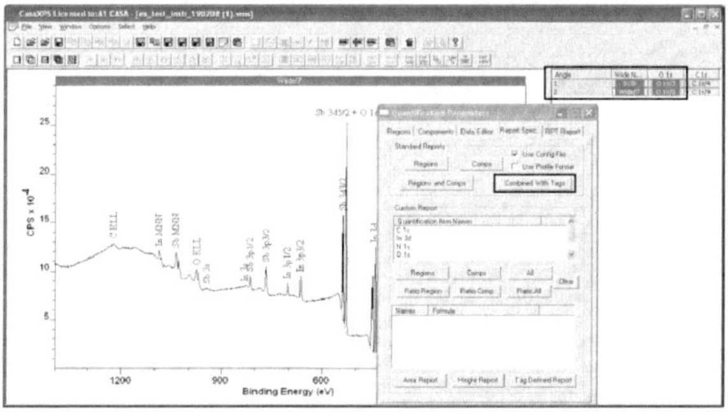

The resulting quantification report includes tables created from both rows of VAMAS blocks. The start of a new table is indicated by the appearance of the experimental variable in the second column. Note, the quantification report is completely defined using a configuration file and so reference to a column in terms of position relates only to reports generated based on the configuration file:

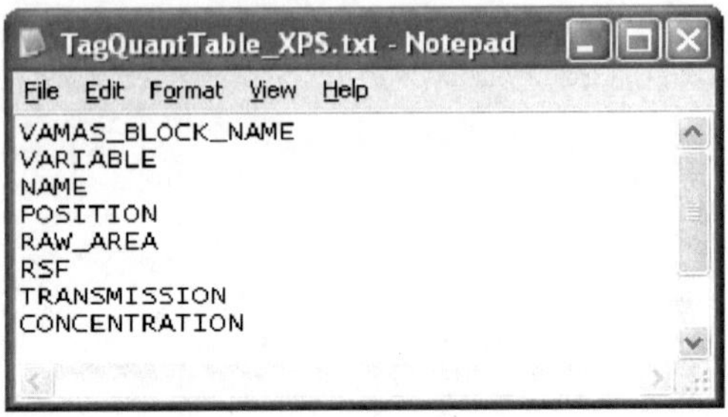

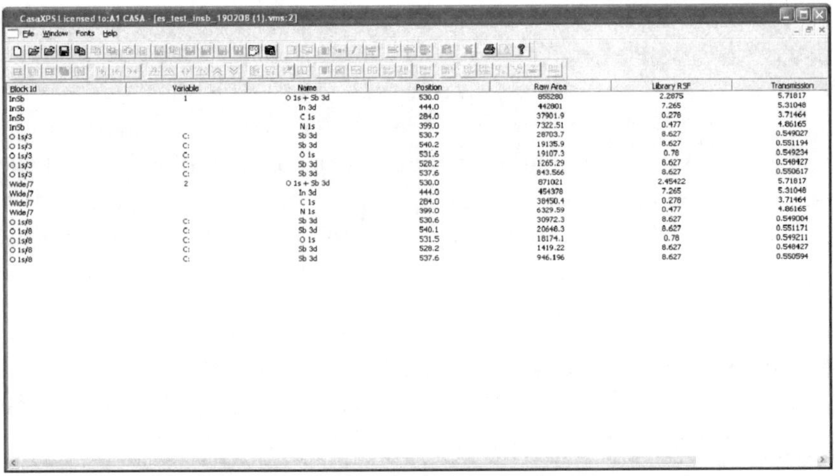

Block Id	Variable	Name	Position	Raw Area	Library RSF	Transmission
InSb	1	O 1s + Sb 3d	530.0	855280	2.2875	5.71817
InSb		In 3d	444.0	442801	7.265	5.31048
InSb		C 1s	284.0	37901.9	0.278	3.71464
InSb		N 1s	399.0	7322.51	0.477	4.86165
O 1s/3	C:	Sb 3d	530.7	28703.7	8.627	0.549027
O 1s/3	C:	Sb 3d	540.2	19135.9	8.627	0.551194
O 1s/3	C:	O 1s	531.6	19107.3	0.78	0.549234
O 1s/3	C:	Sb 3d	528.2	1265.29	8.627	0.548427
O 1s/3	C:	Sb 3d	537.6	843.566	8.627	0.550617
Wide/7	2	O 1s + Sb 3d	530.0	871021	2.45422	5.71817
Wide/7		In 3d	444.0	454378	7.265	5.31048
Wide/7		C 1s	284.0	38450.4	0.278	3.71464
Wide/7		N 1s	399.0	6329.59	0.477	4.86165
O 1s/8	C:	Sb 3d	530.6	30972.3	8.627	0.549004
O 1s/8	C:	Sb 3d	540.1	20648.3	8.627	0.551171
O 1s/8	C:	O 1s	531.5	18174.1	0.78	0.549211
O 1s/8	C:	Sb 3d	528.2	1419.22	8.627	0.548427
O 1s/8	C:	Sb 3d	537.6	946.196	8.627	0.550594

Working with Data Files

The purpose of this section is to review the features in CasaXPS for aiding those working with large sets of samples, where the data are not necessarily identical in nature but nevertheless have a common theme.

For example, a series of measurements might be made on a set of stainless steel samples, where each experiment includes a survey plus a set of high resolution spectra; however, while the spectra always include data from the C 1s, O 1s and N 1s energy intervals, other intervals such as Cr 2p or Fe 2p may also be included in the data files.

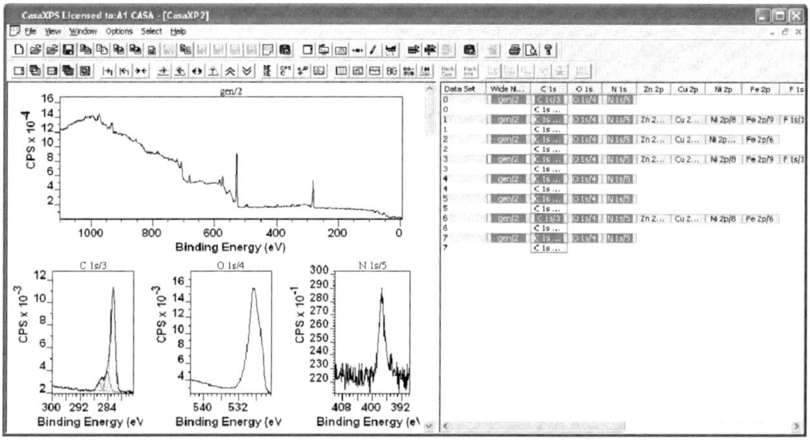

If the data were identical in terms of the number of spectral regions and order of acquisition, and such samples were routinely analysed over an extended period of time, then it would be worth investing the time to setup the required batch processing files. The fact that the data files include variations on a theme means batch processing is not an option. Fortunately, CasaXPS offers many features for manipulating multiple samples and by applying some of the tricks-of-the-trade large sets of data files can be processed with relative ease.

Opening Multiple Files

CasaXPS is designed to manage multiple files all open at the same time. For individual data files the natural means of loading the data into CasaXPS is to have an experiment frame per data file. An experiment frame offers a means of browsing the file contents in terms of VAMAS blocks and visualising the data via display tiles. When the Open menu option on the File menu is selected, the File dialog window permits the selection of more than one file.

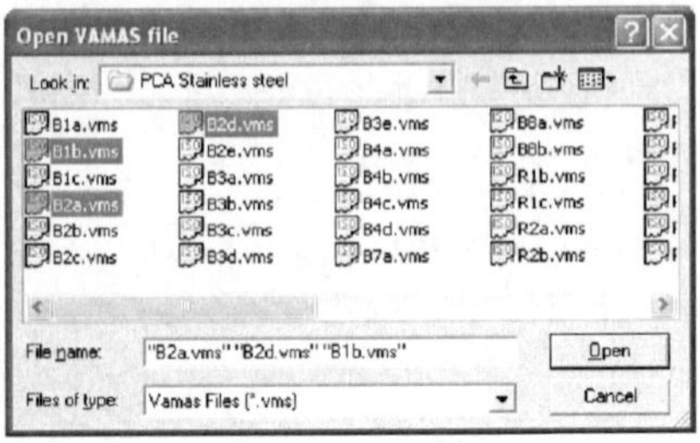

On pressing the Open button on the File dialog window, each of the selected VAMAS files are loaded into separate experiment frames.

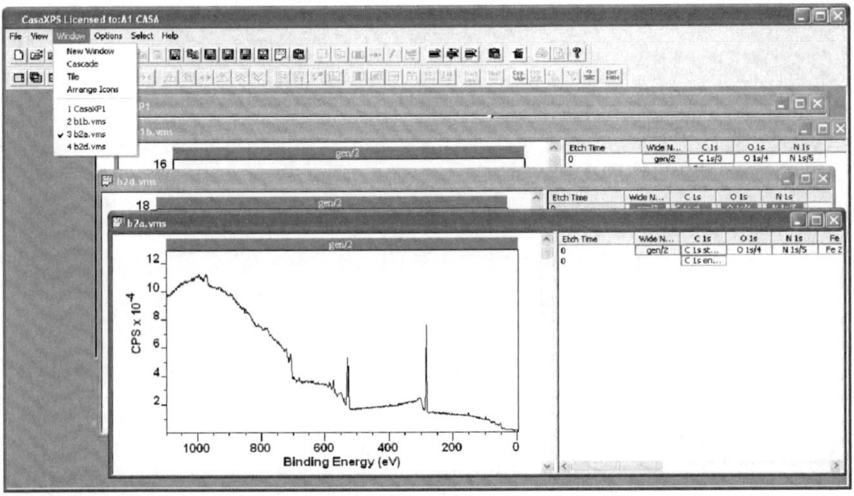

Once the Open File menu item has been selected and the Open VAMAS File dialog is active, the normal operations for making selections in Windows programs are available for choosing the files to be opened. A single file is selected with a left-click of the mouse, which can be followed by holding the Shift or Control keyboard keys down before left-clicking the mouse over a different file. The Shift modifies the left-click action and causes a range-selection to occur, where all the file names between the first and second left-clicked file names become selected. The Control key causes files to be added to the current selection. The following selection made using the File dialog window, in which all the files in the current directory are required, is achieved by first, left-clicking on a file name to ensure the list of files is the active item on the dialog window, then pressing Ctrl-A. All the files in the current directory, subject to the "Files of type" filter, become selected. On pressing the Open button on the dialog an experiment frame, one for each file selected, appears in the CasaXPS main window.

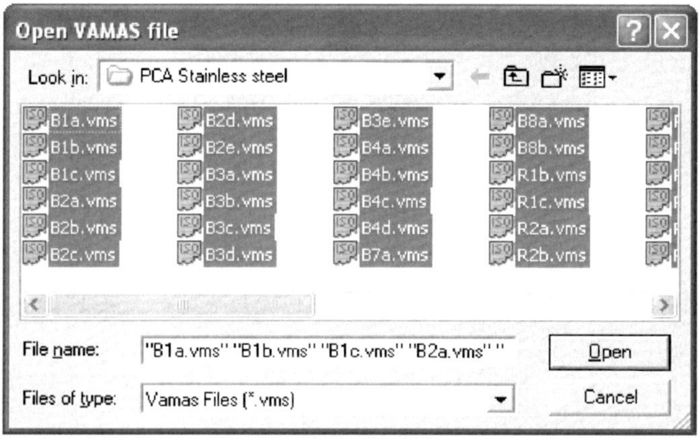

Merging Data into a VAMAS file

Merging Data Files from Disk

The File Menu of version 2.3.15 offers two new options for merging data files. Previously the existing Open and Merge and the Convert and Merge options provided a means of merging a set of files into a single VAMAS file. The files selected via the File dialog window are entered into the new VAMAS file using the alphabetic order of the file names selected. The two new options offer a further selection mechanism in which the order of selection is used to order the data within the new VAMAS file.

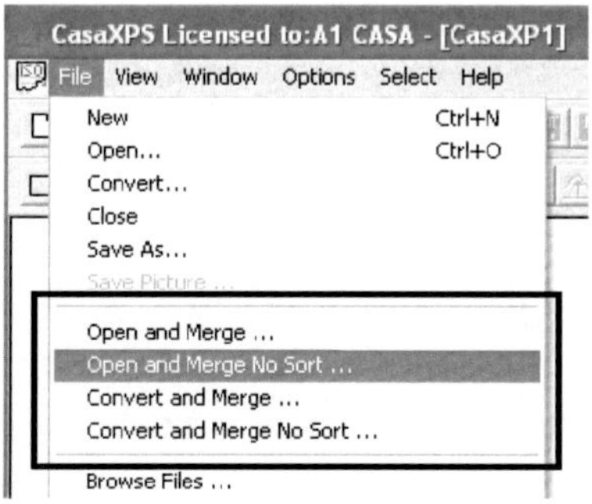

The dialog window invoked by selecting either the **Open and Merge No Sort** or the **Convert and Merge No Sort** menu options on the File menu displays the files in the current directory, from which a selection is made using the mouse and the Control Key. After the selection is complete, on pressing the **Merge** button the selected files are merged into a new experiment frame in the order of the selection via the mouse actions.

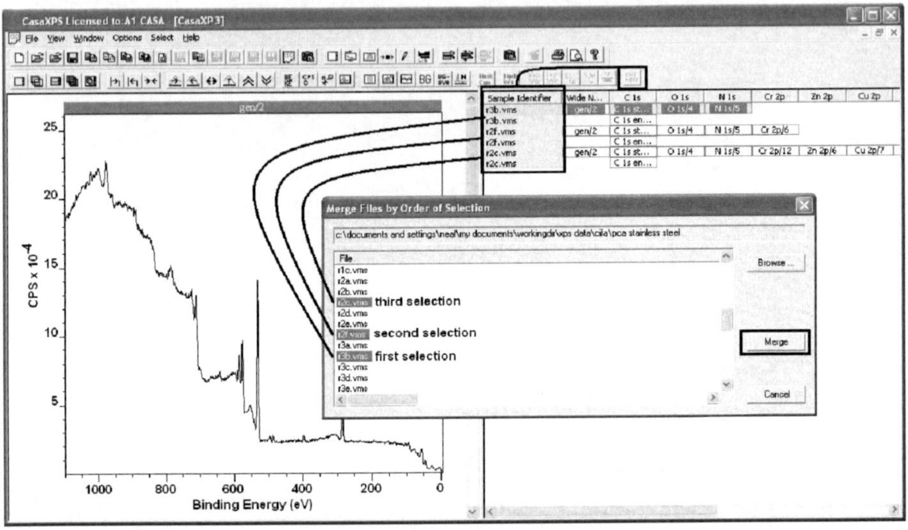

The Browse button invokes the standard File dialog window, which in this context is used to change the current directory. Simply select a file via the File dialog window and press the Open button. The text-field at the top of the dialog is updated with the directory path for the chosen file and the files within the newly selected current directory are listed on the dialog window.

Collecting VAMAS blocks into a single experiment frame offers a means of preparing an overlay display. A display tile is only capable of displaying data from the same experiment frame and it is therefore necessary to merge data from different files before a visual comparison of the data can be made.

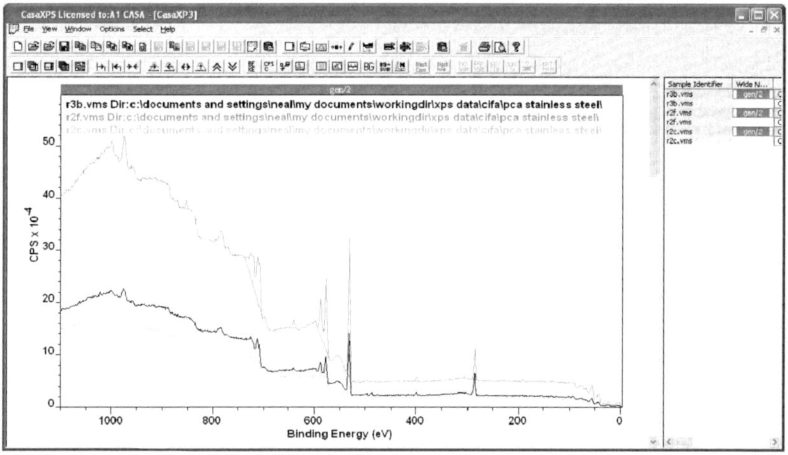

Data selected in the right-hand pane are overlaid in the active tile by pressing the Overlay toolbar button.

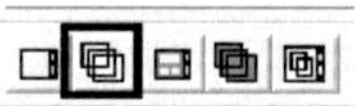

When VAMAS files are merged, the original file name is added to the VAMAS block comment.

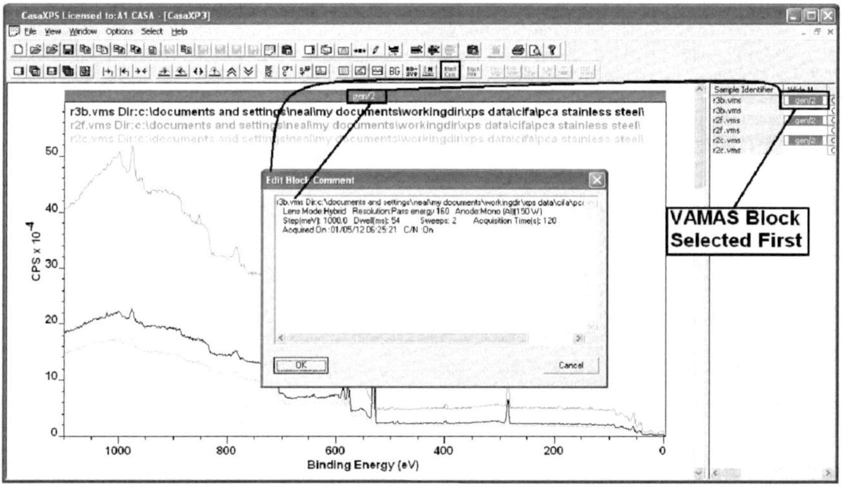

One option for providing a key or legend for overlaid spectra uses the text from the first line in the VAMAS block comment field for each VAMAS block overlaid in a tile. Enabling the display of a key over the data is performed on the Display property page of the Tile Display Parameters dialog window.

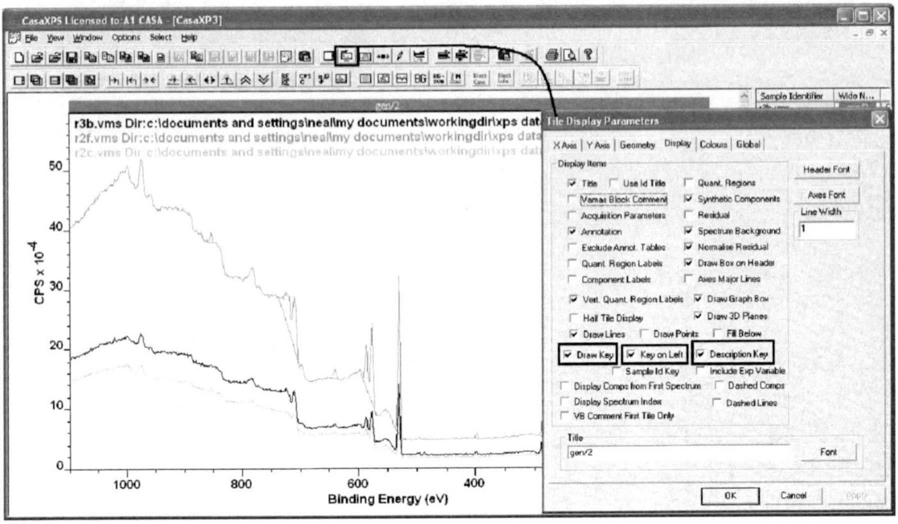

Other options for the text used in the legend include the VAMAS block sample identifier and experimental variable, while the default text derives from the block identifier used to label the VAMAS block array in the right-hand pane.

Moving VAMAS Blocks between Opened Files

VAMAS files already open in CasaXPS provide a source for creating or adding to VAMAS files. The data blocks selected in the right-hand pane are moved to a different experiment frame or appended to the current file using the Copy and Paste VAMAS blocks toolbar button.

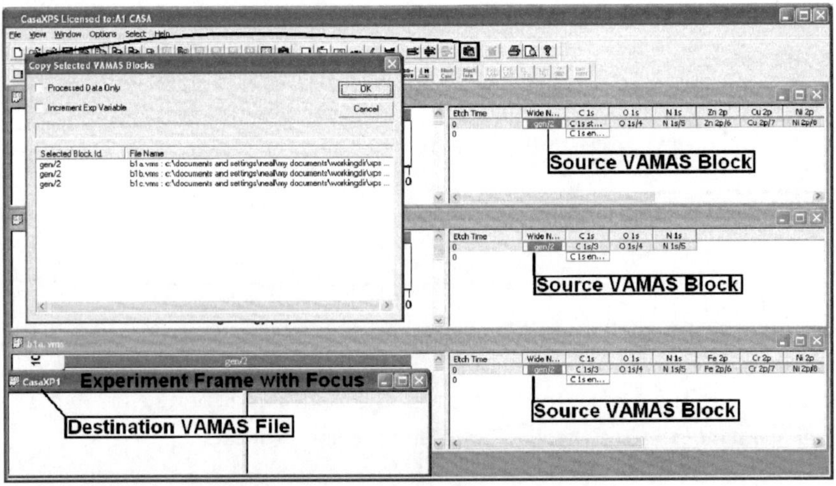

The data blocks listed on the dialog window invoked by the toolbar button are copied and pasted into the destination VAMAS file.

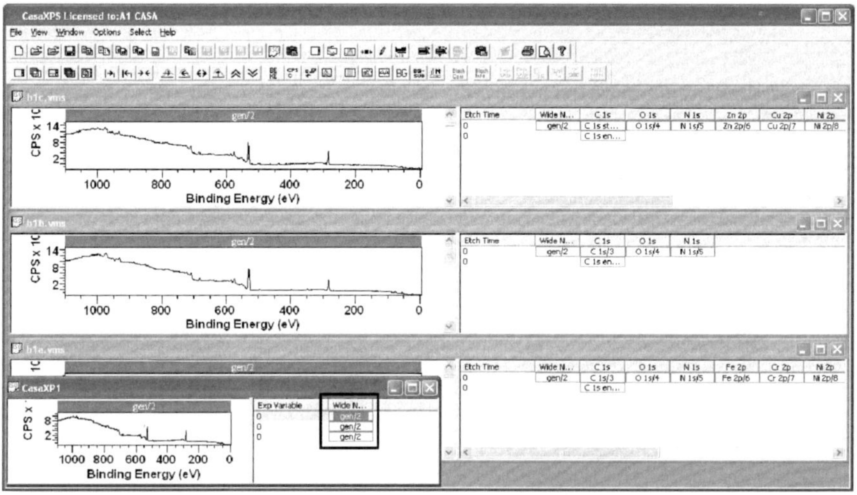

The Selection Mechanism for VAMAS blocks

With large sets of similar data files, the desire is typically to apply the same set of processing operations to each file, prepare the display and print the results. The problem is therefore to manipulate the data such that these operations are as painless as possible. The basis for any operation in CasaXPS is the selection of one or more VAMAS blocks, so before describing the operations, the new selection mechanism for multiple files are described first.

An experiment frame offers two views into a VAMAS file, namely, the left-hand pane in which spectra are displayed in graphical format and the right-hand pane browser. Both play a role in defining the target and source for various operations such as processing and propagating the results of processing to other data blocks. For example, some processing operations depend on both the VAMAS blocks overlaid in the active tile and also the VAMAS blocks selected in the right-hand pane. The active tile is therefore on occasion treated as a secondary selection, where the primary selection is managed by the right-hand pane. Energy calibration for data files collected into a single VAMAS file is an example of an operation requiring two distinct sets of VAMAS blocks. These two sets of VAMAS blocks used in an advanced energy calibration are maintained in the active tile and the right-hand pane.

The logic governing the use of these two selection mechanisms requires some explanation. In general, a single target for a processing operation is defined as the *active VAMAS block* in the *active display tile* of the experiment frame with input focus.

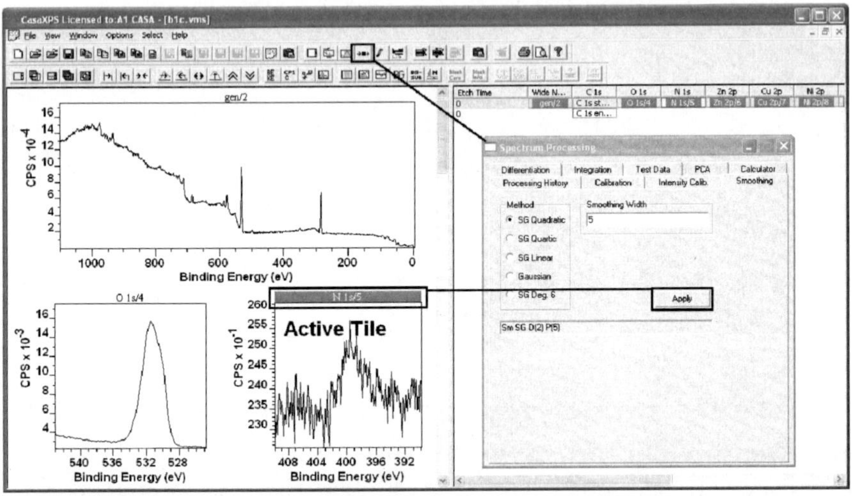

The *active display tile* is the tile displaying data in the left-hand pane of the experiment frame for which the title to the tile is highlighted. When more than one VAMAS block is displayed in the active tile, the *active VAMAS block* is the block selected first in the right-hand pane at the time the data are displayed in the *active display tile*.

Property pages such as those on the Spectrum Processing dialog window and the Annotation dialog window act on a single target data block and therefore the concept of the *active VAMAS block* is central to understand the cause and effect mechanism within CasaXPS. Once a block has been manipulated using the *active VAMAS block*, for sets of similar data the progression from the operations performed on the active VAMAS block to processing equivalent data blocks is to transfer these processing operations by propagation. Hence the requirement to specify a source block and a set of target blocks. The source for a propagation action is specified using the *active VAMAS block* mechanism, while the target blocks are defined using the selection in the experiment frame right-hand pane. Anyone processing XPS depth profiles would routinely use these concepts, where all the selections in terms of *active display tiles* and the right-hand pane are made within a single experiment frame. When multiple files are involved, the definition for the source and target blocks extends to cover selections over many different experiment frames.

The method for selecting data blocks in the right-hand pane of an experiment frame is not limited to a single experiment frame. Provided the Control key is held down, any subsequent selections made by left-clicking the mouse over the array of VAMAS blocks in the right-hand panes adds to the set of currently selected data blocks. The following shows a set of six files where a survey spectrum from each file is displayed in the active tile and is also the current selection in the corresponding right-hand pane.

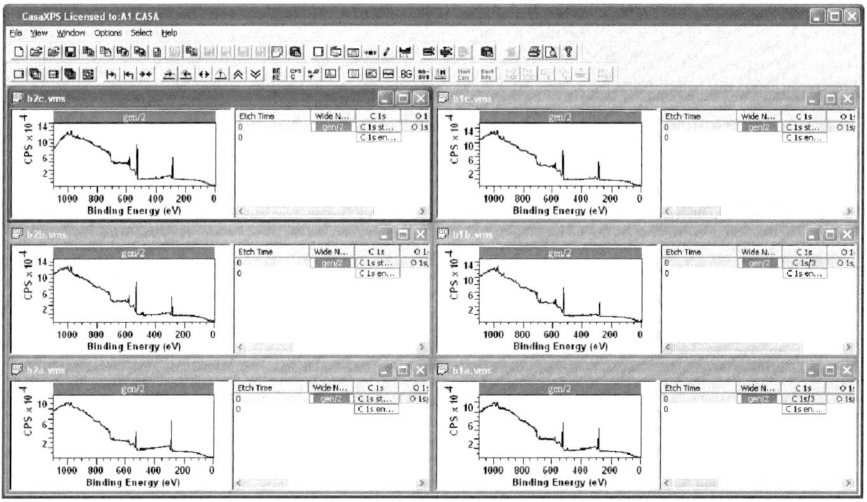

While these data blocks could have been individually selected using the mouse, for larger sets of files, relying on the mouse and the Control key to make such selections is not very time efficient. To improve the ability to select related data blocks across experiment frames, the Select menu of the main window offers options for selecting blocks throughout a set of experiment frames. Function keys have been associated with these menu options so that the selections can be made without excessive mouse movements

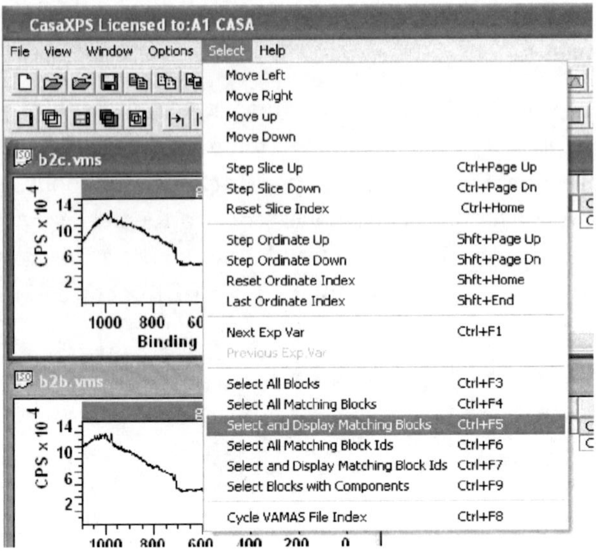

Select All Blocks (Ctrl F3): All data blocks in each experiment frame are selected via the menu option or alternatively hold the Control key down and press the F3 function key on the keyboard.

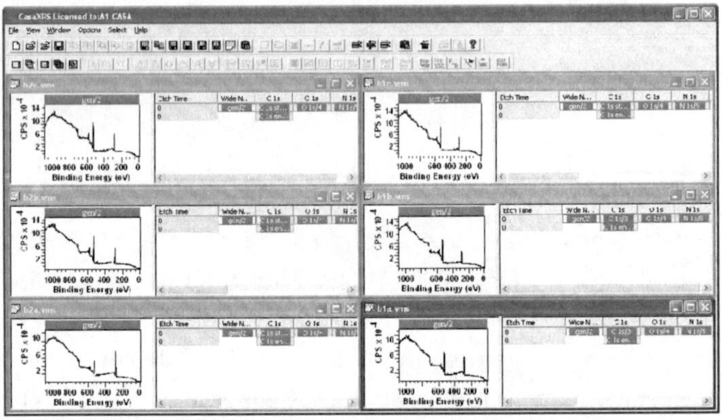

Select All Matching Blocks (Ctrl F4): The selected blocks in the experiment frame with input focus define the species/transition fields used to match against all the data blocks in the current set of experiment frames. The result of pressing the **Select All Matching Blocks** menu option is all data blocks from the current set of experiment frames with identical species/transition fields are added to the current set of selected data blocks. For example, an initial state of a set of files might be as follows:

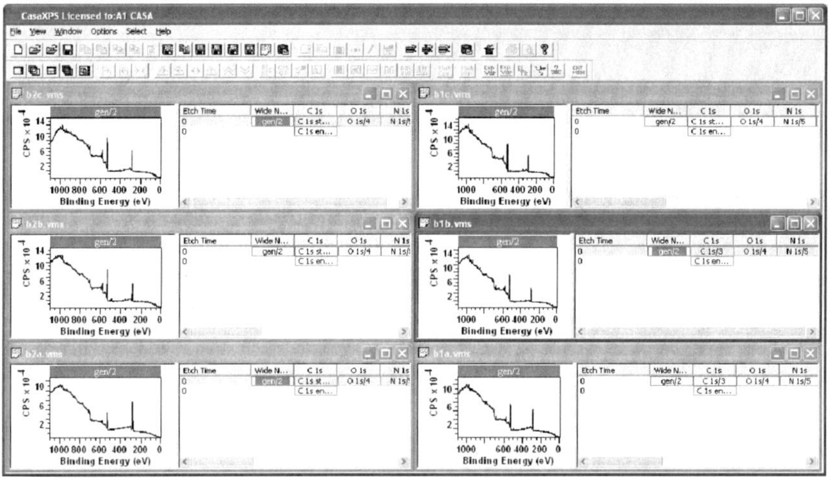

Three of the six survey spectra are currently selected. To add the set of O 1s data blocks to a selection, one O 1s data block from any file must be selected whilst the Control key is held down. The Control key must be held down to prevent the survey spectra from becoming deselected.

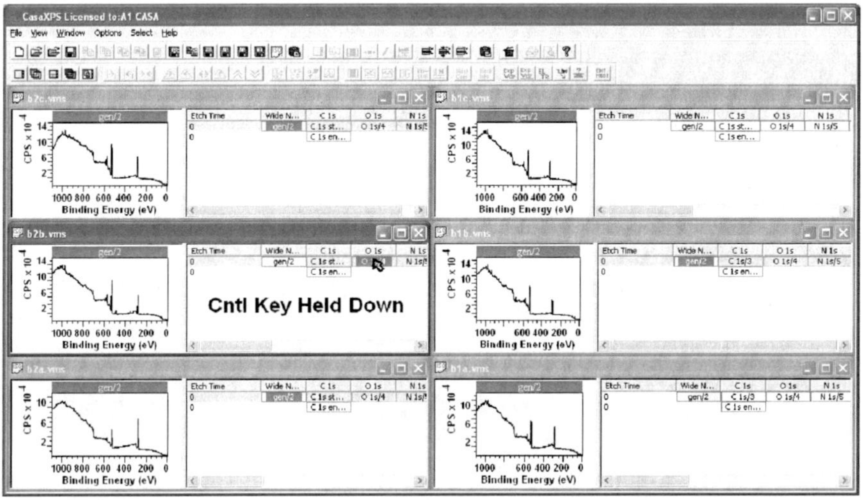

While input focus is still on the experiment frame with the O 1s selected, holding the Control key down and pressing the F4 function key results in the selection of both the existing survey spectra and additional O 1s blocks in every experiment frame. The data displayed in the scrolled list of tiles in each experiment frame are unaffected by the action of the menu option.

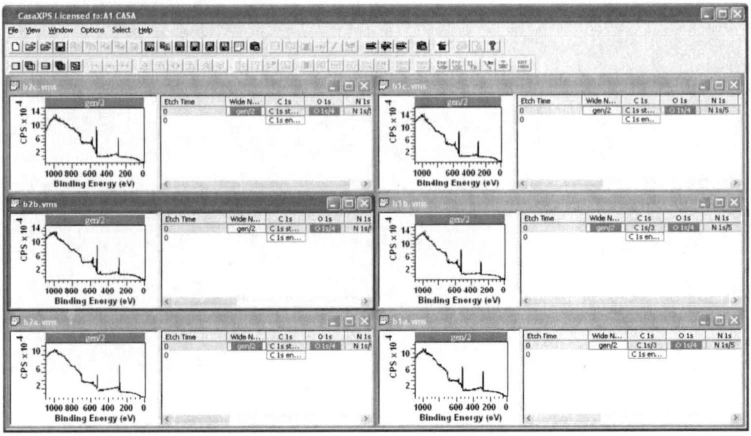

Select and Display Matching Blocks (Ctrl F5): The data displayed in the active tile is affected by the **Select and Display Matching Blocks** menu option. The intention is to change the active VAMAS block in each and every experiment frame using the same selection mechanism as **Select Matching Blocks**. Rather than leaving the survey spectra displayed in the left-hand pane, the consequences of **Select and Display Matching Blocks** menu option is to display the O 1s spectrum for each experiment frame for which the survey is not selected.

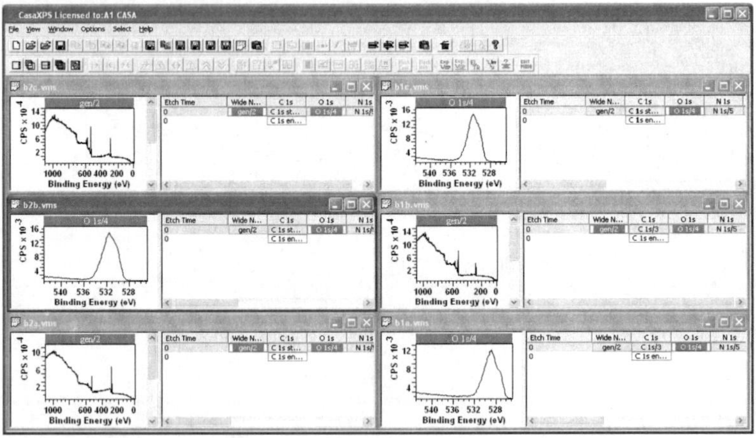

The need to adjust the active VAMAS block is motivated by a new energy calibration option which performs a calibration across files.

Select All Matching Block Ids and **Select and Display All Matching Block Ids** are equivalent to **Select Matching Blocks** and **Select and Display Matching Blocks**.

The criterion used to make the match between the selected blocks and the blocks in the open files differs. A block identifier is the VAMAS block field used to display the array in the right-hand pane. These two additional selection options function by matching the block identifier for the selected blocks in the experiment frame with focus against the block identifiers for all VAMAS blocks in open files and adding to the current selection any VAMAS block found to satisfy the criterion. **Select Matching Blocks** and **Select and Display Matching Blocks** require VAMAS blocks to match species and transition VAMAS fields. The species and transition fields are concatenated to provide the text used in the headings above the array of VAMAS blocks in the right-hand pane. Essentially, only VAMAS blocks with identical headings are selected by the **Select Matching Blocks** and **Select and Display Matching Blocks** menu options.

Select Blocks with Components differs from the other selection options on the Select menu. Only those blocks with components in the experiment frame with focus are selected. VAMAS blocks without components are deselected. The motivation for selecting VAMAS blocks with components derives from peak modelling of ToF SIMS data, where the VAMAS file is organised into a set of VAMAS blocks representing unit mass intervals.

An Example involving the Selection Options: Energy Calibration for Multiple Files

The best way to appreciate the value of these selection mechanisms is to describe an example in which the use of these shortcuts is essential to the efficient analysis of the data.

Charge compensation issues often cause photoelectric lines to appear shifted on a sample-by-sample basis. The following set of O 1s spectrum measured from different samples of similar materials illustrates the problem.

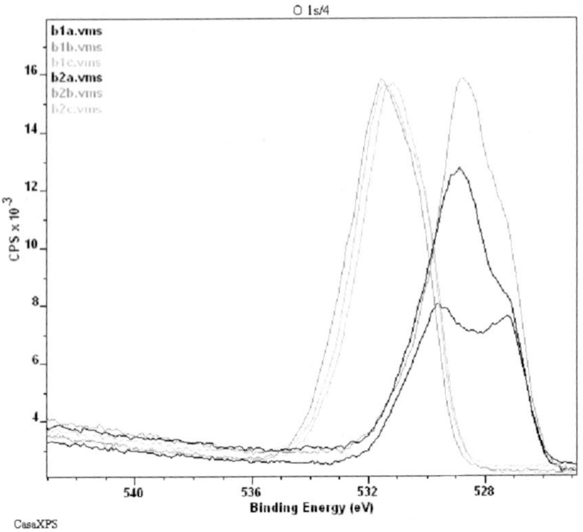

Each set of data is shifted in energy by potentially a different amount and as a result, simply creating a region for one spectrum then propagating the region to the set of spectra maintained in separate data files would typically fail to define the background in an ideal fashion.

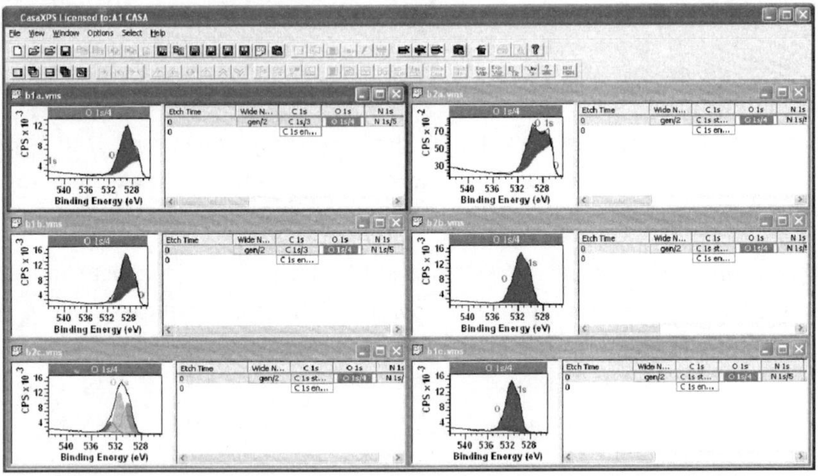

It is therefore advisable to energy calibrate the spectra from each file before performing the propagation of regions and/or components. As a result, two new options on the Calibration property page of the Spectrum Processing dialog window offers a means for calibrating sets of spectra in different experiment frames with a single operation.

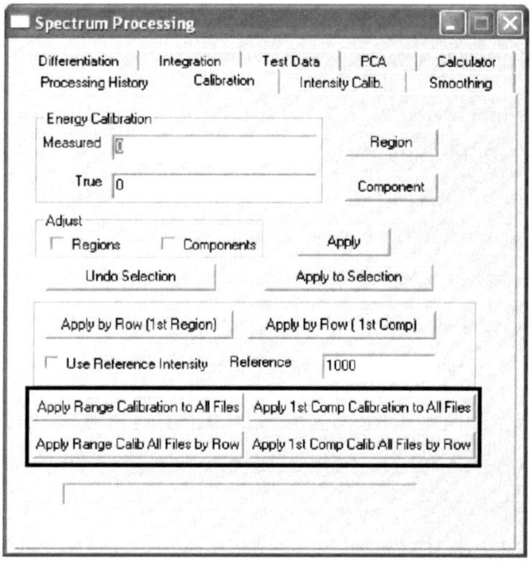

Energy calibration is often performed to ensure the saturated carbon peak appears at binding energy 285.0 eV. For carbon spectra other than data consisting of a single carbon peak, the implication is a peak-model is required to establish the appropriate position for the saturated carbon transition. The problem with data such as the stainless steel spectra is that an energy calibration must exist before a peak model can be propagated to the data with different charge state in the various VAMAS files. Without an initial calibration, the location of the background region and synthetic peaks may be in error by several eV and therefore automatic peak fitting fails to produce appropriate results as exemplified below.

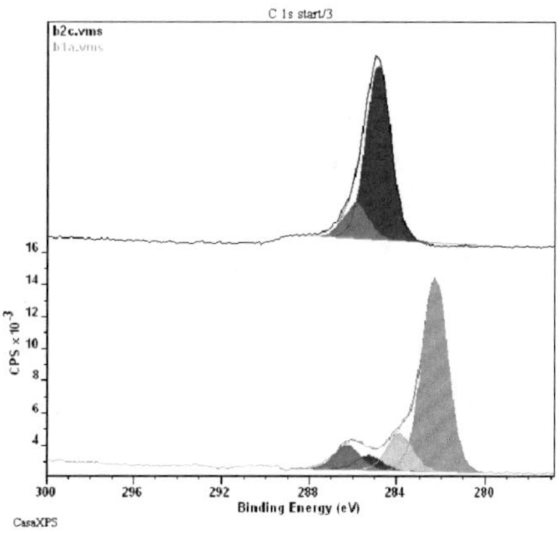

For this reason, the energy calibration is sometimes performed in two stages. First a calibration based on the maximum intensity in a range is performed. Although not perfect, often the range calibration is more than good enough for the application, but in the event that greater precision is required, a second calibration based on the position of a synthetic component is available. The range calibration allows peak models to be copied and fitted to the data in the different files and once these peaks are fitted to the data, the second form of calibration is applied, where the position for one of the synthetic components define the fine adjustment needed to establish the precise energy calibration.

Both calibration buttons for energy-shifting data in multiple files require the use of the selection mechanism. The process of energy calibrating a file centres on identifying a spectrum from which the measured energy position of a peak is computed. Each experiment frame must define a single spectrum, from which the un-calibrated location of a peak is determined and together with the known value, entered in the True field on the Calibration property page, are sufficient to calculate the shift required to correctly position the photoelectric lines in binding energy.

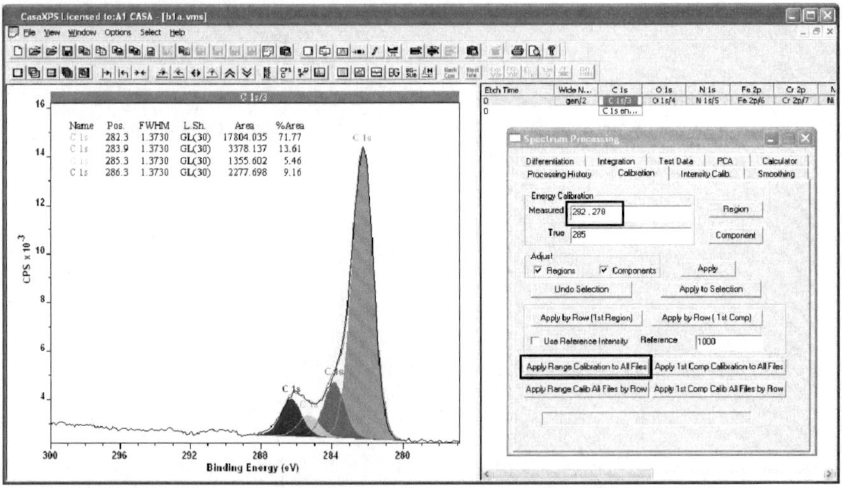

The spectrum used for the calibration calculation in each experiment frame is the *active VAMAS block* for that experiment frame. Hence the existence of the *Select and Display Matching Blocks* menu option described above. The display in each experiment frame can be set to a given species/transition at a click of a button. For example, the C 1s blocks can be used to calibrate the data in each of the stainless steel files therefore in order to perform the calibration each experiment frame must display the C 1s data in the active tile. Simply selecting a C 1s data block in any experiment frame before pressing the Ctrl+F5 key-sequence causes all the C 1s data blocks to highlight and at the same time displayed in the scrolled-list of tiles; thus, making the C 1s blocks the *active VAMAS block* in each experiment frame. In using the *active VAMAS block* to specify the spectrum from which the energy shift is computed, the right-hand pane selection is available for indicating those data blocks to which the calibration must also apply. The Select Matching Block menu option or Cntl+F4 provide the route to changing the selection in the right-hand pane without changing the data displayed in the active tile for each experiment frame.

There is an underlying assumption about the nature of the data in the files under consideration. It is assumed that the spectrum used to perform the calibration is in the first row of the right-hand pane. These data files include two C 1s regions, one acquired at the beginning of each measurement and one acquired after all the other spectra are recorded.

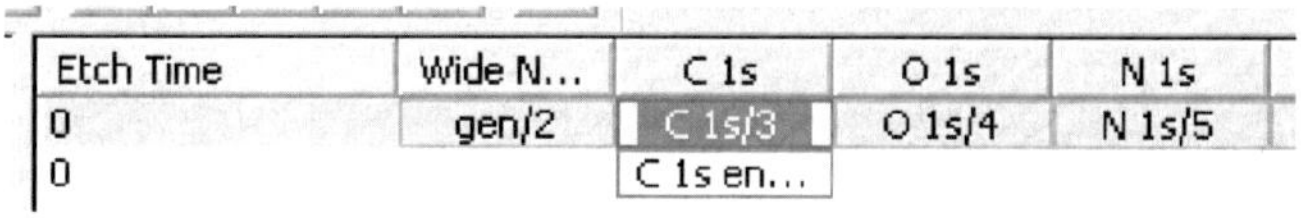

As the data files stand, Ctrl+F5 would always make the first of these two C 1s spectra the *active VAMAS block*. If for any reason it is desired to calibrate using the second C 1s spectrum, it would be necessary to distinguish between the two C 1s spectra by changing the species/transition fields in the VAMAS block information so these two spectra differ resulting in both appearing on the first row in the right-hand pane. An alternative would be to ensure the data are entered into the VAMAS file such that the block identifiers are consistently named throughout the sequence of measurements. If the same block identifiers were used then the Select and Display Matching Block Ids would achieve the desired result without reorganising the VAMAS blocks in the right-hand pane.

The first phase of establishing a rough calibration for all the VAMAS files based on the C 1s spectrum in each file is achieved by:

1. Select a C 1s VAMAS block in one experiment frame and press Cntl+F5. The C 1s spectrum will appear as the active VAMAS block for each experiment frame.

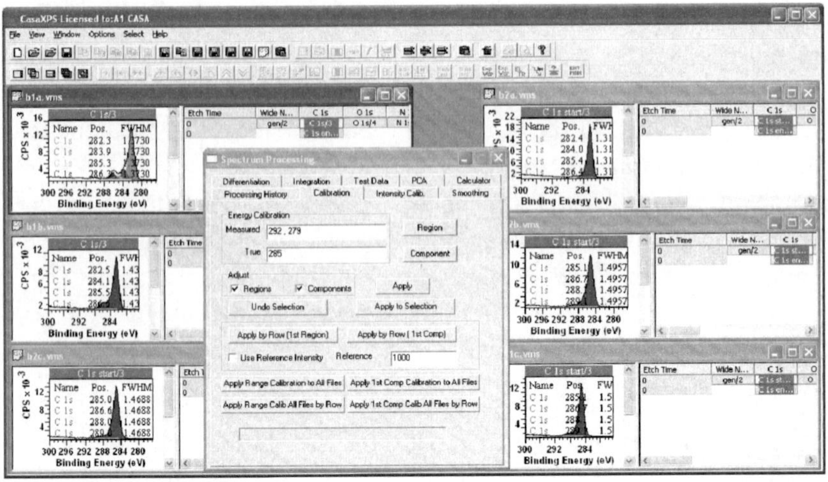

2. Since these data files each contain different numbers of VAMAS blocks, select all the VAMAS blocks using Cntl+F3. A subset of these VAMAS blocks could be targeted using a specific selection in the experiment frame with focus before pressing Cntl+F4.

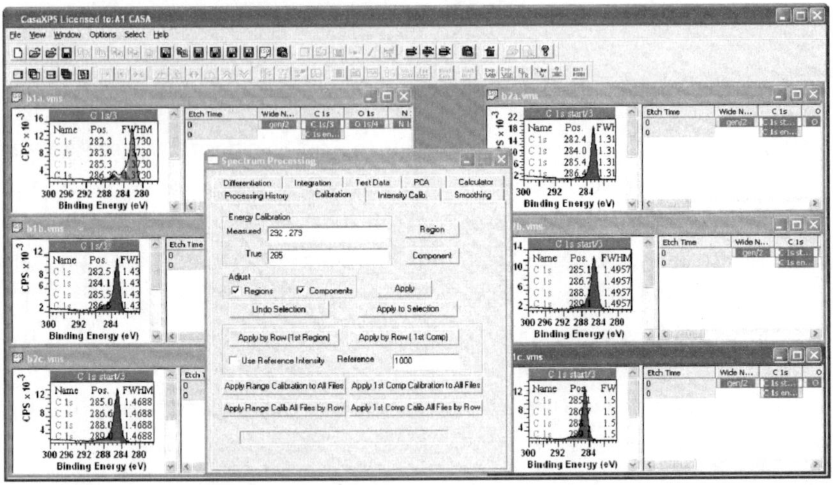

3. Using the Calibration property page on the Spectrum Processing dialog window, enter a range of energies such that the largest C 1s peak displayed in each experiment frame is included in the energy range.
4. Calibrate the entire set of files by pressing the Apply Range Calibration to All Files button on the Calibration property page.

5. Confirm the list of selected VAMAS blocks and files are as intended and press the OK button on the dialog window invoked by pressing the button.

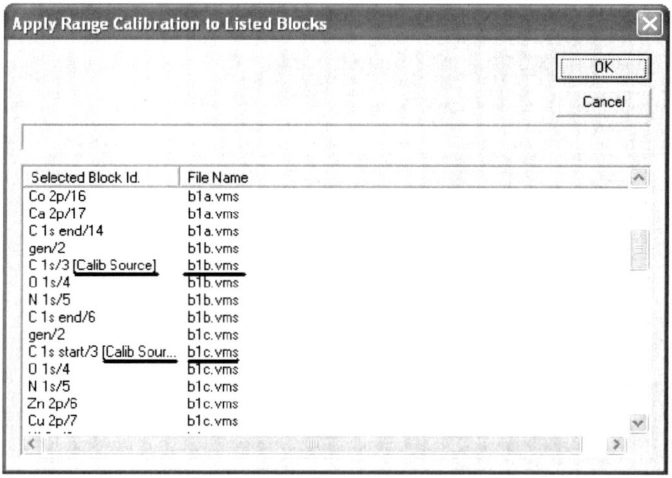

The VAMAS block used to calculate the calibration is indicated for each file involved in the calibration process.

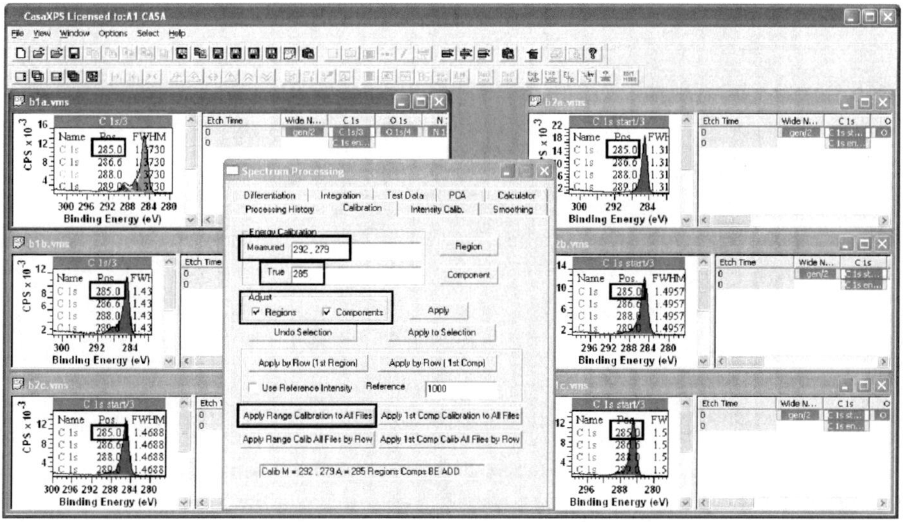

The first approximation to the calibration is now complete. The next step involves propagating the peak model for the C 1s spectrum and recalibrating the data files based on the location of the component representing the saturated carbon peak.

To propagate a peak model prepared for a specific C 1s VAMAS block to the remaining C 1s data:

1. Select the VAMAS block for which the peak model is prepared and press the Cntl+F4 key or use the Select menu. All VAMAS blocks with the same species/transition fields become selected for all files open in CasaXPS.

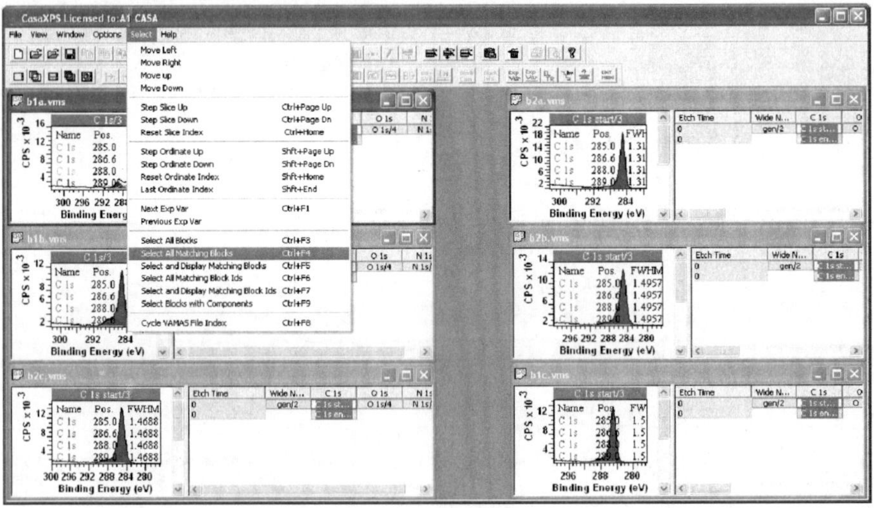

2. Place the cursor over the left-hand pane of the experiment frame displaying the C 1s spectrum for which the peak model is designed and right-click the mouse.

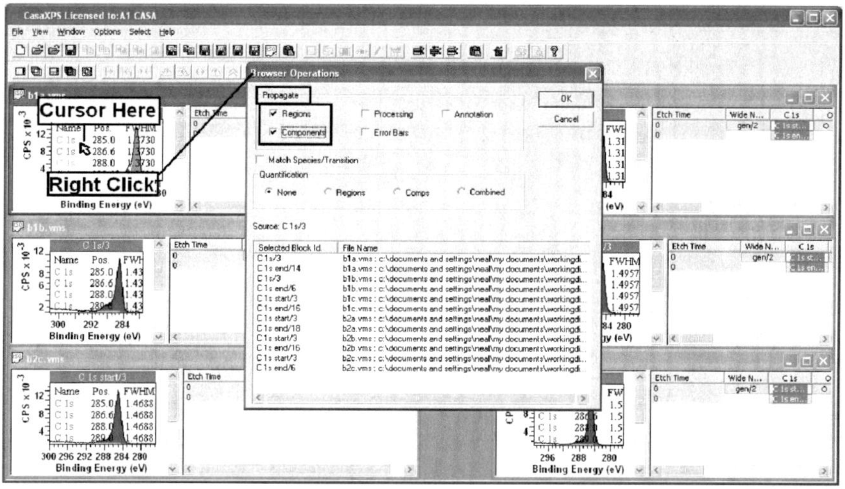

3. Check the Browser Operations window lists the intended target VAMAS blocks and press the OK button.

The propagated peak models are now much improved due to the calibration step prior to performing the propagation. Calibration based on an energy range appropriate for the C 1s data results in a precision of one decimal place for the position of the saturated C 1s peak.

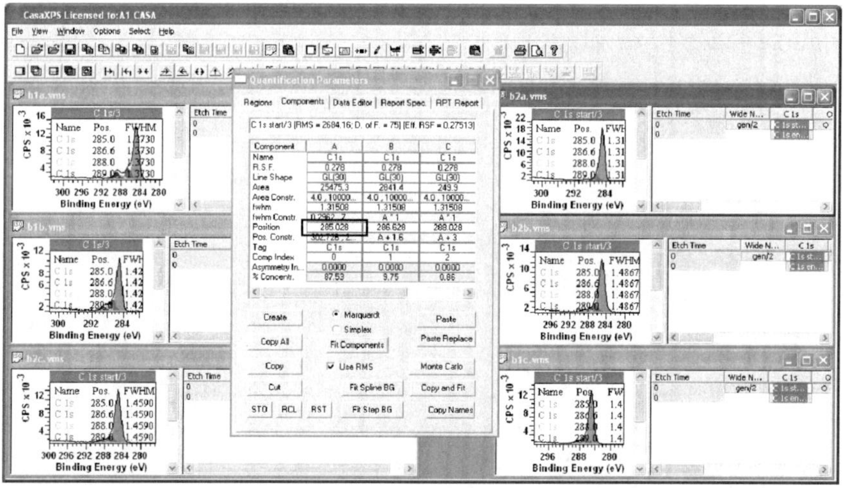

The final improvement in locating the peaks with respect to binding energy is achieved by again displaying in the active tile the C 1s spectra now all modelled using the same components, selecting all the VAMAS blocks in the right-hand panes and re-calibrating the full set of data using the Apply 1st Comp Calibration to All Files button on the Calibration property page. The application of the calibration based on a component position requires the value entered onto the property page for the True field to correspond to the component position in column A, as displayed on the Components property page.

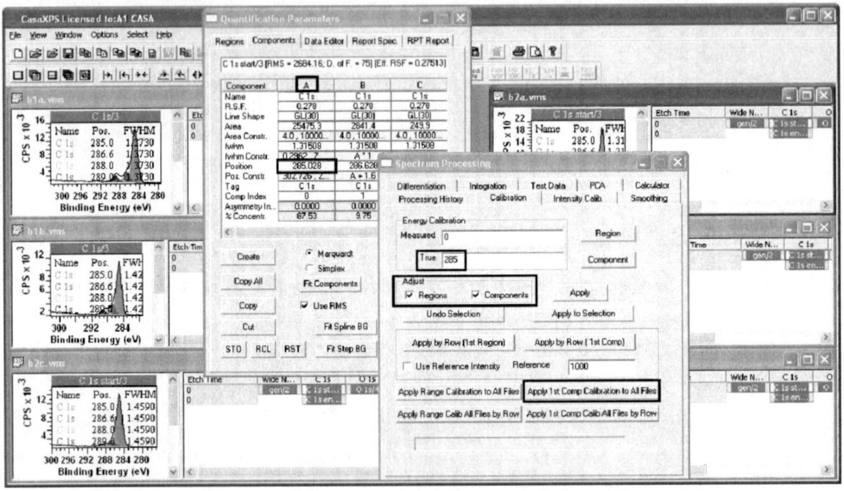

On pressing the Apply 1st Comp Calibration to All Files button, a dialog window lists the selection state with respect to the calibration operation.

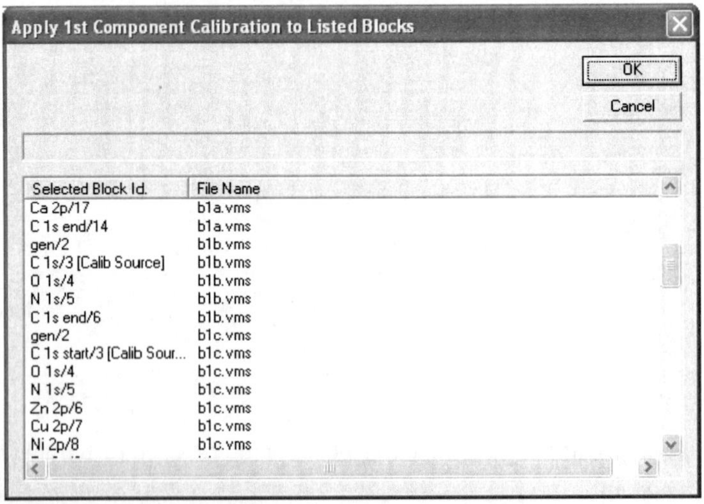

On pressing the OK button on the dialog window, the calibration is performed by calculating the required energy shift for each file based on the first component defined for the VAMAS block displayed in the active tile, and applying the calculated shift for a file to all the VAMAS blocks selected in the file.

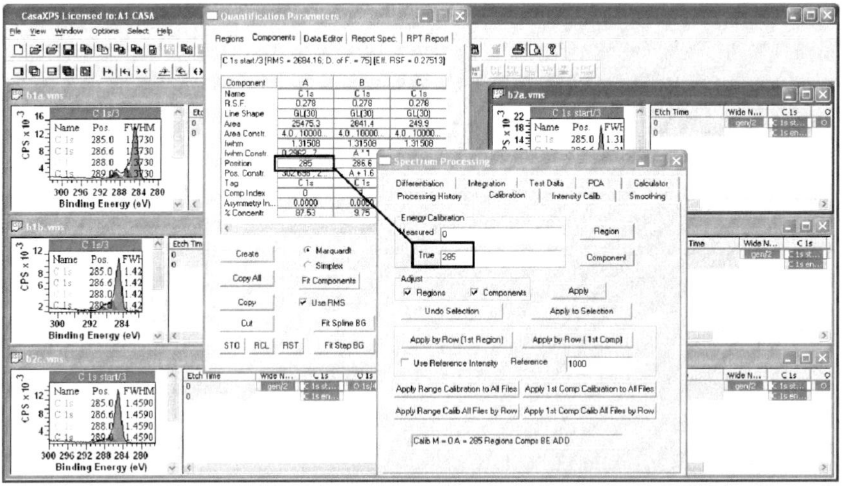

Copying all the data into a new experiment frame and switching to edit mode for the right-hand pane illustrates the result achieved by calibrating the entire data set with respect to the saturated carbon peaks.

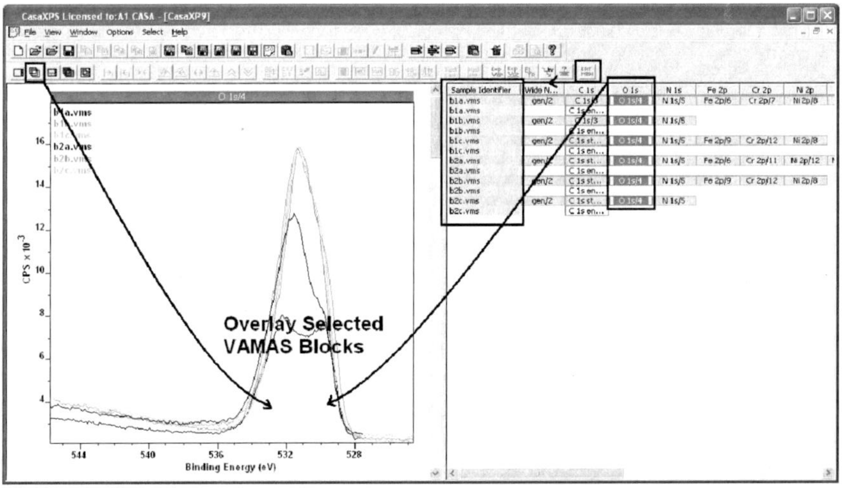

Generating Reports for Multiple Files

While the propagation options permit processing and the transfer of quantification regions and components, the ultimate goal in performing these tasks is to collate the resulting information. Quantification reports may take the form of text-based tables prepared and exported to a spreadsheet program or graphical displays of the spectra including tabulations of atomic concentration and other characteristic information for the samples.

Quantification for sets of files is performed via one of two routes:

1. The Browser Operations dialog window used to propagate regions, components and processing also includes an option for generating a report.

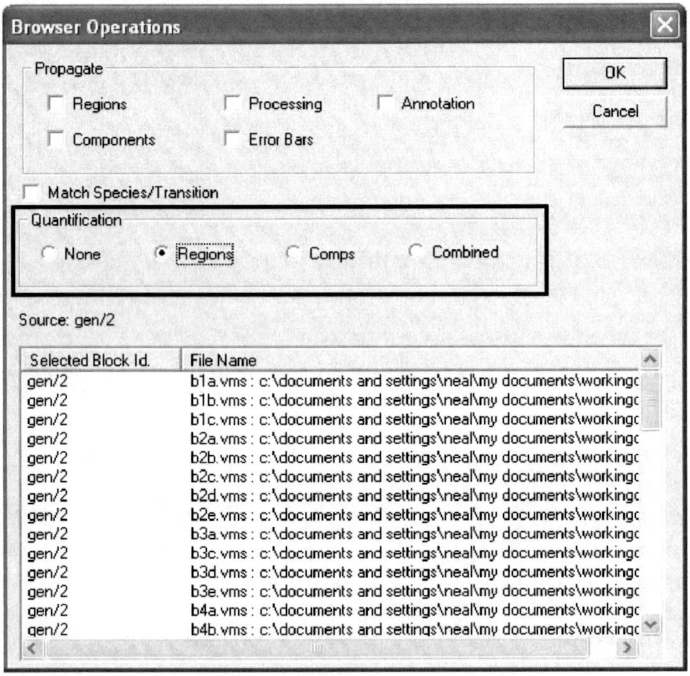

2. Collect the appropriate data together in a new VAMAS file and generate a report via the Report Spec property page.

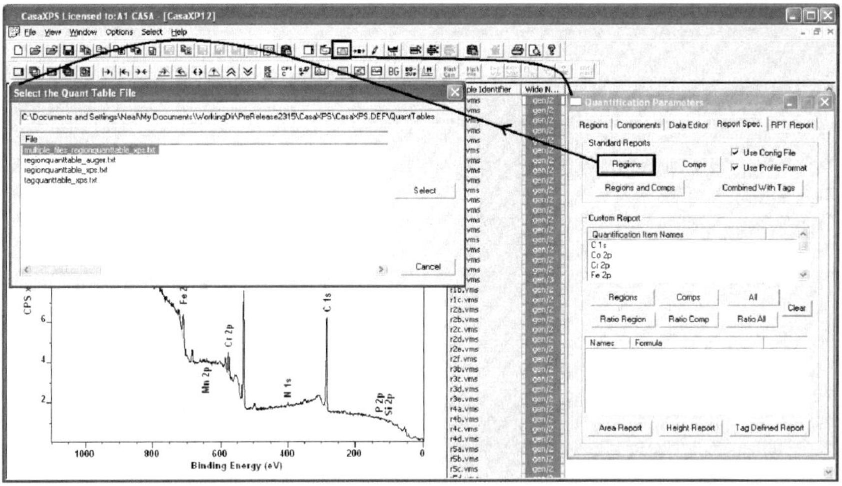

Generating a Report from the Browser Operations Dialog Window

While it is possible to progress directly from propagation of regions and components to report generation, an inspection of the data following propagation is probably advisable before producing a quantification report from the propagated regions or components. A warning message is displayed in the event propagation is followed directly by report generation.

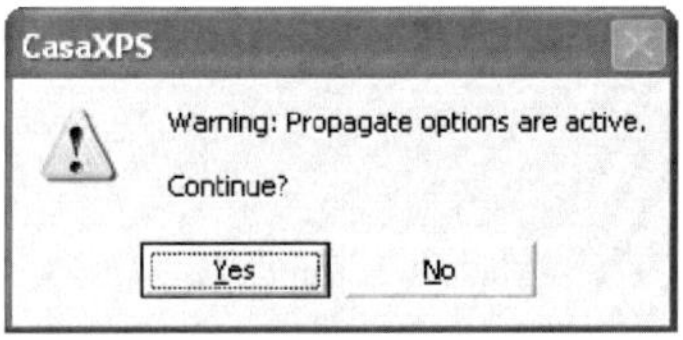

For the example of the stainless steel VAMAS files, processing of the survey spectra might be performed in three steps.

1. Energy-calibrate the survey spectra using the range calibration option described above.
2. Define a set of regions appropriate for all survey spectra in the data set and propagate these regions throughout the opened VAMAS files.
3. Use the propagate dialog window without any propagation options active but with the Region radio button in the Quantification section selected. The result of enabling a Quantification radio button is, on completion, a clipboard dialog window appears offering a quantification report for export to other programs.

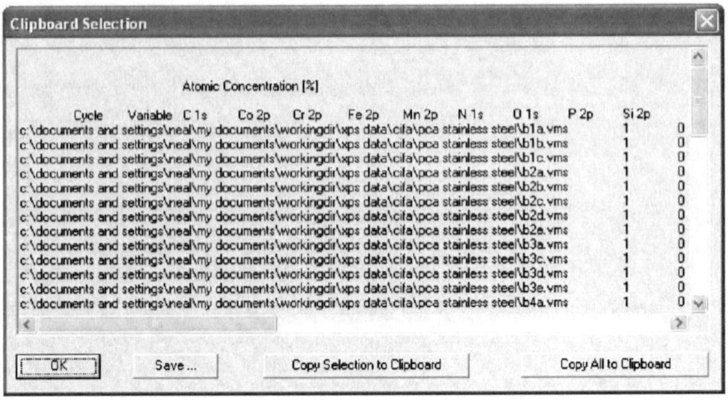

The format for the quantification report includes two tables consisting of atomic concentration values and peak area values corrected for transmission and relative sensitivity.

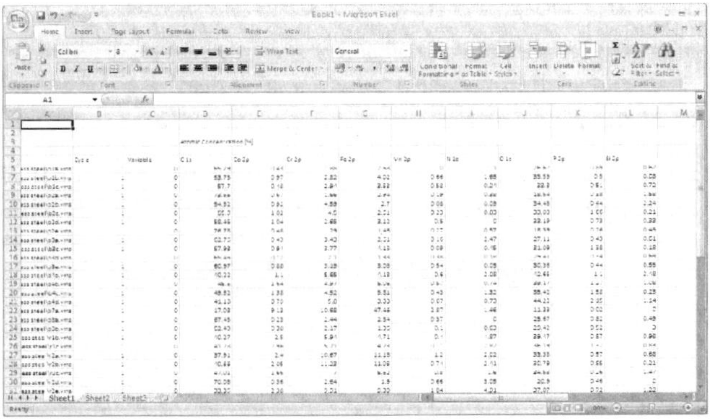

Quantification based on Copying VAMAS Blocks

The alternative method for generating a quantification report from multiple data files involves copying the VAMAS blocks from the files in question into a new experiment frame. The advantage of moving the data into a single experiment frame resides in the additional functionality offered by the Report Spec property page, where the report format can be configured in the case of Standard Reports or profiled using the Custom Report features. Custom reports are discussed in detail in the section on depth profiling XPS data.

Compiling a report based on regions defined for the set of survey spectra from the stainless steel samples again involves creating calibrated spectra populated with quantification regions. These steps can be performed before or after copying the data to a new experiment frame. Maintaining the processing steps within the individual files retains the option of printing the data using specific template formats described below and also the original organisation of the data files is unaffected. Data copied to a new experiment frame is not required to include all the data in the original data files and may only include data specific to the task in hand. For example the new experiment frame may only contain the survey spectra and none of the narrow scan measurements.

The selection mechanisms are used to collect spectra into a new experiment frame. To generate equivalent reports to the one obtained from the Browser Operations window, moving the survey spectra into a new experiment frame is sufficient. Select a survey spectrum in any one of the many files currently open in CasaXPS and use the Select menu Select Matching Blocks to add all data with species/transition fields set to Wide None to the current selection.

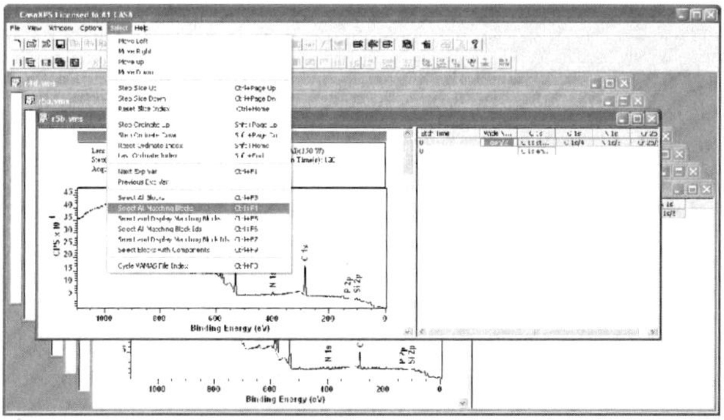

The experiment frames shown above are display using the Cascade menu option on the Windows menu. Holding down the Control key and repeatedly pressing the TAB key on the keyboard cycles through the experiment frames. Using the TAB key in this away sequentially raises each experiment frame in turn to the front of the window cascade and allows the validity of the current selection to be assessed.

A new experiment frame is created using the File menu or by pressing the New toolbar button.

Following the normal procedure for moving VAMAS blocks between VAMAS files, the Copy and Paste VAMAS blocks toolbar button invokes a dialog window listing the selected VAMAS blocks. On pressing the OK button on the dialog, the VAMAS blocks listed on the dialog window are copied into the experiment frame with focus.

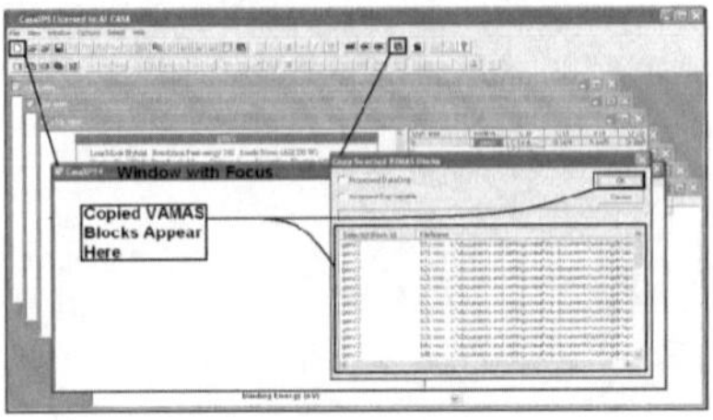

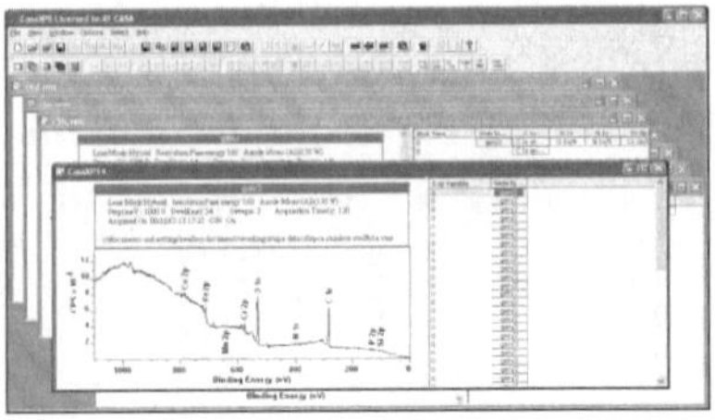

Once collected into a single experiment frame, the survey spectra are used to generate quantification reports using the Report Spec property page. There is, however, a need to switch modes for the right-hand pane from the default ordering in terms of experimental variable values to ordering the data with respect to the row label strings. The VAMAS blocks when copied from the original experiment frame are assigned the VAMAS sample identifier field based on the filename of the original VAMAS file. The sample identifier strings in each VAMAS block represent an alternative row ordering for the array of blocks in the right-hand pane and pressing the Edit Mode toolbar button toggles between these display modes for the right-hand pane.

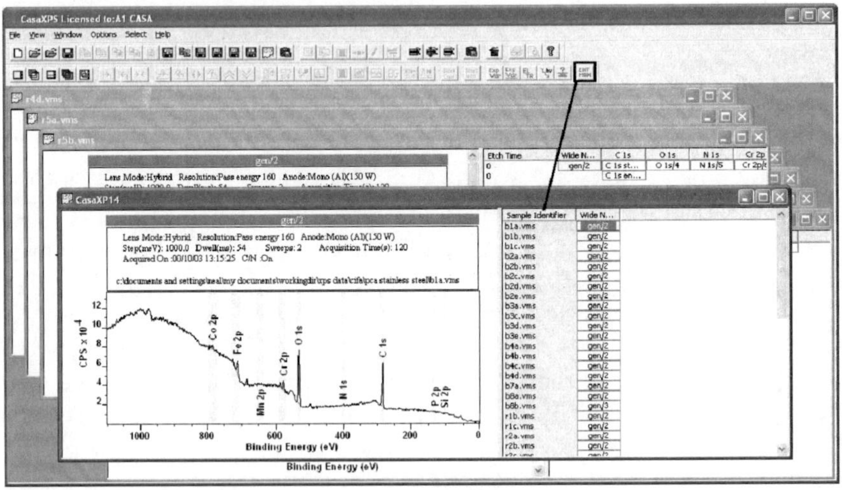

When a report is generated, the state of the display for the right-hand pane determines whether the experimental variable orders the quantification information or the row labels as seen above. Since the experimental variable for each of the original files are all zero, these fail to differentiate the data when viewed in the newly created file. The sample identifiers, on the other hand, provide clear information regarding the source of the data. Additionally, the VAMAS block comment for each spectrum copied to the new file is also updated with the full path for the original file.

A report generated from the new VAMAS file is obtained via the Standard Report using the configuration file:

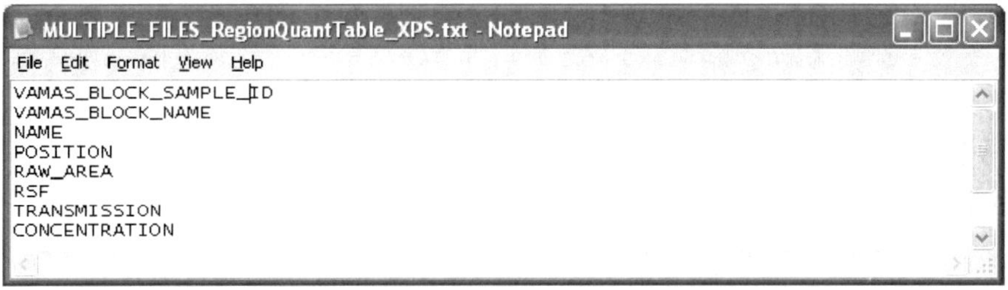

The VAMAS_BLOCK_SAMPLE_ID keyword ensures the report includes the data source information. With the entire column of survey spectra selected in the new VAMAS file, on pressing the Region button on the Standard Report a report indicating the sample composition appears as a report view window.

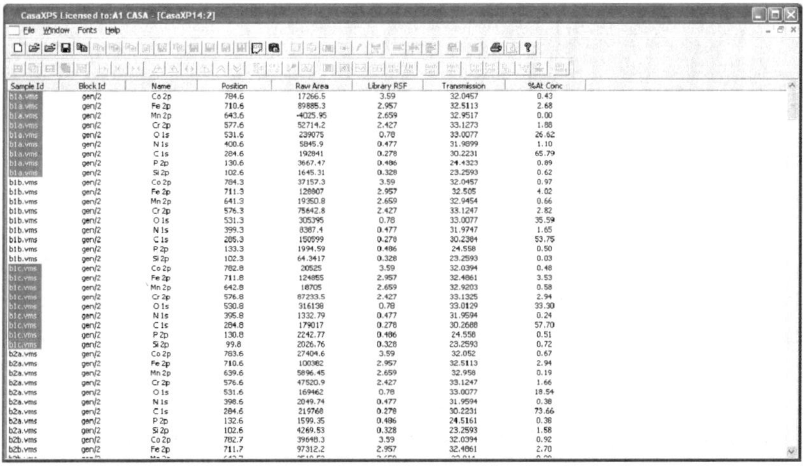

Sample Id	Block Id	Name	Position	Raw Area	Library RSF	Transmission	%At Conc
b1a.vms	gen/2	Co 2p	784.6	17266.5	3.59	32.0457	0.43
b1a.vms	gen/2	Fe 2p	710.6	89885.3	2.957	32.5113	2.68
b1a.vms	gen/2	Mn 2p	643.6	-4025.95	2.659	32.9517	0.00
b1a.vms	gen/2	Cr 2p	577.6	52714.2	2.427	33.1273	1.88
b1a.vms	gen/2	O 1s	531.6	239075	0.78	33.0077	26.62
b1a.vms	gen/2	N 1s	400.6	5845.9	0.477	31.9899	1.10
b1a.vms	gen/2	C 1s	284.6	192841	0.278	30.2231	65.79
b1a.vms	gen/2	P 2p	130.6	3667.47	0.486	24.4323	0.89
b1a.vms	gen/2	Si 2p	102.6	1645.31	0.328	23.2593	0.62
b1b.vms	gen/2	Co 2p	784.3	37157.3	3.59	32.0457	0.97
b1b.vms	gen/2	Fe 2p	711.3	128807	2.957	32.505	4.02
b1b.vms	gen/2	Mn 2p	641.3	19350.8	2.659	32.9454	0.66
b1b.vms	gen/2	Cr 2p	576.3	75642.8	2.427	33.1247	2.82
b1b.vms	gen/2	O 1s	531.3	305395	0.78	33.0077	35.59
b1b.vms	gen/2	N 1s	399.3	8387.4	0.477	31.9747	1.65
b1b.vms	gen/2	C 1s	285.3	150599	0.278	30.2384	53.75
b1b.vms	gen/2	P 2p	133.3	1994.59	0.486	24.558	0.50
b1b.vms	gen/2	Si 2p	102.3	64.3417	0.328	23.2593	0.03
b1c.vms	gen/2	Co 2p	782.8	20525	3.59	32.0394	0.48
b1c.vms	gen/2	Fe 2p	711.8	124855	2.957	32.4861	3.53
b1c.vms	gen/2	Mn 2p	642.8	18705	2.659	32.9203	0.58
b1c.vms	gen/2	Cr 2p	576.8	87233.5	2.427	33.1325	2.94
b1c.vms	gen/2	O 1s	530.8	316138	0.78	33.0129	33.30
b1c.vms	gen/2	N 1s	395.8	1332.79	0.477	31.9594	0.24
b1c.vms	gen/2	C 1s	284.8	179017	0.278	30.2688	57.70
b1c.vms	gen/2	P 2p	130.8	2242.77	0.486	24.558	0.51
b1c.vms	gen/2	Si 2p	99.8	2026.76	0.328	23.2593	0.72
b2a.vms	gen/2	Co 2p	783.6	27404.6	3.59	32.052	0.67
b2a.vms	gen/2	Fe 2p	710.6	100382	2.957	32.5113	2.94
b2a.vms	gen/2	Mn 2p	639.6	5896.45	2.659	32.958	0.19
b2a.vms	gen/2	Cr 2p	576.6	47520.9	2.427	33.1247	1.66
b2a.vms	gen/2	O 1s	531.6	169462	0.78	33.0077	18.54
b2a.vms	gen/2	N 1s	398.6	2049.74	0.477	31.9594	0.38
b2a.vms	gen/2	C 1s	284.6	219768	0.278	30.2231	73.66
b2a.vms	gen/2	P 2p	132.6	1599.35	0.486	24.5161	0.38
b2a.vms	gen/2	Si 2p	102.6	4269.53	0.328	23.2593	1.58
b2b.vms	gen/2	Co 2p	782.7	39648.3	3.59	32.0394	0.92
b2b.vms	gen/2	Fe 2p	711.7	97312.2	2.957	32.4861	2.70

An additional option for preparing the report information place on the clipboard by the Copy toolbar button is the tick-box Use Profile Format on the Report Spec property page of the Quantification Parameters dialog window.

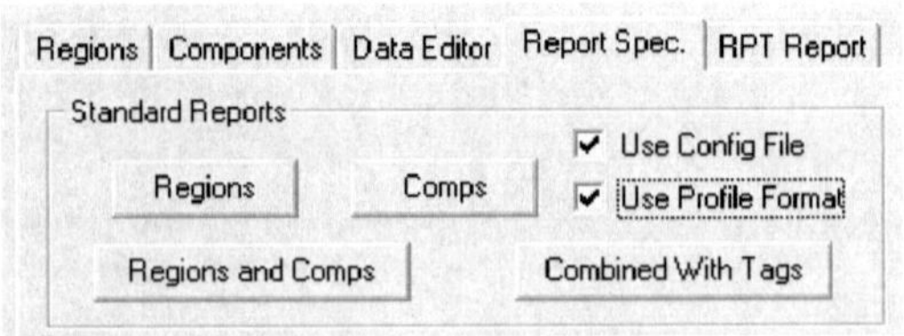

When ticked, the Use Profile Format tick-box makes no difference to the report as shown in the window displayed in CasaXPS, however when the report is copied to the clipboard additional tables are added to the clipboard. These additional tables list the quantification information for the different entities such as area, position FWHM and concentrations ordered in columns rather than the usual rows produced by the Standard Report. After the clipboard contents are pasted into a spreadsheet, the report specified by the configuration file is supplemented by tables ordered by columns rather than by rows.

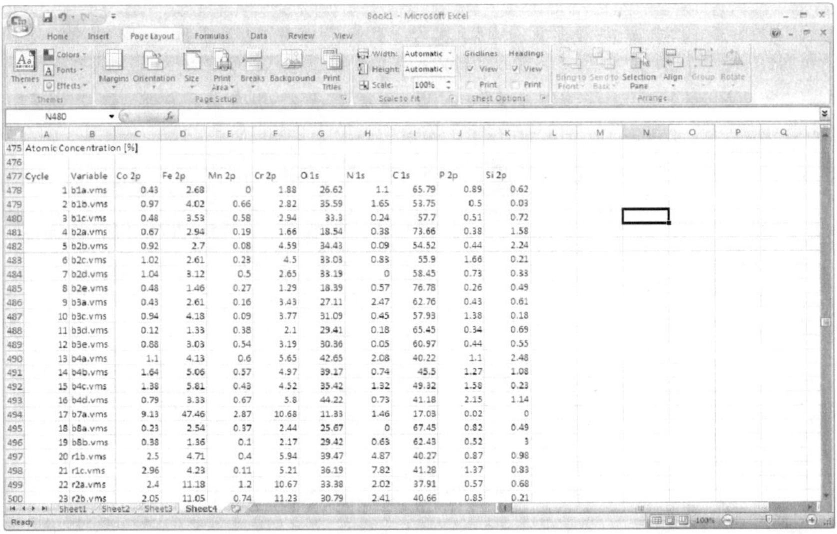

Atomic Concentration [%]

Cycle	Variable	Co 2p	Fe 2p	Mn 2p	Cr 2p	O 1s	N 1s	C 1s	P 2p	Si 2p
1	b1a.vms	0.43	2.68	0	1.88	26.62	1.1	65.79	0.89	0.62
2	b1b.vms	0.97	4.02	0.66	2.82	35.59	1.65	53.75	0.5	0.03
3	b1c.vms	0.48	3.53	0.58	2.94	33.3	0.24	57.7	0.51	0.72
4	b2a.vms	0.67	2.94	0.19	1.66	18.54	0.38	73.66	0.38	1.58
5	b2b.vms	0.92	2.7	0.08	4.59	34.43	0.09	54.52	0.44	2.24
6	b2c.vms	1.02	2.61	0.23	4.5	33.03	0.83	55.9	1.66	0.21
7	b2d.vms	1.04	3.12	0.5	2.65	33.19	0	58.45	0.73	0.33
8	b2e.vms	0.48	1.46	0.27	1.29	18.39	0.57	76.78	0.26	0.49
9	b3a.vms	0.43	2.61	0.16	3.43	27.11	2.47	62.76	0.43	0.61
10	b3c.vms	0.94	4.18	0.09	3.77	31.09	0.45	57.93	1.38	0.18
11	b3d.vms	0.12	1.33	0.38	2.1	29.41	0.18	65.45	0.34	0.69
12	b3e.vms	0.88	3.03	0.54	3.19	30.36	0.05	60.97	0.44	0.55
13	b4a.vms	1.1	4.13	0.6	5.65	42.65	2.08	40.22	1.1	2.48
14	b4b.vms	1.64	5.06	0.57	4.97	39.17	0.74	45.5	1.27	1.08
15	b4c.vms	1.38	5.81	0.43	4.52	35.42	1.32	49.32	1.58	0.23
16	b4d.vms	0.79	3.33	0.67	5.8	44.22	0.73	41.18	2.15	1.14
17	b7a.vms	9.13	47.46	2.87	10.68	11.33	1.46	17.03	0.02	0
18	b8a.vms	0.23	2.54	0.37	2.44	25.67	0	67.45	0.82	0.49
19	b8b.vms	0.38	1.36	0.1	2.17	29.42	0.63	62.43	0.52	3
20	r1b.vms	2.5	4.71	0.4	5.94	39.47	4.87	40.27	0.87	0.98
21	r1c.vms	2.96	4.23	0.11	5.21	36.19	7.82	41.28	1.37	0.83
22	r2a.vms	2.4	11.18	1.2	10.67	33.38	2.02	37.91	0.57	0.68
23	r2b.vms	2.05	11.05	0.74	11.23	30.79	2.41	40.66	0.85	0.21

The row label strings are used to differentiate the information from the spectra provided the report is generated from an experiment frame in which the right-hand pane is displaying the row labels rather than the experimental variable values. The Edit Mode toolbar button toggles the display mode for the right-hand pane between experimental variable and row label arrangement of the VAMAS blocks.

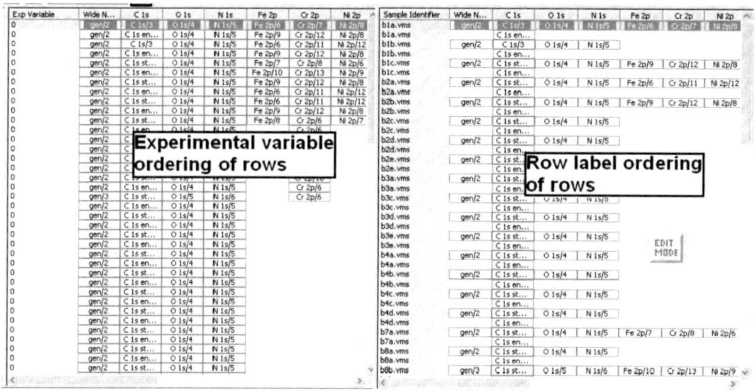

Printing Data from Multiple Files

A visual record for the sample analyses may be desired, where the data from each file must be arranged in a specific format before printing. Given an arrangement of display tiles, the display format may be saved as a tile format file (tff file). Tile format files are lists of display parameters applicable to a specific type of VAMAS file block structure. Data acquired in the same sequence as the file used to prepare the tile format file can be automatically displayed using the tile format file. For the example of stainless steel data sets, while the files are not all identical in terms of VAMAS block numbers, the common theme throughout the set of data files is the first four VAMAS blocks are a survey followed by carbon, oxygen and then nitrogen spectra. A display based on these four VAMAS blocks would therefore be appropriate. Once a display is prepared involving both parameters defined using the Tile Display Parameter dialog window and the Page Tile Format dialog window, the display arrangement is saved to disk using the File menu.

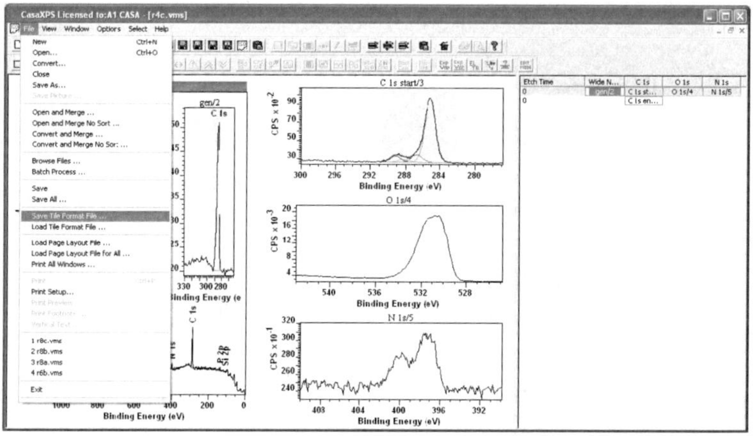

The tile format file may be saved to any directory, however the File menu options for loading a page layout file format offer tile format files from the CasaXPS.PTF directory located in the same directory as the CasaXPS.exe file.

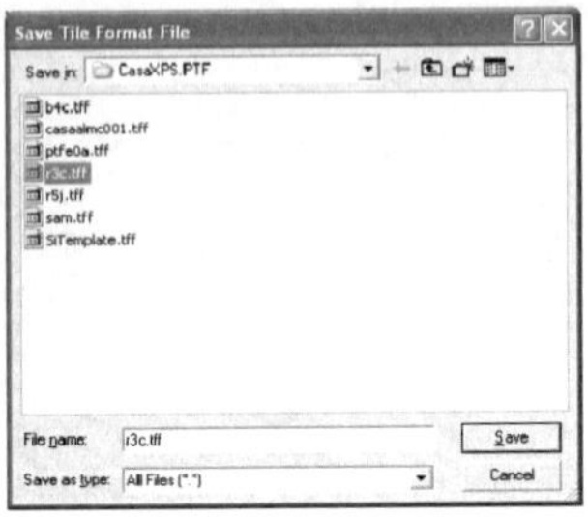

Once saved, the tile format file can be loaded using the File menu option Load Page Tile Format for All.

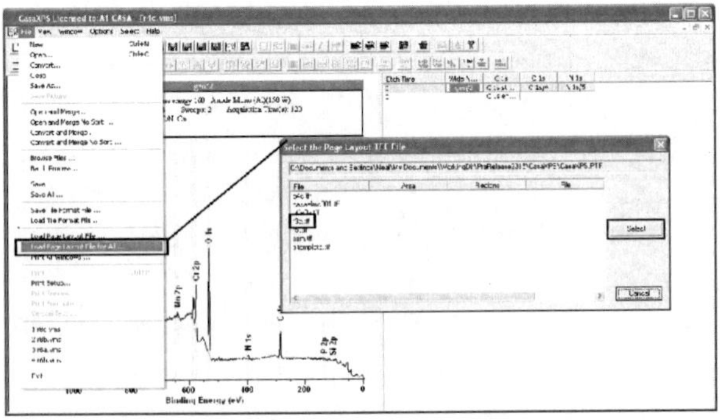

The Load Page Tile Format for All menu option causes tile display for all the open files to be organised according to the display specification saved previously.

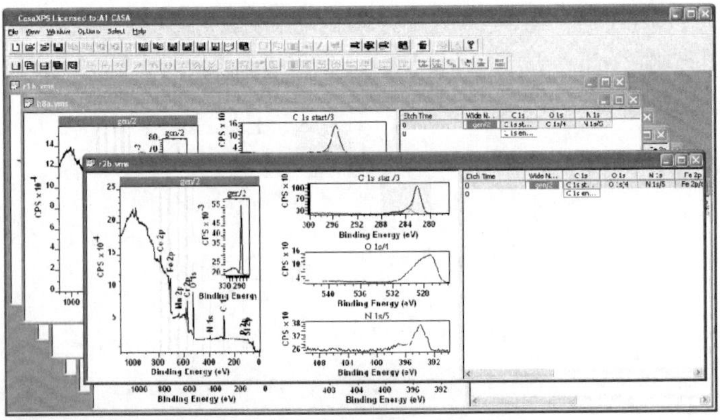

Following formatting either via the tile format file mechanism or by manual means, the entire set of open windows are printed using the Print All Windows menu option on the File menu.

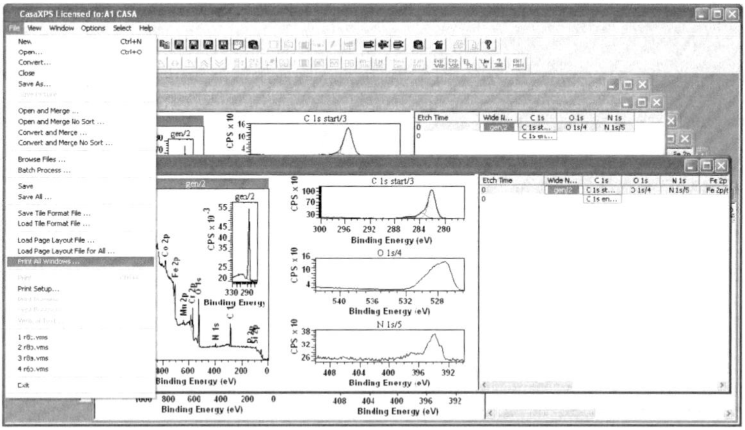

A dialog window indicates the number of files involved in the printing operation and offers an opportunity to cancel the print action.

Window Menu Options

An experiment frame is a view into the open VAMAS file. These experiment frames are managed using the Window menu, from which the experiment frame windows can be cascaded or tiled with the main CasaXPS window. Each experiment frame can also be lowered into an icon or made full sized using the buttons associated with the experiment frame window.

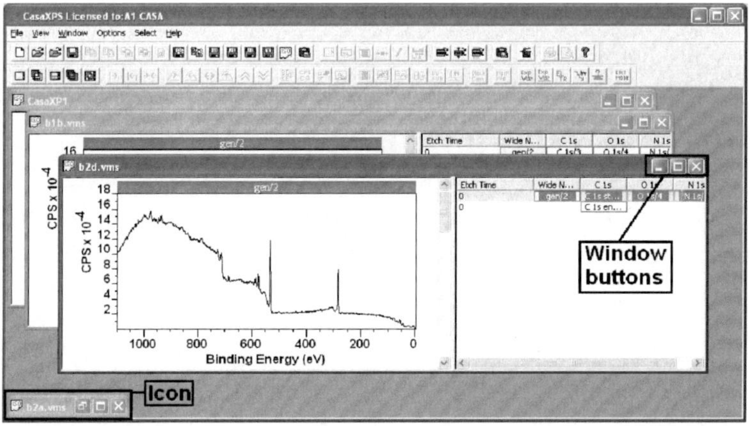

When loaded into CasaXPS, a VAMAS file may have more than one experiment-frame view of the data. The Window menu includes a menu option for creating additional experiment frames and each experiment frame is capable of maintaining a visualisation of the data file. Creating new experiment frame windows provides a means of maintaining a display configuration whilst still retaining the ability to browse the data within the VAMAS file. For example, using the New Window option on the Window menu allows three different tile formats to exist for the same data file:

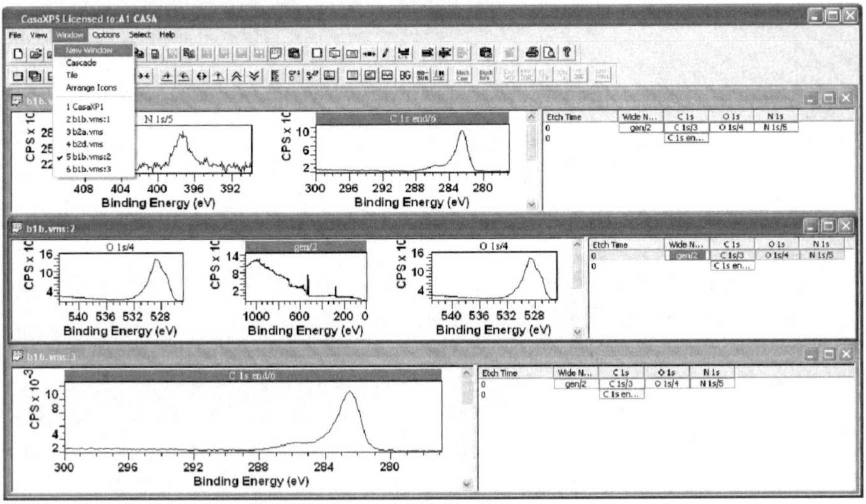

These additional experiment frames appear with a number count following the file name in the window title bar. To remove an experiment frame, close the window using the X window button. The file is closed only when all the experiment frames are close.

Profiling Data within an Experiment Frame

A profile experiment involves taking a measurement, then repeatedly changing the state of a sample before taking a further measurement. A common profiling experiment involves changing the state of the sample by etching with an ion gun.

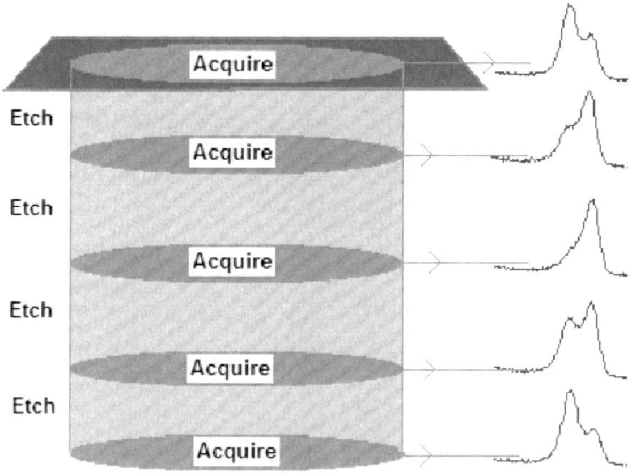

Data sets resulting from these sputter depth profiles order the VAMAS blocks into rows corresponding to the cumulative etch time.

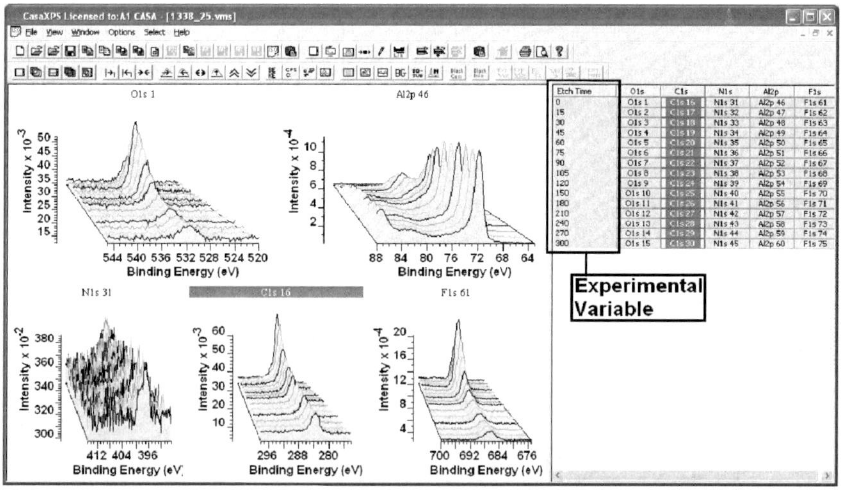

These dramatic changes in spectra due to etching a sample are reasonably characteristic of sputter depth profiles. More subtle changes in spectral shape due to surface reactions are also possible. The example used to illustrate profiling features in version 2.3.15 is based on an experiment in which clean aluminium metal is allowed to oxidise in vacuum. The objective is to monitor the relatively minor changes to the surface chemistry with time.

These data acquired on a Scienta ESCA300 where originally transferred to VAMAS format through CasaXPS using X/Y pair ASCII files. The modern data system for the Scienta instruments uses an IGOR binary format directly imported into CasaXPS.

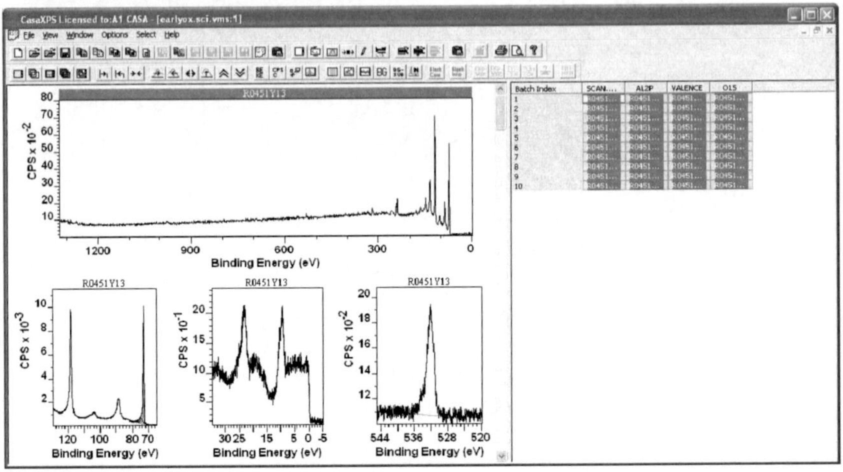

Each file from the original dataset contained four spectra: a survey spectrum and three spectra measured over aluminium 2s and 2p, the valence band and oxygen 1s energy intervals. The objective is to characterise the growth of the aluminium oxide peak. The changes to the aluminium 2p peak over the course of the experiment are relatively small; the metallic doublet attenuates as an oxide peak grows.

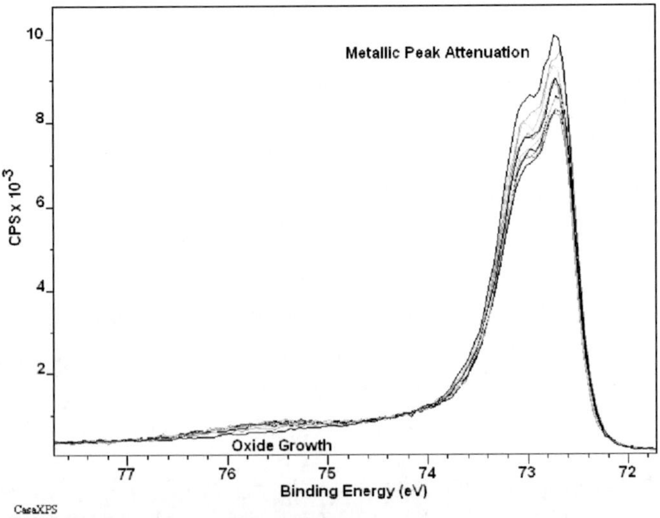

Since the changes in the data are small, to extract information from these data the precision in the calculation must be good. An analysis of these data leading to precise results is developed in the following sections.

A Look at an Experiment via Survey Data

As a first step in the analysis, the survey spectra can be used to provide the general trends in the experiment. An elemental composition profile based on four quantification regions provides an initial perspective of the experiment.

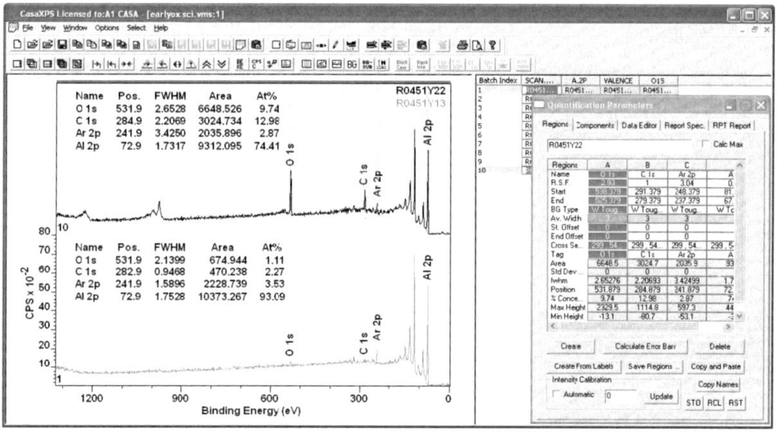

The regions added to the spectrum are best placed by using the data with most overall variation, namely the survey spectrum with experimental index number 10.

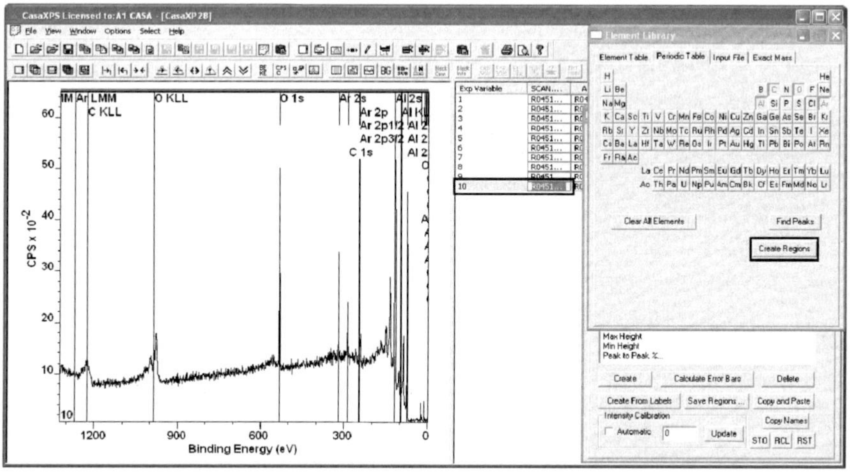

The data clearly include aluminium, oxygen, carbon and argon. The argon in the sample is from cleaning the sample using an argon ion gun source to sputter the aluminium oxide when initially exposing the metallic aluminium surface. Once regions are created for the survey spectrum with experimental variable 10, the regions are propagated to the survey spectra for the remaining experimental variable index numbers. To propagate these regions, select the column of survey spectra in the right-hand pane and, with the cursor over the tile displaying the survey spectrum in the left-hand pane for which regions are defined, right-click the mouse button to invoke the propagate dialog window.

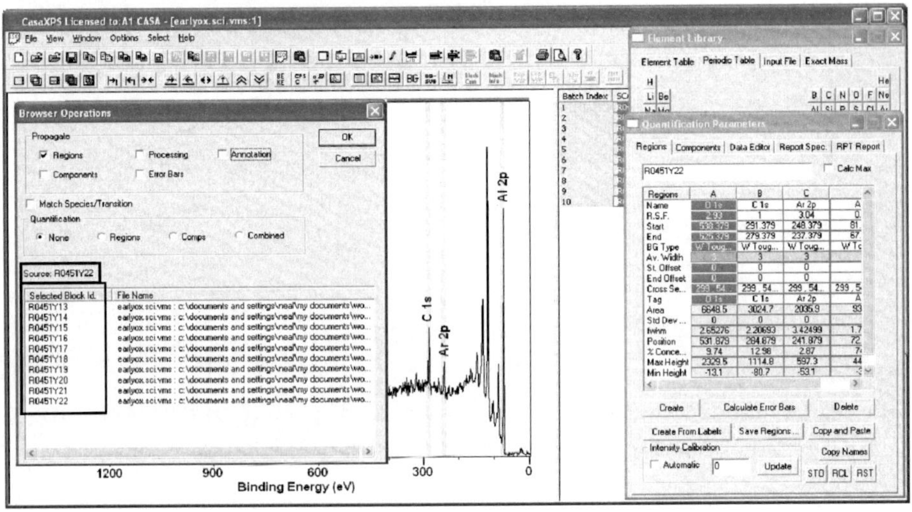

On pressing the OK button on the dialog window, the regions are transferred to the survey spectra selected in the right-hand pane.

Profiling the changes in the regions through the survey spectra is performed using the Custom Report section of the Report Spec property page.

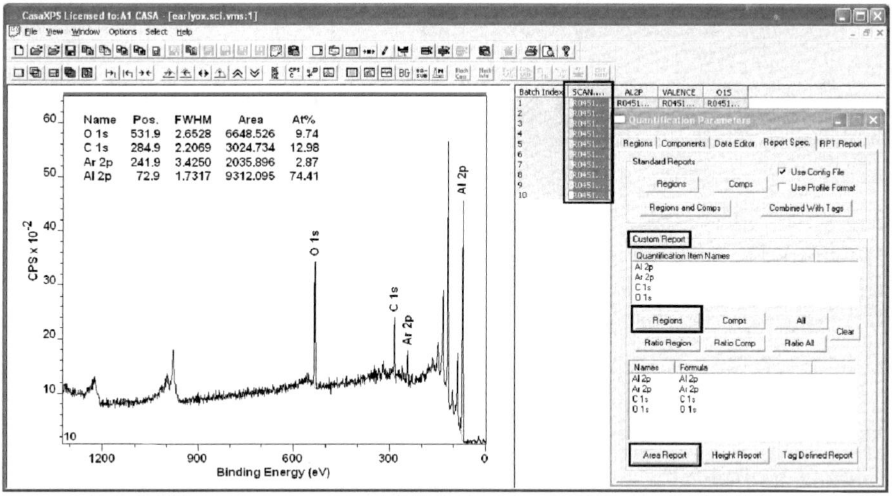

The Custom report, like the Standard Report options, generates text based reports on the basis of the VAMAS blocks selected in the right-hand pane. A Custom Report produces tables of intensities based on the quantification items organised via the Name/Formula table.

Names	Formula
Al 2p	Al 2p
Ar 2p	Ar 2p
C 1s	C 1s
O 1s	O 1s

The formulae for these regions are simply a straight copy of the region name fields; however in general the formulae can be any arithmetic expression involving combinations of the name fields from either regions or components. The buttons between the quantification items table and the names/formula table are only a way of adding entries to the lower table. On pressing the Regions button, the regions appearing in the quantification items table are copied into the names/formula table below.

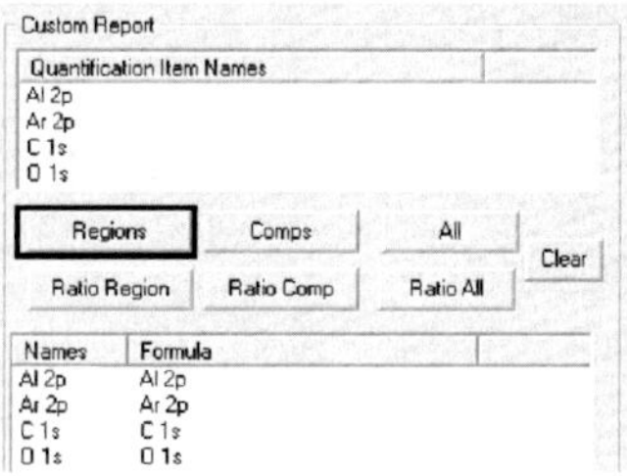

NB the Custom Report does not use the concept of a region or a component used by the Standard Report section, but rather treats intensity measured from regions and components in exactly the same way. Understanding that the Custom Report simply works with quantification items is important, for the following reason. If two or more regions and/or components are assigned the same names, the intensities for these regions and/or components are automatically added together before use with the formulae in the name/formula table. Pressing the Region button in the Custom Report section does NOT limit the report to regions only. The Regions button simply supplies entries to the names/formula table based on regions. If a component of the same name as a region exists with non-zero RSF for both the region and component, the intensities from the quantification items with the same names are automatically summed with the effect of doubling the intensity for the transition involving the said region and component.

In the current example, the survey spectra only use regions therefore pressing the Regions button between the tables in the Custom Report section populates the name/formula table with appropriate entries for profiling the sample as a function of measurement index. The profile report is generated by pressing the Area Report button.

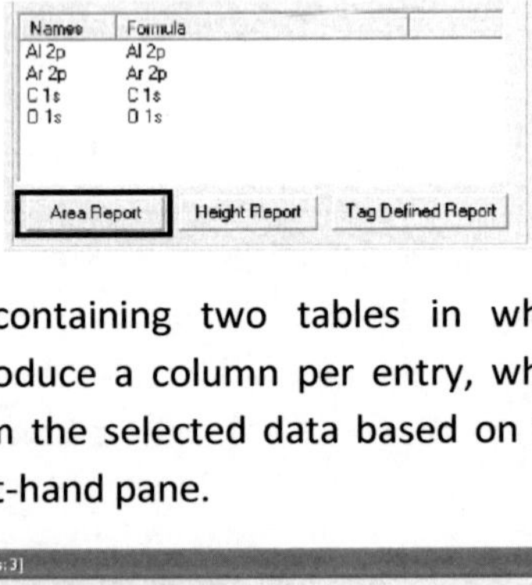

A table is generated containing two tables in which the entries in the names/Formula table produce a column per entry, where the rows within the tables are extracted from the selected data based on the row ordering for the VAMAS blocks in the right-hand pane.

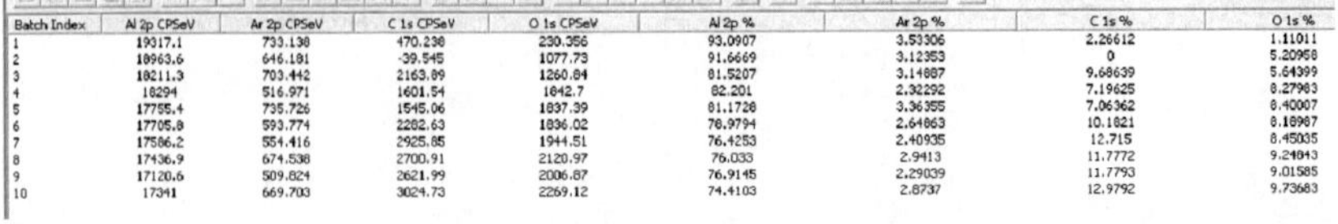

Batch Index	Al 2p CPSeV	Ar 2p CPSeV	C 1s CPSeV	O 1s CPSeV	Al 2p %	Ar 2p %	C 1s %	O 1s %
1	19317.1	733.138	470.238	230.356	93.0907	3.53306	2.26612	1.11011
2	18963.6	646.181	-39.545	1077.73	91.6669	3.12353	0	5.20958
3	18211.3	703.442	2163.89	1260.84	81.5207	3.14887	9.68639	5.64399
4	18294	516.971	1601.54	1842.7	82.201	2.32292	7.19625	8.27983
5	17755.4	735.726	1545.06	1837.39	81.1728	3.36355	7.06362	8.40007
6	17705.8	593.774	2282.63	1836.02	78.9794	2.64863	10.1821	8.18987
7	17586.2	554.416	2925.85	1944.51	76.4253	2.40935	12.715	8.45035
8	17436.9	674.538	2700.91	2120.97	76.033	2.9413	11.7772	9.24843
9	17120.6	509.824	2621.99	2006.87	76.9145	2.29039	11.7793	9.01585
10	17341	669.703	3024.73	2269.12	74.4103	2.8737	12.9792	9.73683

A VAMAS file containing the variation of the report columns plotted against the experimental variable is obtain by selecting the Create Profile menu item from the File menu.

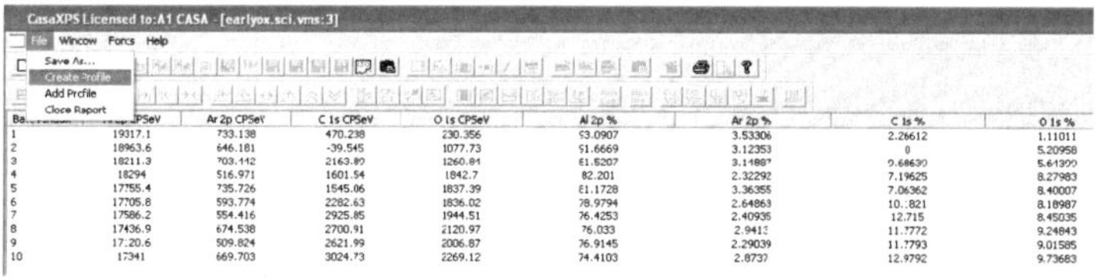

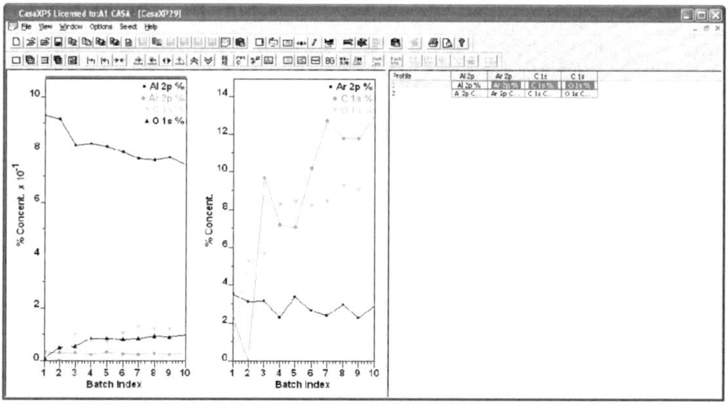

The abscissa used to plot the profile is the experimental variable. The index numbers corresponds to exposure time for the aluminium surface. Since the original data files where without the timing information, the dataset is initially organised with respect to a data set index number. The true experimental variable could be added to the VAMAS file using a toolbar button.

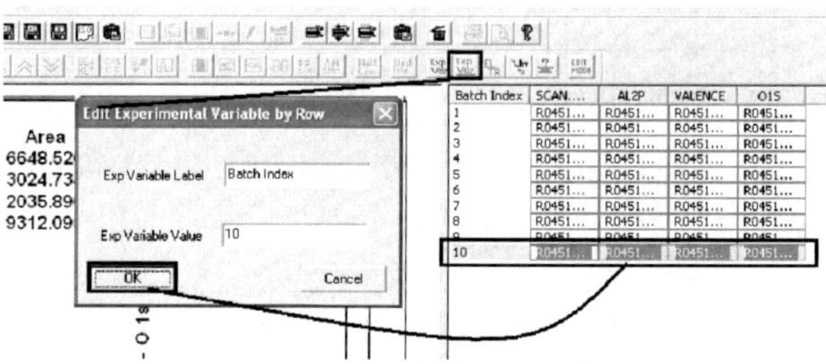

The value entered on the Edit Experimental Variable by Row dialog window modifies those VAMAS blocks selected in the right-hand pane and also reorders the array of VAMAS blocks in the VAMAS file; as a consequence the right-hand pane is reordered with respect to the newly entered experimental value.

Profiling using High Resolution Spectra

While the analysis of the survey spectra shows clear trends within the profiles, the more subtle changes in the high resolution data provide an opportunity to improve the precision of the measurements.

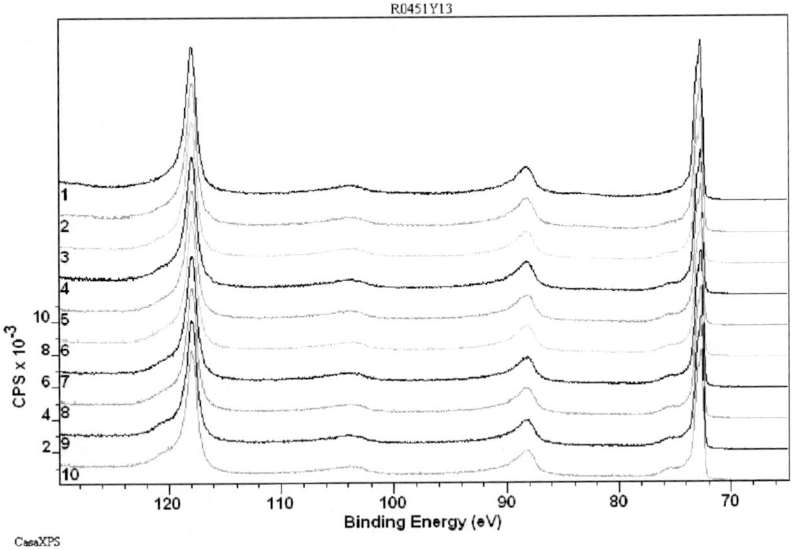

Exposure of the aluminium to the vacuum causes the growth of a chemically shifted peak apparent in both the Al 2s and Al 2p photoelectric lines. The better resolved Al 2p spectra compared to the Al 2s peaks suggests the Al 2p will yield more reliable component intensities. Successfully profiling these types of data requires appropriate lineshapes for the features observed in the data.

The problem usually associated with modelling oxidized metals is determining the extent of the asymmetry expected for the metallic peaks. Without a clear view of the peak structure, determining the asymmetry for the metallic peaks is largely guess work. Estimating the asymmetry from a pure metallic spectrum significantly improves the understanding of the line shape required. Ensuring a spectrum from aluminium is without oxide is far from easy and the potential in any metallic data for multiple peak structures is always a concern. To illustrate the issues consider the case of a Si 2p doublet, where the separation of the doublet peaks is typically

50% greater than that of aluminium. Interpretation of a silicon doublet depends on the decision regarding the amount of asymmetry expected in the elemental silicon peaks. Two peak models one assuming asymmetry and one without could yield very different results for spectra from Si 2p. Both models fit the data identically.

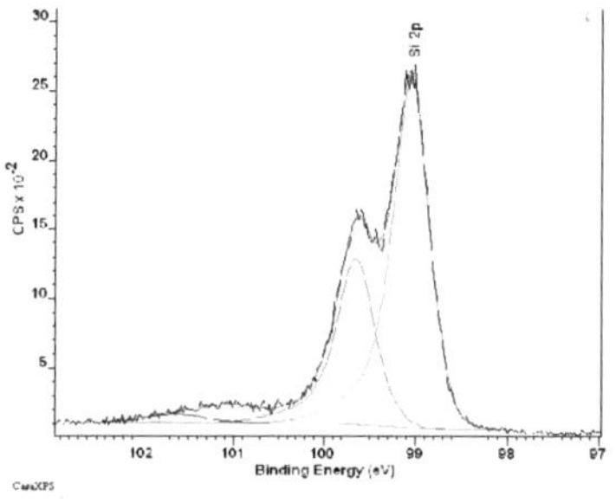

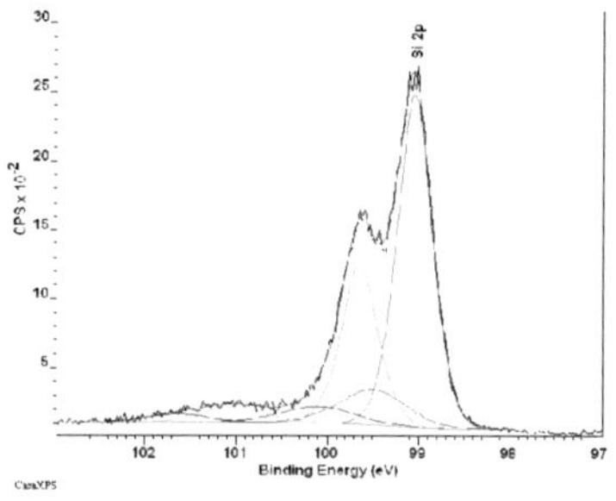

Moving these models into an oxidised silicon sample when supplemented with a GL component representing the oxide produces the following peak model options for the same SiO_2 data.

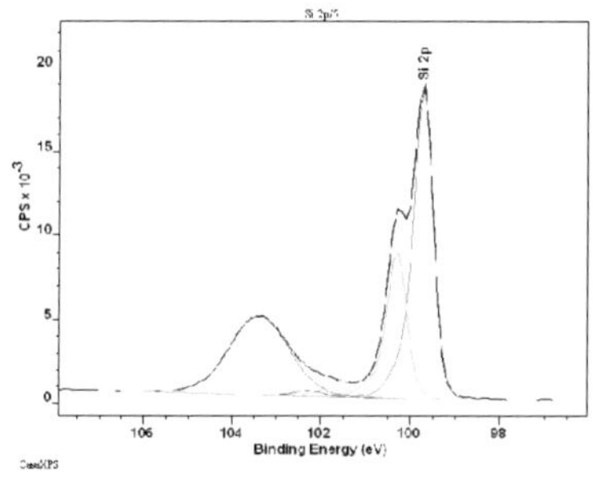

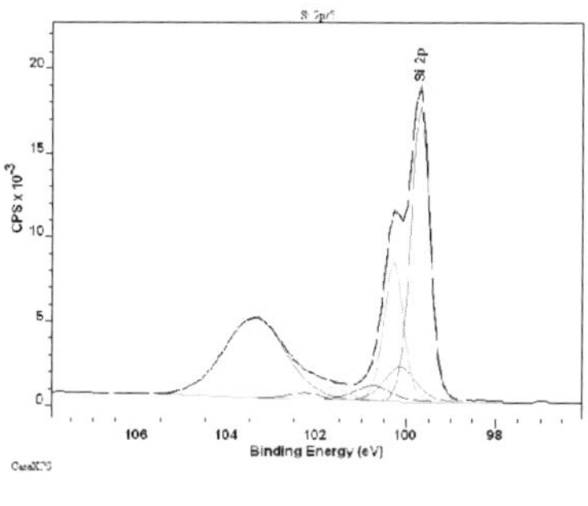

The following discussion is intended as a means of illustrating features in CasaXPS rather than endorsing the analysis techniques employed. In the course of examining the aluminium data, different aspects of data processing in terms of manipulation of spectra and identifying lineshapes are examined as a means to explore CasaXPS.

Asymmetric Lineshapes and Calculating Lineshapes from Data

The problem with modelling asymmetric lineshapes resides in obtaining a target shape to which one of the many functional forms can be matched. While the aluminium spectra begin the measurement from a cleaned aluminium surface the presence of an oxygen peak suggests the Al 2p spectrum still must include a contribution from an oxide peak. The process of deriving asymmetric lineshapes for the Al 2p envelope will be performed making the assumption of a correlation between the intensity of the O 1s peaks and the intensity of the oxide peak included in the Al 2p data. The first calculation is therefore to determine the relative intensity of the oxygen peaks. The intention is to use the proportion of oxygen to remove the Al 2p oxide contribution from the metallic Al 2p peaks and therefore construct a target data envelope to which synthetic lineshapes can be prepared.

Calculating the Relative Intensities for O 1s Peaks

The first step is to find evidence to support the assumption regarding the correlation between the Al 2p oxide growth and the O 1s peak intensity. If the O 1s peak were to change shape as the timed experiment unfolds, the assumption would be doubtful. Demonstrating the peaks are identical in shape throughout the experiment provides a comfort factor in as much as the assumption is not rejected by the test. Visually inspecting the O 1s peaks suggests the peaks are the same shape. Overlaying the O 1s data in the active tile provides a first impression of the O 1s data.

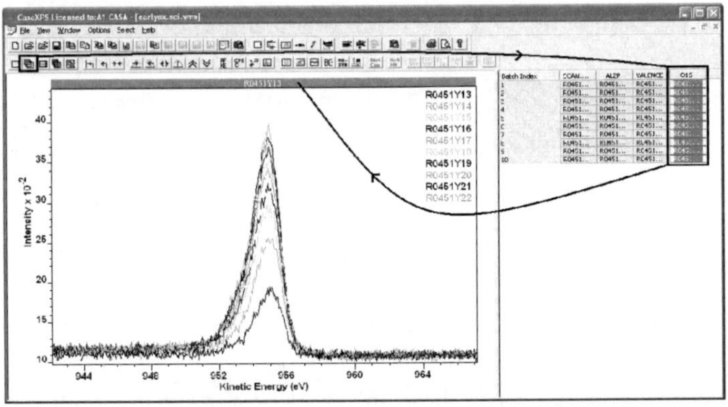

A more rigorous test would be to compare the normalised O 1s intensities. The Calculator property page offers several options for normalising data based on different criteria. The option best suited to comparing the O 1s spectra uses the integrated area of the peaks to determine a normalisation factor for each spectrum. Since normalisation based on peak area is relatively common, the option on the Calculator property page of the Spectrum Processing dialog window offers a button for applying the operation to a selection from the current experiment frame.

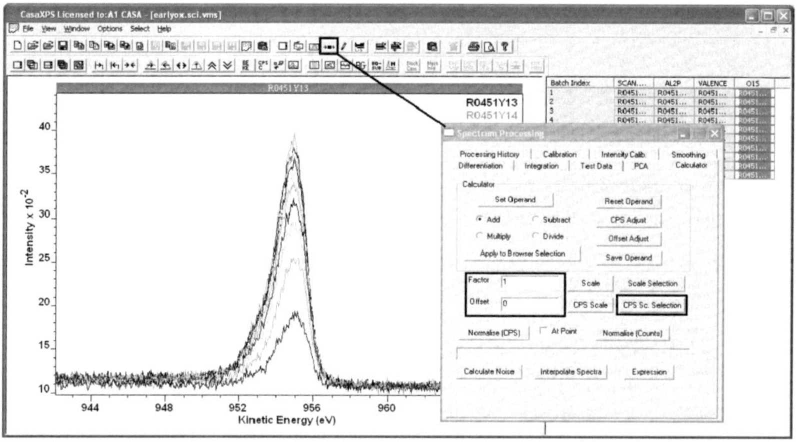

The CPS Scale Selection button on the Calculator property page requires the definition of a region for each of the O 1s spectra. Creating a region on the first O 1s spectrum using the Region property page of the Quantification Parameters dialog window followed by propagating the regions to the other O 1s spectra provides the context for the normalisation operation.

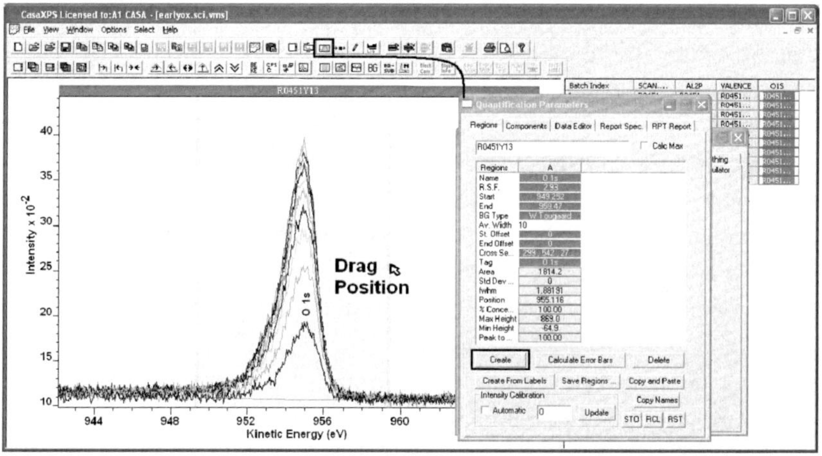

When data are overlaid in the active tile, the VAMAS block first selected in the right-hand pane at the time of pressing the overlay toolbar button (F2 function key) is the data block affected by the Regions property page. The block identifier used to display text for each cell in the right-hand pane and which is also the default text used to display a title for display tiles appears in the text-field at the top of the Regions property page.

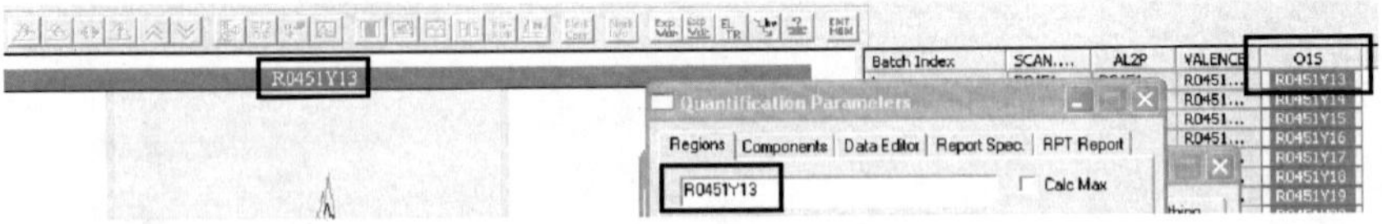

Since the normalisation operation requires a region for each O 1s spectrum, the region created on the active O 1s VAMAS block must be propagated to the remaining O 1s spectra. The propagate dialog window uses the data in the active tile of the experiment frame with focus as the source for the propagation operation and transfers the information from the source VAMAS block to the set of VAMAS blocks selected in the right-hand panes.

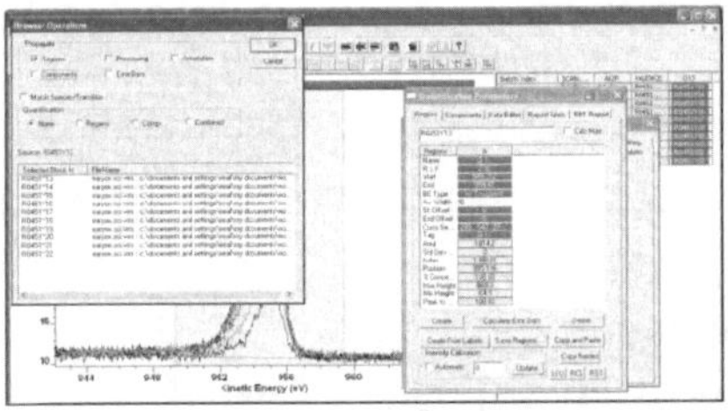

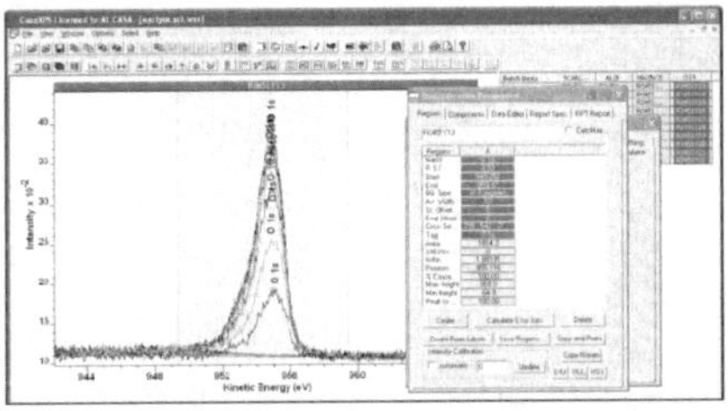

After propagation the O 1s spectra all have regions defined. While it would be possible to apply the normalisation step to the data in the original file, it is sometimes useful to move a copy of the data of interest to a new experiment frame. Processing such as energy calibration may already exist for each O 1s spectrum based on a row-by-row calculation. The normalisation for visual inspection is perhaps a temporary change to the data and not required in general. While processing for VAMA blocks can be reversed, for sets of spectra the custom nature of the energy calibration means care must be taken to only undo the processing operation associated with the normalisation operation. If the data are copied to a new experiment frame before normalisation the original data file need not be temporarily altered and the normalised data are simply discarded when appropriate. The O 1s data are energy calibrated with respect to the rising edge of the valence band spectra, therefore to continue the normalisation operation, the column of O 1s VAMAS blocks will be copied to a new experiment frame.

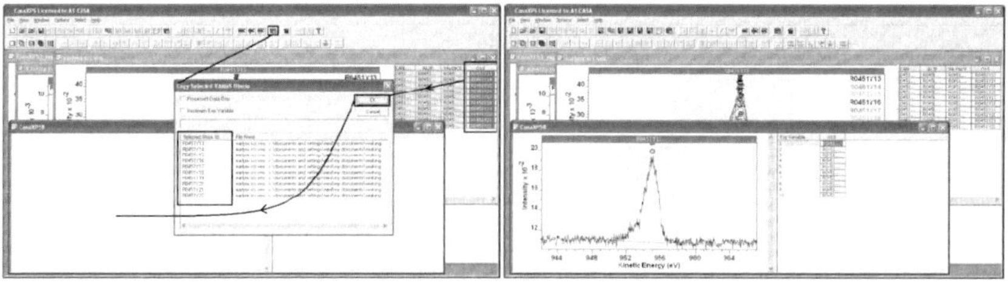

Normalisation and display of the O 1 spectra confirms the similarity of the peak structure.

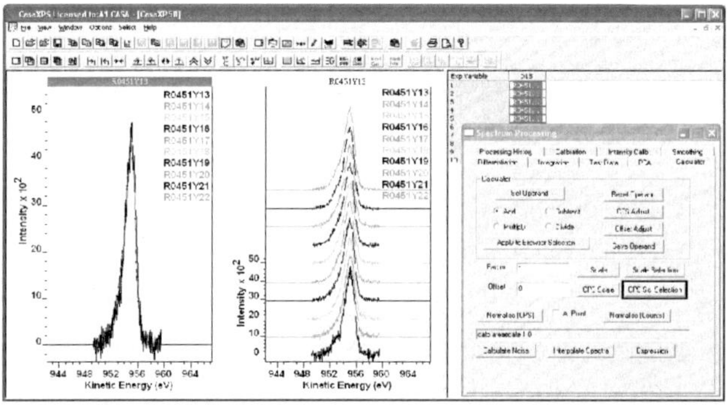

Normalisation of data based on a region transforms the spectra to background subtracted data such that the data envelope is scaled to ensure the peak area measured in CPSeV is unity.

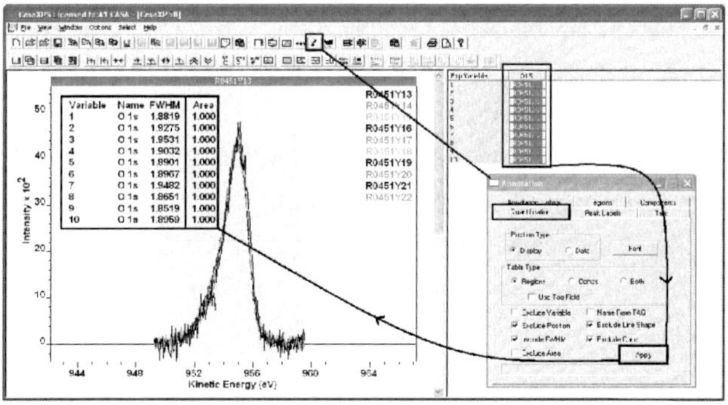

The analysis of the Al 2p data therefore develops under the assumption the O 1s peak is an indicator for the intensity of the Al 2p oxide peak. The O 1s peak areas provide an estimate for the contribution of the Al 2p oxide peak to measured data envelopes. The first Al 2p spectrum, on visual inspection looks predominantly metallic in nature.

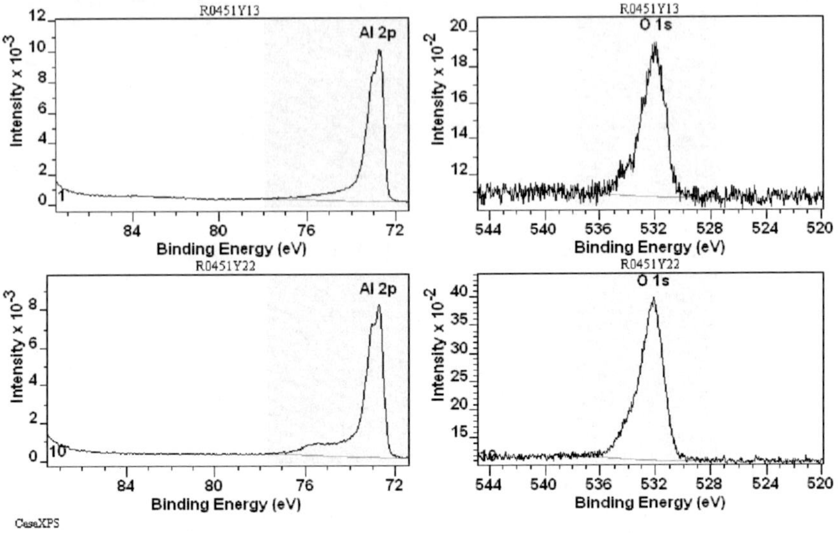

The O 1s peak from the same measurement indicates the Al 2p peak from batch 1 should include 28.4% of the oxide peak in the Al 2p data from batch 10. In an attempt to remove the oxide contribution to the Al 2p data within batch index 1, the data from the Al 2p region with batch index 1 is used to create a lineshape assumed to represent the metallic Al 2p transition and also 28.4 % of the oxide transition observed in batch 10. The lineshape created from the batch 1 Al 2p data when fitted to the batch 10 Al 2p data together with a GL component provides a means of estimating the position and area for an Al 2p oxide peak representing 71.6% of the Al 2p intensity in the batch 10 data. Given the Al 2p oxide peak from the batch 10 data, the spectrum calculator provides a means of removing a calculated proportion of an Al 2p oxide peak from the batch 1 spectrum. The result is an approximation to the lineshape for pure aluminium metal. Regardless of how true the calculated lineshape might be, the description of the data manipulation options, at least, is given a context by the attempted lineshape derivation.

Deriving the lineshape for metallic aluminium initially requires the definition of a lineshape based on data. A background for each spectrum is critical to the process of determining a lineshape. Different backgrounds change the shape of peaks in different ways and therefore a background which least interferes with the peak shapes is preferable. A background based on the Tougaard 2-parameter universal cross-section provides a stable background approximation for all the Al 2p data envelopes. The background type W Tougaard, standing for weighted Tougaard, is calculated using the 2-paramater universal cross-section where the numerator in the cross-section is weighted to ensure the background meets the spectrum at a given intensity at the region limits.

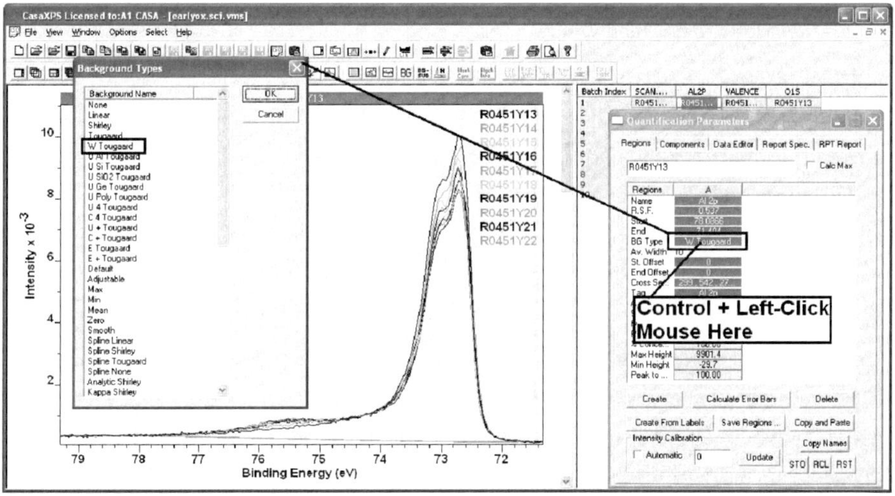

The set of background types available in CasaXPS can be viewed by placing the mouse over the background type field for a region and, before the field is selected for manual entry, left-clicking the mouse with the Control keyboard key held down. If the background field is already in edit mode, i.e. text can be typed into the field, no dialog window will appear.

To extract the data associated with the region defined on the aluminium spectrum, a toolbar button on the SIMS toolbar is used. The SIMS toolbar is made visible using the View menu on the CasaXPS main window.

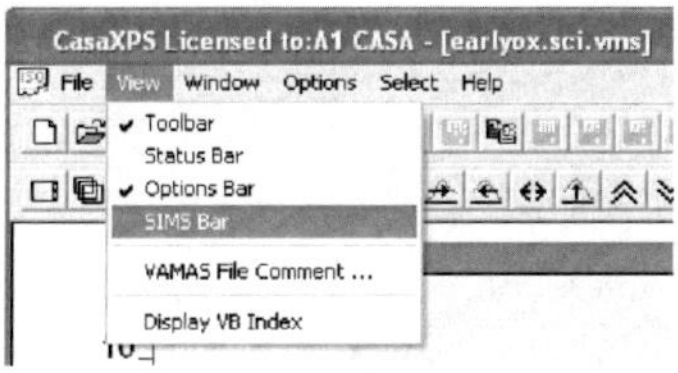

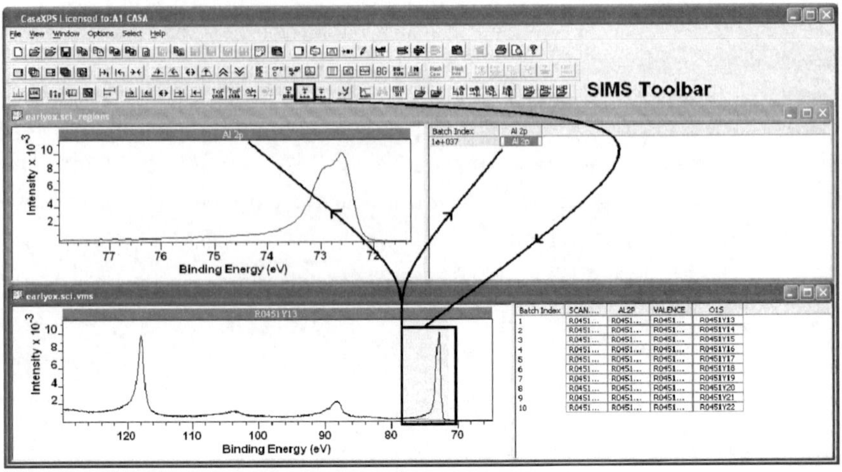

Displaying the batch 1 Al 2p spectrum in the active tile, the SIMS toolbar button indicated extracts data from energy intervals defined by regions and saves the data in a new experiment frame using a separate VAMAS block per region on the original spectrum.

The intention is to use the extracted peak shape as a component in a peak model. Components in peak models are designed to represent the signal above background and therefore the data in the region must be background subtracted using a background typical for the data to which the component is intended for use. Since the background for the Al 2p spectra are calculated using a non-zero Av Width region parameter, the background is partially calculated using data not included in the region interval. The background removed from the Al 2p data envelope is therefore best preformed before extracting the region data. Background subtraction is performed on the Test Data property page of the Spectrum Processing dialog window.

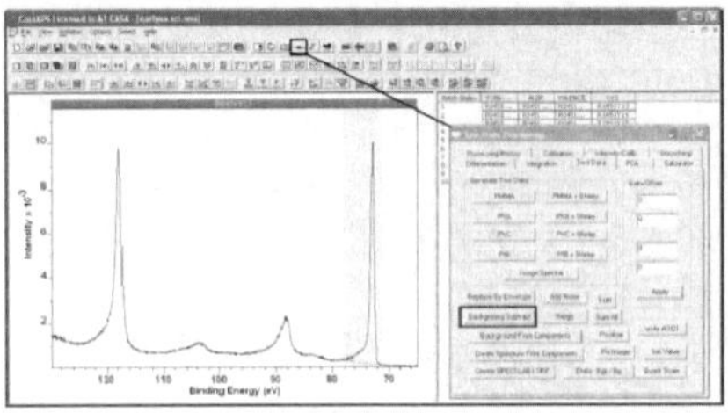

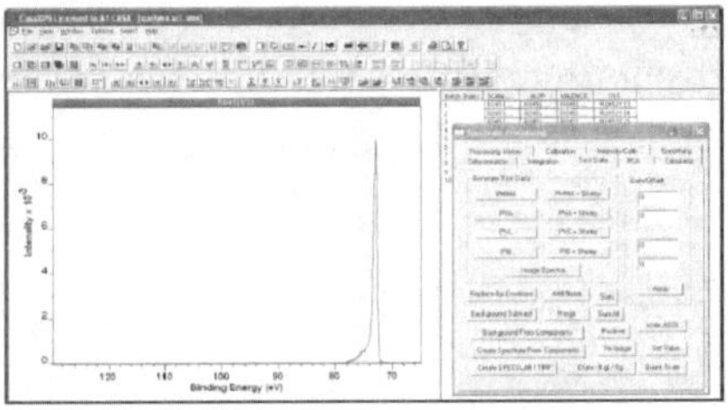

Once the Background Subtract button is pressed, the processing operation subtracts the background intensities from the raw data. Note that for data outside of any regions, the background is defined as the raw data and therefore outside the regions the background subtracted data are all zero.

The lineshape corresponding to the Al 2p region is extracted from these background subtracted intensities using the SIMS toolbar button.

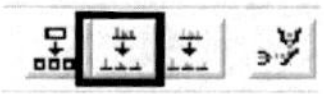

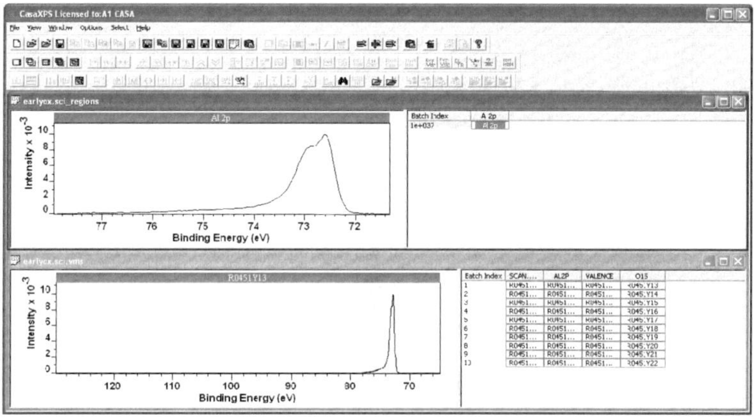

Again, it is probably best to develop the lineshape for the Al 2p data by copying the Al 2p spectra into a new experiment frame together with the newly created background subtracted VAMAS block.

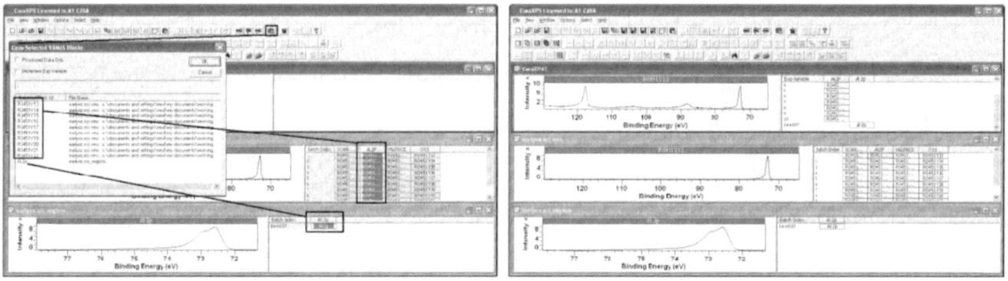

Components based on data are defined using the block identifier for a VAMAS block within the same VAMAS file. The block identifier must begin with the % character and be distinct within the VAMAS file. The data for Al 2p and the VAMAS block created from background subtracted region data are now located in the same experiment frame. The block identifier for the VAMAS block prepared from the batch 1 region must be edited to ensure the data can be successfully used to define a component.

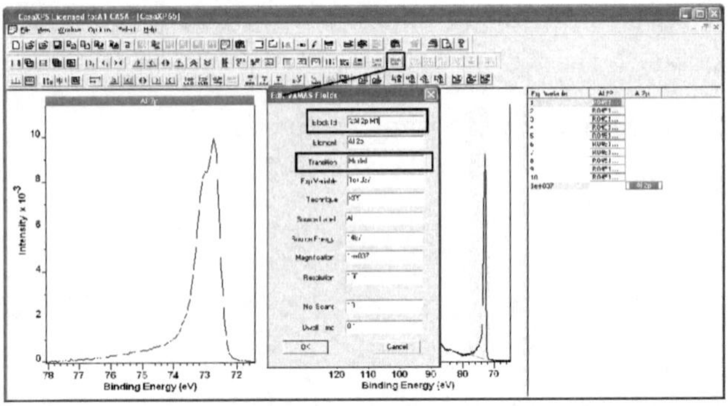

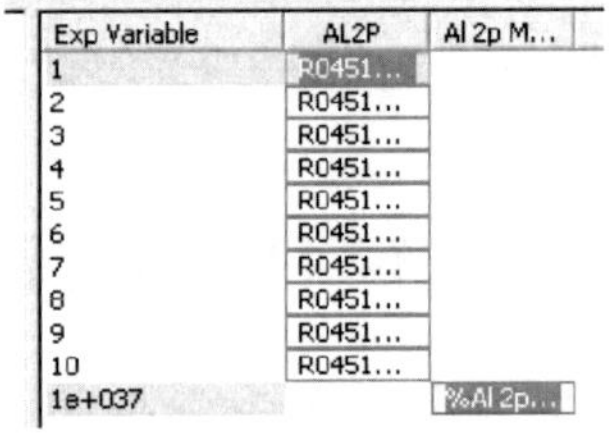

The % prefix to the block identifier causes the normalisation of the lineshape when used in peak models. Without the % character the data would need additional manual processing.

Creating a component based on data simply involves adding a VAMAS block containing the data shape to the file in which the component is required and changing the lineshape parameters to the block identifier string for the VAMAS block containing the lineshape. Since the lineshape for Al 2p was prepared from the data in batch 1, a good place to start would be to verify that the lineshape represents the batch 1 Al 2p data. A region already exists on the Al 2p data, therefore to add a lineshape from the prepared VAMAS block, first create a component. Once created, the lineshape parameter for the component is replaced with the block identifier string for the lineshape VAMAS block.

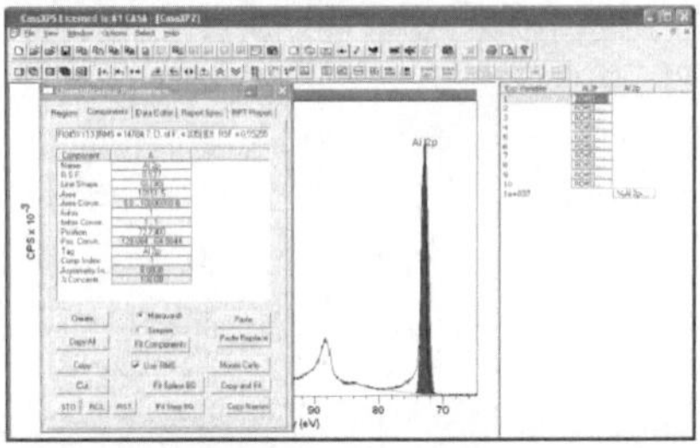

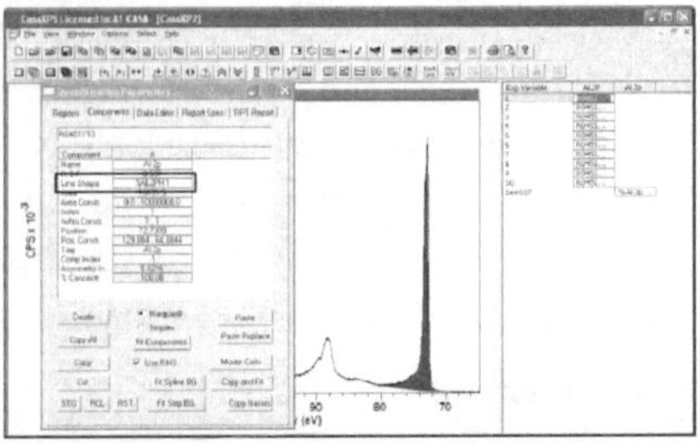

The FWHM for lineshapes based on data should be fixed at unity. Enter the value 1 into the FWHM field followed by entering the # character into the FWHM constraints field for the component using the lineshape. The # character without any numerical value following when entered into a constraint field causes the corresponding parameter to be fixed at the current value. When the new component is fitted to the data from which the lineshape derives, the fit should be near perfect.

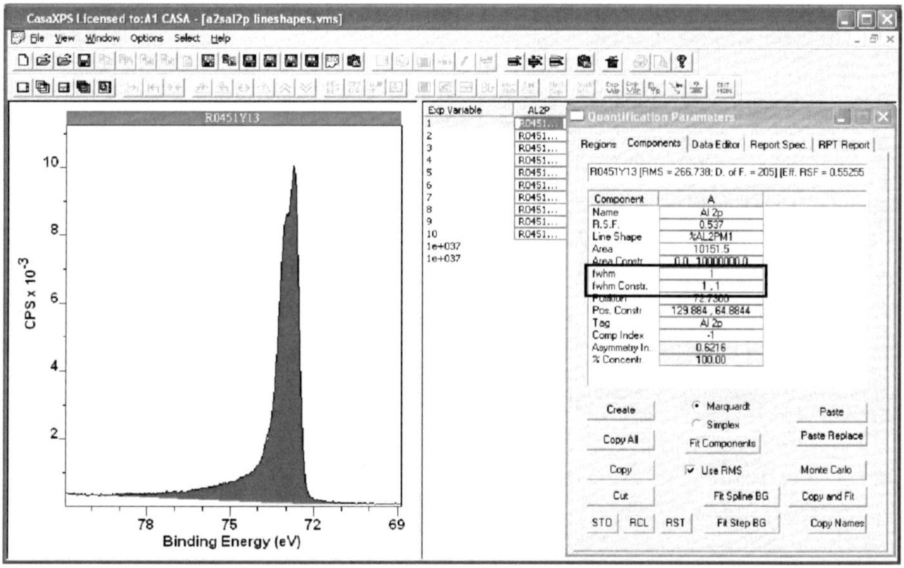

The new lineshape works well with the original batch 1 data. The next step is to model the batch 10 Al 2p data. To move the component defined on the batch 1 Al 2p to the batch 10 data, whilst the batch 1 data is the active VAMSA block, press the Copy button on the Components property page. A copy of the component selected in the table on the Components property page is placed on an internal clipboard for components. The Al 2p data from batch 10 should be displayed in the active tile before pressing the Paste button on the Components property page. The component previously placed on the internal component clipboard is inserted into the component table for the batch 10 data. When passed via the components clipboard, the component added via the Paste button is not fitted to the data, but is supplied exactly as copied from the original data.

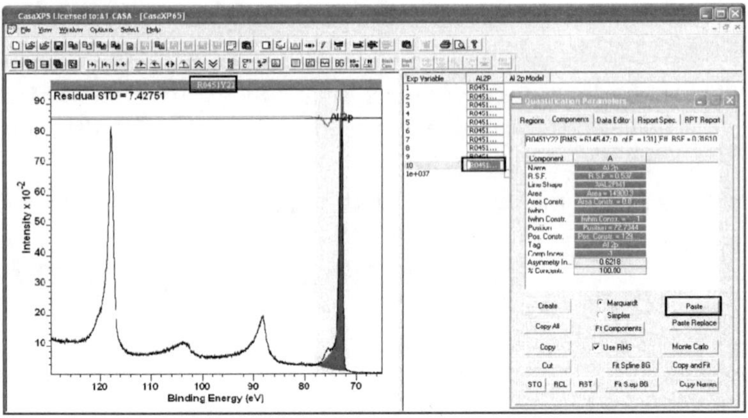

A Gaussian/Lorentzian required to allow for the Al 2p oxide not accounted for by the batch 1 lineshape must be added to the peak model before fitting is performed. The peaks when fitted to the batch 10 data represent the Al 2p metallic doublet plus 28.4% of the Al 2p oxide contribution and a GL peak representing 71.6% of the Al 2p oxide contribution to the batch 10 data.

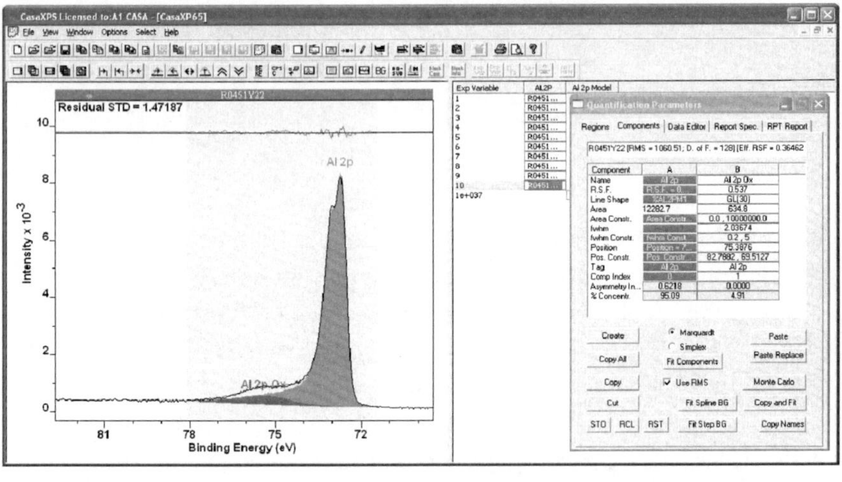

The area parameter for the Al 2p oxide is 634.8. Since this value is expected to correspond to 71.6 % of the true oxide contribution to the Al 2p envelope, a GL function with area parameter equal to 250.3, or 28.4% should be part of the data envelope for batch 1. The procedure is therefore fix the FWHM and position for the GL component in batch 10, move the component to batch 1 Al 2p and set the area parameter to 250.3. If the background plus the 28.4% Al 2p oxide represented by the GL peak are subtracted from the batch 1 data envelope, the remaining signal should be due to the Al 2p metal peaks.

Fix the position and FWHM parameters in the GL component on the batch 10 data by entering # into the position and FWHM constraint fields followed by pressing the Enter keyboard key. The area parameter for the GL peak can be set to 250.3. With the GL component selected on the Components property page, press the Copy button.

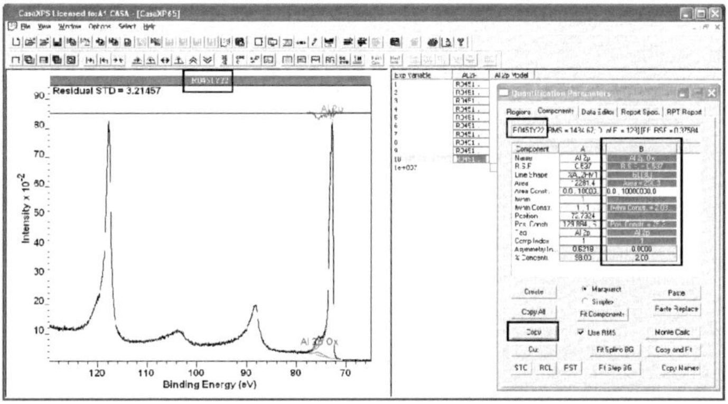

Select and display the spectrum from batch 1 in the active tile. This time, paste the Al 2p oxide peak using the Paste Replace button. The Paste Replace button overwrites the components currently defined on the active VAMAS block with the components on the internal component clipboard.

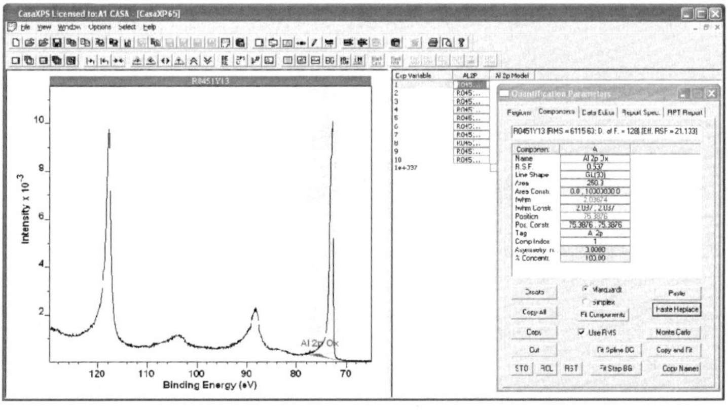

The synthetic envelope for the batch 1 data consists of the background plus the single GL peak positioned and scaled to represent the expected Al 2p oxide peak based on information from the Al 2p oxide peak from the batch 10 data and the relative intensities of the O 1s peaks for the batch 1 and batch 10 measurements. If the synthetic envelope is subtracted from the batch 1 Al 2p data the resulting background subtracted data will approximate the shape of the Al 2p metal doublet pair.

The Test Data property page provides a button labelled Replace by Envelope. On pressing the Replace by Envelope button for the batch 1 Al 2p data when defined with a background spanning the Al 2p data envelope and a single GL peak approximating the Al2p oxide, the resulting data offers a spectrum for the aluminium without the Al 2p metallic peaks.

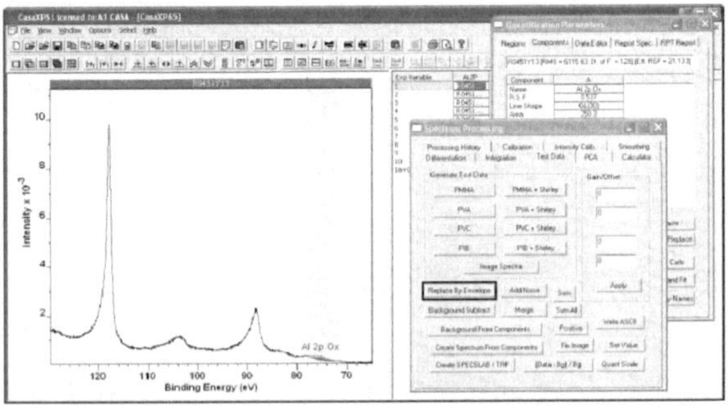

The spectrum prepared without the Al 2p metallic doublet must be subtracted from the unprocessed spectrum to reveal the Al 2p metallic doublet lineshape. The processed data is subtracted from the raw data using the Calculator property page on the Spectrum Processing dialog window. With the data displayed in the active tile, press the Set Operand button. The data from the active tile is loaded into a buffer, indicated by a change of colour for the data in the active tile.

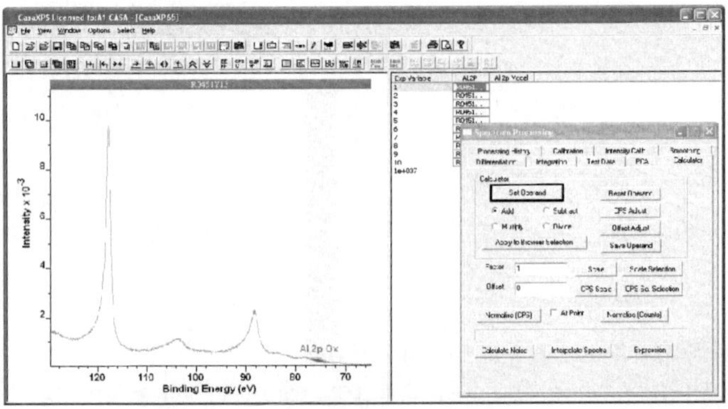

With the buffer loaded from the processed data envelope, the VAMAS block for the batch 1 Al data can be returned to the original spectrum using the Processing History property page. Pressing the Undo button returns the data to the state before the Replace by Envelope button operation.

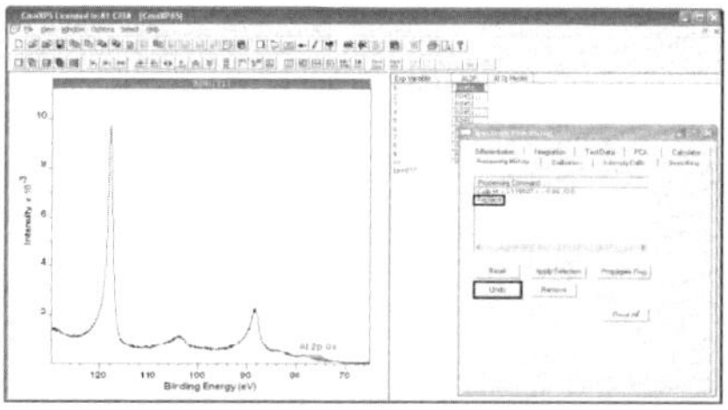

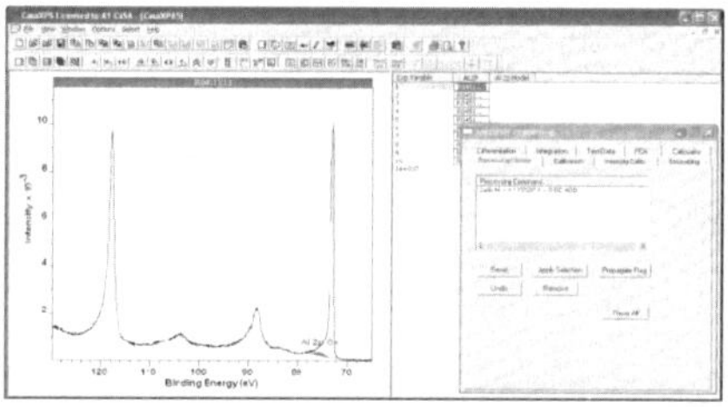

Returning to the Calculator property page causes the trace loaded into the buffer to appear draw over the data currently displayed in the active tile. The trace loaded in the buffer of the calculator can be applied to the selection of VAMAS blocks in the right-hand pane. Only the batch 1 Al data need be selected, the radio button for subtraction enabled and the Apply to Browser Selection button pressed.

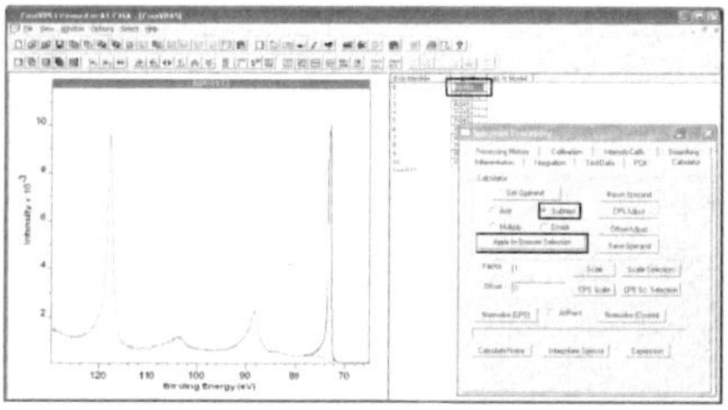

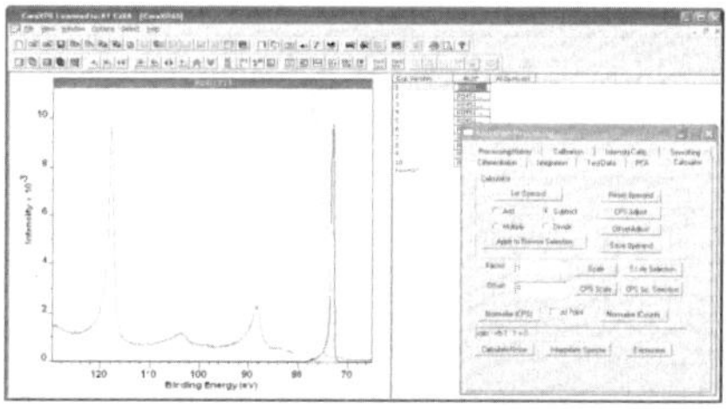

Finally, the SIMS toolbar button for creating VAMAS blocks from regions isolates the Al 2p metallic lineshape.

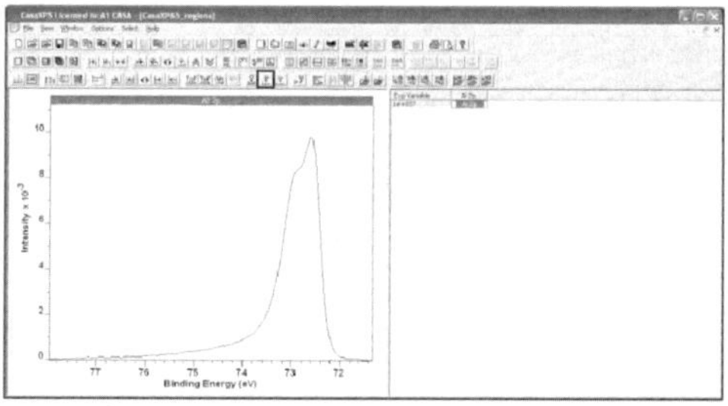

In principle, the computed lineshape offers a means of determining synthetic lineshapes with the correct asymmetry to represent metallic Al 2p peaks. The reason synthetic lineshapes are desired rather than a direct use of the lineshape based on the data is the lineshape based on data alone would be difficult to use with data from different energy resolutions and/or instruments. The synthetic lineshapes are capable of adjusting FWHM based on the two component peaks and are therefore more flexible and general.

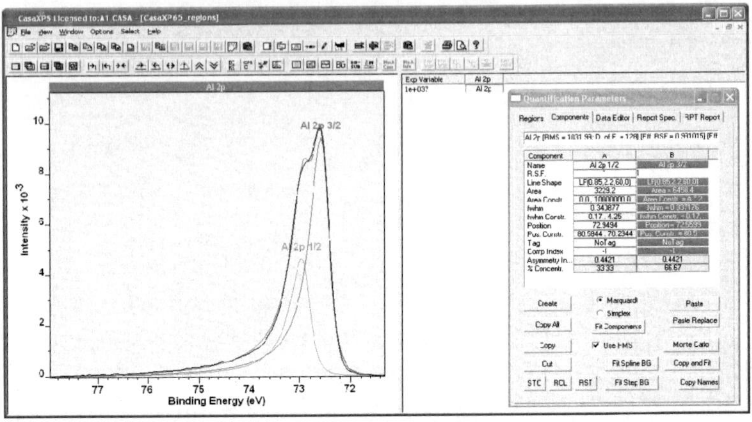

As a test for these newly determined lineshapes for Al 2p doublets, the synthetic peaks developed for data from a Scienta ESCA 300 are used to model data from a Kratos Axis Ultra.

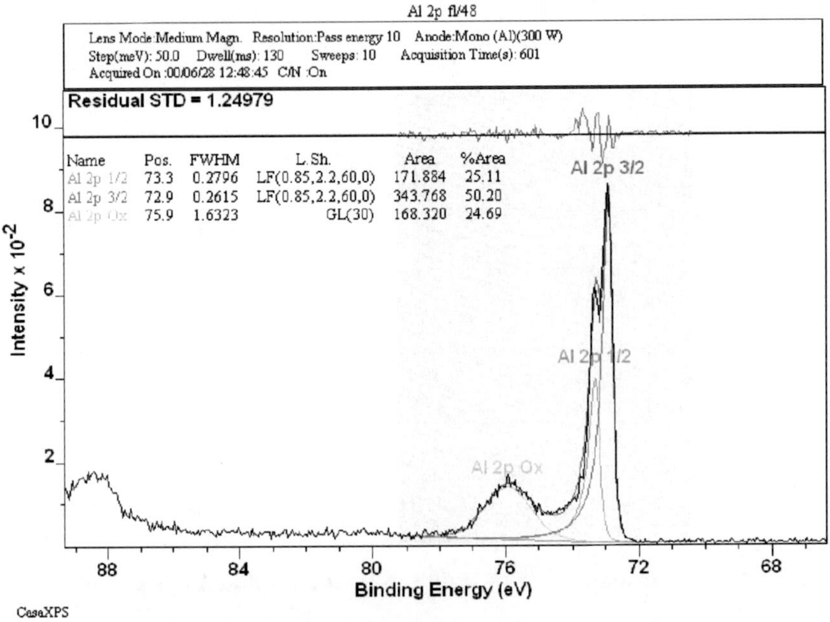

A key feature of the peak model is the LF lineshape. While a Doniach Sunjic profile, in principle, best describes the asymmetry observed in metallic lineshapes, the area beneath the DS lineshape for most values of the asymmetry parameter is infinite. The consequence to XPS of functional forms for lineshapes with infinite area is that the intensity of a peak measured with such a lineshape is arbitrary and must be calibrated for each measurement. The lineshape chosen to describe the Al 2p metallic peaks is designed to offer DS like lineshapes, but includes a damping function for the asymmetry which ensures the area beneath the LF lineshape is finite and therefore suitable for making measurements for peak intensity. The success of the LF lineshapes chosen for the Al 2p peak model can be judged by the effective RSF calculated from the region and the components. For the Al 2p data from the Kratos instrument, using an RSF of unity for each component returns an effective RSF of unity.

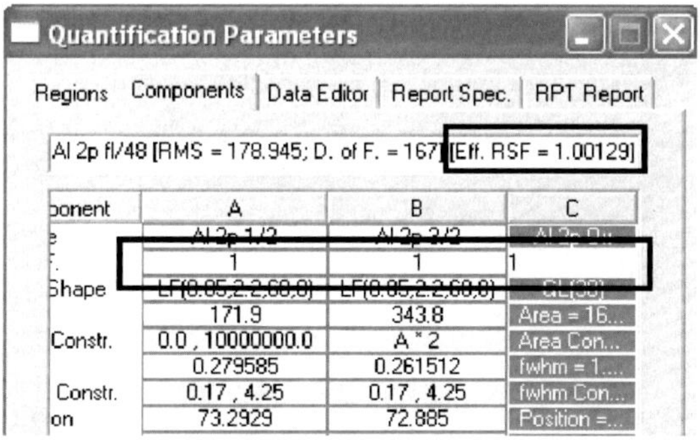

The significance of the effective RSF matching the RSF for the components is the area measured by the region is the same as the area measured by the components in the peak model. If the effective RSF differs from the RSF used in the components, then assuming the peak model fits the data, the lineshapes are failing to calculate the same area for the data envelope as the region.

Applying the peak model to the profile experiment produces a set of fits for the Al 2p interval.

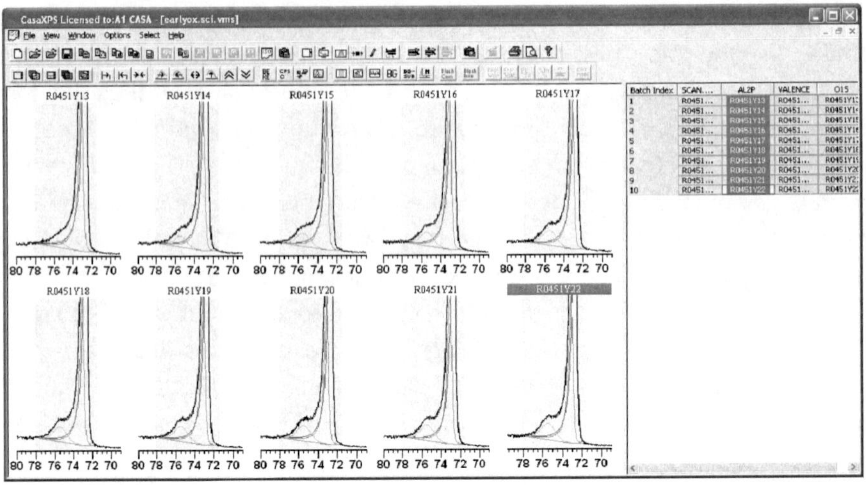

From these peak fits, a profile for the Al 2p oxide peak is calculated using the Custom Report section on the Report Spec property page.

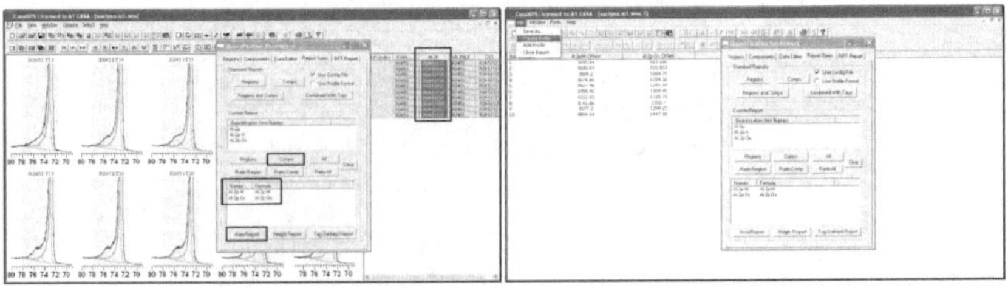

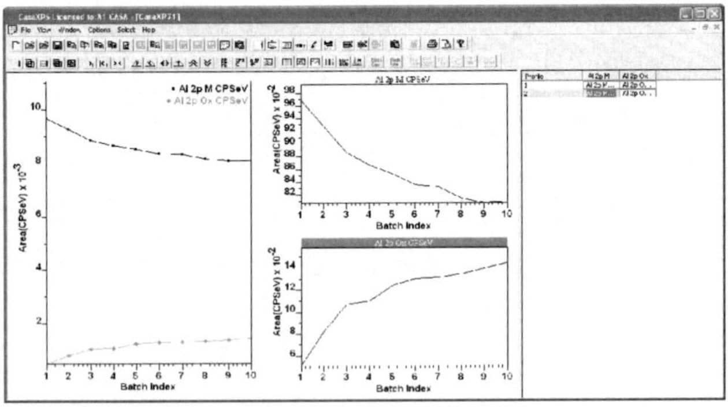

Profiling using Linear Least Squares

A linear least squares procedure offers a means of partitioning a spectrum into component spectra. The component spectra are chosen to embody the transitions responsible for the measured data. Once these component spectra are determined in a least squares sense, the relative contributions of these underlying transitions to the measured data can be identified using quantification regions in exactly the same way any spectrum in the profile is quantified.

The least squares procedure is described in the context of the Savitzky Golay algorithm for smoothing data and differentiating spectra. The essential difference in the least squares decomposition of spectra compared to the Savitzky Golay algorithm is the basis functions are now spectra rather than terms ($1, x, x^2, ...$) in a polynomial. The net result is the same in the sense that a spectrum $\underline{s}$ is expressed as a linear combination of a set of n component spectra $\underline{c}_i$.

$$\underline{s} \cong \sum_{i=1}^{n} a_i \underline{c}_i$$

The coefficients a_i are determined in a least squares sense and the spectrum $\underline{s}$ is therefore decomposed into component spectra $a_i\underline{c}_i$.

When deciding to use linear least squares (LLS) as a means of profiling data, the first question should be: do I have enough knowledge of the data set to construct appropriate basis components? When selecting the $\underline{c}_i$ component spectra, the selected set of component spectra must span, in a mathematical sense, the information content of any spectrum decomposed into these component spectra. Failure to include sufficient component spectra can impair the results. For example, consider three GL peaks and a data envelope consisting of the sum of the three peaks:

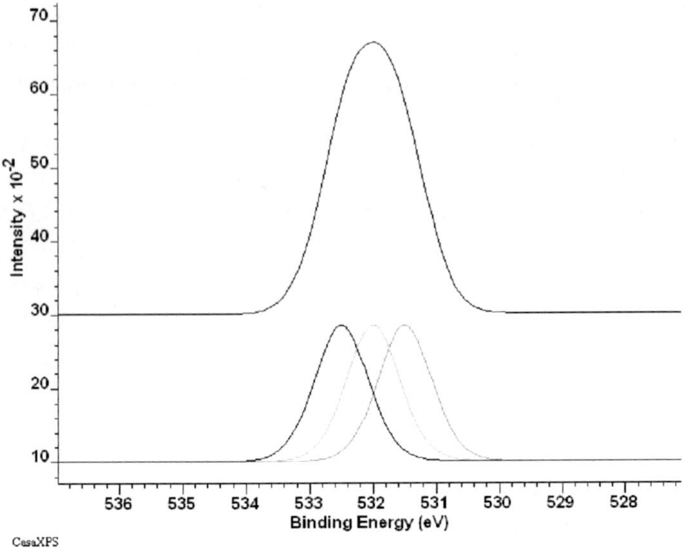

If all three component peaks are used to approximate the data envelope, the least squares criterion returns a perfect match between the data envelope and the linear least squares solution. If however only two of the components are used to approximate the full data envelope in the LLS sense the results are far from ideal.

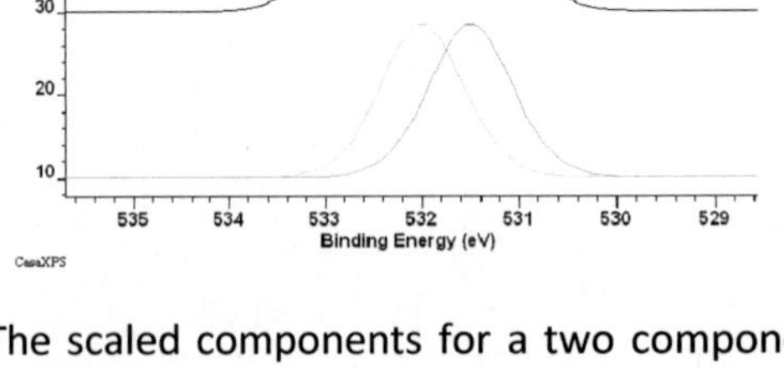

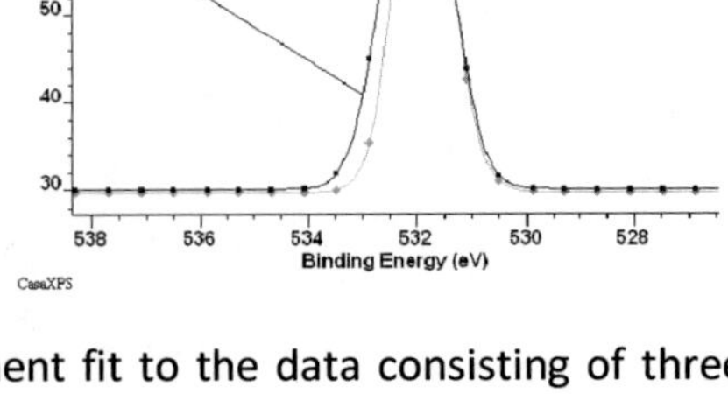

The scaled components for a two component fit to the data consisting of three components yields an over estimate for one component and an under estimate for the contribution of the second component.

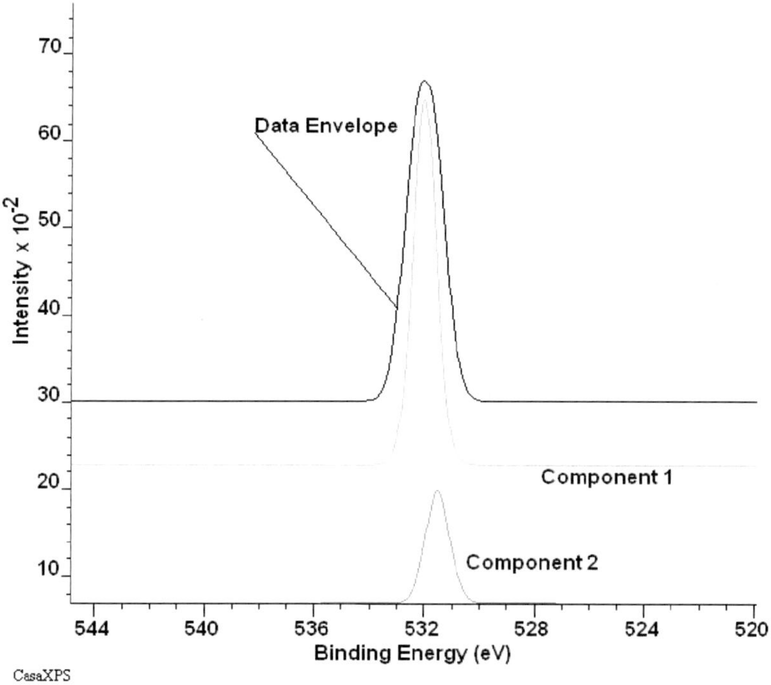

The outcome of a LLS analysis applied to profile data may appear reasonable, but the errors due to the LLS approach are large. The fundamental problem with the LLS approach is the linear approximation of the data by the set of components. If the peak or peaks in the original data shift due to changing charge state, for example, the components will no longer match the data in terms of position and problems ensue. Attempts to fix these problems necessarily lead to introducing non-linear least squares aspects into the LLS algorithm, at which point the wheel is reinvented known an non-linear least squares peak modelling. The bottom line is, to use LLS, the data set must be completely understood in terms of components. There are other issues with linear dependence of component spectra used in the LLS solution. For these reasons, whenever a LLS solution is performed in CasaXPS, the results are delivered such that the user can inspect all aspects of the LLS process.

The aluminium oxidation sequence provides a simple data set with which to illustrate the LLS features in CasaXPS.

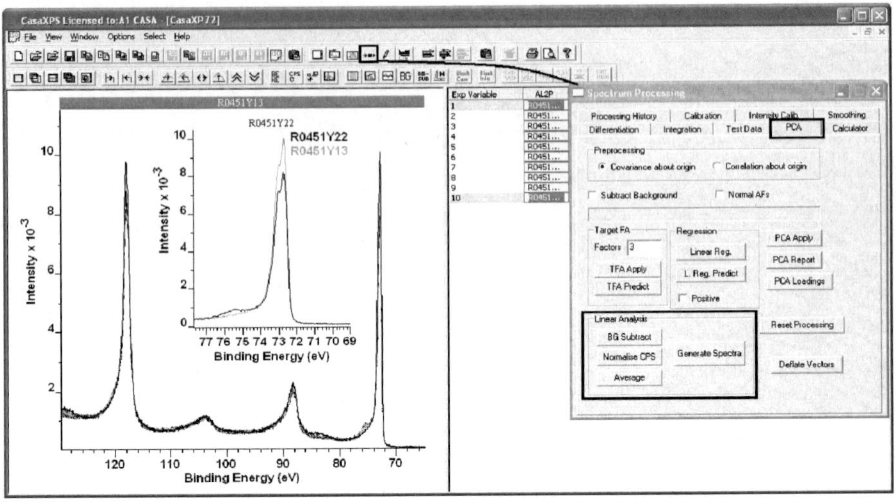

As a first example, consider the data in the aluminium interval as consisting of varying proportions of the data in batch 1 and batch 10. The two spectra from these batches will form the component spectra for use with the Linear Analysis options on the PCA property page of the Spectrum Processing dialog window. Creating a LLS decomposition for a set of data involves displaying the component spectra in the active tile, selecting in the right-hand pane the set of spectra for which a decomposition is desired and pressing the Generate Spectra button on the PCA property page.

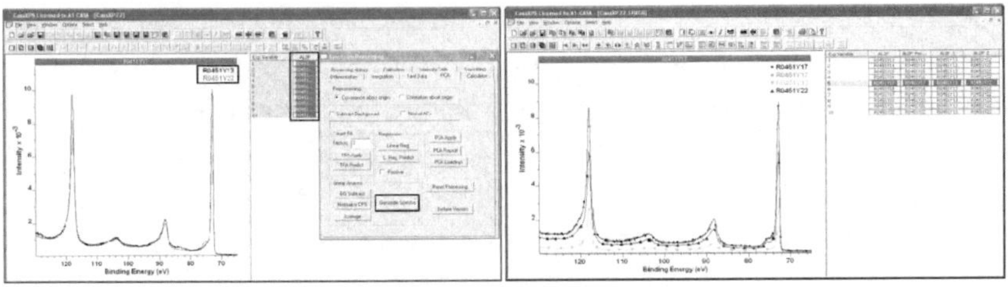

The result of pressing the Generate Spectra button is a new experiment frame in which a row of VAMAS blocks is created for each VAMAS block selected in the original file. Each row includes a VAMAS block for the original data, the LLS solution representing the sum of the scaled component spectra and for each component spectra a VAMAS block containing the scaled component spectra, the sum of which is equivalent to the VAMAS block in the second column.

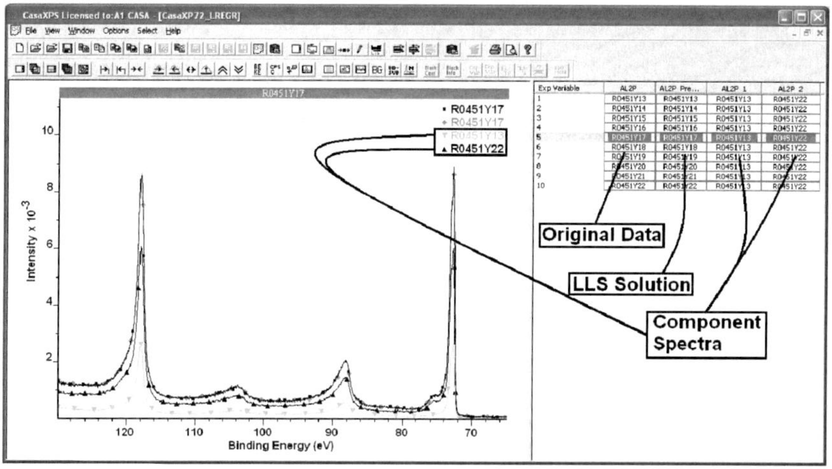

The change from the initial state defined by batch 1 to the final state of batch 10 can be assessed by creating regions on the component spectra generated by the LLS operation.

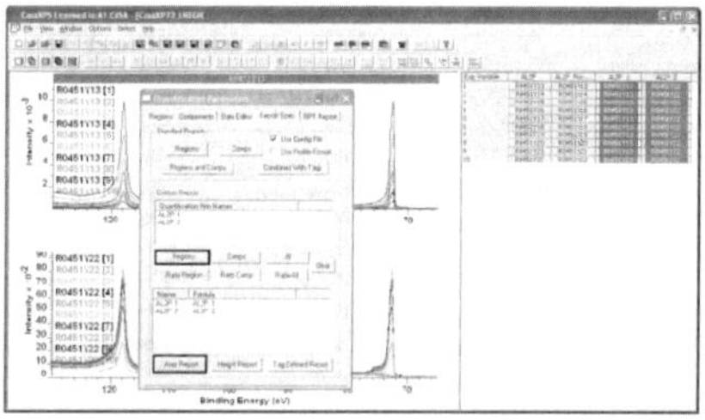

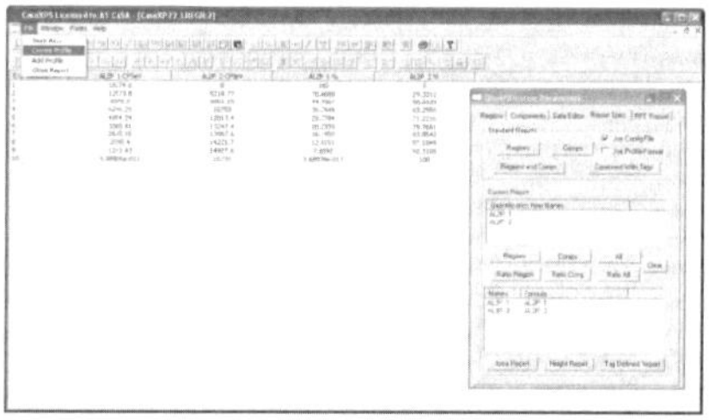

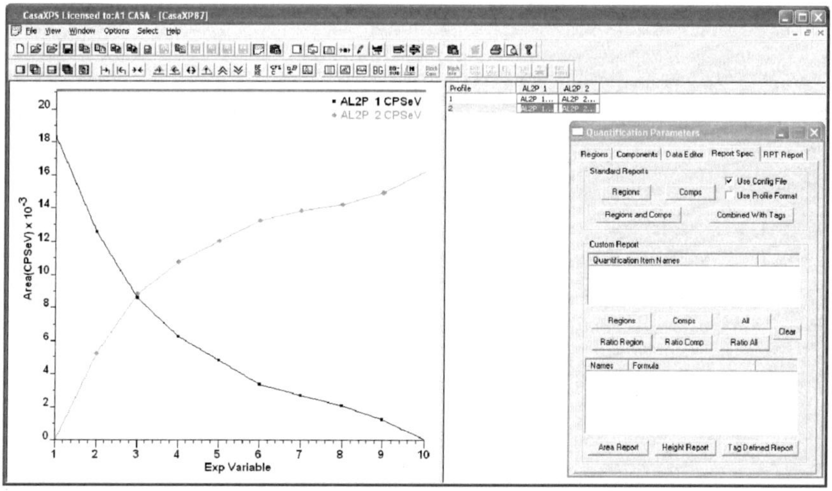

Energy Calibration Options for Rows of Data

A set of measurements such as the aluminium oxidation experiment typically require energy calibration on a row-by-row basis. Spectra acquired under identical acquisition conditions and recorded at the same time are assumed to be equivalent in charge state to one another. Measurements separated in time may differ in charge state and therefore the energy calibration for each of the sets of ten batches should be at least checked for consistency in peak positions. The spectra in the aluminium data set are reasonably well calibrated in energy, but nevertheless the following calibration methods applied to these data illustrate the principle for managing similar file structures.

When positioning peaks with respect to binding energy, the energy of the Fermi level in all conductors connected to ground is taken as zero. Therefore, a method for fitting a step function to an edge provides a tool for calculating the position of a feature offering a reference point when calibrating the energy scale. The valence band data acquired as part of the aluminium data includes an edge which, by way of example, will be used to calibrate the data set.

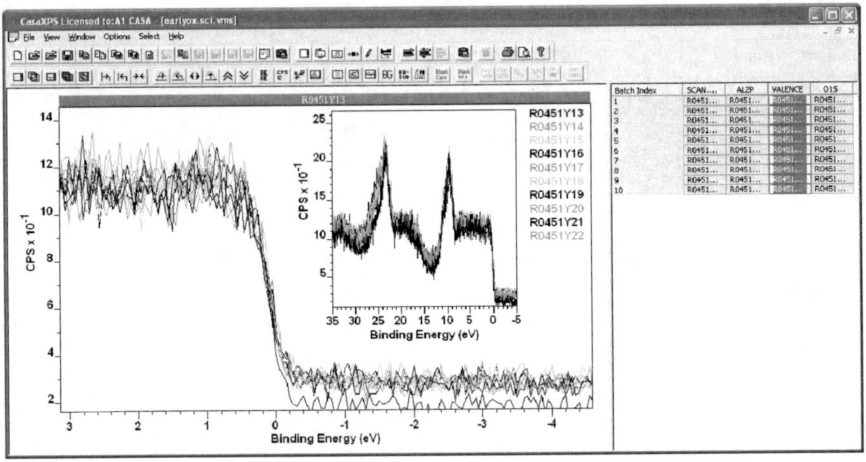

Measuring the position of an edge involves creating a region spanning the rise or drop in the data. The background types Step Up and Step Down provide a means of defining a functional form for which the position and width of the edge can be estimated.

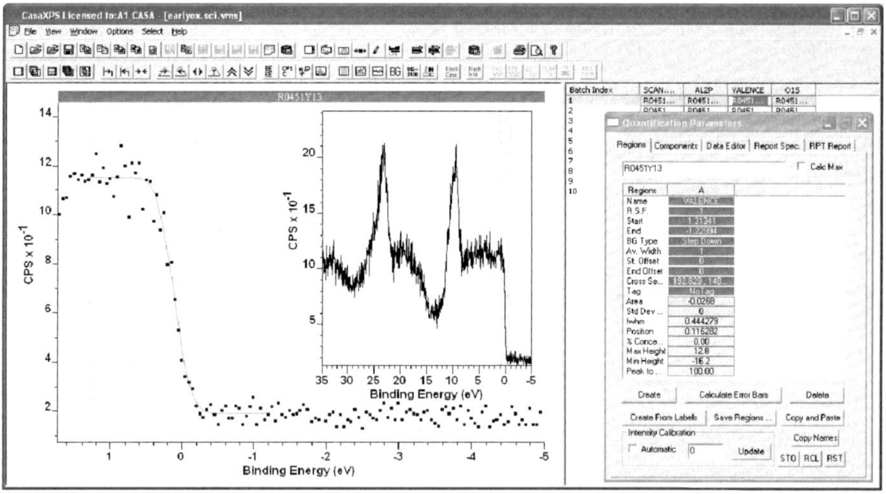

After a region is defined and located close to the edge, changing the background type to Step Down causes the parameters for the step function to be re-initialised with respect to the edge in the data. The step function includes four parameters displayed in the cross-section field for the region on the Regions property page of the Quantification Parameters dialog window. These four parameters may be optimised using a button on the Components property page, where the Fit Step BG button adjusts these parameters in a least squares sense to the edge limited by the region.

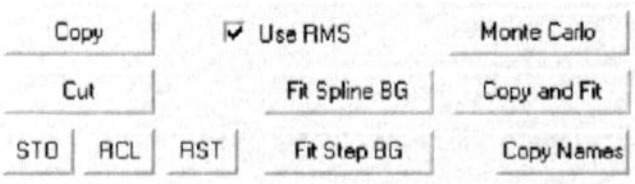

An edge must be defined for each valence band spectrum. The propagation option used to move regions between spectra can again be employed. Propagating a region defined with a step background type also, as part of the propagate operation, fits the region to the data receiving the region.

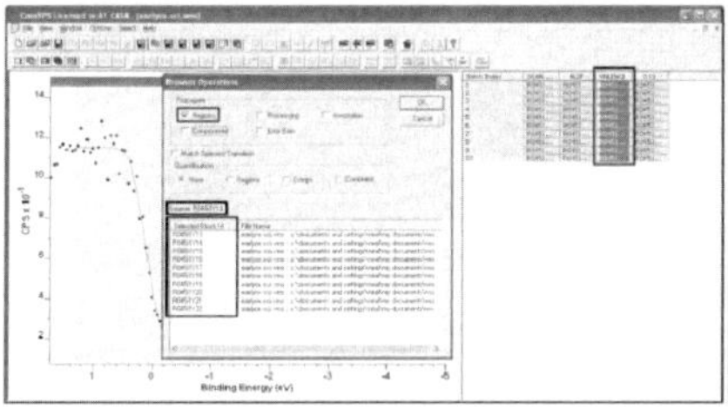

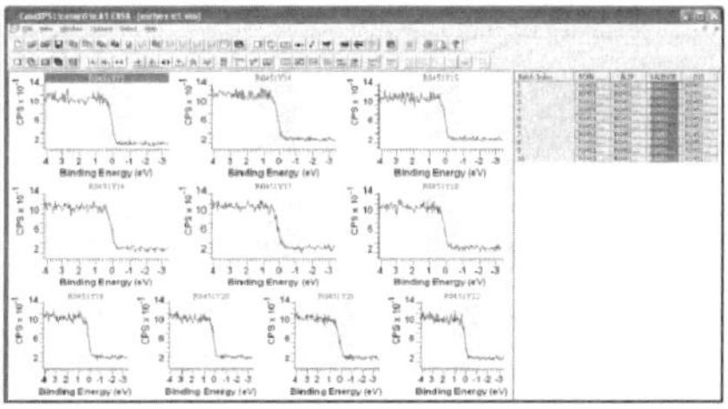

The position determined from the Step Down background for each region can be used to calibrate the spectra for the entire experiment. The Calibration property page includes options for calibrating rows of spectra based on the energy determined from the first region defined on a VAMAS block. Using the right-hand pane to indicate the VAMAS blocks from which the positions are to be computed and entering a value in the True field prepares the property page for a calibration based on the Apply by Row (1st Region) button.

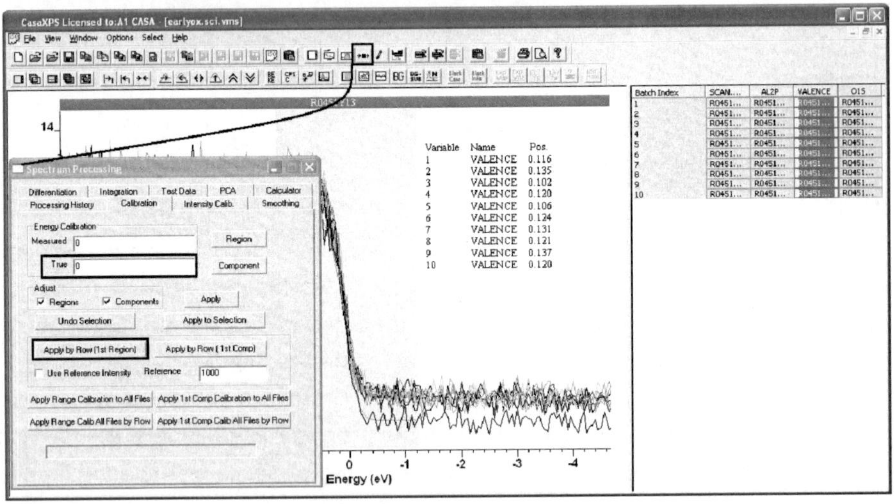

The selected column in the right-hand pane specifies not just the source VAMAS block for the region used in the calculation, but also determines the rows of VAMAS blocks to which the calibration is applied. If a VAMAS block is selected for use with the Apply by Row (1st Region) button, then all VAMAS blocks in the row will be calibrated without exception.

After refitting the step down backgrounds to the shifted data, the positions for the edge measured using the background are all aligned and equal to zero.

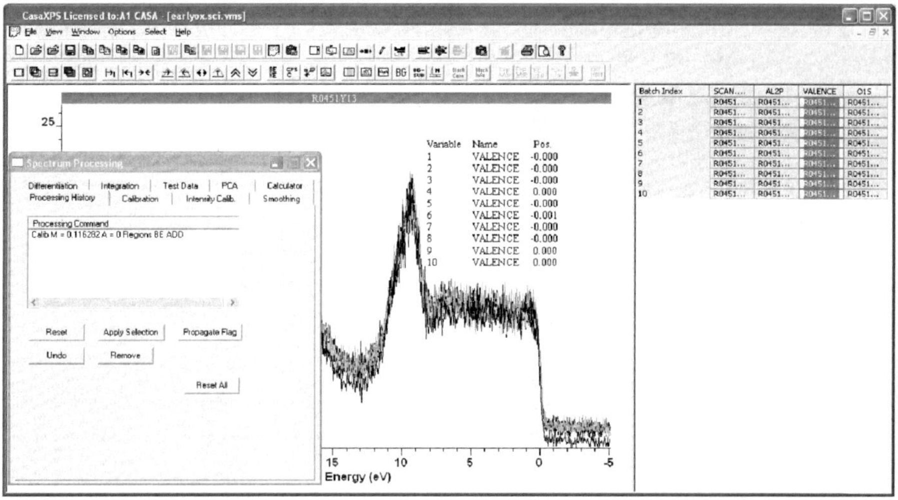

Since each row in the file includes a valence band spectrum and all valence band spectra are selected in the right-hand pane, a processing instruction for the energy calibration operation is added to each VAMAS block in the file. The measured value is determined from the column of selected VAMAS blocks and the true value derives from the text-field on the Calibration property page.

Calibration options involving calibration based on the first region or first component defined on the selected VAMAS blocks, target VAMAS blocks only within the one experiment frame and, all VAMAS blocks within a row for which a VAMAS block is selected are processed.

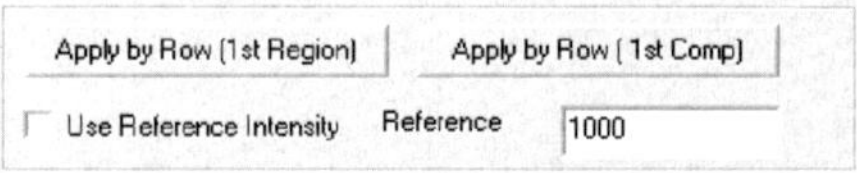

This source and target mechanism should be contrasted with the options on the Calibration property page which act on multiple VAMAS files. The source for determining a calibration shift and the target blocks to which the shift is applied are both selectable for operations designed for multiple files.

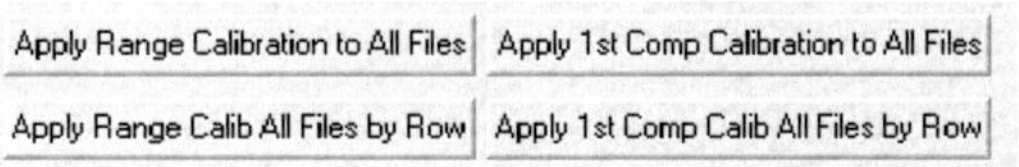

The Calibration property page represents a progression from a simple energy shift determined from and applied to a single VAMAS block to situations in which multiple VAMAS blocks determine a range of energy shifts which are selectively applied to many and different VAMAS blocks throughout a set of files. The number of calibration options of increasing complexity ensures the ease for both the simplest calibrations, yet offering efficient methods for those working with large sets of data.

Spectrum Processing Dialog Window

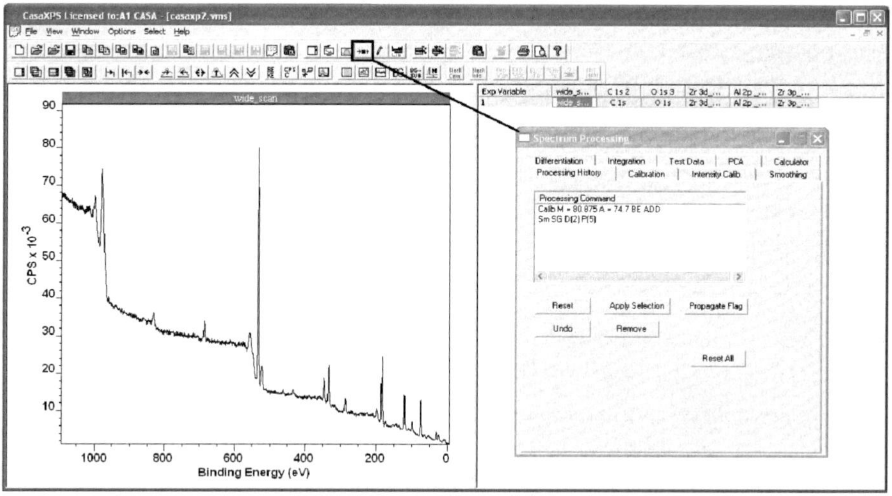

The Spectrum Processing dialog window includes:

1. The Processing History property page: lists processing instructions currently applied to the first VAMAS block displayed in the active tile.

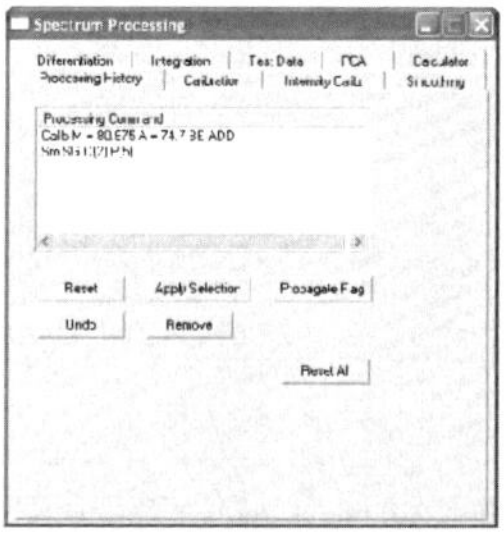

2. Calibration Property page: provides a range of options for energy calibrating data.

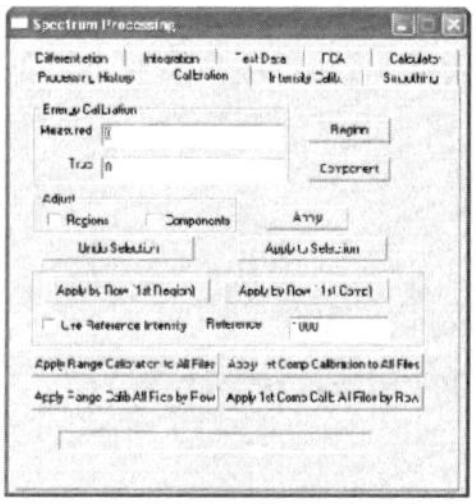

3. Intensity Calibration property page: offering explicit intensity calibration in terms of transmission function and energy corrections applied directly to the data.

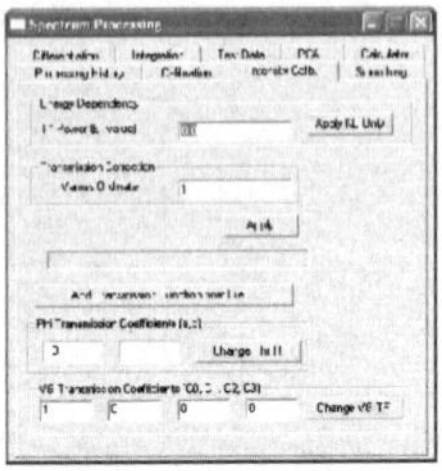

4. Smoothing Property Page: offers a range of smoothing options.

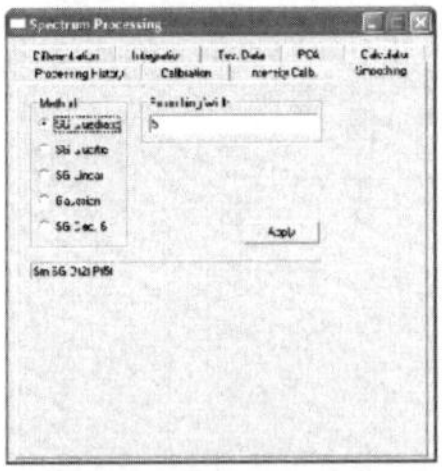

5. Differentiation Property Page: provides Savitzky Golay differentiation of data.

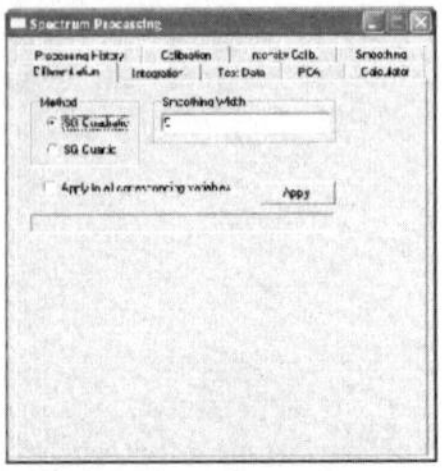

6. Integration Property Page: offers Savitzky Golay integration of data.

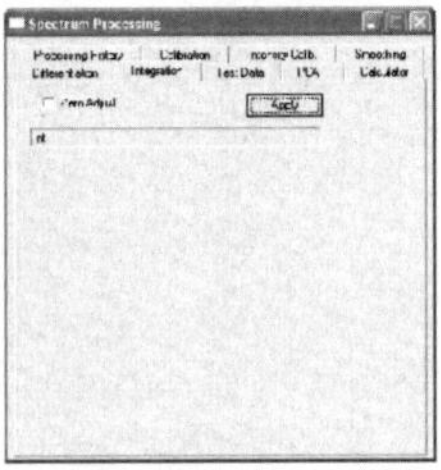

7. Test Data Property Page: offers a wealth of miscellaneous options and is far more useful that the name suggests.

8. PCA property page: includes linear least squares tool for analysing sets of spectra and various PCA options.

9. Calculator Property Page: provides options for combining and scaling spectra.

Processing History

Each time a processing option is applied to the data in a VAMAS block a processing instruction is added to a list maintained by the VAMAS block. When saved to disk, the VAMAS blocks within the VAMAS file save the original raw data together with these lists of processing instructions. Loading a VAMAS file entails reading the data for each VAMAS block and reapplying the processing operations previously saved in the data file.

The Processing History property page lists the set of processing operations maintained by the VAMAS block displayed in the active tile. The processed form of the data is used in the display tiles. To return the data to the unprocessed form, options on the Processing History are used to unwind the processing steps.

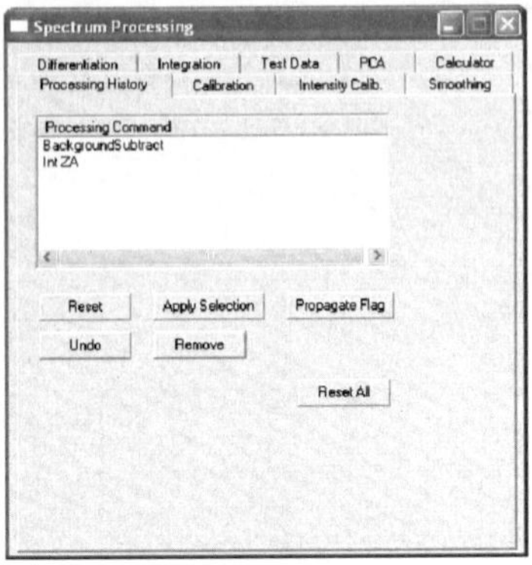

The Undo button progressively unwinds the processing performed on the VAMAS block in the active tile, deleting the processing operation listed at the bottom of the history list. In contrast, the Reset button removes all processing operations in the history list. Two additional options allow processing instructions to be selected before either removing the selected operation or applying only those operations selected in the history list to the data in the active tile.

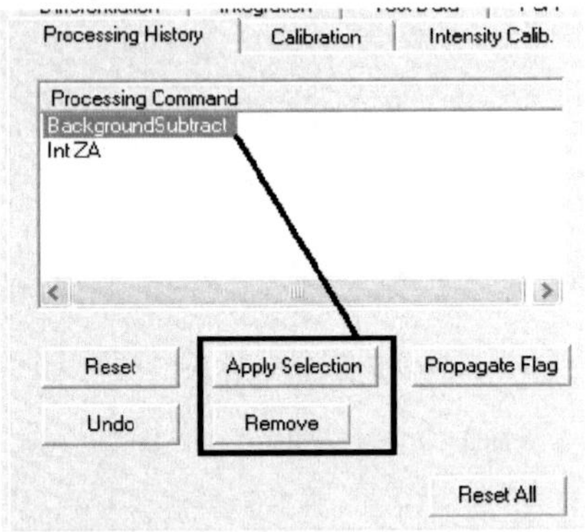

Processing operations can be flag to indicate the operation should not be used when propagating processing to other VAMAS blocks. Energy calibration for a spectrum may not be appropriate for a spectrum to which other operations are required. The Propagate Flag button marks the selected items in the history list using a toggle on and toggle off mechanism. When flagged, the processing operation is not included in any propagation step.

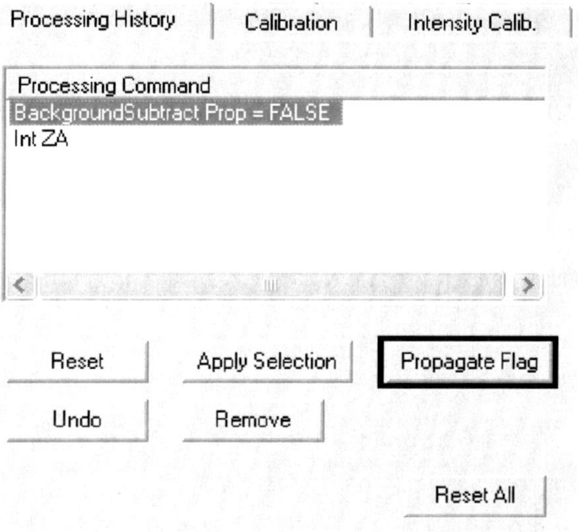

A means of globally cancelling all processing for a set of spectra is by overlaying the VAMAS blocks in the active tile before pressing the Reset All button.

Energy Calibration

The Calibration property page performs energy calibration by calculating an energy shift based on a measured value typically determined from a feature in the spectra and a true value which specifies the expected value for the spectral feature in the data. The True text-field is always used to determine the calibration shift. The Measured text-field may or may not be explicitly utilised depending on the calibration option applied to the data.

The calibration option chosen depends on the number and location of VAMAS blocks involved in the operation.

Calibration of a Single VAMAS Block

For a single spectrum displayed in the active tile, the Apply button on the Calibration property page calculates the energy shift using the Measured and True text-fields. Only the active VAMAS block in the active tile is calibrated by the Apply button.

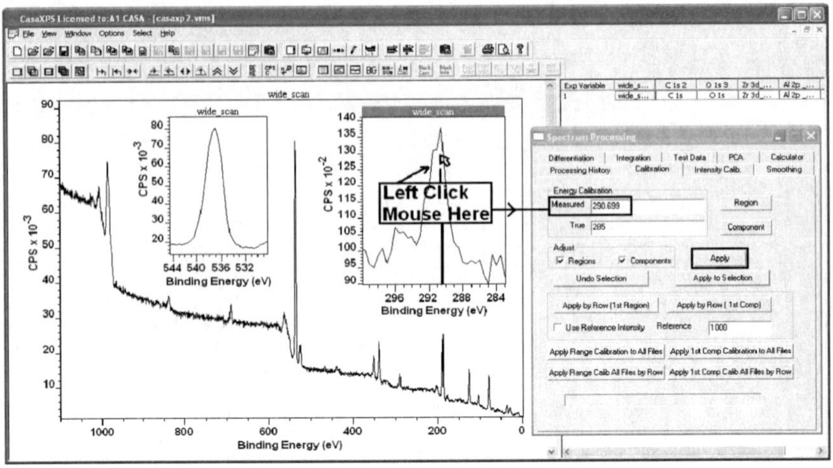

The energy calibration for a survey spectrum is a typical case where only the data in the active tile requires a calibration energy shift.

Energy Calibration for a Set of VAMAS Blocks

The next level in energy calibration is performed for a selection of VAMAS blocks in the right-hand pane and based on the Measured and True values specified on the Calibration property page. The Apply to Selection button is appropriate for sets of narrow scan spectra all acquired under identical operating modes for which a common energy shift is required. All spectra for which the calibration shift is applicable are selected in the right-hand pane before pressing the Apply to Selection button.

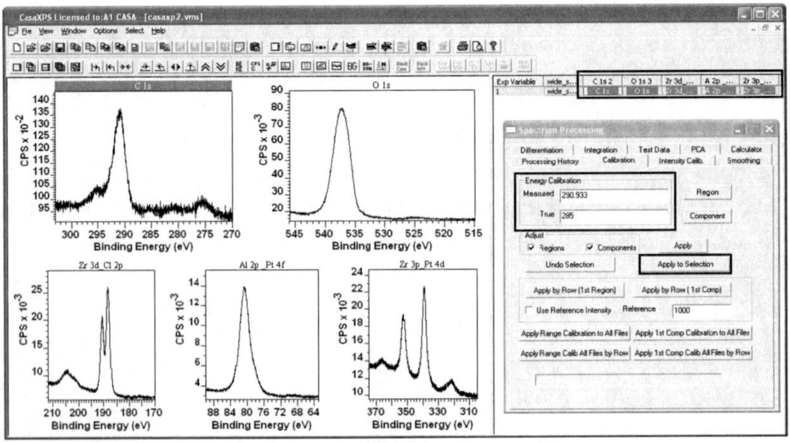

Only the VAMAS blocks selected in the right-hand pane receive the calibration operation calculated from the Measured and True values as a result of pressing the Apply to Selection button.

Entering Values for the Measured and True Parameters

The text-fields on the Calibration property page labelled Measured and True represent the energy typically associated with a spectral feature as measured and following calibration. The simplest way to specify the measured energy is to indicate a position with the cursor on the data displayed in the active tile by left clicking the mouse. The energy corresponding to the cursor position is entered into the Measured text-field. The True text-field is left unchanged.

Using Drag Actions to Define Calibration Parameters

A similar mechanism also updates the True text-field at the same time the Measured is updated. If the Shift keyboard key is held down, the cursor when dragged from one point on the display to another updates the True value with the initial position of the cursor and the Measured text-field with the final position as the drag movement terminates. The Shift key combined with the Calibration property page top-most on the Spectrum Processing dialog window allows an element marker to act as a starting point for a drag operation and the position of the peak to which the element marker corresponds as the end point for the drag motion.

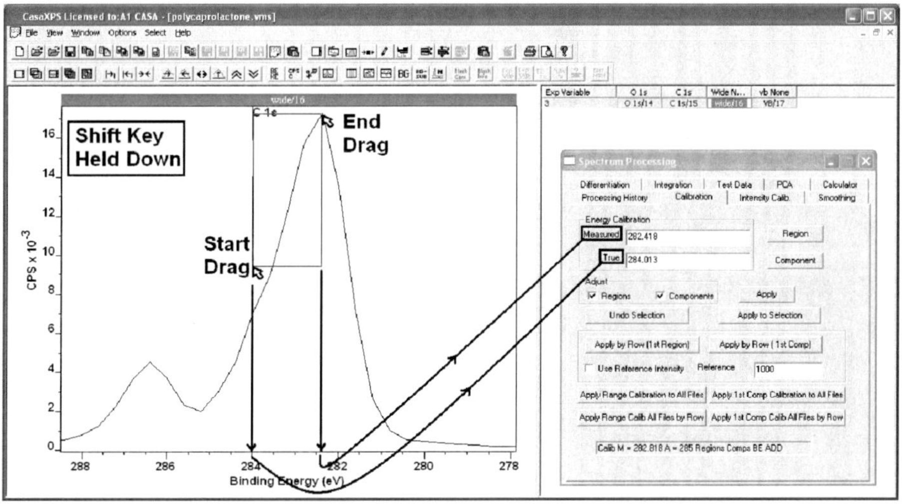

Aligning Overlaid Spectra

A further mode for updating the Measured and True text-fields involves holding down the Control and the Shift keyboard keys while dragging the mouse. The objective is to move one spectrum in energy relative to another. Overlaying two spectra in the active tile provides a visual comparison for the relative positions of two spectra. If the cursor is placed at a position on the active VAMAS block data, holding down both the Control and Shift keys before beginning a drag movement causes the two energies on the Calibration property page to update when the drag operation terminates as a result of releasing the left-mouse button. A shadow spectrum representing the data in the active VAMAS block moves sideways with the mouse movement and can be align relative to the second spectrum in the display tile. On release of the left mouse button, the True text-field is updated with the final position of the cursor and the Measured text-field updated with the initial point at which the drag operation began.

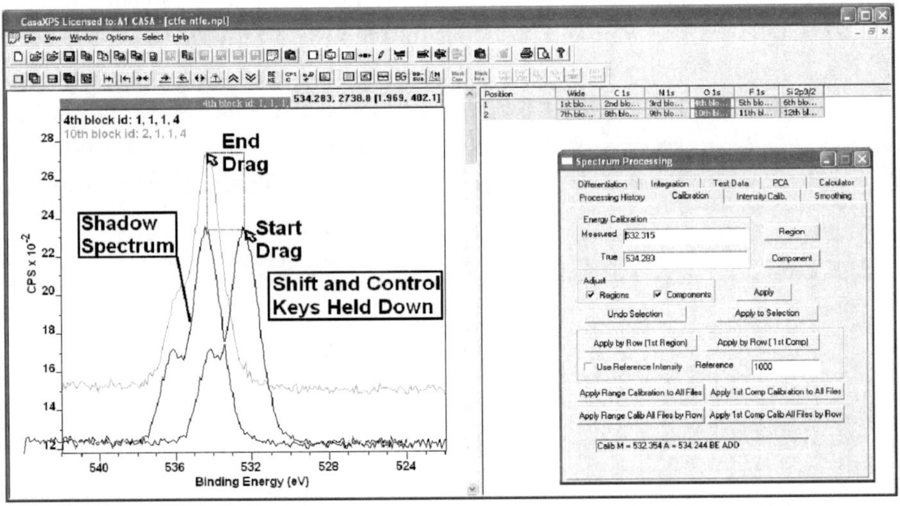

If the second spectrum displayed in the active tile is assumed to be correctly positioned in energy, on pressing the Apply or Apply to Selection buttons causes an alignment in energy between two sets of data acquired under differing charge state conditions.

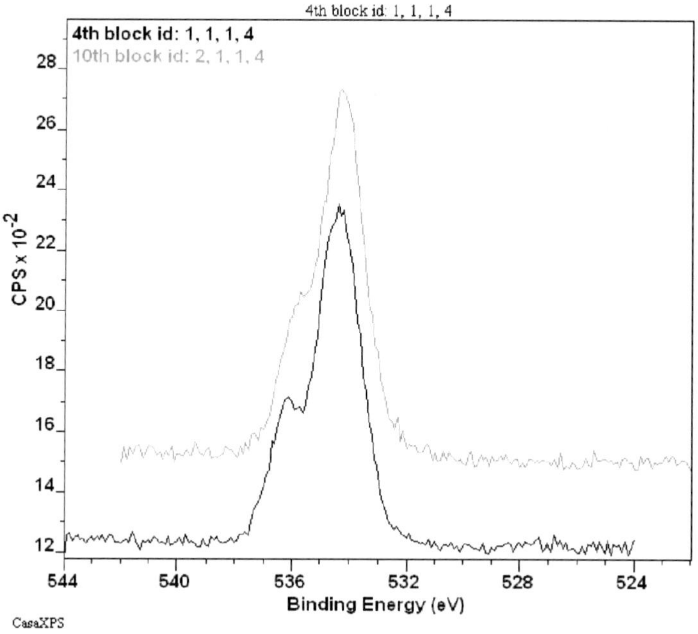

Updating Calibration Parameters from Regions or Components

Two further ways of updating the Measured and True text-fields gather information from either a region or component defined on the active VAMAS block. The position is used to update the Measured value, while the True value is updated by matching the name field from the region or component to a transition in the current element library. Using the Quantification Parameters dialog window, select a region or component by left-clicking the mouse with the cursor over a column of parameters for either a region or component before pressing the Region or Component button on the Calibration property page.

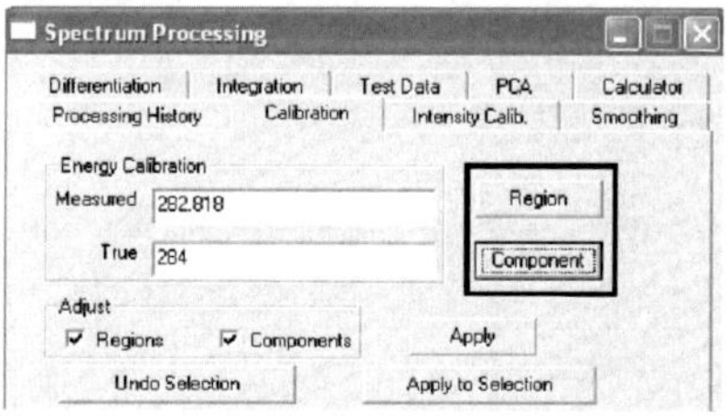

The following picture illustrates the movement of information based on a component. An equivalent operation based on a region produces the same result differing only in the position of the maximum intensity in the region is used rather than the position parameter for the selected component.

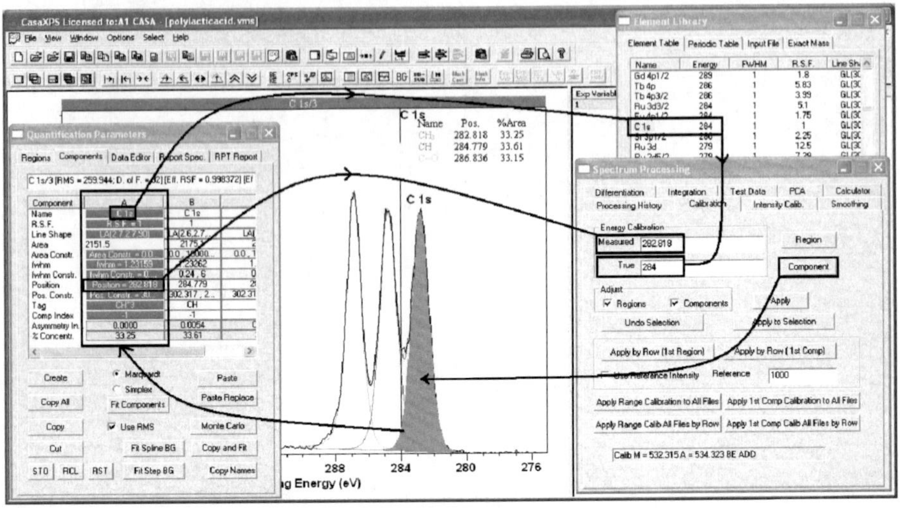

Calibration Defined by a Range of Energies

Rather than calculating an energy value for the Measured parameter from a quantification region, a slightly more crude estimate for the Measured parameter can be obtained by determining the position for the maximum intensity within a range of energies. The motivation for introducing a range option is for efficient processing of many data files. For data where peaks are shifted due to sample charging, propagating regions and components is limited by the extent of these relative shifts in peak positions. A rough charge correction using a range of energies offers a means for aligning the data sufficiently to allow more precise regions and components to be propagated. These better defined regions or components, in turn, can be used to provide a precise calibration for data spread over many files or merged into a single file containing rows of data with potentially different charge states to correct.

A key feature of the range calibration method for single spectra is a range calibration command can be propagated. For example, preparing the calibration parameters for a survey spectrum can easily be made applicable to data of a similar nature. The following illustrates a range calibration for a survey spectrum based on an O 1s peak, which is subsequently propagated to a second survey spectrum. The range calibration calculates the measured value based on the VAMAS block to which the operation is applied.

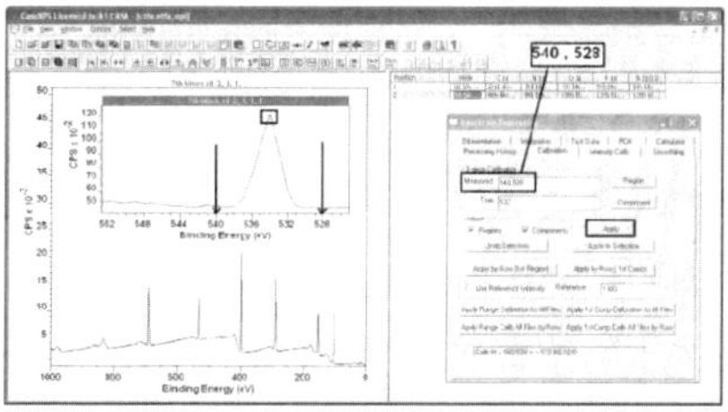

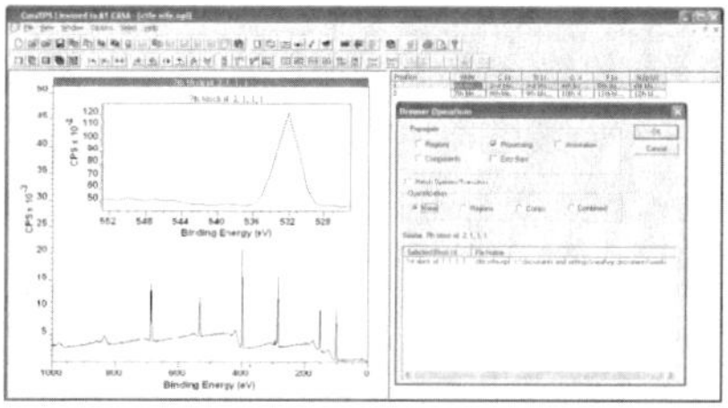

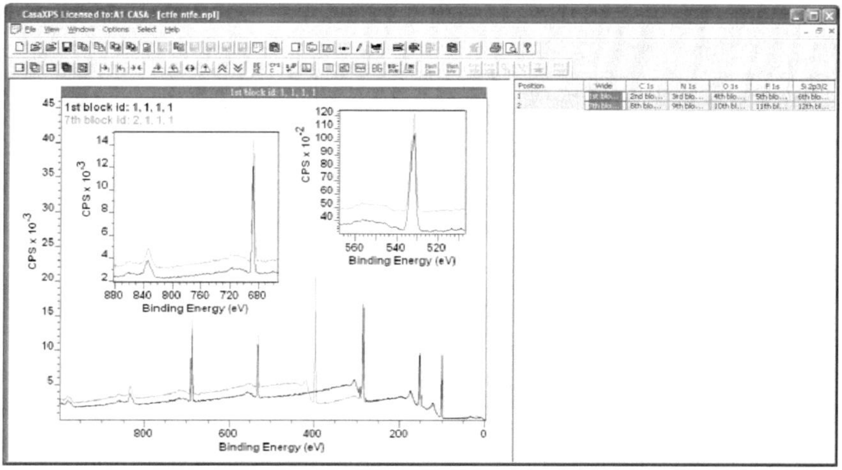

Range Calibration for Complex Datasets

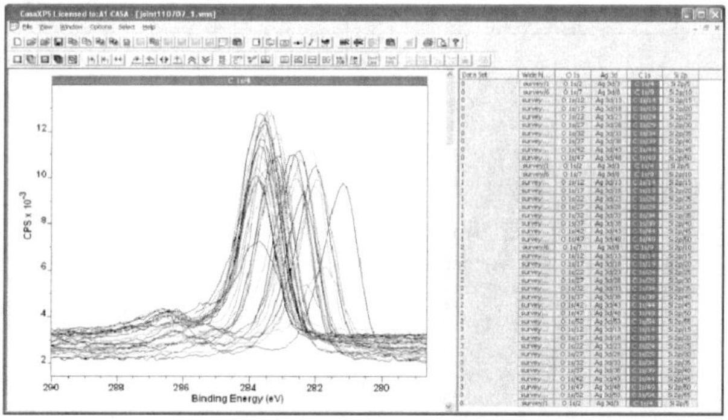

The propagation mechanism uses the processing operations from one VAMAS block and applies the processing to a set of selected VAMAS blocks. The Apply to Selection allows a range calibration operation applied to one VAMAS block, specifically the active VAMAS block displayed in the active tile, to compute an energy shift from the active VAMAS block, and then applies the shift to the set of selected VAMAS blocks. Neither method is applicable to a file containing multiple acquisitions of a similar nature where each set of VAMAS blocks corresponding to an acquisition requiring different calibrations. The propagation operation cannot spread information beyond the selected VAMAS blocks and a range calibration operation established for a C 1s spectrum would make no sense applied to O 1s data. Equally, the Apply to Selection calibration option could be applied manually to each set of VAMAS blocks. For large sets of experiments the procedure for calibrating the data would be time consuming. For these reasons a new mechanism for calibrating complex dataset based on range calibration is offered.

The extension for calibrating sets of spectra using a range calibration requires the specification of the VAMAS blocks to which the range calibration applies and also the set of VAMAS blocks for which an identical calibration is appropriate. A file of experiments is calibrated using the following steps:

1. Select the set of spectra to be used when energy calibrating the data file.
2. Overlay the spectra in the active tile.

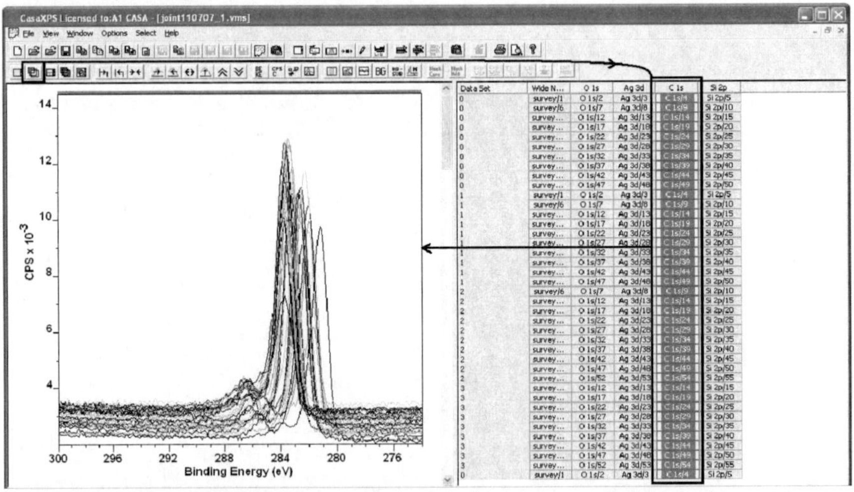

3. Inspect the spectra to ensure the largest peak in each spectrum is appropriate for calibrating the entire profile.
4. Determine an appropriate energy range such that the peaks all lie within the chosen interval.
5. Display the selected spectra one-per-tile.

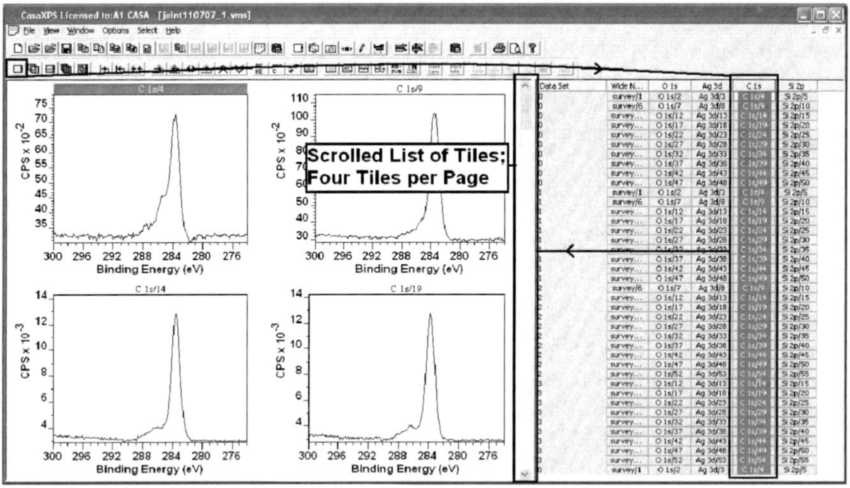

The data displayed in the list of tiles in the left-hand pane of the experiment frame represents the set of data from which an energy calibration is determined.

6. Enter the energy range into the *Measured* text-field on the Calibration property page of the Spectrum processing dialog window. The range is entered in the format “energy comma energy”.
7. Enter the desired position for the largest peak for each spectrum in the scrolled list of display tiles.

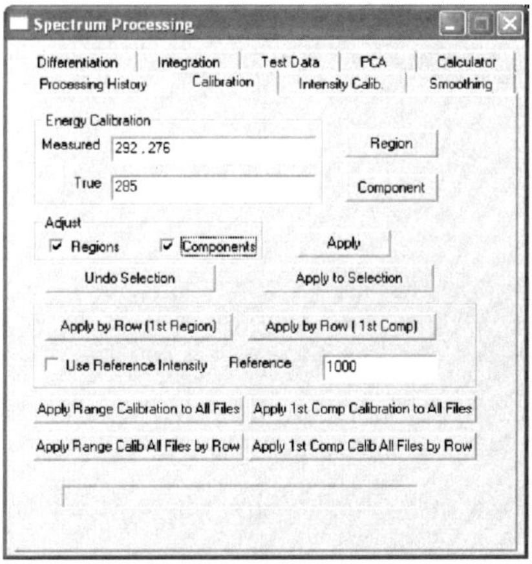

8. Select the VAMAS blocks for which the energy calibration should be performed.

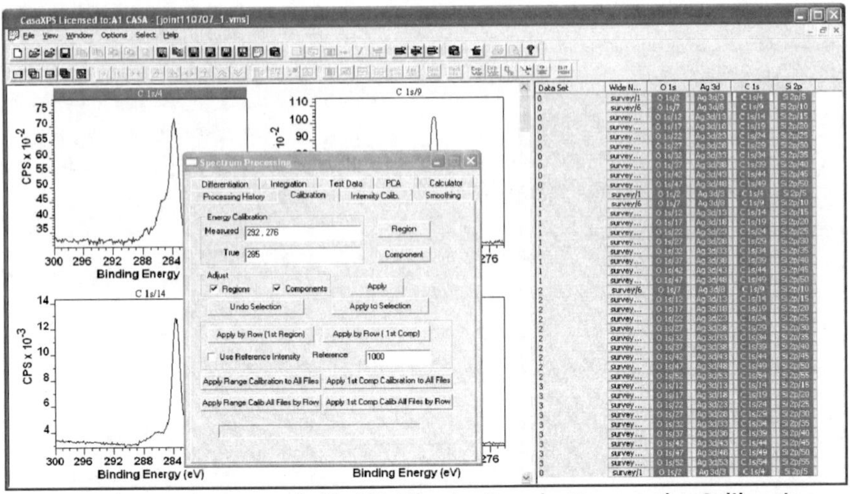

9. Press the Apply Range Calib ALL Files by Row button on the Calibration property page.

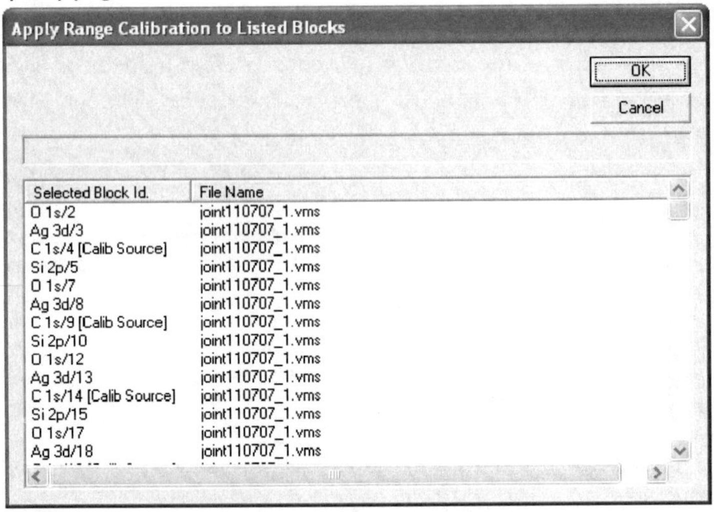

Only those VAMAS blocks selected in the right-hand pane of the experiment frame will be calibrated.

10. Check the list of VAMAS blocks and files and ensure that the appropriate VAMAS blocks are targeted. Press the *OK* button.

11. Confirm that the Calibration has been applied to the data using the Processing History property page of the Spectrum Processing dialog window.

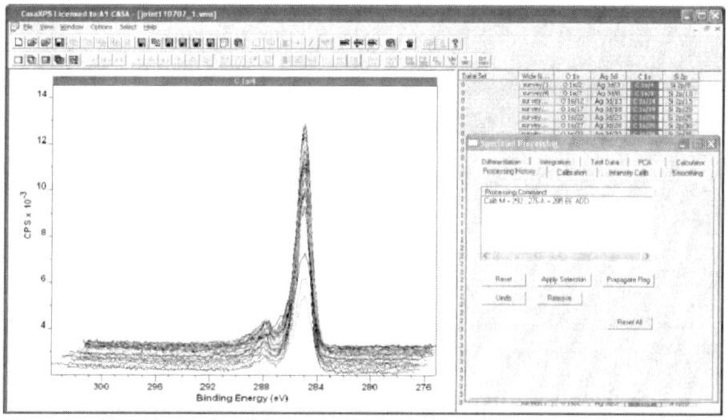

The key point is a calibration is performed on a row-by-row basis using the alignment of the VAMAS blocks in the right-hand pane. These row orientated operations are powerful since it is possible to perform exactly the same global calibration action on not just the experiment frame with focus, but can be applied to any number of VAMAS file open in CasaXPS. The Select menu allows the preparation of multiple experiment frames so that the scrolled-list of tiles for each file defines the source for the calibration command and the selection in the right-hand panes specifies the target VAMAS blocks. These operations are discussed in detail elsewhere in the manual.

Intensity Calibration

The subject of intensity calibration is dealt with in detail elsewhere in the manual. Essentially, the response function for an instrument, known as the transmission function, is often included in the data and when present, can be applied explicitly to data via the Intensity Calib property page. Correcting the data explicitly via the Intensity Calib options is not the normal route to quantifying spectra. The more widely used approach is to apply the transmission correction to the peak areas at the time a quantification report is produced.

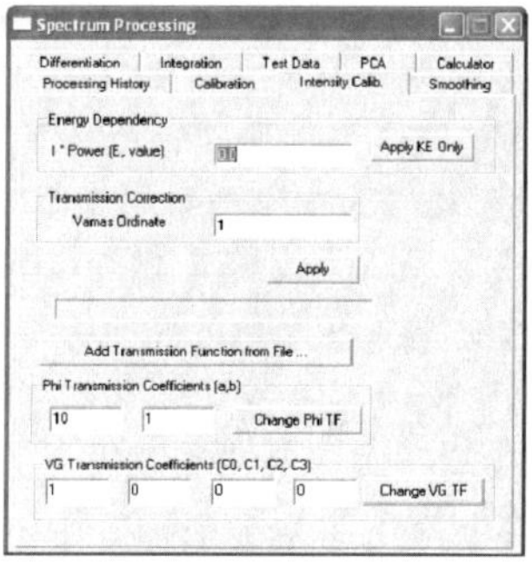

The major disadvantage of applying any intensity corrections directly to the data is the statistical information known for pulse counted data is lost. Chi-square and error analysis performed using Monte Carlo methods are no long meaningful once data is directly modified. Circumstances in which applying the transmission directly to the data might include when calculations are performed based on the background such as techniques developed by Tougaard. The theoretical shapes for backgrounds, in principle, should be computed using data for which the instrumental response is removed.

The transmission function corresponding to the spectral data in a VAMAS block is recorded as a corresponding variable. More than one set of data can be stored in a VAMAS block, each set of data are allocated an ordinate index and the transmission function is typically saved as the ordinate with index equal to unity (index number 1). A spectrum is usually saved in ordinate index zero. The Apply button on the Intensity Calib property page acts on the data in the active tile and divides the data in ordinate index zero by the data in the ordinate index specified on the property page.

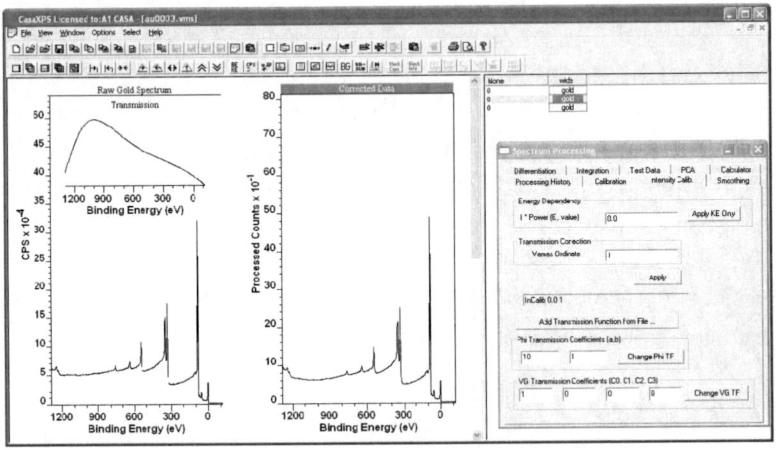

A further correction to the data based on scaling the intensities by the kinetic energy raised to an exponent is also applied when the Apply button is pressed at the same time as the transmission function. A zero value for the exponent used in the energy dependency correction provides the means of making no energy dependency correction. Note the energy dependency is applied to the measured intensity by multiplying by the kinetic energy raised to a power. The correction is typically applied elsewhere by dividing rather than multiplying by the kinetic energy raised to a power. To reproduce the same result in CasaXPS, the value entered will need to be negative. For example, to obtain the quantification for a JEOL XPS instrument, the energy dependency is specified in the JEOL system to be 0.2. To obtain the same correction in CasaXPS, the value must be entered as -0.2.

A transmission function from a file can be added to spectra in CasaXPS. The gold spectrum above is corrected using an NPL transmission function computed for a Kratos Axis Ultra at University of Manchester. The transmission function is supplied in a VAMAS format Q.vms file.

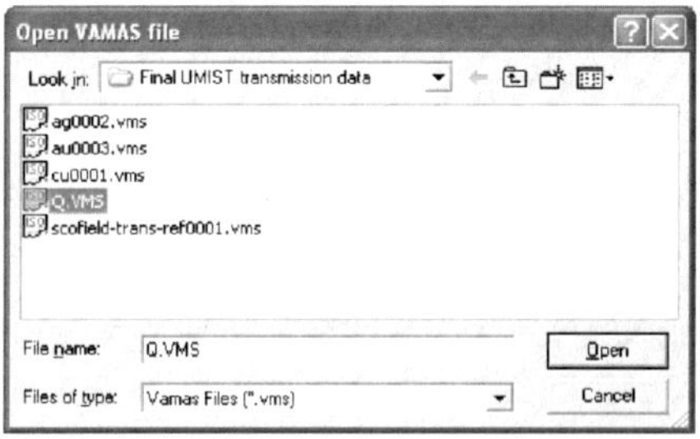

Transmission functions are added to VAMAS blocks via the Intensity Calib property page by selecting the VAMAS blocks in the right-hand pane for which the transmission function is applicable and pressing the Add Transmission Function from File button on the property page:

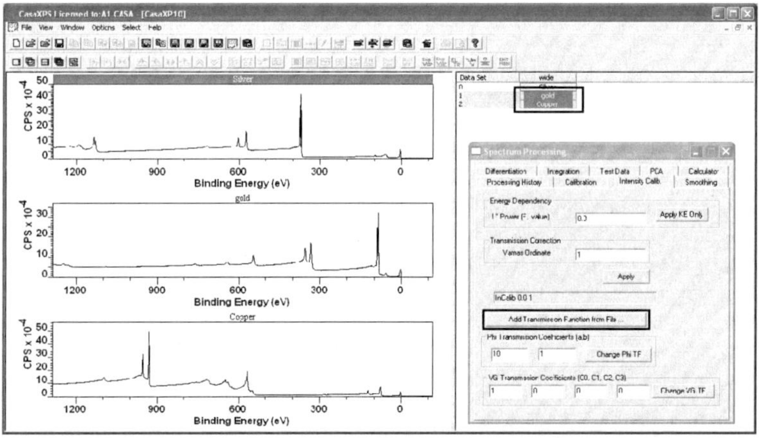

An entry is added to the VAMAS block comment field for each block for which a transmission function is added. The VAMAS block comment can be viewed as a header to the display tile or via a dialog window invoked via a toolbar button.

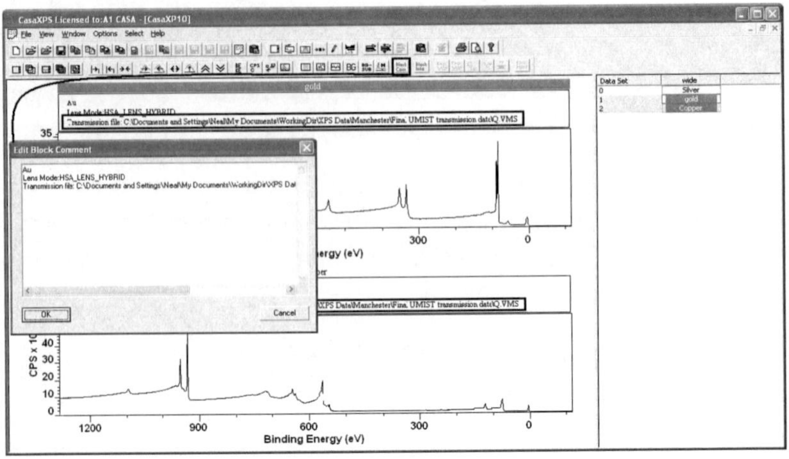

Further inspection of the transmission function is achieved by using the Control + Page Up and Control + Page Down keyboard keys. Pressing the Page Up and Page Down keys modified using the Control key steps the ordinate index for a VAMAS block either up or down. The transmission function is typically stored in the ordinate with index 1, while the spectral data usually appears in a VAMAS block with ordinate index 0.

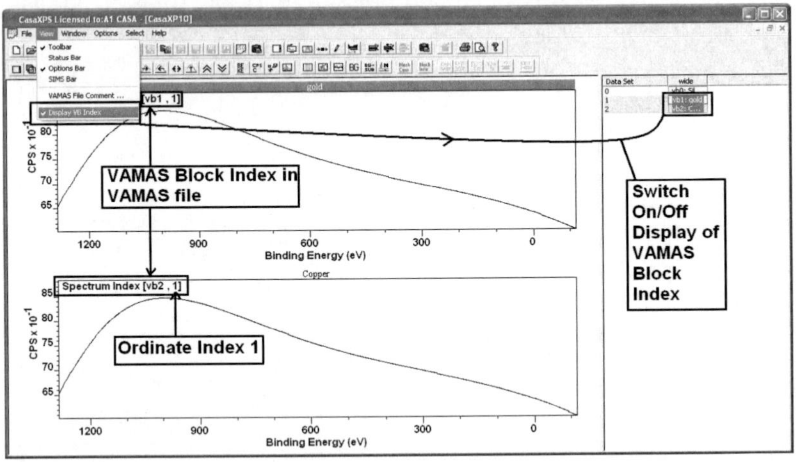

PHI and Thermo data include transmission function information using a functional form. The transmission for data from either MultiPak or Avantage/Eclipse can be adjusted using the appropriate parameters specified on the Intensity Calib property page. Modifications to these transmission functions are typically performed under extraordinary circumstances and are only included in CasaXPS to rectify rare errors in the acquisition process.

Calculator Property Page

Calculator Section

The Calculator section of the Calculator property page represents those options associated with the definition and manipulation of the temporary VAMAS block information referred to as the **operand**.

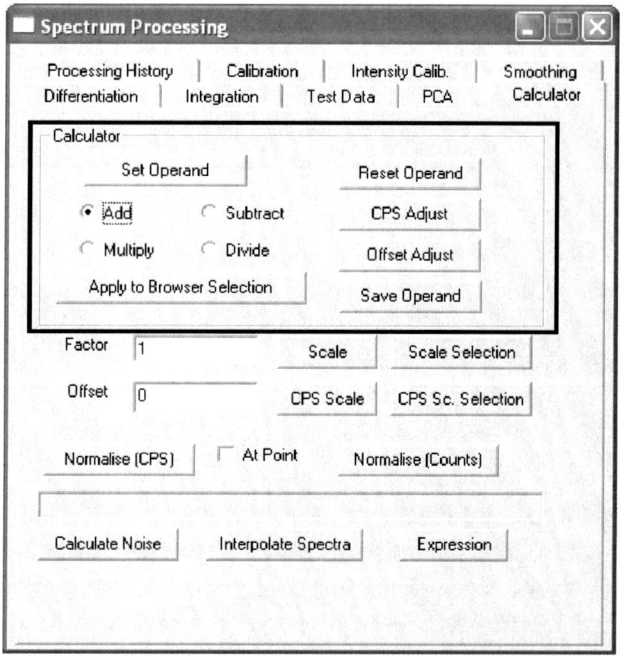

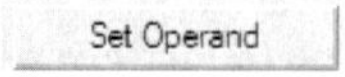

The operand is set from the active VAMAS block (first VAMAS block selected and displayed in the active tile). On pressing the **Set Operand** button, the current temporary VAMAS block maintained by the Calculator property page is replaced by the active VAMAS block. A trace from the operand is displayed in the active tile whenever the Calculator property page is active.

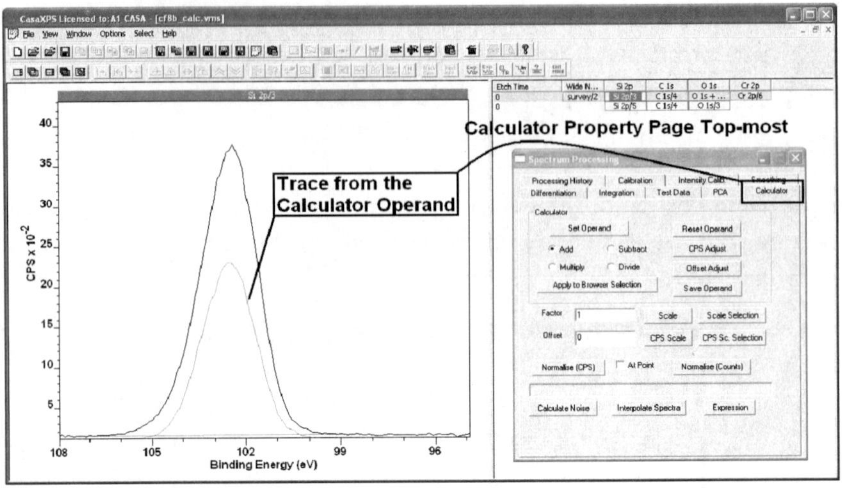

The operand is combined as a right operand with the current selection in the right-hand pane using the operator selected from the radio buttons. The operator must be chosen before the **Apply to Browser Selection** button is pressed.

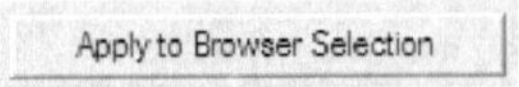

The data from the current operand is used as the right-operand for the chosen operation and is applied to each left-operand corresponding to the VAMAS blocks selected in the right-hand pane of the experiment frame. The result of the operation is stored in the processed data for the selected VAMAS block. Resetting the processing operations using the Processing History property page will restore the raw data, thus undoing the action of the calculator.

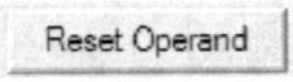

The data held within the operand may be adjusted relative to the spectrum displayed in the active tile. These adjustments can take the form of button actions or mouse controlled offsets, shifts and scaling. When adjusting the operand using the mouse, the Shift-Key must be held down. If the mouse is left-clicked at a point in the active tile whilst holding down the Shift-Key, the operand is offset in order to position the operand trace through the point at which the mouse click was performed. To scale and shift the operand the mouse should be dragged whilst at the same time holding down the Shift-Key. The vertical size of the resulting box determines the scaling applied to the operand data and the horizontal dimension produces a shift in the energy position. Pointing to a data channel on the operand with the Shift-Key held down and then dragging the mouse to the comparable position on the active spectrum will move the operand over the top of the active spectrum.

The action of the Reset Operand button is to scale the data in the operand to match the ordinate range for the active spectrum in the active tile. That is to say, the operand data is force to be visible within the active tile and therefore in a state where the mouse actions can be used to position the operand relative to the active spectrum.

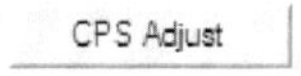

Pressing the CPS Adjust button alters the dwell-time and number of scans within the operand to match the VAMAS block's corresponding active spectrum.

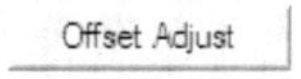

Adjusts the data in the operand to ensure all the ordinate values are non-positive.

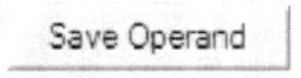

Once an operand has been adjusted appropriately, the VAMAS block maintained by the Calculator property page can be saved to an experiment frame using the Save Operand button.

An Example to Illustrate the Calculator

The first step in any quantification is to define backgrounds to spectral features. The most commonly used backgrounds are linear, Shirley or Tougaard, all of which owe their popularity to ease-of-use rather than the ability of these shapes to adequately describe the background beneath a photoelectric peak. Nevertheless, despite their failings, the desire of most analysts is to apply these algorithms to all peaks used for quantification in a consistent manner and gain virtue by producing repeatable results. Further, the choice of background is often coupled with a particular set of sensitivity factors, so there is a strong desire to reduce all data to an appropriate state in which the preferred background is easily deployed.

The example data chosen to examine the Calculator property page contains a small Cr 2p doublet located on a loss structure resulting from a large O 1s peak. In the absence of the O 1s peak, most analysts might choose to use a Shirley background as a means of defining the intensity from the Cr 2p doublet. However the energy loss structure from the O 1s results in the Cr 2p doublet being tilted with respect to Cr 2p peaks measured in the absence of oxygen. Further, the O 1s loss structure contains minor loss peaks lying within the limits of the Cr 2p doublet.

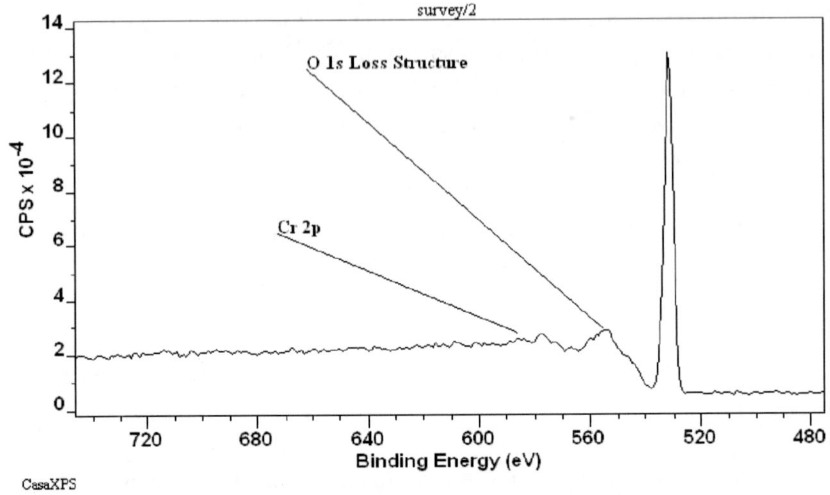

These minor loss peaks are of significant size compared to the chromium doublet. High resolution data provide a closer look at the features associated with the Cr 2p energy interval.

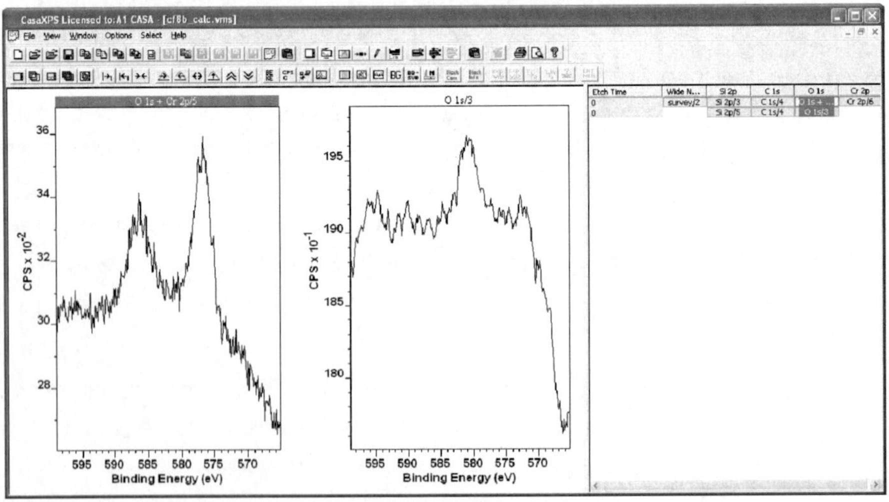

These data are acquired from modified and unmodified surfaces, where the Cr 2p doublet appears in the spectra following the modification of the material. Using the unmodified O 1s loss structure, the hope is therefore to remove the contribution of the O 1s loss structure from the Cr 2p peaks in the modified material. Once the O 1s loss structure is removed from the data, a Shirley background can be used to measure the intensity of the Cr 2p peaks.

The intention is to quantify a set of samples for which silicon, carbon, oxygen and chromium are quantified using narrow scan spectra. The O 1s peaks above illustrate the nature of the problem. The right hand tile displays data taken from the unmodified material and, although the count rates are similar, the data from the modified material differs potentially in magnitude and relative position of the spectral features. Before attempting to remove the distortions from the Cr 2p doublet due to the O 1s loss structure by subtracting the unmodified data from the modified data, the two sets of data must be calibrated in energy and scaled in intensity in such a way as to retain the essential quantification information.

An operation which both normalises data and adjusts the data relative to one another is located on the Calibration property page. The steps leading to the same outcome could be performed using both the Calculator and Calibration property pages; however combining these steps is both more efficient and less error prone. A procedure for normalising a data-set in preparation for use with the Calculator is performed on the Calibration property page of the Spectrum Processing dialog window.

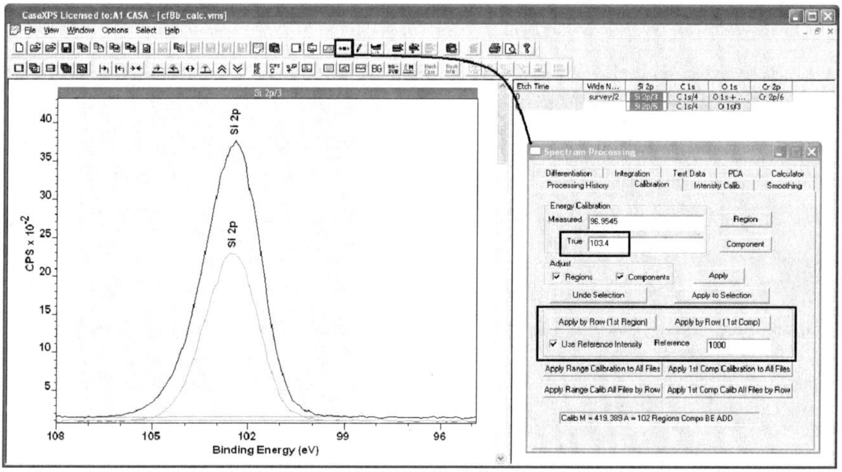

The Calibration property page is defined ready for the application of the operation to the data set, where the Si 2p spectra in each data set are about to be used to compute the necessary adjustments to both intensity and energy. The idea is the two samples are essential equivalent in terms of the Si 2p spectra and that any differences in position and intensity of these two independently acquired Si 2p spectra can be accounted for within the acquisition process. That is to say, if each spectrum within a data set is energy calibrated and intensity scaled using a normalisation constant determined from the Si 2p peak, then provided the same procedure is applied to both data sets, the background characteristics for the Cr 2p data can be accommodated by subtracting the two sets of scaled spectra. Furthermore, making these same adjustments to each spectrum in the data based on the counts per second intensity from the Si 2p data will leave the quantification table invariant with respect to the transformation. The steps to perform these transformations are as follows:

1. Define a quantification region on each of the Si 2p spectra.
2. Enter the position for the Si 2p peak in the **True** text-field on the Calibration property page.
3. Since regions are defined on the Si 2p spectra as part of this procedure, the tick-boxes in the section labelled Adjust for both regions and components should be ticked.
4. Ensure the tick-box labelled **Use Reference Intensity** is also ticked.
5. Ensure only the Si 2p VAMAS blocks are selected in the right-hand pane of the experiment frame.
6. Finally, press the button labelled **Apply By Row (1st Region)**

The consequence of these steps is the creation of a new experiment frame in which each data set now appears as energy calibrated and intensity adjusted spectra. The Si 2p regions defined on the original data set have been used to compute the measured position for the Si 2p peaks and also the intensity of the peaks in counts per sec electron Volts. These computed values for the two Si 2p spectra are used to shift each of the spectra on a row by row basis in the right-hand pane and the intensity of each spectrum is scaled so that the area of the Si 2p peaks in the new experiment frame is equal to the arbitrary value entered in the **Reference** text-field. All peaks in a row are scaled by this same value resulting in rows of data from different samples all scaled so the intensities are directly comparable. The data are now ready for the Calculator.

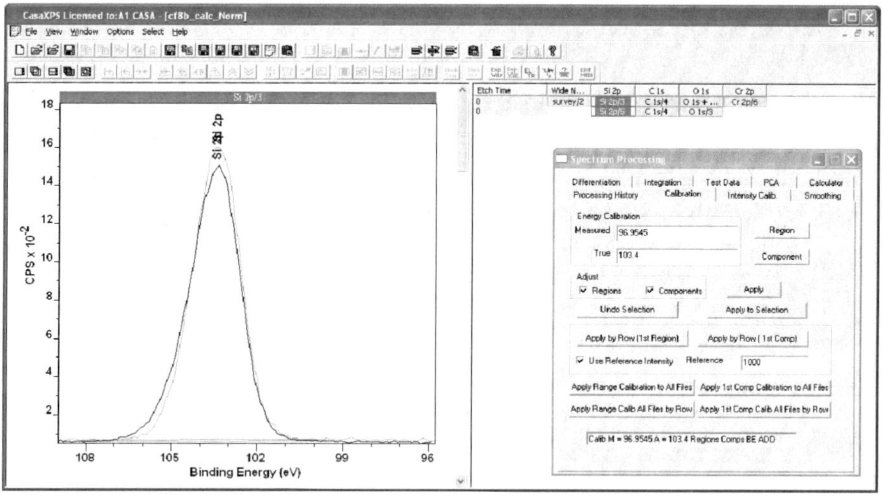

The new experiment frame generated by the calibration step is assigned the same name as the original VAMAS file plus the string _Norm concatenated with the base name of the VAMAS file. The data in the normalised file are scaled in intensity measured in CPSeV, therefore the dwell-time and number of scans fields in the original file are no longer meaningful and so are set to unity in the normalised VAMAS blocks. A further point worth noting is that the area field reported for the Si 2p spectra on the Regions property page of the Quantification Parameters dialog window is equal to the requested scale value, which means that transmission and escape depth corrections are also accounted for during the intensity scaling procedure. The transmission and escape depth parameter are transferred to the new file of scaled spectra so quantification can proceed in an identical fashion to the equivalent computation performed on the original file.

The intensity calibration might equally well be performed based on a synthetic component rather than a quantification region. If the intensity for the normalisation is determined from a synthetic component, it may be a surprise to observe the area parameter from the synthetic component, following the normalisation, is not necessarily equal to the reference intensity, which was the case for normalisation based on regions. Indeed, if transmission and/or escape depth corrections are included in the calculation, the area parameter for the synthetic component used to normalise the spectra will not equal the reference value. This is because the area value seen on the Components property page of the Quantification Parameters dialog window is a parameter for a peak model and is therefore an input value. The values used in a quantification report are output parameters and according to the rules used in CasaXPS, only output values are adjusted for transmission and escape depth, therefore the area reported for a component in a quantification report will agree with the reference intensity used to normalise the spectra. In the case of the quantification region, the area is computed from the data and is therefore an output; hence the transmission and escape depth corrections are already included for the area as determined from the region.

Subtracting the Spectra

The Calculator property page on the Spectrum Processing dialog window offers a range of options for performing arithmetic on spectra. The calculator is structured so that a spectrum is loading into a temporary location associated with the Calculator property page and from this temporary location the data is applied to any number of spectra indicated via the right-hand pane, where the result of the operation is passed into the processed data for each of the VAMAS blocks included in the selection.

The data illustrated below are displayed using a zoomed section of the O 1s regions from both the modified and unmodified materials following the energy calibration and intensity normalisation procedure described above.

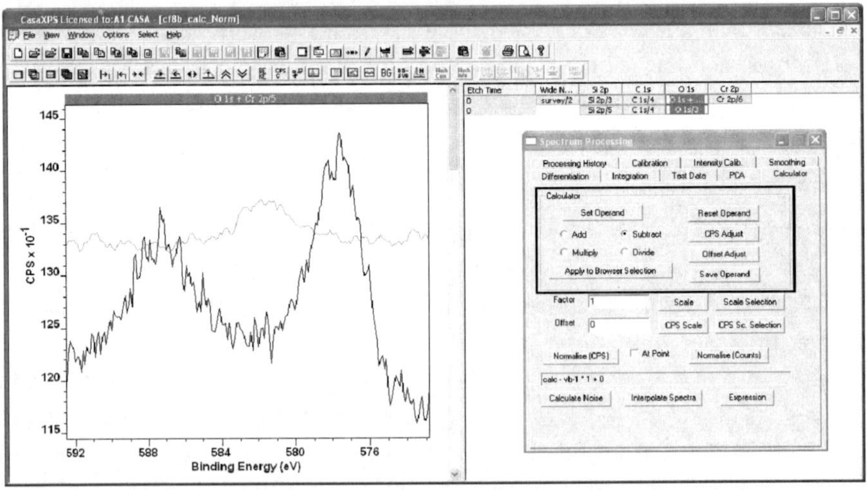

After normalisation, the unmodified background lies above the Cr 2p doublet peaks, although the data are scaled appropriately. The calculator requires the data from the unmodified sample to be loaded into the temporary location and the trace in the temporary location positioned below the Cr 2p doublet by an offset operation. Once prepared, the temporary data can be subtracted from the Cr 2p data to yield a spectrum for which a Shirley background is applicable. Using the normalised experiment frame, the steps within CasaXPS are as follows:

1. Display the O 1s spectrum from the unmodified sample in the active tile and press the Set Operand button on the Calculator property page. The trace associated with the temporary location on the Calculator property page is displayed over the top of the data in the active tile and will continue to be displayed for as long as the Calculator property page is the top page on the Spectrum Processing dialog window.
2. Double-click the Cr 2p narrow scan spectrum VAMAS block from the modified material. The Cr 2p spectrum will display in the active tile and, provided the calculator page is active, the calculator operand will appear also in the active tile.

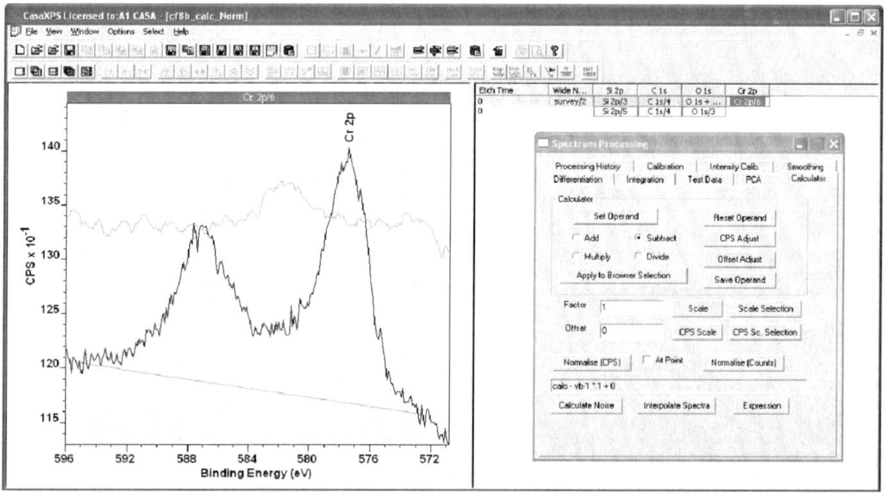

3. Press the **Offset Adjust** button. The action associated with the Offset Adjust button causes a negative offset to be applied to each data channel of the temporary calculator operand. For XPS spectra, this ensures each datum from the calculator operand is below the target spectrum; in this case below the Cr 2p data.
4. Select the Cr 2p VAMAS block in the right-hand pane of the experiment frame. Only those spectra selected in the right-hand pane will be operated upon by the calculator. Furthermore, if the same operation is required for a

set of Cr 2p spectra taken from different samples, say, then selecting all the Cr 2p spectra at the same time permits the action to be applied en masse.

5. Select the type of arithmetic operation required. In this example the radio button for subtraction should be chosen.
6. Press the button labelled **Apply to Browser Selection**. The current processed data in the Cr 2p spectrum is replaced by the section of the O 1s spectrum subtracted from the Cr 2p data.

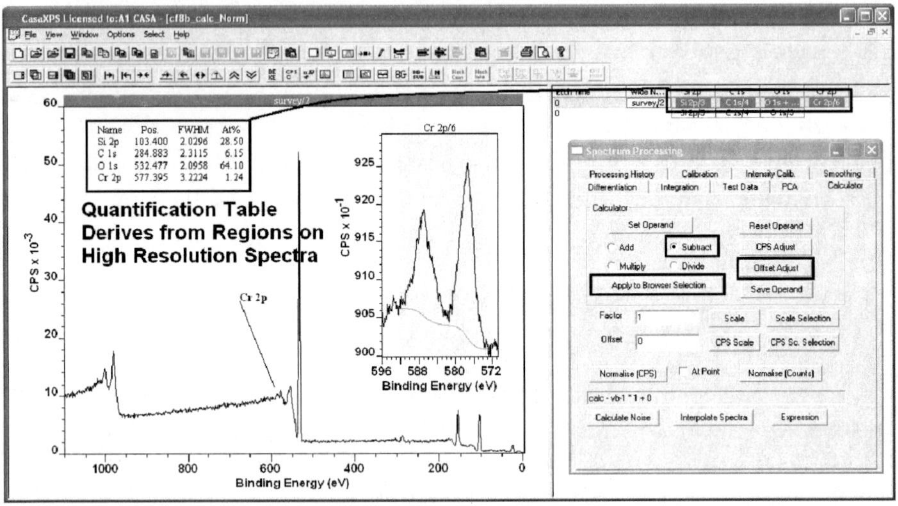

The analysis is completed by defining appropriate quantification regions for the four narrow scan spectra (C 1s, Si 2p, O 1s and the computed Cr 2p data) and creating a quantification table either using the Quantification property page on the Annotation dialog window or the Report Spec property page of the Quantification Parameters dialog window.

A note of caution however, is that any manipulation of the data resulting in intensity adjustments invalidates the use of Monte Carlo error analysis. Uncertainties determined from quantification regions or synthetic peaks require the data to obey Poisson statistics; any scaling of the data will remove the information needed to analyse the errors and therefore error bars cannot be computed for data modified by the calculator.

Normalising Spectra

There are two approaches to normalising XPS spectra:

1. Define an energy bin as the normalisation point and scale all other intensities relative to the intensity at the specified bin.
2. Normalisation with respect to peak area.

Normalisation at a point can be either:

1. Based on the peak maximum.
2. Based on an energy-bin specified using the Shift-Key and the cursor.

Normalisation based on peak area requires the definition of a region. The background subtracted peak area is adjusted to be unity before multiplying by the specified scale factor; the data are left as background subtracted intensities.

Consider two O 1s peaks measured from the same sample at two very different take-off angles. Enhanced surface sensitivity is coupled with reduce signal intensity for the data measured at 70° to the surface normal compared to 0°. A visual comparison of these peaks requires normalisation.

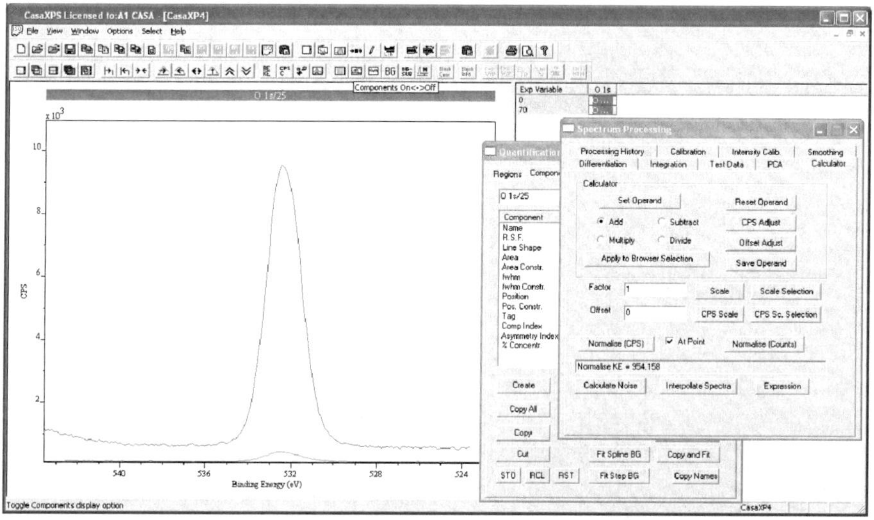

Normalisation based on peak maximum:

1. Display the spectrum in the active tile.

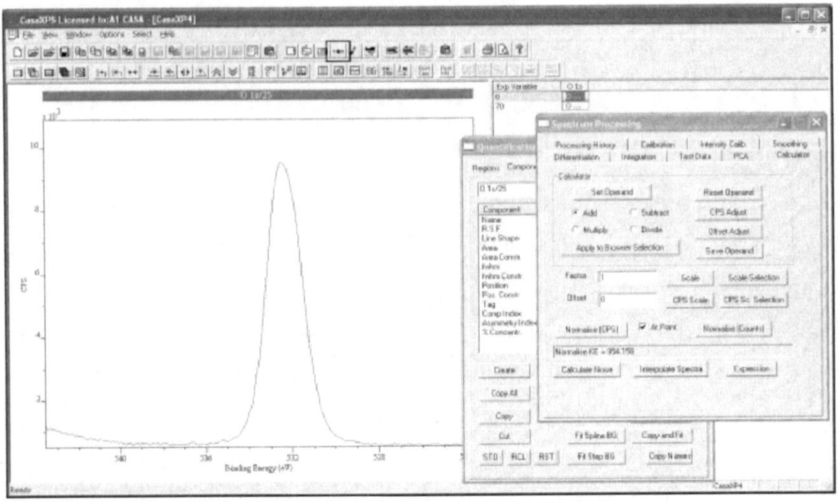

2. Invoke the Spectrum Processing dialog window and select the Calculator property page.

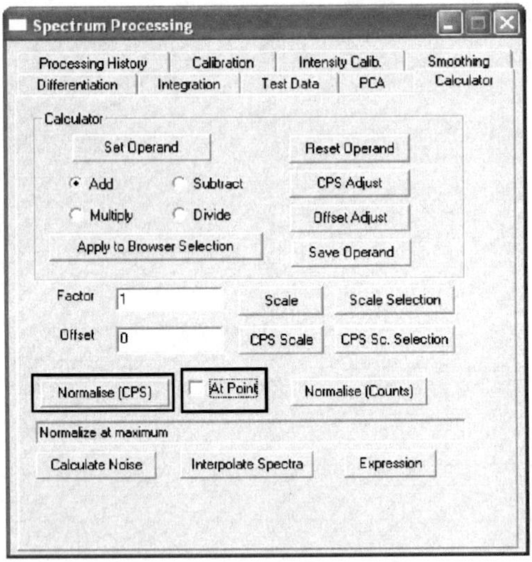

3. Ensure the tick-box labelled At Point is not ticked and press the Normalise (CPS) button.

Observe that the maximum intensity measured in CPS is now unity.

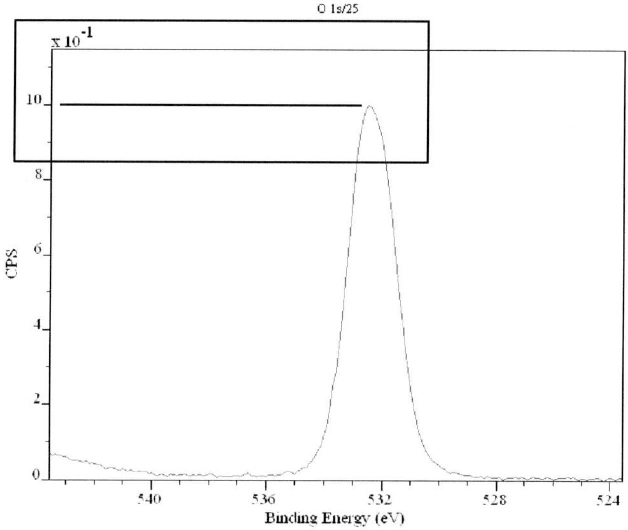

Repeat these steps for the second spectrum and overlay both spectra.

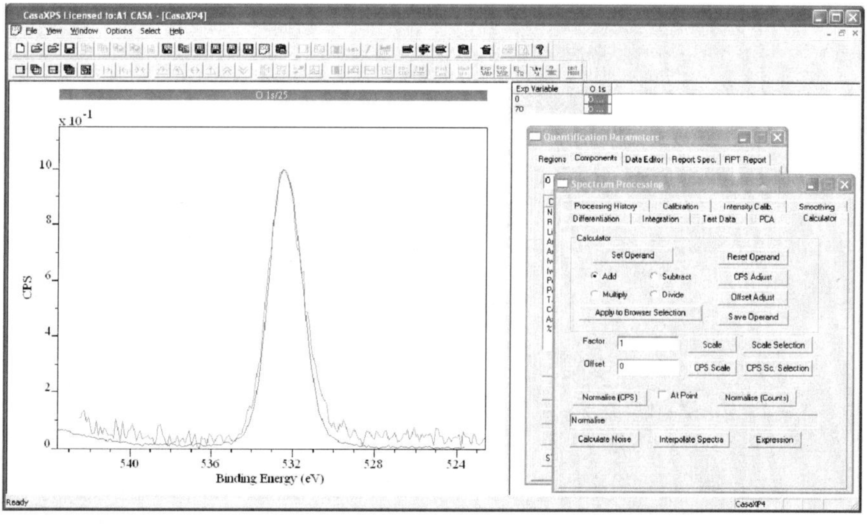

Normalisation based on peak area:

1. Display an O 1s spectrum in the active tile.
2. Using the Quantification Parameters dialog window create a region using the Regions property page.

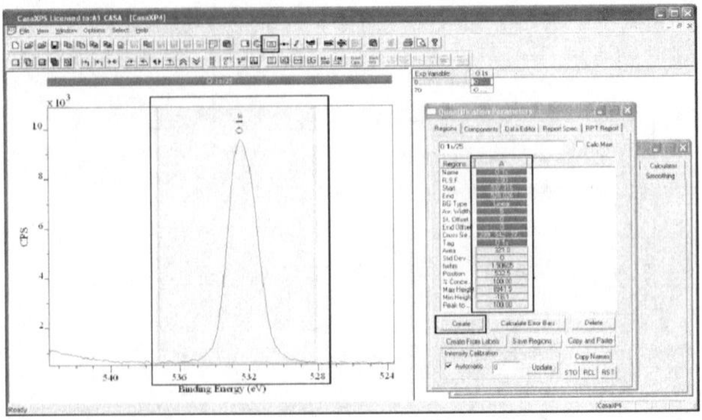

3. On the Calculator property page, ensure the Factor text-field is set to unity and the Offset field is set to zero before pressing the CPS Scale button.

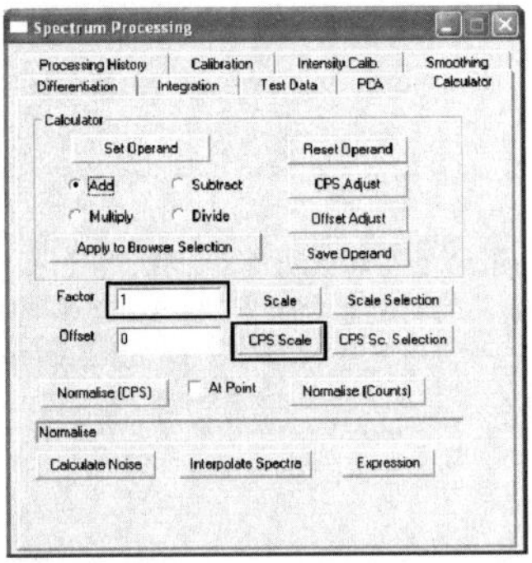

The spectrum is background subtracted and the uncorrected peak area is normalised to unity.

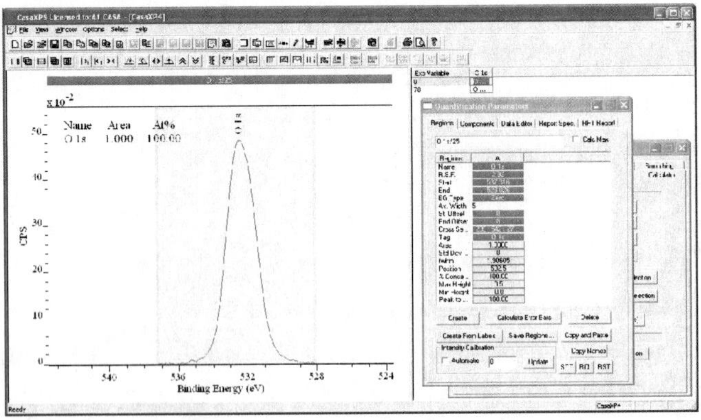

Repeat these steps for both spectra and overlay in the active tile.

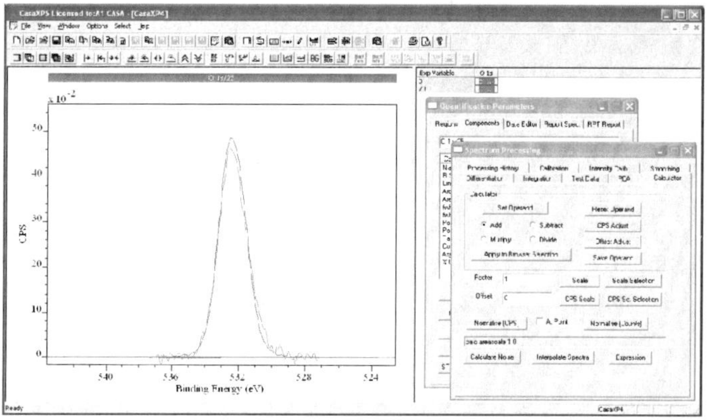

The raw area of the normalised peaks may be specified using the Factor text-field and offset using the Offset text-field. The following display is achieved using the same scale factor but a different offset value applied to the two spectra.

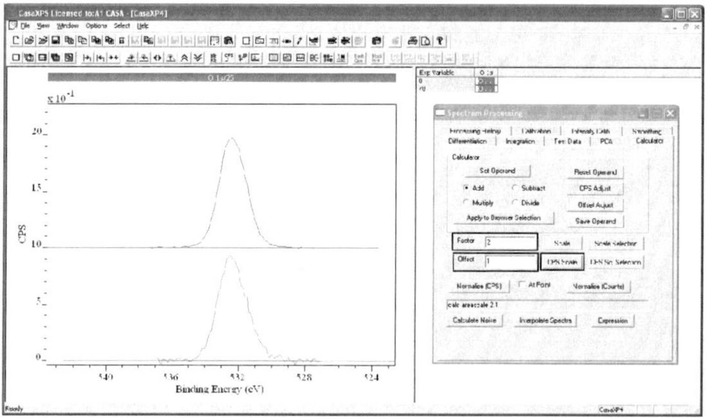

Normalisation Options

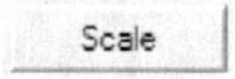

The ordinates within the active VAMAS block are scaled and offset using the values entered into the Factor and Offset text-fields on the Calculator property page. A quantification region must be defined on the spectrum. The background subtracted data is scaled by the value entered in the Factor text-field and added to the background plus the value entered in the Offset text-field.

Analogous to the Scale option, however the data are normalise to the area of the first region defined on the spectrum before scaling is performed. The background is removed from the data and the offset value added to the normalised scaled ordinates.

Normalise (CPS) Normalisation based on a data bin within a spectrum is performed using the Normalise (CPS) button. The action of the button is modified by the tick box At Point. If the tick-box is deselected, the normalisation is performed using the data channel with maximum intensity, however when ticked, the normalisation is performed using a datum indicated by a mouse action. To define the desired position at which the normalization is to be performed, hold the Shift Key down and left-click on the spectrum. The feedback text on the Calculator property page will indicate the value for the energy determined by the Shift-Left-Click action. Each datum in the spectrum is divided by the intensity at the selected bin, where the intensity is measured in counts per second.

Normalise (Counts) Normalisation based on the maximum intensity in a spectrum, where the intensity is measured in counts.

Miscellaneous Calculator Options

Calculate Noise The Calculate Noise option offers a means of visualising the noise in a spectrum. The procedure repeatedly applies a linear least squares fit to a linear polynomial over localised sections of the spectra with the view to minimising the information content at a local level. The difference between the spectrum and the smoothed curve replaces the processed data in the VAMAS block. The procedure is most effective away from peaks.

Interpolate Spectra Two spectra overlaid in the active tile are used to generate a sequence of VAMAS blocks, where the new VAMAS blocks contain data derived from linear interpolation between the two original spectra. Linear combinations of the two spectra are generated where the percentage step size for the interpolating parameter is entered in the **Factor** text-field on the Calculator property page. The original spectra are assign experimental variables of zero and one hundred, so for example, if the Factor text-field is set to "1", then the number of interpolated spectra will be one hundred and one. A new experiment frame is created containing the interpolated spectra.

Expression An arbitrary arithmetic expression combining the data from VAMAS blocks in a given experiment frame is used to create a new VAMAS block within a new experiment frame. Each VAMAS block within a VAMAS file is assigned an index number starting with zero. The individual VAMAS blocks are referenced, when included in an expression, using the VAMAS block index in the format vb0, vb1, vb2, etc. and combined using constants and brackets as seen in the VAMAS Block Expression dialog window.

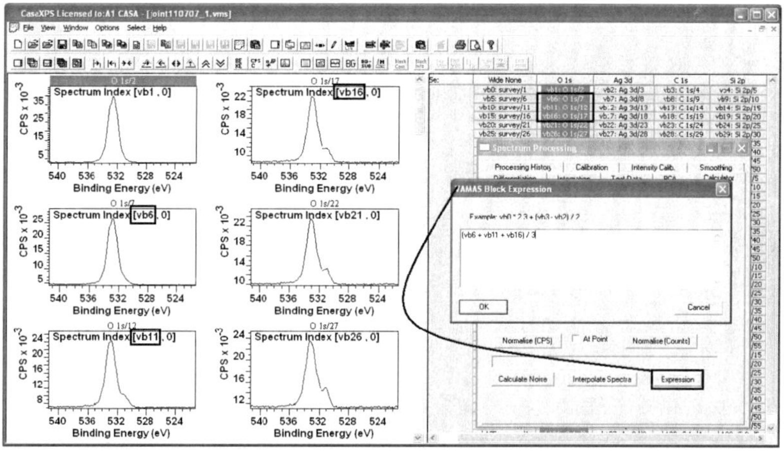

Once an expression is entered into the text-field and the OK button pressed, a new VAMAS block is created in a new experiment frame; the VAMAS block comment  contains an entry indicating the name of the original VAMAS file and the expression used to create the data within the new VAMAS block.

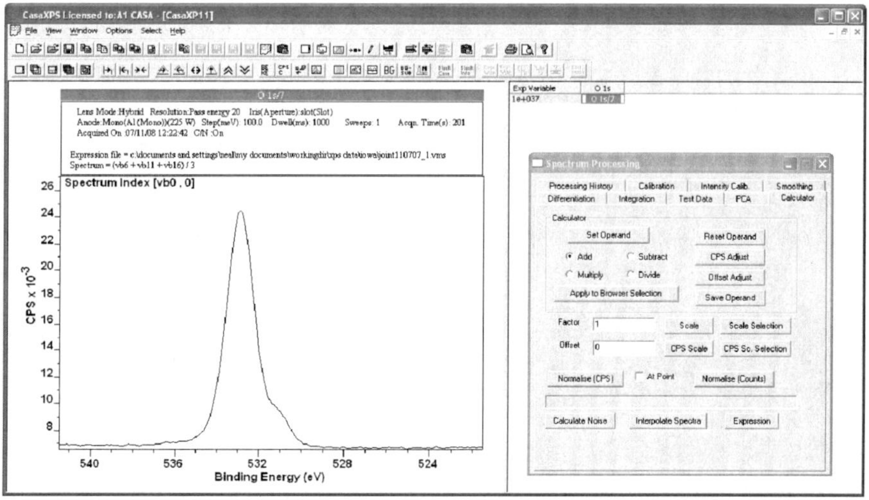

Smoothing, Differentiation and Integration

The techniques used to perform these operations are all based on approximating subsets of the data by polynomials determined in a least squares sense and using the polynomial, the derivative of the polynomial and the integral of the polynomial to approximate these operations for the raw data. The Savitzky Golay method for determining these polynomials is central to these processing options.

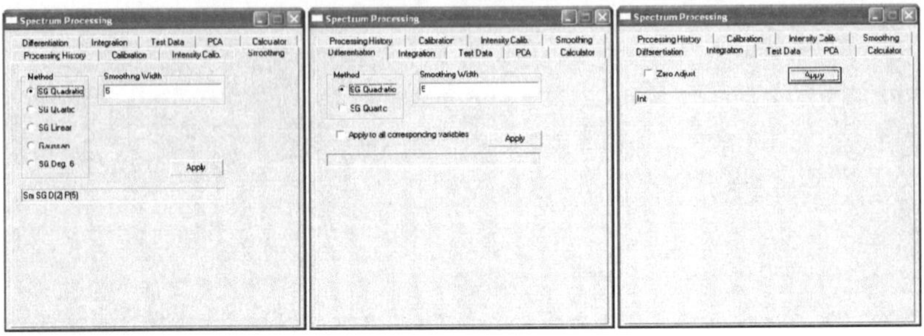

Smoothing Data

Data smoothing based on numerical convolution algorithms are only recommended for data with features significantly broader than the step-size used to collect the data. Progressive smoothing of data can be performed by limiting the number of data channels used per smooth operation when applying the same operation multiple times. The objective in smoothing data is to reduce the influence of noisy without damaging the peak resolution. The following is example of data where the smoothing width is less than the width of the features in the spectrum.

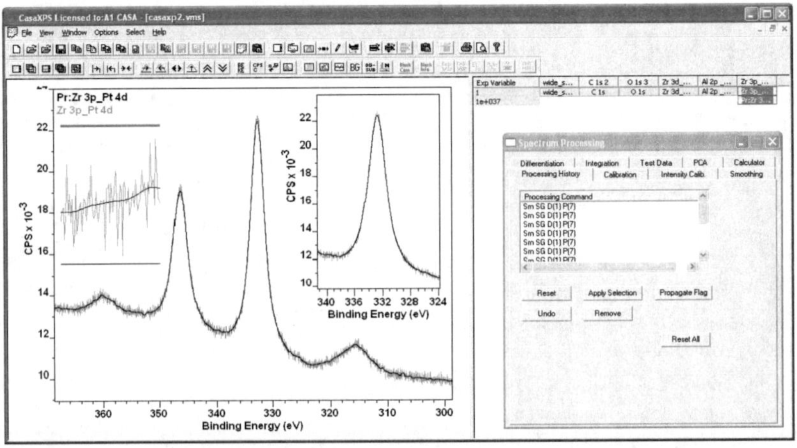

The successfully smoothed data above should be contrasted with a single application of the same linear smoothing operation where the peak width in terms of data channels is too small for the width of the smoothing operation. Even moving to a quadratic Savitzky Golay polynomial rather than a linear polynomial damages the peak shape for data without sufficient data bins spanning a peak.

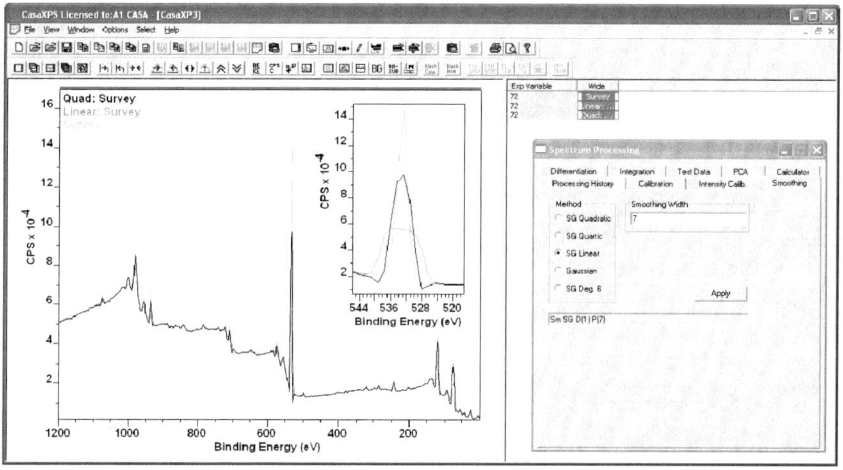

When working with survey spectra, it is better to use the Av Width mechanism as a means of removing the influence of noise on quantification regions and hence synthetic components rather than smoothing the data. The Av Width parameter is located on the Regions property page of the Quantification Parameters dialog window.

Differentiating Data

The need to differentiate spectra stems from Auger data. Historically Auger data were routinely collected as signal differentiated in hardware. Modern Auger instruments tend to collect the data in direct mode where the electrons are directly counted without hardware modification to the signal. Since differentiated signal was commonly used for Auger spectra, a quantification procedure based on measuring intensity using the difference between the peak maximum and the peak minimum was developed using libraries of relative sensitivity factors prepared for these differential forms of the spectra. To permit the continued use of these libraries and to provide continuity with the past, direct Auger spectra are differentiated in an attempt to reproduce the hardware peak shapes suitable for use with these relative sensitivity factors.

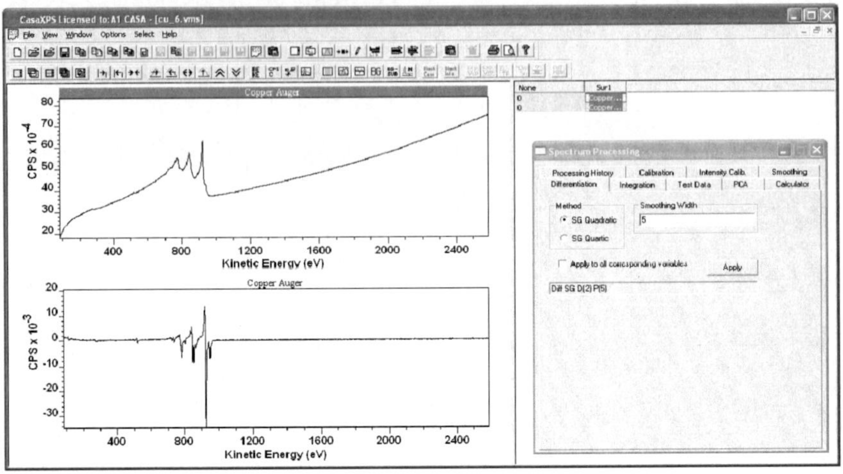

The Differentiation property page uses the Savitzky Golay algorithm to differentiate a spectrum.

Integrating Spectra

The Integration property page offers one of the tools for manipulating spectra. The primary purpose for integrating spectra is, like differentiation, aimed at Auger data. Data supplied in differential form can be, with the aid of other processing options, transformed to direct form.

Hardware differentiate spectra include a background which matters little to peak-to-peak quantification, but if integrated dominates the peak structure to the point of swamping the integrated peak information. To recover the peak information from a spectrum measured in differentiated mode, a background must be removed from the data before integration can yield the desired result. A background suitable for hardware differentiated spectra is based on a linear least squares fit of a linear background. The background is defined using the Regions property page on the Quantification Parameters dialog window with a background type of Regression (abbreviation R). A background is subtracted from the spectral data using the Test Data property page. Thus, defining a region spanning the entire Auger spectrum using background type Regression followed by background subtraction using the Test Data property page and integrating the background subtracted data creates a spectrum equivalent to data collected in direct mode.

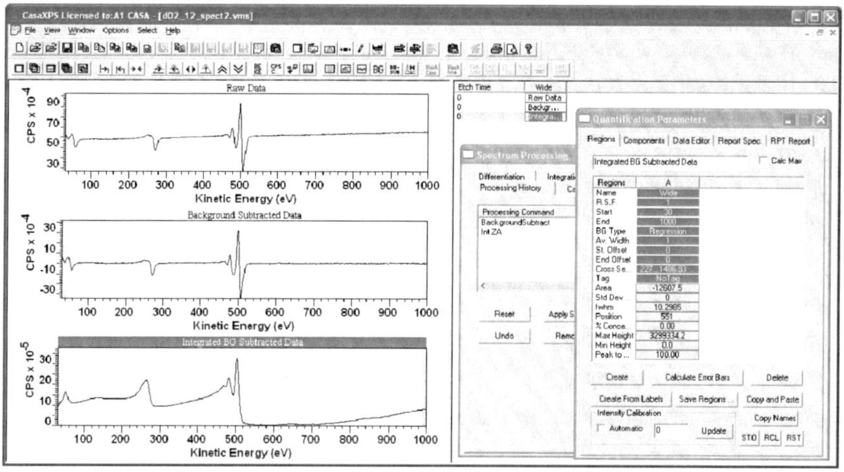

The theoretical basis for these processing options for smoothing, differentiating and integrating spectra is now discussed.

Savitzky-Golay Method

Two options on the Spectrum Processing dialog window commonly used for smoothing of experimental data and the determination of derivatives are performed using the algorithm proposed by Savitzky and Golay (A. Savitzky and M. J. E. Golay, Anal. Chem., 36, 1627 (1964)). The same algorithm employed to differentiate spectra is used to smooth data and therefore it should be clearly understood that the act of differentiating a spectrum using the Savitzky Golay method necessarily includes a smoothing operation.

Theory

The Savitzky-Golay algorithm uses linear least squares to approximate data tabulated at regular intervals by polynomials of various degree.

Given a set of data containing both signal and noise, the initial objective of the Savitzky-Golay method is to replace the raw data by a smoother set of data representing the true signal responsible for the recorded intensities. For a constant underlying signal, the most natural means of estimating the true signal from a set of measurements would be to average the values. The act of averaging a set of values is in fact one example and possibly the simplest applications of the linear-least-squares principle. Spectral data, on the other hand, typically contain peaks superimposed on a background signal and therefore a more subtle use of averaging is required if the essential structure in the data set is to be retained. One way to use the averaging process, but to maintain information relating to the variation in the intensities, is to perform a local averaging for each bin within a spectrum; for example, each data bin could be replaced by the average of three bins, the bin itself and the two bins on either side of the bin. The averaging operation could be applied to a data set via a digital convolution of the data bins with a convolution kernel consisting of the values {1/3, 1/3, 1/3}. These simple, yet often used concepts are at the basis of the Savitzky-Golay method, which in essence applies the least-squares principle to determine an improved set of kernel coefficients for use in a digital convolution, where these improved coefficients are determined, in the least-squares sense, using polynomials rather than, for the case of averaging, simply assuming a constant value determined from a sub-range of data bins. Indeed, the Savitzky-Golay method could be seen as a generalisation of averaging data, since averaging a sub-range of data corresponds to using a Savitzky-Golay polynomial of degree zero.

To illustrate the Savitzky-Golay method, consider the specific example in which five data bins are used to approximate a quadratic polynomial. The polynomial can be expressed in the form:

$$p(x) = a_0 + a_1 x + a_2 x^2$$

where the coefficients a_0, a_1 and a_2 are determined from the simultaneous equations in which the abscissa x is the index for the data bin; the origin is always placed at the central data bin, thus the abscissa values corresponding to each of the data bins are $\{-2, -1, 0, 1, 2\}$:

$$\begin{bmatrix} 1 & -2 & 4 \\ 1 & -1 & 1 \\ 1 & 0 & 0 \\ 1 & 1 & 1 \\ 1 & 2 & 4 \end{bmatrix} \begin{bmatrix} a_0 \\ a_1 \\ a_2 \end{bmatrix} = \begin{bmatrix} d_{-2} \\ d_{-1} \\ d_0 \\ d_1 \\ d_2 \end{bmatrix}$$

or

$$\boldsymbol{A}\underline{\boldsymbol{a}} = \underline{\boldsymbol{d}}$$

where the evenly spaced data bins $\{d_{-2}, d_{-1}, d_0, d_1, d_2\}$ are selected with the target of replacing the value for d_0 with the value for the polynomial at $x = 0$ or $p(0) = a_0$.

Since there are five equations and only three unknowns, the coefficients to the polynomial must be determined in the least-squares sense, where the linearly independent basis functions are *1*, *x* and x^2. The normal equations yield:

$$A^T A\underline{a} = A^T \underline{d}$$

Since A^TA is a square symmetric matrix of rank three, the coefficient vector $\underline{a}$ is determined from $[A^TA]^{-1}A^T$, the top row of which yields the prescription for computing the value of a_0, namely:

$$a_0 = [s_0, s_1, s_2, s_3, s_4] \begin{bmatrix} d_{-2} \\ d_{-1} \\ d_0 \\ d_1 \\ d_2 \end{bmatrix}$$

Thus, for each set of five such data bins, the central bin can be replaced by the value determined for a_0. In other words, a digital convolution using the five point kernel $\{s_i\}$ and the raw data bins results in a smoothed set of data bins, where a linear least squares quadratic polynomial is used to model the data, five channels at a time.

Similarly, the derivative of a spectrum can be computed using the Savitzky-Golay polynomial. Again the intention is to approximate the derivative at a given point in the spectrum using the derivative of the polynomial at $x = 0$. Since $dp(0)/dx = a_1$, the second row of the matrix $[A^TA]^{-1}A^T$ yields a second convolution kernel for computing the derivative of the spectrum and, apart from the difference in the kernel values, the computation of the derivative proceeds in an analogous fashion to that of the smoothing calculation.

The variation on a theme occurs with the integration algorithm. Here, the polynomial is again used in the approximation to the integral of the spectrum, however rather than evaluating the polynomial at the point $x = 0$ the integral between $x = -1$ and $x = 0$ is computed. Completing the integration over a range of data bins is then achieved by summing the set of sub-intervals computed using a convolution kernel determined from all three rows of the matrix $[A^TA]^{-1}A^T$:

$$\int_{-1}^{0} p(x)dx = a_0 - \frac{a_1}{2} + \frac{a_2}{3}$$

Therefore

$$\int_{-1}^{0} p(x)dx = [i_{0,}i_{1,}i_{2,}i_{3,}i_{4}]\begin{bmatrix} d_{-2} \\ d_{-1} \\ d_0 \\ d_1 \\ d_2 \end{bmatrix}$$

Where the i_j in the convolution Kernel are the linear combination of the three terms from each of the rows of $[A^TA]^{-1}A^T$ prescribed by the expression above. To compute the integral with respect to energy requires the multiplication of the convolution integrals by the energy step-size.

The use of the Savitzky-Golay polynomial to evaluate the derivative is essential for noisy data, since an interpolating polynomial would produce an inferior result to that of a least-squares approximation. On the other hand, there is an academic nature to using Savitzky-Golay integration, since simply summing the data bins includes the averaging mechanism required to reduce the influence of random noise on the computed values; however the symmetry of using the same algorithm to compute both the derivative and its inverse is somewhat pleasing.

The theory behind the Savitzky-Golay options, whilst illustrated using a five-point quadratic approximation, can be applied for any odd number of points applied to any degree of polynomial, provided the number of data bins over specifies the information required to compute the polynomial coefficients. CasaXPS offers quadratic, quartic and linear polynomials, while the number of data bins used to process the spectra is specified in a text-field on both the Smooth and also the Differentiate property pages on the Spectrum processing dialog window. Integration is always performed using a five-point quadratic Savitzky-Golay approximation. One further point regarding integration is that integration cannot recover constant offsets lost during differentiation, so there is an option (Zero Adjust) on the Integration property page, which when ticked, ensures the data are all positive following an integration calculation.

Test Data Property Page

The options on the Test Data property page are a collection of miscellaneous tools. Initially created to provide a range of test data aimed at providing data envelopes to which peak fitting and other analysis techniques could be investigated using data of know form, the Test Data property page has developed into a collection of operations to aid a more general understand of algorithms in CasaXPS. For example, the individual steps used to perform a Monte Carlo error analysis for a peak model can be explicitly performed on a spectrum using features on the Test Data property page.

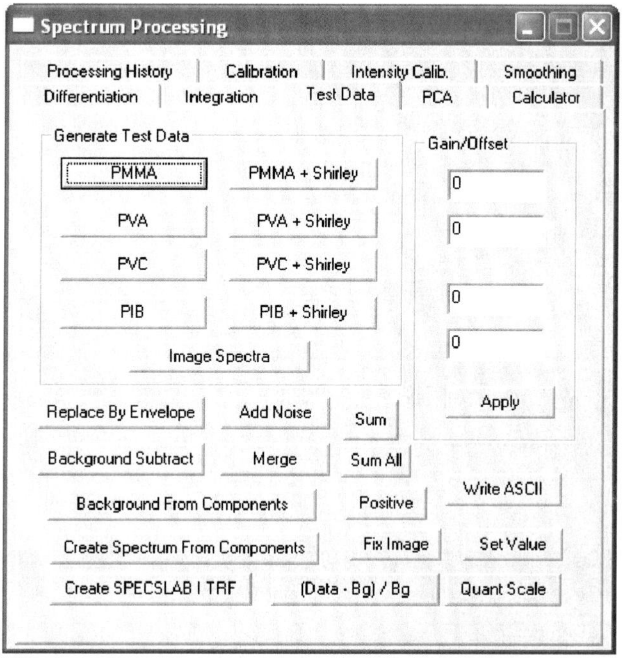

Other features are included on the Test Data property page to provide less commonly used operations on data at the request of users. For example the Fix Image button corrects a problem in image data acquired by one specific instrument and is unlikely to be of general use. Due to the ad hock nature of the Test Data property page, only features of a more general nature will be described.

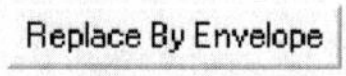

The envelope referred to is the total synthetic envelope consisting of a summation of the background to the data and each of the synthetic components defined on the VAMAS block. Replacing the data with the synthetic envelope offers a means of smoothing data for presentation purposes. For example, a low intensity Cr 2p doublet can be enhanced by fitting components to the data using a non-physical peak model with the view to simply fitting the peak structure.

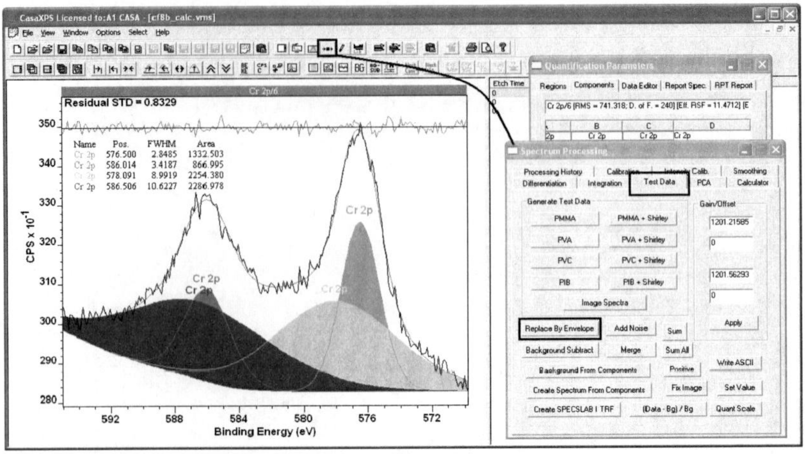

The residual plot displays the normalised difference between the synthetic envelope and the data. The Replace by Envelope button substitutes the raw data with the synthetic envelope calculated from the background plus the four components.

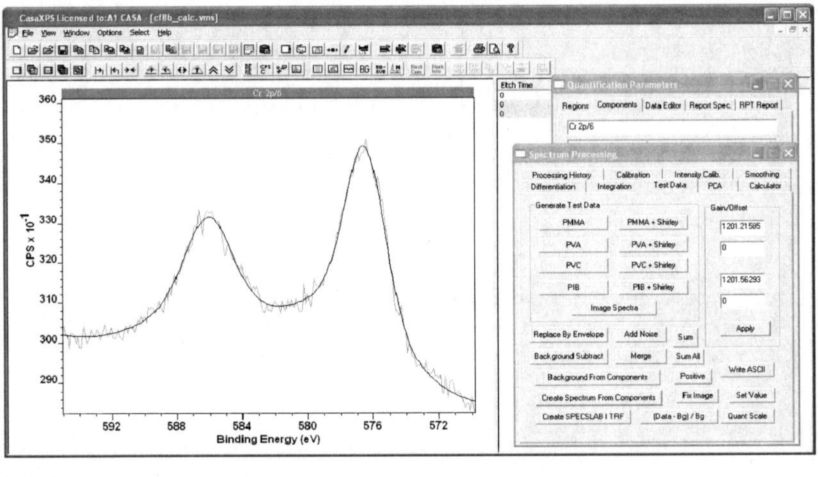

The noise in pulse counted data obeys Poisson statistics. Thus given a smooth data envelope determined from the data as illustrated using the Cr 2p data, the Add Noise button on the Test Data property page allows noise to be introduced back into the processed data. Extracting a smoothed envelope from data followed by adding noise back into the smoothed data lies at the heart of the Monte Carlo method for estimating precision errors in measured quantities.

The Background Subtract button replaces the processed data with the difference between the spectrum and the current background to the spectrum. Since the current background is determined from the set of quantification regions, the operation is also dependent on the regions at the time of application.

A Tougaard background defined for a survey spectrum and the Background Subtract button offer a means to highlighting the peaks in the data. The same data preparation extracts the background curve by pressing the Replace by Envelope button. Since the survey does not include any components, the data envelope is simply the background.

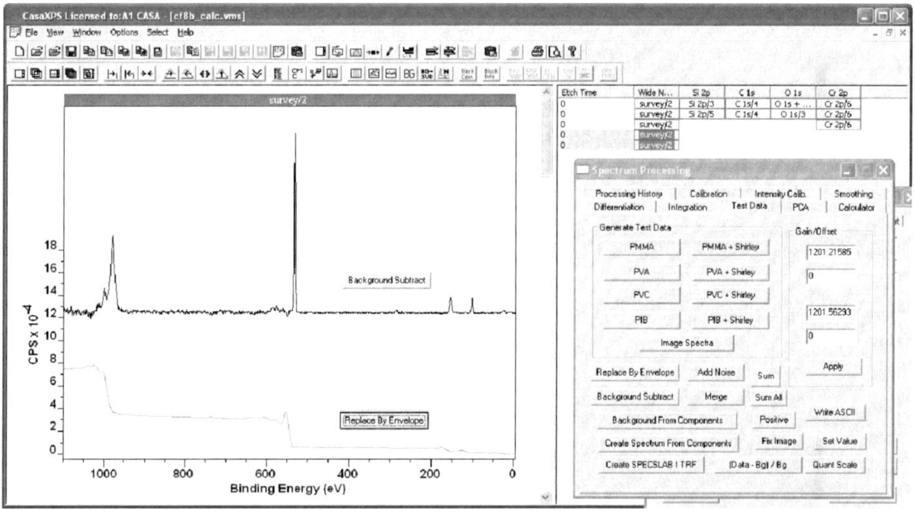

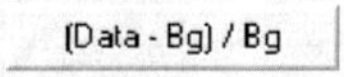

The (Data – Bg) / Bg button acting on the current background generates a background subtracted spectrum scaled by the magnitude of the background. For the SiO_2 survey previously used to illustrate the Background Subtract button, the data are transformed to enhance the peaks with low background intensities.

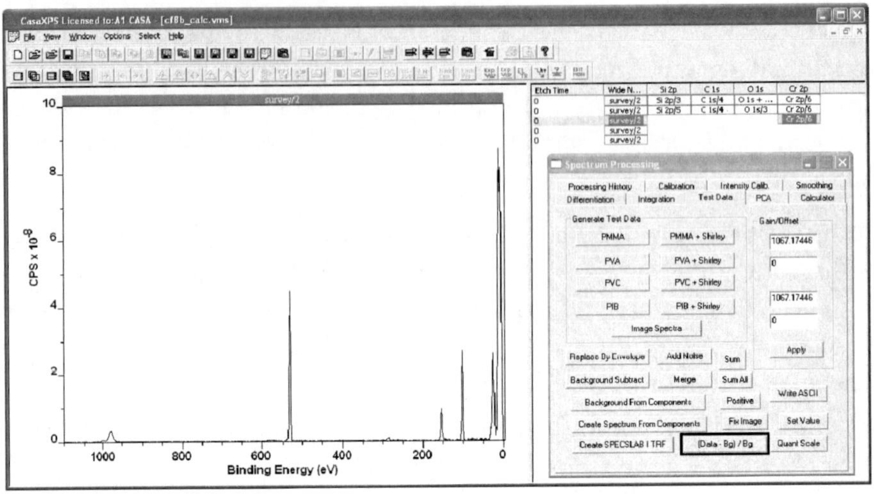

Exporting Background Subtracted Data

1. Using the Quantification Parameters dialog window, prepare the spectrum with a background and synthetic components.

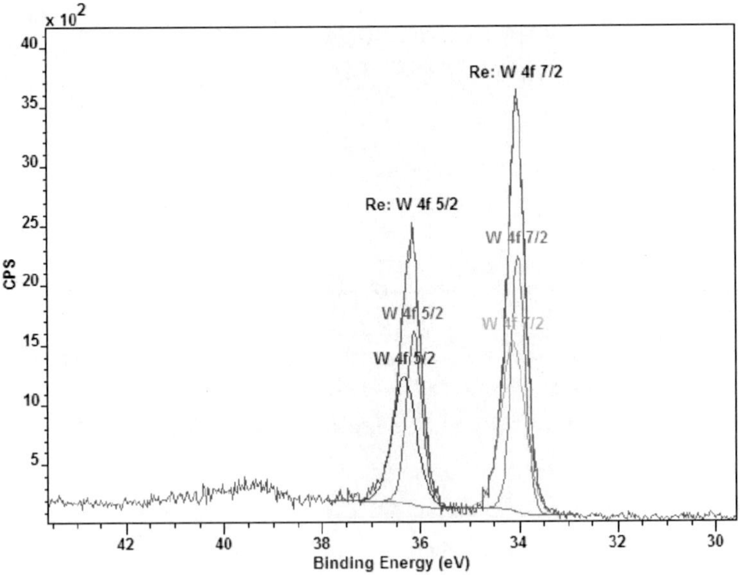

2. Using the Test Data property page on the Spectrum Processing dialog window, press the button labelled Background Subtract.

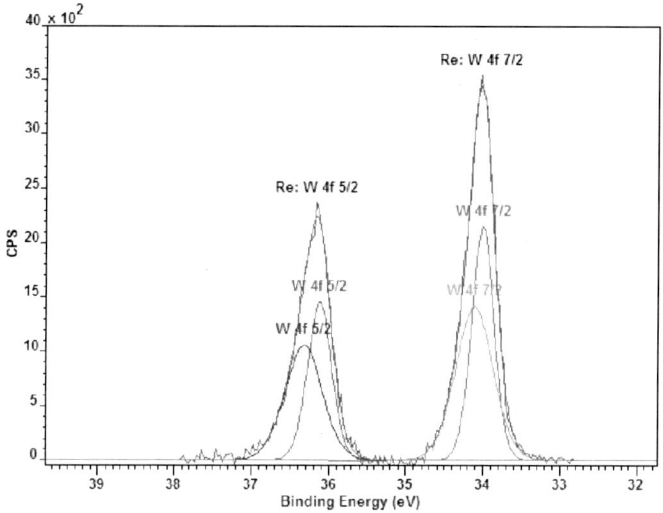

3. Display the data in the Active Tile and press the TAB spaced ASCII to clipboard toolbar button.

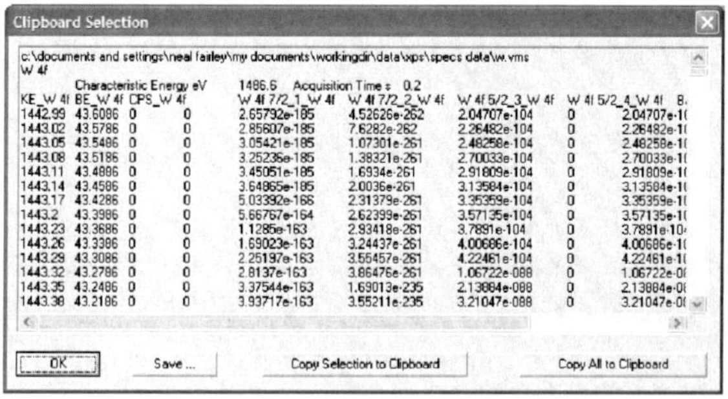

4. Press the Copy All to Clipboard button on the resulting Clipboard Selection dialog window.
5. Paste or Control-V in Excel.

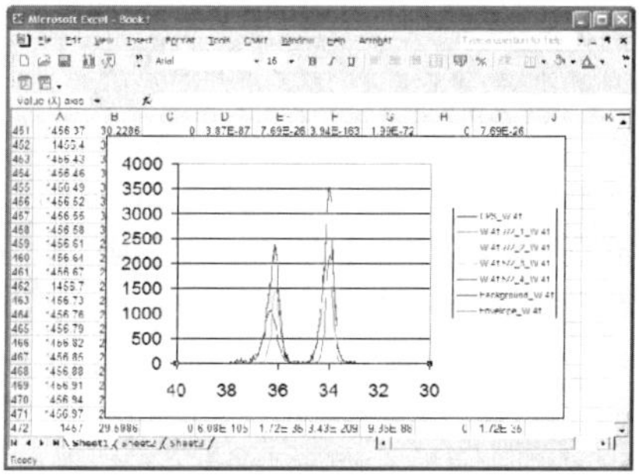

Quant Scale Button

A common requirement is to display spectra from a sequence of experiments in an overlay plot where the intension is to visually inspect the variation in the data with respect to the changing experimental conditions. Data from a sequence of measurements for a silicon sample acquired at different angles of sample tilt result in a range of intensities and relative chemical state contributions to the data envelope. The spectra vary as a consequence of the depth sampled by the analyser with each change in angle. The raw data for five angles are shown below.

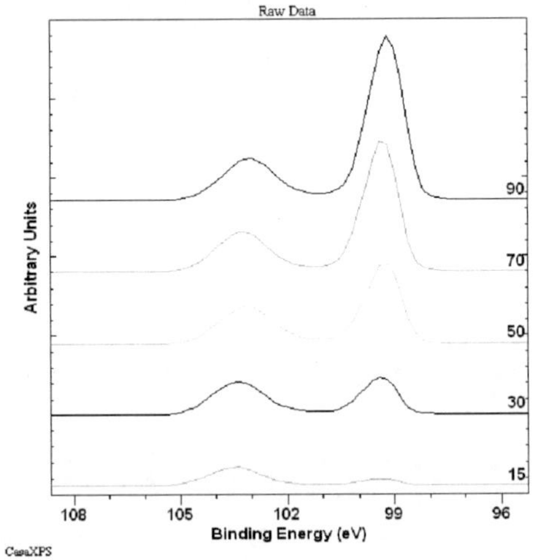

The display shows the relative intensities of the elemental and oxide peaks varying with angle, however the counts per second (CPS) also reduces with angle. One solution often employed to remove the reduction in CPS is to normalise each spectrum with respect to the area of the region defining the Si 2p peaks. The consequence of normalising to the peak area is that the peaks are scaled to provide a uniform appearance and size. While permitting the data to be plotted on the same axis scale, the relative importance of the peak sizes to the sample composition is as misleading as the plot for the raw data. As an alternative to the normalisation offered on the Calculator property page, a further means of scaling the data is offered on the Test Data property page of the Spectrum Processing dialog window. The Quant Scale button on the Test Data property page provides a scaling equivalent to the results obtained from a quantification report. That is to say, the peaks are background subtracted and then scaled based on the total CPSeV adjusted for RSF and transmission corrections.

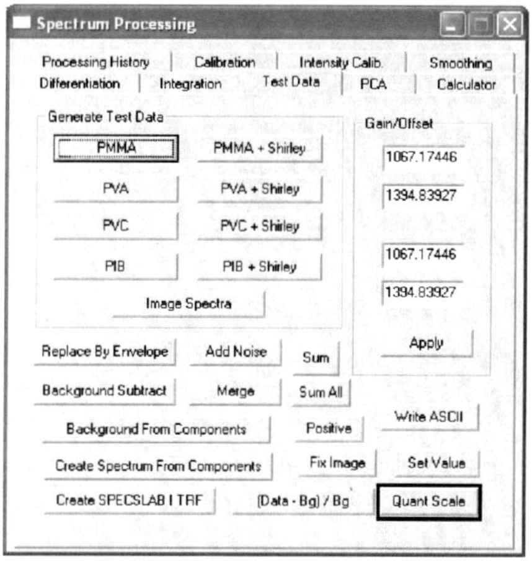

The following plots are an example of the SiO_2 Si 2p peaks shown above as raw data where the left-hand plot displays the Si 2p data quantified relative to the O 1s peaks for each angle. The right hand plot represents the same raw data normalised with respect to the peak area of the Si 2p data envelopes.

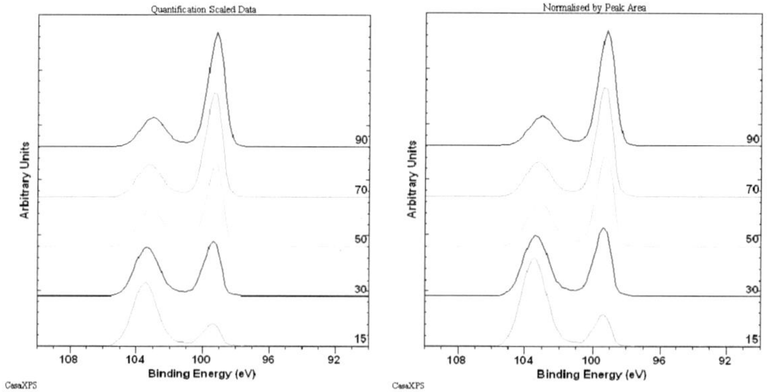

The data in the left-hand plot are visualised with the scaling used to generate quantification reports from regions; a procedure widely accepted as the correct means of comparing XPS data in tabulated format.

To perform a quantification scaling of the data:

1. Prepare quantification regions for each spectrum used in the scaling procedure. The above data required a set of regions defined for the Si 2p data and also the O 1s spectra.

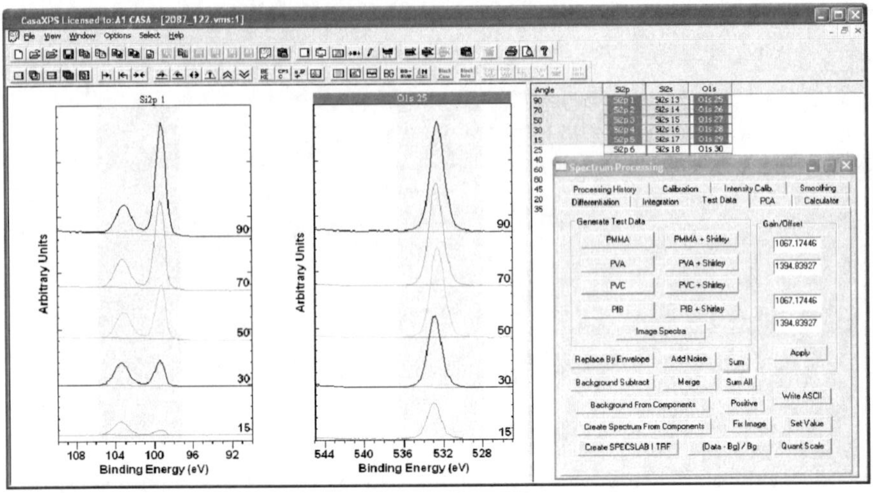

2. Select in the right-hand pane those VAMAS blocks for which regions are prepared.

Angle	Si2p	Si2s	O1s
90	Si2p 1	Si2s 13	O1s 25
70	Si2p 2	Si2s 14	O1s 26
50	Si2p 3	Si2s 15	O1s 27
30	Si2p 4	Si2s 16	O1s 28
15	Si2p 5	Si2s 17	O1s 29
25	Si2p 6	Si2s 18	O1s 30

3. Press the Quant Scale button on the Test Data property page. The spectra are scaled on a row-by-row basis.

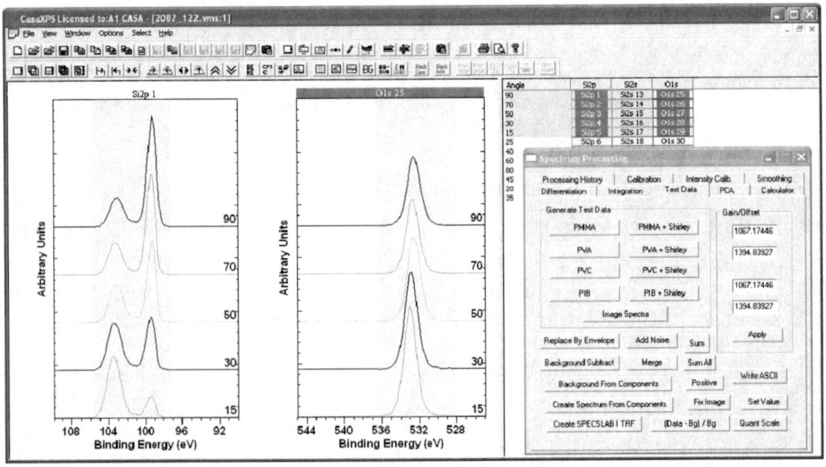

PCA Property Page

Curve synthesis is probably the most widely used method for data analysis employed by XPS researchers. Unfortunately, statistically good curve fits are not always physically meaningful and, in many cases, great care must be exercised when choosing the model to describe the data. Any assistance in understanding the model is therefore of great value and it is with this end Principal Component Analysis (PCA) is offered as a supplementary tool. Factor analysis is a mathematically challenging tool that requires knowledge of matrix algebra coupled with a feel for a statistical approach to data interpretation. A true understanding for the subject can only be obtained by studying the literature and through practical experience. Therefore the material presented here is only an introduction.

Theory behind Principal Component Analysis

Factor analysis is a multivariate technique for reducing matrices of data to their lowest dimensionality by use of orthogonal factor space. The challenge is to identify the number of significant factors (principal components) and use this information to model the data. In XPS the data matrix is composed of spectra where each acquisition channel is viewed as a co-ordinate in an r-dimensional space; r is equal to the number of acquisition channels per spectrum. The problem addressed by PCA in the context of spectroscopy is to determine the number of distinct spectroscopic features present in a particular set of c spectra.

The following example tries to illustrate the nature of the problem using a grossly simplified data set. Consider a set of three spectra; each spectrum has three acquisition channels:

s1 = (4, 3, 6) , **s2** = (2, 3, 2) , **s3** = (2, 0, 4)

The data matrix D corresponding to these three-channel spectra is:

$$D = \begin{pmatrix} 4 & 2 & 2 \\ 3 & 3 & 0 \\ 6 & 2 & 4 \end{pmatrix}$$

These three vectors belong to a 3-dimensional space, however they do not span 3-dimensional space for the following reason. If a linear combination of the vectors **s1**, **s2** and **s3** is used to construct a new vector **v**, then **v** always lies in a plane (a 2-dimensional sub-space of 3-dimensional space). The fact **v** lies in a plane is a consequence of the following relationships between the three spectra:

$$\mathbf{s3} = \mathbf{s1} - \mathbf{s2}$$

Thus a vector **v** formed used a linear combination of the three vectors **s1**, **s2** and **s3**

$$\mathbf{v} = a\,\mathbf{s1} + b\,\mathbf{s2} + c\,\mathbf{s3}$$

can be rearranged in terms of two of the three vectors as follows:

$$\mathbf{v} = a\,\mathbf{s1} + b\,\mathbf{s2} + c\,(\mathbf{s1} - \mathbf{s2})$$

$$\mathbf{v} = (a + c)\,\mathbf{s1} + (b - c)\,\mathbf{s2}$$

Thus, two principal components exist for the set of three spectra.

The analysis of the data matrix in the above simple example has been performed by observation. Unfortunately real spectra are not so simple and spotting the linear relationships between the columns of the data matrix requires a more sophisticated approach. PCA, also known as eigenanalysis, provides a method for identifying the underlying spectra constituting the building blocks for the entire set of spectra. The data matrix is transformed into a new set of r-dimensional vectors. These new vectors span the same subspace as the original columns of the data matrix, however they are now characterised by a set of eigenvalues and eigenvectors. The eigenvalues provide a measure for the significance of the abstract factors with respect to the original data. Various statistics can be computed from these values aimed at identifying the dimensionality of the subspace spanned by the spectra. A detailed discussion relating to the merits of these statistics can be found in E.R. Malinowski. Factor Analysis in Chemistry. Wiley. NY. 1991.

The procedure for calculating the abstract factors has its roots in linear least square theory. In fact the preferred method from a numerical perspective is to form a Singular Value Decomposition (SVD) for the data matrix.

$$D = USV^T$$

Where D is the data matrix formed from c spectra, each containing r channels. U is the same dimension as D, while S and V are c by c matrices. S is a diagonal matrix such that the diagonal elements are the square root of the eigenvalues of the correlation matrix

$$Z = D^T D$$

The abstract factors are computed from US, while the rows of V are the corresponding eigenvectors of Z; the co-ordinates of the eigenvectors represent the loading for the abstract factors and specify how linear combinations of these factors can be used to reproduce the original data. Including all of the abstract factors with the appropriate loading enables the data to be reproduced to an accuracy only limited by the precision characteristic of the eigenanalysis procedure.

The essential feature of the SVD procedure computes the abstract factors so that the factor corresponding to the largest eigenvalue accounts for a maximum of the variation in the data. Subsequent abstract factors are generated such that

1. as much variance as possible is accounted for by each new factor and
2. the newest axis is mutually orthogonal to the set of axes already located.

The procedure therefore computes an orthogonal basis set for the subspace spanned by the original data matrix oriented with respect to the data in a linear least square sense.

In principle, the number of non-zero eigenvalues is equal to the number of linearly independent vectors in the original data matrix. While the statement is true for well posed problems, even the presence of errors due to numerical operations will result in small eigenvalues rather than zero as expected. Numerical errors are an insignificant problem compared to the one presented by the inclusion of experimental error in the calculation. Noise in the data changes the underlying vectors so that almost every data matrix of c spectra with r acquisition channels, where $c \le r$, will span a c-dimensional subspace, even though the underlying vectors should only span fewer than c dimensions.

Various statistics are available for attempting to identify the mostly likely dimensionality of a data matrix. These statistics are designed to aid partitioning the abstract factors into primary and secondary factors. The primary factors are those corresponding to the largest n eigenvalues and represent the set of abstract factors spanning the significant subspace for the data. The secondary factors are those factors associated with noise and, in principle, can be omitted from subsequent calculations. It is not possible to completely disassociate the significant data from the error within the measured data, nor is it clear how to determine the exact number of primary factors based on the statistics. Nevertheless, the basic PCA decomposition offers a more concise perspective of a data set containing multiple spectra and can be used to gain an understanding about the nature of an experiment.

A common desire is to know the number of components required to fit a set of spectra. PCA will not in general provide such information. For example, consider the set of spectra constructed in the image of PMMA, PVA and PVC C 1s spectra. The set of C 1s spectra are a simple linear combination of synthetic spectra created using the Test Data property page and the Expression option on the Calculator property page.

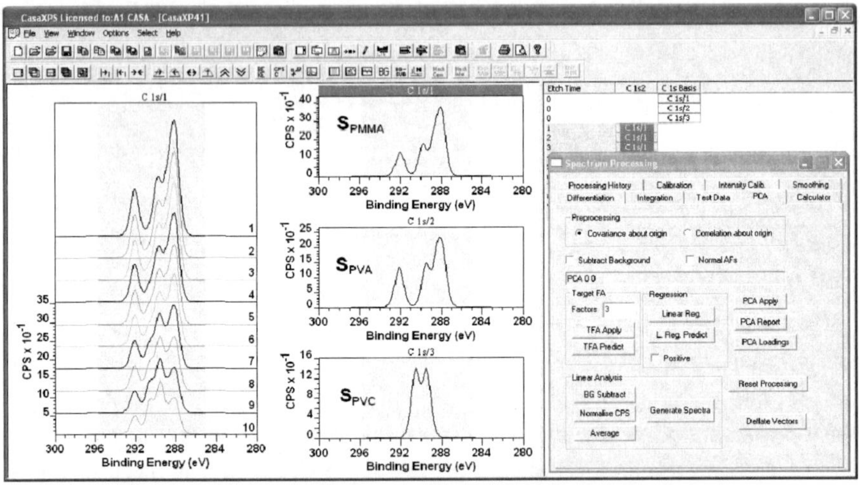

The set of ten C 1s data envelopes are calculated using an expression

$$S_n = nS_{PMMA} + 5S_{PVA} + (11 - n)S_{PVC}$$

For n = 1 to 10. Although each compound is constructed from a number of C 1s peaks (PMMA 4, PVA 4 and PVC 2), the stoichiometry for these compounds masks the true number of synthetic components actually present in the data. Hence the dimensionality of the data might be expected to be three not ten (4+4+2). If fact, the dimensionality should be two even though three spectra were used to construct the test spectra S_n; only two coefficients change throughout the data set, therefore in terms of vector spaces, the spectra all lie in a plane defined by the position vector S_{PVA} and the two direction vectors S_{PMMA} and S_{PVC}. Thus, when a PCA is applied to the set of ten vectors the following table of statistics results.

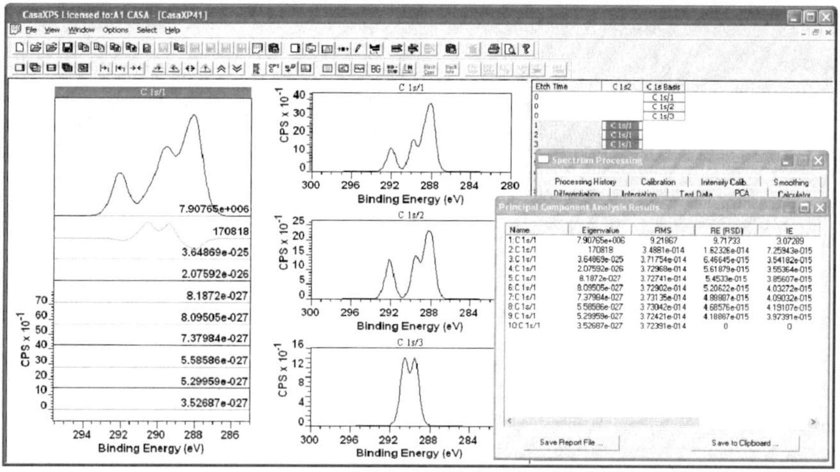

The PCA for the data in the active tile is performed by:

1. Defining a region for each spectrum used in the PCA.
2. Overlaying the spectra in the active tile.
3. Pressing the PCA button on the PCA property page.

The abstract factors replace the processed data for each VAMAS block used in the PCA, which now appear in place of the C 1s spectra in the active tile. A list of eigenvalues corresponding to the abstract factors is also displayed together with the abstract factors in preference to the experimental variable values used when spectra are displayed. Both the appearance of the abstract factors and the relative size of the eigenvalues plus the RMS column on the dialog window invoked by the PCA button suggest only two abstract factors are required to describe the set of ten spectra.

The clarity of the PCA interpretation is due to the use of synthetic data without noise. If data with backgrounds and noise were involved the easy of interpretation would be lost. There is also the small fact that these data are synthetic and therefore completely understood which helps when considering the meaning of the PCA results. For real data, even deciding the number of abstract factors is difficult.

The PCA recovered the nature of the data in a mathematical sense but certainly not in a physical sense. While the PCA failed to predict the number of components used to construct the data set it did highlight that only two of the three components actually changed throughout the sequence of spectra.

Nevertheless, if two of the three underlying spectra PMMA, PVA or PVC were used to model the data using linear least squares (LLS) the results would be flawed.

Linear Analysis

The most commonly promoted technique related to PCA for analysing XPS/AES depth profile data is linear analysis or linear least squares decomposition of spectra into component spectra. While for the right data set LLS provides a quick means of splitting the data into more basic information, LLS is not without dangers for the wrong type of data sets. The success or failure of LLS depends on the choice of component spectra and how appropriate these data are to the data set being analysed.

Linear least squares attempts to model a spectrum $\underline{s}$ using a set of component spectra $\underline{c}_i$ by determining the coefficients a_i in a least squares sense such that:

$$\underline{s} \cong \sum_{i=1}^{n} a_i \underline{c_i}$$

The algorithms used to compute a PCA are strongly related to those used when determining a linear least squares solution. The LLS approach will be investigated using the test data prepare for PCA.

A LLS solution for the test data revolves around the choice for the component spectra. The component spectra are known to be S_{PMMA}, S_{PVA} and S_{PVC}. When all three component spectra are used to approximate the spectra S_1 to S_{10}, the results are as good as can be expected.

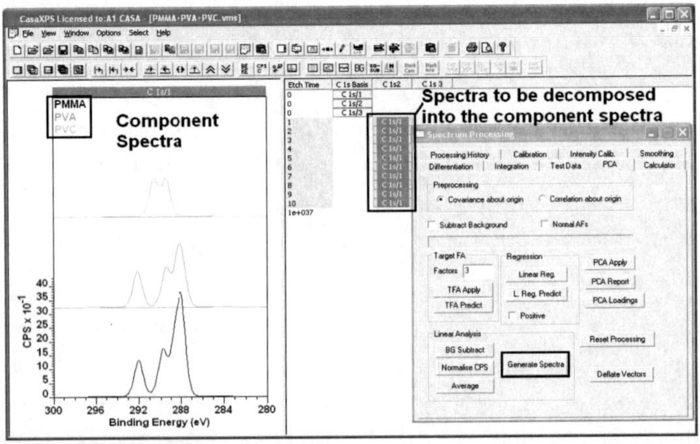

A linear analysis is performed by:

1. Overlaying the component spectra (PMMA, PVA and PVC) in the active tile.
2. Selecting in the right-hand pane the spectra for which the decomposition into the component spectra is required.
3. Pressing the Generate button on the PCA property page.

A new experiment frame is created containing rows of VAMAS blocks, one row for each VAMAS block selected in the right-hand pane. Each row includes VAMAS blocks corresponding to: the original data, processed data computed using a linear combination of the component spectra, and a VAMAS block for each of the component spectra scaled by the coefficients determine by the least squares procedure.

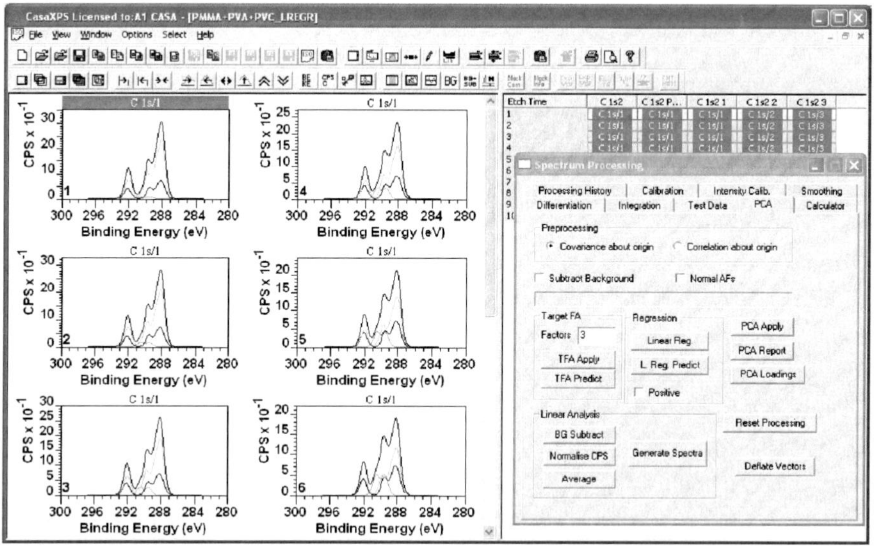

The near perfect decomposition achieved using all three components should be contrasted with the results obtained for a LLS solution where only two of the three component spectra are used.

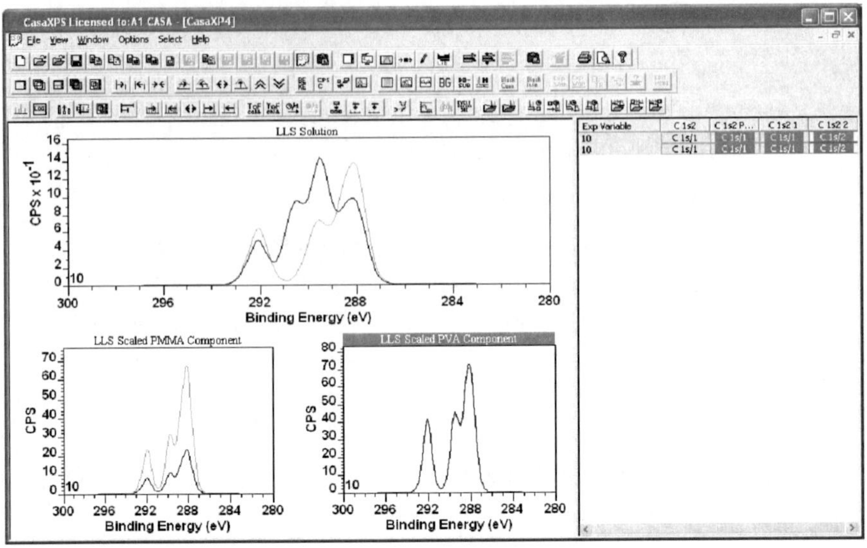

It is not surprising the LLS decomposition using only PMMA and PVA fails to match the accuracy achieve when all three components are included in the calculation. The more concerning element is the increased contribution from the PMMA component when only two components are employed. While the example is chosen to exhibit pathological behaviour, XPS data collected under different conditions will often cause peak shapes to change and more often peaks to shift in energy. Both deformations will effectively increase the dimensionality of the data set and potentially impair the ability of LLS to decompose the data accurately. A shift in the data may cause one component to reduce to zero while another is incorrectly enhanced. The key to successfully using LLS is to have a clear way to inspect the results of the LLS decomposition, hence the creation of multiple VAMAS blocks for each spectrum analysed using the LLS in CasaXPS.

The issues associated with linear least squares decomposition are precisely why peak modelling is essential for XPS data. While poorly defined peak models are equally as error prone, a properly constrained model using chemical and physical information provides the flexibility to account for shifts and shape changes seen in profile data.

An Example of Profiling XPS Spectra using Linear Least Squares to Measure Intensities

A depth profile may produce a set of spectra which vary with etch time in a well prescribed manner. These variations in the data may be identified and quantified by means of fitting known spectra to the sequence of data from the profile using a linear least squares criterion. As a result, the unknown spectra are partitioned into the individual contributions from the known spectra and thereby the chemical state intensities are extracted as a function of depth.

The following data are Cr 2p peaks measured from a sample where the variation in the data is due to ion gun etching of the sample between acquisition cycles.

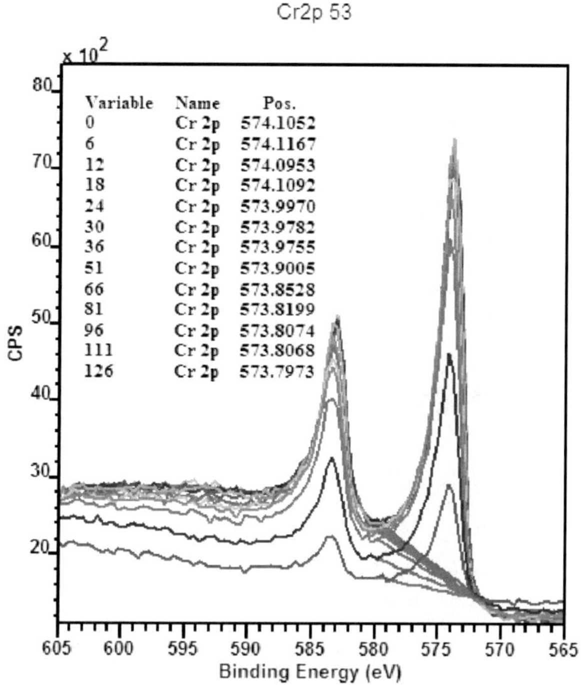

The table of peak positions for the Cr 2p 3/2 transition against etch time suggests the peak maximum moves from 574.1 eV to 573.8 eV as the ion gun removes material from the sample surface. It is postulated that the data throughout the profile can be described by two chemical states of chromium. These two states are assumed to be part of the sequence of spectra, that is, the initial spectra are representative of one state while the spectra at the end of the etch sequence are a good approximation to the second state. This hypothesis can be tested using the linear least square procedure on the PCA property page of the Spectrum Processing dialog window.

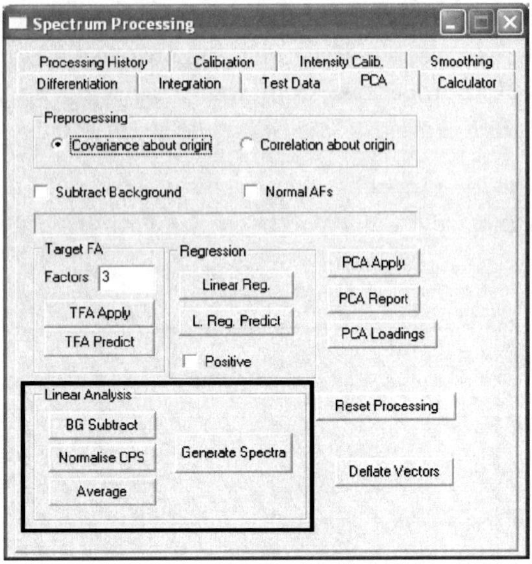

The section of the PCA property page labelled **Linear Analysis** offers buttons for data pre-treatment and also for performing the decomposition of the depth profile spectra into the target spectra chosen to represent the two chemical states.

Decomposition of the Cr 2p Spectra into Two States

The steps leading to the decomposition of the Cr 2p spectra into two states are summarised as follows:

1. Identify the target spectra.
2. Pre-treat the data to remove background influences.
3. Overlay the target spectra in the active tile.
4. In the right-hand pane of the experiment frame, select the spectra for which the decomposition is required.
5. Press the Generate Spectra button on the PCA property page.
6. Collect the decomposed spectra into an experiment frame containing the other data from the profile.
7. Repeat steps 1 to 6 for each set of spectra for which a decomposition by linear least squares is possible.
8. Profile the data using quantification regions defined on the entire data set.

The above sequence of steps will now be described in detail using the Cr 2p data.

Linear Least Squares Analysis of the Cr 2p Spectra

Step 1: Identify the target spectra

The assumption for the set of Cr 2p spectra is each spectrum ***S*** in the sequence of Cr 2p data can be reconstructed from a linear combination of two spectra $\boldsymbol{S_1}$ and $\boldsymbol{S_2}$ as follows:

$$\boldsymbol{S} = a_1\boldsymbol{S_1} + a_2\boldsymbol{S_2}$$

The coefficients a_1 and a_2 are determined in the least squares sense. The spectra $\boldsymbol{S_1}$ and $\boldsymbol{S_2}$ are the target spectra. For the case of this example, the target spectra are assumed to be the average of the first and last three spectra in the acquisition sequence.

To average spectra for use as target spectra, the Average button on the PCA property page can be used.

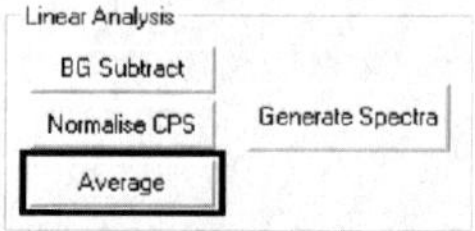

The Average button averages the counts per bin in each of the spectra overlaid in the active tile. Only spectra for which the same number of points and increment are included in the resulting VAMAS block, which is appended to the experiment frame. If the data are not acquired using the same start and energy increment, the Calculator property page can be used to construct the target spectra.

The procedure adopted when constructing a target spectrum uses the counts per bin rather than counts per second. Further, the raw counts per bin are thought to be best employed for this purpose as opposed to normalising the spectra before averaging; scaling of the counts per bin will scale the noise as well as the peak shapes and therefore may introduce exaggerated noise into the average spectrum; the point of averaging spectra is to improve the signal to noise.

Step 2: Pre-treat the spectra to remove background influences

Linear least squares, as the name suggests, is best applied to variations in the data which are linear in nature. The background in XPS is non-linear and often independent of the peak intensity for which the analysis is to be performed. A Cr 2p peak is a good example of these issues as the background to a Cr 2p peak is typically dominated by the nearby O 1s peak to higher kinetic energy, although for this example only the first layer within the profile includes a contribution from an O 1s peak. To reduce the influence of the background on the linear least squares decomposition, the data used in the calculation may be background subtracted.

The background to a spectrum is defined using the Quantification Parameters dialog window available from the top toolbar or the Options menu on the main CasaXPS window. The following picture illustrates a Shirley background applied to the first three spectra in the sequence of Cr 2p data.

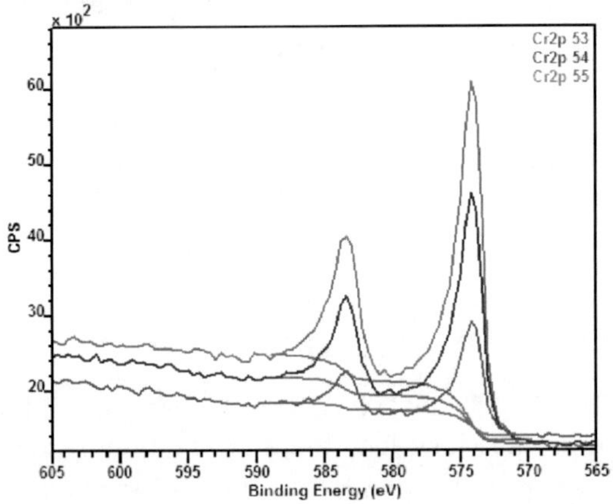

The same start and end energies have been chosen to define the range for which the Shirley background extends. It is clear the Shirley background differs for each of these spectra, particularly in view of the non-physical nature of the first background which cuts through the data between the doublet peaks characteristic of the Cr 2p photoelectron distribution. The standard backgrounds used to process XPS spectra are limited in their description of the true background to the photoelectric peaks, but nevertheless without background removal, the complex nature of the background may adversely affect an analysis.

The definition of the background in CasaXPS is made on a spectrum-by-spectrum basis. It is therefore possible and often desirable to set the limits for the background to differ for each of the spectra to prevent anomalies such as the Shirley background for the first spectrum cutting through the data. Another useful parameter when defining the background is the Av Width. The Av Width specifies the number of data channels to the left and right of the default data channel which when averaged determines the intensities at which the background approaches the data at the region limits. The use of the Av Width parameter reduces the influence of noise on the placement of the background limits and therefore increases the uniformity of the computed background for similar spectra.

To perform the background subtraction, create a region on each of the spectra, display the Cr 2p spectra and target spectra in the active display tile then press the button labelled BG Subtract on the PCA property page.

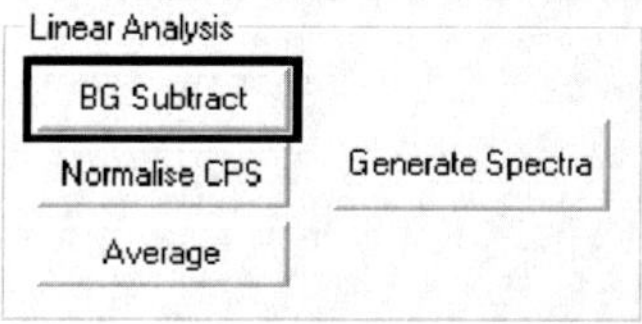

Steps 3, 4 and 5: Prepare the data selection for a linear least squares decomposition

The following picture illustrates the state of the block selection required to perform a LLS analysis for the Cr 2p data using the two target spectra labelled Pr:Cr 2p 53 and Pr:Cr 2p 63.

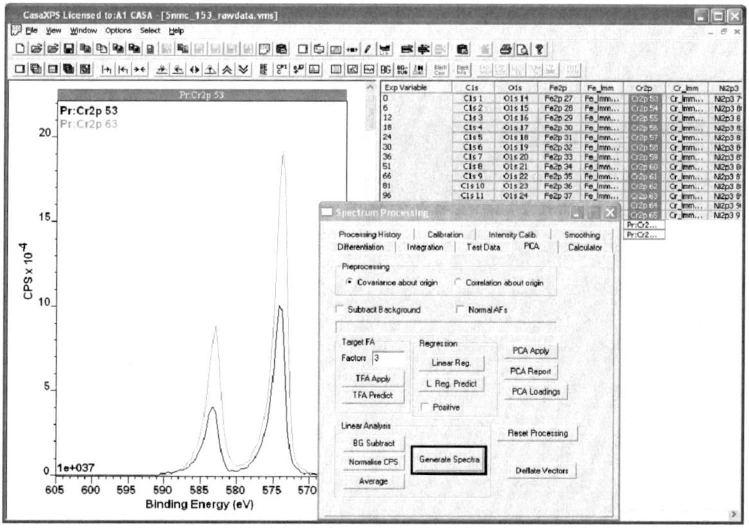

The component spectra are overlaid in the active tile, while the Cr 2p spectra for which the LLS analysis is required are selected in the right-hand pane of the experiment frame. On pressing the Generate Spectra pushbutton on the PCA

property page, a new experiment frame is created containing: 1) the original Cr 2p used in the analysis, 2) the reconstructed spectra computed from a linear combination of the target spectra and 3) each of the component spectra scaled by the factor determined in a linear least squares sense. The scaled component spectra therefore represent the contribution of each of the component spectra to each of the Cr 2p spectra in the profile.

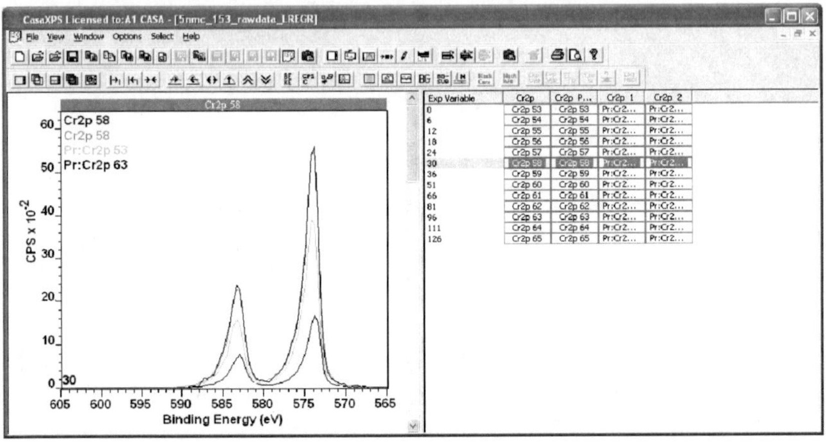

Once the LLS decomposition is available in a new experiment frame the component columns headed Cr 2p 1 and Cr 2p 2 can be copied into an experiment frame containing the spectra required for a profile.

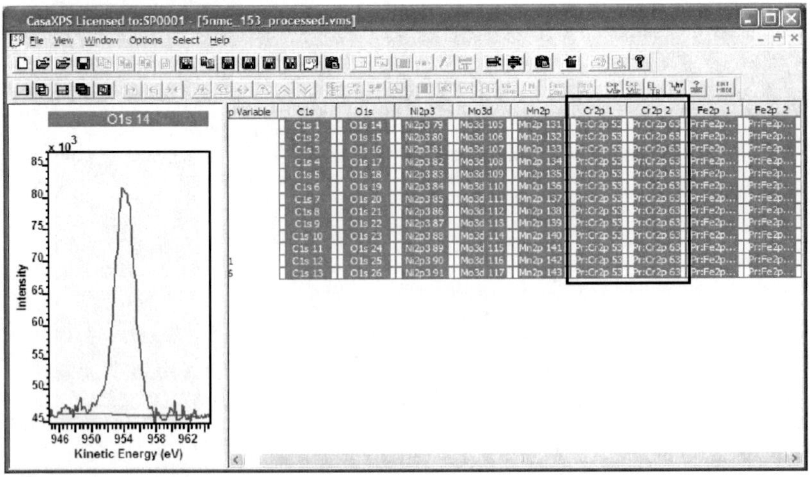

The picture above represents an experiment frame containing all the spectra for which no decomposition via LLS is required together with the two columns from the Cr 2p LLS and two further columns generated in an identical method for the Fe 2p 3/2 spectra. Regions must be assigned to each and every spectrum in the profile. The resulting profile generated using the Custom Report on the Report Spec property page of the Quantification Parameters dialog window follows:

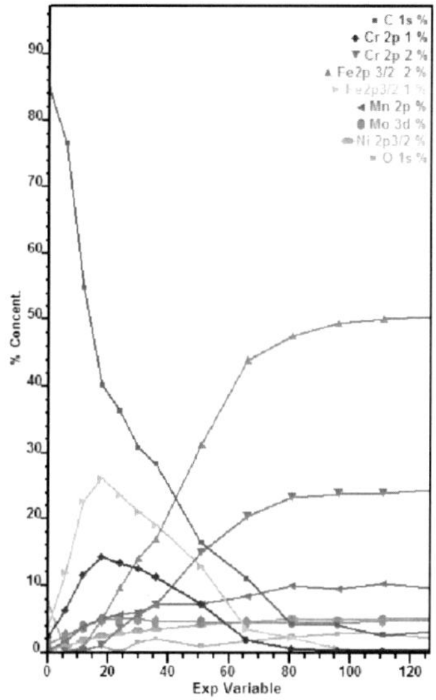

Annotation Dialog Window

The Annotation dialog window is available from the Options menu or via the top toolbar.

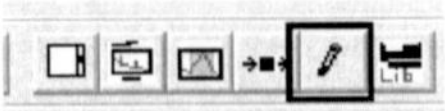

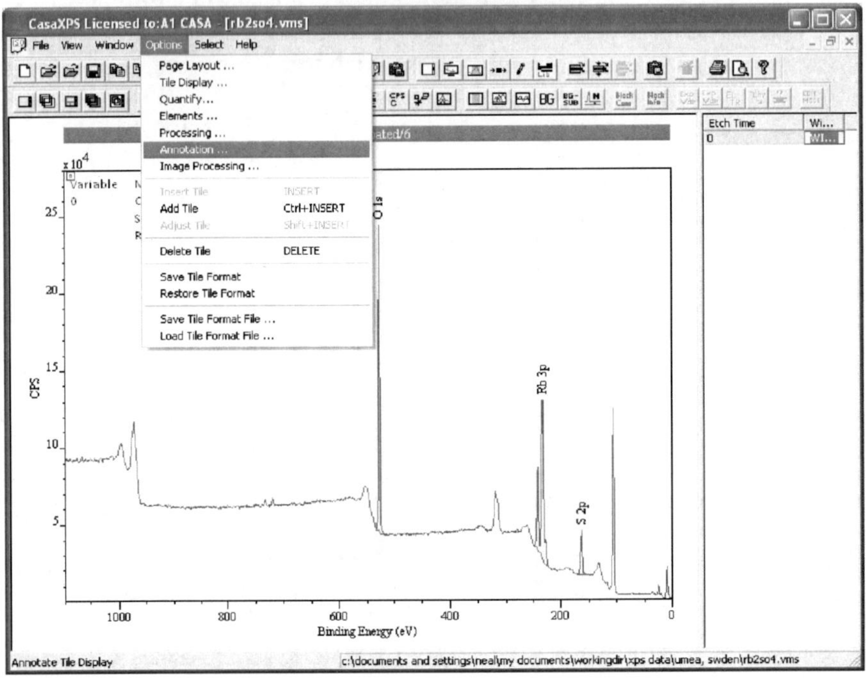

Annotation in CasaXPS is managed via a set of property pages on the Annotation dialog window. Each time a piece of annotation in the form of a table or text is added to a VAMAS block, an entry is added to the Annotation History property page. The Annotation History provides the means of amending and deleting existing annotation associated with a VAMAS block.

Annotation History Property Page

The Annotation History property page on the Annotation dialog window offers a scrolled list of entries reflecting the annotation currently defined on the VAMAS block displayed in the active tile of the left-hand pane for the experiment frame with focus.

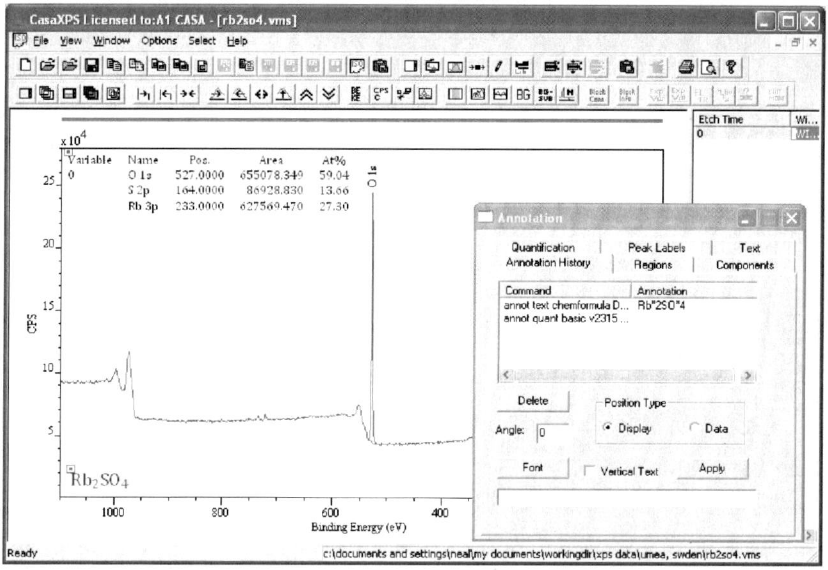

The scrolled list provides a means of selecting an annotation entry with the view to modifying the entry or deleting the entry from the VAMAS block.

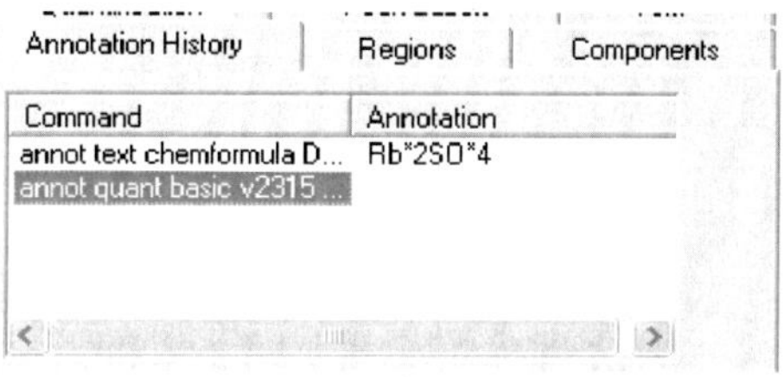

Once an entry in the scrolled list is selected, attributes for the annotation may be adjusted, such as font or text, before pressing the Apply button.

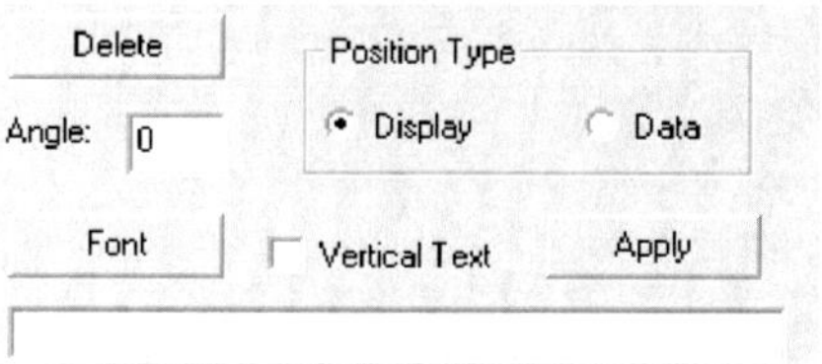

Changing the font used to display a piece of annotation involves:

1. Selecting the entry in the annotation history table.

2. Pressing the Font button below the annotation history table to invoke the Font dialog window.

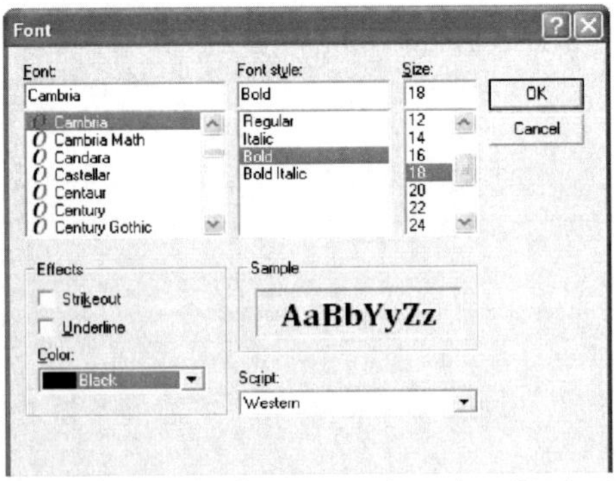

3. Adjusting the Font attributes before pressing the OK button on the Font dialog window, followed by pressing the Apply button on the Annotation History property page.

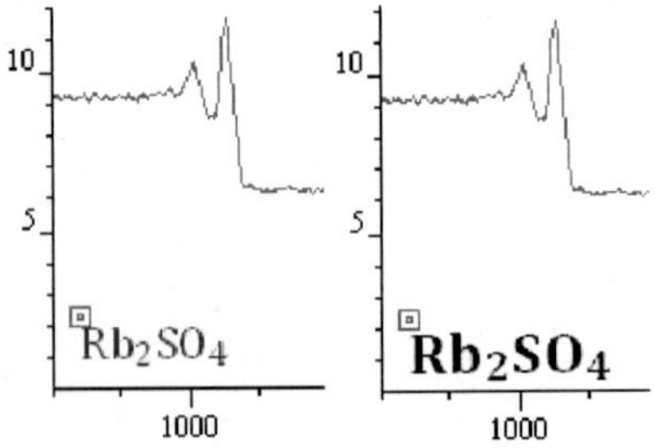

Moving annotation is performed using the box with the dot just above and to the left of a piece of annotation. The box appears only when the Annotation History property page is top-most on the Annotation Dialog window.

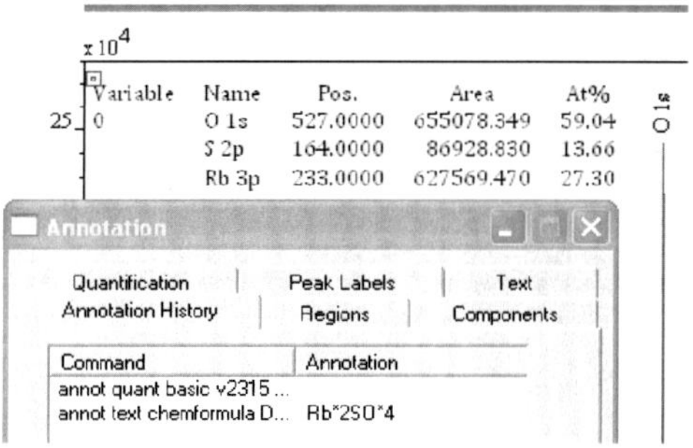

Point at the box and drag the cursor to a new position

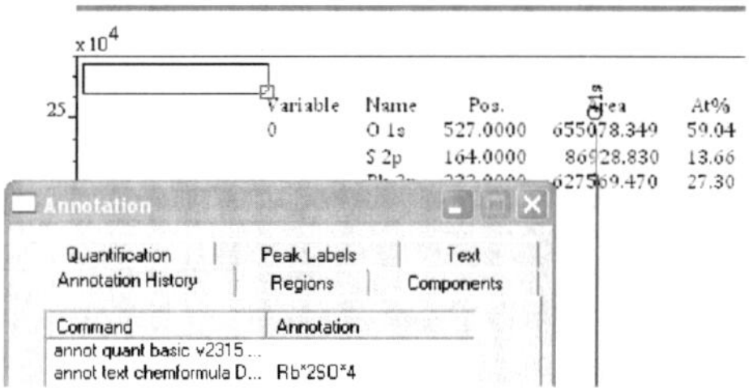

The drag box showing the extent of the movement can be removed by left-clicking outside the zoom box.

Annotation Quantification Tables

The Quantification property page offers a means of displaying a full quantification table over any data displayed in the active tile.

Quantification annotation differs from annotation tables created from the Regions or the Components property pages in that the table displays quantification information from the VAMAS blocks selected in the right-hand pane, whereas tables based on the Regions or Components property pages display quantification information only deriving from the VAMAS block for which the annotation is defined.

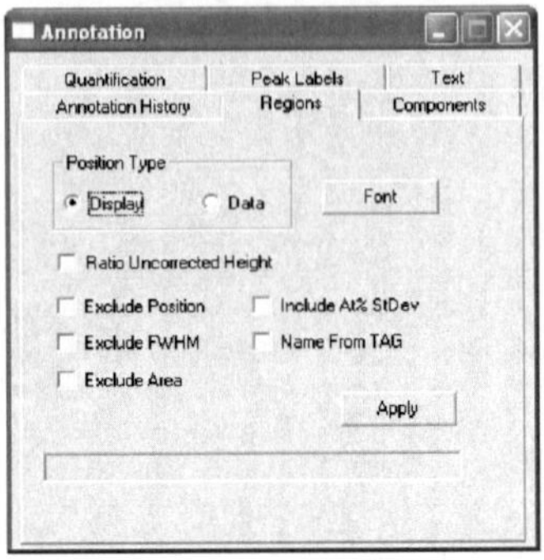

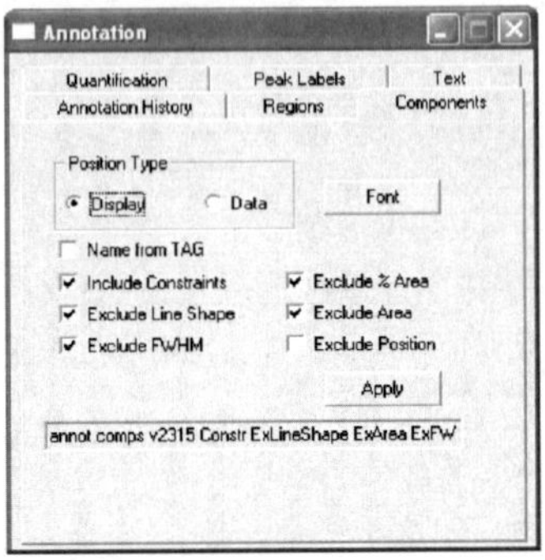

A quantification table derived from a survey spectrum may be displayed over data from a high resolution spectrum. In contrast the Components property page on the Annotation dialog window is used to ensure peak model information derives directly from the high resolution spectrum for which the components are defined.

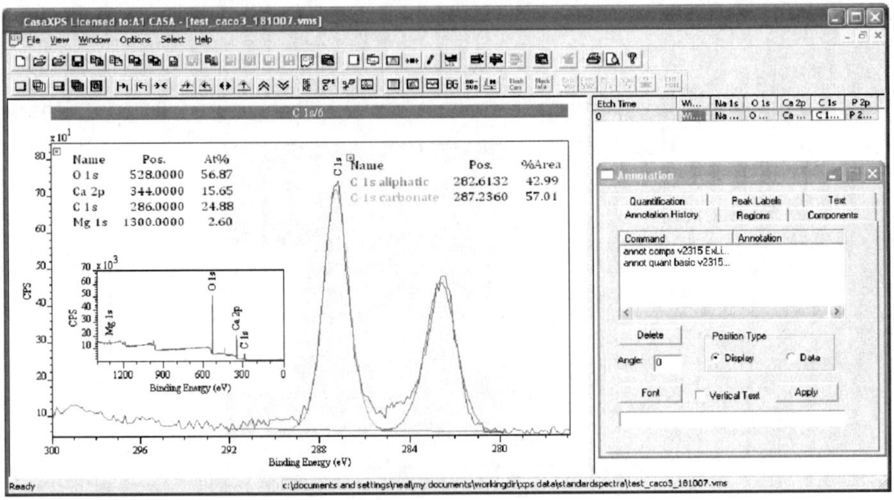

To prepare such a display of information:

1. Select and display the C 1s high resolution spectrum.

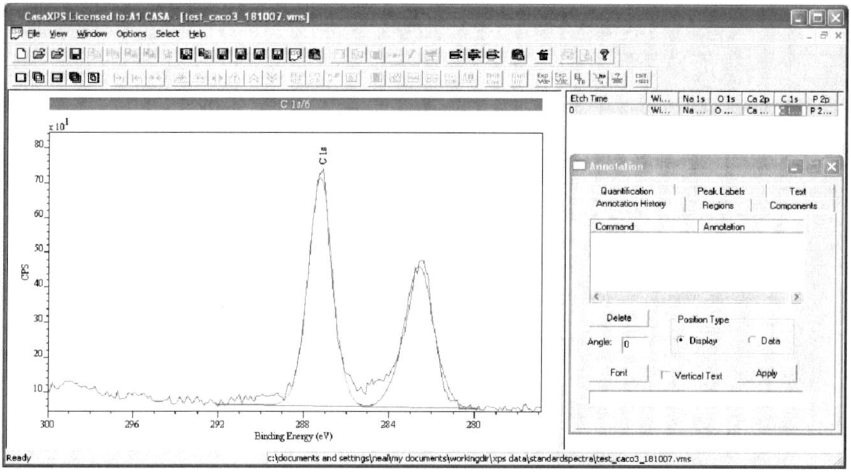

2. Using the Quantification property page to add a quantification table to the C 1s VAMAS block.

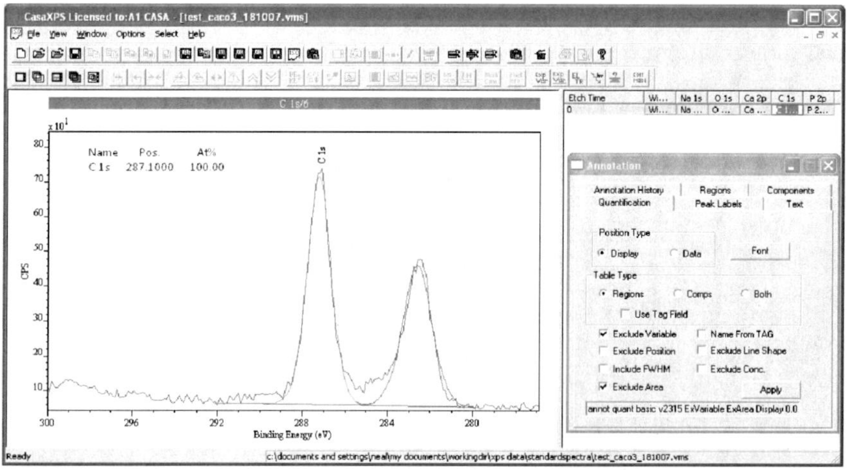

The reason the table currently shows the information from the C 1s high resolution spectrum is because the C 1s VAMAS block is selected in the right-hand pane.

3. Select the survey spectrum in the right-hand pane using a single click with the left mouse button.

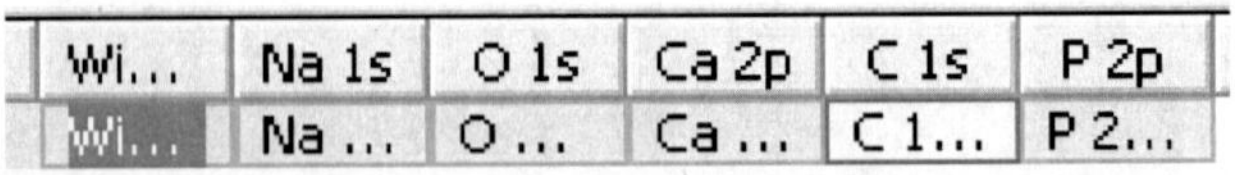

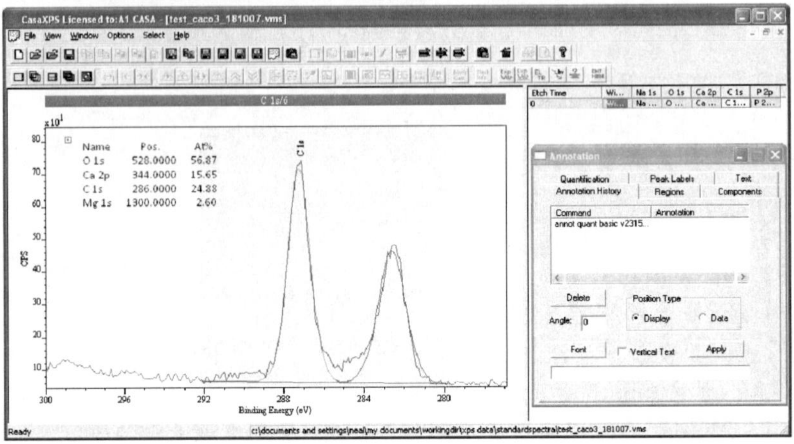

The annotation table based on the survey spectrum now appears over the C 1s data displayed in the active tile.

4. Add a further annotation table using the Component property page on the Annotation dialog window. Move the tables using the box mechanism available when the Annotation History property page is top-most.

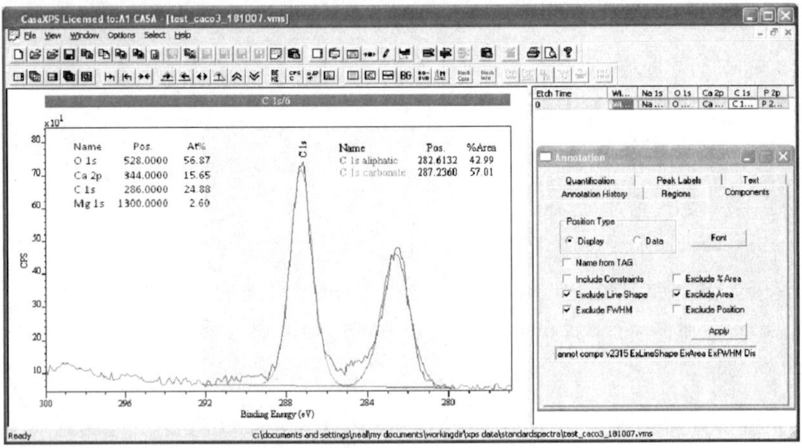

Note that the survey spectrum is selected in the right-hand pane, thus providing the source for the information displayed in the table created using the Quantification property page. The red box with a yellow background associated with the C 1s VAMAS block indicates that the active tile is displaying data from the C 1s VAMAS block. If the C 1s VAMAS is selected instead of the survey spectrum the nature of the table changes to reflect the region information available from the C 1s VAMAS block only.

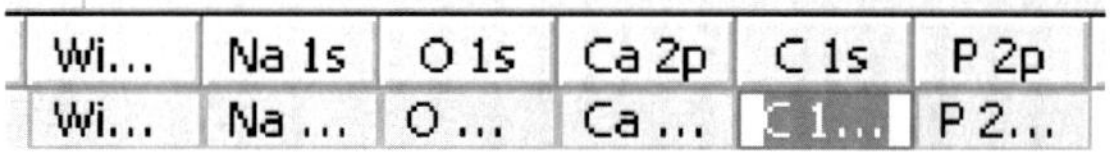

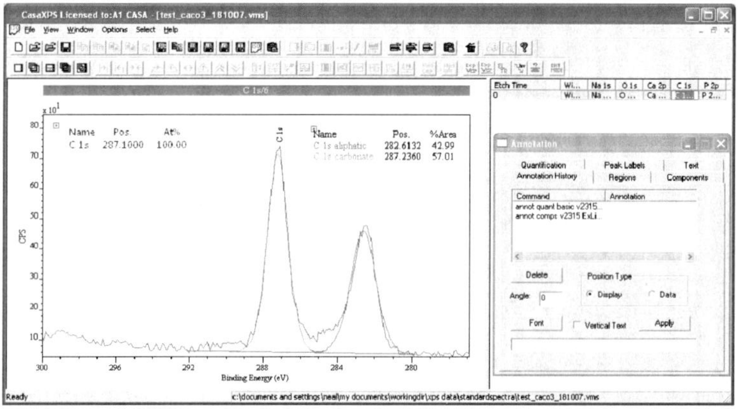

The inset tile displaying the survey spectrum from which the quantification data is derived is achieved as follows.

1. Draw a zoom box indicating the area of the active tile in which the inset should be placed.

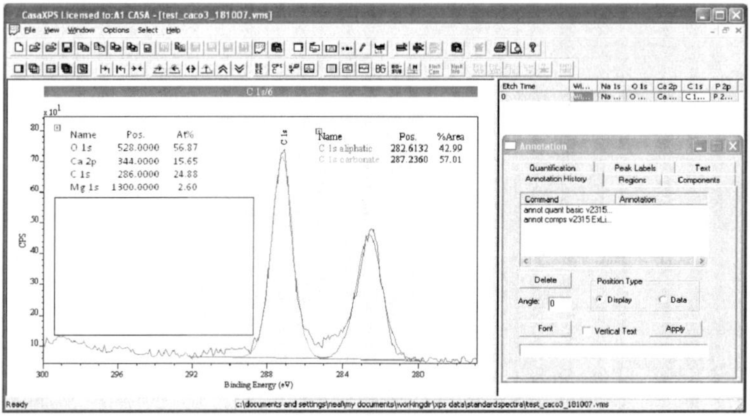

2. Press the Insert key on the keyboard.

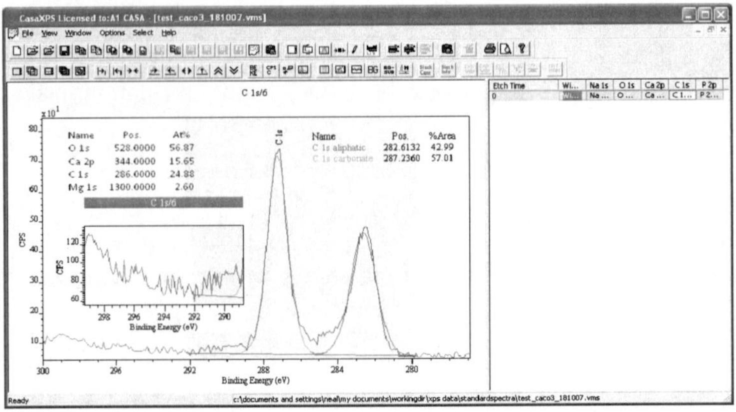

The data initially displayed in the inset tile are from the parent tile; that is, initially the inset tile displays the background intensities from the C 1s spectrum.

3. Select the survey spectrum in the right-hand pane and press the Overlay toolbar button or F2 function key.

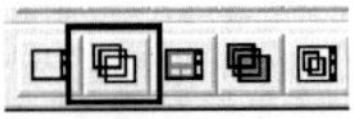

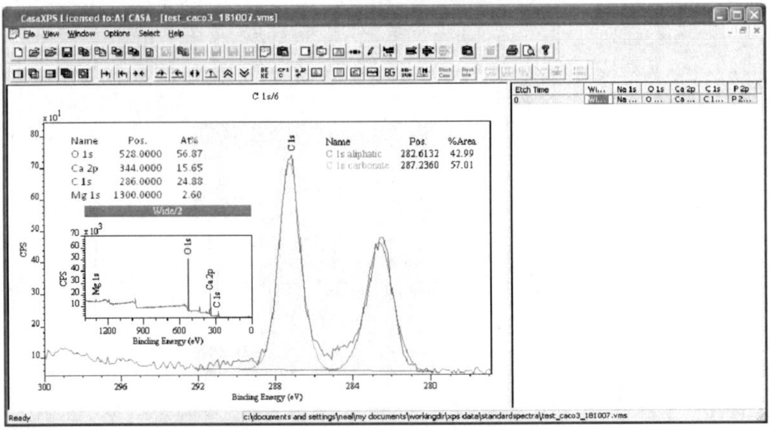

4. Make any adjustments to the display of the survey spectrum in the inset tile using the standard tile display parameters.

Annotation using Formulae

The tables over the C 1s spectrum below illustrates how labels associated with quantification items can be used to convey the chemistry identified by a peak model.

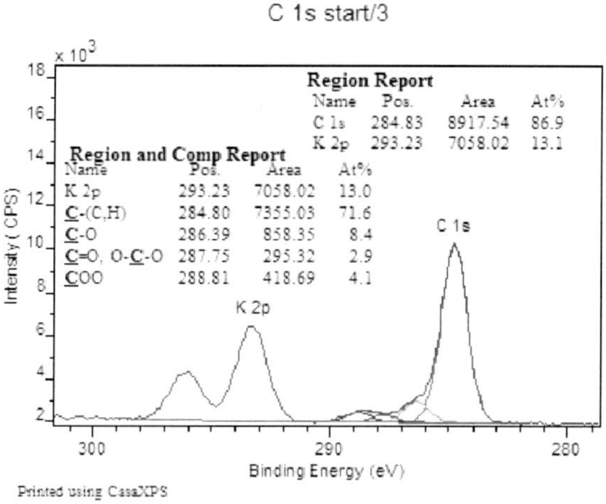

While formulae where previously available as annotation text, version 2.3.15 of CasaXPS enhances these existing formulae and adds similar functionality to the region, components and quantification annotation tables.

The mechanism for adding bold and underlined characters to these formulae is via special characters acting as a prefix. The reason for special ASCII characters rather than the Microsoft Windows font set is to avoid introducing complex binary codes into an ASCII VAMAS data file. The advantages of an easily transported data file format far outweigh the advantages of using the binary control characters required by the Windows philosophy.

The special characters recognised by the annotation are:

_	Underline next character
~	Make the next character bold
\	Make the next character bold and underlined
*	Subscript the next numerical sequence of characters
< and >	Superscript characters between < and > brackets.

The O 1s spectrum is annotated with strings constructed from these special formatting characters. The lower table shows the strings used to construct the formatting for the strings in the top table.

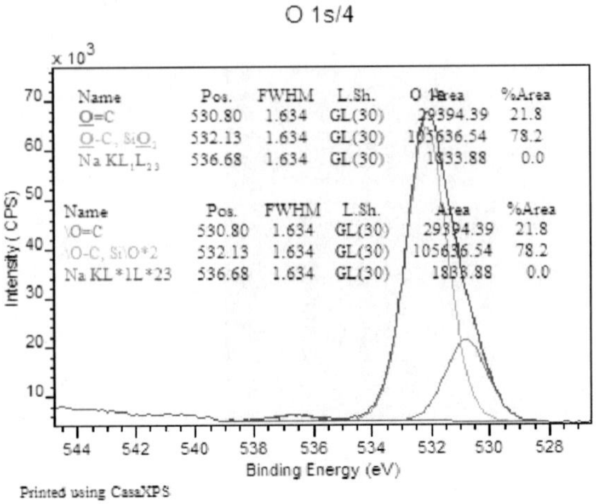

Each region or component includes two strings, namely the Name field and the TAG field.

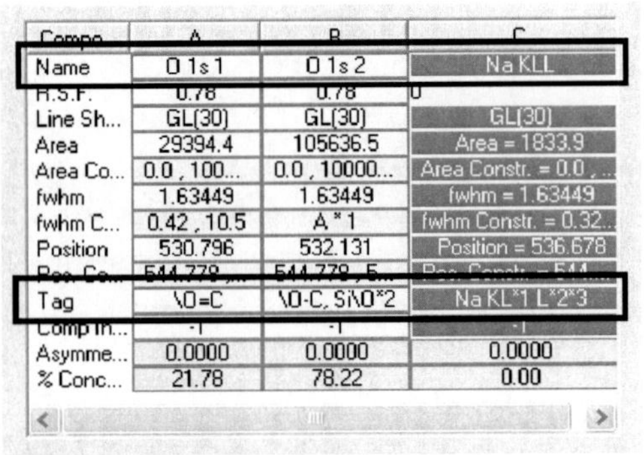

Compo...	A	B	C
Name	O 1s 1	O 1s 2	Na KLL
R.S.F.	0.78	0.78	0
Line Sh...	GL(30)	GL(30)	GL(30)
Area	29394.4	105636.5	Area = 1833.9
Area Co...	0.0 , 100...	0.0 , 10000...	Area Constr. = 0.0 , ...
fwhm	1.63449	1.63449	fwhm = 1.63449
fwhm C...	0.42 , 10.5	A * 1	fwhm Constr. = 0.32...
Position	530.796	532.131	Position = 536.678
Pos. Co...	544.778 , ...	544.778 , 5...	Pos. Constr. = 544...
Tag	\O=C	\O-C, Si\O*2	Na KL*1 L*2*3
Comp In...	-1	-1	-1
Asymme...	0.0000	0.0000	0.0000
% Conc...	21.78	78.22	0.00

Both the Name field and the TAG fields are strings available for introducing formatted text. The Name field is the string typically used when creating quantification reports as well as displaying labels above regions or components. Since the Name field is used in multiple contexts, it is sometimes more convenient to define the formatted string via the TAG field rather than the Name field. Each annotation report table now includes a tick-box used to display the formatted text from the TAG rather than the Name field.

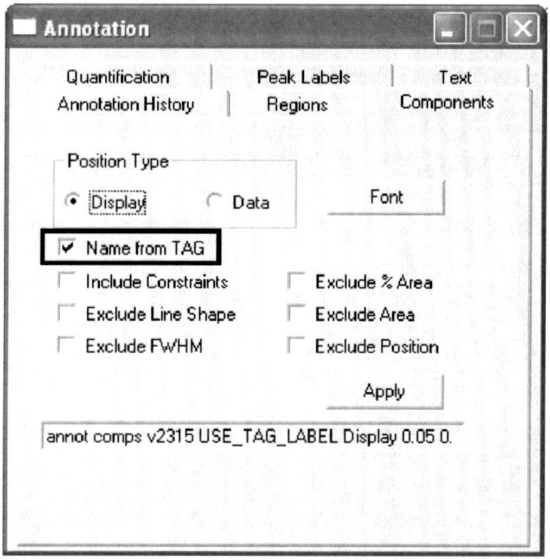

This allows strings suitable for exporting to text-based files to be entered into the Name field while CasaXPS formatted strings can be maintained within the TAG field. As an example, the O 1s spectrum below illustrates a table displayed using the TAG field option to display the formatted text, while the unformatted text in the lower table is displayed via the Name field.

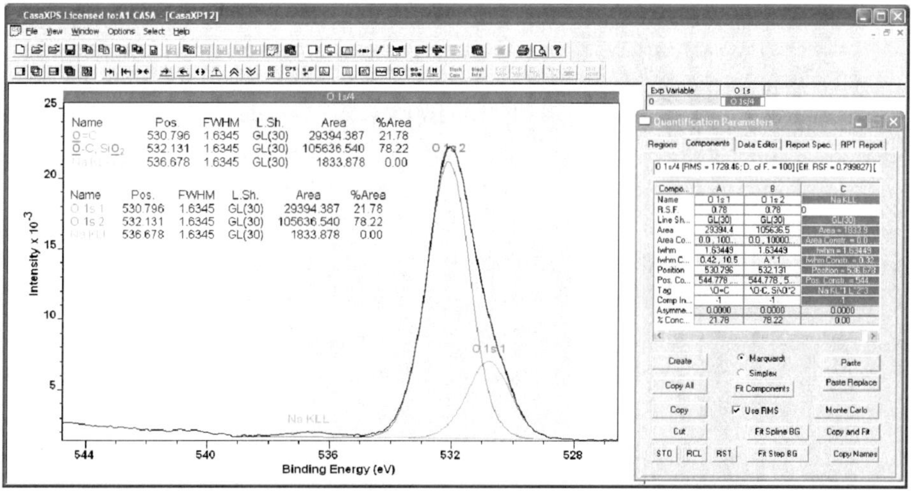

Note: formatted strings will only apply to annotation tables created using version 2.3.15 and above. Data annotated using earlier version of CasaXPS will not exhibit formatted names; thus if formulae are desired, the existing annotation table will require replacing by a newly created component table.

The following Fe 2p spectrum demonstrates formatted text applied via the Text property page of the Annotation dialog window.

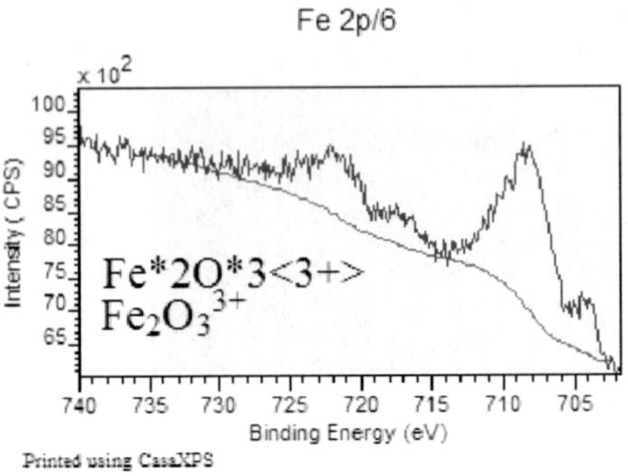

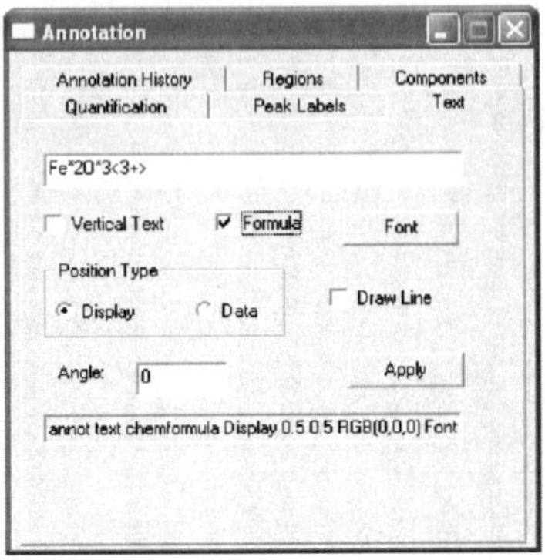

Enhanced Reporting Based on Regions and Components

Annotation tables created from the Quantification and Components property pages of the Annotation dialog window, like quantification reports generated from the Standard Report options on the Report Spec property page of the Quantification Parameters dialog window, will now only include a region in the quantification report provided there are no components defined within the region with non-zero RSF fields. Previously, any quantification item with a non-zero RSF would be included in the quantification report. Thus, to prepare a quantification report using a combination of regions and components it was necessary to use zero RSFs for any region for which the intensity is measured using components. The introduction of the new criterion, namely, that a region is only included provided there are no components in the same energy interval defined by the region, means the RSFs do not need to be adjusted to achieve the desired quantification report. The C 1s/K 2p spectrum illustrates a simple quantification report generated from the spectrum containing both the C 1s signal and also a doublet peak from potassium.

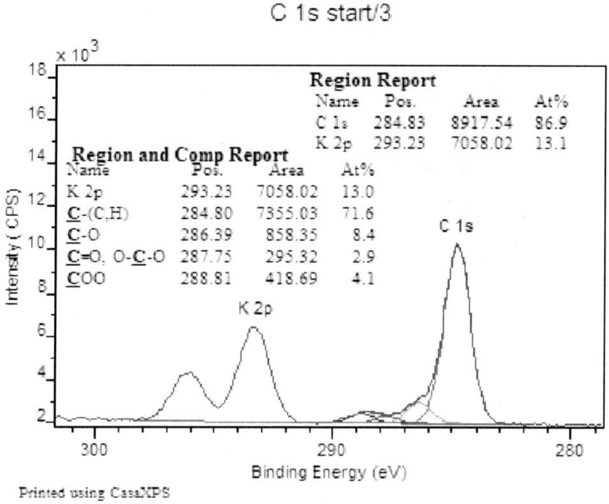

The annotation quantification table containing two entries is calculated from the quantification regions only, while the second quantification table combines the intensities measured from the C 1s synthetic components and also the intensity for the K 2p peak measured using a region. Previously, it would not have been possible to display both of these tables at the same time, since the table containing both regions and components would force the RSF in the C 1s region to be set to zero, thus preventing a meaningful regions-only report.

Quantification Parameters Dialog Window

Regions Property Page

A region is a collection of parameters used to define the background to and identify peaks within a spectrum. The region parameters include a name field used to reference the region in quantification reports, a relative sensitivity factor (RSF) for scaling the peak intensity and the background algorithm applied within the energy interval specified for the region. Armed with these parameters, regions return a set of quantities calculated from the spectral data. The outputs include atomic concentration, peak position, peak area and full width at half maximum (FWHM).

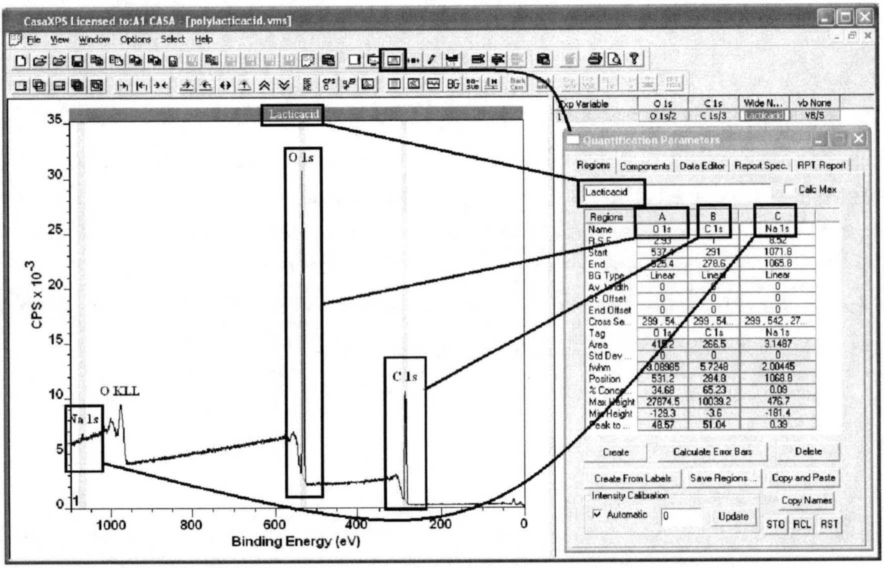

Regions are typically sufficient for elemental quantification of spectra. A report generated from regions may appear over the data displayed in the left-hand pane or tabulated using the Report Spec property page.

The Regions property page displays region information for the active VAMAS block displayed in the active tile. The VAMAS block identifier used in the title for a display tile is displayed in the top text-field on the Regions property page. Each region defined on the active VAMAS block appears as a column of parameters in a table on the Regions property page.

Features relating to the Regions property page are described below.

Creating a Region

The Region property page provides two options for explicitly creating regions.

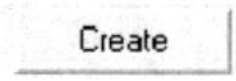

The Create button adds a region to the active VAMAS block. If the element/transition VAMAS fields are correctly set for the VAMAS block as the region is created the name and RSF are extracted from the current element library.

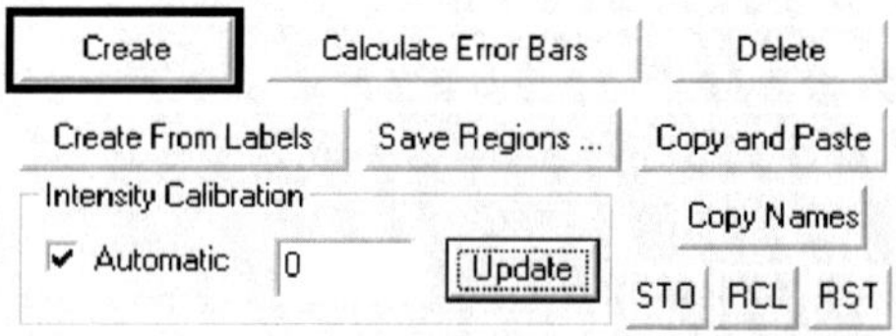

The element/transition fields for the VAMAS blocks concatenated form the string used to head the columns for VAMAS blocks in the right-hand pane.

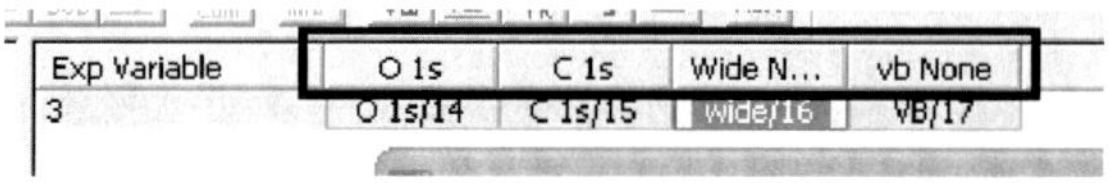

When creating a region, these strings appearing in the right-hand pane headers are matched against the name field displayed on the element library property page. A newly created region will be updated with the name and RSF from the element library provided a match occurs.

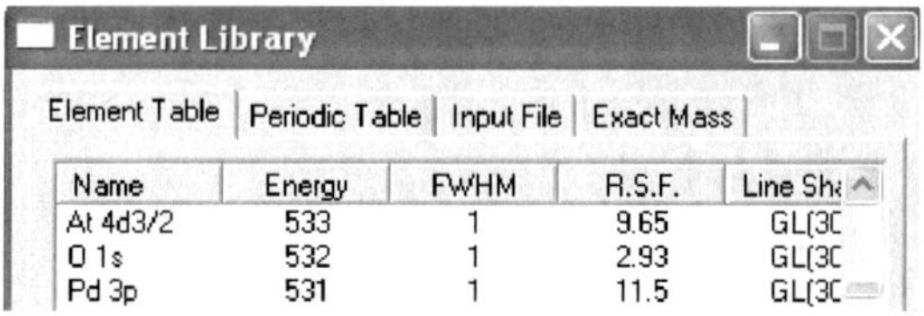

For example, displaying a VAMAS block containing data from the O 1s energy range in the active tile before pressing the Create button extracts the correct RSF for the O 1s peaks.

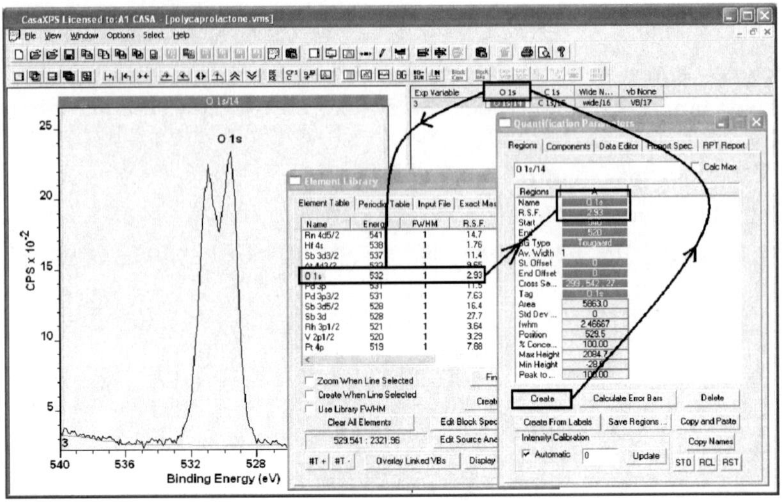

The width of the region created via the Create button is determined by the current energy range used to display the data in the active tile. A natural operation prior to creating a region via the create button is zooming into an energy interval about the peaks of interest. For a survey spectrum the zoom operation is even more appropriate than for a narrow scan spectrum.

Clearly a survey spectrum including multiple elements does not have an appropriate element/transition field therefore the name and RSF fields must be updated after creation of any regions.

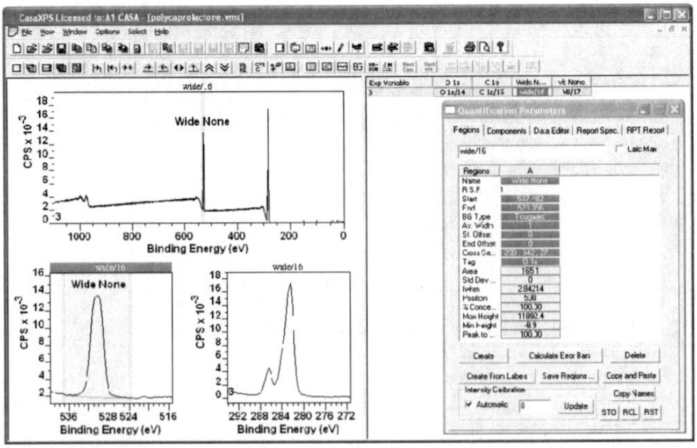

A mechanism for forcing an update of the RSF from the element library for a region facilitates modifications by extracting the RSF using the string entered in the name field for a region. If a name field is entered to match the name field in the element library the RSF is updated provided the name is entered with a # character as a prefix to the name. On pressing the Enter keyboard key, the # character is removed from the entered name and the RSF is updated from the element library.

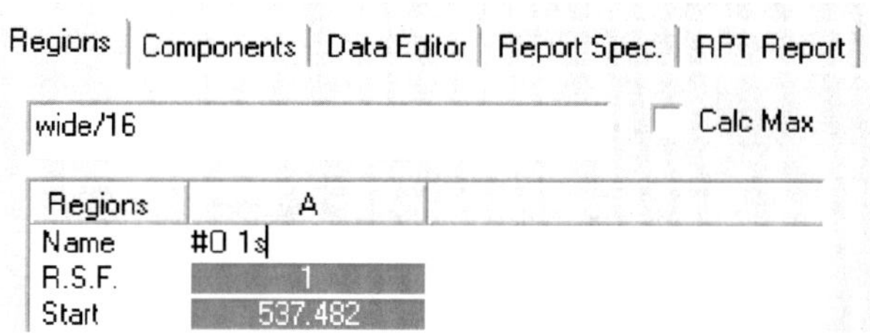

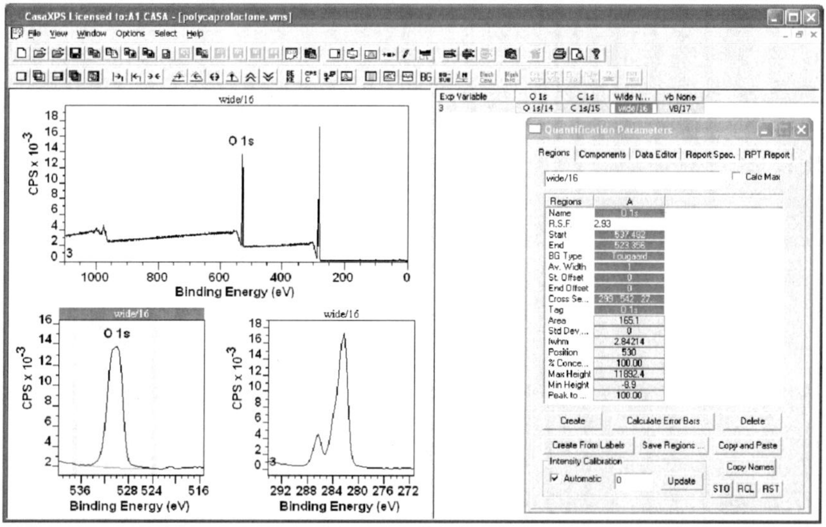

The Create button is typically employed to manually add regions for data where the automatic mechanism fails to provide a complete set of quantification regions. The element library is the more usual route to populating a survey spectrum with regions. The proper use of regions for quantification relies on the information extracted from the element library and hence regions can be created en masse for a survey spectrum via the Create Regions button on the Element Table property page.

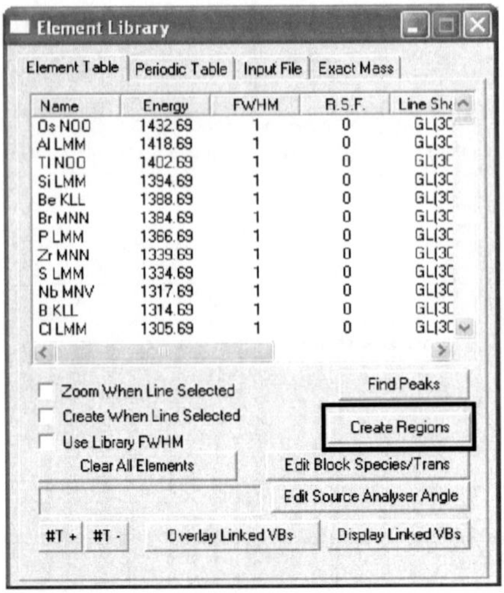

The Regions property page provides the means of adjusting these automatically created regions.

The second option on the Regions property page for creating regions offers one of the automatic methods for populating a survey spectrum with regions.

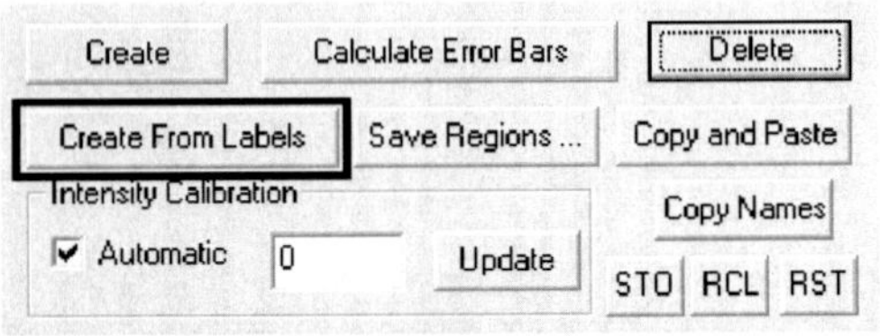

The Create from Labels button coordinates with annotation defined on a survey spectrum to link peaks in the data with transitions from the element library. An analysis based on a survey spectrum might include identifying the peaks suitable for quantifying the sample, followed by labelling features in the data to provide a complete picture showing assignments for all peaks to transitions. The Annotation property page provides a route to labelling peaks based on element markers temporarily placed on the data using the element library. Labelling the peaks using annotation, if performed in two stages, provides a natural means of creating regions. Annotation using the Peak Labels property page is used first to identify the peaks for which regions are required.

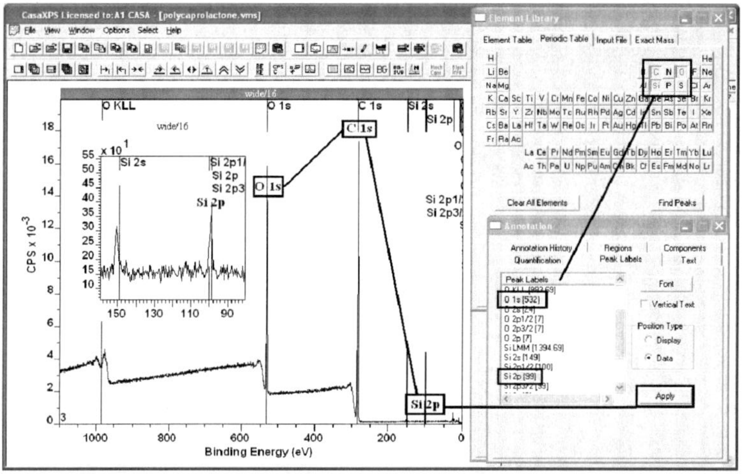

With the set of annotation matching the set of peaks required for quantification, the Create form Labels button, when pressed, uses the peak label annotation to create regions.

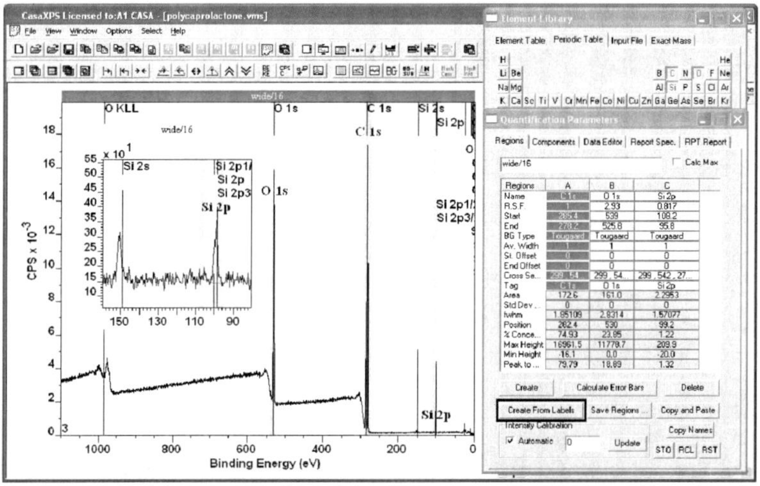

The key point is that peak label annotation is created using transitions identified via the element library; therefore the peak labels provide a link to the transitions responsible for the peaks. As a result, the RSF and names for the regions created from the peak labels are extracted from the element library. Once the regions are created for the first set of annotation labels, additional informative labelling can follow using the Peak Label property page a second time.

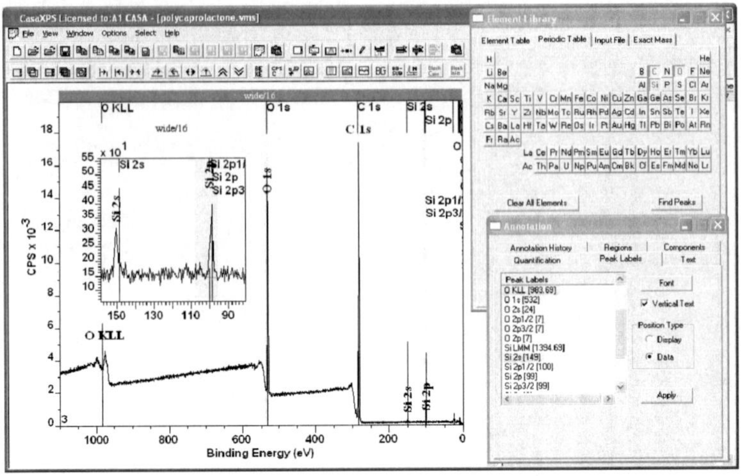

The Annotation property page also offers a means of adding to the display a quantification table based on regions.

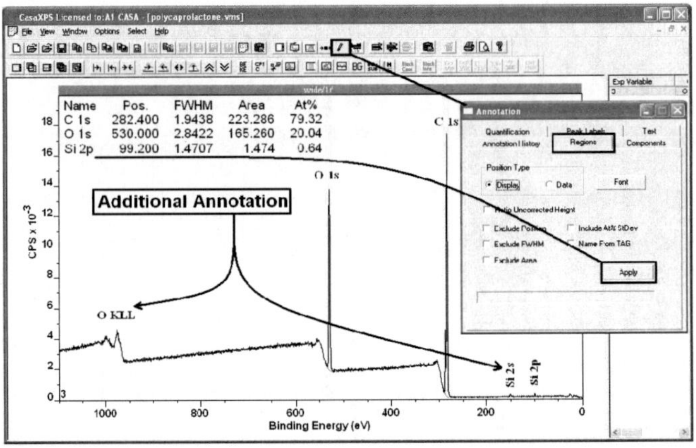

Regions Table

The set of regions defined on the active VAMAS block are displayed as columns of parameters on the Regions property page. A region is selected by left-clicking anywhere among the parameter section of the table or on the heading to the region column. When a parameter in the table is beneath the cursor and the mouse button is pressed, the parameter field becomes a text-edit field. New parameter values entered in these edit fields are only accepted by pressing the Enter keyboard key. Clicking the mouse away from a modified field rejects the newly entered information.

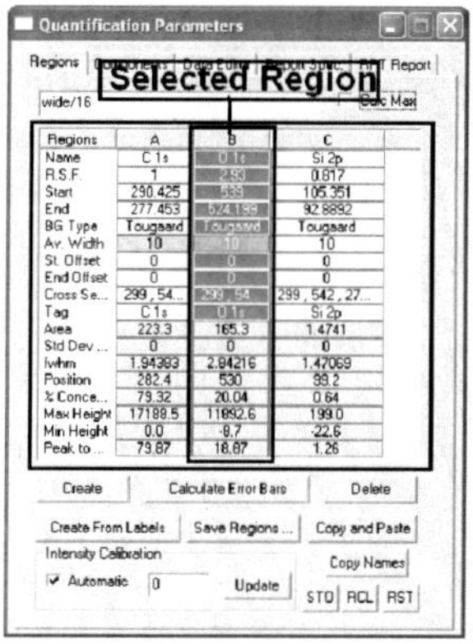

A selected region is marked with the highlight colour. The Delete button on the Regions property page removes a selected region from the active VAMAS block.

The Region Table lists the parameters specifying each region. A unique name identifies the transition associated with each region and provides a label for use in quantification reports.

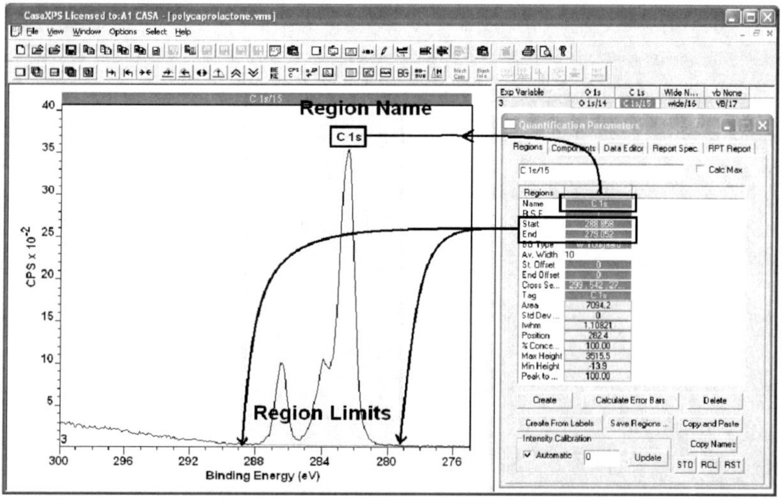

The name parameter is displayed over the data in the left-hand pane under the control of settings on the Tile Display Parameters dialog window. Similarly the region limits as specified by the Start and End parameters define an energy interval optionally marked on the display using a fill colour. These two display attributes are switched on and off via the Display property page of the Tile Display Parameters dialog window.

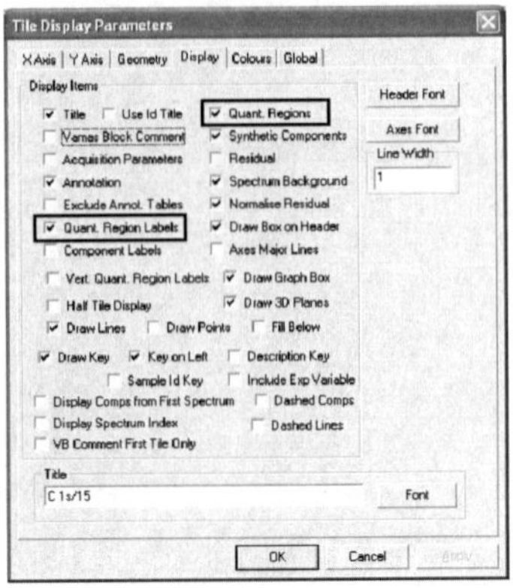

These display options for regions are toggled using a toolbar button.

Pressing the toolbar button changes the state of the display parameters in a sequence. If initially the tile displays a region with the name field and a fill colour marking the region limits, pressing the toolbar button once removes the fill colour from the display leaving the name field displayed. Pressing the toolbar button a second time removes the name label from the display and returns the fill colour to the display. A third time of pressing the toolbar button removes the name field and the fill colour. A final button press returns both the fill colour and the name label to the active tile.

1

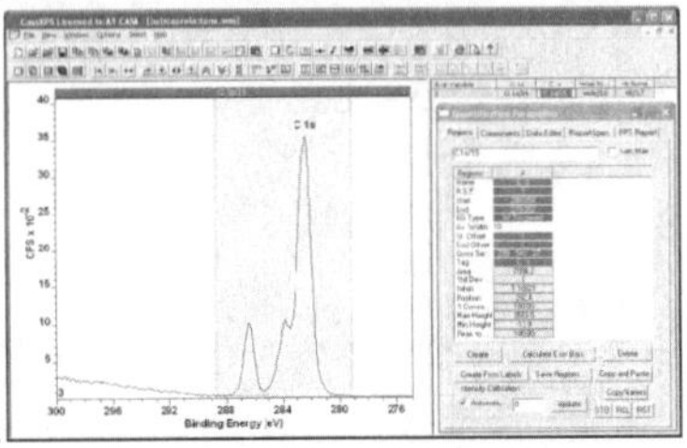

2

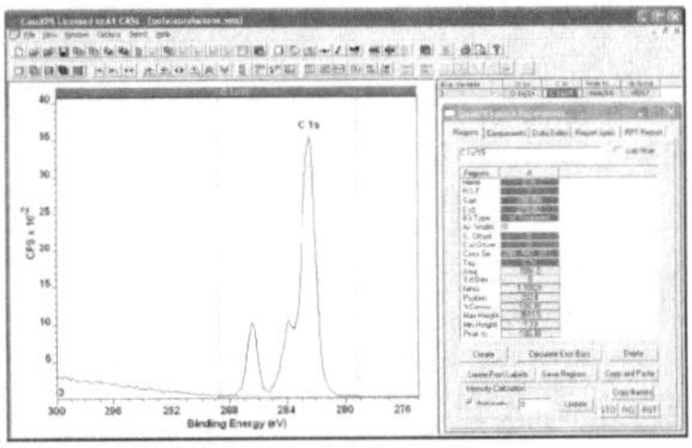

3

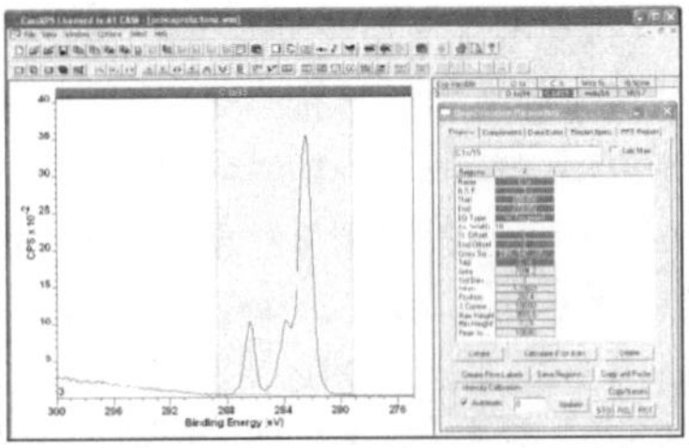

4

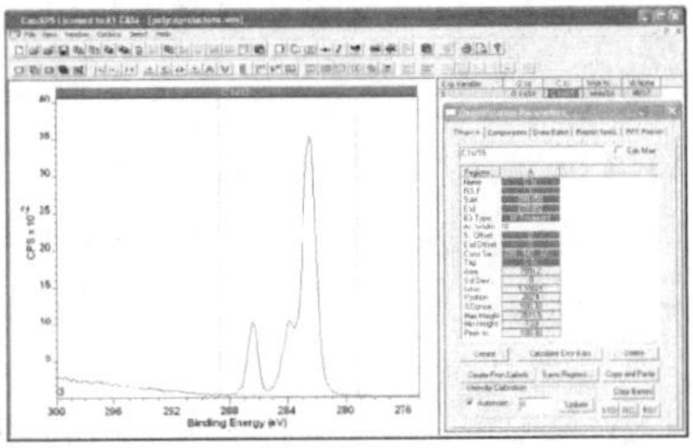

Note that the name field from regions is an alternative route to labelling peaks than using the Peak Label property page on the Annotation dialog window. If more than one label appears displayed over the data associated with a peak, the most likely explanation is the region label from the name field and peak label annotation are being displayed at the same time. The solution is to use the toolbar button to remove the region label from the display.

The primary function of a region is to measure the intensity and therefore the amount of material for an element within the surface of a sample. Peak area simply measured from the spectra is proportional to the amount of substance in the surface, however to quantify a sample in terms of atomic or mass concentration a scaling factor relating the raw peak area to the amount of substance must be supplied. These scaling factors are called relative sensitivity factors and are entered for each region defined on the data.

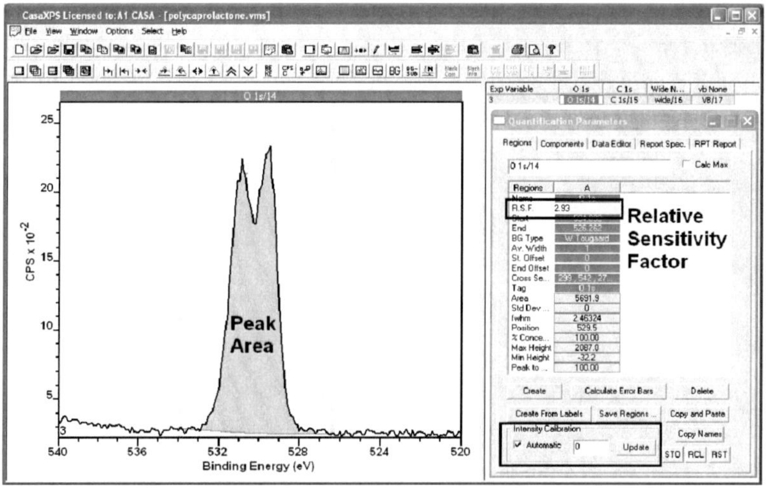

In addition to the relative sensitivity factors, a further adjustment is usually made to the peak area calculated from the raw data to account for instrumental response as a function of kinetic energy of the electrons ejected from the surface. By default these instrumental corrections are automatically applied to the peak area calculated from the data. Data can be quantified with and without these instrumental corrections by un-ticking the Automatic tick-box on the Regions property page and pressing the Update button. If a transmission function is detected in the VAMAS file, the Automatic tick-box will initially be enabled.

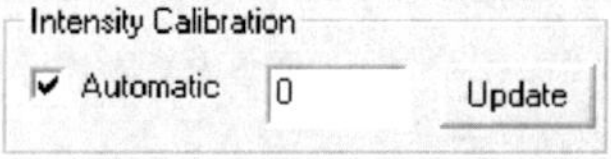

The text-field also included in the Intensity Calibration section corresponds to the KE correction described on the Intensity Calib property page of the Spectrum Processing dialog window. Note, the use of the Intensity Calib property page and the Intensity Calibration section of the Regions property page to correct for transmission could cause the correction to be applied in error twice. The normal method for correcting peak area for transmission is that used by the Region property page, hence it is the default method used without requiring user intervention.

Background Parameters

Potentially up to seven parameter fields determine the background approximation used to remove background signal from resonance peaks. The detail of the many background types are described elsewhere. For the majority of background types, entered via the BG Type field, the extent over which the approximation is applied is limited to an energy interval defined by the Start and End region parameters.

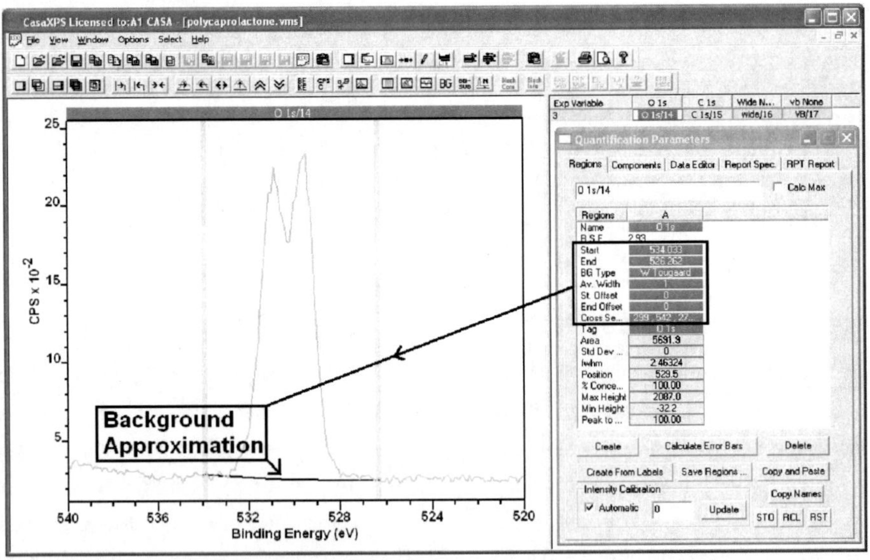

With the Region property page top-most on the Quantification Parameters dialog window, a pair of vertical lines drawn in the active tile indicates the energy for the Start and End parameters. If a mouse drag-action is initiated with the cursor close to either of these vertical lines, the values for the Start and/or End energy are modified under mouse control.

A list of background types is offered in a dialog window invoked by placing the cursor over the current value for the BG Type in a region, holding the Control keyboard key down before left-click the mouse. The dialog appears provided the BG Type field is not already in edit mode. If the BG Type field is already the focus for the key board, indicated by the text cursor, simply selecting a different field returns the BG Type field to a state in which the dialog window can be invoked.

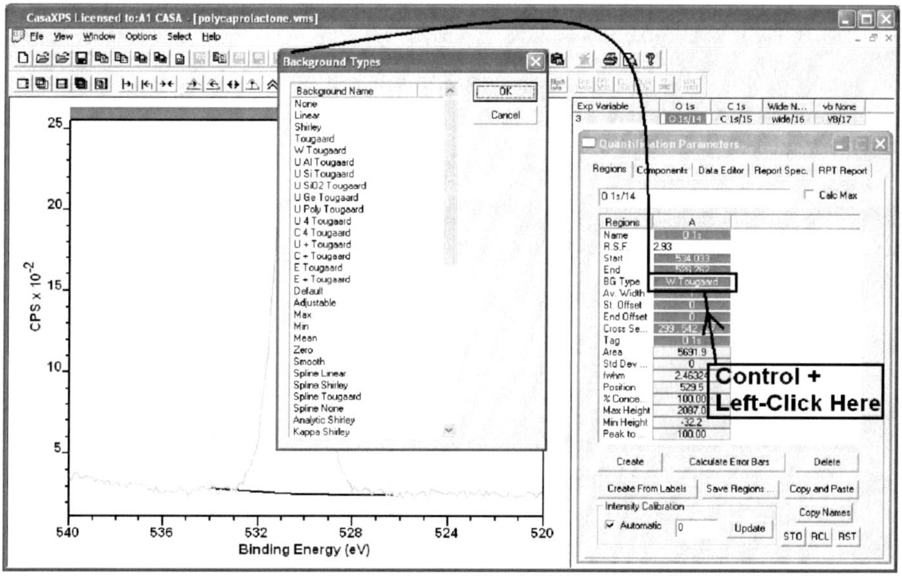

While a wide range of background algorithms are possible, the most commonly used background types can be entered simply using the first character from the background type name and pressing return. Entering l for linear or s for Shirley or t for Tougaard before pressing the Enter keyboard key is sufficient to change the BG Type field.

Av Width Field

The greatest source for precision errors when quantifying peak intensities is the definition of the intensity at which the approximation to the background meets the spectral data. This statement applies equally to both intensities measured via quantification regions or synthetic components. The source of the error lies in the stability of the background algorithm with respect to noise in the data. To reduce the influence of noise on these calculations, the Regions property page allows the specification of a, so called, average width which is labelled Av. Width and is defined as an integer value representing the number of data channels either side of the data channel defined by the start and end energy parameters. Prior to version 2.3.15, the only method used to compute the intensity of the background at these energy limits was a mean average of these data channels defined via the Av. Width parameter. While appropriate for some circumstances, there are situations where simply averaging the data in the mean sense causes a poorly defined background and therefore an alternative method for calculating the intensity of the background at these energy limits is offered in version 2.3.15. The new method for calculating the background intensity at the region limits is based on polynomial least squares fitting to the data channels defined by the Av. Width parameter.

The nature of the problem addressed by the new option is illustrated below, where three different backgrounds are defined for the same data.

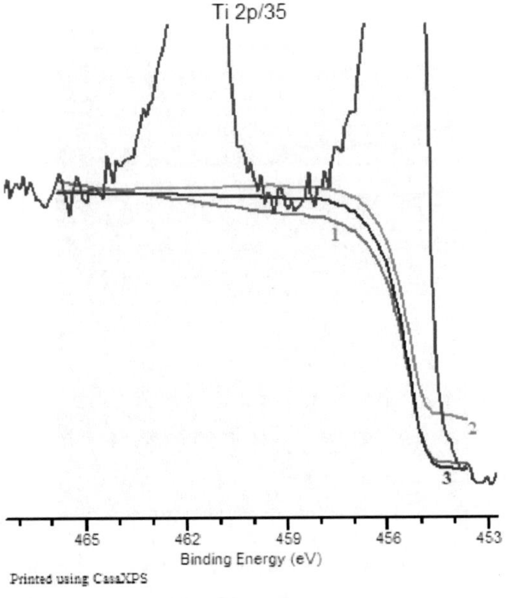

The background labelled 1 represents a pair of backgrounds, one linear and the other Shirley, where the Av Width is set to zero in both regions. That is, the background limits are defined by a single data channel. Obviously, the choice of the single data channels strongly influence the linear background beneath the Ti $2p_{1/2}$ peak and also the Shirley background defined for the Ti $2p_{3/2}$ peak. For a single spectrum, these data channels could be adjusted by eye, but if the data set includes many Ti 2p spectra the task of individually assigning the background limits is both time consuming and also introduces bias into the analysis. It is therefore better to introduce an averaging over several data channels which in principle provides a more representative intensity for the background limits. The background labelled 2 is calculated using 25 data channels in a mean average sense to compute the background intensity limits (Av Width = 12, i.e. 25 = 2*12+1). The number of data channels used in the average may seem extreme, however for noisy data a large number of channels may be required and also, due to the large number of data channels, the resulting background illustrates a problem caused by averaging when the peak intensities are included in the mean average. The right-hand-end of the background labelled 2 is raised above what might be considered appropriate for the data. This occurs because the point at which the background should commence is at odds with the number of data channels used in the mean average. While clearly visible as a problem at the right-hand-end of the regions, the issue is also present in the valley between the two data peaks, where it can be difficult to both position the background limit and also find an appropriate number for the Av Width to eliminate the noise influence. It is precisely for these reasons that situations arise where the mean average needs to be replaced with an average intensity based on a polynomial fit.

The background labelled 3 above is identical in definition to the background labelled 2, with the exception that a polynomial is used to fit the 25 data channels at the region limits. The nature of the polynomial based background limits causes the computed backgrounds to be more stable than the single data channel background and also prevents the sides of the peaks deforming the background resulting from a simple mean average. As with all numerical algorithms, there are circumstances where the polynomial approximation can fail too, but in general the polynomial method provides a solution for situations where a mean average is inappropriate.

The Regions property page illustrates the means of indicating the polynomial method is active; that is, the Av Width parameters are displayed with a different background colour.

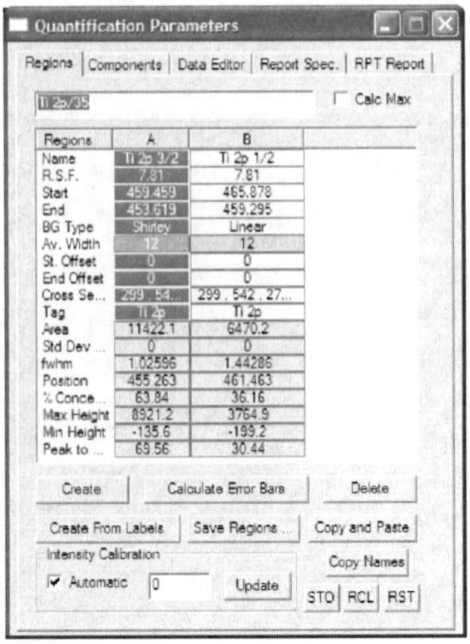

The colour is only displayed for those regions for which the polynomial method is active and can be switched on and off by using the Control-Key as follows. While the Av Width parameter is not an edit field, hold the Control-Key down then left-click the mouse over the Av Width parameter value. A dialog window will appear offering to switch between the methods for calculating the background intensity at the region limits.

The default mode used to calculate the background intensity region limits is that of a mean average. To change the default behaviour to that of fitting a polynomial to the Av Width data channels, an entry must be added to the CasaXPS.DEF/ParameterFile.txt configuration file. To enable polynomial fitting, add the line:

```
av width fit
```

to the ParameterFile.txt file located in the CasaXPS.DEF directory, which in turn is located with the CasaXPS.exe executable file.

It is also possible to configure the default number value for the Av Width parameter. The line:

```
bg average width = <value>
```

must be added to the ParameterFile.txt file, where <value> is a positive integer.

Start Offset/End Offset Parameters

Background algorithms typically are required to approach the intensity of the spectral data at the limits of the region energy interval. The Av Width parameter provides options for altering the definition of the spectral intensity by averaging data channels to determine the appropriate intensity for the background at the region limits. Regardless of the computed intensity for the spectrum at a region's limits, the two offset parameters provide a further means of adjusting the background intensity for these two energies. The Start and End Offset parameters are a percentage reduction in the background intensity from the value calculated for a zero offset percentage.

The Start and End Offset limits are useful when defining backgrounds for data with some defect.

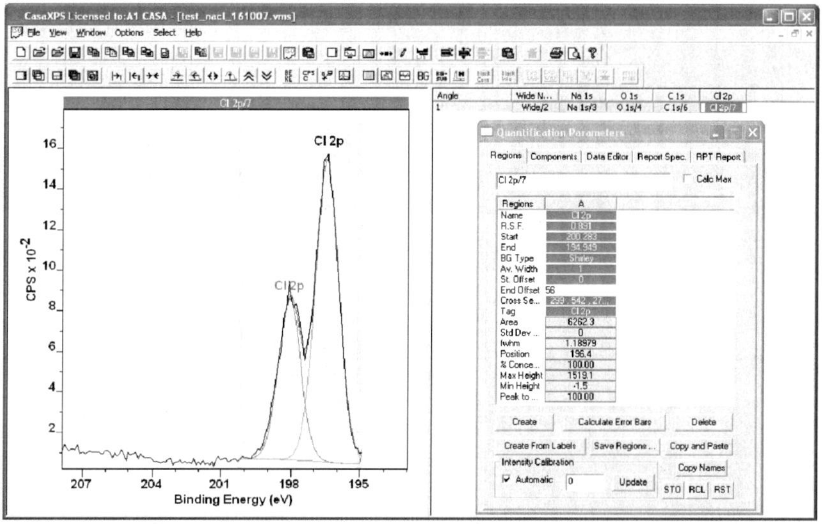

The data for the Cl 2p doublet is incomplete so a background intensity based on the last data channel would be incorrect; however offsetting the intensity for the background at the right-hand end of the region permits a meaningful peak model to be defined. The offset is selected in the case of the Cl 2p data to produce the expected 2:1 ratio for the intensities of the synthetic doublet 2p peaks.

Cross Section Field

Four numerical parameters are offered by the Cross-section parameter field. The name cross-section relates to the use of these four parameters with various

Tougaard background energy loss cross-sections. The meaning of these four parameters depends on the type of background specified via the BG Type field. Some of these meanings for the cross-section parameters are discussed in the following section.

TAG Field

The TAG is an alternative string with which a region can be identified. An equivalent field appears in the parameter list for components and these two parameters fields, one for a region and one for a component serve as a means of linking components to regions for quantification purposes. The TAG strings when assigned keywords alter the information extracted from a region by the Custom report on the Report Spec property page. See the section on the Report Spec property page for more details on the subject of keywords and TAG strings. The subject of quantification using TAG strings is also dealt with in detailed discussions elsewhere in the CasaXPS manual.

STO, RCL and RST Buttons

Constructing a peak model for a data envelope is typically a sequence of trial and error steps guided be a combination of physics, known chemistry about the sample and experience. Forcing a set of synthetic components to obey rules of this nature requires the use of constraints, typically built in response to feedback from the optimisation step. To assist the development of peak models three buttons have been a added to both the Regions and Components property pages of the Quantification Parameters dialog window, namely STO, RCL and RST.

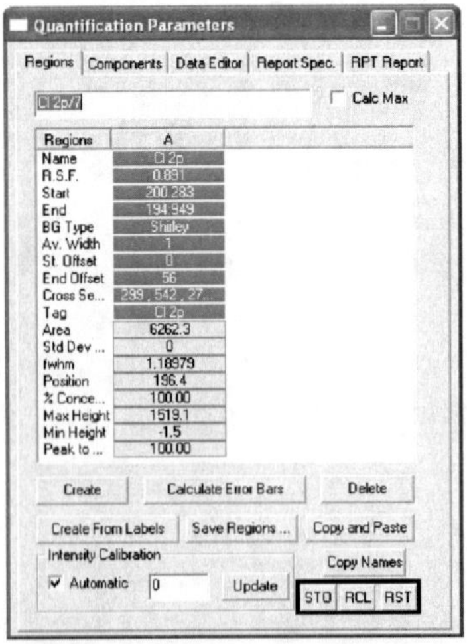

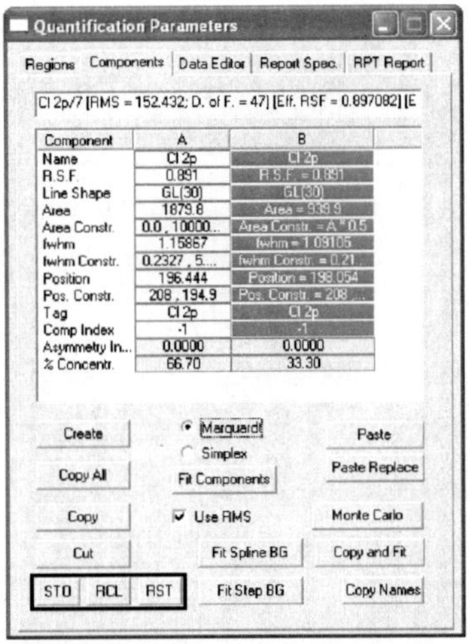

The function of these buttons is to allow the current state of a peak model to be entered onto a list of peak models using the STO or Store button, then if necessary, recalled to the current model using the RCL or Recall button. The RST or Reset button allows the list of peak models to be reduced to the current peak model defined by the Region and Component property page tables.

Each time the Fit Components button is pressed on the Components property page a new entry is added to the list of peak models, which includes both the synthetic components and the current set of regions defined on the VAMAS block. A separate list is maintained for each individual VAMAS block for the duration of the VAMAS file whilst being processed within CasaXPS. That is, the list of peak models is not saved to file, but acts as a support during the creation of the final form for the peak model.

Transferring Regions within a VAMAS File

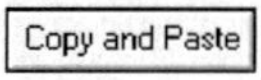

A common desire is to prepare a set of regions on one spectrum before transferring the regions to selected spectra for which the regions are equally appropriate. The propagation mechanism permits regions and components to be propagated within a file or from one file to many other files containing suitable data. There are however occasions where visual inspection of the data helps guide the development of an analysis for a single experiment involving multiple acquisitions. Movement of regions based on the contents of display tiles supplements the global propagate options to allow a set of display tiles to specify the data from which spectrum the regions are defined and to which spectra the regions are transferred.

By way of example, consider the following file containing a depth profile experiment. The data are collected from a multilayer sample where the layers alternate between silicon oxide and titanium oxide, thus the O 1s peak shifts in energy according to the layer structure as a function of etch time. Positioning a region for the O 1s peak therefore depends on the etch time and the state of the ion gun etch crater. As a result, it may be deemed best to position the region limits appropriately to the O 1s peaks via a visual inspection of the data.

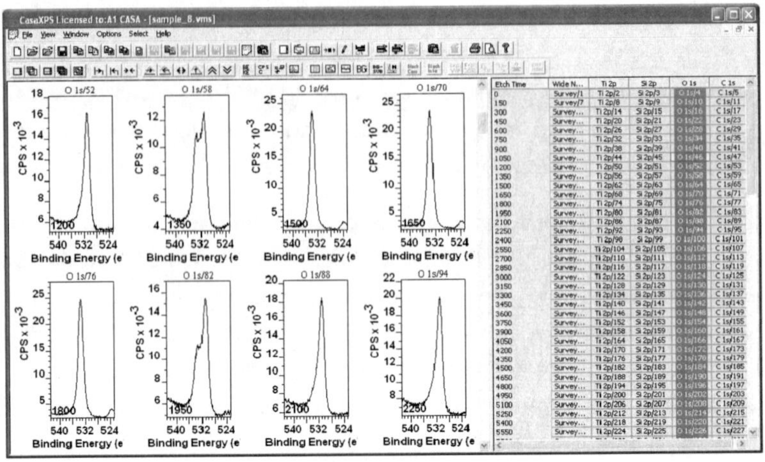

A region defined appropriately for the SiO_2 O 1s peak provides an adequate definition for data measured from depths where titanium is not a significant component in the spectra. However the same region prepared based on the data with block identifier O 1s/70 at etch time 1650 when propagated to all O 1s spectra fails to define reasonable backgrounds for data other than SiO_2 surfaces.

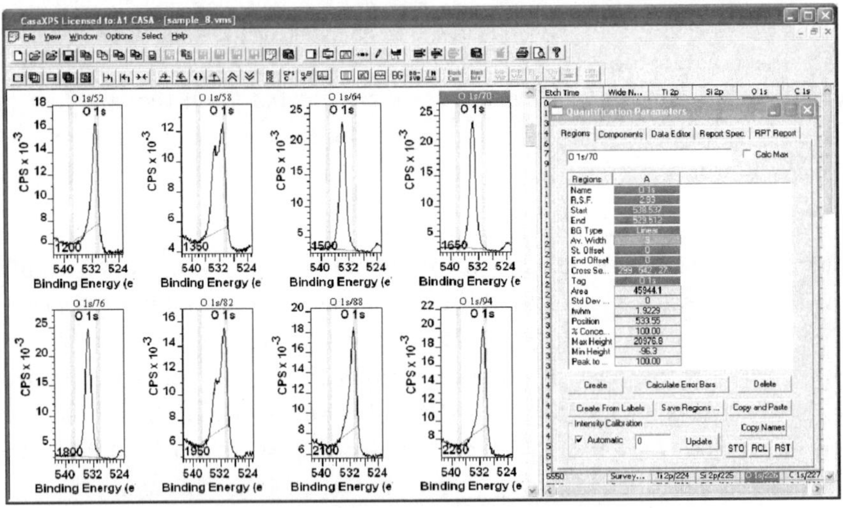

The set of O 1s spectra will need partitioning into spectra with and without the influence of titanium. Selecting the SiO_2 layers requires visual inspection. The selection in the right-hand pane can be developed by adding to the current selection using the Control keyboard key and left-clicking the mouse with the cursor over a tile in the left-hand pane.

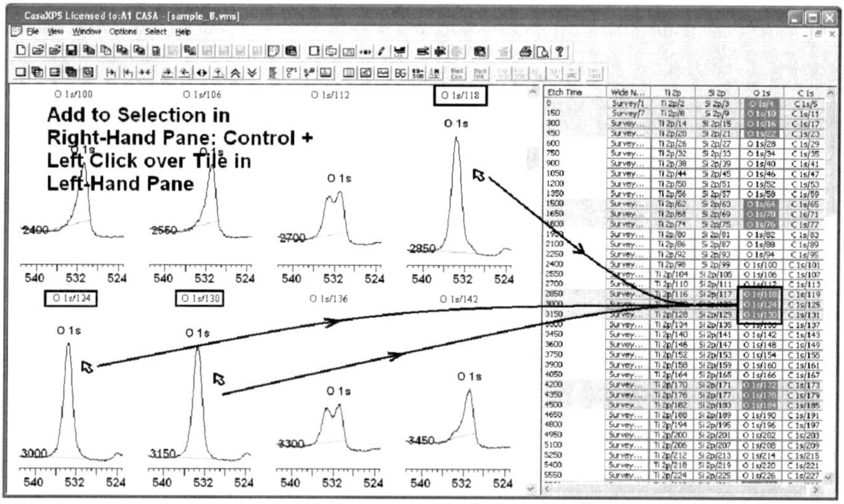

Once the O 1s spectra corresponding to the SiO_2 layers are selected in the right-hand pane, a pair of display tiles can be used to maintain two sets of mutually exclusive set of spectra either belonging to the set of SiO_2 layers or belonging to the complementary set of spectra. A display in which two tiles displaying overlay plots for two sets of spectra provide more than a visual perspective for these data, but also maintain a record for the data blocks used to create the overlay plots. The state of the display is saved to a temporary buffer via the Options menu. At a later time the display state can be recovered via the Restore Tile Format option on the same menu.

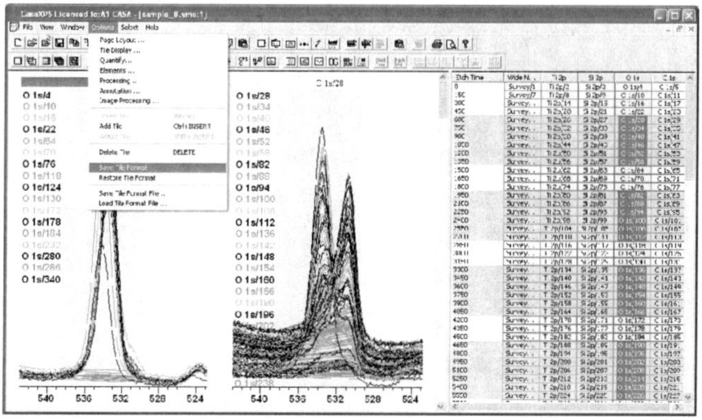

The VAMAS file is now prepared for use with the Copy and Paste button on the Regions property page.

The Copy and Paste button copies regions defined on the spectrum in the active tile to spectra displayed in the left-hand pane scrolled list of display tiles. To adjust the set of regions defined on the O 1s spectra containing a titanium component involves:

1. Display the O 1s spectrum one per tile in the left-hand pane.

To display the spectra corresponding to a collection already overlaid in a tile requires the selection in the right-hand pane to reflect the select used to create the tile of overlaid spectra. Returning the right-hand pane to a previous state is achieved by first deselecting all the VAMAS blocks in the right-hand pane before placing the cursor over the tile displaying the spectra and holding down the Control keyboard key left-clicking the mouse.

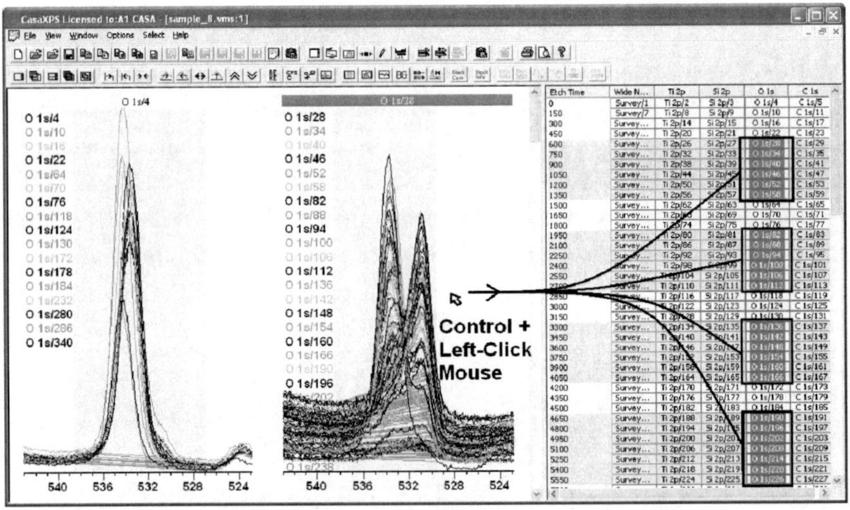

Having re-established the selection in the right-hand pane to only include the O 1s containing a mixture of chemical states, the data are displayed one per tile by pressing the Display toolbar button.

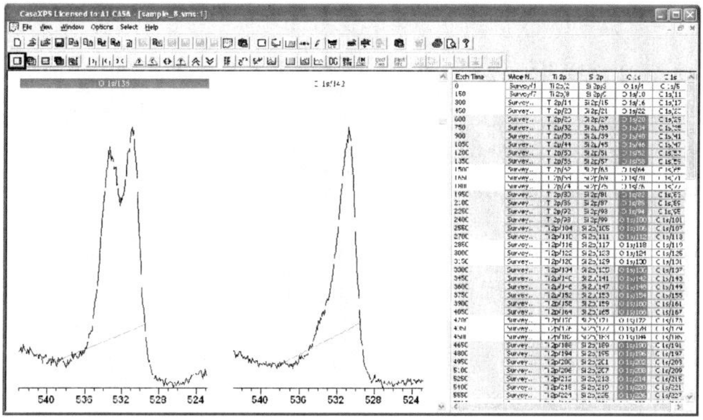

2. Adjust the region on one of the tiles as appropriate and press the Copy and Paste button.

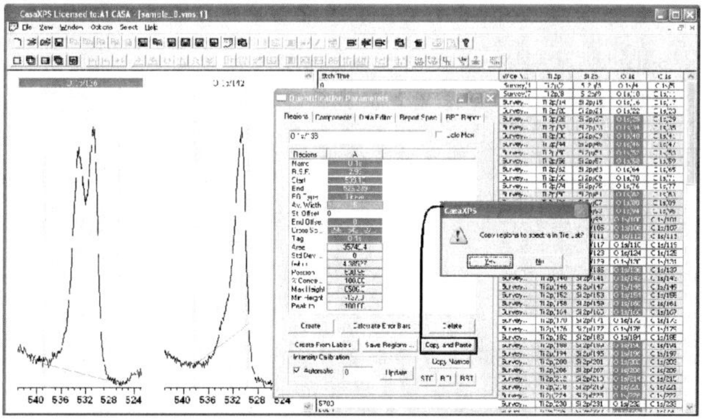

3. A dialog window requests confirmation for the transfer of the regions to the data in the display list. To proceed, press the Yes button on the dialog window then scroll through the data in the left-hand pane to verify the results visually.

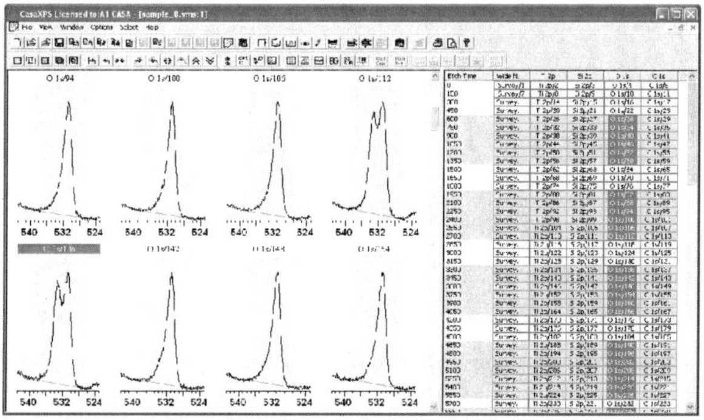

The Copy and Paste button on the Regions property page only transfers region information. Components defined on the target spectra are left unaffected. Specifically, not fitting is performed as part of the Copy and Paste operation. An equivalent button on the Components property page provides a means of transferring and fitting components using the same source and target definition.

In conclusion, the difference between the propagate mechanism using the Browser Operations dialog window and the Copy and Paste button on the Regions property page lies in the method used to specify the source and target VAMAS blocks. The Copy and Paste button uses the active VAMAS block as the source for the regions while the set of tiles displayed in the left-hand pane defines the set of target VAMAS blocks.

The name field appears in the final report generated from region information. Ideally the name used for a region would be specified at the time of creation, but there are times when the name used for a region needs to be changed. While the name could be changed in a region before propagating the region to other spectra, if the region limits have been carefully designed, propagating a single region may undo work previously done in positioning regions appropriately for the peak structures. The above example using a multilayer sample and O 1s peaks is a case in point. The regions are prepared based on two subsets of O 1s spectra and simply propagating a region to all would negate the previous preparation for the regions. The Copy Name button offers a means of propagating the region name field only. All other fields are left unaltered by the operation. The source for the Copy Name button is the VAMAS block in the active tile.

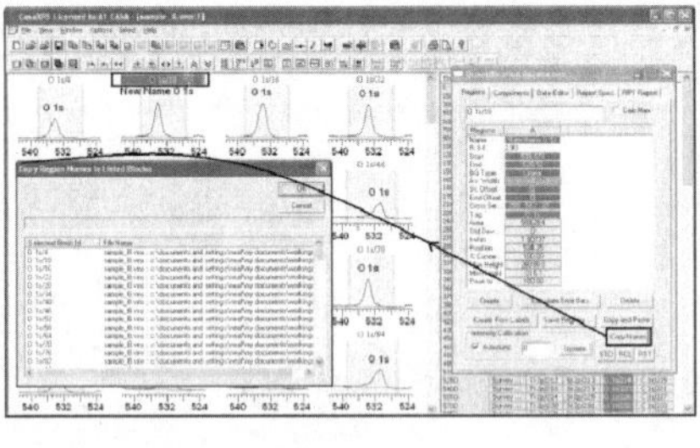

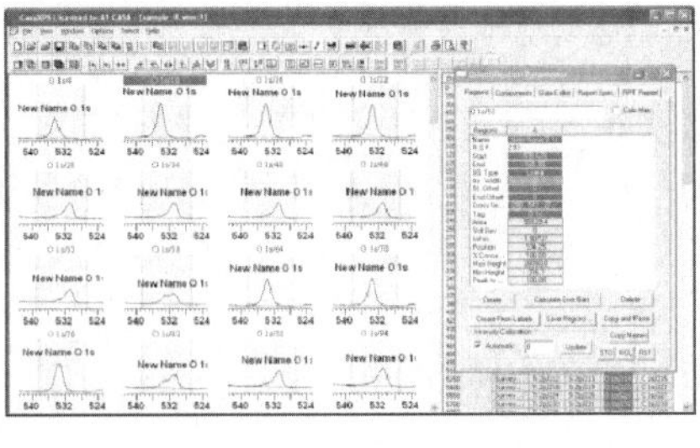

Outputs from a Region

One of the primary reasons for defining regions is to condense the information in spectra into succinct tables of characteristic values so data from different samples can be compared. The outputs from a region include the peak area, the peak position and the FWHM. These are all included in the region table on the Regions property page. The regions table also offers a row for the atomic concentration, however the percentage atomic concentration only makes sense for survey spectra where sufficient regions are defined to characterise the elemental composition.

The peak position for a region is by default measured from the data channel with maximum intensity in the region. A tick box labelled Calc Max modifies the peak position calculation which when ticked causes the peak position to be calculated from the maximum of a quadratic polynomial approximating the peak top.

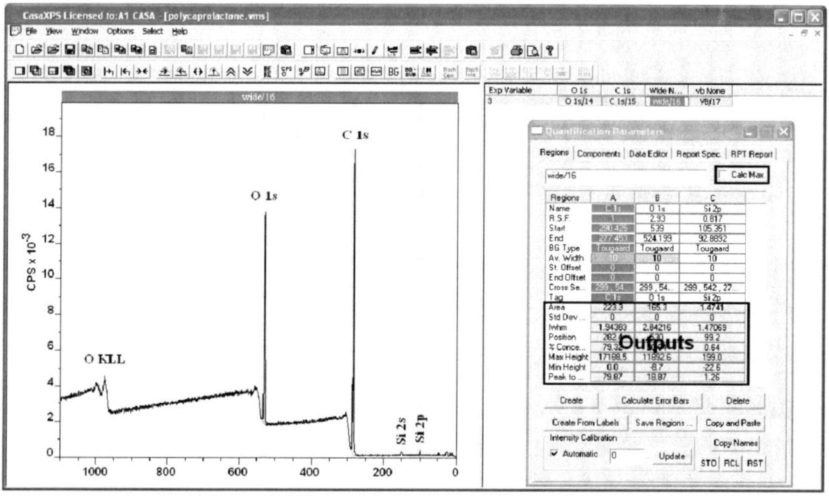

Background Types

Tougaard Backgrounds

The synthetic line-shapes are very dependent on the availability of background subtraction algorithms to complement their use. If a background is incorrectly removed from a spectrum then the merit of attempting to model the result with theoretically correct synthetic line-shape is less clear.

Tougaard and co-workers have devoted much time to understanding the backgrounds in XPS spectra. The transport of electrons through a material after excitation by x-rays can be described by equations involving a one-sided convolution of the recorded data with an energy-loss probability distribution. This loss function offers a prescription by which electrons leaving the sample with an initial energy may have their characteristic energy altered by the interactions with the surface. Each material has a characteristic loss function of varying complexity and Tougaard has written many papers describing methods for establishing both generally applicable approximations (so called, universal cross-sections) and specific forms for individual materials.

The principal methods used by Tougaard for calculating the loss functions are theoretical dielectric response models and empirical estimates computed from spectra acquired using reflected energy-loss spectroscopy (REELS). Tougaard follows these calculations by fitting the results to a rational function which models the resonance structure in the calculated loss-functions and allows the essential distribution to be described by a simple formula. These loss-functions are defined in terms of four parameters, three of which describe the shape of the rational function and one to allow for various band gaps in different materials. Tougaard refers to the distribution below as a three-parameter universal cross-section and has established values for a number of materials including aluminium, silicon, silicon dioxide and others. The form of this universal cross-section is

$$U(T\colon B, C, D, T_0) = \begin{cases} \frac{BT}{(C-T^2)^2+DT^2} & T > T_0 \\ 0 & T \leq T_0 \end{cases} \quad (1)$$

A set of backgrounds specified by Tougaard are implemented in CasaXPS:

U Ge Tougaard short form U Ge: Three-parameter cross-section determined for germanium.

U Si Tougaard short form U Si: Three-parameter cross-section determined for silicon.

U SiO2 Tougaard short form U SiO2: Three-parameter cross-section determined for silicon dioxide.

U Al Tougaard short form U Al : Three-parameter cross-section determined for aluminium.

U Poly Tougaard short form U Poly: Three-parameter cross-section determined for polymers.

U 4 Tougaard short form U 4: Custom three-parameter cross-section where the parameters are entered on the Regions property page in the Cross Section text-field. The four numerical values entered in a comma separated list correspond to B, C, D and T_0 in the energy-loss function above.

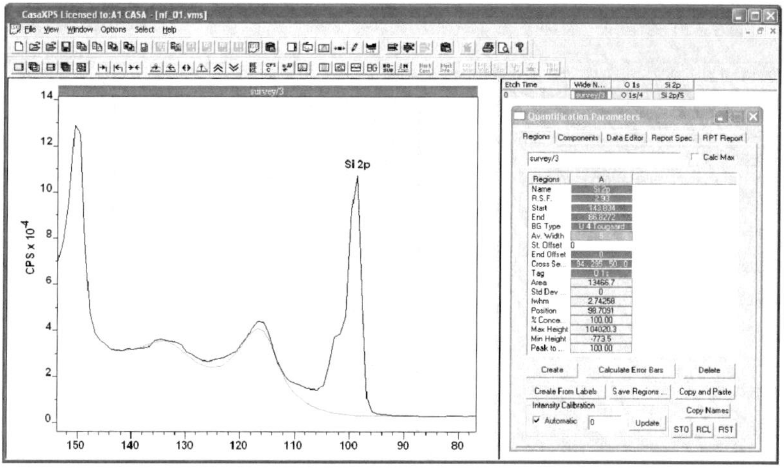

C 4 Tougaard short form C 4: Alternative custom three-parameter cross-section where the parameters are entered on the Regions property page in the Cross Section text-field. The four numerical values have the same meaning as those found in the U 4 Tougaard form; however T_0 is used to shift the resonance structure rather than simple acting as a cut-off limit. It is therefore possible to retain the shape of the distribution but move the position of the maximum without changing the C and D parameters.

Adjusting the Three-Parameter Universal Cross-Section

The rational function for the three-parameter cross-section is defined in terms of three constants B, C and D. This approximation is the quotient of a linear polynomial and a quartic polynomial; however the denominator determines the position and strength of the resonance in the cross-section. The parameters C and D both determine the position, width and height of the resonance, but to a first order (small D) the position is influenced by the square root of C and the sharpness of the cross-section is determined by the size of D.

C Value Background Type and the Universal Cross Section

A Tougaard background calculation using a universal cross-section is defined as follows:

$$F(E) = J(E) - \int_{E}^{E_{max}} J(E')U(E' - E{:}B,C,D)dE' \quad (2)$$

Where *F(E)* is the background subtracted spectrum, *J(E)* is the measured spectrum and *U* is the universal cross-section in Equation (1) defined in terms of the parameters B, C and D. The integral in Equation (2) states mathematically the way the measured spectrum *J(E)* is combined with the loss function *U* via an integral to establish the background shape. The background shape is scaled by the parameter *B* so that the background and measured spectrum match at some point below a peak in the data. For a given spectrum *J(E)*, the size of *B* will depend on the intensity of the peak under consideration and also the background loss structure in the measured spectrum.

When the objective is to calculate the background to the measured spectrum, the interplay between the peak intensity above background and the *B* parameter is not so important. However, the C Value background type attempts to provide parameters which, in some sense, characterise the samples in question and therefore the calculation of the background to a spectrum is broken down in to steps for which the *B* parameter is made independent of the measured peak intensity. Rather than calculating the background shape using *J(E)*, a synthetic lineshape is defined, *P(E)*, and associated with a cross-section defined using Equation (1). The equation for the background becomes:

$$L(E) = c_0 Y_0(E) + c_1 Y_1(E) + c_2 Y_2(E) \qquad (3)$$

$$Y_0(E) = \int_E^{E_{max}} \hat{P}(E') \hat{U}(E' - E{:}\, 1, C, D) dE' \qquad (4)$$

For *i = 0,1,...*

$$Y_{i+1}(E) = \int_E^{E_{max}} Y_i(E') \hat{U}(E' - E{:}\, 1, C, D) dE' \qquad (5)$$

Where $\hat{P}(E')$ and $\hat{U}(T{:}\, 1, C, D)$ are normalised forms of *P* and *U* above. The coefficients c_0, c_1 and c_2 are determined in the least-squares sense such that *L(E)* matches the spectral data. By adopting these heuristics, the *B* parameter when set equal to c_0 can be viewed as an approximation to the intensity of the photoelectric peak required to generate the observed background.

C Value Background Type uses a slightly different form to the Tougaard universal cross-section:

$$U_c(T{:}\, B, C, D, T_0) = \begin{cases} \frac{B(T-T_0)}{(C-(T-T_0)^2)^2 + D(T-T_0)^2} & T > T_0 \\ 0 & T \le T_0 \end{cases} \qquad (6)$$

The T_0 parameter shifts the functional form so the shape for the Tougaard loss-structure can be moved by specifying different T_0 values without the need to alter the C and D parameters.

A C Value background type is constructed for a spectrum using three of the four parameters in the cross-section field for a region.

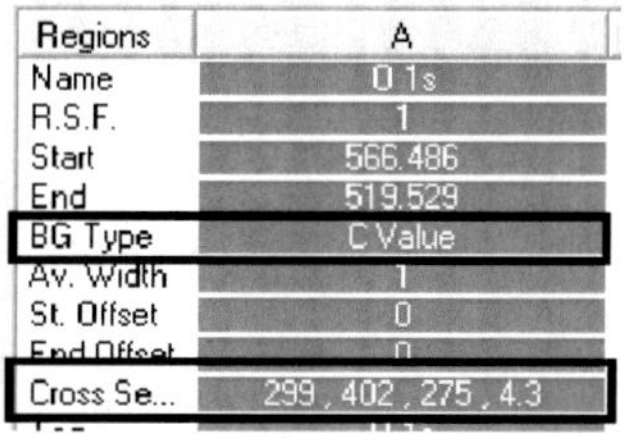

The cross-section parameters above are prepared for an O 1s peak measured from a sample consisting of a thin film of SiO_2 on Si.

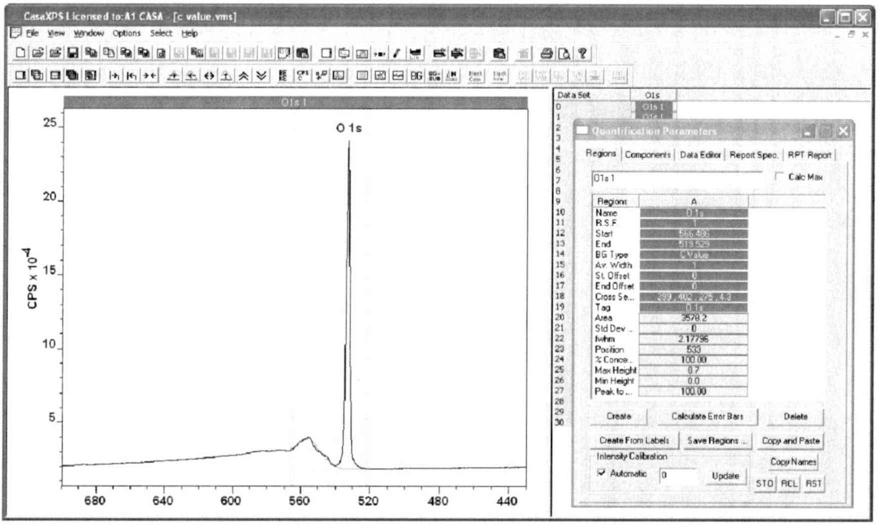

While the C Value background visually approximates the loss-structure, the difference between the C Value background type and other backgrounds is the output parameter values. The Area output field provides an estimate for the intensity of the one-loss peak, while the Max Height output field displays the ratio of the one-loss peak intensity to the zero-loss peak intensity. The ratio of the one-loss peak intensity to the zero loss peak intensity is a measure for the scattering of the electrons at the surface and can be used to compare samples for similarity in structure. For example, a set of O 1s data measured from samples of SiO_2 thin films on Si (C. van der Marel, Philips Research Laboratories, Eindhoven, NL) result in the following characteristic values for the ratio offered in the Max Height field.

Ratio of One-Loss to Zero-Loss Peak Intensity	Film Thickness (nm)
0.541564	2
0.583905	3
0.715352	4
0.76064	4.5
0.795741	5
0.919354	8
0.724685	4
0.834605	6
0.876449	7

Assuming an exponential attenuation in intensity for electrons emitted from a thin film, the following relationships apply for the zero loss intensity I_0 and the one-loss intensity I_1

$$\frac{I_0}{I_0^\infty} = \left(1 - e^{-\frac{p}{a}}\right) \qquad (7)$$

$$\frac{I_1}{I_1^\infty} = \left(1 - e^{-\frac{p}{a}}\right)^2 \qquad (8)$$

Thus

$$\frac{I_1}{I_0}\frac{I_0^\infty}{I_1^\infty} = \left(1 - e^{-\frac{p}{a}}\right) \qquad (9)$$

Where p is the distance travelled by the electrons within the surface.

Plotting the SiO_2 data in terms of film thickness against $-\ln\left(1 - \frac{I_1}{I_0}\frac{I_0^\infty}{I_1^\infty}\right)$ demonstrates a correlation between film thickness and the information from the C Value background type.

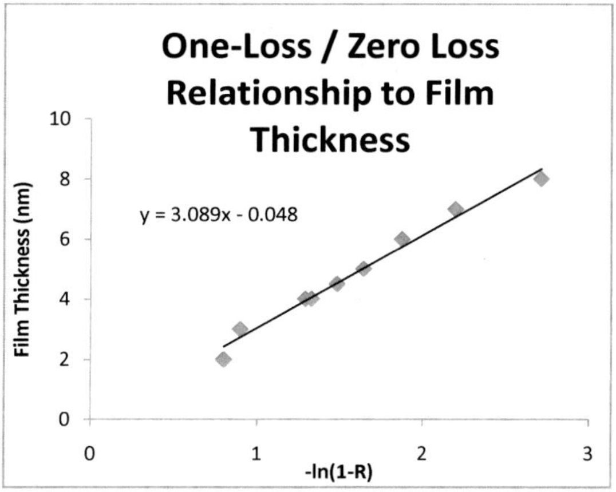

The significance of using an intensity ratio to monitor film thickness relates to XPS imaging. The intensity for a peak as a function of position varies due to instrumental factors. One approach to removing these instrumental factors is to quantify the surface by measuring intensities for each element in the surface. For imaging data, acquiring a complete set of transitions for a surface required to perform the quantification calculation is potentially very time consuming. Using the background for a single peak offers an alternative measurement regime less time consuming yet also capable of accounting for signal variations across an image due to instrumental factors.

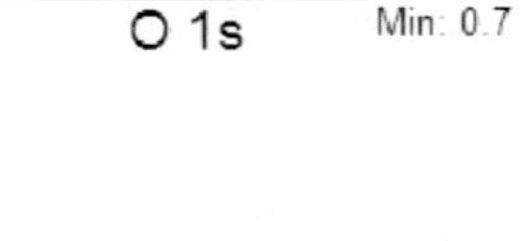

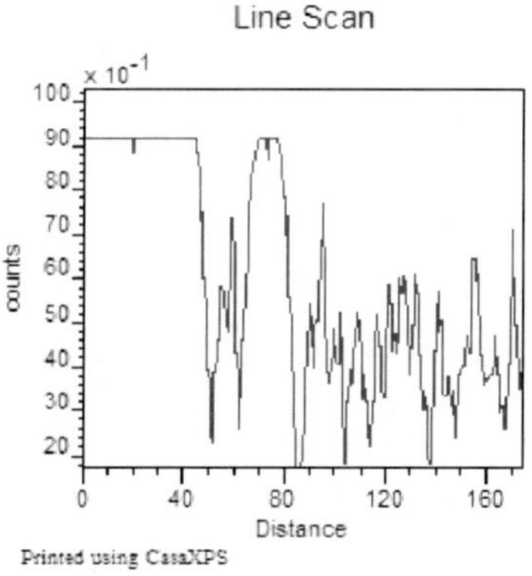

The background to the photoelectric peak indicates the proximity of the material to the surface. A rapidly rising background following a peak indicates electrons from the same transition are scattered to a greater extent than a peak for which the background rises then falls rapidly. The amount of scattering is an indicator of the depths from which the electrons are emitted. These qualitative statements are transformed into semi-quantitative values through the C Value background. Consider a homogenous silicon dioxide sample:

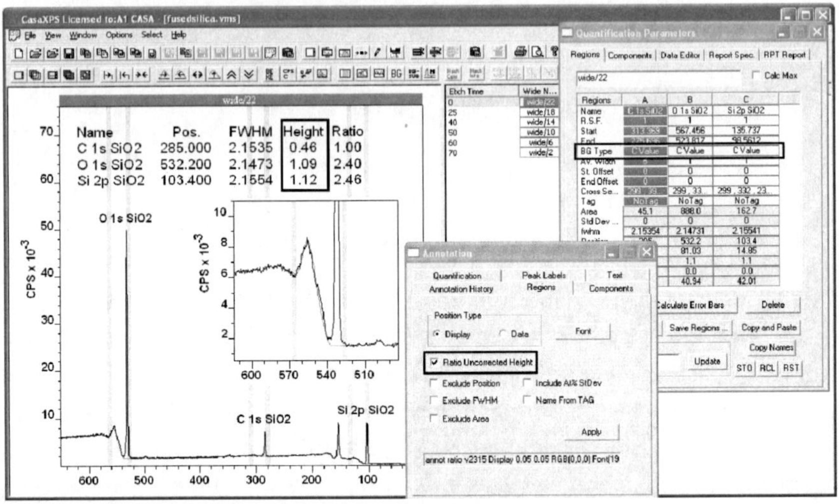

The ratio of the one-loss to the zero-loss intensities are reported in the Max Height region output fields. These can be added to the display as annotation using the Regions property page on the Annotation dialog window. Ticking the tick-box labelled Ratio Uncorrected Heights causes the region table to include the Height output. The column headed Ratio is literally the ratio of the height values relative to the first region displayed in the table and should be ignored for results from the C Value background. The significance of the Height column in the annotation table is the O 1s and Si 2p background intensity relative to the zero-loss peak is of similar size and close to unity. The equivalent value for the C 1s background and peak is about half the corresponding values for the O 1s and Si 2p. The implication is therefore the carbon is at the surface above the SiO_2 material and represents a thin film of contamination.

A similar analysis of a survey spectrum for a more complex sample provides evidence for sample structure.

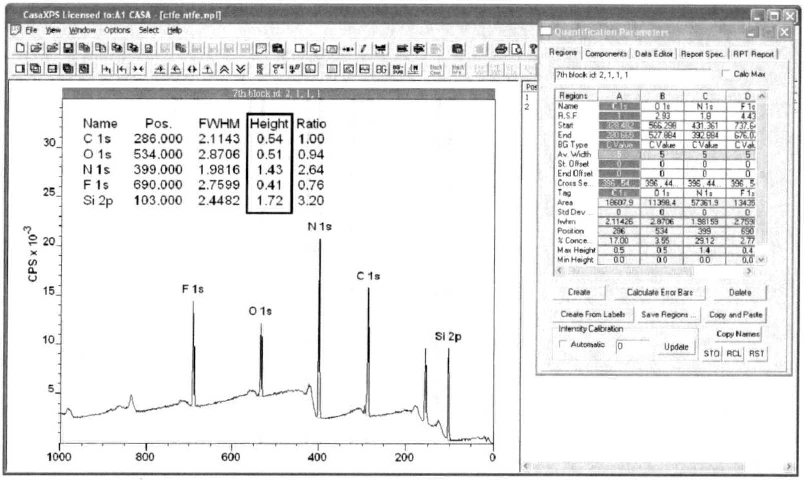

The region table over the survey spectrum supports carbon, oxygen and fluorine all appearing as a thin film over silicon and nitrogen. The one-loss to zero-loss values suggest more scattering for electron energies characteristic of N 1s and Si 2p than for the carbon, oxygen or fluorine. Visual inspection of the survey spectrum would also support these conclusions as the loss structures for the three elements with ratios of about 0.5 are short lived in intensity, while the N 1s and Si 2p loss structures influence a far wider range of energies.

Converting qualitative assessments about survey spectra to quantitative values is a key step in developing expert systems.

The key to successfully characterising a background using the C Value background type is determining an appropriate Tougaard loss-function. Since the algorithm for calculating the background involves a linear least squares solution for Equation (3), an inappropriate loss-function may produce badly fitted background shapes and therefore meaningless one-loss intensities.

Spline Backgrounds

Spline backgrounds offer a flexible tool for constructing backgrounds to data for which the commonly used background type fail. Creating a background based on a cubic spline is essentially an interactive operation and as such represents a custom solution for a particular piece of data. While not recommended for normal XPS data, circumstances occasionally dictate that any solution is better than no solution, hence the spline background is offered as a last resort rather than a first.

Constructing a spline background involves the cross-section field on the Regions property page together with the Start and End Offset fields, providing a total of six knots per region. From a user's perspective, the spline knots are adjustable parameters equally spaced across the energy interval permitting the construction of a smooth curve representing the background shape. There are three spline background types: spline linear, spline Shirley and spline Tougaard. The only difference between these background types is the initial shape for the background. On creation the initial shape approximated by the spline function is either a linear, Shirley or Tougaard background shape. The follow illustrates the step for creating a spline linear background.

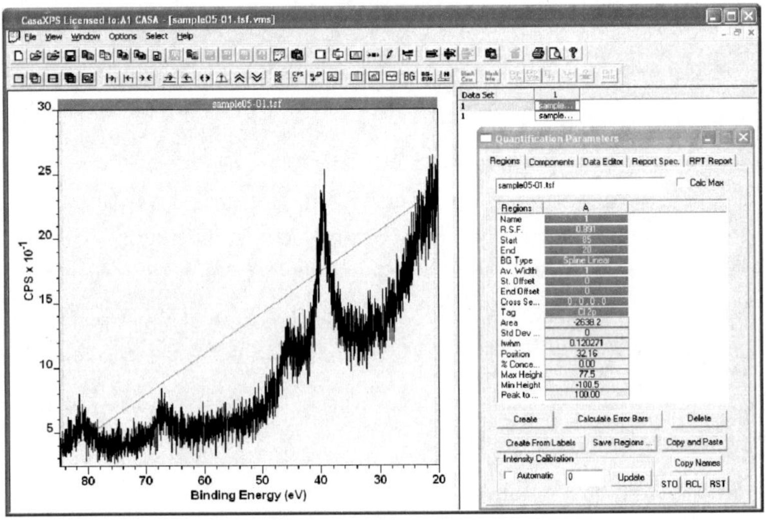

On pressing the create button on the Regions property page a region is created for the data in the active tile. The BG Type may be specified by entering the characters sl before pressing the Enter keyboard key. The BG Type field is updated with the strings Spline Linear and a dialog window offers the option to update the spline parameter fields.

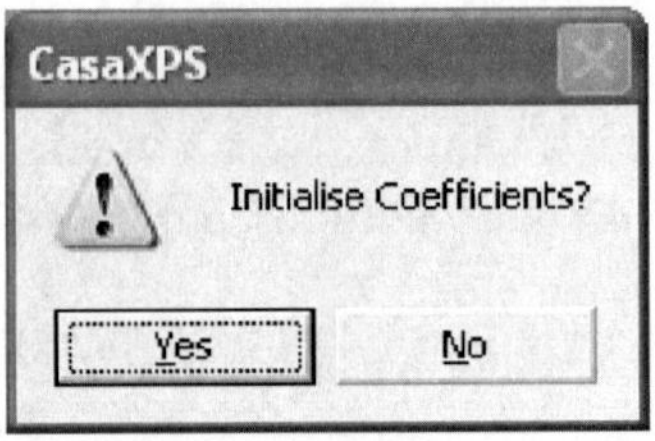

The dialog only appears if the BG Type actually changes to a new BG Type. If the BG Type is already Spline Linear the spline parameters are left unchanged from the previously used values. Adjustments to the spline parameters are performed under mouse control. Since flexible backgrounds are more often adjusted in conjunction with manipulating synthetic components, the adjustments to the spline parameters are performed with the Components property page top-most on the Quantification Parameters dialog window. Place the cursor at a position anywhere on the current spline linear background and drag the cursor vertically.

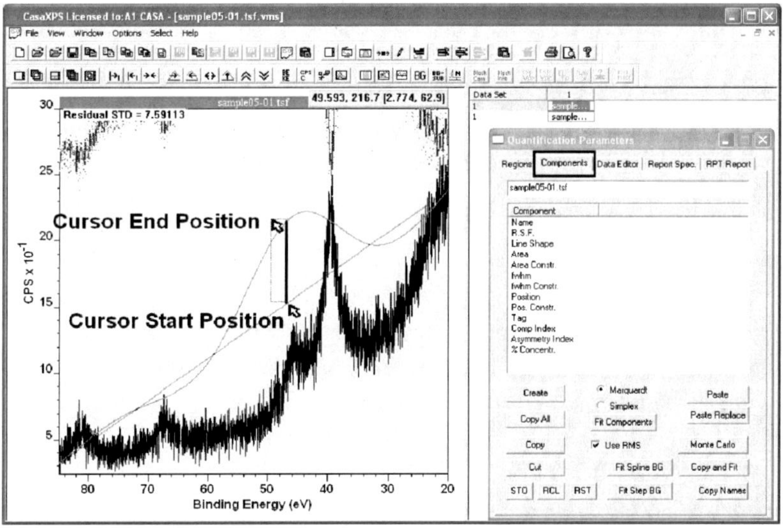

The drag action alters one of the knots in the spline background resulting in a smooth deformation of the background curve.

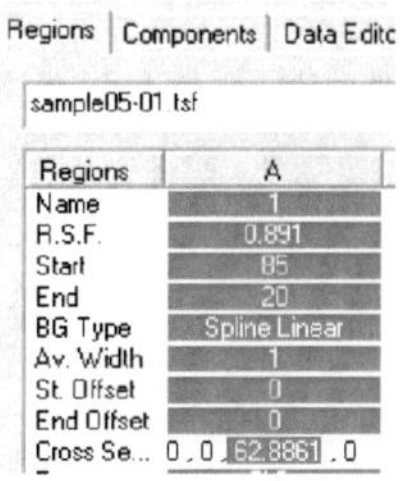

The new value for the spline knot can be traced by observing changes to either the cross-section or the Start or End Offset parameters. Further adjustments to different spline knots are achieved by moving along the spline background and making a series of minor alterations to the background shape until a satisfactory background is obtained.

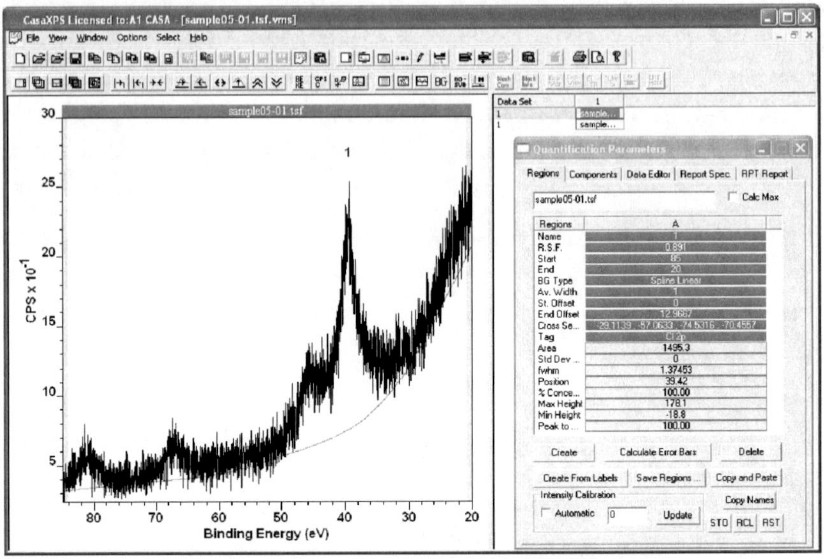

Edge Measurements using a Complementary Error Function

The Heaviside step function $H_c(x)$ is the mathematical description for an ideal edge.

$$H_c(x) = \begin{cases} 1 & x > c \\ 1/2 & x = c \\ 0 & x < c \end{cases}$$

Physical edges however are less well defined, where the shape observed in measured data is often a blend of the underlying edge structure and also the instrumental response inherent in the measurement process. One means of defining the Heaviside step function is to define the function as the following limit:

$$H_c(x) = \frac{1}{2}\lim_{t\to 0} erfc\left(\frac{c-x}{t}\right)$$

When viewed as a limit involving the complementary error function, the complementary error function *erfc* provides a means of understanding the observed data. The parameters t and c can be related to a Gaussian used to compute the *erfc* function.

$$erfc\left(\frac{c-x}{t}\right)=\frac{2}{\sqrt{\pi}}\int_{x}^{\infty}e^{-\left(\frac{c-y}{t}\right)^{2}}dy$$

While the *erfc* function models the shape of the measured edge, the deviation from an ideal edge is characterised by the width of the Gaussian used in the integral and the position of the edge is the centre of the same Gaussian.

A further observation cementing the relationship between the Heaviside step function and the complementary error function is that the complementary error function can be viewed as a convolution of a Gaussian with the Heaviside step function. A convolution is again the mathematical tool used to blend the contributions of two distributions to form an observed data envelope. For example, the Voigt function used to describe photoelectric line-shapes is a convolution of a Gaussian with a Lorentzian function. The latter representing the life-time broadening of a transition, while the former attempts to introduce an instrumental influence on the observed peaks in an XPS spectrum.

Fitting a complementary error function to an edge, in a least squares sense, provides a tool for characterising a step in the data. Modelling a step using the complementary error function is performed in CasaXPS by using one of two background types. The backgrounds are defined using four parameters as follows:

$$BG(KE)=\frac{a_0}{2}erfc\left(\frac{a_1-KE}{a_2}\right)+a_3$$

Where a_0 measures the magnitude of the step, a_1 identifies the location of the step, $(2\sqrt{\ln 2})a_2$ is the full width at half maximum (FWHM) of the Gaussian used to compute the complementary error function and a_3 represents a constant offset. These four parameters are specified using the four values displayed in the Cross Section fields on the Regions property page. After the region is created using either the Step Up (Su) or Step Down (Sd) background types, the a_i can be optimised by pressing the Region column button on the scrolled-list on the Regions property page.

The following is an example of the Step Down background type used to model the valence band edge in an XPS spectrum. The Step Down background is a reflection in the vertical line $KE= a_1$ of the Step Up background.

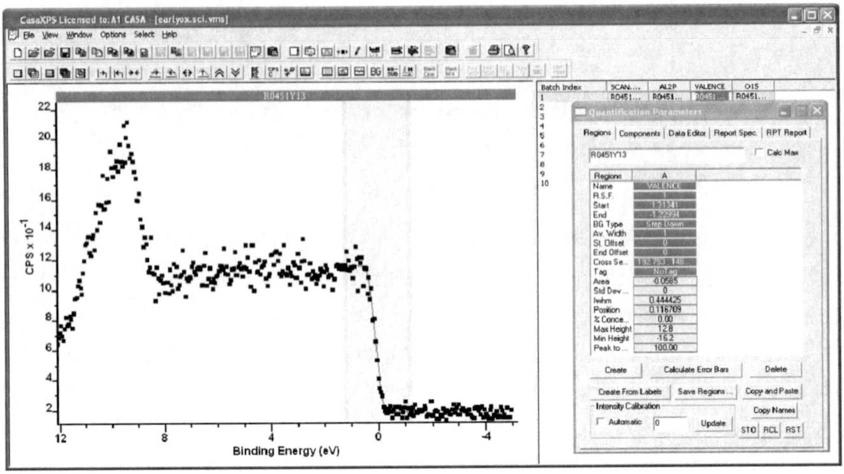

Once fitted to the data, the Step Down or Step Up background types report the position of the edge a_1 and the FWHM $(2\sqrt{ln2})a_2$ on the Regions property page.

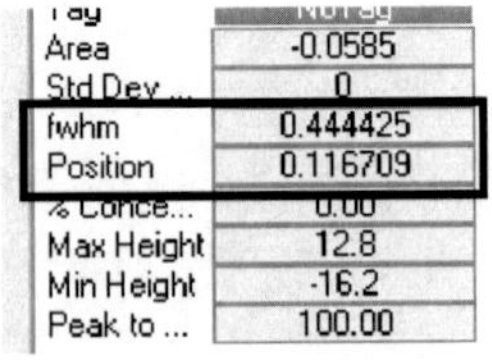

A further parameter sometimes of interest is the position of the intersection of the horizontal offset line y = a_3 with the line representing the linear portion of the step. When approximated using the complementary error function, a line representing the linear portion of the step can be defined as the tangent line at the position of the edge. The intersection of the tangent line with the horizontal offset line occurs at $KE = a_1 \pm a_2$ where the ± refers to the Step Down or the Step Up background type. Given that the background type is either Step Up or Step Down, the intersection of these two lines is reported as the Position Constraint in a configured Regions Standard Report, where the field POSITION_CONST must be added to the RegionQuantTable.txt file in the CasaXPS.DEF directory. Alternatively a_1 and a_2 can be extracted from the second and third entries in the Cross Section field on the Regions property page.

Step background types can be propagated to other spectra using the Browser Operations dialog window.

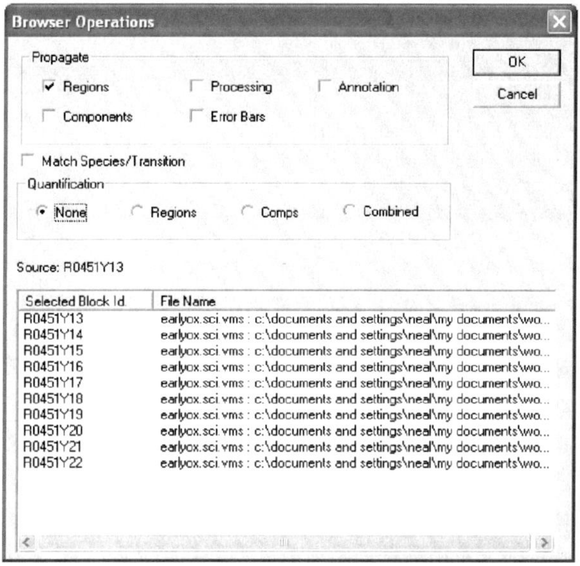

The region defined on the VAMAS block displayed in the active tile is propagated to other similar spectra by first selecting the VAMAS blocks in the right-hand pane, then right-clicking the mouse over the tile displaying the spectrum for which the Step region is defined. Step background types are different from other background types in that the background is both copied to the target data and also a non-linear least squares optimization determines the four coefficients as part of the propagation.

Components Property Page

When quantifying XPS data, peak modelling is an essential tool without which both elemental and chemical analysis would often fail. The following spectrum represents a case in point.

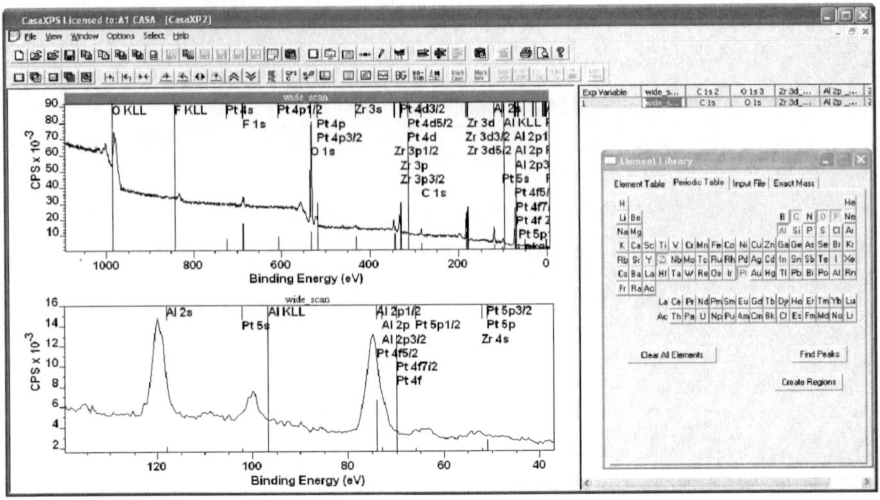

The sample includes aluminium and small amounts of platinum. The only platinum peaks of sufficient strength to measure the contribution from platinum to the spectrum are obscured by the Al 2p peak. A peak model is therefore required to compute atomic concentrations for the surface composition. Peak models are constructed using the Regions property page to define backgrounds and the Components property page to specify collections of synthetic peaks.

The Component property page consists of a header text-field, a component table and a set of action buttons.

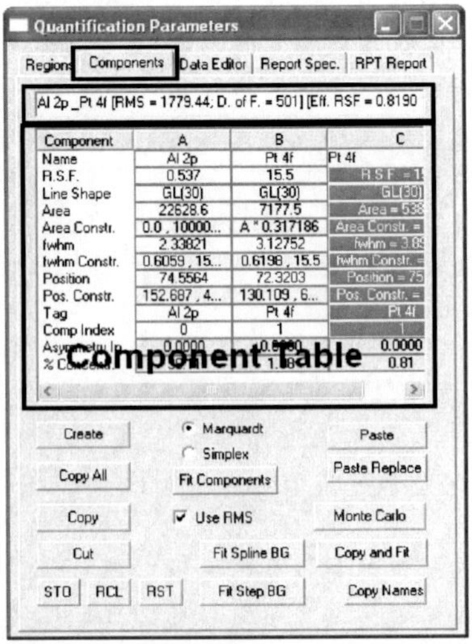

A table of components lists the set of components defined for the active VAMAS block displayed in the active tile. The block identifier for the active VAMAS block is displayed in the text-field at the top of the Components property page.

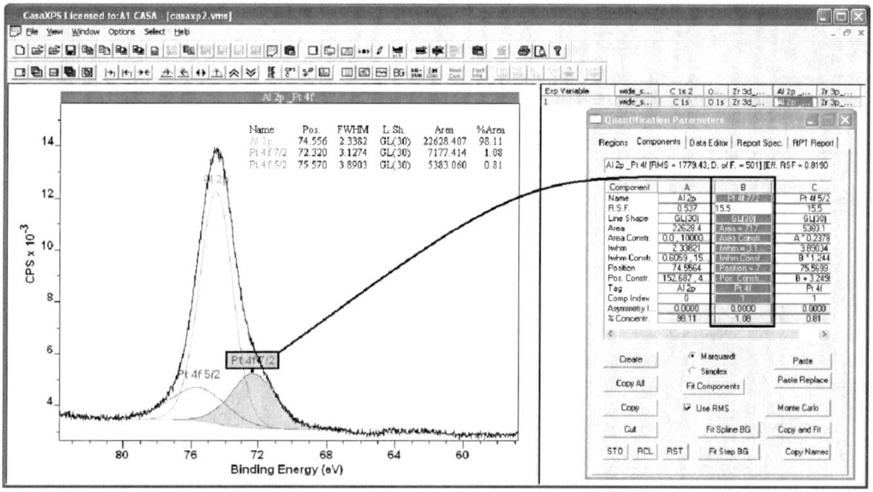

The headings above each set of component parameters are an integral part of the peak model. The characters not only label the components but are used to define constraints on the model parameters essential to ensure physically meaningful solutions when automatically fitted to the data.

Component	A	B	C
Name	Al 2p	Pt 4f 7/2	Pt 4f 5/2

Components are defined using a name field performing the same role as the name field in regions. In fact, the Custom Report on the Report Spec property page treats information gathered from regions and components identically and refers to either a region or a component name as a quantification item name.

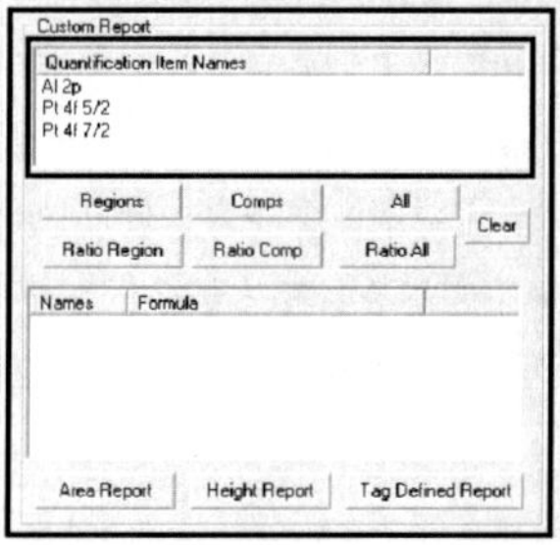

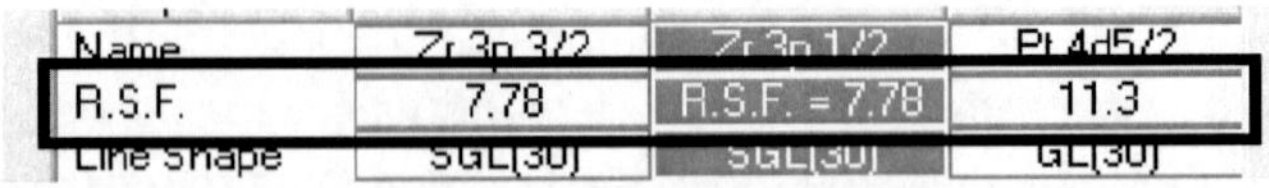

When quantifying XPS spectra, relative sensitivity factors (RSF) are used to scale the measured peak areas so that variations in the peak areas are representative of the amount of material in the sample surface. An element library typically contains lists of RSFs for XPS transitions. For some transitions more than one peak appears in the data, so called doublet pairs. In the case of the default CasaXPS library, three entries are available for each set of doublet peaks: one entry for the combined use of both doublet peaks in a quantification table and two entries for situations where only one of the two possible peaks is used in the quantification. A common cause of erroneous quantification is the inappropriate use of these optional RSF entries.

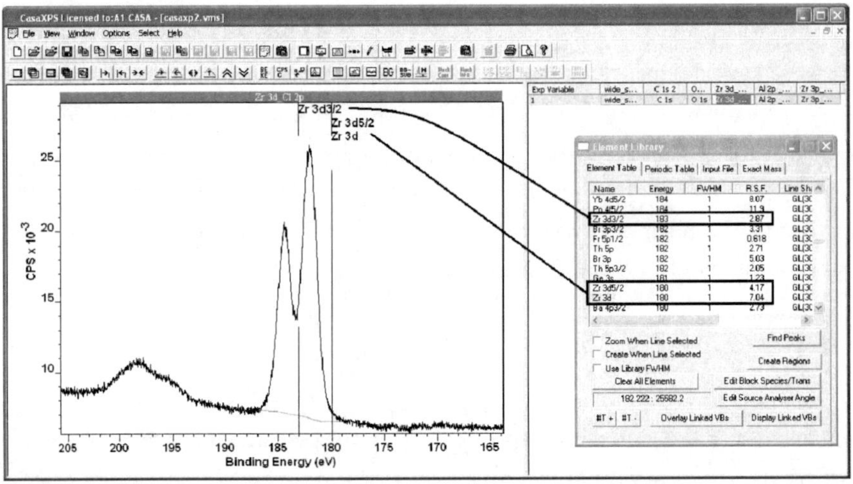

A good illustration of the issues involved with doublet peaks and RSF assignment is found in samples containing platinum, zirconium and aluminium. The Zr 3p doublet pair and the Pt 4d peaks can overlap preventing an easy estimate for the peak intensities using regions alone. The more natural peak with larger RSF values for platinum coincides with the Al 2p peaks. The problem is therefore to select peaks for which computed intensities are reliably determined and assign appropriate RSFs to these raw peak areas.

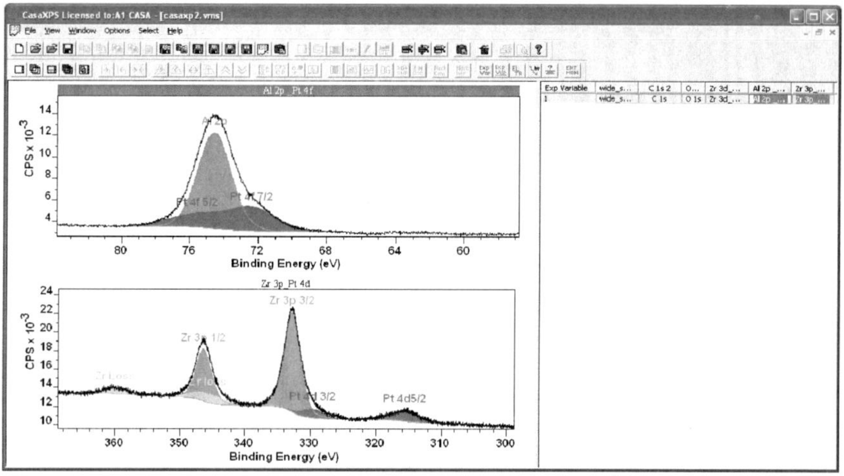

A discussion of how these peak models were determined will be deferred until later allowing focus to be placed on the assignment of RSFs to the component peaks. For the sake of argument, quantification will be based on the narrow scan spectra including C 1s, O 1s, Al 2p/Pt 4f and Zr 3p/Pt 4d. Regions are used for the C 1s and O 1s data, while peak models are required for the Al 2p/Pt 4f data.

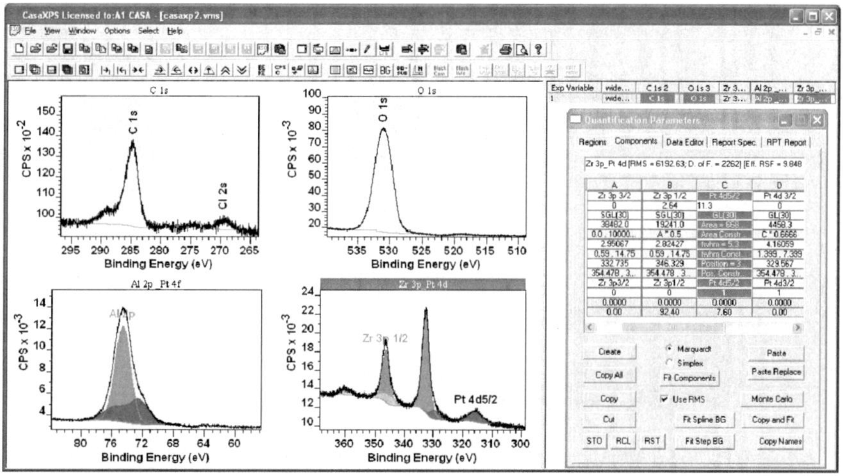

While the peak models include many components, only the components used in the quantification are assigned non-zero RSFs. The Al 2p component represents both peaks for the Al 2p doublet and therefore is assigned the total RSF for Al 2p. Zirconium measured using the Zr 3p 1/2 transition only must be assigned the RSF for just the Zr 3p 1/2 peak of the Zr 3p doublet. Similarly since only the Pt 4d 5/2 peak is used in the quantification calculation the corresponding specific RSF must be used. All other component RSFs should be zero. Peak areas are divided by the RSF for the peaks. It is important to scale the peaks chosen using the corresponding RSF for the transition. If only one peak from a doublet pair is used to quantify an element the chosen RSF must match the component assignment.

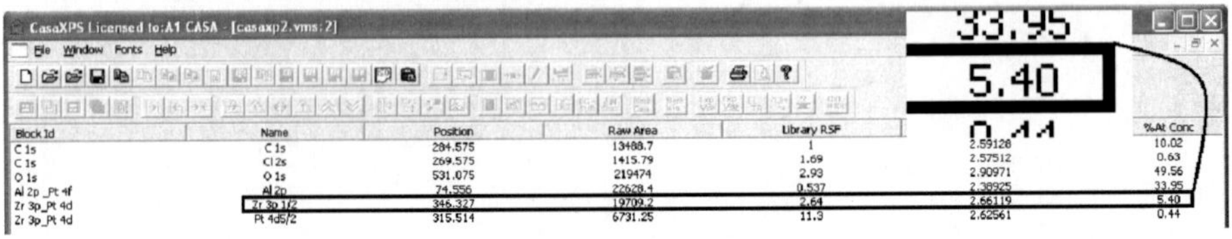

If as an alternative both peaks from the Zr 3p are included in the quantification calculation, the RSF for both components must be assigned the total RSF for the Zr 3p transition. The following quantification report is entirely equivalent to the above report based on only one of the Zr 3p peaks. The only difference between the two tables is an entry for both peaks appear in the quantification table and to obtain the total atomic concentration for zirconium these two entries must be summed.

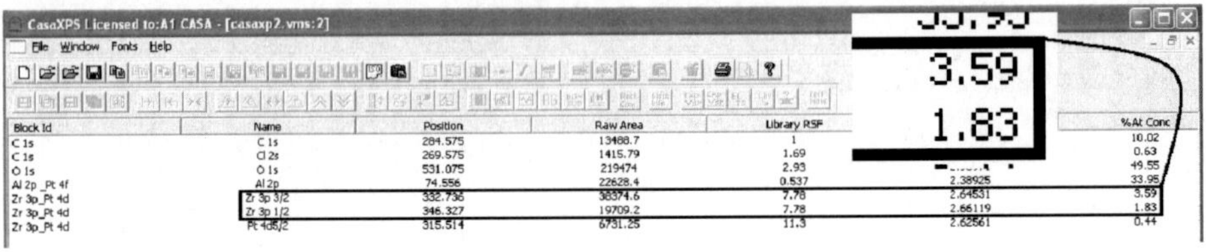

The key point when choosing the RSF for a component in a doublet pair is to base the choice on the number of components used in the quantification table, not the individual assignment for the components.

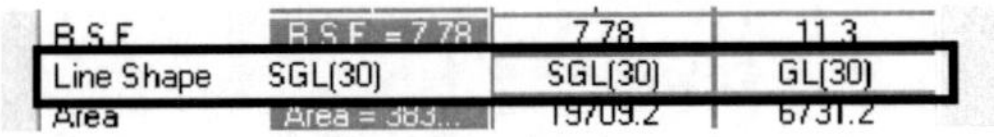

The lineshape parameter is a string used to specify the functional form used to calculate the shape for a component. The various lineshapes used for different transitions are discussed in detail elsewhere. The format for the strings used to specify lineshapes include a name together with the appropriate parameters for the name specified. Many lineshapes involve a Lorentzian blended with a Gaussian form:

Gaussian:

$$G(x{:}\,e,f,m) = exp\left(-4ln2\left(1-\frac{m}{100}\right)\left(\frac{x-e}{f}\right)^2\right)$$

Lorentzian:

$$L(x{:}\,f,e,m) = \frac{1}{1+4\frac{m}{100}\left(\frac{x-e}{f}\right)^2}$$

Lorentzian Asymmetric Lineshape

$$LA(x{:}\,\alpha,\beta,f,e) = \begin{cases}[L(x{:}\,f,e,100)]^{\alpha} & x \le e\\ [L(x{:}\,f,e,100)]^{\beta} & x > e\end{cases}$$

Asymmetric Tail function:

$$T(x{:}\,s,k,e,f) = \begin{cases} s\ exp\left(-k\left(\frac{x-e}{f}\right)\right) & x \le e\\ 1 & otherwise\end{cases}$$

Lorentzian Asymmetric Lineshapes Convoluted with a Gaussian

LA(a,b,n): $LA(x{:}\,a,b,f,e)$ numerically convoluted with a Gaussian characterised by the integer n.

LF(a,b,w,n): Damped version of LA lineshape limited by width parameter w.

Symmetric Gaussian Lorentzian Line Shapes

Product of a Gaussian with a Lorentzian

GL(m): $GL(x{:}\,e,f,m) = G(x{:}\,e,f,m)L(x{:}\,e,f,m)$

Sum or linear combination of a Gaussian with a Lorentzian

SLG(m): $SGL(x{:}\,e,f,m) = \left(1-\frac{m}{100}\right)G(x{:}\,e,f,1) + \frac{m}{100}L(x{:}\,e,f,m)$

Gaussian-Lorentzian Asymmetric Line Shapes

GL(m)T(k): $GL(x{:}\,e,f,m) + \left(1-GL(x{:}\,e,f,m)\right)T(x{:}\,1,k,e,f)$

SGL(m)T(k): $SGL(x{:}\,e,f,m) + \left(1-SGL(x{:}\,e,f,m)\right)T(x{:}\,1,k,e,f)$

GL(m) SL(s,*l*): $$GL(x\colon e, f, m) + \big(1 - GL(x\colon e, f, m)\big)T(x\colon s, 13.8/l, e, f)$$

SGL(m) SL(s,*l*): $$SGL(x\colon e, f, m) + \big(1 - SGL(x\colon e, f, m)\big)T(x\colon s, 13.8/l, e, f)$$

These lineshapes and others such as the Doniach Sunjic asymmetric lineshape are described in ***Walton et al ISBN 978-0954953317***.

Area = 22628.4	7177.4	5383.1
Area Constr. = 0.0 , 1...	A * 0.317186	A * 0.23789
fwhm = 2.33821	3.12744	3.89034
fwhm Constr. = 0.605...	0.6198 , 15.5	B * 1.244
Position = 74.5564	72.3203	75.5699
Pos. Constr. = 152.6...	130.109 , 6...	B + 3.2496

The parameters used to fit components to spectral data are peak area, FWHM and position. Each of these parameters is accompanied by constraint parameters. Without constraints many peak models would fail to recover physically meaningful values for the parameters used in the optimisation step. It is therefore essential to manage the optimisation parameters using the constraints to enforce a sufficiently rigid model which guides the mathematical least squares solution to a physically meaningful result.

Constraints are defined using the column headers to the component table on the Components property page.

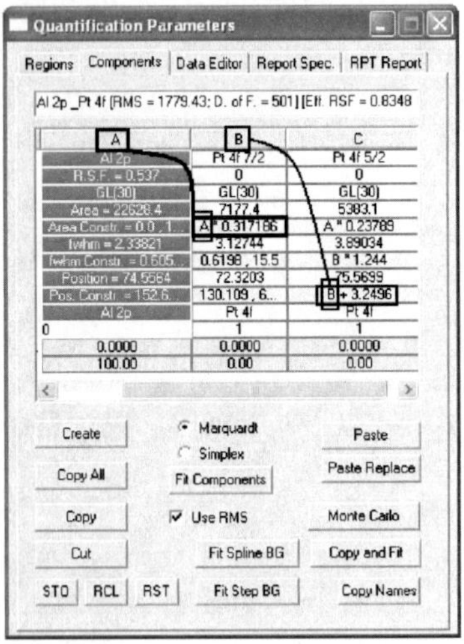

An area constraint of the form A * 0.5 entered into a component in column B forces the peak area for the component in column B to be half the area of the component in column A. Similarly, an offset between a peak in column C and a peak in column B could be specified by entering B + 3.2496 in the position constraint field in column C. FWHM constraints are identical to the format used for area constraints.

Constraints are released using the # character. If a constraint field is replaced by the # character followed by a numerical value, the constraint is defined as the current value plus and minus the value entered following the # character.

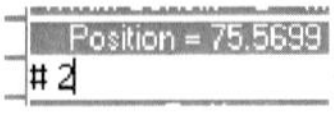

75.5699 + 2 , 75.5699 - 2

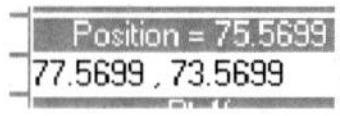

To illustrate the use of constraints, consider the problem of measuring the platinum signal from the Pt 4f doublet.

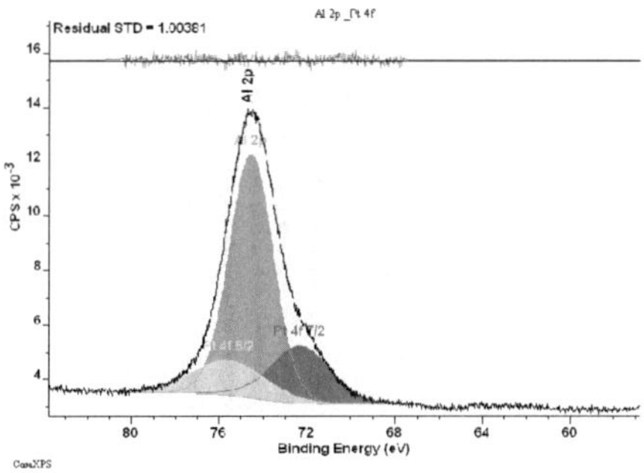

Clearly these peaks are highly correlated and therefore using an approximation to both lineshapes and background, selecting peak areas based on optimised parameters without constraints leads to a mathematical solution. From a physical perspective the peak model is worthless even though the fit to the data is very good with a residual stdev below unity.

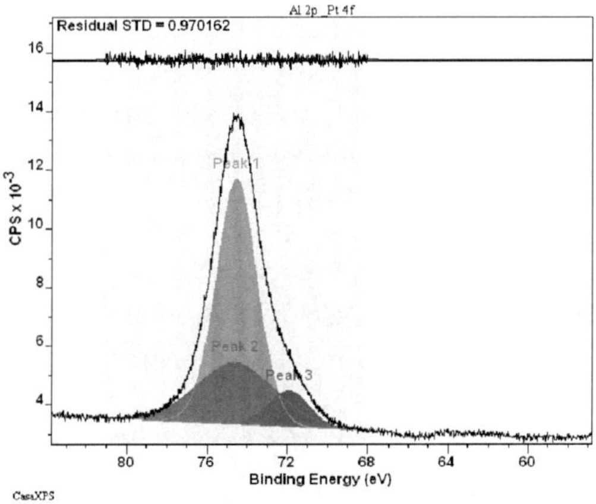

Peak 1 in some sense approximates the Al 2p signal, but Peaks 2 and 3 are clearly not representative of a 4f doublet pair. The most obvious failings are the intensity ratio and FWHM for the two peaks intended to represent the Pt 4f doublet peaks. Transitions with an angular momentum of 3 split in the ratio 3:4 due to spin-orbit coupling, therefore the area for the Pt $4f_{7/2}$ peak should be about 4/3 larger than the Pt $4f_{5/2}$ peak. Further, a typical pair of 4f peaks results in a greater FWHM for the $4f_{5/2}$ peak compared to the $4f_{7/2}$peak. Attempting to calculate the intensity of the Al 2p and Pt 4f peaks based on an unconstrained peak model is less than satisfactory. A first attempt to improve the peak model would be to introduce area constraints for the Pt 4f peaks.

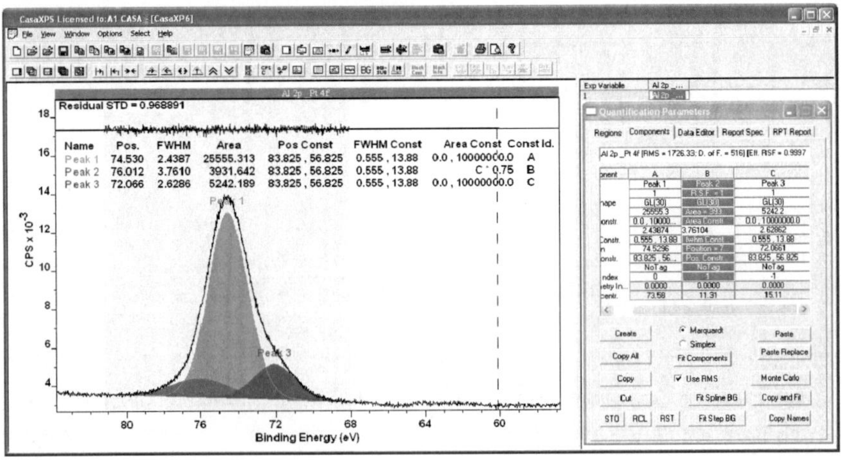

The area constraint C * 0.75 entered for the peak in column B on the Components property page has the effect of enforcing the expected ratio for the Pt 4f peaks. When fitted to the data using the area constraint for the Pt 4f peaks, a new solution results which reassuringly restores the expected behaviour for the FWHM for these peaks. The more information added to the peak model, the more reliable the peak intensities become. If the relative positions for the Pt 4f peaks were known, these could be added to the model.

Using information gathered from other VAMAS blocks can also be useful in constraining peak parameters. For the current example, the Al 2s peak is without interference and although not measured using a narrow scan spectrum, a survey spectrum for the sample does provide information about both the Al 2s and Al 2p/Pt 4f peaks. The expected ratio for the Al 2s to Al 2p peaks is 1:0.713 (using Scofield cross-sections; empirical relative peak areas for the Al 2s to Al 2p ratio would be better measured using the same operating mode to acquire the spectra under analysis) and imposing area constraints for a model involving two regions in which one part of the model area is well defined will enhance the modelling process.

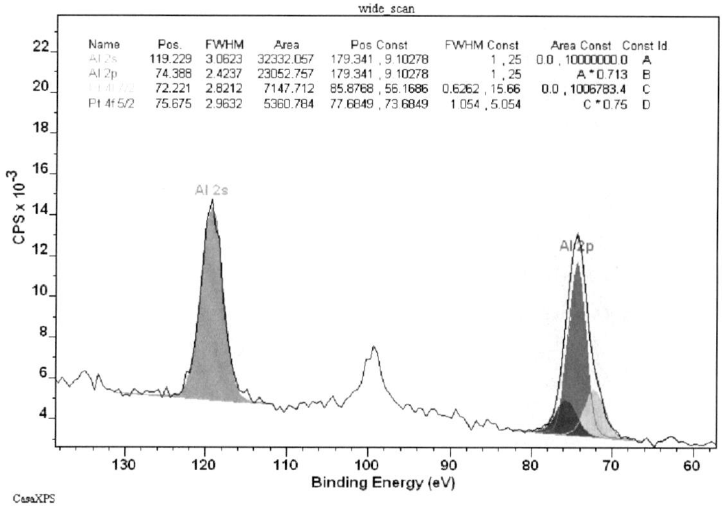

The fixed relationship between the Al 2s and Al 2p peak areas helps to define the area for the Pt 4f peaks overlapping the Al 2p peak. Once the Al 2p peak intensity is established, the relative intensity for the Al 2p and Pt 4f peaks can be fixed using area constraints with the view to moving the model to the narrow scan spectrum so quantification can proceed based on just narrow scan data.

Moving a Peak Model between VAMAS blocks without immediately fitting to the data involves using the Copy, Copy All, Paste and Paste Replace button on the Components property page.

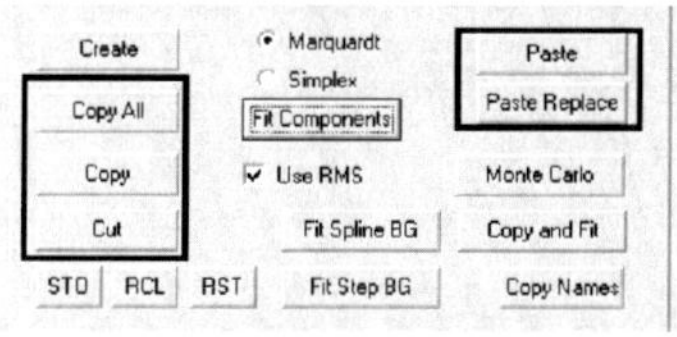

A set of peaks constructed on the survey spectrum is moved to a narrow scan spectrum by first displaying the spectrum with the components in the active tile before pressing the Copy All button.

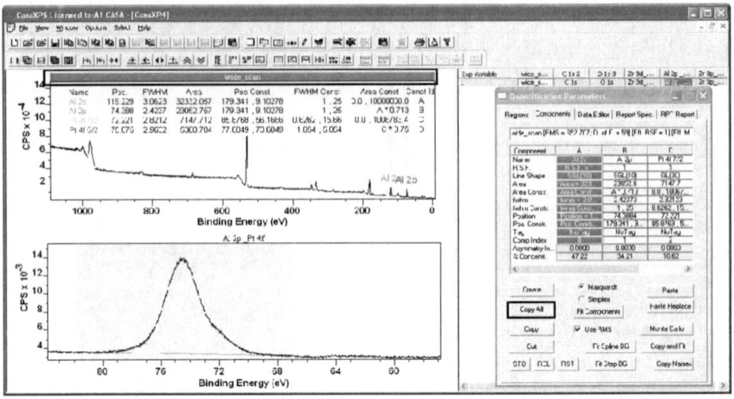

After switching the focus to the tile displaying the spectrum for which the components are required, pressing the Paste button adds the components previously copied to any components already defined on the active VAMAS block or Paste Replace causes the components on the active VAMAS block to be replaced by the components on the component clipboard. For the current exercise, no components are defined on the narrow scan spectrum so either of the Paste options works in the same way, namely the components placed on the clipboard are added to the spectrum without fitting to the data.

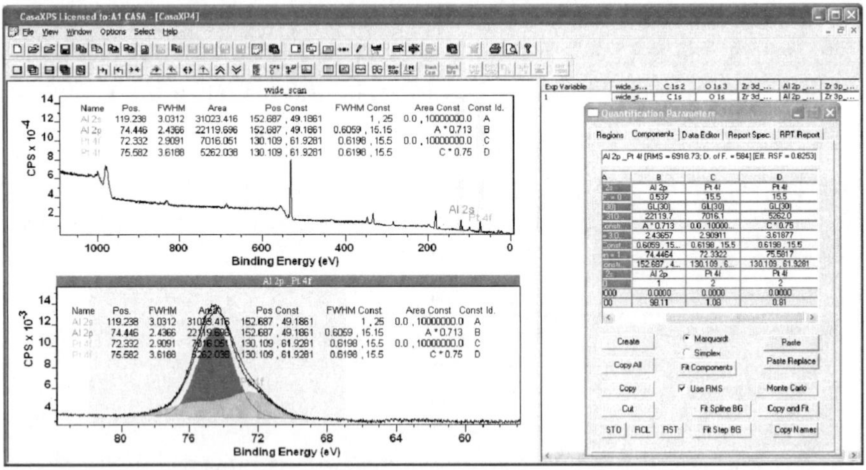

The set of peaks copied onto the narrow scan spectrum include the Al 2s component in column A. The components of interest are the Al 2p and both of the Pt 4f doublet peaks. It is therefore necessary to delete the Al 2s component from the narrow scan spectrum before fitting the model to the data. Further, the objective is to copy the Al 2p and Pt 4f peaks determined using the Al 2s peak on the survey and maintain the intensity relationship from the survey data for the Al 2p peak and the Pt 4f peaks. Thus area constraints must be adjusted to permit the Al 2s component to be removed and enforce the relative area between the Al 2p and Pt 4f peaks.

The Cut button is used to delete a component. The Cut button also placed the component removed from the model onto the component clipboard replacing the current contents of the clipboard. Before the Al 2s component can be delete, all constraints linking parameters from other components to the Al 2s component must be released. This restriction on removing a component prevents critical components to a constrained model from being removed by mistake. Since the Al 2p peak area is constrained to the area of the Al 2s component, the area constraint for the Al 2p must be released. The easiest way to remove the constraint is to enter #1000000 in the area constraint field in the Al 2p component. The # character followed by a large number simply ensures the area for the Al 2p component can optimise within an excessively large range. Once all constraints relying on the Al 2s peak are broken, the Al 2s component is deleted by selecting the component on the Components table before pressing the Cut button.

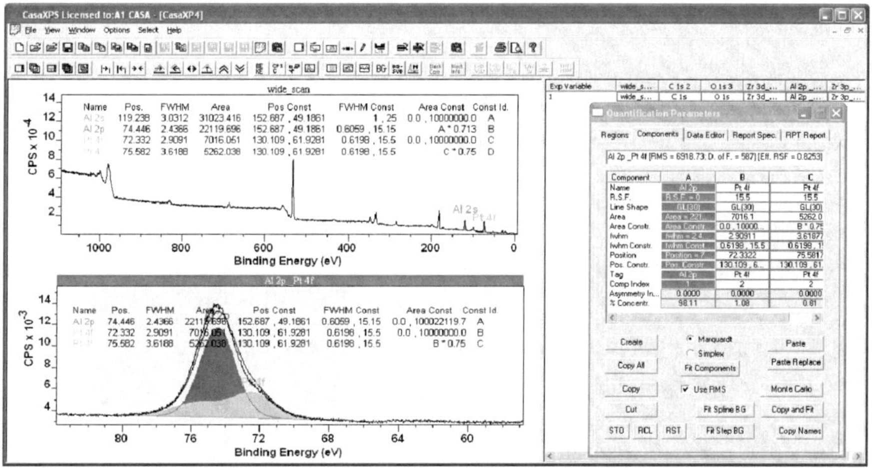

The final adjustment to the constraints for the remaining three components is designed to fix the relative intensities for the Al 2p component and the Pt 4f peaks. The Pt 4f peaks are already constrained to be in the ratio 3:4. The problem reduces to fixing the area of the peak in column B to maintain the same relative area with the Al 2p component now in column A. To enter a constraint to maintain a current relationship between two constraints in a peak model, simply enter the column header into the constraint field without any numerical factor or offset. Thus to fix the current area relationship between the Al 2p component in column A and the Pt 4f component in column B, enter A into the area constraint field and press Enter. A factor based on the current parameter values is computed and entered into the area constraint field in column B.

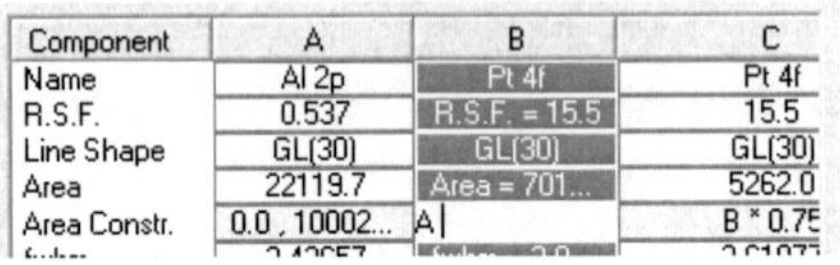

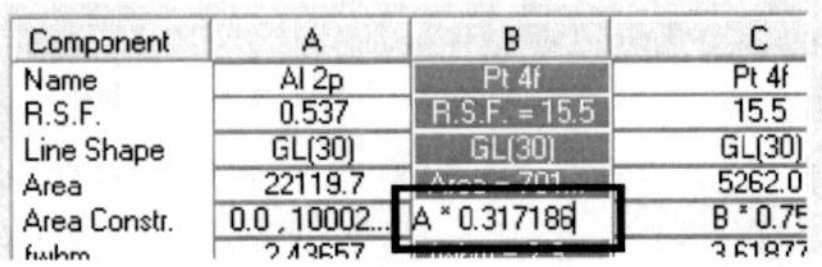

Since the component in column C is already constrained to column B, the relative area for all the peaks is now fixed and allowed to vary within the limits defined by column A. The peak model can now be fitted to the narrow scan data whilst maintaining the relative area for the Al 2p to Pt 4f peaks determined from the survey spectrum.

It is worth pointing out that the survey spectrum was acquired using a larger step size than the narrow scan spectrum The energy resolution for the analyser was the same so the survey and the narrow scan data are more comparable than most. The norm would be to acquire the survey at a lower energy resolution providing greater sensitivity at the cost of wider peaks. Fitting components to the survey made sense in the context of these data.

The newly constrained peak model when fitted to the data provides an improved estimate for the Pt 4f peak intensity. Using quantification regions to measure the intensity for the C 1s, Cl 2s, O 1s and Zr 3d peaks, and components to measure the peak intensities for the Al 2p and Pt 4f peaks, the Report Spec property page Standard Report generated from the Regions and Comps button offers an alternative way to quantify the sample.

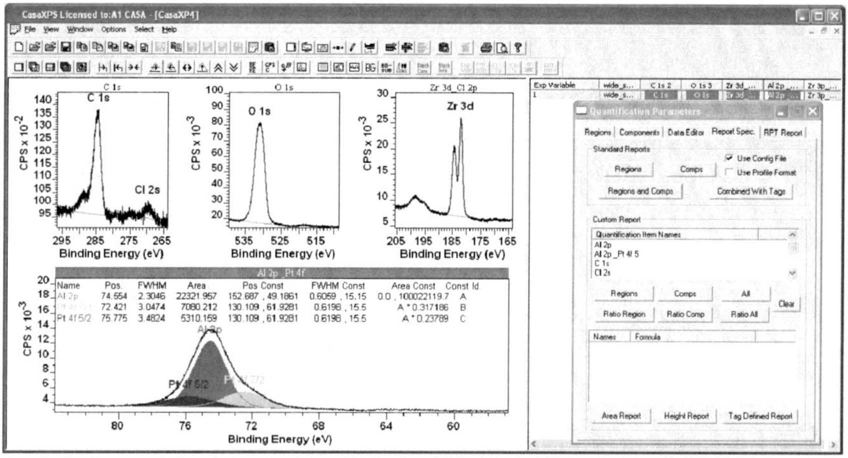

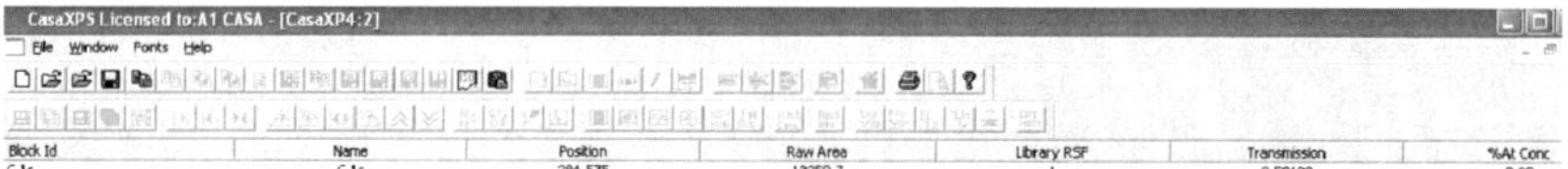

CasaXPS Licensed to:A1 CASA - [CasaXP4:2]

Block Id	Name	Position	Raw Area	Library RSF	Transmission	%At Conc
C 1s	C 1s	284.575	13259.7	1	2.59128	9.80
C 1s	Cl 2s	269.575	1263.22	1.69	2.57512	0.56
O 1s	O 1s	531.075	220864	2.93	2.90971	49.63
Zr 3d_Cl 2p	Zr 3d	182.100	55136.2	7.04	2.48655	6.03
Al 2p _Pt 4f	Al 2p	74.554	22322	0.537	2.38925	33.33
Al 2p _Pt 4f	Pt 4f 7/2	72.421	7080.21	15.5	2.38742	0.37
Al 2p _Pt 4f	Pt 4f 5/2	75.775	5310.16	15.5	2.39028	0.27

The data in the Zr 3p/Pt 4d VAMAS block includes additional complications in the form of both overlapping peaks and also structure in the zirconium background.

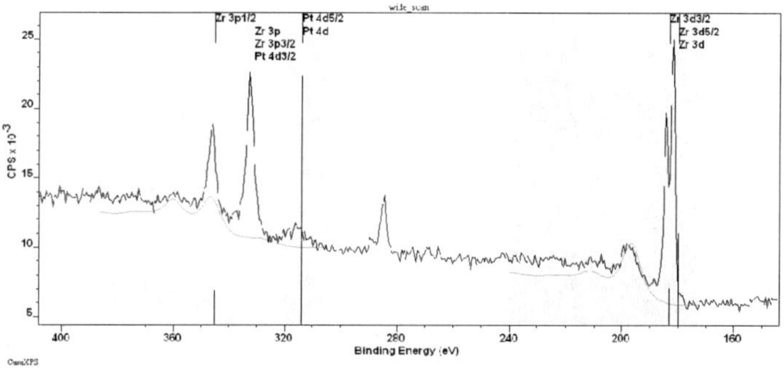

A C 4 Tougaard background type constructed for the Zr 3d peaks when applied to the Zr 3p peaks illustrates the potential issues with the Zr 3p peaks when attempting to quantify the sample.

The choice of platinum peaks is also relevant to the quantification results not merely due to uncertainty in RSF values for different transitions from the same element, but because platinum shows evidence of being physically below the surface layer. The survey spectrum shows no sign of peaks for the Pt 4s and Pt

$4p_{1/2}$ transitions. These transitions appear with lower kinetic energy for the ejected electrons than the Pt 4f electrons and therefore the assumption is these peaks are attenuated due to scattering processes, whereas the Pt 4f transition corresponding to more energetic electrons are evident due to the increased depth from which the electrons with higher kinetic energy can emerge from the surface without scattering.

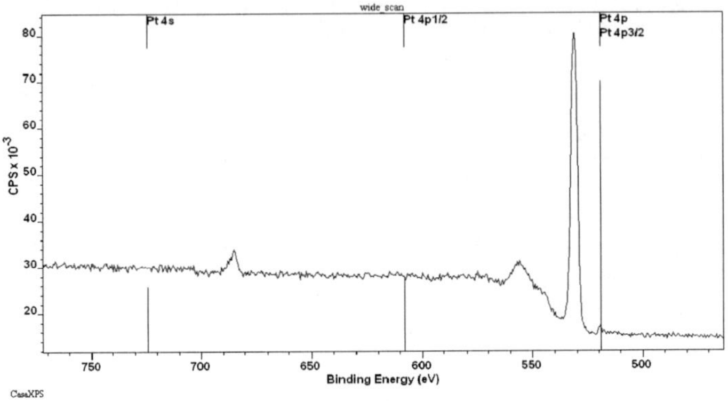

The survey spectrum is processed to remove the x-ray satellite line for the O 1s peak to reveal a small Pt $4p_{3/2}$ peak. Satellite subtraction is performed on the Data Editor property-page on the Quantification Parameters dialog window.

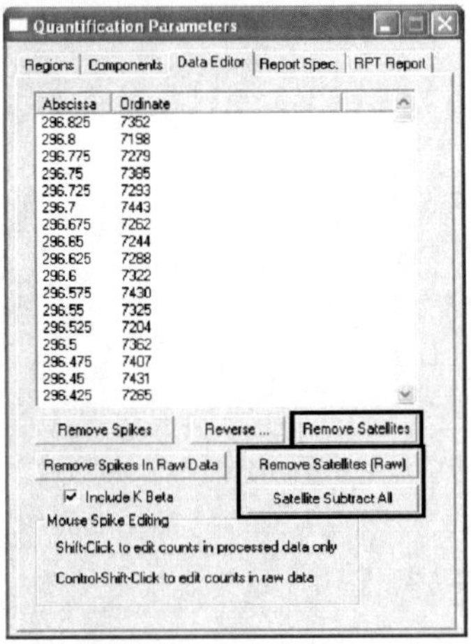

Removing x-ray satellite peaks from data acquired with unfiltered x-ray sources requires a region for each photoelectric peak in the spectrum and the correct assignment in the VAMAS block for the anode material used in the x-ray gun. The buttons on the Data Editor property-page act on the data displayed in the active tile. The options Remove Satellite and Remove Satellite (Raw) differ in the consequences for the data in the VAMAS block displayed in the active tile. The VAMAS blocks whilst loaded into CasaXPS maintain both a copy of the original data, referred to as raw data, and a copy of the data following any processing operations performed on the data. When processing is undone in CasaXPS, the processed data is updated with the raw data. Satellite subtraction offers the ability to modify the raw data directly which once performed cannot be undone without reloading the unsaved version of the file. If saved following modification of the raw data, the raw data is lost to the file too. Applying the satellite subtraction using the Remove Satellite button retains the option to undo the satellite subtraction via resetting the processing history. Performing the same operation using the Remove Satellite (Raw) button updates the raw data and cannot be rectified via the Processing History property page.

The third option Satellite Subtract All allows satellite subtraction to be applied to all the VAMAS blocks overlaid in the active tile. A dialog window asks if the operation should apply to the processed or raw data.

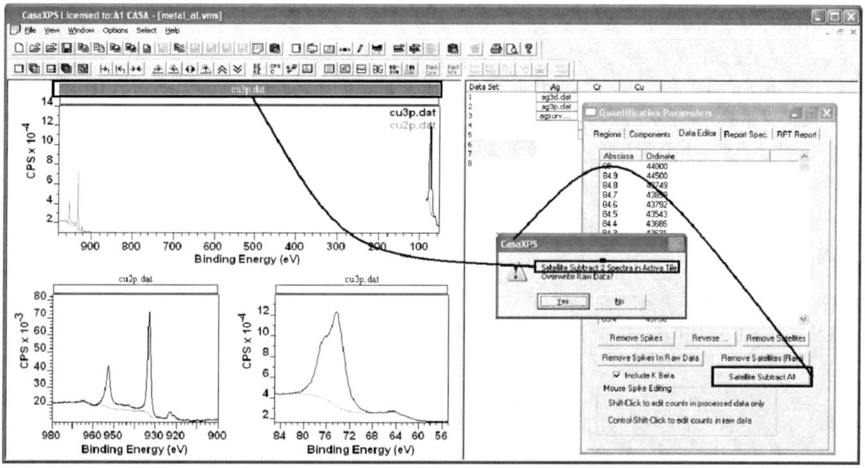

Following satellite subtraction in which the raw data is replaced, the VAMAS block comment is updated with a string to indicate the data are now processed.

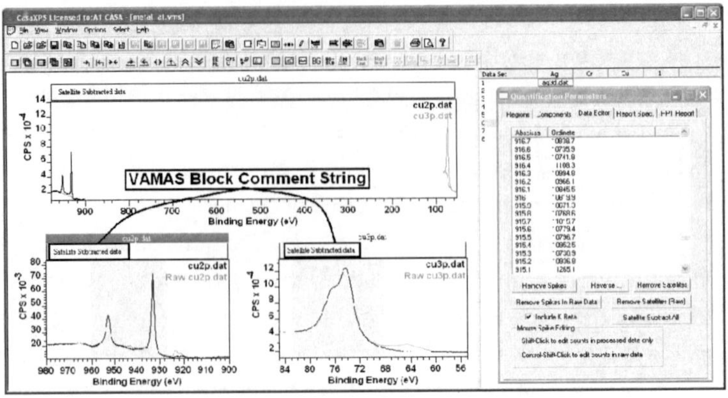

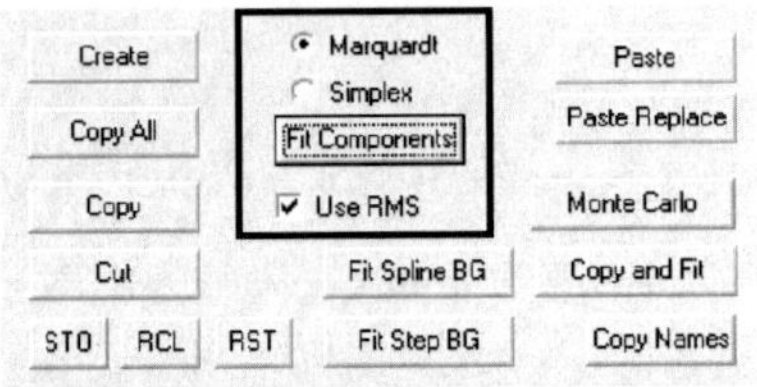

Fitting a peak model to data is achieved via the Fit Components button on the Component property page. The optimisation parameters are adjusted using either a Marquardt-Levenberg algorithm or via optimisation based on the Simplex method for non-linear least squares to minimise the residual between the synthetic data envelope and the spectral data. A tick-box switches between minimising the root mean square (RMS) and the chi square.

Each time the Fit Components button is pressed, before adjusting the model parameters the current state of the model, both regions and components, are saved to a list of peak models. At any point in time, the current state for the peak model can be added to the list of peak models by pressing the STO button.

Pressing the RCL button causes the list of peak models to be recovered one at a time, most recent first. A third button RST resets the list to the current peak model and clears the list of all other models.

Optimisation is also performed using the Copy and Fit button. The Copy and Fit button is an alternative means for transferring components between spectra within the same experiment frame. The Copy and Fit option, primarily designed for fitting sets of spectra where the peak model spans multiple VAMAS blocks worth of data (***Walton et al ISBN 978-0954953317***), also provides useful functionality for general data within a file. Transferring component models using the Copy and Fit button is performed without altering the regions defined on the data. While similar selective operations are possible via the propagate option, the default operation of the propagate mechanism is to transfer regions whenever components are propagated. A configuration entry (propagate components only) can be added to the CasaXPS.DEF/ParameterFile.txt configuration file to allow the propagation of components only.

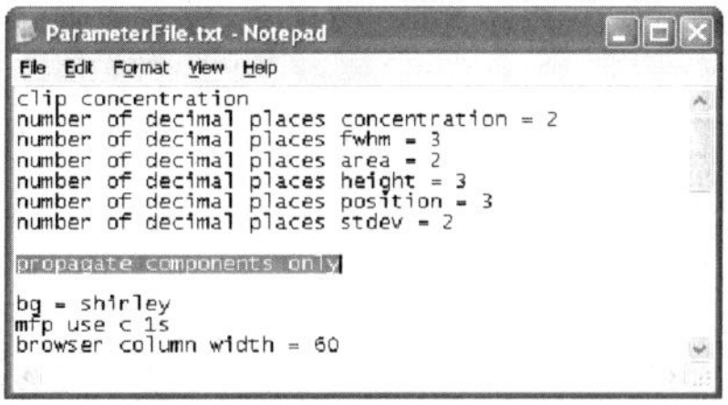

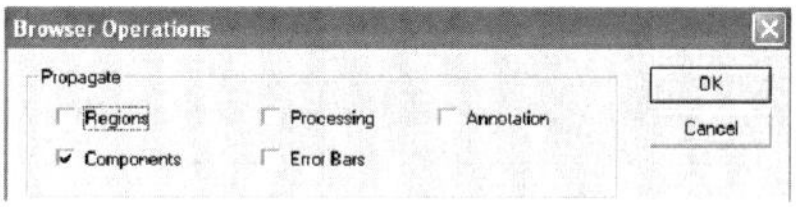

The difference between the Copy and Fit button and the propagate mechanism is the VAMAS blocks must be in the same experiment frame whereas the propagate mechanism allows components to be transferred and fitted to data across multiple files open in CasaXPS. The Copy and Fit button takes the components defined on the active VAMAS block in the active tile and transfers the components to the set of VAMAS blocks in the set of display tiles appearing in the left-hand pane, one VAMAS block per tile.

The following data set includes a sequence of O 1s spectra corresponding to oxides of silicon and titanium. Regions are defined on the data using a partition of the O 1s data into those clearly bonded with silicon and a second set where the titanium is also a significant component of the spectra. Since the regions are different for each of these two sets of spectra any peak model developed for the O 1s data must be copied to the full set of O 1s spectra without altering the region definitions.

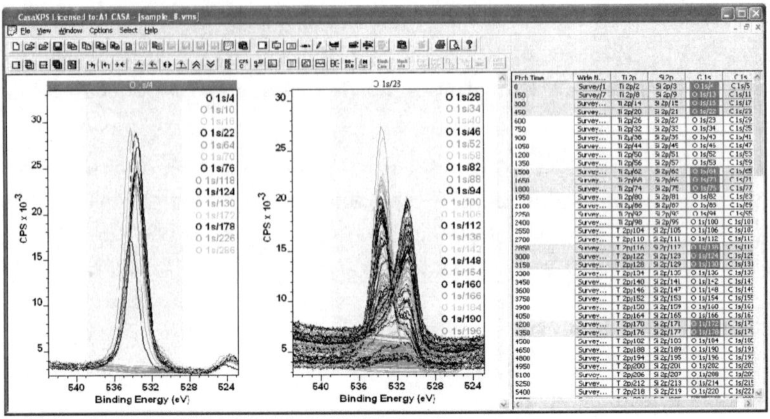

The Copy and Fit button offers a means of creating peak models for each O 1s spectrum in the depth profile without undoing the work performed in setting up the regions.

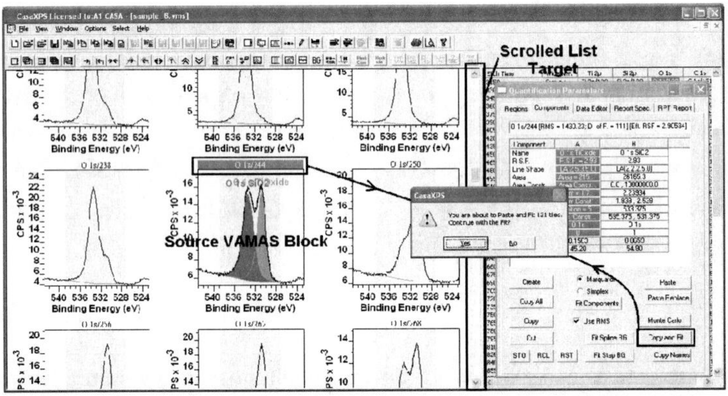

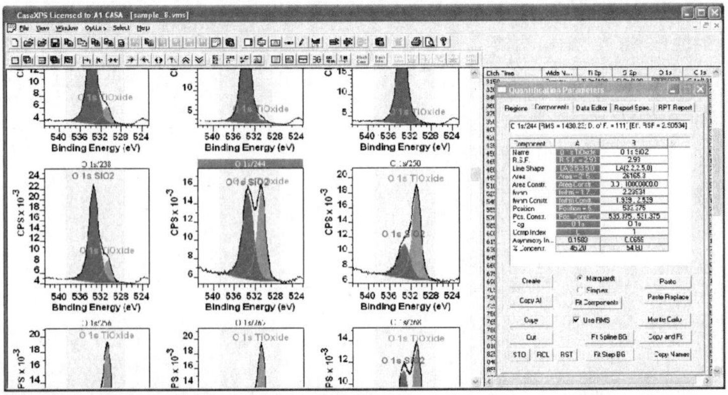

Profiling the data set based on regions defined on the titanium, silicon and carbon, plus two components for the oxygen leads to the following profile generated from the Custom Report.

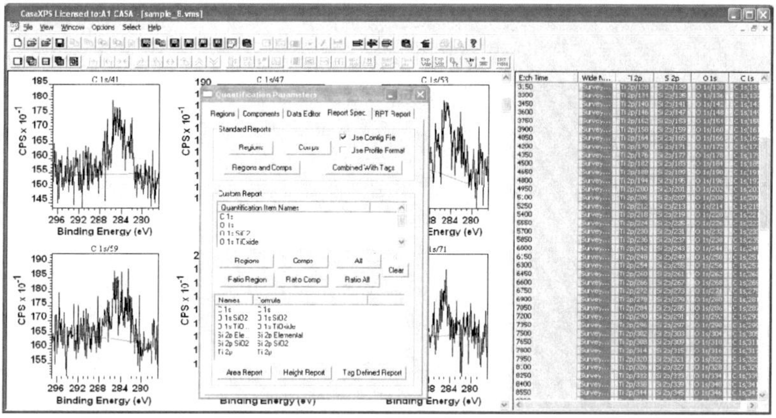

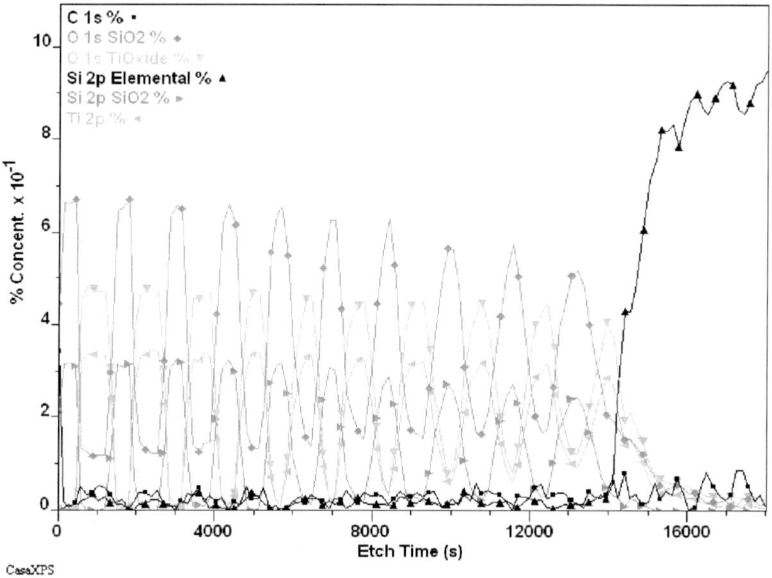

Profiles analysed using peak models is by far the best route to extracting tends in the data. The alternative often suggested is to use PCA based linear least squares (LLS). While a solution for the O 1s can be obtained using linear least squares, the O 1s peaks move in energy as a function of etch time and therefore the overly rigid models required by LLS alter the intensities for the O 1s peaks depending on how well the chosen component spectra accommodate the O 1s spectra in the profile. For example, the O 1s peaks during the initial etch cycles experience differing charging conditions and therefore the LLS solutions based on a representative O 1s peak from the SiO_2 layers fails to provide a good fit for these data. The LLS solution clearly underestimates the O 1s peaks below:

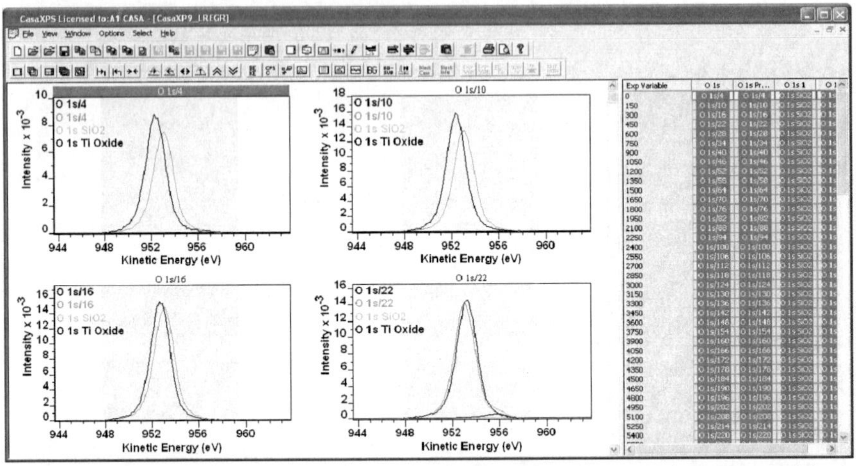

Problems with the LLS solutions also exist for interfacial data. The VAMAS block O 1s/58 below results in an underestimate for the O 1s signal from silicon, again as a result of shifting peaks.

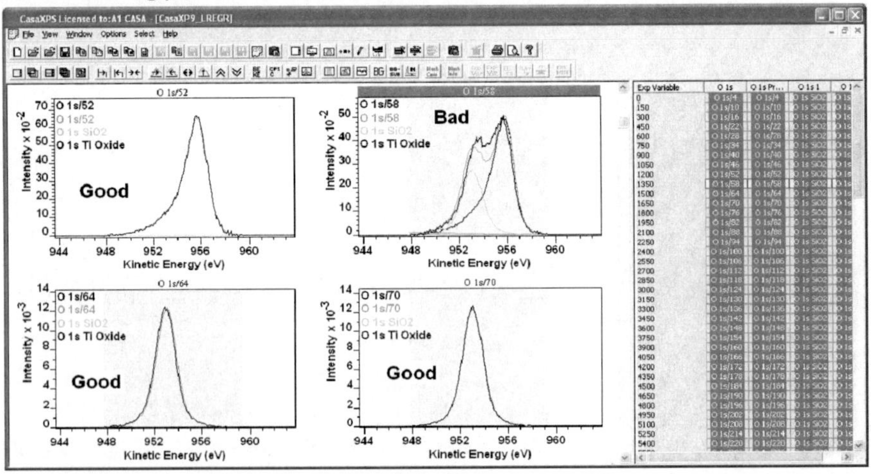

The flexibility of a peak model fitted using non-linear least squares produces a more accurate estimate for the O 1s peaks.

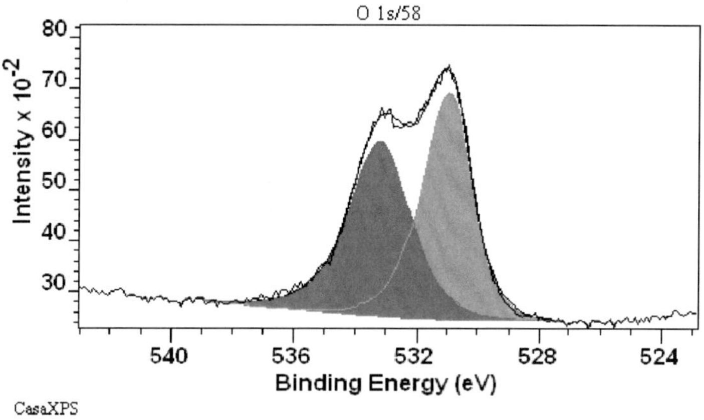

The real advantage of developing a peak model over LLS is the worst case scenario for a peak model is all parameters in the model are constrained to be fixed except for the peak area parameters. Under these circumstances the solution for the peak model would yield identical results to the LLS. Adding back freedom to the position and FWHM parameters relaxes the peak model to accommodate shifts and other variation in the data due to the measurement environment, and so the possibility of an accurate solution is always open when modelled using synthetic components.

A further point worth making is, if at any point in a profile the signal is deemed to be zero but noise in the spectra causes a residual intensity for a given element, the RSF for the regions or components used to measure the signal can be set to zero, thus forcing the spurious signal to zero too. The general flexibility offered by regions and components permits the profile data to be illustrative and well as quantitative, without the danger sometimes experienced by LLS of masking genuine features in the experiment.

When preparing a profile, an easy error to make is not assigning the region and component names ultimately desired for the final quantification results. For example, when a region or component is initially created the name from the element library for the transition is the most likely string entered automatically into the corresponding name fields. These name fields are used by the Custom Report designed for generating profiles and since region and component areas assigned the same name are automatically summed by the Custom Report it is essential names for regions and component should differ.

Otherwise when profiled using the Custom Report, the area for a region and components with the same name measuring the same peak envelope result in doubling the intensity of the transition. A sequence of carefully prepared peak models assigned inappropriate names can be remedied using the Copy Names button on the Components property page.

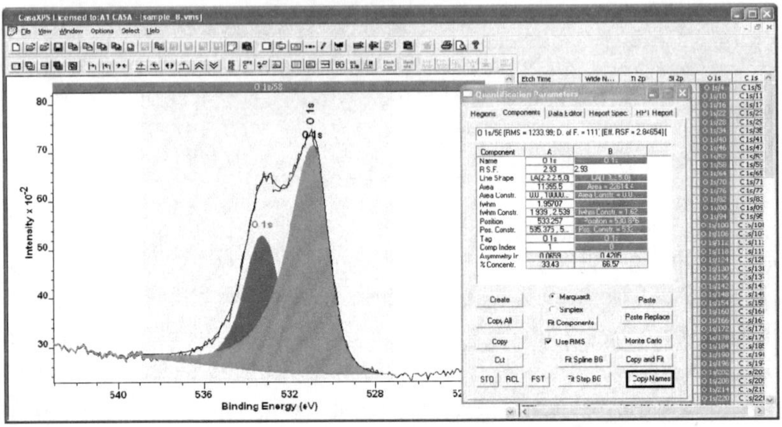

The same means is used of specify the target set of spectra as the propagate mechanism. The source for the component names is the active VAMAS block for which components are tabulated on the Components property page. Modifying the name fields on the Components property page provides the source for a new naming convention for a set of components. On pressing the Copy Name button a dialog window lists the set of VAMAS blocks currently selected in the right-hand pane or panes of open VAMAS files. The name field for components are updated by pressing the OK button on the dialog window. No other component parameters are altered by the action of the Copy Name button.

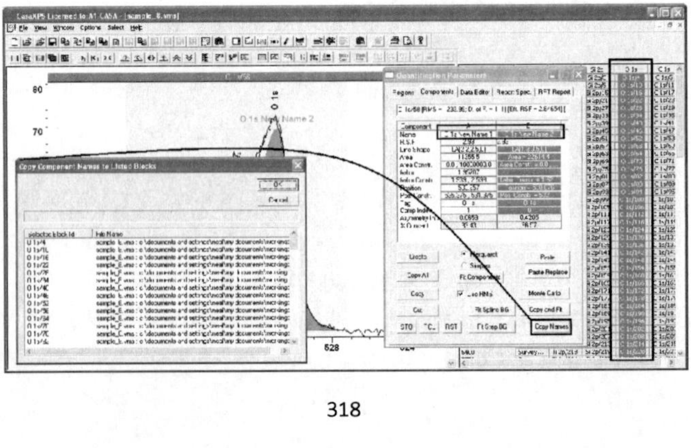

Monte Carlo Error Analysis for Peak Models

Monte Carlo error analysis is an option for analysing the implications of peak constraints. In principle the technique provides as error estimate for the precision with which fitting parameters are determined by the optimisation process given the expected noise in the data. The reality for modern instruments is less clear as detector systems become more complex and count rates are calculated from multiple data streams thus altering the nature of noise for pulse counted data. At best Monte Carlo or any computationally based error estimates are only precision rather than accuracy based. Particularly for peak models, a very precise calculation for a set of peak parameters is of little virtue if the peak model is grossly inaccurate in its description of the physical processes responsible for the data envelope. A far more realistic approach to error statistics from peak models is using the results to improve the stability of models rather than claim precision for computed values.

Consider the peak model used to estimate the intensities for aluminium and platinum:

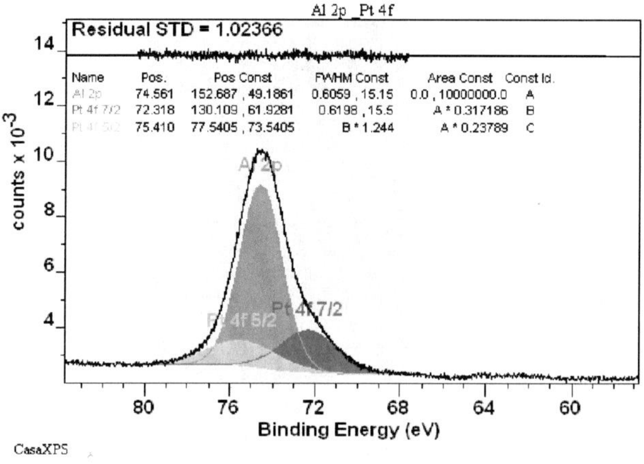

The constraints are integral to determining the position, FWHM and peak area. If a Monte Carlo error analysis is performed for the three component model above the results for the peak positions are as follows:

Component Name	Position	STD DEV
Al 2p	74.561	0.004948
Pt 4f 7/2	72.318	0.025664
Pt 4f 5/2	75.41	0.10245

After examining the standard deviation in the component positions the uncertainty in the Pt 4f 5/2 peak is an order of magnitude larger than the uncertainty in the other two peaks. The table therefore suggests noise may be a factor when determining the positions for these peaks if the model as it stands were applied to similar data with poorer noise statistics. If the constraints are altered to force the relative positions of the Pt 4f peaks to maintain a fixed value, the same table appears to show the position parameters are less sensitive to noise.

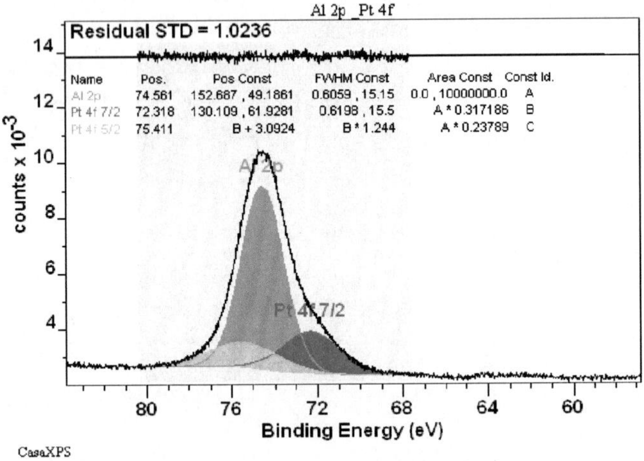

Component Name	Position	STD DEV
Al 2p	74.561	0.003849
Pt 4f 7/2	72.318	0.030876
Pt 4f 5/2	75.411	0.030876

These stronger constraints require more physical knowledge but clearly establishing the separation for the Pt 4f peaks improves the stability of the model. Creating a rigid model probably improves the reliability for all quantities determined for aluminium and platinum. The trick is to balance the construct of a model to both provide sufficient flexibility to prevent spurious least squares solutions but rigid enough to be insensitive to noise. Monte Carlo error analysis is very useful in achieving these goals.

The Monte Carlo button on the Components property page offers the means to investigate a peak model.

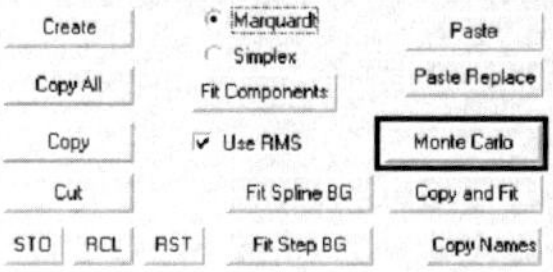

To obtain an estimate for the uncertainty in fitting parameters, the model is displayed in the active tile before pressing the Monte Carlo button on the Components property page. A progress dialog window appears showing the current state of the Monte Carlo simulation and provides a means of terminating the computation sequence.

On completion two dialog windows appear presenting the results of the Monte Carlo calculation. These two dialog windows offer an error matrix and the set of simulation results from which the error matrix is calculated. These tables of results can be placed on the clipboard and transferred to a spreadsheet program for further analysis.

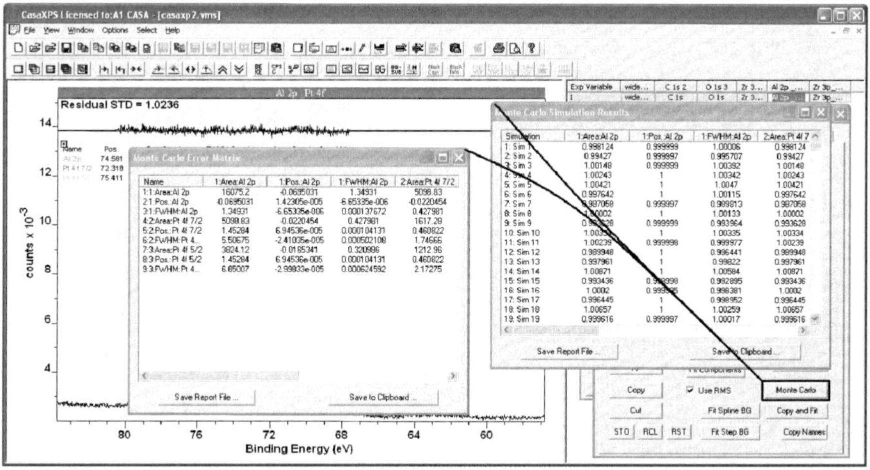

The error matrix when copied to a spreadsheet program includes an additional column in which the standard deviation for each parameter in the peak model is presented.

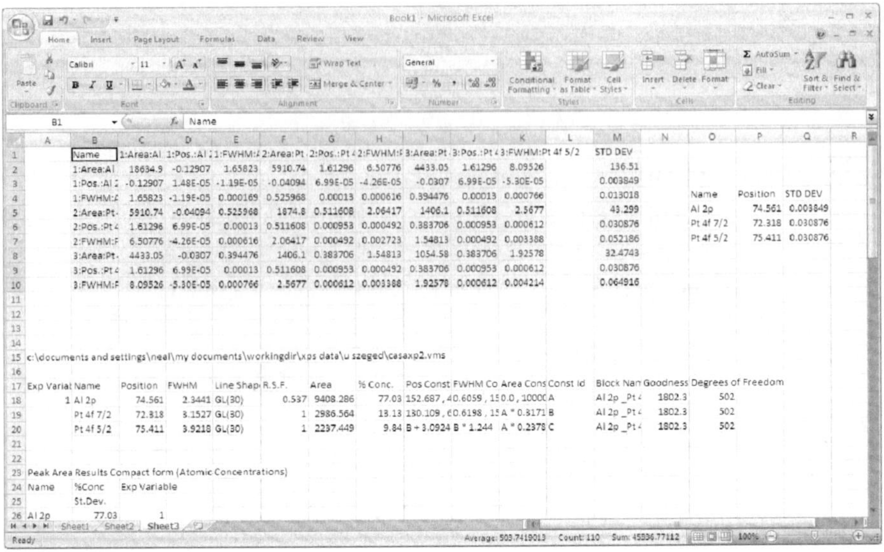

Name	1:Area:Al	1:Pos.:Al	1:FWHM:	2:Area:Pt	2:Pos.:Pt	2:FWHM:	3:Area:Pt	3:Pos.:Pt	3:FWHM:Pt 4f 5/2	STD DEV
1:Area:Al	18634.9	-0.12907	1.65823	5910.74	1.61296	6.50776	4433.05	1.61296	8.09526	136.51
1:Pos.:Al	-0.12907	1.48E-05	-1.19E-05	-0.04094	6.99E-05	-4.26E-05	-0.0307	6.99E-05	-5.30E-05	0.003849
1:FWHM:	1.65823	-1.19E-05	0.000169	0.525968	0.00013	0.000616	0.394476	0.00013	0.000766	0.013018
2:Area:Pt	5910.74	-0.04094	0.525968	1874.8	0.511608	2.06417	1406.1	0.511608	2.5677	43.299
2:Pos.:Pt	1.61296	6.99E-05	0.00013	0.511608	0.000953	0.000492	0.383706	0.000953	0.000612	0.030876
2:FWHM:F	6.50776	-4.26E-05	0.000616	2.06417	0.000492	0.002723	1.54813	0.000492	0.003388	0.052186
3:Area:Pt	4433.05	-0.0307	0.394476	1406.1	0.383706	1.54813	1054.58	0.383706	1.92578	32.4743
3:Pos.:Pt	1.61296	6.99E-05	0.00013	0.511608	0.000953	0.000492	0.383706	0.000953	0.000612	0.030876
3:FWHM:F	8.09526	-5.30E-05	0.000766	2.5677	0.000612	0.003388	1.92578	0.000612	0.004214	0.064916

Name	Position	STD DEV
Al 2p	74.561	0.003849
Pt 4f 7/2	72.318	0.030876
Pt 4f 5/2	75.411	0.030876

c:\documents and settings\neal\my documents\workingdir\xps data\u szeged\casaxp2.vms

Exp Variat	Name	Position	FWHM	Line Shap	R.S.F.	Area	% Conc.	Pos Const	FWHM Co	Area Cons	Const Id	Block Nan	Goodness	Degrees of Freedom
1	Al 2p	74.561	2.3441	GL(30)	0.537	9408.286	77.03	152.687 , 4	0.6059 , 15	0.0 , 10000	A	Al 2p _Pt	1802.3	502
	Pt 4f 7/2	72.318	3.1527	GL(30)	1	2986.564	13.13	130.109 , 6	0.6198 , 15	A * 0.3171	B	Al 2p _Pt	1802.3	502
	Pt 4f 5/2	75.411	3.9218	GL(30)	1	2237.449	9.84	B + 3.0924	B * 1.244	A * 0.2378	C	Al 2p _Pt	1802.3	502

Peak Area Results Compact form (Atomic Concentrations)

Name	%Conc	Exp Variable
	St.Dev.	
Al 2p	77.03	1

More details about Monte Carlo error analysis are available in The Casa Cook Book.

RPT Report Property Page

While originally designed for batch processing applications, quantification reports defined by RPT files are available from the Quantification Parameters dialog window. The RPT Report property page allows a previously defined RPT file to be applied to those experiment frames for which at least one block is selected. The options on the Select menu help to select blocks across experiment frames and once the appropriate experiment frames are so identified, pressing the Generate Report button on the RPT Report property page permits the appropriate RPT file to be loaded. On completion, a report dialog window corresponding to the RPT file and the selected experiment frames appears.

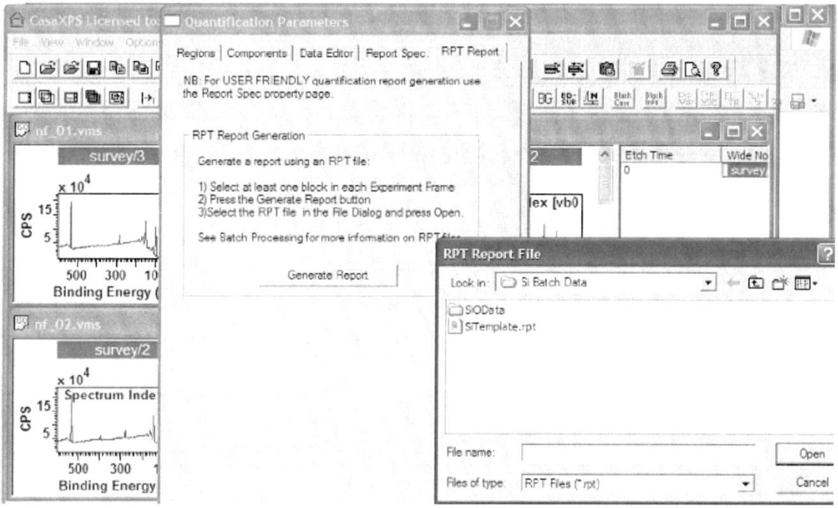

A simple text edit program such as Notepad can be used to prepare the RPT file. Once a program has been associated with the rpt file extension, right-clicking the mouse over the RPT file in the File dialog window and selecting the Open option will invoke the chosen text editor. The RPT Report property page not only offers a means of creating a very specific report for a particular type of experiment, but also provides a means of creating and testing RPT files in preparation for use with batch processing.

It is important to realize that an RPT file is specific to a particular experiment. The order of the VAMAS blocks in the experiment frame is important and therefore any file included in the reporting process must conform to the rigid format defined in the RPT file. Further before applying the RPT file, all processing and quantification items must be previously created on the target data with exactly the appropriate definitions for the RPT file. While flexible with respect to the quantification information tabulated, the RPT mechanism is very inflexible with respect to the data and data treatment.

RPT Configuration File Entries (Batch Processing)

The RPT mechanism is the most flexible means in CasaXPS of tabulating results computed from quantification regions and/or synthetic peak models. However, the cost of using this tool is that the resulting table must be defined in very basic terms. An RPT file defines the columns of a report using the VAMAS file block structure and the ordering of the quantification regions and components within the blocks of data.

A VAMAS file consists of a header section followed by a set of data blocks. Within CasaXPS, the order of these blocks is maintained using an index number beginning at zero illustrated below.

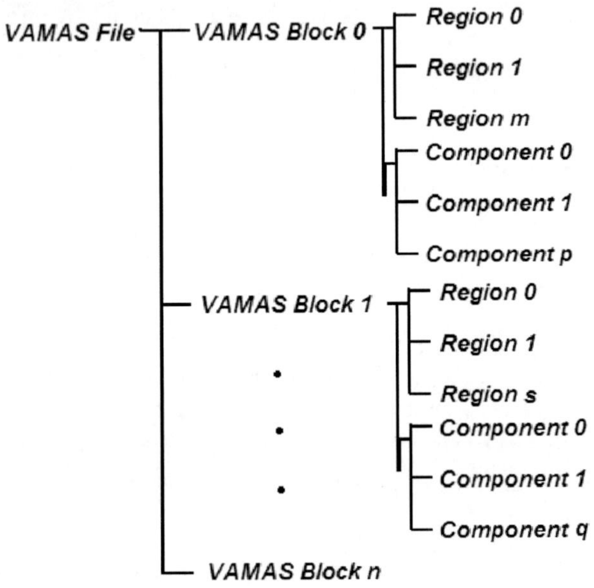

Each data block referenced by index (e.g. vb0, vb1, vb2, ...) includes ordered lists of quantification regions and components, also illustrated above, which are again referenced using the index within a VAMAS block for a given region or component (e.g. r0, r1, r2, ... and c0, c1, c2, ...). To identify a specific piece of information from a region or component, the datum of interest is defined using the VAMAS block index, a keyword string and either the index string for the region or component.

For example, data in a file containing three VAMAS blocks are prepared to include regions and components. The spectra from the file illustrated below are displayed such that the VAMAS block index appears in the top left-hand corner of the graphical area (an option on the Tile Display dialog window) from which it is clear the data can be referenced by vb0 for the survey spectrum, vb1 for the O 1s spectrum and vb2 for the Si 2p spectrum. The survey spectrum has three quantification regions defined on it, while the O 1s and Si 2p spectra each have a single region defined. In addition, the Si 2p data are fitted using a peak model in which four synthetic components are used.

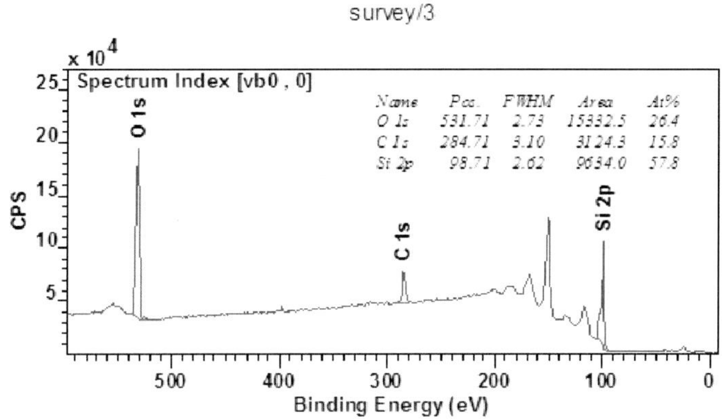

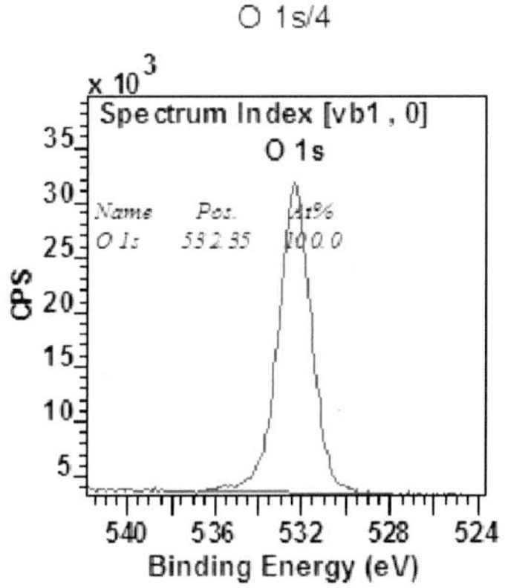

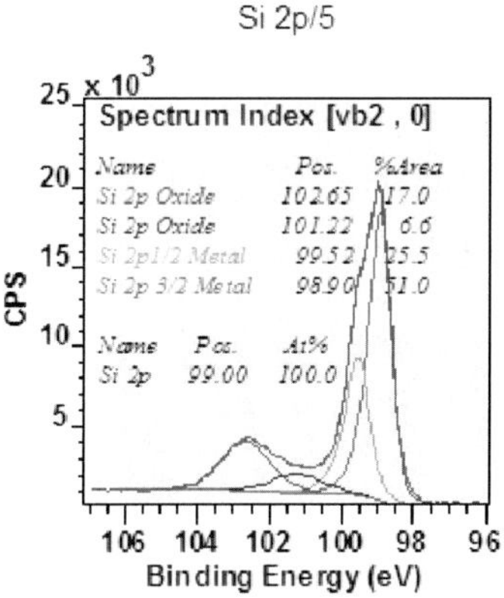

The order assigned to the regions and components is defined by the column on either the Region or Component property page in which a given region or component appears, respectively.

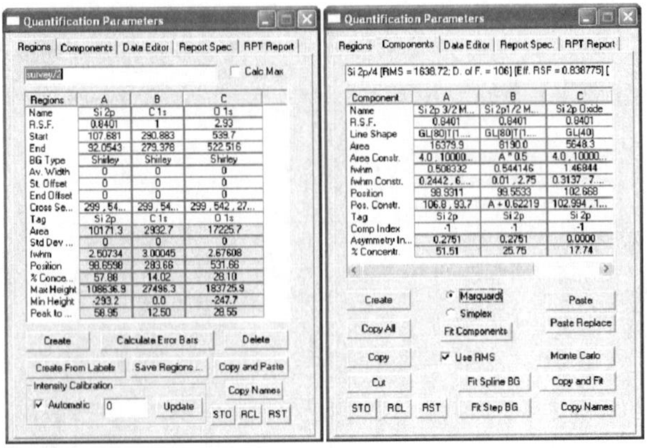

The regions and components on the Quantification Parameter dialog window always appear in the order in which the items are created. The order important to the RPT file definitions is defined by the Quantification Parameters dialog window, which may for example differ from the order used in quantification reports and annotation. The order used to list regions and components in annotation is subject to configuration. To specify the transmission and RSF corrected intensity from the second component defined on the Si 2p VAMAS block the string vb2;INTENSITY;c1 would be used in the RPT file.

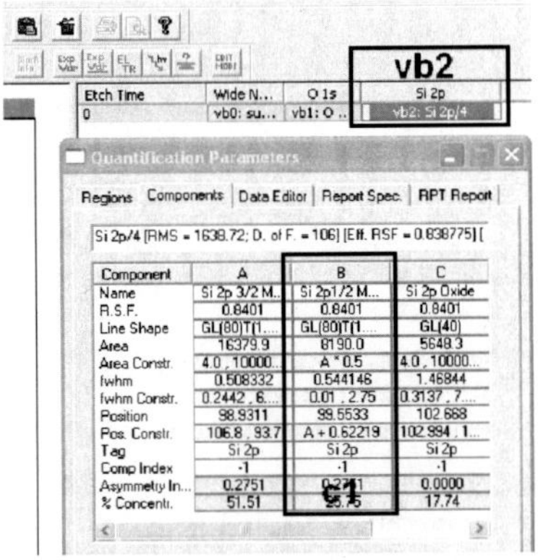

That is, since the index for the VAMAS blocks begin with zero, ***vb2*** identifies the third VAMAS block in the file and similarly ***c1*** indicates the component in column B of the list on the Components property page. The O 1s intensity from the survey spectrum would be identified using the string vb0;INTENSITY;r2. This is because the O 1s region on the survey spectrum appears in column C, while to reference the O 1s intensity from the narrow scan spectrum the region would be identified using vb1;INTENSITY;r0.

Batch Processing

CasaXPS offers a very simple yet powerful tool for transferring quantification and processing to other data via the propagate mechanism. Batch processing is only used to process large sets of identical samples.

Batch processing is aimed at situations where a set of essentially equivalent samples require identical data reduction steps. The objective is to provide a simple sequence of user interactions resulting in a report as well as optionally printing of the spectra in a predefined format.

Batch processing offers:

- Automatic data conversion to the ISO 14976 (VAMAS) file format.
- Data reduction steps bases upon a previously processed VAMAS file.
- Printing after formatting the data using a .tff file.
- Generation of a report based upon a report specification file.

Once the necessary configuration files are defined, the whole procedure amounts to selecting the template file and the raw data directory, then waiting for the results.

Overview

The configuration files used as part of the batch processing feature appear in a directory called CasaXPS.BAT in the same directory as the executable file CasaXPS.exe (other CasaXPS directories such as CasaXPS.DEF and CasaXPS.HLP may also appear in the same directory). For each set of samples for which batch processing is required there will be at least one file in the CasaXPS.BAT directory, the so called ***template file***. A template file is merely a .vms file containing a set of VAMAS blocks in the same order and number of as will be present in the data files acquired from each of the samples being analysed. Any processing, annotation, regions and components required for each sample should be applied to the data in the template file. When the batch processing is invoked, these operations from the template file are applied to each file in a target data directory.

Accompanying the template file, are optionally two files with the same base-name but with file extensions .tff and .rpt. The .tff file must contain information generated from the template file relating to the tile display format required when printing the data. If printing is not required, then the CasaXPS.BAT directory should not contain a corresponding .tff file to the template file. Similarly, the .rpt file is an ASCII file specifying the format for a row of data in the final quantification report. If no .rpt file corresponding to the template file exists in the CasaXPS.BAT directory, a default report is generated once batch processing is complete. Defining the display state used for printing the spectra is described elsewhere.

The objective for the .rpt file is to allow all the quantification items derived from the regions and components to be made available in a report, where these quantities can be combined using any arithmetic combination thereof including functions such as SQRT, LOG (natural log i.e. base e), EXP, SIN and COS. With the aid of these mathematical functions, intensities may be used to compute values for, say, over-layer thicknesses as well as error bars for such calculations. The emphasis is on exporting the data for use elsewhere, for example a spreadsheet program where the ultimate report may includes conditional display colours, more involved computation and/or graphical display, all previously defined on one sheet using data taken from a data entry sheet accepting the format defined by the .rpt file. The following describes defining the .rpt files.

Setting-up the .rpt File

The .rpt file is an ASCII file best prepared in a simple program such as Notepad. Keywords and defined strings are used to annotate the report and extract the quantification details from the processed data files. The syntax for entries in the .rpt file appears in the following table:

newline	Inserts a new line in the header section of the report
header;<text-string>	Defines a text string for use as a header to the report. Each header so defined appears in a separate cell when pasted into a spreadsheet.
text;<text-string>	Defines a text string that will appear embedded in the report and is repeated for each row.
blank	Inserts a blank cell in the ultimate spreadsheet.
vf;FILE	If defined, the filename for the original file for the sample entered in a row.
vf;vmsfile	The base-name of the VAMAS file from which the current row in the report is defined.
vf;DESC	If defined, the file description for the sample entered in a row.
vf;DATE	The date when the data in the row was acquired.
vf;BATCH	If defined, the batch identification string for the

	row of data
vf;header;dir	Enter the data directory name into the header section of the report.
vb<index>;<keyword>	Extracts information from a VAMAS block defined using the VAMAS block index (an integer) and a keyword (see following table). The VAMAS block indices run from 0 to the number of blocks in the file minus one.
vb<index>;<keyword>;r<index>	Extracts information from a Region in a VAMAS block defined using the VAMAS block index (an integer) and a keyword (see following table) followed by the letter r (for region) and the region index within the VAMAS block. The VAMAS block indices run from 0 to the number of blocks in the file minus one. The region index runs from 0 to the number of regions in a VAMAS block minus one. The region order is defined by the columns in the Regions property page.
vb<index>;<keyword>;c<index>	Extracts information from a Component in a VAMAS block defined using the VAMAS block index (an integer) and a keyword (see following table) followed by the letter c (for Component) and the component index within the VAMAS block. The VAMAS block indices run from 0 to the number of blocks in the file minus one. The component index runs from 0 to the number of components in a VAMAS block minus one. The component order is defined by the columns in the Components property page.

Keywords used to define quantities in the RPT entries are defined in the table below.

FIT	Goodness of fit metric (Chisq or RMS)
EXP_VAR	Experimental Variable assigned to the VAMAS Block
BLOCKID	Block identification string for VAMAS Block
SAMPLEID	Sample identification string for VAMAS Block
INTENSITY	Intensity measured in CPSeV (area under peak)
POSITION	Binding Energy of the peak maximum
FWHM	Full Width at Half Maximum
STDEV	Error in measured intensity for peak area. (Regions only)
MAX_HEIGHT	Intensity at maximum counts (depends on technique)
MIN_HEIGHT	Intensity at minimum counts (depends on technique)
RSF	Relative Sensitivity Factor used to compute Intensity
PEAK_TO_PEAK	Difference in maximum and minimum intensity within a Region.
MASS	Mass value in Daltons (amu) assigned to a Region or Component.

The syntax definitions shown in the above tables are illustrated using NotePad, where an example .rpt file demonstrates how the individual quantification items are referenced and provides examples of arithmetic expressions involving intensities and standard deviations. Note the use of the SQRT function, which allows the uncertainty in the ratio calculation to be determined.

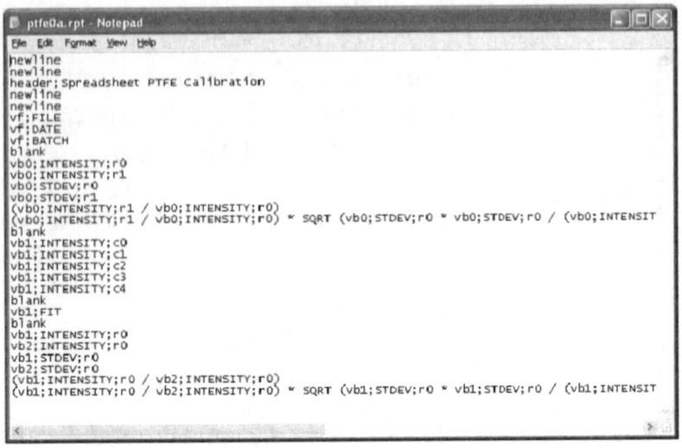

Energy Calibration Feature designed for Batch Processing

Calibration of spectra is typically different between samples and therefore a mechanism for instructing the calibration to proceed based upon the location of a peak from within a new file is required. To this end, a range of energies may be specified for the measured calibration energy.

Given a range of energies for the measured value, the exact energy used in the calibration for each sample is determined from the corresponding peak for which the range calibration is applied in the template file. If the Apply to Selection option in used, then the other spectra so calibrated will include a reference to the spectrum used to initiate the energy calibration.

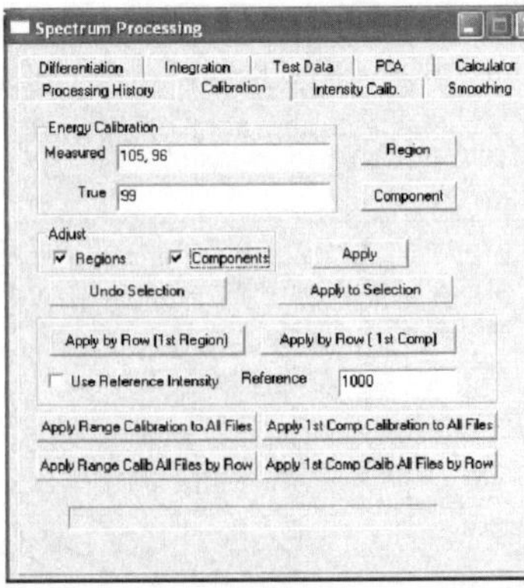

The value determined for the Measured field is computed from the data within the specified range. Note the energies specified using the range syntax refers to the original bins assigned at acquisition time. That is, previous calibrations do not alter the data bins used by the new calibration mechanism. Furthermore, the value so determined is obtained by interpolating the data via a quadratic polynomial, where a linear least square criterion is used to determine the polynomial.

An Example; Batch Processing without Printing and using the Default Report File

In this example, a set of samples representing a sequence of self assembling mono-layers on gold, are analysed using identical acquisition and processing procedures. While the propagate option in CasaXPS is well suited to such tasks, the processing of these data can be achieved with minimal user interactions via the batch processing mechanism. The principal virtue of the batch mechanism resides in the ability of an experienced scientist to set-up the prescription for analysing the samples, after which a person with less XPS experience or even limited experience of using CasaXPS can generate a report in three easy steps.

Defining the Batch Processing

It is important each sample is analysed with the same sequence of acquisition steps. That is, the resulting files must contain identical acquisition regions in terms of number and VAMAS block order within the files. A representative VAMAS file is prepare with all the required processing and saved in the directory CasaXPS.BAT located in the same directory as the executable file CasaXPS.exe. Since the default report will be used for these samples the report specification file is not required, the absence of which in the CasaXPS.BAT directory is the flag to use the default report. Also, the similar absence of a .tff file with the same base-name as the .vms file prevents any printing of spectra during the batch processing.

The template file consists of four VAMAS blocks, where the Au 4f region is used to energy calibration all four regions in the file. The new range calibration procedure described above is employed to calibrate the data.

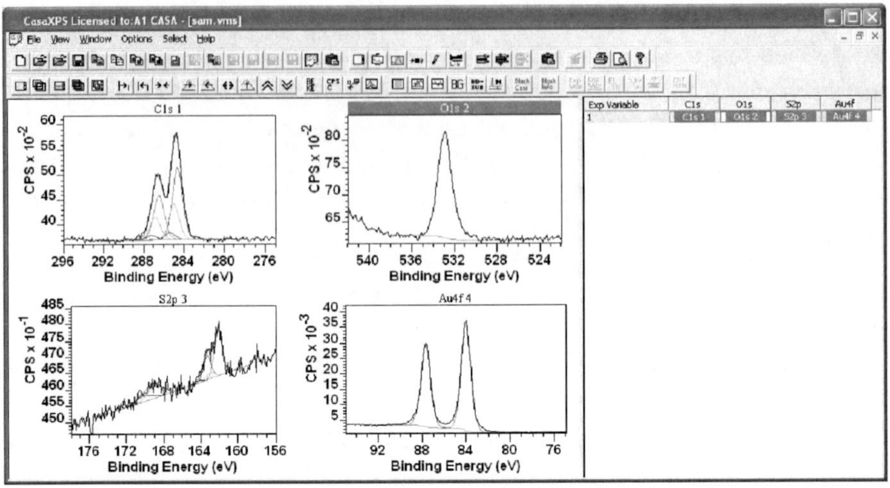

Applying the Batch Processing

After acquisition, the data files should be collected into a separate directory. In this example the data has been acquired using a PHI Quantum and therefore a set of .spe binary files generated. These .spe files must be stored in a directory with no other .spe files other than those measured from the intended sample set. Three simple steps are then required to process a set of files.

1. From the File Menu, select the Batch Processing menu item.

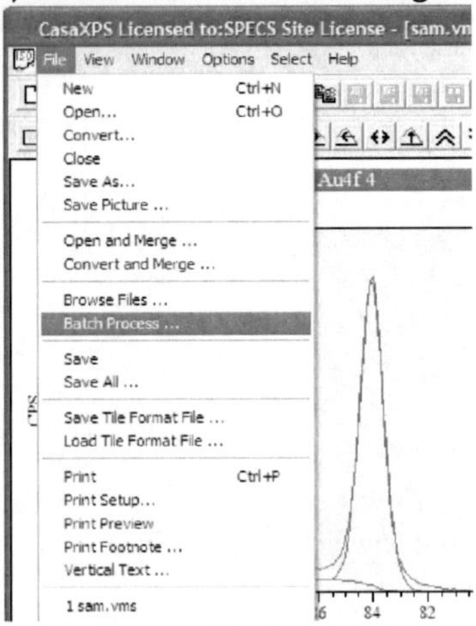

2. Select the appropriate template file from the list offered on the dialog window and press the Apply Template button.

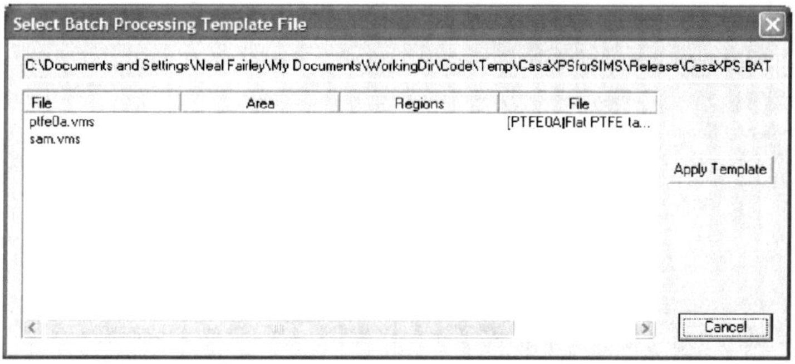

3. Select one of the .spe files within the File Dialog window and press Open.

It is now a case of waiting for the results to appear in a clipboard selection dialog window.

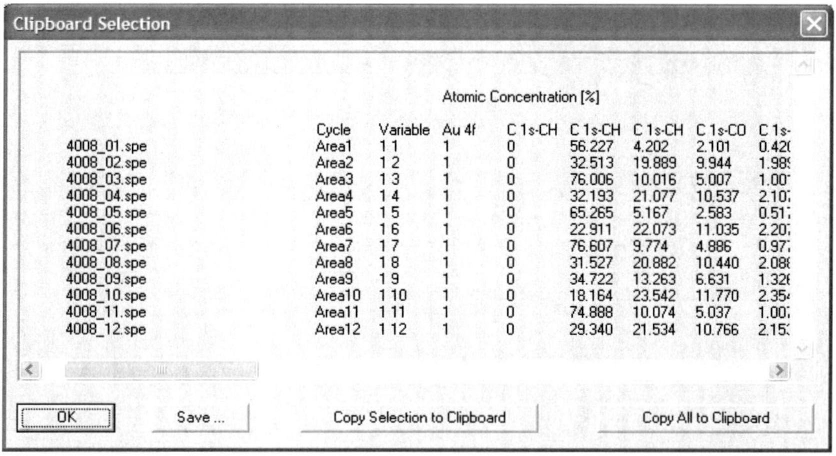

The default report is a TAB spaced file which can be copied via the clipboard into a spreadsheet program or alternatively the report can be saved to file.

An Example: Batch Processing with Printing and .rpt File

In this example, a sequence of measurements is made across the surface of a silicon wafer where the ratio of elemental silicon to silicon oxide is required. For each sample the atomic concentration determined from regions on the survey spectrum are combined using formula in a .rpt file; also the intensities for the silicon states, measured using a peak model, are processed from the data and the ratio computed as part of the report. A template .vms file must be prepared:

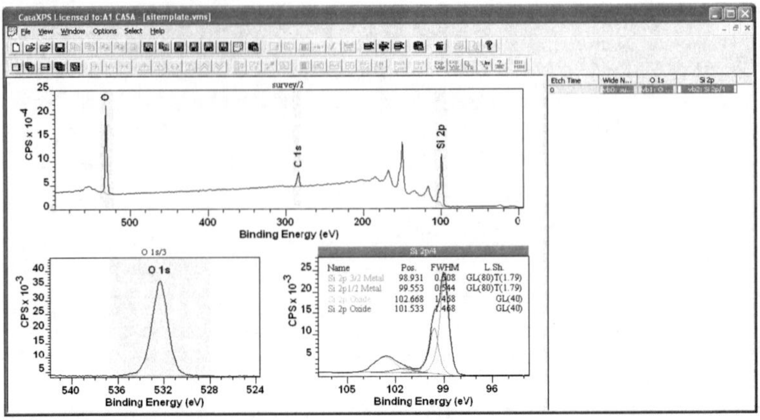

A tff file for the display state is also prepared as well as a .rpt configuration file defining the report format.

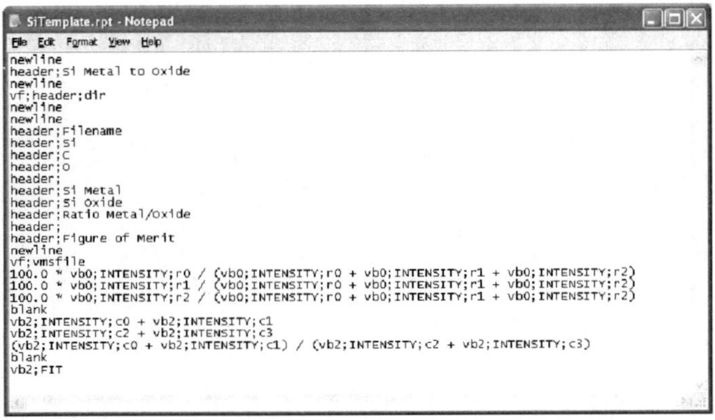
SiTemplate.rpt - Notepad

```
newline
header;Si Metal to Oxide
newline
vf;header;dir
newline
newline
header;Filename
header;Si
header;C
header;O
header;
header;Si Metal
header;Si Oxide
header;Ratio Metal/Oxide
header;
header;Figure of Merit
newline
vf;vmsfile
100.0 * vb0;INTENSITY;r0 / (vb0;INTENSITY;r0 + vb0;INTENSITY;r1 + vb0;INTENSITY;r2)
100.0 * vb0;INTENSITY;r1 / (vb0;INTENSITY;r0 + vb0;INTENSITY;r1 + vb0;INTENSITY;r2)
100.0 * vb0;INTENSITY;r2 / (vb0;INTENSITY;r0 + vb0;INTENSITY;r1 + vb0;INTENSITY;r2)
blank
vb2;INTENSITY;c0 + vb2;INTENSITY;c1
vb2;INTENSITY;c2 + vb2;INTENSITY;c3
(vb2;INTENSITY;c0 + vb2;INTENSITY;c1) / (vb2;INTENSITY;c2 + vb2;INTENSITY;c3)
blank
vb2;FIT
```

All three files in the CasaXPS.BAT directory have the same base-name and the inclusion of the .tff and .rpt files causes the printing of the spectra and the generation of the report, respectively.

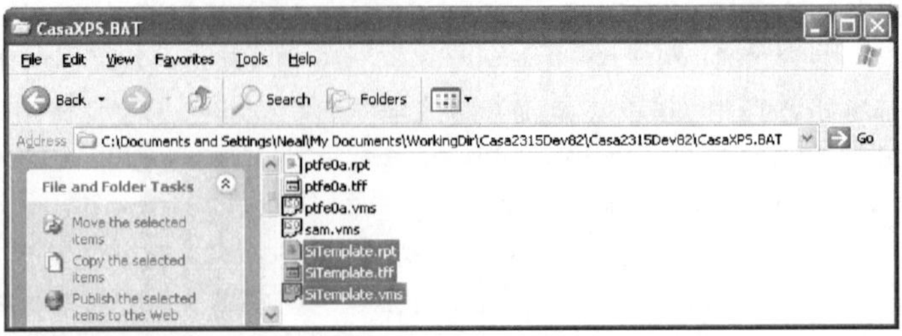

The steps for batch processing with printing together with a custom report are identical to the steps described above. The only difference is the additional .tff and .rpt files are required.

A batch of twenty sets of spectra was acquired on an Axis Nova in the Kratos Applications Lab. where each experiment was performed at a different location on the silicon sample along a line scan. The silicon wafer had previously been etched at specific locations. Such analyses can be set up by an experienced XPS analysis and left to a technician for batch processing the results.

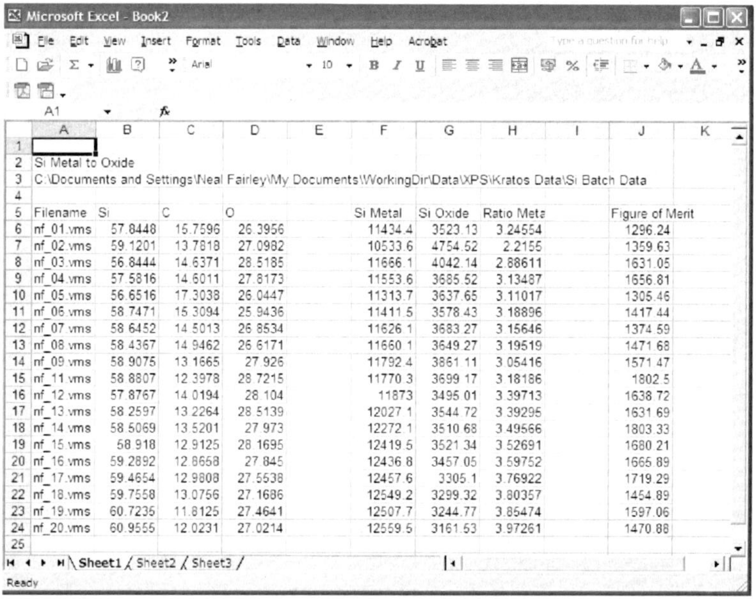

	A	B	C	D	E	F	G	H	I	J	K
1											
2	Si Metal to Oxide										
3	C:\Documents and Settings\Neal Fairley\My Documents\WorkingDir\Data\XPS\Kratos Data\Si Batch Data										
4											
5	Filename	Si	C	O		Si Metal	Si Oxide	Ratio Meta		Figure of Merit	
6	nf_01.vms	57.8448	15.7596	26.3956		11434.4	3523.13	3.24554		1296.24	
7	nf_02.vms	59.1201	13.7818	27.0982		10533.6	4754.52	2.2155		1359.63	
8	nf_03.vms	56.8444	14.6371	28.5185		11666.1	4042.14	2.88611		1631.05	
9	nf_04.vms	57.5816	14.6011	27.8173		11553.6	3685.52	3.13487		1656.81	
10	nf_05.vms	56.6516	17.3038	26.0447		11313.7	3637.65	3.11017		1305.46	
11	nf_06.vms	58.7471	15.3094	25.9436		11411.5	3578.43	3.18896		1417.44	
12	nf_07.vms	58.6452	14.5013	26.8534		11626.1	3683.27	3.15646		1374.59	
13	nf_08.vms	58.4367	14.9462	26.6171		11660.1	3649.27	3.19519		1471.68	
14	nf_09.vms	58.9075	13.1665	27.926		11792.4	3861.11	3.05416		1571.47	
15	nf_11.vms	58.8807	12.3978	28.7215		11770.3	3699.17	3.18186		1802.5	
16	nf_12.vms	57.8767	14.0194	28.104		11873	3495.01	3.39713		1638.72	
17	nf_13.vms	58.2597	13.2264	28.5139		12027.1	3544.72	3.39295		1631.69	
18	nf_14.vms	58.5069	13.5201	27.973		12272.1	3510.68	3.49566		1803.33	
19	nf_15.vms	58.918	12.9125	28.1695		12419.5	3521.34	3.52691		1680.21	
20	nf_16.vms	59.2892	12.8658	27.845		12436.8	3457.05	3.59752		1665.89	
21	nf_17.vms	59.4654	12.9808	27.5538		12457.6	3305.1	3.76922		1719.29	
22	nf_18.vms	59.7558	13.0756	27.1686		12549.2	3299.32	3.80357		1454.89	
23	nf_19.vms	60.7235	11.8125	27.4641		12507.7	3244.77	3.85474		1597.06	
24	nf_20.vms	60.9555	12.0231	27.0214		12559.5	3161.53	3.97261		1470.88	
25											

Report Spec Property Page

Standard Reports

Standard reports are configurable row-orientated reports generated from survey and/or narrow scan spectra measured from the same surface. Creating a quantification report involves:

1. Creating quantification regions and/or components for each peak used to characterise the sample.
2. Selecting in the right-hand pane the VAMAS blocks containing the spectra for which regions are defined.

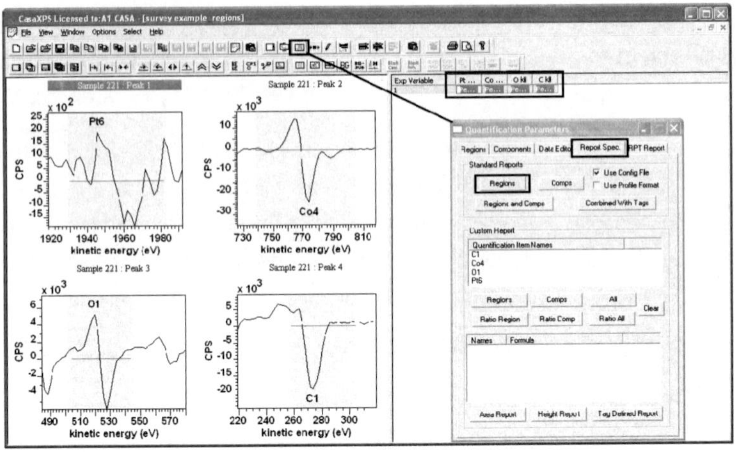

3. Invoking the Quantification Parameters dialog window and selecting the Report Spec property page.
4. Pressing the button labelled Regions in the Standard Report Section on the Report Spec property page.

When the Regions button is pressed, if the Use Config File tick-box is ticked a configuration file is used to define the information appearing in the text report. A detailed discussion regarding these configuration files is presented in a later section. The report generated from one specific configuration file appears as a text report in CasaXPS.

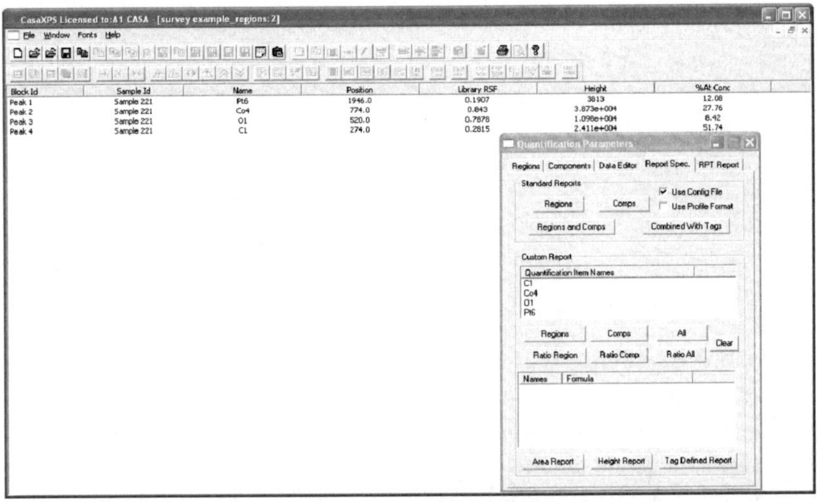

A quantification report generated from the standard report options is copied through the clipboard by pressing the Copy toolbar button or Control-C at the time the text report window has focus in CasaXPS.

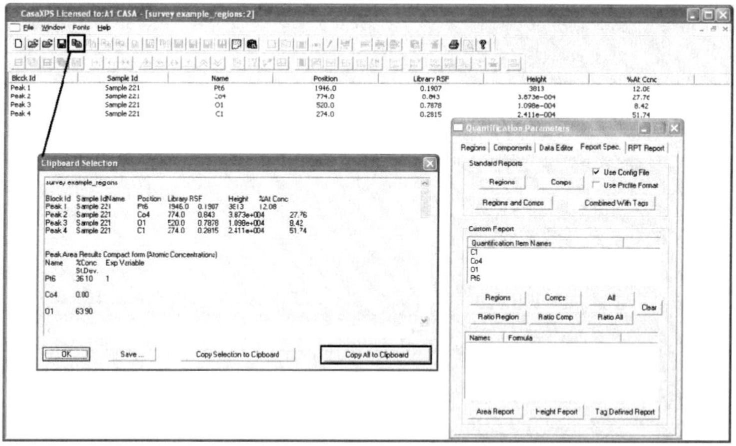

Any program capable of accepting text via the clipboard can be used to further manipulate the data. The data placed on the clipboard includes a variety of tabulation formats.

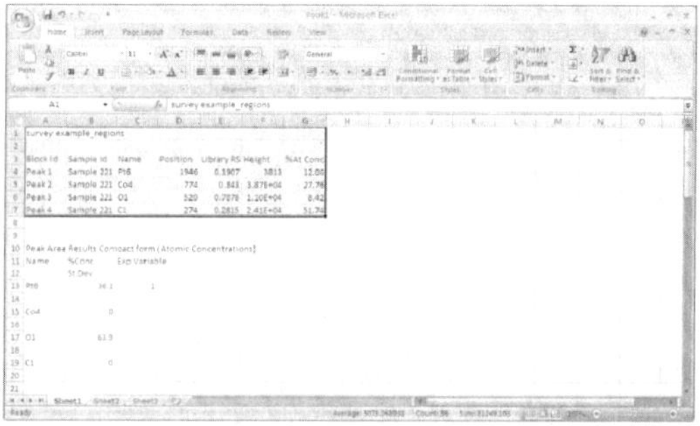

Configuration Files for Standard Reports

The configuration files for the standard report are constructed from a set of keywords entered into an ASCII file one keyword per line. The keywords are:

Keyword	Description
VARIABLE	Experimental Variable value from the VAMAS block or Row Label when in Edit Mode
NAME	Region or component name.
POSITION	Peak position.
FWHM	Peak full width at half maximum

AREA	Peak area correct for transmission and energy dependence but not RSF
RSF	Relative Sensitivity Factor
CONCENTRATION	% Atomic Concentration
ERROR_BAR	Std Deviation in % atomic concentration for regions
START	Quantification region lower limit
END	Quantification region upper limit
PEAK_TO_PEAK	Intensity for peak to peak Auger Peak intensity maximum to minimum XPS/SIMS peak height above background
PEAK_TO_PEAK_CONC	% Concentration measured using peak to peak intensity
LINE_SHAPE	Synthetic line-shape for a component
AREA_ERROR_BAR	Std Deviation in peak area measured using a quantification region.
TRANSITION_TAG	Tag string from region or component
POSITION_CONST	Component position constraint string
AREA_CONST	Component area constraint string
FWHM_CONST	Component FWHM constraint string
COLUMN_LABEL	Column character appearing above a region or component on the respective property page
DEGREES_OF_FREEDOM	Degrees of freedom used to compute the figure of merit from least squares fit.
VAMAS_BLOCK_NAME	VAMAS block identifier
CENTROID	Position of the centroid of a peak
MASS	Mass assigned to a region or component
MASS_CONC	% Mass Concentration
SIGNAL_TO_NOISE	Std Dev for noise distribution
CORRECTED_AREA	Peak area corrected by the total sensitivity factor
TOTAL_SENSITIVITY_FACTOR	Combined factor from RSF, Transmission and energy dependence factors
TRANSMISSION	Transmission function value at peak maximum
MEAN_FREE_PATH	Kinetic energy dependence factor
RAW_AREA	Uncorrected integral of background subtracted signal
PEAK_PLUS	Peak intensity above background
PEAK_MINUS	Peak intensity below background
SIMS_PEAK_AREA	Summation of data channel
VAMAS_BLOCK_SAMPLE_ID	VAMAS Sample Identifier string

Notepad or any other means of creating an ASCII file can be employed to create the configuration files.

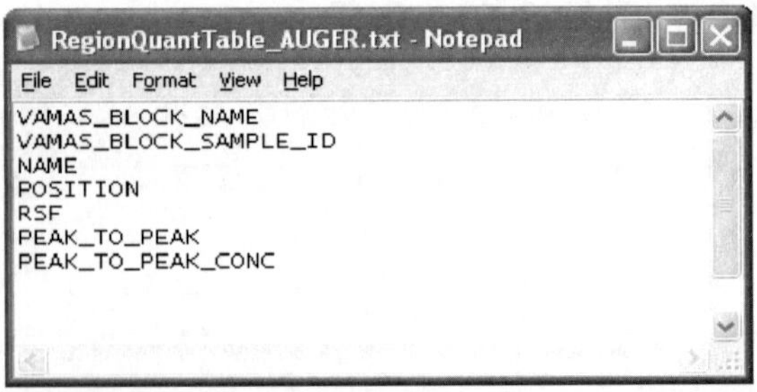

The configuration file used to generate the standard report is located on the disk relative to the directory containing the CasaXPS.exe executable file. Within the same directory as the CasaXPS.exe executable file is a directory called CasaXPS.DEF. Default display settings enabled on starting a new CasaXPS session are also saved in the CasaXPS.DEF directory.

Each type of configuration file for the standard report options is identified by key names; specifically, the file called RegionQuantTable.txt provides the configuration information for the columns in the standard report generated when the Regions button in the standard report section is pressed. Similarly, other configuration files with key names are associated with the other reporting options in the standard report section. These configuration files are used by default each time a standard report is requested and are most appropriate for those users requiring a fixed format for each report generated.

A further feature allows a choice of configuration files. If a directory exists in the CasaXPS.DEF directory by the name of QuantTables, then on pressing a standard report button the user is offered a list of configuration files. The report format is dependent on the choice made from the list.

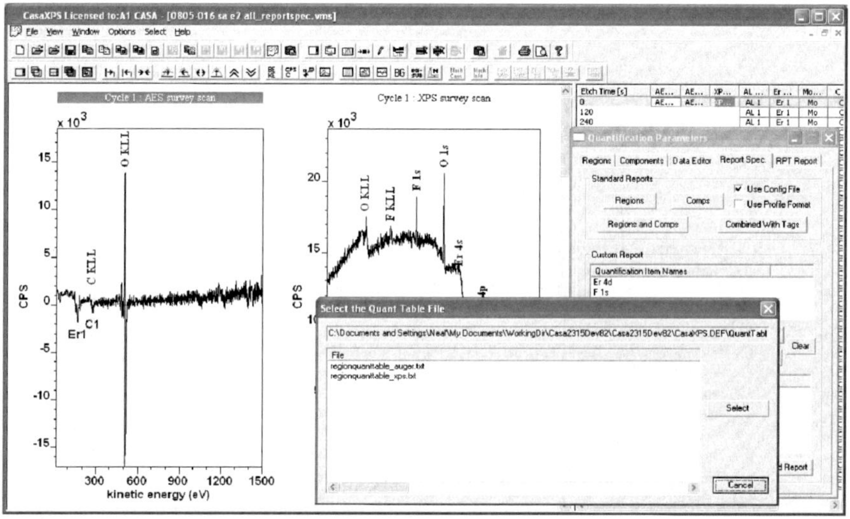

Since all files in the directory CasaXPS.DEF/QuantTables are offered in the dialog window, the names of the files within the QuantTables directory are unimportant and therefore the correct configuration file for the type of data must be selected.

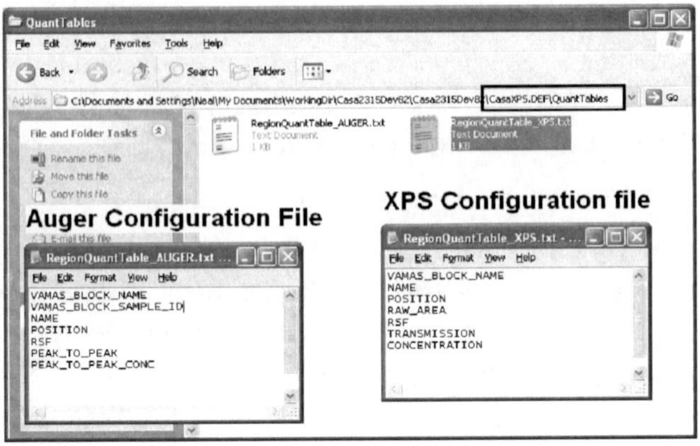

To quantify the Auger survey:

Select in the right-hand pane the VAMAS block containing the AES survey spectrum and press the Regions button from the Standard Report section.

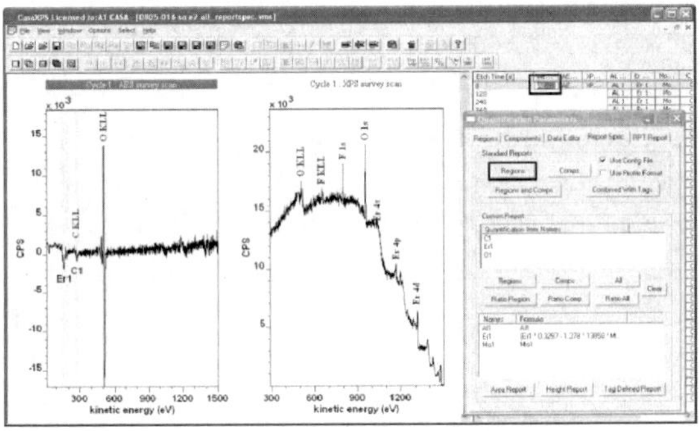

On the resulting dialog window, select the configuration file from the list and press the Select button. The quantification table appears with column headings defined by the configuration file.

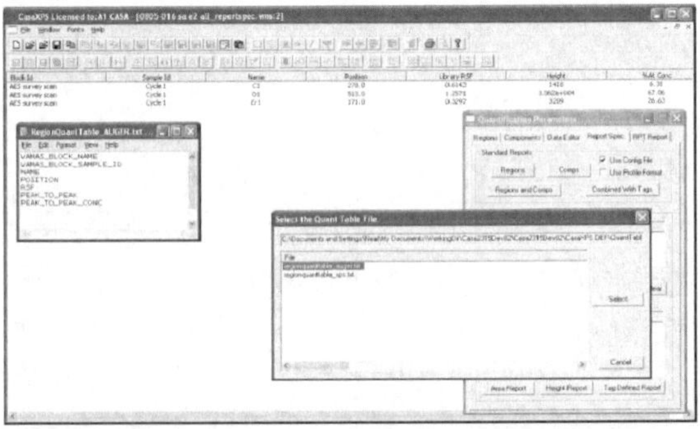

A different report is obtained from a similar sequence of steps for the XPS survey spectrum recorded from the same sample and located in the same VAMAS file. By selecting the configuration file prepared for XPS data an appropriate report is selectively produced; XPS spectra are typically quantified using peak area after background subtraction rather than the peak-to-peak approach of Auger spectra.

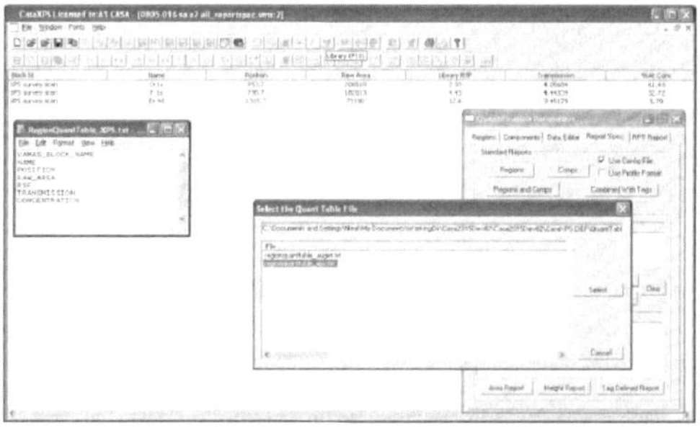

In the event no selection is made from the dialog window invoked by pressing the Regions button, the default configuration file for the Regions button is used to generate the report. The default configuration file for the Regions button on the Standard report is located in the CasaXPS.DEF directory with the key name RegionQuantTable.txt.

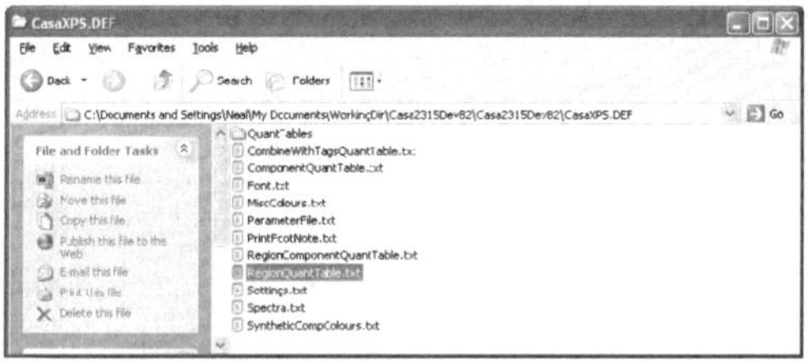

The selection dialog window only appears if the QuantTables directory exists in the CasaXPS.DEF directory. The default configuration file for the Regions button is automatically used if the CasaXPS.DEF directory is prepared *without* the QuantTables subdirectory.

Custom Reports

Custom reports are not configurable and data are presented in columns with each row of the table associated with an experimental variable. The intention is to provide a means of profiling changes in spectra with respect to etch time or angle or any parameter that varies throughout the course of an experiment.

The Custom Report, like the Standard Report, only applies to the current selection in the right-hand pane of the experiment frame. Regions and components are treated identically within the custom report and are referred to as quantification items, where both forms of these quantification items are identified by the name fields used in the definition of the regions and components. When a VAMAS block is selected in the right-hand pane, all the region names and component names are collected into a list displayed under the heading Quantification Item Names.

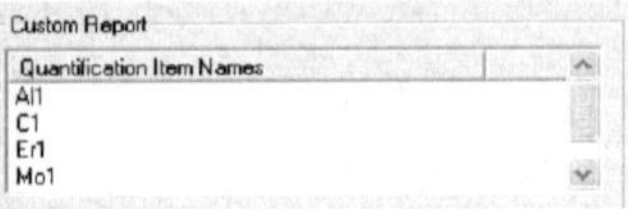

Only quantification item names appearing in the Quantification Item Names list are used in the custom report.

Auger data provided by Tyne R. Johns (Sandia National Laboratories)

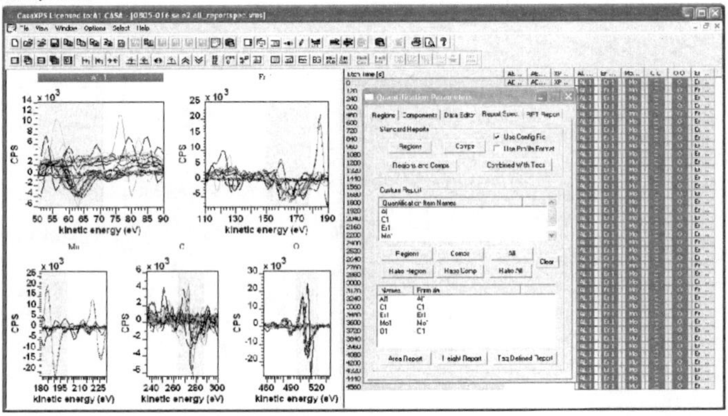

A custom report is defined in terms of the currently active quantification item names using the Name and Formula table.

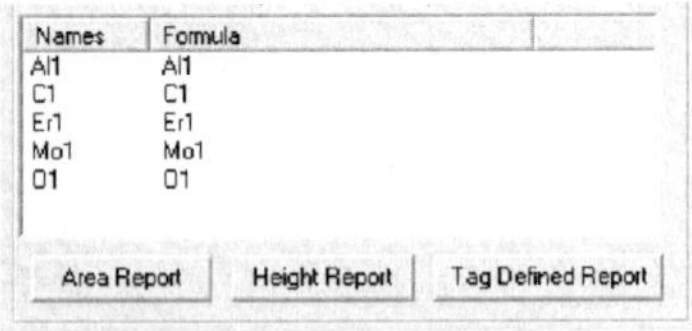

The Names and Formula table can be initially populated using the set of buttons between the two tables. Pressing the Regions button between the Quantification Item Names table and the Names and Formula table causes the set of unique region names currently displayed in the Quantification Item Names table to be transferred to the Names and Formula table. The Names and Formula entries can be edited by right-clicking the mouse with the cursor over a name entry in the lower table.

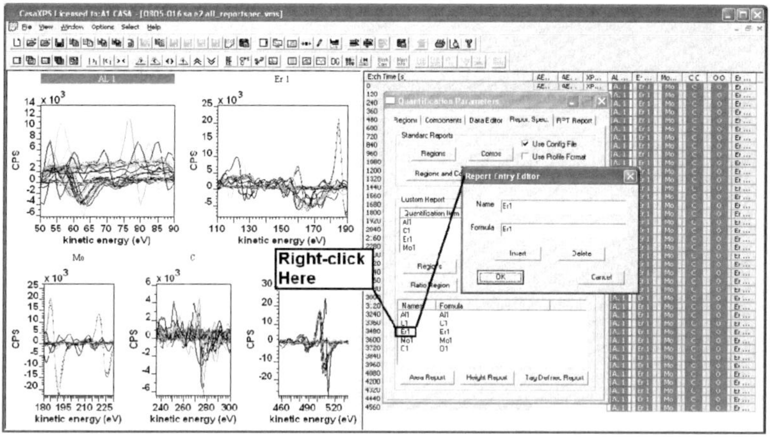

The function of the buttons between the two tables is to provide an initial state for the Names and Formula table. Although the action apparently loads the Names and Formula table using information from Regions, for example, it is important to note that any component with the same name as a region will also be included in the custom quantification report regardless of whether the Region button was initially pressed. The objective for the custom report is to provide a flexible means of combining intensities from both regions and components, so to differentiate between regions and components different names should be used.

A further word of warning is that any quantification item with identical names will be summed together. This feature makes it doubly important that regions and components should be assigned different names. The consequence of not using unique names for regions and components is the intensities will effectively be doubled for any spectrum for which a region defines the background for a component. Peak fitting with components is rarely performed for Auger spectra, so this warning is less important for Auger as for those using XPS, but nevertheless, custom reports will sum regions with identical names therefore an awareness of the mechanism is important.

For the purposes of profiling the data currently being used as an example, initially a custom report simply based on the region names is sufficient. To create the Names and Formula entries:

1. Select the VAMAS blocks containing the quantification regions previously prepared.

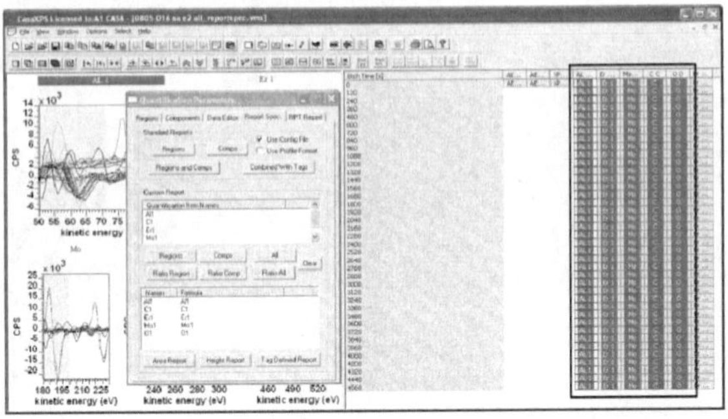

2. Press the Regions button between the two tables in the custom report section.

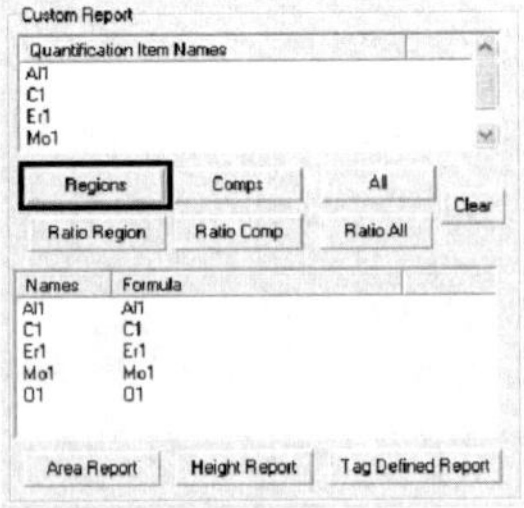

3. Since the data are in derivative form and therefore peak-to-peak intensities and RSFs are in use, press the Height Report button in the custom report section.

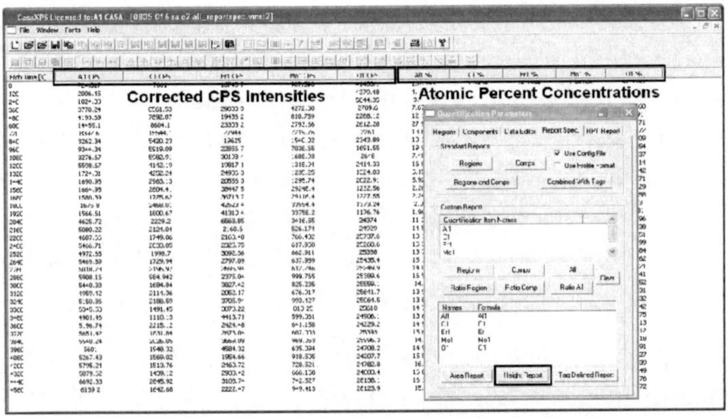

The resulting quantification table represents two sets of traces, namely, a set of corrected peak intensities in CPS and a set of atomic concentrations expressed as a percentage. These data may be placed on the clipboard using the Copy toolbar button (or Control-C) and pasted into plotting software or further manipulated in CasaXPS. A VAMAS view of the profiles is obtained either as a separate VAMAS file or within the current spectrum file using the File menu offered while the report window has focus.

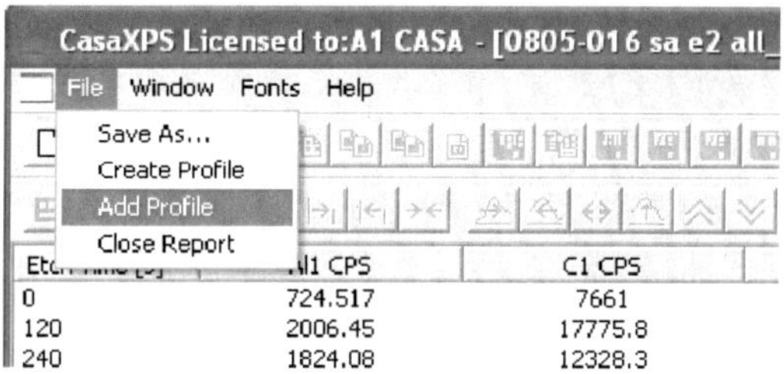

The Create Profile menu option causes a new experiment frame to appear containing two rows of VAMAS blocks. The top row corresponds to the atomic percentage columns in the quantification report, while the second row in the new experiment frame corresponds to the RSF corrected peak-to-peak intensities.

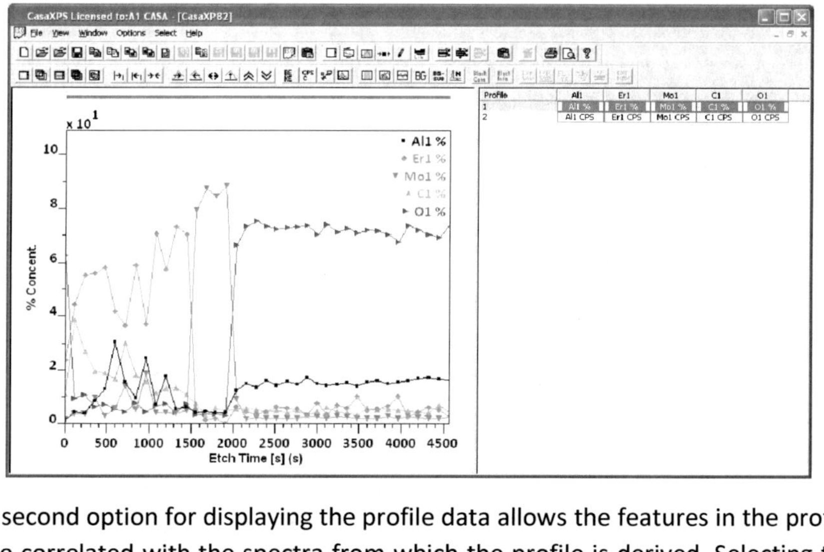

The second option for displaying the profile data allows the features in the profile to be correlated with the spectra from which the profile is derived. Selecting the Add Profile menu option from the File menu causes the profile data to be added to the original VAMAS file containing the spectra. When a profile is added to the spectral data, a string is added to the display of the spectra in the active tile.

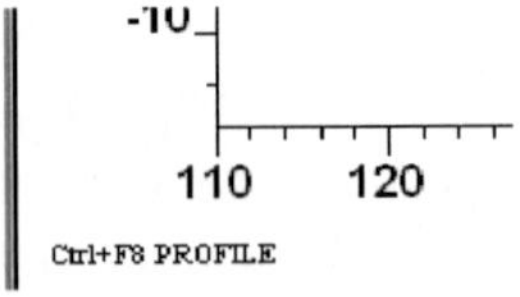

The string Ctrl+F8 Profile indicates that holding down the Control key on the keyboard and pressing the F8 function key cause the display to switch from spectra to the most recently added profile data.

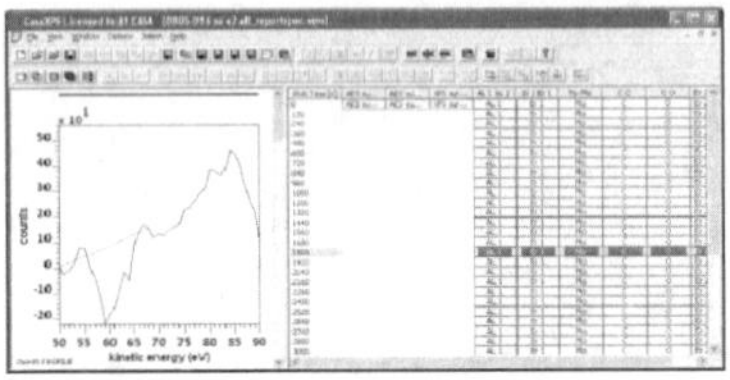

Crtl+F8

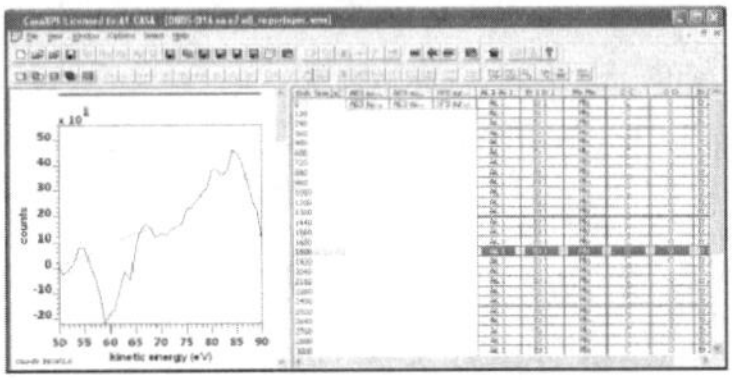

A raw Auger depth profile may therefore be viewed in spectrum format, where rows of spectra ordered with respect to etch-time, or processed profile format, where traces computed from the spectra are plotted against etch-time. The Control+F8 key stroke not only switches between the two perspectives of the data, but also changes the display of the spectra based on the position of the cursor when viewed in profile format, or the displayed position of the cursor in the profile format based on the selection in the right-hand pane when viewed in spectrum format. The row currently selected in the spectrum format of the profile, and therefore the etch time, translates into to position of the cursor on the profile format of the data. Similarly, a cursor placed on the profile format of the data becomes a selected row of spectra when the Control+F8 action is pressed causing the display to revert back to the spectrum format.

It is also possible to indicate a range of spectra via the normal selection mechanism in the right-hand pane of the experiment frame displaying the spectra. On pressing Ctrl+F8, a pair of vertical cursors indicates where in the profile the selected spectra correspond in the profile. Again, if a pair of vertical cursors is placed on the profile trace, on switching back to the spectrum form of the data, the range of spectra indicated by the cursors on the profile becomes selected in the right-hand pane of the spectrum form of the data.

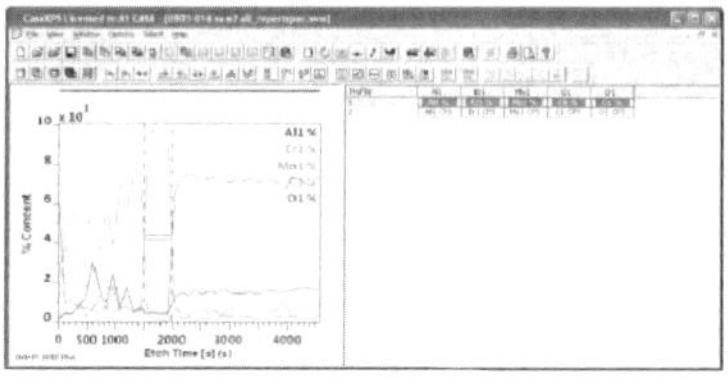

Crtl+F8

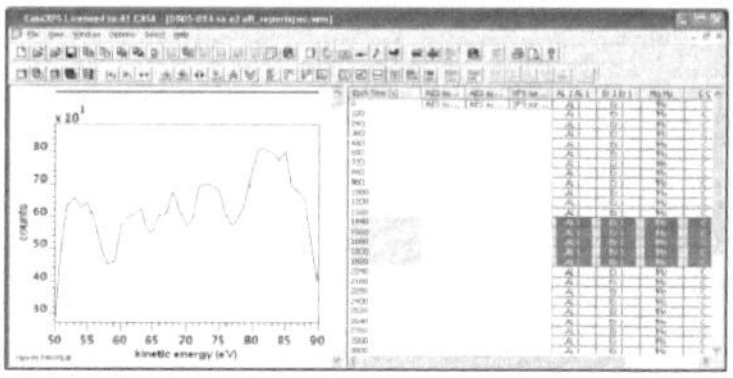

To mark the profile with a pair of cursors, hold the Shift key down while dragging the cursor across the active tile displaying the profile. On releasing the mouse button, the drag box marks the position of the two cursors.

Mass Concentration

Quantification based on Regions and Components

Creating a quantification report based on both regions and components requires:

1. The creation of regions with appropriate mass assignment.
2. The creation of components with appropriate mass assignment.
3. The set of spectra all positioned in the same row in the right-hand pane of the experiment frame.
4. A configuration file RegionComponentQuantTable.txt defined in the CasaXPS.DEF directory including entries for the mass and mass concentration values.
5. The use of the Standard Report button Regions and Comps.

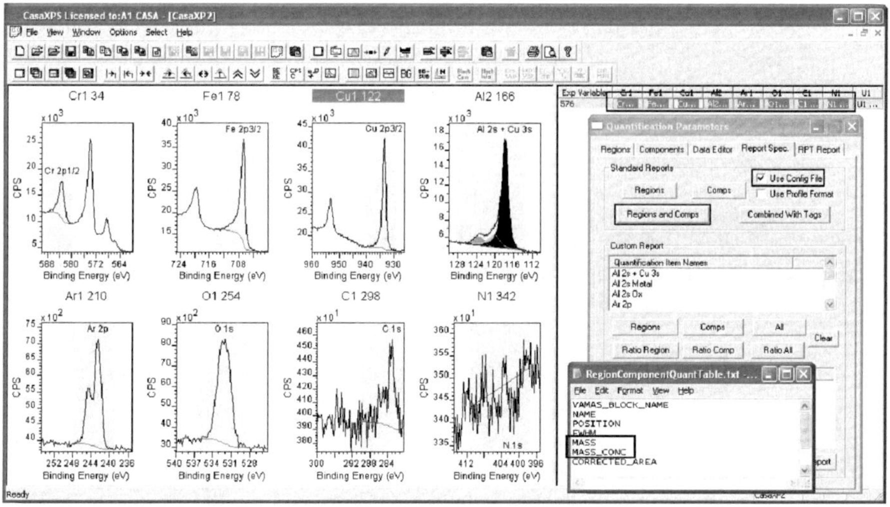

Create Regions with Appropriate Mass Assignment

Creating a region with appropriate mass assignment requires the uses of:

1. The Quantification Parameters Dialog Window.
2. The Element Library
3. The spectrum displayed in the active tile.

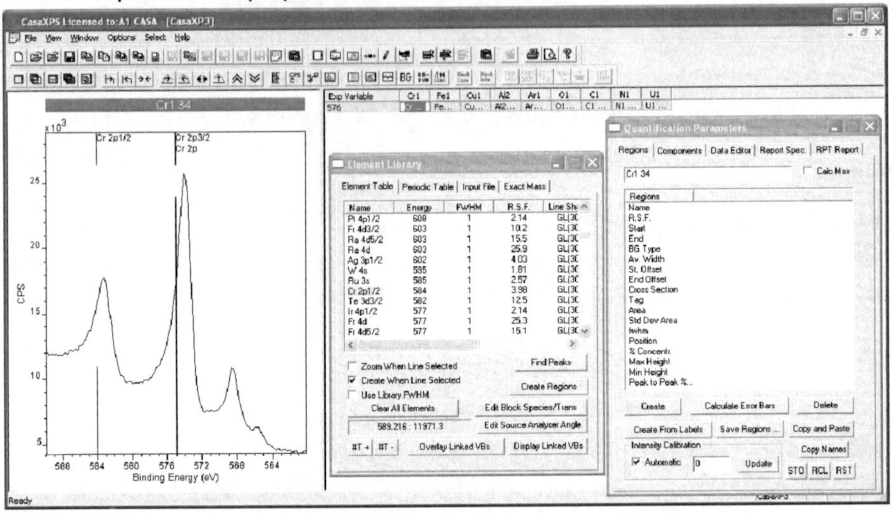

A region may be created in a number of ways; however the important fact for generating mass concentration reports is the region is created using the element library. Regions created via the element library are assigned the average mass for the element and without the use of the element library to identify the element responsible for the spectrum the mass assignment cannot be made with certainty.

When a region is created via the Create button on the Regions property page, the VAMAS block fields for the species and transition provide a string used to search the element library for the entry with appropriate RSF and mass for the spectrum.

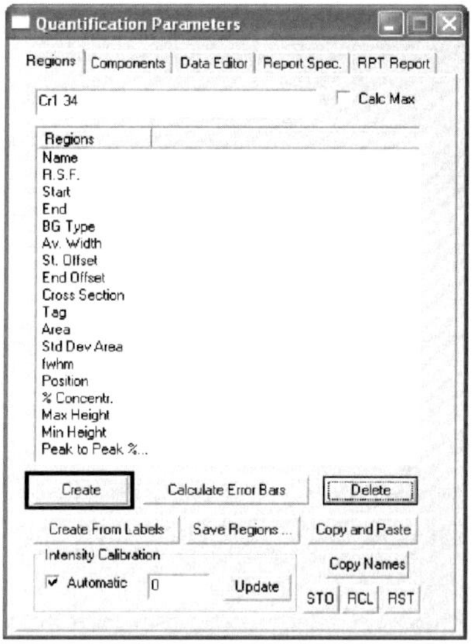

The easiest way to create a single region on a high resolution spectrum is to first ensure the species/transition fields are correctly assigned prior to pressing the Create button.

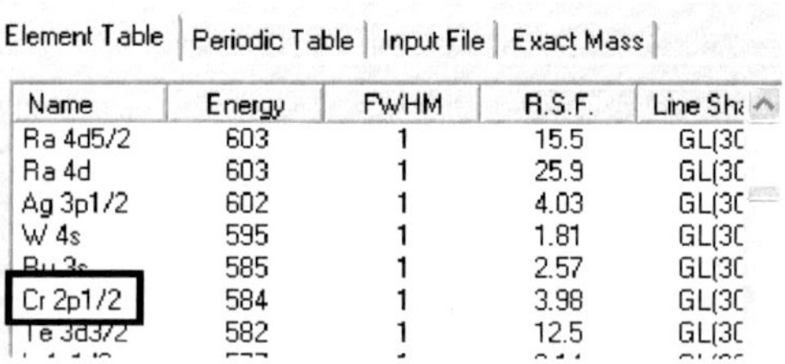

The element library entry must match the species/transition fields for the VAMAS block containing the data. The example data displays the strings constructed from the species/transitions for the VAMAS blocks as headers above the array of data blocks in the right-hand pane. Initially these strings do not match the current library entries.

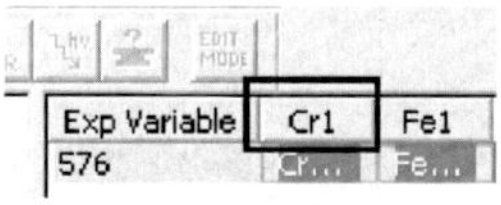

Assigning the correct species/transition fields for a VAMAS block can be achieved using the Element Table property page.

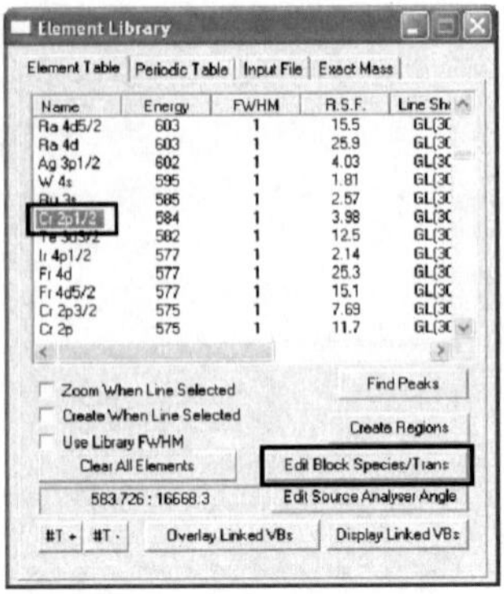

With the VAMAS block displayed in the active tile, select the transition from the element table scrolled list then press the Edit Block Species/Trans button on the Element Table property page. A dialog window appears offering the element and transition based on the selected entry in the element library.

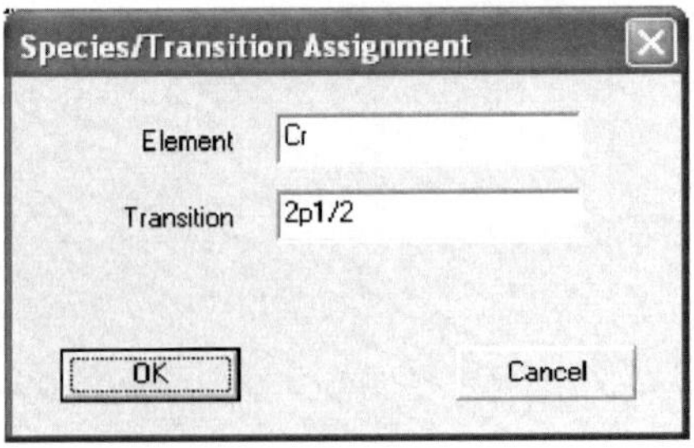

The right-hand pane of the experiment frame is updated with the new values from the dialog window.

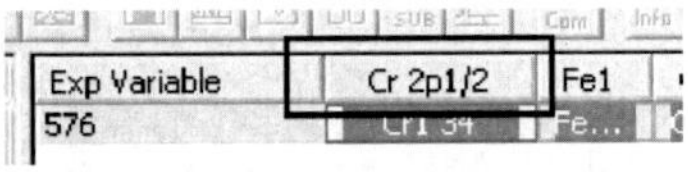

On pressing the Create button on the Regions property page, a new region is created on the data in the active tile.

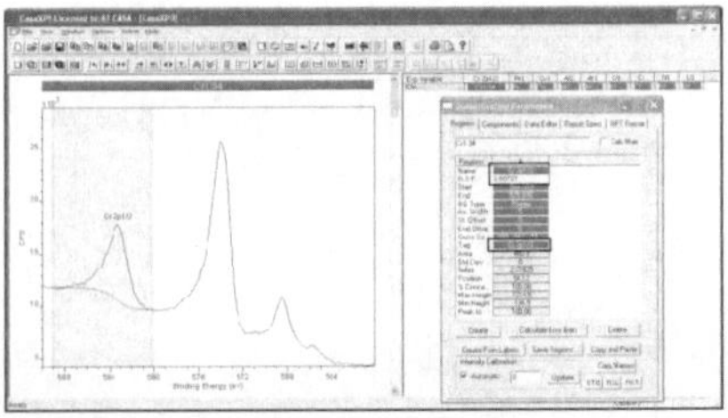

The new region is updated with the name and tag fields updated using the species/transition fields from the element library. The RSF field is also entered from the library entry matching the species/transition fields. Although not explicitly displayed, the average mass for the element is entered into the region parameters too.

The start and end energy limits for the newly created region are determined from the current display settings for the active tile. These may need adjusting to ensure the region RSF and peak area match one another.

Updating an Existing Region

A region already defined on a VAMAS block may need to change the RSF or a reassignment of the average mass parameter. To force a region to update the RSF and average mass, enter the name field from the element library entry into the name field of the region preceded by the # character. On pressing return, the string matching the name field entered into the region causes the RSF and tag fields to be updated from the library.

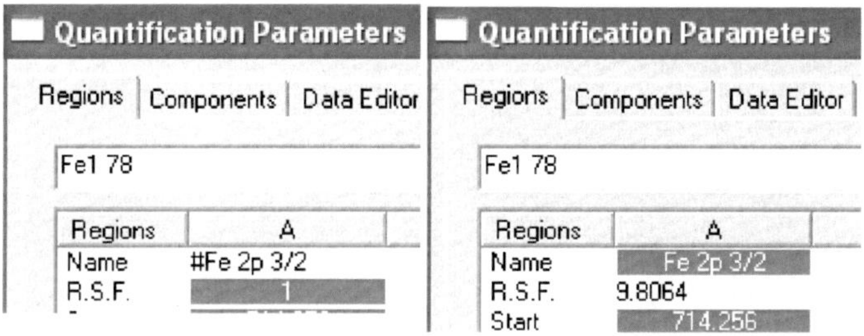

Before **After**

The average mass for the region is also updated on pressing the Enter key on the keyboard.

Create Components with Appropriate Mass Assignment

The creation of components is performed on the Components property page of the Quantification Parameters dialog window.

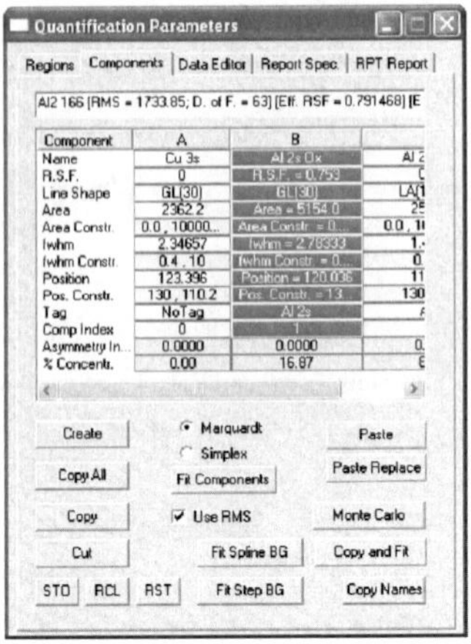

Components are subject to identical issues as regions and are managed in an identical way to that describe above for the creation of regions. The only difference between the values updated from the element library for components compared to regions is the line-shape field for components. When a component is created from the element library, the line-shape stored in the library is also updated from the library.

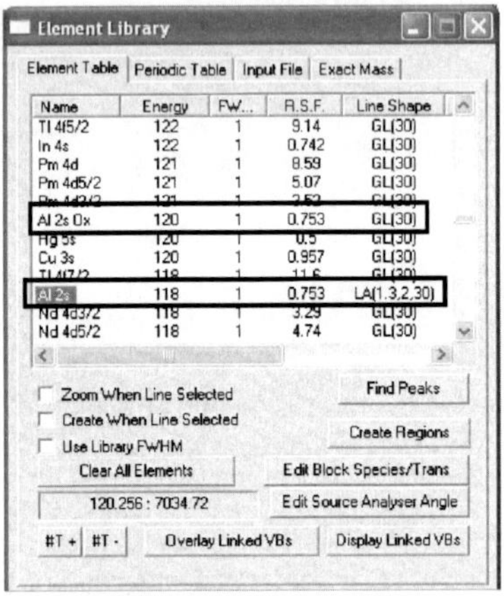

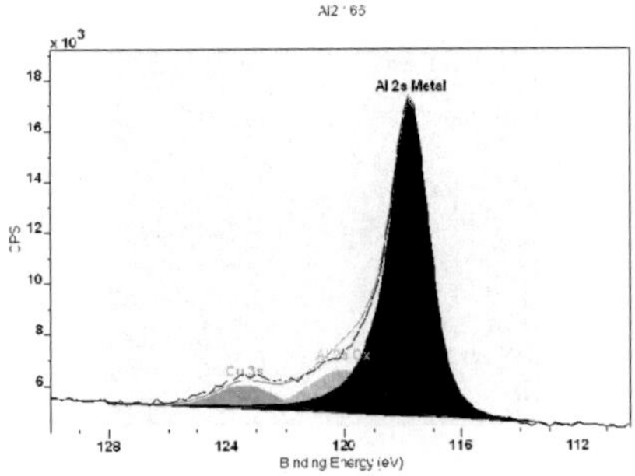

Quantification Report

A quantification report in which the mass concentration is included requires the use of a configuration file and the Standard Report section of the Report Spec property page on the Quantification Parameters dialog window.

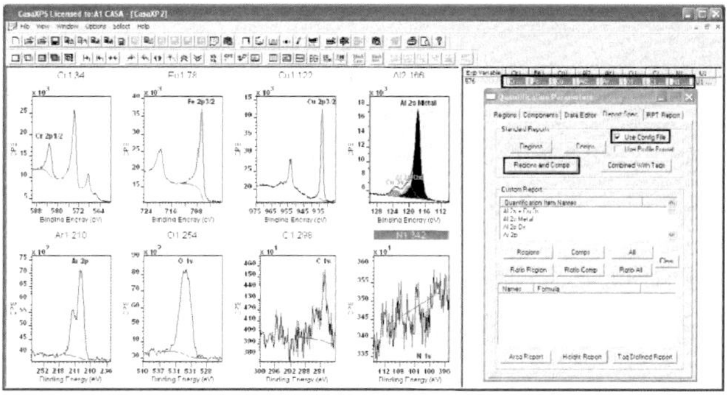

Regions and components must be prepared for each of the high resolution spectra used in the quantification. Any components required to model the data but not required as part of the quantification should have the RSF set to zero.

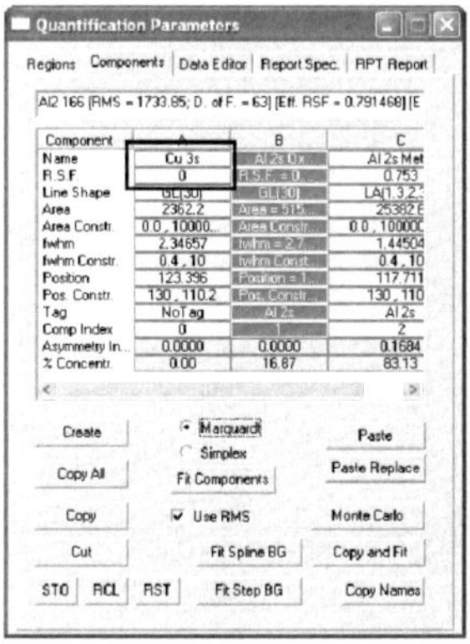

All regions or components with RSF set to zero will be excluded from quantification tables generated by the Standard Report. For example, it would be incorrect to include the Cu 2p 3/2 region and also the Cu 3s component from the Al 2s peak model. The RSF for the Cu 3s component is therefore set to zero.

To generate a quantification report using both regions and components from a set of high resolution spectra:

1. Select the VAMAS blocks containing the spectra in the right-hand pane.

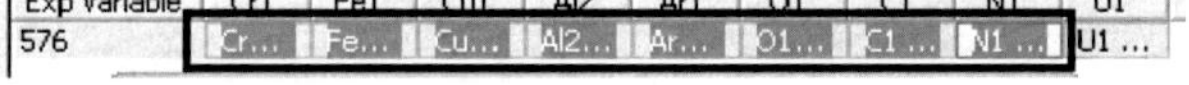

2. Tick the Use Config File tick-box

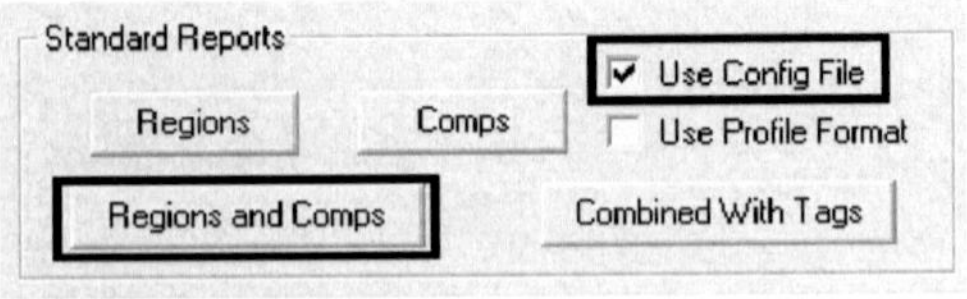

3. Press the Regions and Comps button in the Standard Reports section of the Report Spec property page.

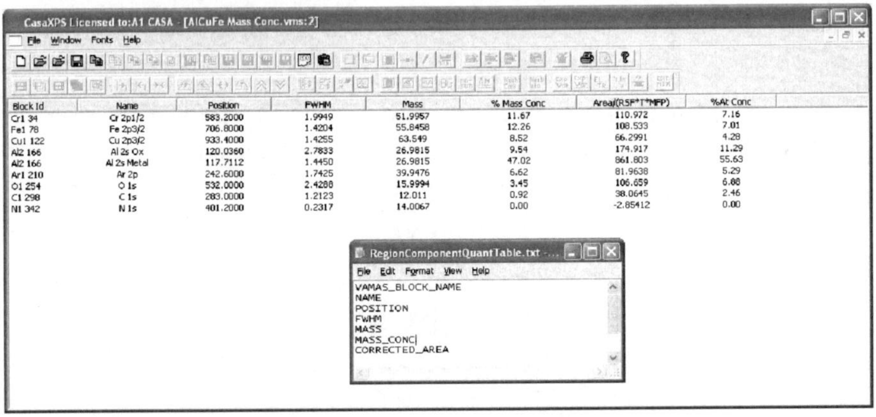

Block Id	Name	Position	FWHM	Mass	% Mass Conc	Area/(RSF*T*MFP)	%At Conc
Cr1 34	Cr 2p1/2	583.2000	1.9949	51.9957	11.67	110.972	7.16
Fe1 78	Fe 2p3/2	706.8000	1.4204	55.8458	12.26	108.533	7.01
Cu1 122	Cu 2p3/2	933.4000	1.4255	63.549	8.52	66.2991	4.28
Al2 166	Al 2s Ox	120.0360	2.7833	26.9815	9.54	174.917	11.29
Al2 166	Al 2s Metal	117.7112	1.4450	26.9815	47.02	861.803	55.63
Ar1 210	Ar 2p	242.6000	1.7425	39.9476	6.62	81.9638	5.29
O1 254	O 1s	532.0000	2.4288	15.9994	3.45	106.659	6.88
C1 298	C 1s	283.0000	1.2123	12.011	0.92	38.0645	2.46
N1 342	N 1s	401.2000	0.2317	14.0067	0.00	-2.85412	0.00

Standard Reports using Tags

Motivation

Spectra may include numerous photoelectric and Auger peaks, some of which overlap and therefore prevent a simple compositional analysis of the sample surface. The following spectrum is an example of data acquired at pass energy 160 on a Kratos Axis Ultra, where the K 2p and C 1s peaks overlap.

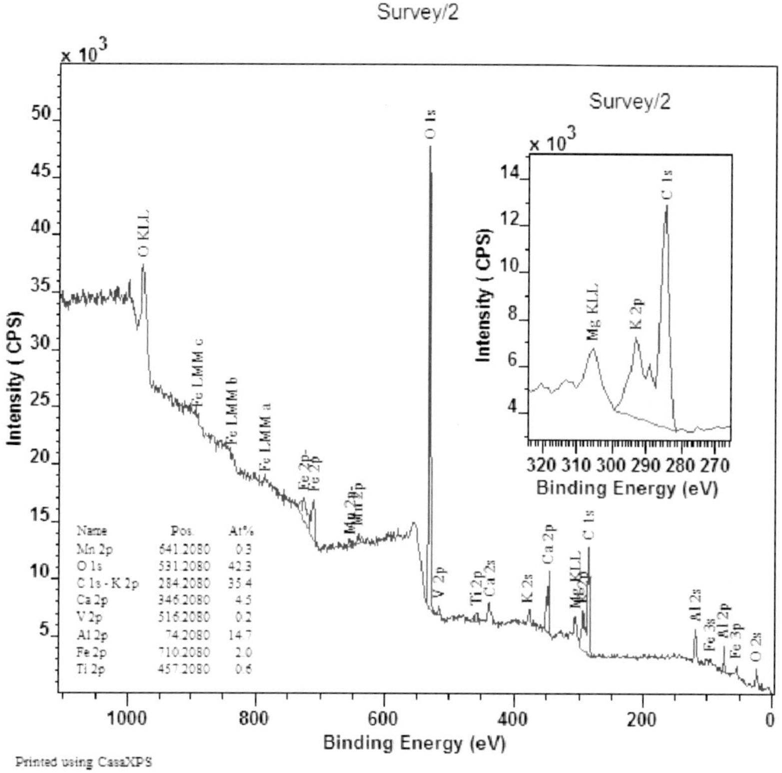

The advantage of acquiring data at high pass energies, namely enhanced signal-to-noise for a given acquisition time, is lost when the spectral features can only be separated using less sensitive pass energies with better energy resolution. For the example spectrum above, a simple elemental concentration measurement based on integration regions is impeded by the overlapping K 2p and C 1s peaks. The quantification problem arises because the RSF for the combined envelope is depended on the relative proportions of the two elements. The concentration for the overlapping peaks must be obtained by applying an effective RSF computed from an appropriate peak model, which may require higher resolution spectra. The following high resolution data for the carbon and potassium region provides a means of computing the effective RSF for the survey spectrum above.

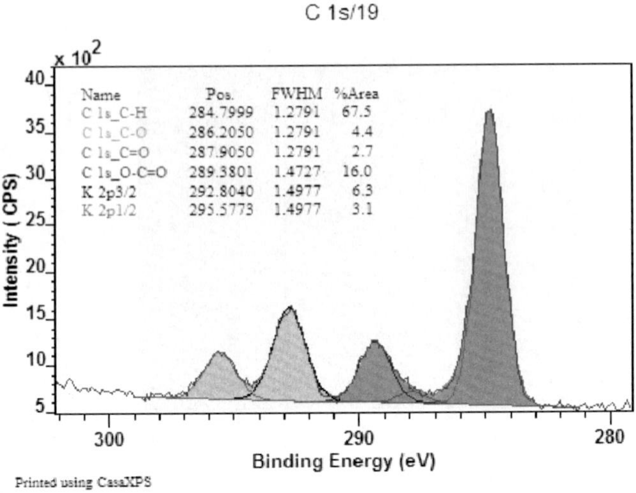

The better resolved peaks illustrates clearly the mixing of peak areas and differing RSFs for the transitions involved in the potassium and carbon envelope, and allows the computation of the weighted RSF for the overlapping envelope in the survey spectrum. Determining a weighted RSF from the high resolution data therefore permits the partial quantification of the sample via the survey data. That is, the quantification table over the survey spectrum determines the combined contribution to the atomic concentration from the overlapping peaks, thus allowing the remaining entries in the table to report true atomic concentration values.

The following discussion describes how to calculate the effective RSF and the use of Tags as a means of combining the survey spectrum with high resolution data to obtain a full quantification of the sample without the need to acquire high resolution spectra for each transition in the quantification. The obvious advantage of limiting the number of high resolution spectra is that of time spent collecting the data.

A new feature in version 2.3.14 is the introduction of a configuration file for the standard report generated using Tags. An example highlighting the use of mass concentration will be used to describe the new configuration file.

Quantification using Tags

A full quantification for the survey data requires the use of a peak model to differentiate the contribution to the quantification table from the K 2p and the C

1s transitions. As an example, these data are useful because quantification can be performed in either of two ways, namely:

1. Using the high resolution spectrum to construct a well defined peak-model that can be readily adapted to the data from the survey spectrum, therefore directly quantifying the contributions from the regions and synthetic components computed from the survey spectrum alone.
2. Use the proportions for the K 2p and C 1s peaks from the high resolution spectrum to compute an effective RSF for the K 2p/C 1s region, followed by generating a Tag report containing the partial quantification table augmented with a subdivision of the K 2p/C 1s region as prescribed by the peak intensities from the high resolution spectrum.

Observations:

1. While the data are sufficiently well separated in this example to permit a fit of the peak-model from the high resolution data to the survey spectrum, in general, peaks may overlap in ways that the survey spectrum produces poor precision when fitted to synthetic components.
2. Without the high resolution K 2p/C 1s spectrum, it would be difficult to confidently prepare a peak model based entirely on the K 2p/C 1s region from the survey; therefore both methods rely on the high resolution spectrum to perform the quantification.
3. The survey spectrum was acquired using a pass-energy of 160 eV while the high resolution spectrum structure is due to a smaller step-size and a pass-energy of 40 eV. Issues associated with changes in the transmission efficiency between these two operating modes, even with transmission calibration, prevents quantification begin performed directly using both spectra, that is mixing intensities measured from the two different operating modes in the same quantification table. Theoretically, a properly calibrated instrument should allow quantification using data from different operating modes, in practice, mixed mode quantification is not recommended.

Quantification using Regions and Components

The Standard Report options on the Report Spec property page offer the means to quantify spectra based on Regions only, Components only as well as mixing intensities from Regions with Components in the same report. Ordinarily, performing a peak fit to poorly resolved data is imprecise so would not generally be employed for survey spectra; however for the example data set in question, the availability of the high resolution spectrum provides a means of characterising a peak model which can be copied, constrained and fitted to the K 2p/C 1s region as shown below. The principal reason for performing the quantification using both regions and components is to illustrate the equivalence of quantification using Tags to the more common use of regions or components. The second survey spectrum shown in the right-hand pane of the experiment frame is simply a copy of the first survey spectrum. The two survey spectra are identical apart from the quantification items defined on the two data blocks.

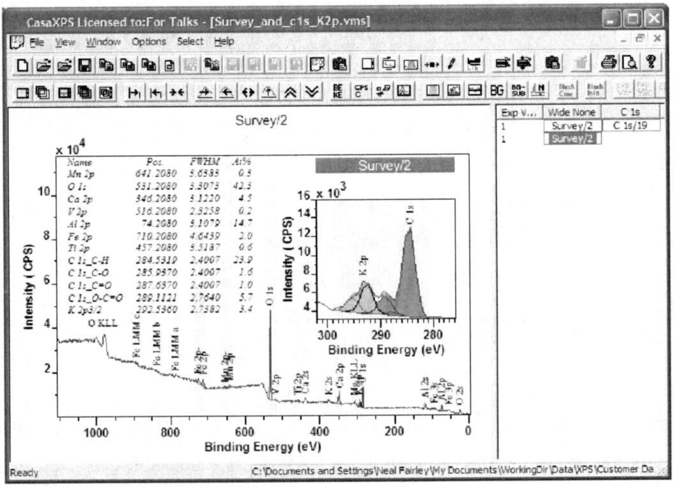

The peak model created for the high resolution spectrum is constrained to the extent that only the relative positions of the six synthetic components and their relative FWHM are allows to be optimised when fitting the model to the K 2p/C 1s region on the survey spectrum. The constraints used in the peak model are tabulated as follows.

Name	Pos Const	FWHM Const	Area Const	Const Id
C 1s_C-H	302.208 , 279.108	0.28 , 7	0.0 , 10000000.0	A
C 1s_C-O	A + 1.4051	A * 1	A * 0.0650981	B
C 1s_C=O	A + 3.1051	A * 1	A * 0.0398136	C
C 1s_O-C=O	A + 4.5802	0.28 , 7	A * 0.237488	D
K 2p3/2	A + 8.0041	D * 1.017	A * 0.370313	E
K 2p1/2	A + 10.777	D * 1.017	A * 0.185157	F

The report generated from the Standard Report button **Regions and Comps** using the survey spectrum using the constraints developed for the high resolution data are presented below.

Tag	Exp Variable	Name	% Mass Conc	Mass	%At Conc
Mn 2p	1	Mn 2p	0.9	54.938	0.3
O 1s		O 1s	34.9	15.9994	42.3
Ca 2p		Ca 2p	9.4	40.078	4.5
V 2p		V 2p	0.4	50.9415	0.2
Al 2p		Al 2p	20.5	26.9815	14.7
Fe 2p		Fe 2p	5.7	55.8458	2
Ti 2p		Ti 2p	1.4	47.8784	0.6
Mixed		C 1s_C-H	14.8	12.011	23.9
Mixed		C 1s_C-O	1	12.011	1.6
Mixed		C 1s_C=O	0.6	12.011	1
Mixed		C 1s_O-C=O	3.5	12.011	5.7
Mixed		K 2p3/2	6.8	39.1019	3.4

The configuration file RegionComponentQuantTable.txt located in the CasaXPS.DEF directory is displayed in a Notepad window was used to create the above quantification table.

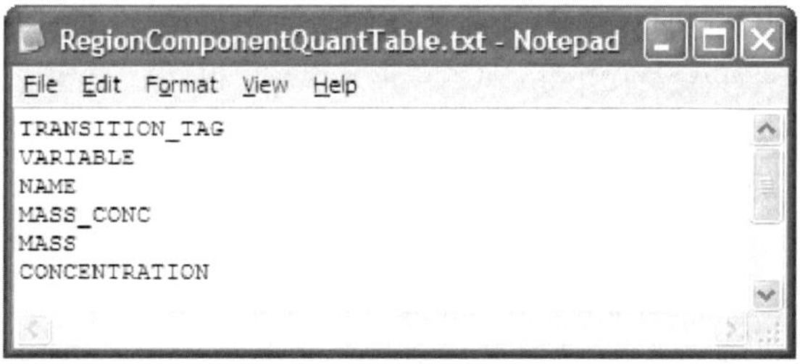

The advantage of generating the quantification from regions and components is library RSFs can be directly applied to each region or component in the table. These quantification results use the default CasaXPS library and therefore the RSFs in the quantification are Scofield cross-sections. Since the data are taken from a Kratos Axis Ultra, the Kratos RSF table matching the Kratos transmission function should have been used in practice. For the purpose of the present discussion, the accuracy of the quantification is not important, only the precision of the calculation.

Quantification using Combine with Tags

An equivalent quantification for the data can be performed using the Tag mechanism. A configuration file, CombineWithTagsQuantTable.txt, identical in contents to the one shown above is defined for the Combine with Tags button. The configuration file is shown open in Notepad. All the Standard Report configuration files are located in the CasaXPS.DEF directory.

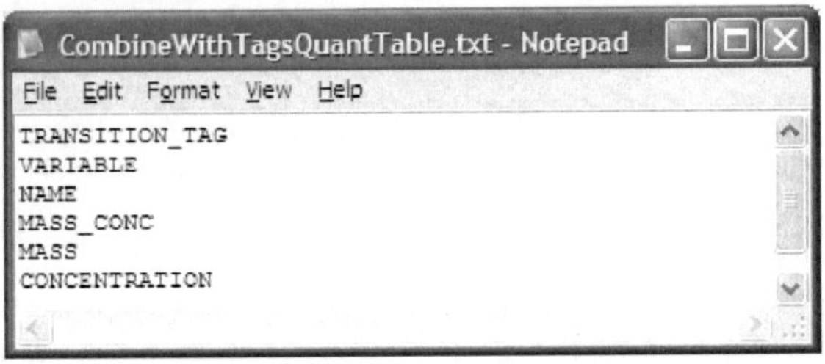


```
TRANSITION_TAG
VARIABLE
NAME
MASS_CONC
MASS
CONCENTRATION
```

Since more than one VAMAS block are used, namely, the survey spectrum and the high-resolution spectrum, both must appear on the same row in the right-hand pane of the experiment frame, and both VAMAS blocks must be selected in the right-hand pane before pressing the **Combine with Tags** button on the Report Spec property page. The resulting quantification table generated using the Tag mechanism is shown below, where the only difference between the tables is the additional entry labelled C 1s – K 2p with Tag set to Mixed. The preparation of the region with the name C 1s – K 2p is central to generating the quantification report and will be discussed in more detail below.

Tag	Exp Variable	Name	% Mass Conc	Mass	%At Conc
Mn 2p	1	Mn 2p	0.9	54.938	0.3
O 1s		O 1s	34.9	15.9994	42.3
Mixed		C 1s - K 2p	26.7	14.5917	35.4
Ca 2p		Ca 2p	9.4	40.078	4.5
V 2p		V 2p	0.4	50.9415	0.2
Al 2p		Al 2p	20.5	26.9815	14.7
Fe 2p		Fe 2p	5.7	55.8458	2
Ti 2p		Ti 2p	1.4	47.8784	0.6
Mixed	C:	C 1s_C-H	14.8	12.011	23.9
Mixed	C:	C 1s_C-O	1	12.011	1.6
Mixed	C:	C 1s_C=O	0.6	12.011	1
Mixed	C:	C 1s_O-C=O	3.5	12.011	5.7
Mixed	C:	K 2p3/2	6.8	39.1019	3.4

The idea behind the Tag mechanism is an intensity measured from the survey spectrum can be linked to a peak-model from a high resolution spectrum. The concentration from the survey spectrum is divided between the components fitted on the high-resolution spectrum and reported in the quantification table as a list of concentrations summing to the concentration for the region from the survey spectrum with the same Tag string as the components. For example, in the table above the region labelled C 1s - K 2p is assigned the Tag Mixed. The components from the corresponding energy interval measured using the lower pass energy are also assigned the Tag string Mixed. The actual Tag string is not important so long as the one used is different from any other Tag strings used for other regions and components contributing to the quantification report. Regions not part of the quantification report should be assigned the string NoTag; for example the region used to create the peak model on the high resolution spectrum should be assigned a Tag field of NoTag.

To summarize the creation steps used to generate the Tag report:

1. Each element for which a photoelectric transition can be uniquely identified on the survey spectrum, a region must be created from the

element library. The reason the element library is explicitly stated is that when a region is created via the element library, not only is the RSF and the Tag field updated, but also the average mass for the element is added to the region information. The quantification table includes the mass concentration and to ensure each entry has the appropriate mass, the table also includes a column displaying the mass specified for each quantification item.

2. For the same reason, the set of peaks used to model the transitions from the high resolution data must also be created using the element library.
3. The Tag field for the region on the survey spectrum and the components from the high resolution spectrum must all be assigned the same unique Tag string. For this example the word Mixed was chosen, but any string would do provided it is different from the string NoTag and unique to the one region on the survey spectrum and the set of corresponding components on the high resolution spectrum.
4. The RSF for the C 1s-K 2p region must be computed from the peak model for the high resolution spectrum and manually entered into the region RSF field on the Regions property page. The effective RSF for a peak-model is displayed in the text-field at the top of the Components property page. The value for the effective RSF can be copied and pasted from the Components property page into the RSF field on the Regions property page.

The effective RSF is a weighted average of the RSFs used in the components in the peak model, where the weighting is determined from the relative intensities of the components and provides a scaling for the region intensity measured from the survey spectrum. The effective RSF allows the partial quantification of the survey spectrum using regions only. Similarly, when reporting the mass concentration, an effective mass is required for the intensity associated with the C 1s-K 2p region on the survey spectrum. An effective mass, like the effective RSF, is computed from the peak model defined on the high resolution spectrum and displayed in the text-field at the top of the Components property page.

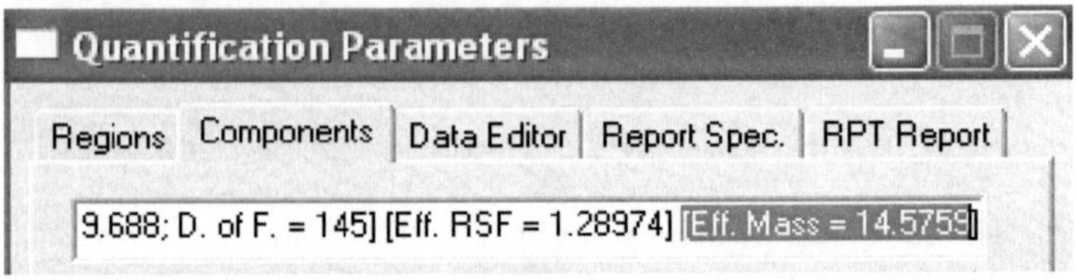

5. For quantification reports which include the mass concentration, such as the one above, the region defined on the survey spectrum accounting for the overlapping peaks must be assigned the effective mass computed from the Component property page. The effective mass is displayed to the right of the effective RSF and typically requires the use of the cursor and arrow keys on the keyboard before the effective mass string is made visible. The effective mass can be selected from the text-field then copied and pasted into the Tag field for the corresponding region on the survey spectrum. The format for the keyword string entered into the Tag field is Mass = <real number>. On pressing the Enter key on the keyboard, the mass so specified is updated in the region and the previously assigned Tag string is returned to the Tag field. If the Tag field does not return to the previously assigned Tag string, then the mass failed to be updated due to a syntax error.

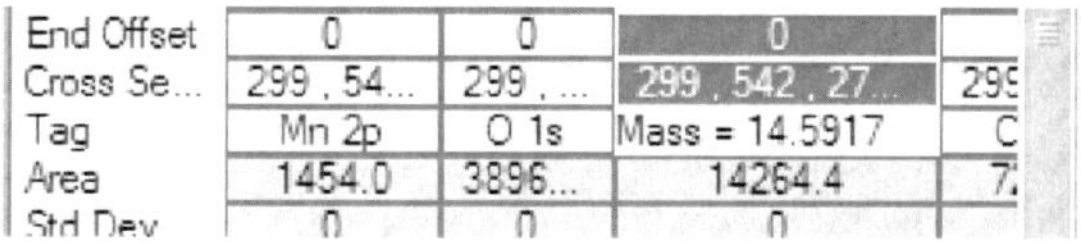

End Offset	0	0	0	
Cross Se...	299 , 54...	299 , ...	299 , 542 , 27...	29[illegible]
Tag	Mn 2p	O 1s	Mass = 14.5917	C
Area	1454.0	3896...	14264.4	7.
Std Dev	0	0	0	

6. The report is generated by pressing the Combine with Tags button on the Report Spec property page located in the Standard Report section.

While the quantification using Tags is more complicated than the report using regions and components, often overlapping peaks are difficult to fit using a survey spectrum so Tags provide a means of obtaining quantification which would otherwise be difficult to perform.

Toolbars

The following description represents an overview of the features and options within CasaXPS viewed from the perspective of the toolbar buttons, dialog windows and related menu items. The toolbar buttons are an important part of the user interface and provide short-cuts to many of the actions performed on the dialog windows.

The toolbar buttons are initially displayed at the top of the Main Program window and are activated or deactivated by left-clicking the mouse with the cursor over either the left-hand pane or the right-hand pane of an experiment frame.

Toolbars activated for left-hand pane:

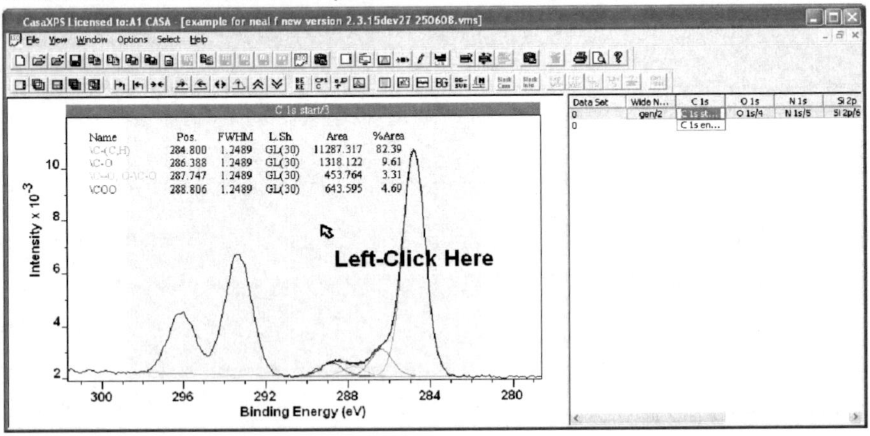

Or Toolbars activated for right-hand pane:

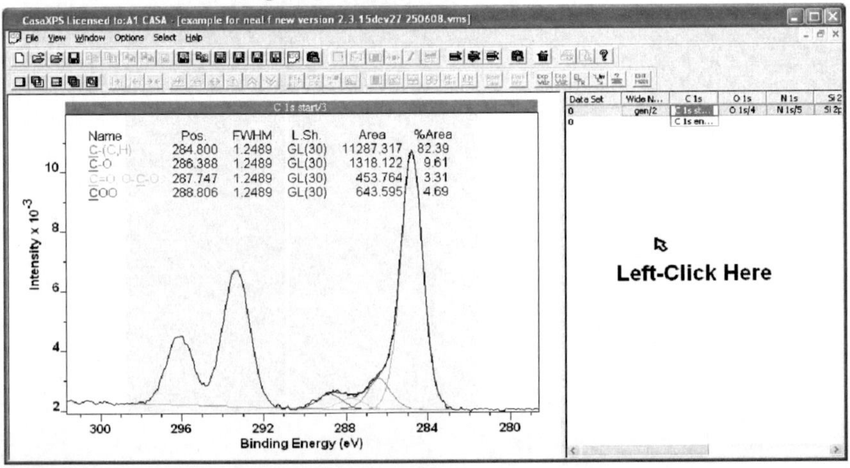

There are three possible toolbars.

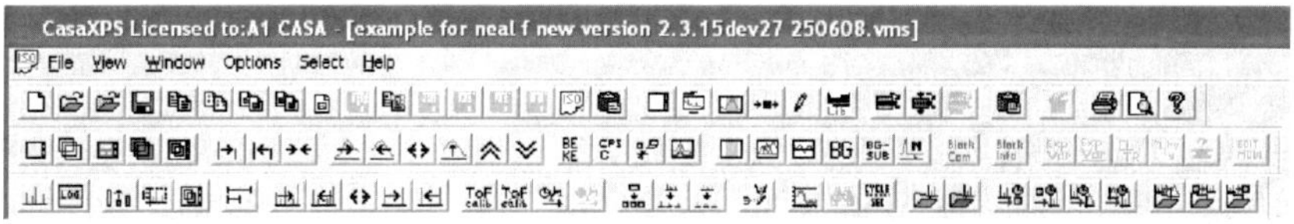

Anyone of these toolbars can be moved and re-positioned using the mouse or hidden from view using the toggle menu items on the **View** menu.

Toolbar Buttons

Toolbar buttons are grouped within a toolbar based on the type of actions performed by the buttons. The toolbar buttons and associated dialog windows are discussed in the context of these groupings.

Toolbar options for transferring data into and out of CasaXPS

Left-hand pane active:

Right-hand pane active:

 Creates a new empty experiment frame.

The New toolbar button creates an empty experiment frame. Data from other open VAMAS files can be moved into an empty experiment frame, which can serve as a temporary work area for analyzing data or form the basis for collecting useful results for saving separately from the original data files. Copying VAMAS blocks between experiment frames is facilitated by the Copy/Paste VAMAS blocks toolbar button.

 Open one or more VAMAS files into individual experiment frames.

A File dialog window appears in which one or more VAMAS files can be selected within a directory. On pressing the Open button, the data in the selected VAMAS files are displayed in separate experiment frames, one experiment frame per selected VAMAS file. (See the **Open and Merge** options on the File menu for a means of collecting multiple VAMAS files into a single experiment frame.)

 Converts data from non-VAMAS format to VAMAS format.

Data in a wide range of file formats can be converted to VAMAS format via the **Convert to VAMAS file** File-dialog window.

There are two strategies for converting data files, where either the individual files are converted on a per file basis or alternatively a directory of data files are converted by a single action. The method used for any given format depends on the philosophy behind a given data format and how closely this philosophy matches the design of the ISO 14976 file format. The general rule for choosing the strategy is that individual files are converted whenever the individual files contain the experimental context for multiple acquisitions from a sample (e.g. a survey plus one or more high resolution spectra). Converting a directory of files approach applies to data such as VG Eclipse data, where each spectrum appears in a separate file within a directory.

The general approach to converting file formats is to supply a file extension using a File dialog window. For example, a directory of files containing X/Y pairs in ASCII format can be converted en masse into a single experiment frame by providing a new file name with a .dat file extension via the File Dialog window. The base name for the file name is not important, however the .dat extension to the specified file name causes the conversion to proceed on the basis that all the file in the current directory are ASCII X/Y pairs. A new VAMAS file is written into the current directory, so it is important that the user has write permission for the directory in question.

 Save as

 Copy to clipboard

When an experiment frame is the sub-window with focus, the Copy button places a bitmap on the clipboard. The image drawn into the bitmap is formed from the page of tiles for which one tile is the active tile.

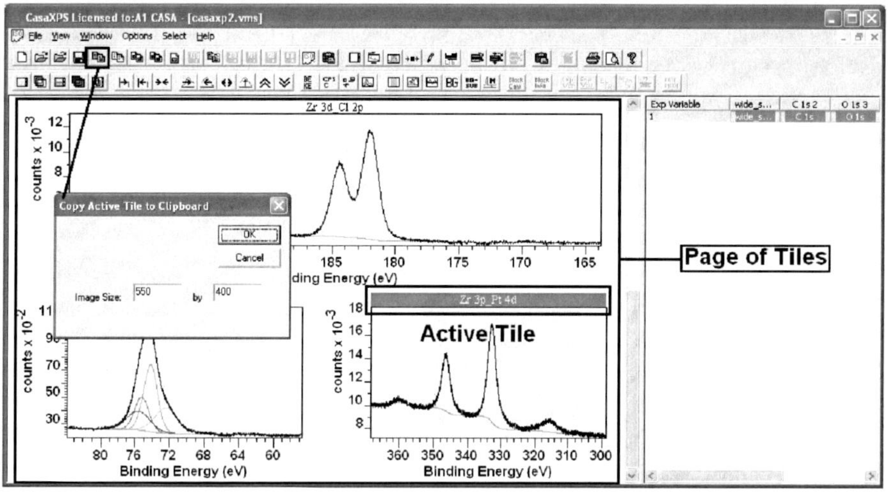

Once on the clipboard, the bitmap can be pasted into any program such as Microsoft Paint, Word, Excel or any other program accepting bitmaps from the clipboard. On pressing the Copy button, a dialog window appears in which the dimensions in pixels for the bitmap is specified. The page of tiles is scaled to fit the size of the bitmap defined by the dialog window.

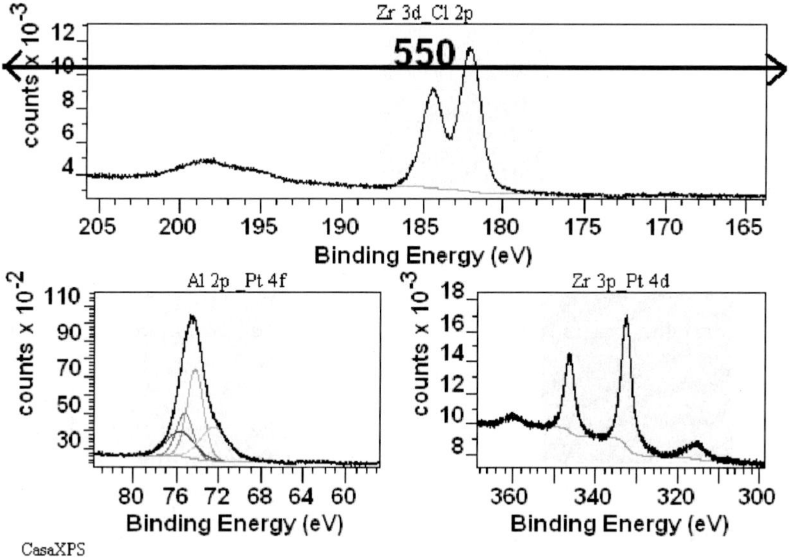

If a report frame is the sub-window with focus, then pressing the Copy button results in a text dialog window, from which the tabulated information in the report can be placed onto the clipboard in a Tab spaced format suitable for spreadsheet programs.

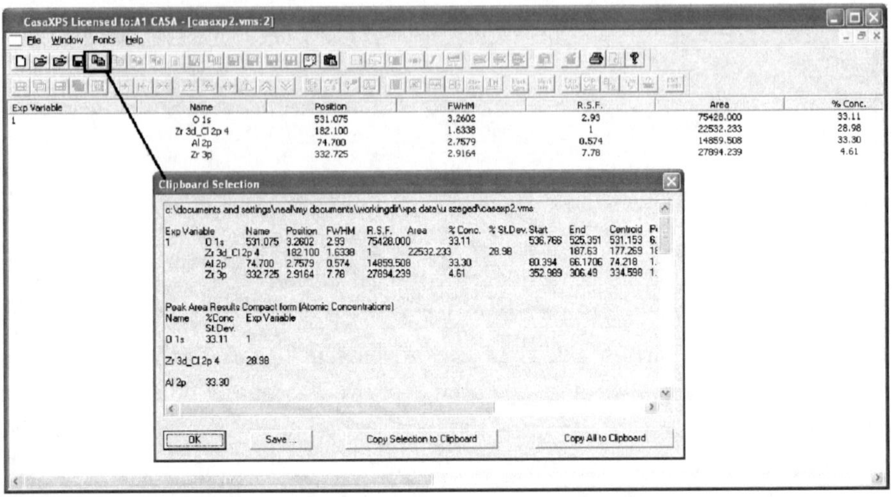

Copy Page of Tiles.

Provides the identical functionality to the Copy toolbar button, but differs in the method used to determine the size of the bitmap placed on the clipboard. The dimensions of the bitmap are determined from the pixel dimensions of the left-hand pane. The scaling for the tile display currently within CasaXPS is used to create the bitmap.

 Copy EMF to clipboard from Active Tile

Using the drawing instructions for the active tile, copy an Enhanced Meta File to the clipboard.

Enhanced Meta Files are a mechanism used by Microsoft to transfer graphical information between programs. An EMF can be displayed in any program capable of interpreting these drawing instructions and so, in principle, an EMF is a compact method for transferring pictures between Microsoft programs. The EMF files generated by CasaXPS are created using the Microsoft Visual C++ compiler, however the underlying standard has changed over the years resulting in anomalous behaviour when a CasaXPS EMF is displayed in different versions of Word (for example). Switches for modifying the behaviour of the EMF file are included in CasaXPS, however it is not possible to create an EMF that works in Word 97 and also in Word 2000. The two main inconsistencies between different versions of Word are 1) the positioning of vertical text and 2) mirror text display. The former can be adjusted using the **Vertical Text** menu item on the File menu to force the vertical text to appear correct for one version of Word; unfortunately, if a Word document is subsequently sent to a person with an incompatible version of Word, the graphic, if left as an EMF insert, will appear incorrect to the observer. For this reason, the use of EMF files is not recommended for general use.

The problem of positioning vertical text is not confined to EMF visualization. An analogous issue exists for some printer drivers and therefore the Vertical Text menu item dialog window invoked from the File menu also provides a solution to the incorrect placement of vertical text on printed output.

 Copy Scrolled List to Clipboard as an EMF

Using the drawing instructions for the entire set of tiles in the left-hand-side of the experiment frame, copy an EMF to the clipboard. See the above discussion relating to EMF from the active tile for caveats.

The following example is a graphic create using the Copy Scrolled List to Clipboard button, however the image has been converted to a bitmap via Microsoft Paint before including in a Word document. The use of the bitmap is to fix the display obtained from the EMF and therefore ensures the display is not corrupted by the version of Word used to display this document.

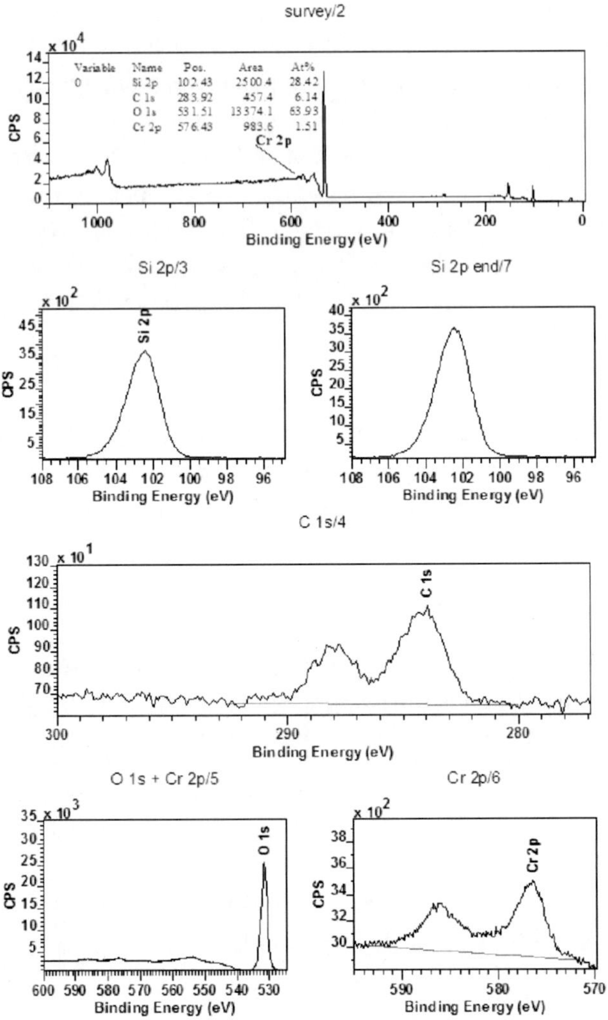

Save TAB spaced ASCII file

Data in a format suitable for import to Excel, Sigma Plot or Origin is output to an ASCII file using the Save TAB spaced ASCII file button. The resulting text file is created from those VAMAS blocks currently selected in the right-hand pane of the experiment frame, where separate tables are formatted from the data in each selected VAMAS block. The tables include the binding/kinetic energy, spectral intensities, background, each synthetic component in any peak model defined on the data and the total synthetic envelope. The table for each VAMAS block output includes columns using both counts-per-second and counts-per-bin.

Copy TAB spaced ASCII to Clipboard

Tabulated data in a similar format to that generated by Save TAB spaced ASCII file is placed on the clipboard with the view to transferring into a spreadsheet or plotting program using the paste mechanism. The source for the data, however, is the spectrum in the active tile rather than the selected VAMAS blocks in the right-hand pane. Note that while the data displayed in a Clipboard Selection dialog window may appear misaligned, the columns of data are separated by tab spaces and will paste into most spreadsheets property aligned. The Clipboard Selection dialog window also allows the information to be saved to a text file.

Save PHI

VAMAS formatted spectra can be exported in PHI Multipak format.

Save data as individual VAMAS files

Both buttons save the selected VAMAS blocks as a set of VAMAS files, where each VAMAS block becomes a separate file. Some programs are not capable of using VAMAS files unless the most basic use of the VAMAS format is employed to save the data. These two buttons provide alternative means of saving the VAMAS formatted data in an attempt to aid the exchange of data between programs. These options may be useful, for example, if spectra are required as input for the NPL transmission correction software.

Save in QUASES format

QUASES format relates to the program written by Sven Tougaard. A dialog window is invoked which offers two options for exporting the data:

1. The **Use Browser Selection** tick-box is ticked. For each selected VAMAS block a QUASES formatted ASCII file is generated, where the file name of the new file(s) indicates the VAMAS block index and corresponding variable index for the source data.

2. The **Use Browser Selection** tick-box is *not* ticked. The VAMAS file is assumed to be ordered consistent with spectra generated from an image

data-set. A range of VAMAS blocks and corresponding variables are defined using two pairs of indices entered on the dialog window, such that when the OK button is pressed, the QUASES files are created based on the specified indices rather than the currently selected VAMAS blocks.

 Paste VAMAS formatted data from clipboard

Some acquisition systems, such as SPECSLAB II place data on the clipboard in VAMAS format. If the clipboard is loaded with VAMAS formatted data then pressing the Paste button on the toolbar will cause the data to appear in a new experiment frame in CasaXPS. A temporary file is used to keep a copy of the data on disk, however the data must be saved to an appropriate file following the paste operation or the VAMAS file will be lost.

 Paste data from clipboard

If VAMAS formatted data is placed on the clipboard, then pressing the Paste data toolbar button performs the same task as the Paste VAMAS formatted data paste button, however a File dialog window requires a disk file to be associated with the experiment frame.

The Paste data button also allows data from RBD's Auger Scan Software to be pasted from the clipboard into CasaXPS. The data appears in a new experiment frame and must be saved to a disk file at a later stage.

Toolbar options for invoking dialog windows

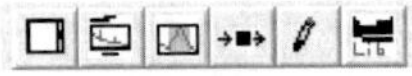

The primary dialog windows for manipulating data are invoked using these toolbar buttons. The Options menu also provides access to these same dialog windows.

Page Layout

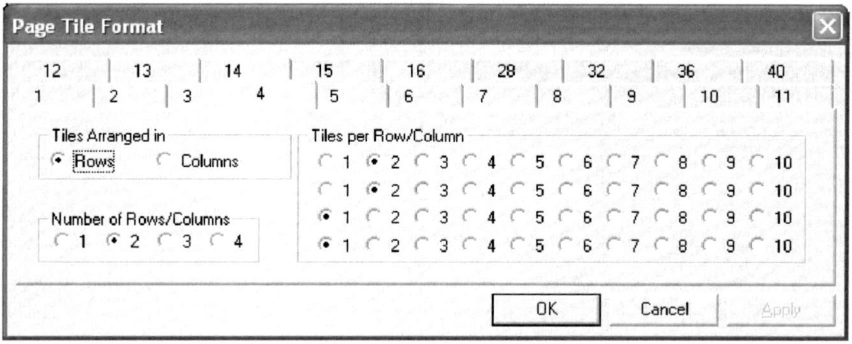

The scrolled-list of tiles in the left-hand pane of an experiment frame represents a sequence of pages. On pressing the Print toolbar button, spectra are printed using the tile layout currently used to view the data in the scrolled-list. A page corresponds to the set of tiles visible at any one time in the left-hand pane. The Page Tile Format dialog window offers a set of default layouts for one or more display tiles per page. Each property page on the dialog window defines an array of non-overlapping display tiles, where initially the number of tiles in the array corresponds to the value used to label the property page. The format defined by a property page can be adjusted using the three sets of radio buttons. A format is defined by specifying the number of rows of tiles, then for each row the number of tiles to appear in each row. The number of rows can be selected from the **Number of Rows/Column** radio buttons. For each row from a possible maximum of four rows, the number of tiles within a row is assigned using the **Tiles per Row/Column** radio buttons. As an alternative, the definition for the tiles per page can be made using columns rather than rows. Switching the page layout between rows and columns is performed using the **Tile Arranged in** radio buttons.

The following page layout shows four tiles arranged using three rows with one, two and one tile per row. The format display using arrange in rows and then arrange in columns is compared.

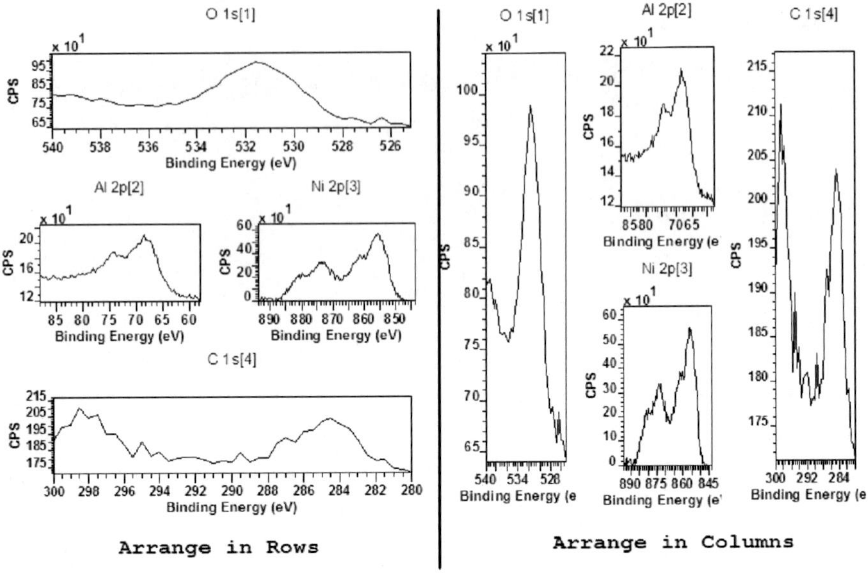

Tile Display Parameters

The Tile Display Parameter dialog window offers a set of property pages for altering the appearance of the active tile.

X Axis Property Page

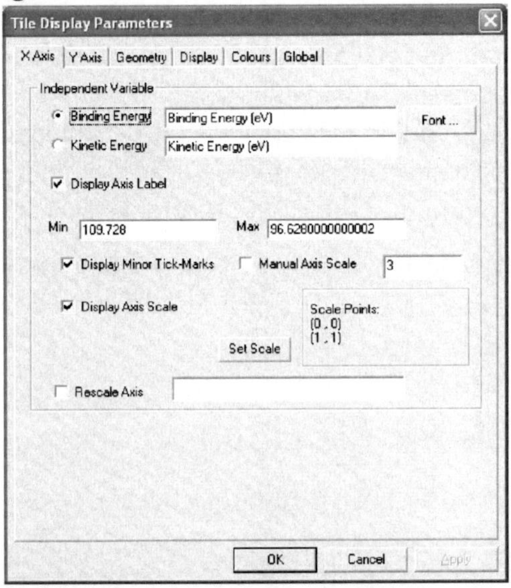

For display purposes, two strings are offered on the X Axis property page and are associated with the choice of binding or kinetic energy display for the energy axis. The convention in XPS is to display the binding energy axis as a decreasing energy scale; however if the core electrons are viewed as lower in energy than the more excited valence band electrons, then it is clear the convention for the binding energy scale is simply missing a minus sign. Thus both kinetic energy and binding energy scale should be seen as increasing energy scales. Binding energy is more commonly used for XPS because the positions of photoelectric lines with respect to the binding energy scale are independent of the x-ray photon energy. The opposite is true for Auger lines, that is, Auger lines always appear at the same positions on the energy scale with respect to the kinetic energy of the ejected electron. Hence AES data is displayed using the kinetic energy scale.

When a spectrum is plotted, the chosen energy type determines which of the two strings are displayed as the label to the X-axis. The font for the X-axis label is defined using a standard Font dialog window invoked by the Font button on the X-Axis property page. Once a font is chosen from the Font dialog window, it is necessary to press the OK or the Apply button on the Tile Display Parameters dialog window before the font in the active tile is changed. The energy range over which the spectrum is displayed is determined from the values entered in the Min and Max fields. The font used to display the X-axis numbers is also used to display the Y-axis numbers, therefore the button to make adjustments to the font used on the axes is located on the Display property page rather than on either the X-axis or Y-axis property pages.

It is also possible to reduce the complexity of the display by either removing the X-axis scale entirely or limiting the tick marks on the X-axis to only the major values. These options are available as tick-boxes on the property page.

Y Axis Property Page

The Y axis label and intensity range are analogous to the X axis property page; however there is an additional label associated with displaying the data using arbitrary units. The tick-box labelled Arbitrary Units removes the numerical scale from the intensity display and adds a third string as the Y axis label in preference to both the strings associated with the counts per second and counts per bin radio buttons. Arbitrary units are useful when the data has been normalized in some way.

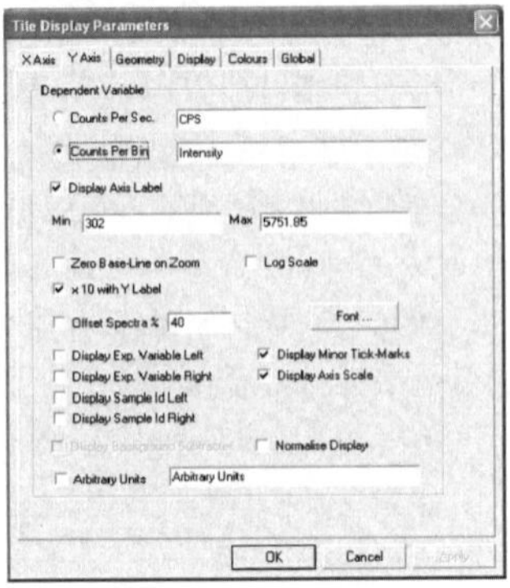

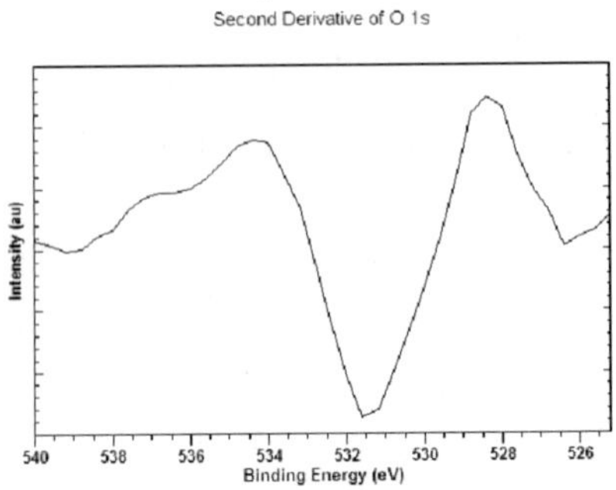

Two frequently used options on the Y axis property page are the **Normalise Display** and **Offset Spectra** tick-boxes (also available from the toolbar buttons and). These options are often used when visually comparing overlaid spectra, where the Offset Spectra tick-box creates a set of vertically offset plotting areas within the display tile and the **Normalise Display** tick-box adjusts the intensities of each spectrum displayed in the tile relative to the intensity of the first spectrum selected via the right-hand pane of the experiment frame.

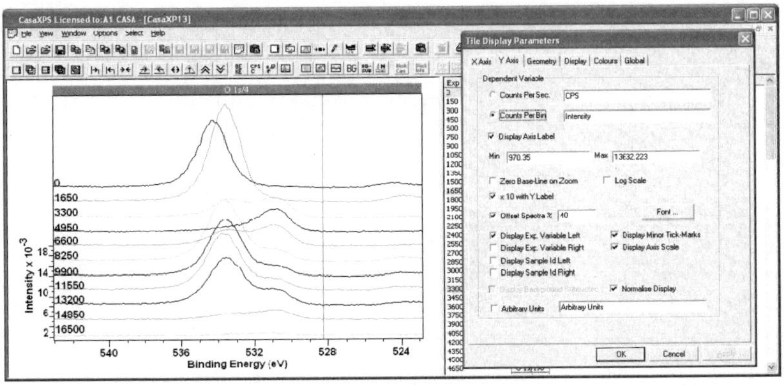

The relative size of the plotting areas and consequently the offset between these plotting areas is specified via the % text-field adjacent to the Offset Spectra tick-box. The value entered in the text-field specifies the percentage size of the plotting areas relative to the size of the axes box in the display tile. If the **Normalise Display** option is also used, a vertical line marks the point at which the data is scaled, where the scaling is performed so that the traces all pass through the same point intersecting the vertical line. The position of the vertical line can be adjusted by holding the Shift-key down and then left-clicking the mouse with the cursor indicating the desired tie point. When printed, the vertical line is not included on the output. The following is a bitmap from a display using a 50% offset

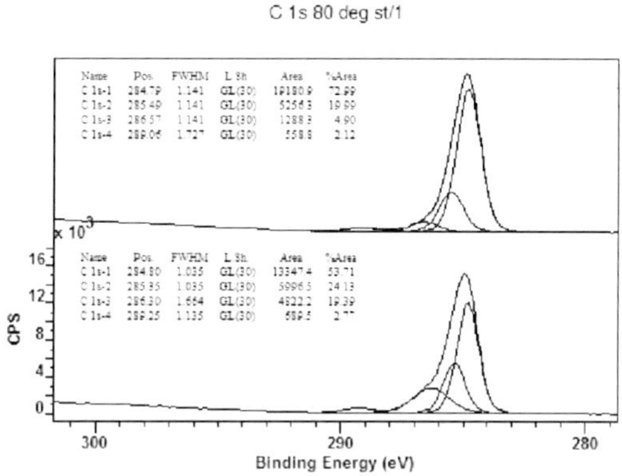

Zero Base-Line on Zoom and **Log Scale** are two tick boxes aimed at SIMS data; the former modifies the behaviour when using the mouse to zoom into a peak. The default zoom behaviour uses the dimensions of both the width as well as the height of the zoom rectangle drawn following dragging the cursor over a display tile. If the cursor is located inside the defined zoom box when the left mouse button is clicked, provided the **Zero Base-Line on Zoom** tick box is *not* ticked, the intensity range defined by the zoom box is used to redisplay the data. Alternatively, if the **Zero Base-Line on Zoom** tick box is ticked, then only the upper-most boundary of the zoom box defines the maximum intensity when the data is redisplayed; the lower limit to the intensity scale is always zero.

Geometry Property Page

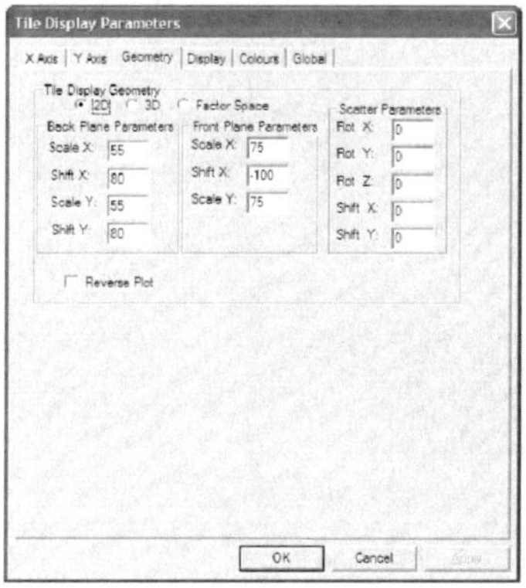

The Geometry property page provides the means to switch between the normal 2D graphical display used to display spectra overlaid on a single pair of axes and a 3D plot, where the axes are offset in both X and Y directions to provide a depth to the display. The spectra are positioned within the display determined by the values assigned to the experimental variable for each spectrum. When a set of spectra are plotted using the 3D option, the size and location of the axes used to draw the data are defined in terms of the Front Plane and the Back Plane. When overlaid spectra are drawn, the first spectrum in the list of selected blocks is drawn on a pair of axes positioned and scaled using the Scale X, Scale Y and Shift X parameters in the Front Plane Parameters section. Similarly the last spectrum in the list of selected blocks is drawn using a pair of axes positioned and scaled according to the same parameters as the Front Plane, but with the additional parameter of Shift Y. All other spectra within the selected blocks appear at axes positioned and scaled using a linear interpolation between these two defining planes. The parameters are percentage based, for example, Scale X 75 represents a set of axes where the size of the X direction is ¾ the size of the box which otherwise would have been used to plot the data in 2D mode. Once the Front and Back planes are shrunken down to some percentage of the surrounding box, the position of the reduced axes are defined using the convention that -100 positions the shrunken plane all the way to the left of the surrounding box, while +100 shifts the shrunken plane entirely to the right. The following 3-D plot shows a display where the Front plane is scaled in both X and Y using 75 and shifted in X by -80.

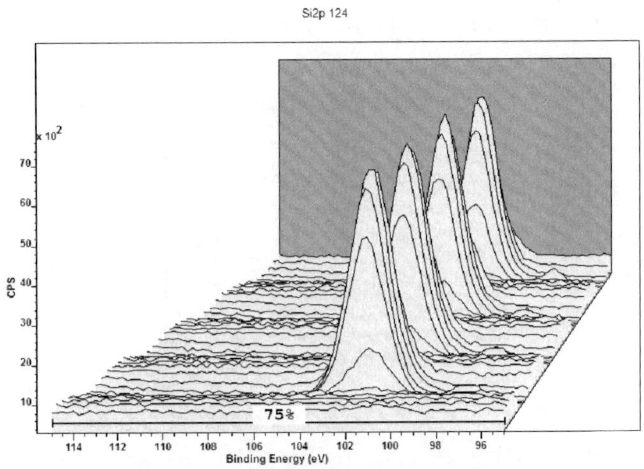

The toolbar button  toggles between the three display-modes 2D, 3D and Factor Space.

Display Property Page

The display characteristics of the active tile are adjusted using the Display property page. The extensive array of tick-boxes permits the inclusion or exclusion of information on the drawing area. Some display properties are also toggled using toolbar buttons , where pressing these toolbar buttons cycles through various combinations of the tick-box setting. For example, pressing the  button initially removes the background colour used to define the range over which a quantification region computes a background, a second press returns the background colour previously removed but removes the region name label and a third press removes both region colour and also the region name string from the display. A fourth button press returns both the region colour and also the region name label. These toolbar button actions could be explicitly defined using the two tick-boxes **Quant. Regions** and **Quant Region Labels** on the Display property page.

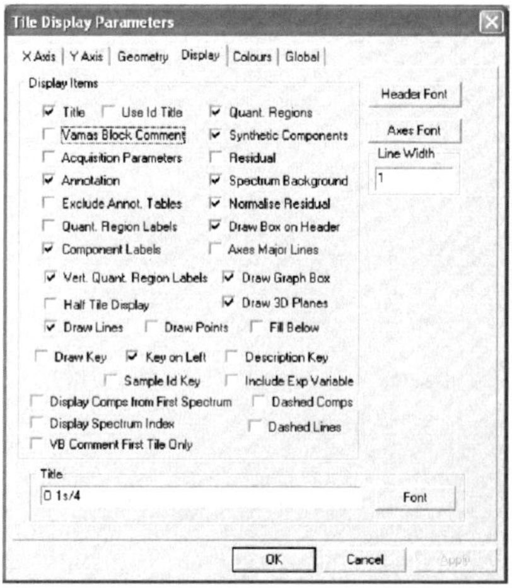

The Display Tick-Boxes

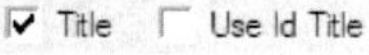

When ticked, the Title tick-box causes the title string to be displayed above the plotting area in a tile. The source for the title is either the text-field on the Display property page 

or if the Use Id Title tick-box is ticked, then the title is constructed from the Block identifier and Sample identifier strings in the source VAMAS block. The font for the title string is also defined using a standard Font dialog window. Note, the font specified through the Font dialog window only takes effect following pressing of the OK or Apply buttons on the Tile Display Parameters dialog window.

Vamas Block Comment When ticked, the comment text lines maintained by the VAMAS block are displayed above the graph area. The display of the VAMAS block comment is modified for sets of tile by the VB Comment First Tile Only tick box. The set of tiles displayed in the left-hand pane only includes the VAMAS block comment for the first display tile, the remaining tiles are positioned as if comments were present, but without the comment text. An equivalent display can be achieved by individually setting the display parameters for the tiles displayed in the left-hand pane, the difference being in the positioning of the tile array with respect to the comment text.

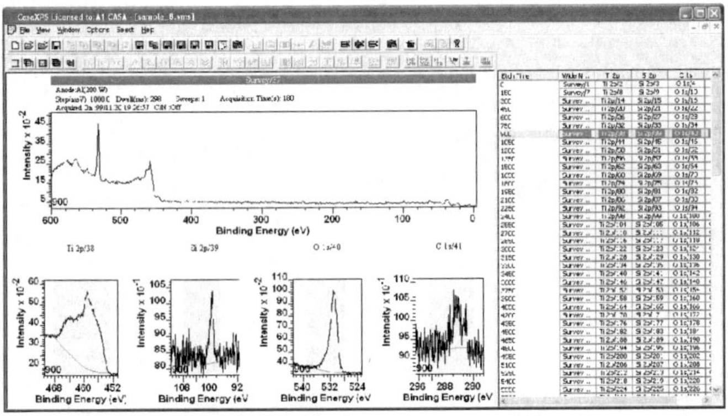

Acquisition Parameters When ticked, the acquisition parameters for the data displayed in the tile are printed above the graph area.

Header Font The font used to display both the VAMAS block comment text and the acquisition parameters is altered using the Font dialog window invoked by the Header Font button. As always, a new font only takes effect when the Apply button is pressed on the Tile Display Parameters property page.

Annotation When ticked, the annotation defined by the Annotation dialog window is displayed on the data in the tile. Note, not all text on the display derives from the Annotation dialog window, e.g. component and region name text.

☐ Exclude Annot. Tables When ticked, annotation tables such as components, regions and quantification tables are not displayed in the tile. This parameter is automatically enabled for inset tiles.

☑ Quant. Region Labels When ticked, the name fields from any quantification regions are displayed on the spectra. Labels from quantification regions do not derive from the Annotation dialog window and are therefore unaffected by the Annotation tick-box above. The toolbar button alters the state of the tick-box

☐ Component Labels Text labels for each component displayed in a tile deriving from the name fields for individual components can be turned on and off. The mechanism for switching these component labels on and off is selecting the components via the table on the Components property page of the Quantification Parameters dialog window. When a component is selected, by left-clicking a given column on the Components property page, the tick-box on the Display property page becomes enabled and the selected component label is toggled on or off. The set of component labels currently displayed can all be turn off by un-ticking the Component Labels tick-box on the Display property page. The labels only appear in a tile when the Component Labels tick-box is ticked.

☑ Vert. Quant. Region Labels When ticked, the labels for the quantification regions, if enabled, are printed in a vertical direction.

☐ Quant. Regions When ticked, a rectangular area defined by the energy limits to a quantification region is displayed on a spectrum using a different background colour to the default tile background colour. These colours are defined using the Colour property page on the Tile Display Parameters dialog window. The  toolbar button alters the state of the tick-box.

☑ Synthetic Components When ticked, components defined on a spectrum are displayed. The toolbar button also toggles the display of the component by altering the state of the Display tick box.

☐ Residual When ticked, the residual plot representing the difference between the data and the total synthetic envelope is plotted along the top of the tile.

☑ Normalise Residual When ticked, the residual plot is normalized with respect to the expected noise in the data. Poisson counting statistics imply the noise and therefore the un-normalized residual is largest where the counts are highest. Normalizing the residual produces an even appearance to the residual plot regardless of the counts per bin. If the counts per bin are unknown, then the residual should be plotted with the Normalise Residual button un-ticked.

☑ Spectrum Background When ticked, the background to the spectrum computed from the quantification region parameters is displayed on the graph.

☐ Draw Box on Header When ticked and header information from the VAMAS comment and/or the acquisition parameters are enabled, a box or boxes are drawn around the displayed header information between the title and the axes box.

☐ Axes Major Lines When ticked, for each major tick mark on the axes, horizontal and vertical dashed lines are drawn.

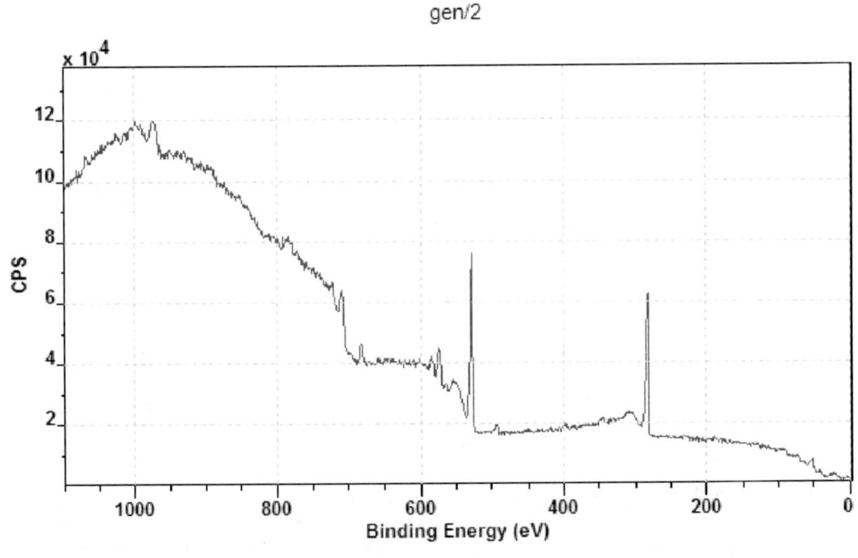

☑ Draw Graph Box When ticked, the rectangle defining the drawing area in a tile is drawn. When disabled, the data are drawn using ordinate and abscissa axes only.

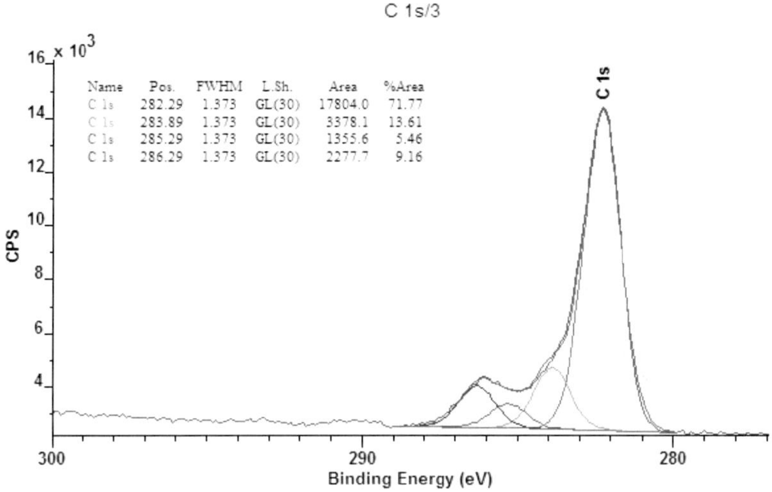

 When ticked, the graphical area used to display the data is reduced to half the size of the tile area. While the graph itself appears in the top half of the tile, annotation defined on the VAMAS block can be moved below the graphical area as shown below, where both a table of components and text have been placed outside the graphical area used to plot the spectrum.

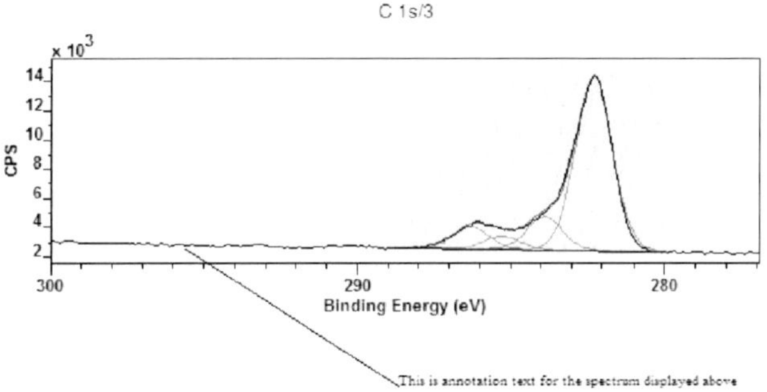

Name	Pos.	FWHM	L.Sh.	Area	%Area
C 1s	282.29	1.373	GL(30)	17804.0	71.77
C 1s	283.89	1.373	GL(30)	3378.1	13.61
C 1s	285.29	1.373	GL(30)	1355.6	5.46
C 1s	286.29	1.373	GL(30)	2277.7	9.16

 When ticked, two rectangular planes, beneath and at the rear of the spectra are filled with a colour defined on the Colour property page. If un-

ticked the display appears as seen below. Note, the 3-D plot is drawn using the Draw Graph Box un-ticked, thus only axes appear on the 3D plot.

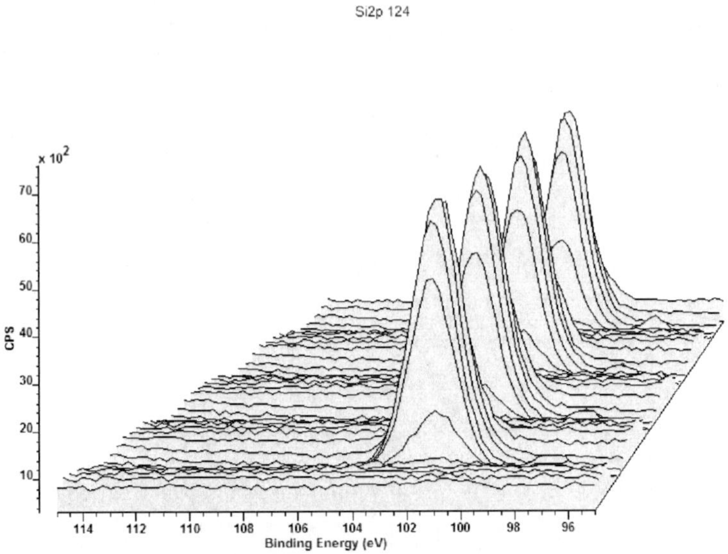

☑ Draw Lines When ticked, a spectrum is drawn using the data points connected by line segments.

☐ Draw Points When ticked and Draw Lines is not ticked, the data points appear as symbols without connecting line segments, one symbol per data point. If tick together with Draw Lines, a reduced number of symbols are drawn at regular intervals and the data points are connected using line segments.

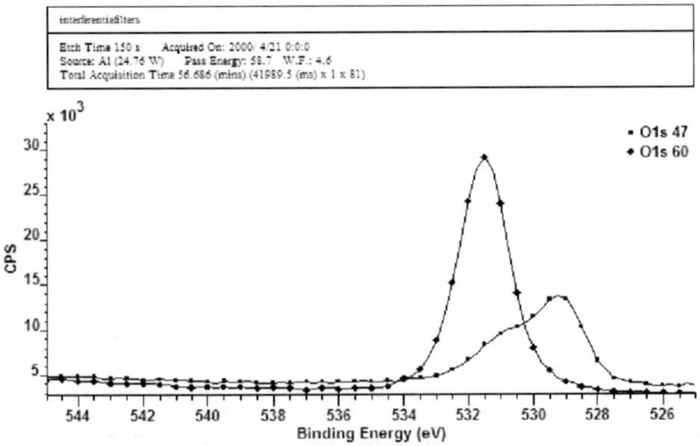

Fill Below The **Fill Below** tick box results in different plots depending on the state of the **Draw Lines** and **Draw Points** tick boxes. If the **Draw Lines** tick box is ticked at the same time as the **Fill Below** tick box, then the area between the graph and the X axis is filled with the colour determined from the **3D Fill** button on the Colour property page. An alternative drawing mode results if the **Fill Below** tick box is ticked and the **Draw Points** tick is ticked whilst the **Draw Lines** tick box is not. Under these circumstances, the data points are used to draw sticks from the data point to the X axis as shown in the Inset Tile below.

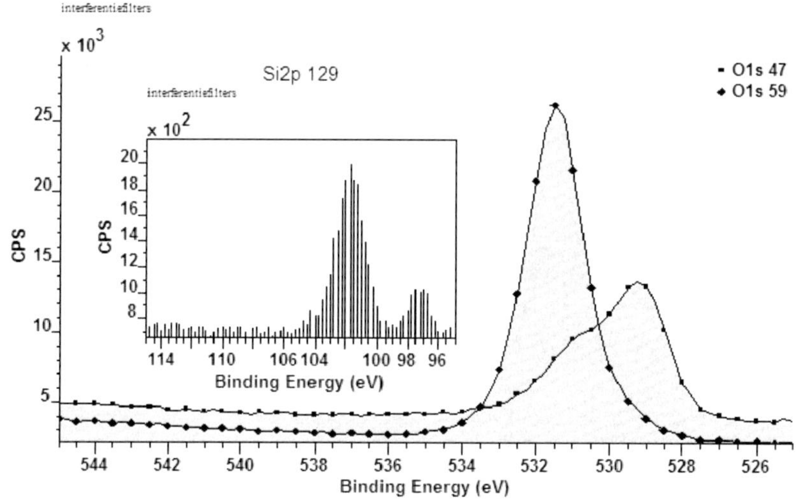

Draw Key When ticked, a key or legend is added to the display of two or more spectra. The default source for the text is the Block Id for the VAMAS block containing the data and is therefore the string used to display the VAMAS block in the right-hand pane of the experiment frame. The block identifier can be adjusted using the following toolbar buttons: Block Info or ?.

Key on Left When ticked, the key or legend is positioned in the top-left side of the graphical area; otherwise the key appears in the top-right-hand side of the graphical area.

Description Key When ticked, the text appearing in the key or legend derives from the first line of the VAMAS block comment Block Com.

☐ Sample Id Key When ticked, the text appearing in the key or legend derives from the Sample Id VAMAS block field. The Sample Id text may appear as an alternative to the Block Id or in conjunction with the Description Key tick box text.

☐ Include Exp Variable When ticked, the current experimental variable is appended to the text appearing in the key.

☐ Display Comps from First Spectrum When ticked, synthetic components defined on the first spectrum of several spectra displayed in a tile are displayed over the data. This tick box is used when fitting a set of linked components spanning multiple acquisition regions.

☐ Display Spectrum Index When ticked, an index with respect to the VAMAS file displayed in the experiment frame appears in the top-left-hand side of the graphical area. Data in VAMAS files are specified by two indices, the VAMAS block index and the corresponding variable index within a given VAMAS block. Displaying data derived from the corresponding variables is achieved by holding the Control Key down and pressing the Page Up and/or Page Down buttons on the keyboard. Control Home and Control End move to the first and last corresponding variables in a VAMAS block. The transmission function for a spectrum, if present in the VAMAS block, appears as the second corresponding variable indexed 1.

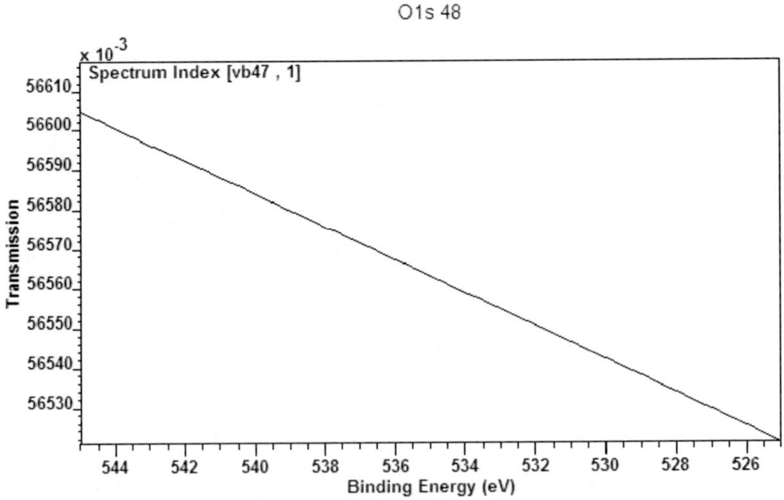

Dashed Comps Dashed Lines When tick and the line width is one or zero (Line Width 1), the synthetic components or the spectra are drawn using a range of line styles.

Axes Font The font used to display the numerical values associated with the X and Y axes are adjusted using the resulting Font dialog window. The font only takes effect following pressing the OK or the Apply button on the Tile Display Parameters dialog window.

Colour Property Page

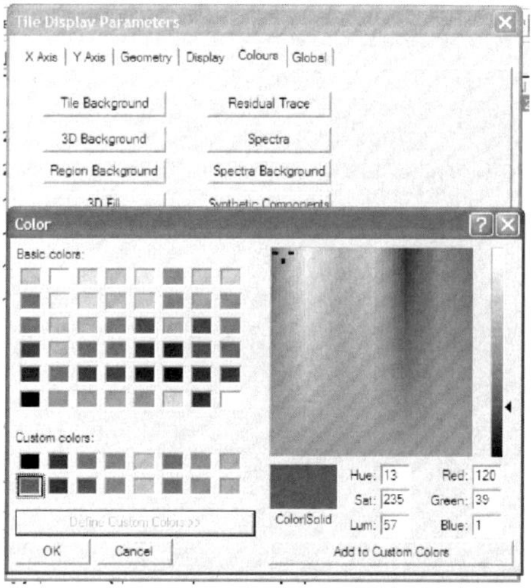

The Colour property page offers a means for adjusting the colours used to display spectra and related information in the display tiles. The set of buttons on the property page all use the standard Microsoft Color dialog window, however two modes of operation are used depending on whether the button selected adjusts one colour or a set of colours. If one colour is involved, for example the Tile Background colour, then simply selecting a colour from any of the colour squares on the Color dialog window and pressing the OK button will alter the parameter, however the colour displayed by the tile is only updated once the OK or Apply button is pressed on the Tile Display Parameter dialog window. The alternative mode involves sets of colours rather than individual colours. For Example, a range of colours are used to display overlaid spectra, therefore the important colours are those appearing in the Custom Color palette on the Color dialog window. There are sixteen colours available for definition via the extended section of the

Color dialog window and these colours are used to display overlaid spectra in the order top-left to top-right, then bottom-left to bottom-right. The button labelled Define Custom Colors, when pressed, reveals a mechanism for making adjustments to the current palette of Custom Colors. Click a colour square from the set of Custom Colors, adjust the colour using the cursor over the large coloured square, then press the Add to Custom Colors button. Once all the changes to the custom color palette are made, press the OK button on the Color dialog window. Again, the tile display is only updated once the OK or Apply button is pressed on the Tile Display Parameters dialog window.

Display modes for components using colour options are also controlled using tick-boxes on the Colour property page. Components are assigned a component index number which when enabled using the tick boxes on the Colour property page provide means for displaying related components with a common colour.

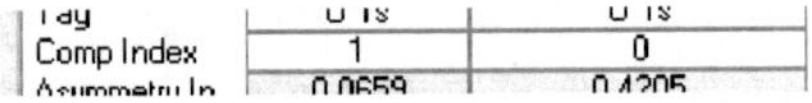

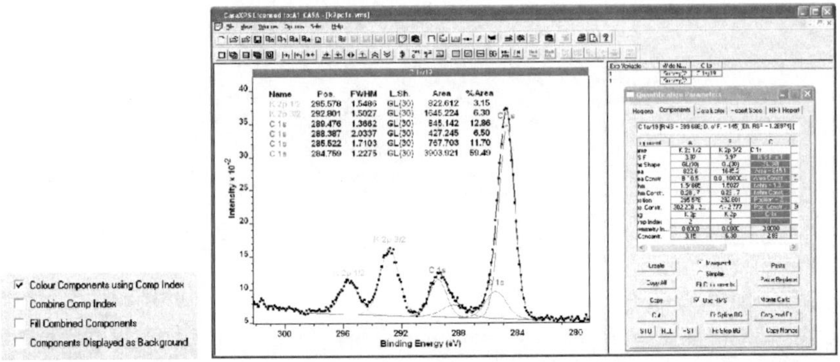

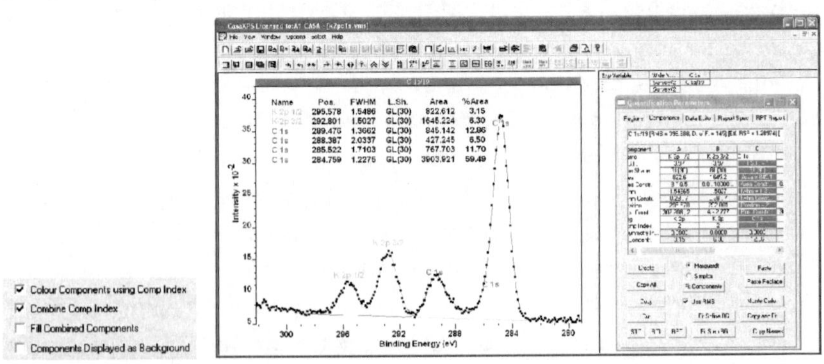

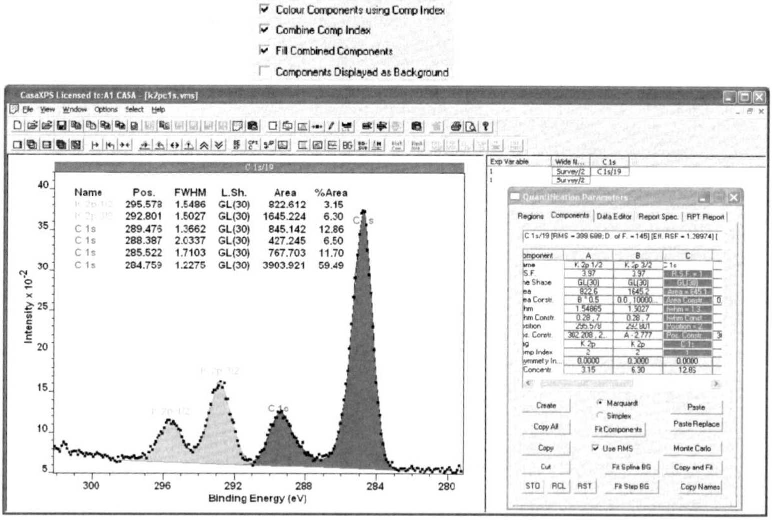

Components Displayed as Background is for situations where a component is included in a peak model to represent a relatively shape loss structure. To emphasis the role played by these background-type components, the display for the peak model can be made to show primary peaks sitting on top of background components. The components considered to be background structures are assigned a component index of -1, while the photoelectric peaks are positive integers.

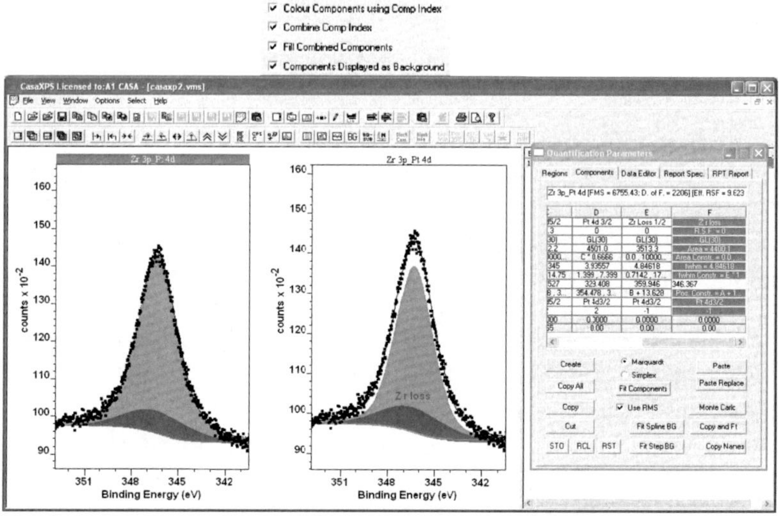

Global Property Page

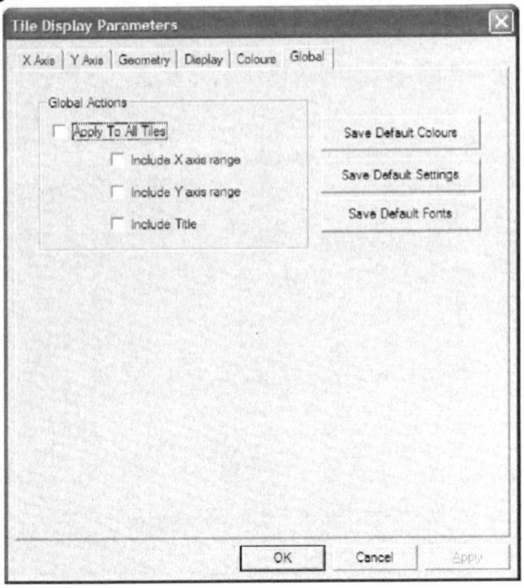

The Tile Display Parameter dialog window alters the display settings for the active tile. If however, the settings prepared and applied to the active tile are also applicable to other tiles currently displayed in the left-hand pane of the experiment frame, then the Global property page can be used to apply these new settings to all the tiles in the scrolled list in the left-hand pane.

When applying certain display setting to a range of tiles, not all the display settings are necessarily appropriate. For example, if two tiles exist displaying an O 1s and a C 1s peak, then although the desire to unify the spectrum colour used to display both spectra is valid, accepting a single range of energies for the X axis is not. Similarly, the intensity range may be inappropriate as well as unifying the title. These display settings are generally excluded when the display settings are applied to a range of tiles, however to accommodate the situation where these parameters require updating too, there are a set of tick-boxes which when tick, explicitly specify that these parameters should also be applied together with all the other tile display parameters.

The Global property page also offers a means of saving default settings for the tile display between CasaXPS sessions. The directory containing the CasaXPS.exe program also contains a directory called CasaXPS.DEF, in which a set of configuration files are stored. Once the tile display in terms of fonts, colours and display options is established for the active tile, pressing the buttons on the

Global property page will save most display settings to disk. On restarting CasaXPS, the saved display settings are read and used to display the data.

Quantification Parameters Dialog Window

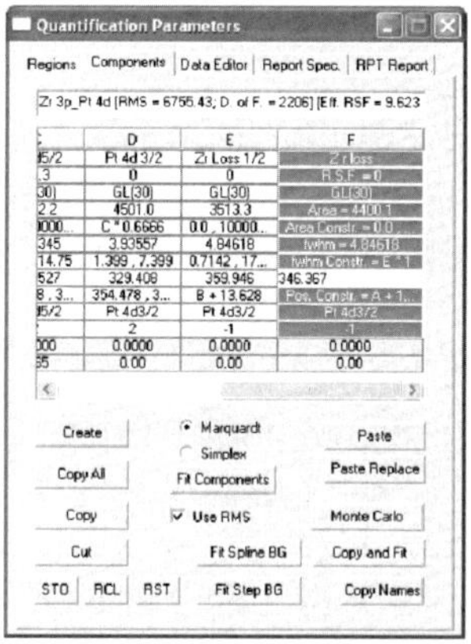

Quantification regions, synthetic components, data editing, satellite subtraction and the generation of quantification reports are all featured on the Quantification Parameters dialog window. The Quantification Parameters dialog window is central to the analysis of spectra; so much so that entire chapters are devoted to the uses and implications of the options on this dialog window.

Spectrum Processing Dialog Window

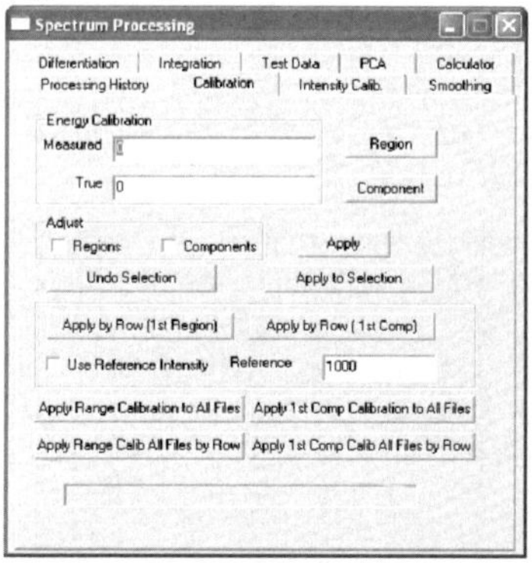

The Spectrum Processing window has become a misnomer since both spectra and images are manipulated via options on this window. The property pages on the Spectrum Processing dialog window are predominantly for processing spectra, but nevertheless certain features are also useful for manipulating images, most notably the processing history.

When data within CasaXPS are manipulated in any way, the original raw data are saved in memory and the displayed data derives from the processed data. Operations performed on the data via the Spectrum Processing dialog window are recorded using a list of instruction known as the processing history. The processing instructions for a piece of data are listed on the Processing History dialog window, from which the processing can be modified and re-applied to the raw data. Making any adjustment to the processing history involves returning the processed data to the initial raw data, then re-application of each command in the processing history list. Note, not all processing commands can be applied in this way. For example, any calculator operation cannot be re-applied because the computation requires the knowledge of other VAMAS blocks within a file or even from other files and therefore cannot be performed in a *safe* manner. If data are processed via other means, for example image arithmetic or altered using the Data Editor property page on the Quantification Parameters dialog window, then the raw data can be reinstated by pressing the Reset button on the Processing History property page.

The set of property pages on the Spectrum Processing dialog window include options with sufficient depth of content to require sections and chapters devoted to their use.

Annotation Dialog Window

Annotation for spectra is managed using an analogous mechanism to the processing history. Each piece of annotation, when applied to a spectrum, is added to an annotation history, which appears in a list on the Annotation History property page and can be adjusted or deleted using options on the property page.

Annotation can take the form of quantification tables, created using options on the Quantification, Regions and Components property pages or text for labelling the data. The uses and issues associated with the use of annotation tables is discussed elsewhere.

Annotation is added to a spectrum by pressing the Apply button found on each of the property pages on the dialog window. A new entry will appear in the Annotation History list each time an Apply button is pressed. If the annotation so created does not appear on the display, check the state of the Annotation tick-box on the Display property page of the Tile Display Parameters dialog window. To see the annotation within a tile, the tick-box must be ticked. In addition to listing the set of annotation defined on a spectrum, the Annotation History property page allows various attributes associated with the annotation to be changed. For example, the font used to display text is altered by selecting an item in the scrolled-list, then choosing a new font via the Font dialog window invoked by the Font button, followed by pressing the Apply button on the Annotation History property page.

Moving annotation is also performed when the Annotation History property page is the active page on the Annotation dialog window. Under these circumstances, each piece of annotation displayed on a spectrum is also accompanied by a small square with a dot inside the square, which appears near the top left-hand side of annotation tables. Dragging the cursor starting at one of these squares causes the annotation to move to wherever the drag motion ends.

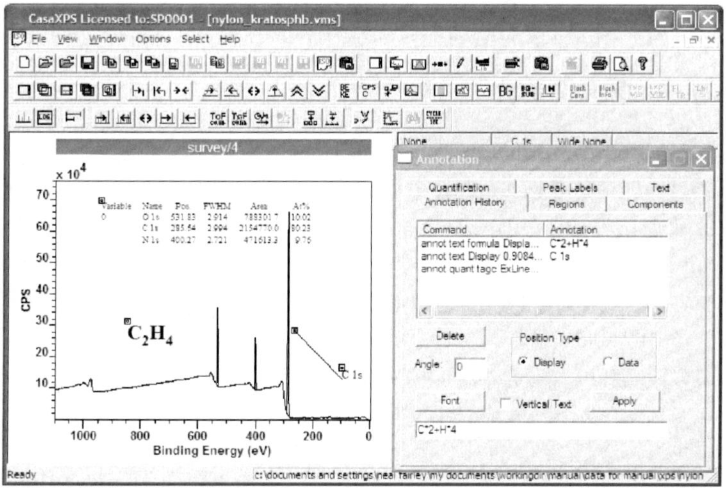

Element Library Dialog Window

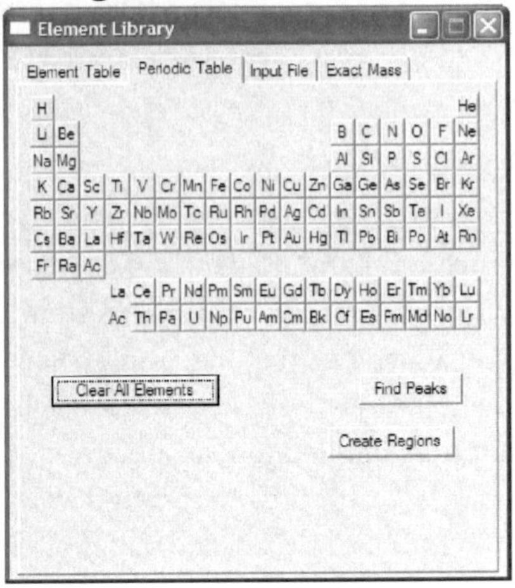

The Element Library dialog window provides the means to qualitatively assess the composition of a survey spectrum. A combination of a scrolled-list of transitions (Element Table property page) linked to the energy scale of a spectrum and selecting elements from the Periodic Table property page permit transition markers to appear over the data. By matching these markers to the peaks, the composition of a surface can be assessed. A complete description of the Element Library can be found elsewhere.

Toolbar option used to propagate a set of commands to other spectra within a file or to spectra in other files

Processing, quantification regions, synthetic components and annotation prepared on a spectrum can be propagated to other spectra requiring the same actions. Once the analysis of a spectrum is complete, spectra within the same file or from other files can be selected (using the right-hand pane of the experiment frames open in CasaXPS) and by giving focus to the active tile displaying the prepared spectrum before pressing the propagate toolbar button. The processing etc associated with the active tile is transferred to the selected VAMAS blocks. The Browser Operations dialog window invoked by the toolbar button displays the block identifier of the source VAMAS block and also a list of the target VAMAS blocks. The types of action to propagate are chosen using tick-boxes in the Propagate section of the dialog window.

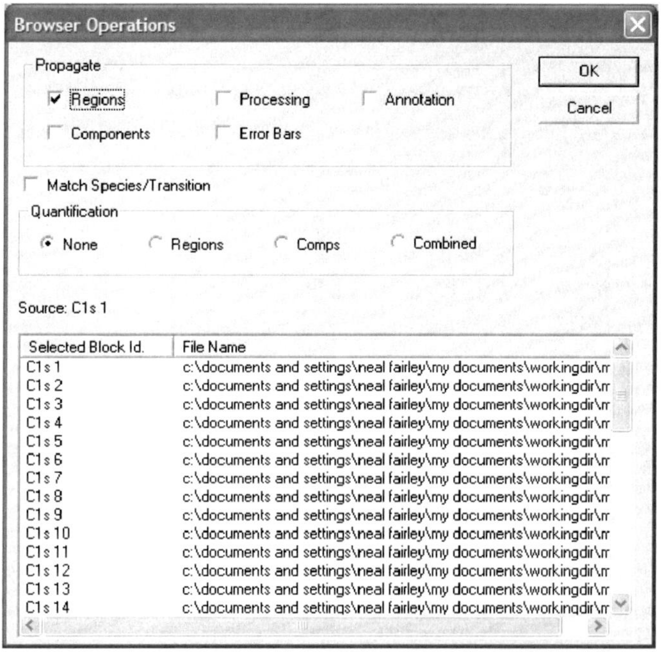

Add to and Deleting VAMAS Blocks from an Experiment Frame

VAMAS blocks can be moved between experiment frames by first selecting the VAMAS blocks using the right-hand pane of experiment frames, passing focus to the experiment frame to which the data are to be transferred, then pressing the toolbar button. A dialog window appears listing all the VAMAS blocks currently selected. On pressing the OK button on the dialog window the data are copied into the experiment frame with focus. The tick-box labelled **Processed Data Only** switches between copying the raw data plus the processing commands from each of the source VAMAS blocks and copying the processed data only. The consequence of ticking the Processed Data Only tick box is the new VAMAS block has no record of the processing steps used to prepare the data and only contains the processed data. For example, if the desire is to copy satellite subtracted data to a new file, the satellites can be removed using the temporary data manipulation option and once all operations have been performed successfully, the satellite subtracted data copied to a new experiment frame using the **Processed Data Only** tick box, thus providing a permanent record of the processed spectra.

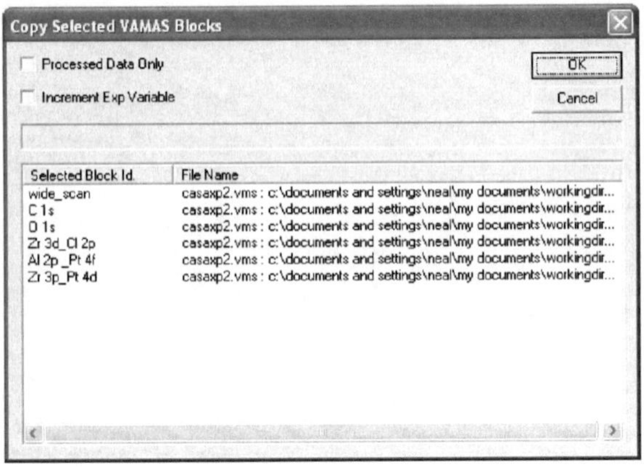

Similarly, VAMAS blocks can be deleted from the current experiment frame with focus. Simply, selecting the VAMAS blocks in the right-hand pane of the experiment frame and press the delete toolbar button ultimately removes the selected VAMAS blocks from the experiment frame. A confirmation dialog window will offer a second chance to reconsider the action, however should the delete action be confirmed, the selected VAMAS blocks are permanently removed from the experiment frame.

An alternative strategy for collecting VAMAS blocks from more than one file is to use the **Open and Merge** menu option on the File menu. The use of the menu option requires all the VAMAS files to be gathered together in a directory. A selection of files all located in the same directory can be made using the Merge VAMAS Files dialog window invoked by the Open and Merge menu option. Use of the Shift key and the Control Key allows multiple files to be selected prior to pressing the Open button. Each file selected will appear in the same new experiment frame, where each set of VAMAS blocks from the original individual files are assigned a unique index value as the experimental variable.

Print and print preview toolbar buttons

All the display tiles currently loaded into the left-hand pane of the experiment frame are printed when the Print toolbar button is pressed.

It is worth noting that, if Adobe Acrobat is installed on the PC running CasaXPS, the Adobe Acrobat Distiller option appears as a possible printer on the Print dialog window. The Adobe Acrobat Distiller allows the display tiles in the scrolled list to be converted to PDF format and saved to disk.

 About CasaXPS toolbar button

Offers the current version number and also allows the licensing information to be entered for a PC.

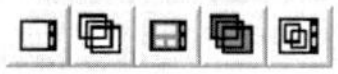 Toolbar buttons for displaying VAMAS blocks in the scrolled list of display tiles

These toolbar buttons are used to display VAMAS blocks selected in the right-hand pane as tiles of graphs organised in the left-hand pane of the experiment frame. The first step is to select the VAMAS blocks using the right-hand pane of the experiment frame, then these selected data are displayed by pressing the appropriate toolbar button for the desired action.

 For each VAMAS block selected in the right-hand pane of the experiment frame a new display tile is create. A new scrolled list is created in the left-hand pane of the experiment frame in which a tile is created for each of the selected VAMAS blocks and one spectrum/image appears in each tile. The display settings last in use are applied to initialize the newly created tiles.

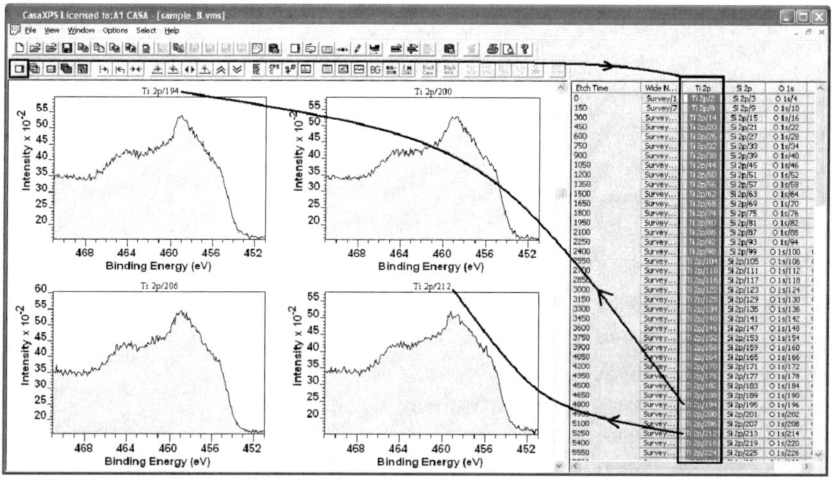

 One or more spectra/images are overlaid in the active tile. Select the VAMAS blocks in the right-hand pane of the experiment frame then select the active tile from the possible tiles already displayed in the left-hand pane. On pressing the toolbar button, the data from the selected VAMAS blocks are displayed overlaid in the active tile. To alter the data in a given display tile, simply left-click the tile,

select the VAMAS block and press the toolbar button. When more than one VAMAS blocks are selected, the order in which the blocks are selected in the right-hand pane determines the order for the data in the active tile.

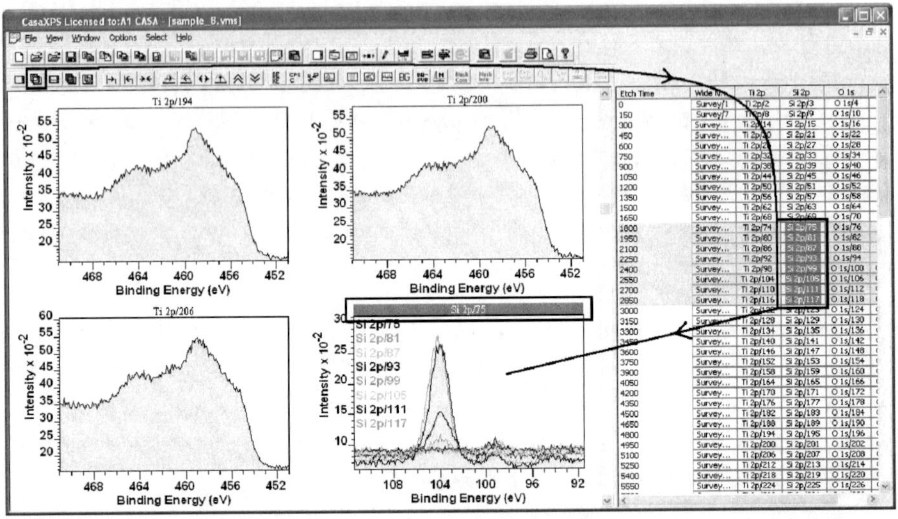

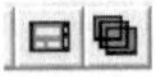 Identical in operation to the 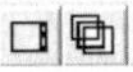 toolbar buttons, respectively, however the current energy and intensity ranges, if possible, are used to display the data.

 Using the selected VAMAS blocks, this toolbar button initializes the scrolled list of tiles in the left-hand pane of the experiment frame, creating a new tile for each row of VAMAS blocks selected within the right-hand pane of the experiment frame. These new tiles are themselves initialized by overlaying the data from each row of VAMAS blocks selected at the time the button is pressed.

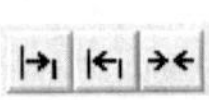 Toolbar buttons for manipulating the zoom list.

 Zooms the energy and intensity displayed via a rectangle specified using the mouse. Using the left mouse button, drag out a box over a spectral feature of interest. On pressing the toolbar button the axes are rescaled to the ranges for energy and intensity defined by the zoom box previously marked in the graphical area of the tile. Each new such zoom action causes an additional zoom state to be added to the current zoom list.

After zooming into a region of a display tile, pressing this toolbar button steps back through the list of zoom states. Repeatedly pressing the Zoom out toolbar button cause the zoom state to appear in a cyclical order.

Reset or re-initialize the zoom-list. If a spectrum already has quantification regions defined, then pressing the Reset toolbar button initializes the zoom list using the energy intervals extracted from the start and end parameters defined for the quantification regions.

Toolbar buttons for moving the current display zoom-state in energy and intensity.

Toolbar buttons for toggling through display options, e.g. switching between binding and kinetic energy for the abscissa. Continuing to press a button ultimately returns the display to the original display state.

VAMAS Fields

Toolbar buttons for invoking dialog windows for editing/viewing VAMAS block information such as the VAMAS block comment and experimental acquisition fields.

Edit VAMAS Block Comment

Each VAMAS block includes as set of comment lines. These comment lines are edited in CasaXPS using the dialog window invoked by the toolbar button. The comment lines can be added to display tiles in the form of a header and the first line of the comment can also be used to create a key or legend for overlaid spectra.

To edit the VAMAS block comment lines, display the data from the VAMAS block in the active tile before pressing the toolbar button. The current comment lines for the VAMAS block are displayed in a text-edit window ready for editing, after which the results can be saved in the VAMAS block by pressing the OK button on the dialog window.

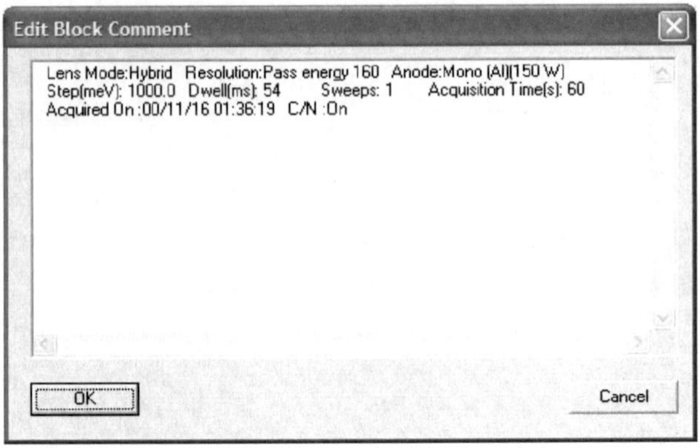

Edit VAMAS Block Fields

Experimental information is collected in each VAMAS block. These VAMAS block fields take many forms and while in theory should be fully defined by the original data file these details may be incomplete. For this reason, some of the VAMAS block fields are offered for viewing and editing on a dialog window. Several of these VAMAS fields are also offered for editing on other more specific dialog windows; however the Edit VAMAS Fields dialog represents the most general means of modifying the experimental information for a specific VAMAS block.

To view or modify the VAMAS fields, display the VAMAS block in the active tile then press the toolbar button. The most common fields requiring adjustment are the Block Id, the Element and Transition fields plus the experimental variable value. Care should be exercised with other field as these may affect quantification and energy calibration.

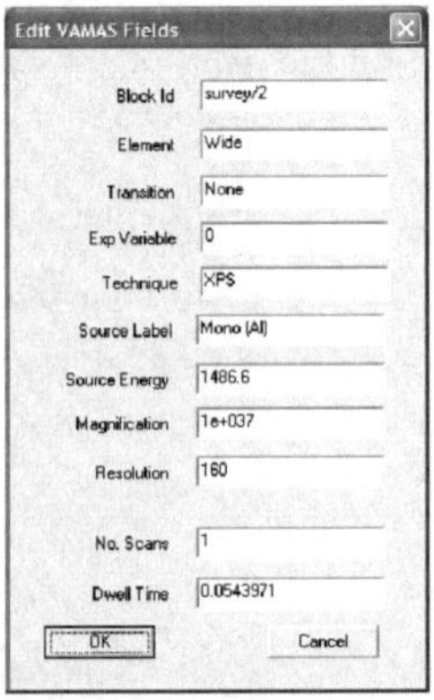

Further Edit Dialogs for VAMAS Fields

Experimental Variable

The toolbar button in question offers a means of globally altering the value for the current experimental variable in all VAMAS blocks in a file. The radio buttons specify the nature and type for the experimental variable.

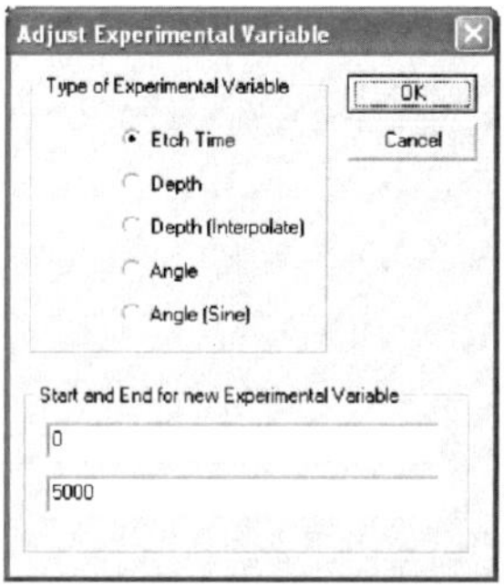

As an example, consider a depth profile in which narrow scan spectra are repeatedly acquired interleaved by etch cycles of a given duration. The following right-hand pane presents the data from such a profile experiment, however ultimately the idea is to plot the trends measured from the spectra as a function of depth rather than etch-time.

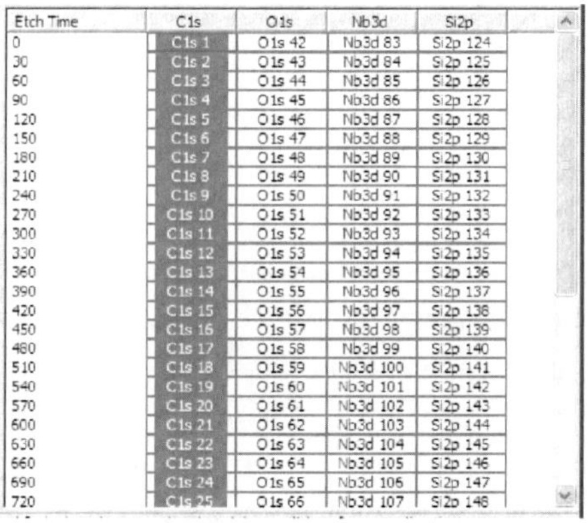

Etch Time	C1s	O1s	Nb3d	Si2p
0	C1s 1	O1s 42	Nb3d 83	Si2p 124
30	C1s 2	O1s 43	Nb3d 84	Si2p 125
60	C1s 3	O1s 44	Nb3d 85	Si2p 126
90	C1s 4	O1s 45	Nb3d 86	Si2p 127
120	C1s 5	O1s 46	Nb3d 87	Si2p 128
150	C1s 6	O1s 47	Nb3d 88	Si2p 129
180	C1s 7	O1s 48	Nb3d 89	Si2p 130
210	C1s 8	O1s 49	Nb3d 90	Si2p 131
240	C1s 9	O1s 50	Nb3d 91	Si2p 132
270	C1s 10	O1s 51	Nb3d 92	Si2p 133
300	C1s 11	O1s 52	Nb3d 93	Si2p 134
330	C1s 12	O1s 53	Nb3d 94	Si2p 135
360	C1s 13	O1s 54	Nb3d 95	Si2p 136
390	C1s 14	O1s 55	Nb3d 96	Si2p 137
420	C1s 15	O1s 56	Nb3d 97	Si2p 138
450	C1s 16	O1s 57	Nb3d 98	Si2p 139
480	C1s 17	O1s 58	Nb3d 99	Si2p 140
510	C1s 18	O1s 59	Nb3d 100	Si2p 141
540	C1s 19	O1s 60	Nb3d 101	Si2p 142
570	C1s 20	O1s 61	Nb3d 102	Si2p 143
600	C1s 21	O1s 62	Nb3d 103	Si2p 144
630	C1s 22	O1s 63	Nb3d 104	Si2p 145
660	C1s 23	O1s 64	Nb3d 105	Si2p 146
690	C1s 24	O1s 65	Nb3d 106	Si2p 147
720	C1s 25	O1s 66	Nb3d 107	Si2p 148

The simplest way to convert the etch-time to depth is to enter the initial and final depths for the crater etched during the course of the experiment, select the Depth radio button on the dialog window, and then press the OK button. The Depth option assumes the rows are equally spaced in depth, however this is not always true. The etch-time between acquisition cycles may not be uniform and therefore a second option Depth (Interpolate) uses the etch time to compute the depth increments between acquisition cycles. The former method is used when the rows are assigned an experimental variable value which does not correspond to etch-time, for example if a set of data were collected from a set of X/Y pair ASCII files without the required etch-time information; in which case, the initial experimental variable may be data set index.

Two other options for setting the experimental variable are Angle and Angle (sine). The former assigns a range of linearly spaced values to the existing rows, while the latter generates row values which are the sine of a linear sequence of steps determined by the start and end values in the range text fields.

Edit Experimental Variable by Row

The experimental variable fields in a VAMAS block help to define the context for an acquisition. Within CasaXPS, the VAMAS blocks are aligned in the right-hand pane of the experiment frame using the value from the current experimental variable from each VAMAS block and since data can only be quantified with respect to each other when the corresponding blocks all appear in the same row in the right-hand pane, it is important to be able to make adjustments to these values. Experimental variables values, such as those above, appear in a natural sequence of increasing etch-times; however, not all such sequences necessarily increase with row position and generally, CasaXPS does not assume any ordering for the VAMAS blocks with respect to these values. The only assumption is that VAMAS blocks with the same experimental variable should appear, whenever possible, on the same row in the right-hand pane. Provided all VAMAS blocks with the same experimental variable have distinct species/transition fields, the blocks when viewed in the experiment frame will appear in the same row. There is a subtle but important difference between the **Edit Experimental Variable by Row** dialog window and all other means of changing an experimental variable value in a block, namely, the VAMAS blocks within the underlying file structure are re-ordered with respect to the newly assigned experimental value, whereas all other adjustments to these same values leave the underlying order of the blocks unchanged. Forcing the order for the blocks to change is useful in situations where the structure of the file does not properly reflect the experiment and sadly, not all file formats contain the full context for an experiment, thus necessitating such adjustments.

To change one or more experimental variables in a set of VAMAS blocks, select the appropriate set of blocks in the right-hand pane and press the toolbar button. A new label for the experimental variable heading may be entered and the new value assigned via the dialog window. On pressing the OK button, the value is assigned to the selected VAMAS blocks and the full set of blocks is reordered to reflect the numerical ordering in the context of the new values.

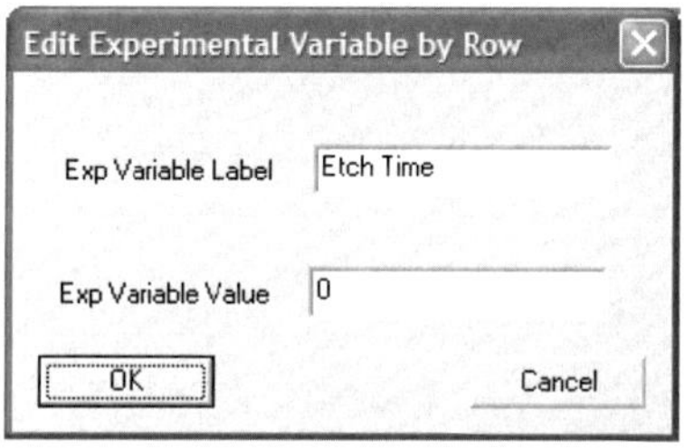

Element Transition or Species Transition VAMAS fields

Element/transition or species/transition VAMAS block fields for the current selection in the right-hand pane are adjusted using the strings entered in the Element and Transition text-fields on the dialog window. The alignment into columns of the VAMAS blocks displayed in the experiment frame is determined from the Species and Transition block strings. A new column appears for each VAMAS block with distinct pairs of these strings. For example, two blocks identified as Si 2p and Si 2p/1 would appear in separate columns in the right-hand pane of the experiment frame, therefore the use of these strings becomes important for rearranging data in preparation for quantification.

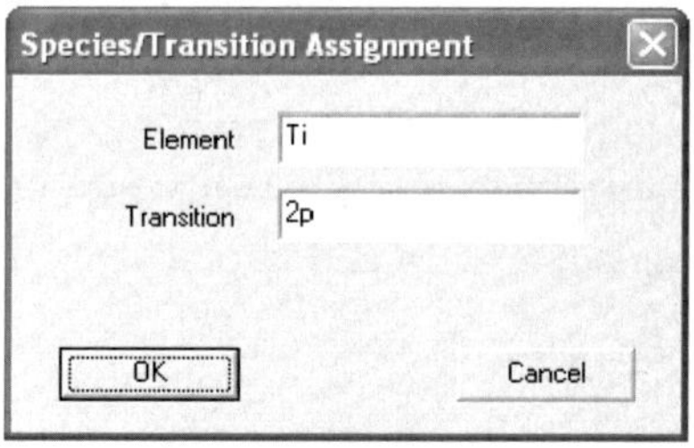

X-ray gun and Analyser Information

Other information often missing for data converted via X/Y pair ASCII files relate to the x-ray anode type (Source Label), photon energy (Source Energy), electron optics magnification and pass energy or retard ratio (Resolution). Again, these values can be assigned to the current selection of VAMAS blocks in the experiment frame, however when assigning a new x-ray source, be sure all the spectra selected have the same Magnification and Resolution settings.

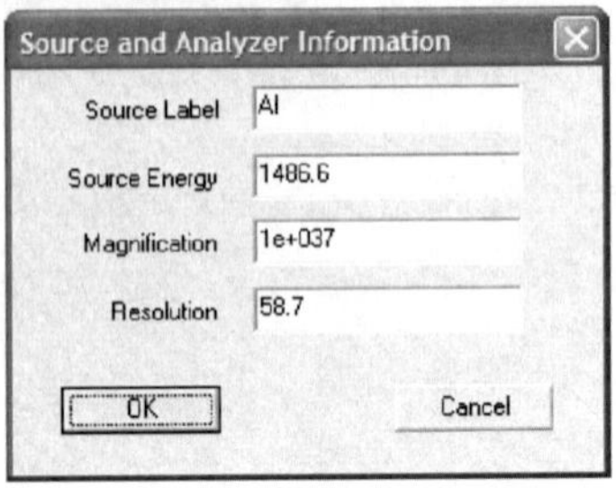

Edit VAMAS Fields Based on a General Selection.

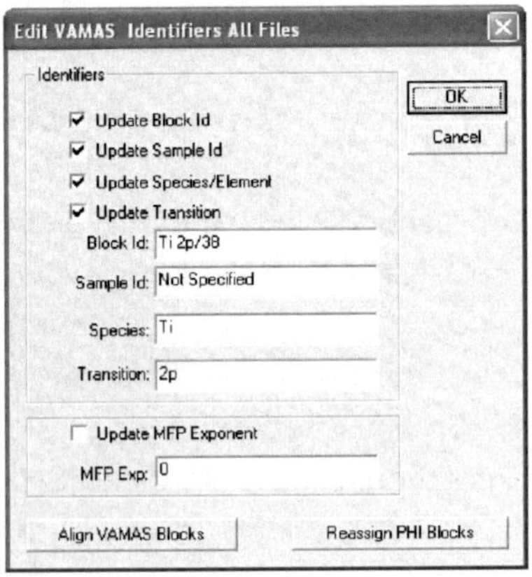

The Block Id is the string that appears in the array of rectangles representing the VAMAS blocks in the right-hand pane of an experiment frame. In addition to the Block Id, the Sample Id is a further string entered into each VAMAS block offering a means of characterizing the data using a text string. The Sample Id is used to construct legends for overlaid spectra and also aligning the VAMAS blocks in the experiment frame when Edit Mode is enabled.

The dialog window offers strings and tick-boxes so that a choice can be made with respect to which of the strings are used when the OK button is pressed. The VAMAS blocks updated with the new values can be selected in as many experiment frames as desired. That is to say, the assignment is not restricted to the blocks selected in the experiment frame currently with focus.

Right-Hand Pane Display Mode

The Edit Mode toolbar button switches the state for the first column in the right-hand pane of the experiment frame between using the experimental variable to order the rows and the strings held in the Sample Id. When pressed once, the experimental variable values are replaced by a set of row labels and these row labels may be edited simply by double-clicking the mouse with the cursor over a row label.

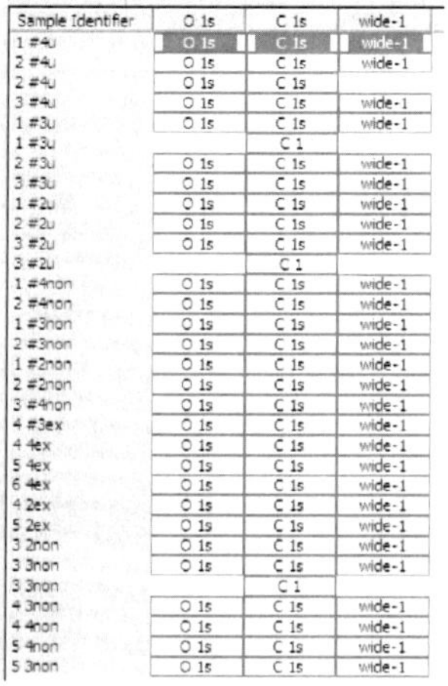

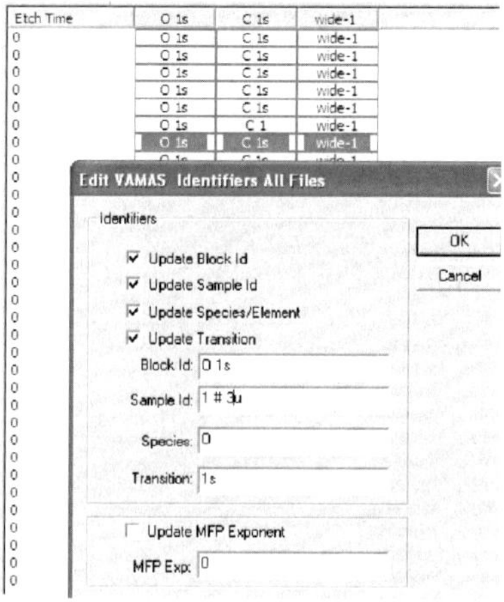